Continental Drift

Britain and Europe from the End of Empire to the Rise of Euroscepticism

In the aftermath of the Second World War, Churchill sought to lead Europe into an integrated union, but a little more than seventy years later Britain is poised to vote on leaving the European Union (EU). Benjamin Grob-Fitzgibbon here recounts the fascinating history of Britain's uneasy relationship with the European continent since the end of the war. He shows how British views of the United Kingdom's place within Europe cannot be understood outside the context of decolonisation, the Cold War and the Anglo–American relationship. At the end of the Second World War, Britons viewed themselves both as the leaders of a great empire and as the natural centre of Europe. With the decline of the British Empire and the formation of the European Economic Community, however, Britons developed a Euroscepticism that was inseparable from a post-imperial nostalgia. Britain had evolved from an island of imperial Europeans to one of post-imperial Eurosceptics.

Benjamin Grob-Fitzgibbon currently works as a Foreign Service Officer (Diplomat) for the United States Department of State. Prior to joining the Foreign Service, he held the Cleveland C. Burton Professorship at the University of Arkansas, where he was also director of the Program in International Relations. He has held a Visiting Fellowship at Wolfson College, Cambridge, and has also taught at Duke University and North Carolina State University. His previously published works include *The Irish Experience during the Second World War: An Oral History* (2004); *Turning Points of the Irish Revolution: The British Government, Intelligence, and the Cost of Indifference, 1912–1921* (2007); and *Imperial Endgame: Britain's Dirty Wars and the End of Empire* (2011).

Continental Drift

Britain and Europe from the End of Empire to the Rise of Euroscepticism

Benjamin Grob-Fitzgibbon
United States Department of State

CAMBRIDGE
UNIVERSITY PRESS

CAMBRIDGE
UNIVERSITY PRESS

University Printing House, Cambridge CB2 8BS, United Kingdom

Cambridge University Press is part of the University of Cambridge.

It furthers the University's mission by disseminating knowledge in the pursuit of education, learning, and research at the highest international levels of excellence.

www.cambridge.org
Information on this title: www.cambridge.org/9781107071261

© Benjamin Grob-Fitzgibbon 2016

This publication is in copyright. Subject to statutory exception and to the provisions of relevant collective licensing agreements, no reproduction of any part may take place without the written permission of Cambridge University Press.

First published 2016

Printed in the United Kingdom by TJ International Ltd. Padstow Cornwall

A catalogue record for this publication is available from the British Library.

Library of Congress Cataloging-in-Publication Data
Grob-Fitzgibbon, Benjamin John.
Continental drift : Britain and Europe from the end of empire to the rise of Euroscepticism / Benjamin Grob-Fitzgibbon.
Cambridge, United Kingdom : Cambridge University Press, 2016. | Includes bibliographical references and index.
LCCN 2016002543 | ISBN 9781107071261 (hardback : alkaline paper)
LCSH: Great Britain – Relations – Europe. | Europe – Relations – Great Britain. | Great Britain – Foreign relations – 1945– | Imperialism – History – 20th century. | Skepticism – Political aspects – Great Britain – History – 20th century. | Group identity – Political aspects – Great Britain – History – 20th century. | Political culture – Great Britain – History – 20th century.
LCC D1065.G7 G76 2016 | DDC 327.4104–dc23
LC record available at http://lccn.loc.gov/2016002543

ISBN 978-1-107-07126-1 Hardback

Cambridge University Press has no responsibility for the persistence or accuracy of URLs for external or third-party Internet Web sites referred to in this publication and does not guarantee that any content on such Web sites is, or will remain, accurate or appropriate.

For my family,
   Amanda, Sophia, Isabel and Kieran

Contents

Acknowledgements	*page* ix
List of abbreviations	xii
Introduction	1

Part 1: Imperial Europeans 11

1	A world undone	13
2	Mr Churchill's Europe	34
3	Mr Bevin's response	60
4	The German problem	79
5	A disunited Europe?	99
6	The continental surprise and the fall of the Labour government	123
7	The realities of government	153
8	Perfidious Gaul	178
9	The decline and fall of the imperial Europeans	202

Part 2: Post-imperial Eurosceptics — 223

10 At sixes and sevens — 225

11 Towards the Common Market — 249

12 The rise of the anti-Marketeers — 277

13 Empire eclipsed, Europe embraced, Britain rejected — 301

14 Entering the promised land? Britain joins 'Europe' — 332

15 Seasons of discontent — 367

16 Half-hearted Europeans — 400

17 Mrs Thatcher, John Major and the road to European Union — 423

Conclusion: Post-imperial Britain and the rise of Euroscepticism — 461

Notes — 471
Bibliography — 561
Index — 582

Acknowledgements

This book was researched and written whilst a Visiting Fellow at Wolfson College, Cambridge, where I spent the academic year 2013–14. At Wolfson, I am thankful to the president Sir Richard Evans, the senior tutor Dr Jane McLarty and the registrar Michelle Searle for their hospitality, as well as to the staff at the Lee Library, where I spent many hours. Beyond Wolfson, I am grateful to the staffs at the University Library and the Churchill Archives Centre, each of whom contributed greatly to this book. At Cambridge University Press, I am indebted to my editor, Michael Watson. I first discussed this book with Michael in Edinburgh in 2012. He immediately grasped what I wished to do and has been supportive of the project ever since. I am grateful for his patience, encouragement and insightful commentary. I must also thank the two outside readers chosen by the Press, who read both the proposal and the completed manuscript and offered suggestions that have made this a better book.

I was able to spend the year in Cambridge thanks to the support of the University of Arkansas and the financial assistance of the Cleveland C. Burton endowment, from which I held the Burton Professorship. I am grateful to the History Department chairs who have supported this project, Lynda Coon and Kathy Sloan, as well as to the Deans of the Fulbright College of Arts and Sciences, Robin Roberts and Todd Shields. I have been blessed with good friends and colleagues at Arkansas who have given me encouragement throughout this process. In the History Department, I am grateful to Laurence Hare, Joel Gordon, Jim Gigantino and especially Calvin White, Jr. In the wider university community, I have benefited from the friendship of my fellow British expatriates, particularly Carl Smith and Fiona Davidson, and from my friend down the corridor, Jill Geisler-Wheeler. Beyond Cambridge and Arkansas, I am thankful for the hospitality given to me by St Antony's College, Oxford, where I stayed whilst in Oxford, and to the staff of the Bodleian Library there. In Birmingham, I benefited from the attention of the staff at the Cadbury Research Library, and in London I am thankful for the staff at the British Library and, as always, the National Archives in Kew. I would be remiss were I not also to publicly mention my friends and colleagues Martin Farr (University of Newcastle), Mikki Brock (Washington and Lee University), Karly Kehoe (Glasgow Caledonian University), Quince Adams (Texas A&M University), David Cannadine (Princeton University) and Alex Roland (Duke University), each of whom continue to provide me with guidance and support.

I have sought and kindly received permission from the following institutions and individuals to quote from materials for which they hold the copyright: the Keeper of Special Collections Dr Chris Fletcher at the Bodleian Library, Oxford; Curtis Brown, London, on behalf of the Beneficiaries of the Estate of Winston S. Churchill; the Director of Special Collections at the Cadbury Research Library, University of Birmingham, Sue Worrall; the Margaret Thatcher Foundation; Miles Gladwyn; Lady Avon; Jan Williams, on behalf of the Trustees of the Harold Macmillan Book Trust; the Churchill Archives Centre, Churchill College, Cambridge; Evelyn Abrams; Lord Norwich; Lord Howard, on behalf of the Trustees of the Estates of the Late J. Enoch Powell; Lady Jay of Paddington; and Lady Duncan-Sandys. My thanks go to each of these individuals and institutions. Despite my best efforts, I was unable to contact some copyright holders of material used in my book. Should these individuals notify the publisher of any omissions, I would be more than happy to seek permission from them and duly acknowledge such permission in all future printings of this work.

Finally, I am thankful for the support of my wife Amanda and my three children Sophia, Isabel and Kieran. More so than in my previous books, my family was by my side throughout the research and writing of this one, as they came with me to Cambridge. This meant that archival visits were bookended by family walks along the Backs, across Grantchester Meadow and to Jesus Green and our local park, Histon Road Rec'. Weeks of writing were interrupted by delightful trips to Northumberland, the Lake District, Dorset, and London, and at the weekends I was distracted from the intricacies of Britain's European policy by the grounds and houses of the National Trust and the beauties of the English countryside. Due entirely to the company of my wife and children, *Continental Drift* was by far my most enjoyable book to write, and I would not have had it any other way. I look forward to having them by my side in all of our adventures to come.

Postscript: Since completing this book, I have left my position as a faculty member at the University of Arkansas to instead work for the US Department of State as a Foreign Service Officer (diplomat). It goes without saying that this work was completed in its entirety in my capacity as a university professor. The views expressed in this book are those of the author and not necessarily those of the US Government.

Abbreviations

ABMS	Mark Abrams Papers
AELAdd	Anthony Eden Additional Papers
AMEJ	Julian Amery Papers
AMEL	Leopold Amery Papers
AP	Avon Papers
BDOEE	*British Documents on the End of Empire*
BDPO	*Documents on British Policy Overseas*
Bodleian	Bodleian Library, University of Oxford
BT	Board of Trade
BW	British Council
CAB	Cabinet Office
CAC	Churchill Archives Centre, Churchill College, Cambridge
CHAR	Chartwell Papers
CHUR	Churchill Papers
CO	Colonial Office
CRL	Special Collections Department, Cadbury Research Library, University of Birmingham
DO	Dominions Office
DSND	Duncan Sandys Papers
DUFC	Duff Cooper Papers
ENZG	Paul Einzig Papers
GLAD	Gladwyn Papers
FCO	Foreign and Commonwealth Office
FO	Foreign Office
HSC	Head of State Correspondence

KNNK	Neil Kinnock Papers
LBJ	Lyndon B. Johnson Presidential Library, Austin, Texas
MS	Sir Evelyn Shuckburgh Papers
MS Castle	Barbara Castle Papers
MS Eng. Hist. c.	Sir Neil Martin Papers
MS Howe	Geoffrey Howe Papers
MS Macmillan	Harold Macmillan Papers
MS Wilson	Harold Wilson Papers
NSF	National Security File
PLDN	Plowden Papers
POLL	Enoch Powell Papers
PREM	Prime Minister's Office
SPRG	Nigel Spearing Papers
T	Treasury
Thatcher MSS/THCR	Margaret Thatcher Papers
TNA	The National Archives, Kew
WLFF	Michael Wolff Papers

INTRODUCTION

On the afternoon of 7 May 1948, Winston Churchill addressed the 750 delegates at the first Congress of Europe. 'This is not a movement of parties but a movement of peoples', he declared. 'If there is rivalry of parties, let it be to see which one will distinguish itself the most for the common cause'. Everyone had been invited to the Congress 'in his individual capacity, nevertheless this Congress, and any conclusions it may reach, may fairly claim to be the voice of Europe'. Its delegates included 'statesmen of all political parties, leading figures from all the Churches, eminent writers, leaders of the professions, lawyers, chiefs of industry and prominent trades-unionists'. Their common cause was a united Europe. Churchill, their Honorary President, implored them to 'pull together and pool the luck and the comradeship'. If they did so, then all of Europe might 'move into a happier sunlit age'.[1]

Churchill was speaking in the Hague not as the leader of the Conservative Party and His Majesty's Loyal Opposition, nor as a former British Prime Minister, but as a citizen of Europe. The British delegation that he led included the Liberal Peers Lord Layton and Lady Violet Bonham-Carter; the trade unionist Bob Edwards and Labour MPs Kenneth Lindsay and Leslie Hale; and the Conservatives Leopold Amery, Robert Boothby, Lady Rhys-Williams and Henry Hopkinson.[2] These Britons were joined by other European dignitaries such as Léon Blum, Jean Monnet, Paul Reynaud, Konrad Adenauer, Paul-Henri Spaak and Paul van Zeeland, names that would soon become synonymous with the cause of European unity. Even the Vatican sent a representative.[3] With British cross-party support and delegations from fifteen other European countries, the Congress adopted a political program that committed its delegates to work towards a 'parallel policy of closer political union', which would 'sooner or later' involve 'the renunciation or, to be more accurate, the joint exercise of certain sovereign powers'.[4] In the economic sphere, it agreed that 'The nations of Europe can only be saved by a complete economic union, providing a single market for labour, production and trade'.[5] Finally, the Congress declared that 'No scheme for European Union would have any practical value without the effective participation of Great Britain. The United Kingdom is an integral part of Europe'.[6] A future European Union would be both politically and economically integrated with Great Britain at its heart.

It is hard to imagine, some seventy years later, that in the aftermath of the Second World War, Britain – an imperial Britain, closely allied with the United States and grappling with the beginnings of the Cold War – sought to lead Europe into an integrated Union. It is perhaps harder still to fathom that it was that imperialist *par excellence* Winston Churchill who first popularised the phrase 'the United States of Europe' and encouraged the French, Germans and other Europeans to put aside their differences and instead work together in common cause. When, in November 2013, the President of the European Commission, José Manuel Barroso, called for British Prime Minister David Cameron to show the type of political courage and vision displayed by Churchill – quoting his 1948 statement that 'We must aim at nothing less than the Union of Europe as a whole' – he was met with resistance from prominent British Eurosceptics. Nigel Farage, leader of the United Kingdom Independence Party (UKIP), even accused Barroso of 'hijacking a single phrase by Churchill', of taking it out of context to 'paint him as a fan of political union in Europe'.[7]

In the midst of the 2010 General Election campaign, the Liberal Democrat leader Nick Clegg argued that the rise of UKIP and the Eurosceptic wing of the Conservative Party could best be explained as a reaction to the loss of empire. Whilst for the European continent the creation of the European Union (EU) was an 'absolute blinding triumph of peace over war, of democracy over tyranny', for Britain it was an 'admission of weakness'. Continued British hostility to the European project, Clegg suggested, was inextricably linked to British nostalgia for the days of empire.[8] The Liberal Democrat leader was not alone in this view. Three years earlier, Stuart Hall – founding editor of the *New Left*

Review and a leading British cultural theorist – claimed that 'The very notion of Great Britain's "greatness" is bound up with empire. Euroscepticism and Little Englander nationalism could hardly survive if people understood whose sugar flowed through English blood and rotted English teeth'.[9] That Euroscepticism was wrapped up in conceptions of race and imperialism was self-evident to Clegg and Hall; why that was so is less clear.

Some popular Eurosceptics have encouraged such criticism from the Left. For example, Daniel Hannan, Conservative Member of the European Parliament for south-east England, has frequently interspersed his commentary on the iniquities of the EU with praise for the Empire.[10] Concurrently, known apologists for the British Empire such as historians Niall Ferguson and Andrew Roberts have written widely on their opposition to deeper British integration with the European continent, condemning the EU as undemocratic and unaccountable.[11] Even Bagehot – the *Economist*'s esteemed columnist on Britain – has noted the link between contemporary Euroscepticism and imperial longing.[12] For the political class and Fourth Estate, it is a commonplace that the rise of Euroscepticism has gone hand in hand with the decline of the British Empire. For academics, however, the worlds of empire and the post-war British relationship with the European continent have remained tucked away in disciplinary silos, and never the twain shall meet.[13]

Given the integrated nature of British imperialism and Britain's place in Europe, it is perhaps surprising that these two elements of a common story have been treated so separately by the academic community, yet there is a distinct divergence.[14] On the one hand, there is a vibrant debate over the end of the British Empire, one which is increasingly interested in the effect that British imperial decline has had on the United Kingdom itself.[15] On the other, there is an historiographical community that explores the United Kingdom's entry into the European Economic Community (EEC), albeit one that is chiefly concerned with examining why Britain has remained 'on the side-lines' of Europe.[16] These two communities have not, for the most part, interacted. For one camp, the Empire and its decline is the chief focus of their studies; for the other, the various institutions and organisations that have worked towards European integration. The only area upon which the two seem to agree is that decolonisation had very little to do with British approaches to Europe and vice versa.[17] This self-imposed isolation of 'imperialists' from 'Europeanists' is not only a trend in recent historiography. On the contrary, it long pre-dates the establishment of the EU and its predecessors.[18] It is a strange irony that, in the press and amongst politicians, there is an assumption that the decline of empire and Europe (particularly the rise of Euroscepticism) have gone hand in hand, whereas for historians there is an equally strongly held contention that empire and Europe have had nothing whatsoever to do with each other!

What are we to make of this? Writing of her experiences as an undergraduate at Bristol University in the late 1960s and early 1970s, Linda Colley found history to be 'thoroughly compartmentalized', with British history, imperial history, American history and European history all operating 'along parallel tracks' that did not meet.[19] Thirty years later, this compartmentalisation was still present, and Colley joined David Armitage in his lament of 'the persistent reluctance of British historians to incorporate the Empire into the history of Britain'.[20] Although historians have, since the 1980s, begun to explore the impact of empire on the British Isles – pioneered in large part by John MacKenzie and his remarkably successful Studies in Imperialism book series – there has nevertheless remained a hesitancy (conscious or unconscious) to extend this study of the imperial impact to an exploration of Britain and the European continent. It is telling that in MacKenzie's series of close to one hundred books, none explicitly explores the relationship between an imperial Britain and the European continent.[21]

If imperial historians have tended to marginalise the effects of empire on Europe (and the decline of empire on Britain's relationship with European integration in the post-war period), then historians of Britain's interactions with the continent have ignored the British Empire all together.[22] This is in part because it does not form part of *their* story of growing European unity.[23] Their search through time to find signs and developments which may (or may not) foretell what is a distinctly modern phenomenon (the EU) points to a larger problem in the literature on Britain's relationship with Europe in the twentieth century. When exploring the dynamics of this complex association, historians have tended to adopt the views and language of modern policymakers, whereby 'Europe' has become synonymous with 'the European Union' and its predecessors. Consequently, to explore Britain's relationship with 'Europe' has come to mean exploring the United Kingdom's relationship with those countries and institutions that make up the EU. It is perhaps inevitable under such circumstances that the main conclusions historians have reached are that Britain has remained distant from 'Europe' (read, the 'EU') and that Britain's interactions with 'Europe' have had little to do with the Empire/Commonwealth. Yet for those Britons living in the 1940s, '50s and '60s, operating without the benefit of historical hindsight, it was by no means clear that 'Europe' was indeed limited only to the particular administrative organs of the European Coal and Steel Community and later the EEC. 'Europe' was far broader than most historians have defined it to be; British considerations of their own place within that Europe were far more complex.

Yet there is perhaps a broader reason for the neglect of Europe by most British historians and nearly all imperial historians, one which rests on notions of British insularity and – dare I say it – cultural arrogance, marked most clearly by the once universal (and still common) usage of 'England' and 'English' for 'Britain' and 'British', without much thought to Scotland, Wales and Ireland.[24] This attitude, often unintentional, has been extended beyond England and the United Kingdom to the European continent. In his inaugural lecture as Regius Professor of History at the University of Cambridge, Richard Evans highlighted this trend with a summary of recent attempts to define English historiography, demonstrating persuasively that, despite a deep British historiography on European history, still the assumption persists of an inherent Anglo-centrism.[25] Like Linda Colley, he sees as significant the 'fact that "British" and "European" History remain essentially separate in UK universities',[26] concluding that it is 'in many ways rather artificial to oppose the study of British History to the study of European..... [O]ur national identity coexists, as in fact it has always done, with many kinds of identity too, local, regional, immigrant, European, "Western"... Europe is an essential part of this wider picture'.[27]

It is the purpose of this book to retell the story of Britain's postwar relationship with the European continent, keeping the broader context of British foreign affairs and Britain's place in the world firmly in view. It argues that Britain's relationship with the European continent has been intimately shaped by the government's handling of the end of empire, by the public's changing perceptions of Britain's place within the world and by the nation's search to define what it means to be British (and European) in the aftermath of both war and empire. It suggests that, in the immediate post-war world, British politicians, civil servants and the public at large viewed British identity as both an imperial one and a European one. There was no contradiction between being an imperial power, part of the English-speaking Atlantic world and a European nation. This identity shaped their approaches to domestic and international policy, their management of the end of empire and their engagement with the European continent following the Second World War. However, from the mid-1950s through the early 1970s, this identity and the worldview it inspired was challenged; challenged by the decline of empire and ultimate decolonisation, by the establishment of the EEC on an understanding of Europe that most Britons by and large did not share and by a Cold War that drew the United Kingdom ever closer to the United States. These challenges were accentuated by a change on the European continent itself, with a shift to a European identity that was no longer based on imperialism/colonisation and was increasingly sceptical about an Atlantic worldview. To complicate matters further, this idea of Europe went through various iterations from the 1940s to the 1960s – both within the United Kingdom and on the continent – ensuring that not only were the core belief systems of Britons in flux during these years, but that the very concept of Europe itself also was constantly changing and evolving.

Throughout the mid-1960s, successive British governments sought to realign their vision of Europe with that of the six member-states of the EEC; however, this necessarily meant a readjustment of their concept of the Commonwealth and Britain's place in the world. With this readjustment came an increasing split with the ideologies and identities of the British public. British entry into the EEC in 1973 occurred at an economically difficult time, with an oil crisis imminent and rising food prices placing increasing strain on the British economy. Despite a successful referendum in 1975 confirming Britain's membership in the Community, many Britons began to suspect that it was the decline of empire in combination with entry into the EEC that had thwarted Britain's place in the world. By choosing Europe over empire, they held, Britain had lost its way; only by distancing itself from Europe and re-embracing Britain's imperial values could the British people reignite the flame of greatness that had been extinguished. Margaret Thatcher, although not the founder of this ideology, was quick to recognise its political potency. It was during the Thatcher years of 1979–90 that the Conservative Party moved from being the party of

Europe to the party of Euroscepticism. Whilst Britain had an empire and empires were largely the preserve of Europeans, British foreign policy rested firmly on the concept of an imperial Europe with Britain leading the way; when, in the 1960s, the loss of empire, combined with a redefining of what it meant to be 'European', separated notions of imperialism from European-ness, a Euroscepticism was born that became impossible to separate from nostalgic neo-imperialism.

This book, then, is the story of the British and Europe, from the end of empire to the rise of Euroscepticism. At the close of the Second World War, many Britons believed that the United Kingdom's responsibility was to lead not just the British Empire and Commonwealth but Europe also. By doing so (and by keeping intact their 'special relationship' with the United States), Britain could move towards a post-war concept of world governance and society with Britain firmly holding the reins. For Britons in these years, greater integration with the European continent was not an alternative to empire but an opportunity to extend their imperial mission alongside and in collaboration with the strengthening of Commonwealth ties. Seventy years later, the Empire is long gone, the Commonwealth has lost its political significance and the United Kingdom's reputation in Europe is largely as an Atlanticist brake on European ambitions. How the British evolved from being a nation of imperial Europeans to one of post-imperial Eurosceptics is the subject of this book.

* * *

To understand Britain's post-war vision of its place in Europe and the world, we must turn first to the pre-war era. That the United Kingdom has throughout its history revelled in its island nature, physically removed from the rest of Europe, is indisputable. The unique geography of the British Isles has shaped its political, social, economic and cultural development, leading to an earlier conception of a unified state than was the case on the European continent and a common national identity at a comparatively early stage of its evolution.[28] The historian R. W. Seton-Watson – writing in 1937 – argued that 'Britain's hybrid position as part of Europe, and yet in some respects outside it served [throughout its history] as a natural stimulus to overseas commercial and political development – trade following the flag – and to reliance upon a strong navy'.[29] Britain's island geography ensured that it developed a naval tradition, which in turn made it a natural competitor in the quest for empire.[30] Furthermore, unlike its neighbours on the continent, the British Isles had a natural separation and protection from invasion which allowed it to escape the necessity of developing a large land army. For this reason, Britons adopted certain national attributes, such as a reverence for 'English liberty' and commerce, that were less prevalent on the continent.[31] Consequently, throughout much of the late eighteenth, nineteenth and early twentieth centuries, there was a connection in the British mind between liberty and imperialism that was far less developed on the continent.

In others ways, however, Britain was unquestionably European in its outlook and history. In its earliest times, it knew nothing beyond the continent – indeed, was peopled *from* the continent – and its past was inextricably linked with its European neighbours; once extra-European expansion began, the very Otherness of those elsewhere in the world encouraged the development of a concept of European 'race' with which the British firmly identified. Throughout the eighteenth and nineteenth centuries, the United Kingdom was no closer or further removed from France in its foreign relations than was Prussia (and Germany thereafter), and the Isles had a more interconnected history with the Netherlands – despite the sea that separated them – than the Netherlands had with its more immediate continental neighbours to the south and east.[32] Until the twentieth century, the British and German peoples 'never fought each other', and their 'traditions of political co-operation were reinforced by dynastic, cultural, religious and economic ties'.[33] Yet an integrated demographic, economic and religious history was not the only element holding Europe together.

From the seventeenth century onwards, European-ness and imperialism became synonymous. To be European *was* to be imperial. European rivalry – particularly among the British, French, Dutch, Spanish and Portuguese – encouraged mercantilist economics and eventually more explicit imperial expansion. Although the Protestant Reformation drove a religious wedge (indeed, wedges) through and within the European nations, there was a discernible 'European' approach to the rest of the world, held as much by Britons as by those on the continent.[34] Throughout the eighteenth century and into the era of the French Revolutionary and Napoleonic Wars (1789–1815), there could be no doubt that Britain was at once a European power and an imperial power, both waging war with other European states for supremacy within Europe whilst at the same time engaging in intense competition with those very same powers for control of the extra-European world. Britain after 1815 emerged as the victor in a Europe that was a 'far less competitive one than in the preceding two centuries'; however, this did not cause the government to withdraw from the continent.[35] On the contrary, it developed a policy of manipulating the European continent into a 'balance of power', which allowed Britain a free hand to pursue its imperial ambitions. This was not a rejection of a European role for the United Kingdom, as some historians have suggested, but rather a continuing recognition that Britain would always have a responsibility in Europe when conflict arose; only by ensuring peace and stability on the continent could Britain pursue its imperial interests outside it.[36]

Following the Crimean War of 1853–56 and the cabinet's 1864 refusal to intervene against Prussia in its clash with Denmark, the government did indeed withdraw from active intervention on the European continent. Nevertheless, there continued throughout the premierships of Gladstone and Disraeli certain 'inherited traditions' from the mid-Victorian era, not least of which were 'rival claims to the manifest British moral leadership of Europe'. The Whigs and Liberals believed it was the duty and responsibility of Britain to establish 'under British auspices a concert of powers sharing a common liberal ideology'; the Cobdenites saw in Europe a natural habitat for their free-trade economics, where a common non-interventionist foreign policy and open markets could bring lasting peace and friendship to the European peoples; and the Conservatives asserted that continued British leadership in Europe stemmed from Viscount Castlereagh's achievements after the Napoleonic Wars, when he had worked to achieve a conservative consensus amongst the restored European monarchies.[37] 'Splendid Isolation' (as it later came to be known) was therefore less a rejection of a British role in Europe than an affirmation that Britain's place in the world – as Europe's leading power – was necessarily larger than the European continent and thus primarily concerned with Britain's extra-European interests.[38] By 1902, even this belief was falling out of fashion, leaving the British government's policy of (relative) isolation from the European continent in effect for less than forty years.[39]

Even during these years of self-imposed exile, the government had continued to act very much as a *European* imperial power, for example, during the combined Anglo–French endeavours to open the

Suez Canal or at the 1884 Berlin Conference, when representatives from Great Britain, France, Germany, Austria-Hungary, Italy, the Netherlands, Belgium, Portugal, Spain, Russia, Sweden-Norway, Denmark and the Ottoman Empire came together to partition Africa into European colonies and dependencies.[40] Writing in 1897 – the year of Queen Victoria's Diamond Jubilee – the Prime Minister, Lord Salisbury, claimed that a federated Europe was 'our sole hope of escaping from the constant terror and calamity of war, the constant pressure of the burdens of an armed peace, which weigh down the spirits and darken the prospects of every nation in this part of the world. The Federation of Europe is the only hope we have'.[41] Some seventy years later, another Prime Minister – Harold Macmillan – wrote that Salisbury's vision was an example of 'thinking in larger terms' than just the 'British Empire [which had] reached its apogee of glory and power'.[42]

When the Second World War erupted in 1939, it did so against the backdrop of two centuries of British foreign policy in which European and imperial considerations were carefully balanced, often inextricably linked. Since the founding of the United Kingdom (and before), Britain's chief rivals had come from within Europe, and it was against other European states – primarily France – that Britain had 'Othered' itself to prove its national uniqueness.[43] Yet, throughout it all, there was a grudging recognition of a shared heritage and common European imperial outlook that caused seemingly opposed powers to join forces, particularly when the beneficiary of such cooperation was a European power rather than an extra-European one. If anything, the Second World War only heightened the sense that Britain's past, present and future was linked to the European continent. If Britain and the British Empire were to survive in the post-war world, they would do so only by leading a larger Europe.

Britain, an island set apart, for many decades the head of a great empire, was (and has always been) a European nation also. As the dynamics of world power shifted following the Second World War, Britain's imperial heritage and its role in Europe were placed under the microscope like never before. Whereas once it had been taken for granted that Britain was both imperial *and* European, the events of the war years shook the British Empire and the European continent, providing Britain with an opportunity to re-examine its relationship with each amidst the rubble that was left. It is here that our story begins.

PART I
IMPERIAL EUROPEANS

1 A WORLD UNDONE

For the first time in six years, floodlights cast shadows across London's streets, brightly illuminating Nelson's Column in Trafalgar Square, the great clock at Westminster and Buckingham Palace. The brilliance of the White Ensign, the Union Flag and the Blue Ensign on the Cenotaph contrasted with the grime-caked stones behind, a continuing reminder of Britain's industrial revolution. Despite the lateness of the hour, crowds still converged around the great monuments, and bonfires burned in many of London's open spaces, more than a few with effigies of Hitler sitting on top. The bells of churches across the capital continued to ring, competing with the sporadic fireworks and making sleep impossible, even if it were desired.[1]

The eighth of May 1945 had been a full day for the Prime Minister, beginning in the early hours of the morning with his radio address to announce Germany's unconditional surrender. There had followed an attendance in Parliament for Question Time, a procession to the Church of St Margaret for an impromptu service of thanksgiving, further pronouncements in the House of Commons and then, at four o'clock, an audience with the King.[2] Some hours later, the Right Honourable Winston Churchill stepped onto the flag-draped balcony of the Ministry of Health, causing an enormous roar from the crowds who had been waiting expectantly for their leader to speak. Wearing his war-worn boiler suit, his polished top hat balanced incongruously on his head, Churchill addressed them through a loudspeaker: 'God bless you all. This is your victory!' At this, many voices in the crowd interrupted to correct him, 'No – it is *yours*'.[3] The Prime Minister finished his evening sometime after ten o'clock with a return appearance on the balcony to lead the crowd in a roaring rendition of 'Land of Hope and Glory'.[4]

VE Day was a celebration in Britain, but the elation of Germany's unconditional surrender could not last long. Europe lay in ruins, Japan remained undefeated and the empire that had sustained Britain throughout its long war was showing signs of fatigue and restlessness. Even those with the greatest reason to rejoice could find little energy to do so. Field Marshal Lord Alanbrooke, Chief of the Imperial General Staff and, as chairman of the Chief of Staffs' Committee, Churchill's foremost military advisor, wrote in his diary on 7 May that he simply couldn't 'feel thrilled', instead experiencing 'infinite mental weariness'. Despite the celebrations occurring throughout the country, Alanbrooke's 'most acute feeling' was 'one of deep depression' and he spent 9 May – a national holiday – at his home tending to his goats and chickens.[5] Churchill himself warned the nation on 13 May that there was 'still a lot to do' and that Britons 'must be prepared for further efforts of mind and body and further sacrifices to great causes'.[6] John Colville, Churchill's long-time private secretary, feared that 'Victory has brought no respite. The P.M. looks tired and has to fight for the energy to deal with the problems confronting him'. In the days following Germany's surrender, Colville found Churchill 'overpowered' and 'weighed down by the responsibility and uncertainty'.[7]

The problems facing Britain were grave indeed. Three quarters of a million homes that had been destroyed or severely damaged during the war had yet to be rebuilt and there was 'huge disruption to public services'. Britain's national debt sat at a record £3.5 billion yet the country was in desperate need of reinvestment after the austerity of war. Neville Chamberlain's social reforms of the 1930s had been left unfinished and, still in 1945, 7 million houses had no hot water supply, 6 million lacked an inside toilet of any kind and 5 million had no fixed bath.[8] And putting aside the fact that Britain and its empire remained at war with Japan, the Prime Minister also had political problems. After five years of coalition government under a Conservative leader, the rank and file of the Labour Party was growing restless. Churchill, whilst not immune to party feelings, thought it best for the coalition to continue until after Japan's defeat, a sentiment shared by the leader of the Labour Party Clement Attlee and his closest colleague Ernest Bevin, both of whom sat in the wartime coalition government. Yet Attlee and Bevin were overruled by the National Executive Committee at their party conference in Blackpool, which on 21 May put before its members a proposition that the coalition be dissolved by October whether or not Japan was defeated. After a near unanimous vote in favour, Churchill dissolved the coalition immediately, formed a Conservative 'caretaker' government and called for a General Election to be held on 5 July.[9] The campaign quickly descended into partisan bickering and 'business as usual'; the electorate as a whole was left 'jaded and sceptical' at such political posturing whilst so many Britons were still fighting overseas. As one Fulham resident put it early in the campaign, 'The war's got us down, what with the bombing and the blackout, and the worrying about coupons and queues, women like me haven't the mind to take to politics'.[10] By June, Colville sensed 'the first intoxication of victory' was 'passing. The [political] parties are creating bitterness, largely artificial, in their vote-catching hysteria'.[11]

If Britain had at least felt the 'intoxication of victory' without ever carrying the weight of Nazi occupation, the same could not be said of the European continent, across which dawn broke on 9 May not with a national holiday but with signs of devastation everywhere. Whether destroyed by bombers from the air or by the ground forces as they steadily advanced and retreated from Normandy and Sicily, bridges, housing, hospitals, schools and cultural monuments that had stood the test of time prior to the war were all reduced to rubble in what observers called 'biblical annihilation'.[12] In Hamburg, Germany, for example, 3,000 aeroplanes had dropped 18,000 tons of bombs, destroying 40,383 houses and 263,000 flats – 48 per cent of all homes in the city – and causing 36,662 casualties.[13] In Dresden, the damage was worse; on the night of 13–14 February 1945 alone, 85 per cent of the city was destroyed, including more than 70,000 residences, 640 shops, 200 factories, 64 warehouses, 24 banks, 19 hospitals, 39 schools, 31 hotels, 3 theatres, 18 cinemas, 11 churches and the Dresden Zoo.[14] In Warsaw, 90 per cent of all buildings were razed by the retreating Germans, and in the small town of Wiener Neustadt near Vienna, just eighteen houses remained from a pre-war population of 45,000.[15]

It was not only the physical damage in Europe's great cities that presented a problem. Observers estimated that as much as 10 per cent of Europe's population – some 60 million people – had been displaced from their homes, creating the largest refugee crisis in world history.[16] Reginald Roy, a Canadian soldier serving with the Cape Breton highlanders, wrote in his diary of travelling through Holland during the first two weeks of May 1945 and seeing 'thousands of people swarming in all directions', as if a 'big stick had been poked into an anthill'.[17] Robert Reid, a BBC war correspondent attached to Patton's army, told his listeners that the 40,000 refugees who moved along the roads of the Moselle valley in Germany reminded him 'of those coloured plates you remembered seeing as a child in the family bible at home', of the Israelites searching for the Promised Land. The displaced peoples he saw were, he believed, 'one of the most serious problems now facing Europe'.[18]

Whereas for Britain the blackouts and Blitz had helped foster a myth of national defiance, the tragedy of Dunkirk transformed into a triumph and Churchill's 'the Few' coming to symbolise British greatness after the Battle of Britain, there was no such silver lining for the continent. For Britons, the war had demonstrated the virtues of a strong patriotism and confirmed their status as an 'island race' set apart. For Europeans on the continent, the war had shown only the dangers of unchecked nationalism and the folly of drawing lines on a map.[19] Many Britons nevertheless shared a commonality with their fellow Europeans over the tragedy of the war and a desire to prevent such destruction in the future. In the General Election campaign, Churchill told supporters in Woodford that European interests were 'an essential part of our interests'.[20]

It was not the first time the Prime Minister had characterised British interests as European interests, nor would it be the last. Churchill saw in Europe a continent which, whilst given to competition and internal strife throughout its history, nevertheless shared with Britain a comparable imperial outlook and a wider Christian heritage that had through the ages combined to form, shape and enhance Western civilisation. It was no secret to his friends and admirers that Churchill had been throughout his career both a staunch imperialist and a statesman with an intense interest in the European continent. His many public letters and commentaries throughout the 1920s and '30s had demonstrated as much.[21] Yet it was not until 1938 that Churchill spelled out in clear terms his vision for Europe and the Empire. On 28 May of that year, Churchill penned an article for the *News of the World* that would forever associate his name with the European continent, asking, 'Why not "The United States of Europe"?' He lamented that 'Never before have three hundred and eighty millions of the strongest, most educated, and most civilised parent races of mankind done themselves so much harm'. It was not only the ancient and irrational hatreds that dismayed him but the 'tangled growth and network of tariff barriers designed to restrict trade and production', which contrasted so greatly with the United States of America where 'free interchange of goods and services over the widest possible area' had led to its 'rapid accretion of material wealth'. Churchill's solution to these problems was a United States of Europe, drawing from the historical examples of past times when 'Rumanians lived on the Tyne and Spaniards on the Danube as equal citizens of a single State'. Churchill argued that a unified European empire, where a person could 'realise himself as French, German, Dutch, or Hungarian, and simultaneously as a European', would 'once united, once federalised, or partially federalised, once continentally self-conscious – Europe with its African and Asiatic possessions and plantations – constitute an organism beyond compare'.

Churchill was ambivalent about Britain's role in this newly created United States of Europe. He recognised the inherent Europeanness of British history with his reference to Rumanians on the Tyne, yet also suggested that British policy had to be 'determined by her dominant conception of a united British Empire'. The British people were European, of this Churchill had no doubt, yet Britain also had unique extra-European responsibilities as Europe's largest imperial power. European interests were British interests – 'Everything that tends to make Europe more prosperous and more peaceful is conducive to British interests' – yet British interests went beyond purely European interests. Churchill therefore concluded that Britain was 'with Europe, but not of it. We are linked, but not comprised. We are interested and associated, but not absorbed'. Britain must 'further every honest and practical step which the nations of Europe may make to reduce the barriers which divide them' but must also work for a 'proportionate growth of solidarity throughout the British Empire', so that Britain – both European and sitting outside Europe – could safeguard its unique island history whilst recognising its common European heritage.[22]

Five months after Churchill wrote his essay, the then-Prime Minister Neville Chamberlain returned from Munich having met the German Fuhrer Adolf Hitler to forge 'peace in our time'. Churchill publicly warned against the dangers of allowing Hitler to annex the Sudetenland of Czechoslovakia and called for Western European unity, arguing that 'If the French Republic and the British Empire were necessary to each other in days of war and in days of success, they are still more necessary in these times when conditions are so different'.[23] Churchill's warning did little good, however, and Chamberlain's appeasement was unable to prevent a German invasion of Poland and the start of the Second World War in September 1939. When Churchill became Prime Minister on 10 May 1940, he proposed an Anglo–French Union to combat the menace they both faced, telling his war cabinet on 16 June that he had seen the French General Charles de Gaulle the previous day, who had impressed upon him that 'some very dramatic move' was necessary to ensure that the French government did not succumb to National Socialist overtures.[24] The Prime Minister put before his cabinet a draft proclamation to be delivered to the French government proposing an 'indissoluble union' between Britain and France, whereby France and Great Britain would 'no longer be two nations, but one Franco–British Union' with a 'common citizenship' and 'joint organs of defence, foreign, financial and economic policies'. For the duration of the war, there would be a single Franco–British war cabinet, and the two parliaments would be 'formally associated' until such time that the constitutional details of the merger could be completed. The cabinet made clear that 'the Union included the whole British Commonwealth of Nations and the French Empire'[25] and unanimously approved Churchill's proclamation after only a very brief discussion. Unfortunately, with one eye to appeasing the Third Reich and the other to the possible spoils of Nazi occupation, the French cabinet rejected the proposal, Marshall Philippe Pétain icily asking why France should want to 'fuse with a corpse'.[26] Within a week, the French government had surrendered to Germany and the fascist French Vichy Regime soon governed France on Germany's behalf.[27]

That France and Britain would take two very different paths for the subsequent five years of war was inevitable, given that one was living under occupation and one was not. For Britain, this was a time when a strong national unity had by necessity to overshadow all other identities and loyalties and when the very survival of the nation was dependent on a heightened sense of patriotism; for France and the Low Countries, the rise of Germany's National Socialist government and its occupation of their lands taught only the dangers of nationalism.[28] Even so, a young Harold Macmillan, in response to a question on war aims in October 1939, wrote, 'if western civilisation is to survive, we must look forward to an organisation, economic, cultural, and perhaps even political, comprising all the countries of western Europe'.[29] In late 1940 – as Britain stood alone under continual German bombardment – the Foreign Secretary Anthony Eden suggested that after the war it might be necessary to construct 'some form of European federation', which would 'comprise a European defence scheme, a European customs union and [a] common currency'.[30]

Consequently, although Churchill turned increasingly to the United States for alliance in the face of the European collapse, he did not ignore the exiled European governments. In the autumn of 1942, he wrote to Anthony Eden that his 'thoughts rest[ed] primarily in Europe – the revival of the glory of Europe, the parent continent of the modern nations and of civilisation. ... Hard as it is to say now, I trust that the European family may act unitedly as one under a Council of Europe'. He acknowledged that Britain would 'have to work with the Americans in many ways, and in the greatest ways', but that 'Europe is our prime care'.[31] He also listened to the pleas of Norway's Trygve Lie and Holland's Eelco van Kleffens who asked for Britain to establish a post-war European security system that would prevent the rise of future autocratic governments, and he met with Belgium's Paul-Henri Spaak who argued that Britain should lead Western Europe towards greater political and economic unity once Germany was defeated.[32] And, as important as Norway, Holland and Belgium were to Churchill, France loomed even larger. Not only was France the greatest of the Western European powers and thus likely to hold a commanding position in any post-war European system, France was also a colonial power which, like Britain, understood the imperial mission of European states. The *Entente Cordiale* that had brought France and the United Kingdom together after centuries of animosity was, after all, a colonial understanding, and, unlike Britain's American ally, France understood that equality and freedom were not always best manifested in immediate national self-determination. In a post-war world in which the United States would inevitably hold more power than ever before, it was essential for Britain to develop partners within Europe who would stand firm against any American anti-imperial impulses.

This message was reinforced following the appointment of Duff Cooper as British Representative to the French Committee of National Liberation in Algiers in late 1943. Cooper, at times a civil servant, Guards officer and parliamentarian, had made his name in 1938 when, on the day after Chamberlain's Munich declaration, he had resigned his position as First Lord of the Admiralty, telling Parliament that 'I have ruined, perhaps, my political career. But that is a little matter; I have retained something which is to me of great value – I can still walk about the world with my head erect'.[33] Churchill immediately passed Cooper a note from the backbenches congratulating him on a speech that was 'one of the finest Parliamentary performances I have ever heard'.[34] It was the first of more than 4,000 letters Cooper received following his resignation.[35] When Churchill became prime minister two years later, he immediately brought Cooper back into the cabinet as Minister of Information, Resident Cabinet Minister in Singapore and then Chancellor of the Duchy of Lancaster.

When the Foreign Secretary Anthony Eden offered him the position in Algiers, it was with the rank of ambassador and the expectation that he would continue as British Ambassador in Paris upon the liberation of France. Eden selected Cooper because of his close links to General Charles de Gaulle and because he shared his view that de Gaulle was the future of France, the man to whom 'the whole people of France would turn'.[36] For this same reason, however, Churchill was unconvinced that Cooper was the right man for the job, having developed distrust and hostility towards de Gaulle over the past three years. Consequently, before Churchill would confirm his appointment, he wrote to Cooper, laying out his vision for post-war Anglo–French relations: 'The help of Britain and the United States is essential to the building up again of a strong France which we both agree is a prime British interest'. However, de Gaulle had 'contracted a deep antipathy to both these countries'. The general was 'Fascist-minded, opportunist, unscrupulous, ambitious to the last degree', whose coming to power in a liberated France could only lead to 'a considerable estrangement between France and the Western Democracies'. Churchill feared that de Gaulle would do his utmost to split Great Britain from the United States and, failing that, to 'split them both from Russia'. This would result in a Europe more fragmented after the war than before. Consequently, de Gaulle could not become France, and France could not become de Gaulle. The future of France was too important to British interests to allow it to become severed from the United Kingdom and its allies.[37] Cooper replied that he would 'do all in his power to strengthen the [French] Committee [in Algiers] with a view to rendering it independent of any individual'. He added, rather cheekily, that 'an individual who had the reputation of being pro de Gaulle and no longer deserved it might prove a very suitable British envoy to the French Committee'.[38] Churchill was persuaded that Eden's judgment was correct and on 11 November 1943 he announced that Cooper would be appointed, to arrive in Algiers immediately in the New Year.

The relationship between Churchill and de Gaulle remained tense throughout the war. In the New Year (1944), the Prime Minister sent to de Gaulle an invitation for them to meet when Churchill passed through Algiers, which offended de Gaulle because the invitation was sent as if Churchill were 'in his own country and not in de Gaulle's'.[39] When they met on 12 January, 'Winston was in a bad mood .... and not very welcoming'.[40] This only further aggravated de Gaulle, who believed that Churchill was treating him in a manner unbecoming a statesman. Nevertheless, the tone soon softened and the meeting 'throughout was friendly'.[41] At its close, the General invited Churchill to review the French troops, during which there were cries of 'Vive Churchill' and 'Vive de Gaulle'. Once the Prime Minister departed, de Gaulle told those gathered that there had been a 'rebirth of the French army and [a] renewal of the Anglo–French alliance'.[42] After an inauspicious beginning, Churchill's visit turned out to be a 'great success', and Cooper wrote in his diary that the Prime Minister was 'very much moved' by the review and left in a 'heavenly mood – very funny and very happy'.[43]

Cooper was encouraged by this and set about his task of improving Anglo–French relations with renewed energy. He recognised as well as anybody that there were certain inherent differences between the French and the British[44] but was nevertheless convinced that following the end of the war the United Kingdom would have to give as much attention to the European continent as it gave to the Empire. On 30 May – just days before the Allied invasion of Normandy – he sent to Eden a long dispatch laying out his expectations for the post-war world and what he believed Europe's position within it would be. He cautioned against any British impulse towards isolation and warned that although the United States would undoubtedly continue as an important friend, 'the interests of the two countries were too divergent to render an [permanent] alliance between them expedient'. More importantly, Britain could not turn its back on Europe, given that 'our country, more than ever in the past, [is] a part of the Continent'. He predicted that security would be the foremost concern of most Europeans, and, for this, they could turn either to the Soviet Union or to Britain. Given that 'Russia, when Germany was eliminated, would present the gravest potential menace to the peace of the Continent', it was crucial that Europe should turn to Britain for leadership rather than to the Soviet Union. Since many European countries would follow France's lead, Anglo–French relations were of the utmost importance. The best way to ensure a European turn to Britain was to propose a 'federation of the western seaboard of Europe', including the United Kingdom, which – having practically 'the whole continent of Africa … at their disposal' – would become the 'strongest' of the three world powers: the United States, the Soviet Union and Europe.[45]

Eden, with an eye to Britain's wartime alliances with both the United States and Russia, thanked Cooper for the 'masterly way in which [he] had dealt with an issue of profound significance' but suggested that a federation of Western European countries would increase rather than decrease any danger from the Soviet Union, 'if indeed such a danger existed', and might offend the United States.[46] Exasperated, Cooper sent a second dispatch in August – five days after Paris was liberated – suggesting that as the United Kingdom would emerge from the war 'with greater honours than any other country', the 'leadership of Europe will await us'. He repeated his belief that British leadership should involve, at a bare minimum, both a political agreement and a defence scheme between Western European powers and cautioned that the United Kingdom might 'miss this opportunity' if its government were to 'hesitate to adopt a positive policy through fear of incurring the suspicion of Russia on the one hand or the disapproval of America on the other'. It was essential, he argued, that the British government not 'allow the formation of our European policy to wait either upon the ukases of the Kremlin or the votes of the American Senate'.[47]

In response to Cooper's dispatches, Eden contacted Lord Halifax, the British ambassador in Washington DC, to ascertain what the American government's response would be towards a Western European bloc including the United Kingdom. Halifax replied on 16 September 1944, assuring Eden that although the United States traditionally disliked 'blocs', a Western European bloc would be 'formed of countries with similar political structure, namely Western democracies, and of a similar development of economic and social civilisation'. It was therefore unlikely that the United States would raise many objections, particularly if the United Kingdom was involved, since 'Great Britain is regarded as the natural leader of Western Europe'. If anything, the United States would 'welcome any radical departure from the past which would point towards a degree of unification in Europe and hence, to American eyes, away from the fragmentation of the Continent'. If British leadership of an integrated Europe could guarantee continental stability, thus ensuring that the United States need not enter another European war, so much the better.[48]

Eden also sought advice from Oliver Stanley at the Colonial Office, Oliver Lyttelton at the Ministry of Production and Harold Macmillan, Minister Resident in the Mediterranean, all of whom supported Cooper's proposal. When the Foreign Secretary dug deeper into some of the issues Cooper had raised, he, too, began to see the reality of a post-war Soviet threat. He became particularly concerned after de Gaulle visited Moscow in December 1944, a visit that seemed to suggest that Cooper's fears of a split within Europe might come to pass, with the French drifting East rather than West. For this reason, he persuaded Churchill to lobby Stalin against a Franco–Soviet pact being signed, arguing that, following the war, he hoped the 1942 Anglo–Soviet alliance might be converted into a tripartite Franco–Anglo–Soviet pact. Stalin, however, was lukewarm about the British proposal and de Gaulle – accusing Churchill of meddling – immediately signed a Franco–Soviet pact that excluded Great Britain. Churchill instantly regretted his approach to Stalin, fearing that the Soviet rebuff had weakened Britain's hand against both the Soviet Union and France; consequently, he ordered Eden to make no more overtures for an Anglo–French post-war alliance.[49]

Having heard nothing from Eden, Cooper wrote again to the Foreign Secretary in March 1945. Now officially installed in Paris as the British Ambassador to France, he had become concerned following a telegram from Sir Hughe Knatchbull-Hugessen, the British Ambassador to Belgium, which revealed the apprehension felt by some Belgians of a 'French penetration and domination' of Europe following Germany's defeat. Sensing that Europe's leaders were already beginning to turn towards considerations of the post-war peace, Cooper argued that the time was right to push for the 'formation of a group of Western European democracies' including France but led by Britain.[50] Referencing Belgium's fears, he wrote that 'throughout our history the Low Countries have been of greater importance to the life of England than any other portion of the globe's surface' and suggested that the

United Kingdom ought to 'go to war rather than allow them to fall into the hands of a great power who might harbour aggressive intentions'.

Knatchbull-Hugessen had made it clear that it was 'to Great Britain that Belgium looks for leadership and security'. Cooper was convinced that 'Holland will soon be looking in the same direction'. He closed his letter with a stark warning to Eden: 'If we again hesitate to give that leadership, as we hesitated between the two great wars, the Powers concerned will be compelled to look elsewhere. ... [T]hey would prefer an alliance with Great Britain and France which would guarantee their independence and integrity rather than with France alone. ... But we must beware lest reluctance on the part of Great Britain to take a decision, or delay in taking it, drive those who would be our friends into the arms of others and leave us in a position of dangerous isolation'.[51]

Cooper's fears were only heightened the next month, when the French government began to increase its troop numbers in Syria and Lebanon where the British Army also had a substantial garrison. Foreign Office representatives in the Levant feared that this could only lead to trouble and instructed Cooper to go at once to see de Gaulle to demand an explanation.[52] He found de Gaulle in a 'most unyielding mood'. The General was convinced that British policy was to 'oust the French from the Levant' and Cooper was 'unable to dissuade him from this view'.[53] Consequently, he wrote to Eden on 4 May, expressing his 'considerable doubts about the wisdom of our present policy in the Levant' and reminding the Foreign Secretary that the British government had 'undertaken to recognise the pre-eminent position of France in the Levant and ... also undertaken that Syria and Lebanon shall receive their independence'. He warned that the present situation of French and British troops existing side by side would in time 'lead to grave trouble' and that the governments needed to instead forge a common Anglo–French policy. Unless the British government was willing to 'adopt the policy which we have repeatedly denied to be ours, that of getting the French out [of the Levant]', the only path remaining was to 'get out ourselves'.[54]

Within weeks, de Gaulle attempted to further reinforce French garrisons in Syria. When the Syrians objected, French forces bombarded Damascus, reducing much of it to rubble. Following protests from the Syrians, the British government unilaterally placed Syria under British martial law.[55] The government would go only so far to work with its

European ally; in the final analysis, British interests would always come first. For Cooper, the declaration was 'most regrettable', but he acknowledged that 'de Gaulle has brought it upon himself'.[56] It was not until 1946 that the situation was eventually resolved, with a joint British and French withdrawal from the Levant and the granting of independence to Syria and Lebanon.[57]

In the meantime, the war in Europe came to a close, although this left much unresolved. Despite himself, Duff Cooper's eyes filled with tears at the sound of the church bells ringing out on VE Day, which he later confessed were tears of sadness as much as joy: 'The Duke of Wellington was right when he said that a victory is the greatest tragedy in the world except a defeat'.[58] By that time, Churchill's stance on Europe and its place in the post-war world had become clear. He recognised that Britain's future lay as much in Europe as it did in the Empire, an assessment largely shared by Anthony Eden and Harold Macmillan. And whilst Churchill had gone further than other Britons in calling for a United States of Europe in 1938, his vision of a Britain that was at once imperial and European was not too far removed from the thinking of previous generations of Britons.

This view was only encouraged by the voluminous correspondence he received following the surrender of Germany, for example, from American President Harry S. Truman who declared that Britain had liberated 'the oppressed people of Europe',[59] and from King Haakon VII of Norway who conveyed to Churchill 'and to the British people my admiration and sincere gratitude for the magnificent part played by Great Britain in the defeat of all enemy forces'.[60] He was encouraged, too, by British civil servants such as Orme Sargent (soon to be Permanent Under-Secretary of the Foreign office) who wrote in early July 1945 that Britain, as the weakest of the 'Big Three', had to lead Western Europe as well as the Commonwealth in order to 'compel our two big partners to treat us as an equal'.[61] Sargent's influential memorandum laid out in clear terms an analysis that Churchill himself had developed over the past decade. Britain must lead Europe, yet such leadership could not undermine its concurrent role as head of the Empire and Commonwealth or its relationship with the United States. As Sargent wrote, 'To be a leading influence in each of those areas – Washington, the Commonwealth, and Western Europe – depend[s] on retaining a leading influence in the other two'.[62] Britain could not be either 'in' Europe or 'out' of Europe; it had to be both.

It was with this strongly held belief in the future greatness of both the British Empire and Britain's role in Europe that Churchill campaigned during the 1945 General Election, which had been triggered by the dissolution of the coalition. It was because of the strength of his convictions that he felt all the more aggrieved when the electoral results came in on 26 July 1945. The Labour Party had secured 393 seats to the Conservatives' 197, and Winston Churchill was Prime Minister no more.

* * *

One of the first to express his condolences to the Prime Minister on his defeat was Harold Macmillan, who was promoted Air Secretary following the collapse of the coalition government but lost his parliamentary seat in the face of the Labour landslide. He wrote to Churchill on 27 July, expressing that 'whatever may happen to me in the future will seem stale and shadowy compared to the pride of having played some part – however small – under your leadership'.[63] Others were not so gracious. Field Marshal Lord Alanbrooke wrote in his diary that 'It is probably all for the good of England in the long run' and mocked that 'If only Winston had followed my advice he would have been in at any rate till the end of the year! But what was my advice to him a mere soldier!!!'[64] Duff Cooper, likewise, remarked that 'the removal of Winston...will make my task [in France] easier' and noted his 'delight' at the defeat of fellow Conservatives Louis Spears and Alec Cunningham-Reid, each of whom had opposed his policy of Anglo–French cooperation in the Levant.[65] He also commented on Ernest Bevin, the most likely Labour candidate for Foreign Secretary, with whom he had 'always been on good terms' and who would thus have 'no personal reason for...wanting to get rid of me'.[66]

In Ernest Bevin, the new Prime Minister Clement Attlee had selected a man who greatly contrasted with his predecessor as Foreign Secretary. Noted for his striking good looks and aristocratic pedigree (his mother was Sybil Francis Grey of the famous Northumberland Greys and his father a baronet), Anthony Eden was blessed with an education at Eton and Christ Church, Oxford. Bevin, a full-framed, overweight man with increasing health problems, never knew his father and began work at the age of eleven as a labourer before becoming a lorry driver and eventually secretary of the Bristol branch of the Dockers' Union.[67] Throughout the First World War, Eden served as a commissioned officer in the army and won the Military Cross at the Battle of the Somme; Bevin argued that his role as a Trade Union organiser was as essential to the war effort as if he had put on a uniform, and he made repeated calls for the government to give greater recognition to the importance of organised labour in any victory.[68] Shortly after the war's close, Bevin co-founded the Transport and General Workers Union; Eden opposed the General Strike of 1926.[69] Whilst Eden held an aristocratic reserve and deference for the existing social order, Bevin was described by his private secretary Roderick Barclay as a man who had 'obtained freedom from any social or other prejudices', was 'boyish' with a 'strong sense of humour', and who, when meeting George VI, would 'put a large hand on the King's back and lead him to a corner where he would tell him some story which usually evolved roars of laughter'.[70] Eden was first elected to Parliament as a Conservative MP in 1923 and progressed loyally and rapidly through the ranks; Bevin did not enter Parliament until he was offered ministerial office in Churchill's coalition government in 1940. To his death, Bevin 'felt stronger loyalty towards his old Trade Union colleagues than towards the Labour Party as a whole'.[71]

Yet, despite their differences, Eden was not dismayed by the change of power, writing to Sir Alexander Cadogan, the Permanent Under-Secretary at the Foreign Office, that he was 'very glad that Bevin is to be my successor. He is the best man they have'.[72] Others shared this assessment. Lord Woolton – who became Chairman of the Conservative Party in 1945 – wrote that Bevin was 'the Churchill of the Labour Party and people had confidence in his common sense'.[73] Nevertheless, July 1945 was a difficult time for a transition of power to occur, with the ongoing Potsdam conference in which Attlee and Bevin rushed to replace Churchill and Eden in their meetings with Stalin and Truman. There was little Bevin could do at the conference to influence the agreement, which had already largely been drawn up. Nevertheless, it proved to be a useful meeting. Bevin saw with his own eyes Soviet Red Army troops in the ruins of Hitler's Chancellery and heard Stalin say, 'In politics one should be guided by the calculation of power'.[74] This, combined with a cold reception from Truman, convinced Bevin that the strong Transatlantic relationship of the previous four years might not survive the end of the war in the Pacific and that Britain's chief threat came from the Soviet Union dominating Europe, directly threatening Britain's traditional foreign policy of balancing continental power. Without an assurance of American aid, only a combination of states in Western Europe, under British leadership, could hope to arrest the expanding power of Russia.[75] His analysis was therefore remarkably similar to Duff Cooper's, whom he left in place at the British Embassy in Paris.

Immediately upon his return from Potsdam, Bevin convened a meeting with Foreign Office officials to discuss British policy towards Western Europe. He suggested that collaboration with Western European countries must form the 'cornerstone' of post-war British policy and revealed a 'grand design' to build economic, political and military cooperation. This design necessarily started with France, which, as the continent's largest democracy and a fellow colonial power, understood both Britain's role in Europe and its imperial interests. Once an agreement with France was secure, cooperation could be expanded to include the Low Countries, Scandinavia and, in time, Italy.[76] This did not mean that Bevin dismissed the centrality of empire to British interests, however. As his speech in the House of Commons on 20 August made clear, the British Empire was still 'central to Britain's position as a world power'.[77] Lord Halifax wrote to Bevin following his speech to say that his words had impressed American public opinion, which had feared a socialist revolution in Britain following the Labour victory, to the extent that many newspapers had declared that Bevin 'no more than Churchill would preside over the liquidation of the Empire'.[78]

Nevertheless, the new Foreign Secretary shared Churchill's belief that in the post-war world empire was not enough; Britain had to lead Europe also. This was a long-held conviction for Bevin, who had suggested in his union journal in 1938: 'The great colonial powers of Europe should pool their colonial territories and link them up with a European Commonwealth, instead of being limited to British, French, Dutch or Belgian concessions as is now the case. Such a European Commonwealth, established on an economic foundation, would give us greater security than we get by trying to maintain the old balance of Power'.[79] Like many of his contemporaries, Bevin was both an imperialist and a European.

Another European imperialist, Duff Cooper, was disappointed not to see greater movement towards European integration following the end of the war. In March 1946, he wrote to Bevin restating his earlier ideas and warning that 'Politicians and private people in this country

[France] are frankly puzzled as to the attitude of Great Britain. ... Members of my staff and I are plied with questions to which we find difficulty in replying. Do we want an alliance with France? Why do we do nothing about it? What is our view as to the future of Germany? Have we lost interest in Europe and do we believe that nothing matters but the United States?' There was, he suggested, only one solution. The time had come 'to count our friends, to fortify them and to bind them closely to our side'. Of these friends, 'France remains, despite her failures and perplexities, potentially the strongest and the richest on the continent. ... An Anglo–French alliance would form a potent magnet for others who are now looking round rather wildly in search of security and salvation'.[80]

Bevin shared Cooper's basic belief in the necessity of an Anglo–French alliance, but the situation was not as simple as Cooper made out. This was because Bevin's 'grand design' for Western Europe had been derailed on 21 August 1945, less than two weeks after he had unveiled it at the Foreign Office, when American President Harry S. Truman announced without warning that Lend-Lease would end.[81] Lend-Lease had been finalised in August 1941 at the Atlantic Conference in Placentia Bay, Newfoundland, when Churchill and Roosevelt met to discuss the future course of the war. In addition to issuing the Atlantic Charter – a statement of combined war aims – the leaders launched talks aimed at assisting the British through their economic woes, Churchill having admitted to Roosevelt in late 1940 that the nation was close to bankruptcy.[82] Lend-Lease was a program whereby the United States increased its own production and then lent or leased to the British government the surplus not needed in America. The United States government became, as one historian put it, 'both the treasury and the production facility for the Allied cause'.[83] By the close of the war, the United Kingdom was utterly dependent upon supplies from the United States for its national survival, its own industries entirely retooled from the export market to defence manufacturing.[84] The abrupt ending of Lend-Lease was a cruel blow indeed.[85]

In addition to Lend-Lease, during the war, the British government had also requisitioned all overseas investments with any liquidity whatsoever and sold them in the United States and Canada, totalling £1,118 million over the course of the war (a quarter of Britain's pre-war wealth). For the balance still remaining after Lend-Lease and the off-loading of foreign investments, the government incurred debts of

£3,555 million, particularly to Commonwealth countries.[86] What was the world's greatest creditor nation prior to the war had become the world's greatest debtor at its close. There was little the United Kingdom could fall back on, since in the early years of the war the government had traded many of its overseas bases for aged destroyers from the then-neutral United States.[87] And the situation showed no signs of relief; in 1946, the United Kingdom's deficit ran at £750 million.[88]

Following Truman's announcement of the ending of Lend-Lease, Attlee informed the House of Commons that Britain was now in a 'very serious financial position', and the famed economist John Maynard Keynes described it as 'without exaggeration a financial Dunkirk'.[89] In a memorandum to the cabinet, Keynes concluded that 'there is no source from which we can raise sufficient funds to enable us to live and spend on the scale we contemplate except the United States'. The alternative, he wrote, was 'a sudden and humiliating withdrawal from our onerous responsibilities with great loss of prestige and acceptance for the time being of the position of a second-class Power, rather like the present position of France'. He continued: 'From the Dominions and elsewhere we should seek that charity we could obtain. At home a greater degree of austerity would be necessary than we have experienced at any time during the war. And there would have to be an indefinite postponement of the realisation of the best hopes of the new Government'.[90] Britain would no longer be a great imperial power and the strongest European state, but would be turning to its former subordinates throughout the Commonwealth for whatever assistance they could give. Its only solution lay in the generosity of the American government.

Consequently, Keynes travelled to the United States with cap in hand to seek a grant-in-aid of $6 billion to cover the debts Britain had incurred fighting the war. He returned instead with a loan of $3.75 billion amortised over fifty years with an annual interest rate of 2 per cent.[91] In return for these 'generous' terms, the British government supported the Bretton Woods Agreement and American plans for a world trading system with convertible currencies. The government promised to introduce sterling convertibility by mid-1947 at the latest.[92] Brendan Bracken warned Paul Einzig, the *Financial Times* parliamentary lobby correspondent, that 'most Members of Parliament did not understand the implications of Bretton Woods', adding that 'nobody who has any knowledge of America will welcome such a development'.[93] His cautionary words were prescient. Under the terms of the loan, sterling was initially set at a fixed exchange rate of $4.03 to the pound. However, when in July 1947 it was made freely convertible against the dollar (as stipulated under the terms of the loan), there was a run on the pound; during the first twenty days of August alone the British Treasury lost $650 million.[94] The American Loan simply transferred Britain's debts from the Commonwealth to the United States; it was not until December 2006 that the final payment of $86 million was sent from the British Exchequer to the United States.[95] The costs of war bit deeply, indeed, paid for by generations.

It was not only in the economic sphere that Bevin faced challenges beyond Western Europe. He had been cautiously optimistic after meeting Stalin at Potsdam, telling the House of Commons that free elections would be held in Poland before the end of the year and would soon follow in Romania, Bulgaria and Hungary. Yet, at the first Conference of Foreign Ministers held in London in September 1945, Soviet Foreign Minister Vyacheslav Molotov informed Bevin that Soviet troops would remain wherever they were currently stationed, including in Poland, with Russia regarding the Eastern part of Europe as its natural sphere of influence.[96] This placed the British government in an especially difficult position in Germany, where it had hoped to reunite the various occupation zones as soon as was practicable. A policy of quick reunification was particularly attractive because the British sector was costing the cash-strapped Treasury colossal amounts to administer, £80 million in the first year alone.[97] The Soviet stance in London ensured there would be no quick resolution to the problem of occupied Germany.

Further afield, in Palestine, the revolt launched by Menachem Begin and the *Irgun Zvai Leumi* on 1 February 1944 was renewed on 1 November 1945 when the Irgun severed the Palestinian railway line in 242 places, sank three police naval vessels and detonated bombs at the main railway station in Jerusalem, destroying the station-master's office and badly damaging seven locomotives.[98] Since the Labour Party's victory in July, the American administration had placed increasing pressure on Attlee and Bevin to lift the restrictions of the 1939 White Paper, which had placed caps on Jewish immigration into Palestine. This pressure had culminated in a press conference on 16 August 1945 when President Truman informed the world's media that he had 'asked Churchill and Attlee to allow as many Jews as possible into Palestine'.[99]

Truman wrote to Attlee two weeks later, including with his letter a report from Earl G. Harrison, the dean of the University of Pennsylvania Law School and a US Congressman, which suggested that to alleviate the refugee problem in Europe an additional 100,000 Jews ought to be allowed to settle in Palestine.[100] Attlee curtly replied that the British government had problems across its empire, that, on the whole, it 'endeavoured to avoid treating people on a racial basis' and that they had 'the Arabs to consider as well', especially those in British India, which contained 'ninety million Moslems, who are easily inflamed'.[101]

The Irgun, recognising that Britain's policy under Labour promised to be little different from that of the Coalition before it, relaunched its campaign of violence to force Britain to withdraw from Palestine so that a Jewish state could be declared. This campaign of violence only stiffened Bevin's resolve, both as an imperialist in defence of the Empire and in his search for a European third force that would prevent British reliance on the United States. As Moshe Shertok, head of Palestine's Jewish Agency wrote, 'Bevin's anger and fury against the United States are unimaginable'. According to Shertok, Bevin said, 'I cannot bear English Tommies being killed. They are innocent'. When Chaim Weizmann, president of the World Zionist Organisation, reminded him of the millions of Jews who had been killed and were still dying in refugee camps, Bevin retorted, 'I do not want any Jews killed either, but I love the British soldiers. They belong to my class. They are working people'.[102]

In India itself, where Attlee's 'ninety million Moslems' resided, the combination of the Congress Party's 'Quit India' movement and Quaid-i-Azam Jinnah's calls for a new Muslim state of Pakistan was also placing pressure on the British government. On 19 September 1945, the British Viceroy Sir Archibald Wavell announced in New Delhi that the government would soon convene a 'Constitution-making body' to resolve the issues raised during the war, but Jinnah responded that the Muslim population would settle for nothing less than the partition of India into separate Hindu and Muslim states.[103] The response from the Congress Party was equally cold, and Wavell warned the cabinet on 6 November that the government must be prepared for 'the use of considerable force of British troops ... the declaration of martial law; the detention of a large number of persons without trial ... and the suppression for an indefinite period of the Congress Party'.[104] As in Palestine, in India, the British Empire seemed to be coming apart at the seams. It is little wonder that John Colville described Britain in late 1945 as entering a 'new terrifying era'.[105]

When Duff Cooper wrote to Bevin in March 1946 to draw his attention back to Western Europe, the situation in the Empire, with the Soviet Union and in Anglo–American relations had little improved; if anything, it had deteriorated. On 13 March – six days before Cooper's memorandum arrived on Bevin's desk – the Foreign Secretary informed the cabinet defence committee that he now considered the Mediterranean and Middle East rather than Europe Britain's most immediate security interest, a marked change from his view just six months before. The Mediterranean, he explained, was the area 'through which we bring influence to bear on Southern Europe, the soft underbelly of France, Italy, Yugoslavia, Greece, and Turkey'. If the British government withdrew from the Mediterranean, 'Russia will move in, and the Mediterranean countries, from the point of view of commerce and trade, economy and democracy, will be finished'. He did not need to remind the committee that the United Kingdom remained the 'last bastion of social democracy', uniquely placed between 'the red tooth and claw of American capitalism and the Communist dictatorship of Soviet Russia'. If the British Empire fell, a moderate and ordered way of life would be lost forever, and, without that, there was little point in pursuing policies of further cooperation in Europe. It was the Empire and all that it stood for that gave Britain the right to lead Europe.[106] And in 1946, that empire was resting on very shaky ground indeed.

2 MR CHURCHILL'S EUROPE

If Ernest Bevin felt bound by the heavy shackles of ministerial office, Winston Churchill was enjoying the freedom of opposition. He had, perhaps understandably, fallen into a deep depression after the General Election and although remaining as Conservative Party leader had spent more time at Chartwell, his family estate, than at Westminster. After a holiday to Italy, however, his spirits revived somewhat and, in November 1945, he travelled to France and Belgium.[1] Speaking at the French Institute in Paris, Churchill gave the first hints of his vision for post-war Europe, hoping that 'a new and happier Europe may one day raise its glory from the ruins we now see about us' and, perhaps flattering his French audience, that 'in this noble effort the genius, the culture and especially the power of France should play its true and incontestable role'.[2]

Four days later, speaking to a Joint Meeting of the Belgian Senate and Chamber in Brussels, Churchill went further. The time had come, he said, for Europe to shed its violent past. He heralded his own 'British island', which had 'repeatedly in the last four hundred years headed victorious coalitions against European tyrants', for once again holding the 'proud but awful responsibility of keeping the Flag of Freedom flying'. He spoke of Britain's 'special associations' – the British Empire, the Atlantic Alliance, and with Soviet Russia – and argued that they formed interlocking 'circles' under the umbrella of the United Nations, none prevailing over the other, and all coming together 'in such a way to make it indivisible and invincible'. Given the tragedies of the two world wars and the destructive capabilities of the atomic bomb, the only possible path to peace was for all states to come together 'under the guardianship of a world organisation'. Within this organisation, Churchill could see 'no reason' why 'there should not arise the United States of Europe, which will unify this Continent in a manner never known since the fall of the Roman Empire'.[3]

Leo Amery, a close friend of Churchill's since the Boer War, wrote to him immediately after the speech, saying that Britain could 'give a real lead to Europe and the world in this matter'.[4] For Amery to be moved in this way was significant, for he was a man known more for his ardent support of the Empire than for his sympathy with Europe. Having served as First Lord of the Admiralty and Colonial Secretary prior to the Second World War, in 1940, Churchill appointed him Secretary of State for India, a position he held until losing his parliamentary seat in the General Election of 1945.[5] Amery included with his letter a speech he had delivered at the University of London on 26 November, titled 'British Links with Europe'. He argued that Europe, rather than being 'merely a geographic expression', was instead a 'moral and cultural entity with a character and life of its own ... which has been built up on the three-fold foundation of Greek freedom, Roman law and order and Christian ethics'.

Although Britain lay outside Europe due to its 'very characteristic culture of [its] own' and its membership in 'an equal partnership of nations [the Commonwealth] distributed all over the world', Britain was nevertheless 'a nation of the European family intimately linked with Europe throughout our whole history'. In religion, philosophy, politics, literature, art and trade it was impossible to separate the history of Britain from that of the European continent, and British security was intimately tied to European stability. After the travesties of the Second World War, peace would only come to Europe through the 'creation of some sort of European union or association as the visible expression and focus of a new European patriotism'. It was up to Britain to take the lead in laying its foundations. Amery concluded that it was the 'duty' of the British Empire, as one born from Europe's heritage, to 'make our contribution to the saving of the old home of this world's greatest civilisation, to the rebirth of Europe as one of the world's great world units'.[6]

Nevertheless, beyond Amery's letter, Churchill received very few other responses to his Brussels speech, and, for the next year, his mind was elsewhere. He spent much of his time working on his *magnum opus*, his six-volume history of the Second World War, which he began writing in Italy in September 1945.[7] Travels throughout the United Kingdom and Europe followed, and, in the New Year, he embarked upon a trip to the United States. In an absence from Parliament that would today be unthinkable for a Leader of the Opposition, Churchill remained in the United States and Cuba for close to three months, only returning to London on 26 March. Whilst there, he travelled at the request of President Truman to the small town of Fulton, Missouri, to deliver a speech at Westminster College, uttering the now-famous words: 'From Stettin in the Baltic to Trieste in the Adriatic, an iron curtain has descended across the [European] Continent'. This was 'not the Liberated Europe we fought to build up', and only a closer Anglo–American unity could put it right: 'If the population of the English-speaking Commonwealth [could] be added to that of the United States with all that such co-operation implies in the air, on the sea, all over the globe and in science and in industry, and in moral force, there will be no quivering, precarious balance of power to offer its temptation to ambition or adventure. On the contrary, there will be an overwhelming assurance of security'.[8]

If Churchill's Fulton speech was later seen by historians as the beginning of the post-war 'special relationship', nothing was further from the truth at the time. *The Times* (London) criticised the dichotomy Churchill described between Communism and Western Democracy, arguing that they had 'much to learn from each other'.[9] In the United States, the response was universally hostile. The *Chicago Sun* accused Churchill of seeking 'world domination, through arms, by the United States and the British Empire';[10] the *Nation* claimed that Churchill had 'added a sizeable measure of poison to the already deteriorating relations between Russia and the Western Powers'; and the *Wall Street Journal* suggested that 'The United States wanted no alliance or anything that resembles an alliance, with any other nation'.[11] President Truman, in the face of the media furore, claimed at a press conference that he did not endorse Churchill's view and denied having seen an advanced copy of the speech, a blatant lie since he had read the words the night before and told Churchill they were 'admirable and would do nothing but good'.[12] To further his point, Truman instructed his Secretary of State, Dean Acheson, to miss a reception held for Churchill the following week in New York, which he had been scheduled to attend.[13]

When Churchill returned to Britain, he found his relationship with Bevin had become strained. He had given no advance warning of his Fulton Speech to anyone in the Labour Party and, although Bevin was largely in agreement with Churchill's analysis of the Soviet threat, the speech had started a fire-storm in the parliamentary Labour Party, with ninety-three Labour MPs tabling a motion of censure against Churchill.[14] Bevin was also increasingly frustrated at Churchill's continued interventions on British policy in Western Europe, the former Prime Minister telling representatives of the States-General of the Netherlands on 9 May 1946 that he hoped there would soon be built a 'world instrument of security' in which 'the Western democracies of Europe' would draw together 'in ever closer unity and association'. He repeated his words from Brussels that 'I see no reason why, under the guardianship of the world organisation, there should not ultimately arise the United States of Europe'.[15] When Churchill spoke to the House of Commons less than a month later, he shocked those present on both sides of the aisle with a call for the former Axis countries to be brought back into the European fold, asking if Parliament was willing, as following the First World War, to inflict 'the utmost severities ... on the vanquished'. Leaving his fellow parliamentarians with no doubt as to where he stood on the issue, he told them, 'Let Germany live. Let Austria and Hungary be freed. Let Italy resume her place in the European system. Let Europe arise again in glory, and by her strength and unity ensure the peace of the world'.[16]

Once again, the ardent imperialist Leo Amery wrote to Churchill, remarking that 'Somehow or other we must help to rebuild this old home of civilisation which we call Europe, first of all up to the present iron curtain, and eventually, I hope, up to the Curzon Line, which is the real frontier between Europe and Asia'.[17] Churchill was buoyed by Amery's support and, on 8 June 1946, wrote to Duff Cooper in Paris asking if he might visit.[18] Cooper agreed, and, in early July, Churchill travelled once again to the continent, stopping briefly in Luxembourg before travelling to Metz, France. By this stage, he had become firmly committed to the European cause and wrote to Viscount Cecil of Chelwood of his temptation to accept the pre-war offer from Aristide Briand to succeed him as President of the Pan-European Union. He explained: 'I have a feeling that an immense amount of pro-British sentiment, in Western Europe at any rate, could be evoked by my working in this association' and added that the 'United States of

Europe movement... might become very big indeed, and a potent factor for world peace'.[19] In France, he renewed his calls for a united Europe, telling his audience at Metz that the Second World War had 'woven our two peoples together in a manner indissoluble and inviolable'.[20]

Upon returning to the United Kingdom, the Conservative leader's belief that only Europe could ensure its own security was confirmed when, on 1 August 1946, President Truman signed into law the McMahon Act forbidding the United States government from sharing further any of its nuclear secrets with any other country, including Great Britain. This was a direct reversal of the Quebec Agreement signed between Churchill and Roosevelt in 1944 and seemed to realise Duff Cooper's earlier fears of an America that would turn its back on the United Kingdom once the war was over.[21] Feeling worn by the state of world affairs, Churchill departed England on 23 August for three weeks' holiday in Switzerland, spending his time painting and working on his war memoirs with no official engagements. Churchill broke his seclusion only once, travelling on 16 September to Geneva to meet with the President and Committee of the International Red Cross and from there to Berne before finally arriving in Zurich on 18 September, where he was scheduled to give a speech at the University of Zurich.

Churchill chose as his topic 'the tragedy of Europe' and repeated his sentiments that if Europe – 'the fountain of Christian faith and Christian ethics... the origin of most of the culture, arts, philosophy and science both of ancient and modern times' – if this Europe 'were once again united in the sharing of its common inheritance, there would be no limit to the happiness, to the prosperity and glory which its three or four hundred million people would enjoy'. The only way to 're-create the European family', Churchill argued, was to 'build a kind of United States of Europe'. In clearer language than he had used to this point, he proclaimed that 'If Europe is to be saved from infinite misery, and indeed from final doom, there must be an act of faith in the European family'. This act of faith, he said, must be a 'partnership' between France and Germany, with France restored to the 'moral leadership' of Europe and Germany given absolution for its recent sins. This United States of Europe should be one where 'Small nations will count as much as large ones and gain their honours by their contribution to the common cause'. Once France, Germany and the smaller European nations were reconciled spiritually – as must happen – the first step would be to form a 'Council of Europe' where all European governments would come together in common cause. Great Britain and the British Commonwealth would be 'the friends and sponsors of the new Europe' and would 'champion its right to live and shine'.[22]

If these last lines seemed to suggest that the United Kingdom might sit outside this United States of Europe, Churchill clarified his position shortly thereafter in an article in *Collier's Weekly*. He wrote that Great Britain, 'lying in the centre of so many healthy and beneficent networks, is not only the heart of the British Empire and Commonwealth of Nations, and an equal partner in the English-speaking world, but it is also a part of Europe and intimately and inseparably mingled with its fortunes'. He wrote of what '*we*' have to do. All those living in Europe 'have to learn to call themselves Europeans, and act as such so far as they have political power, influence or freedom. If we cannot get all countries, we must get all we can; and there may be many. Once the conception of being European becomes dominant among those concerned a whole series of positive and practical steps will be open'. He repeated his call for the establishment of a 'Council of Europe' but also advocated 'some common form of defence' and a 'uniform currency'. He wrote, 'As we have to build from chaos this can only be achieved by stages. Luckily coins have two sides, so that one can bear the national and the other the European superscription. Postage stamps, passports, trading facilities, European social reunions for cultural, fraternal and philanthropic objects will flow out naturally along the main channel soon to be opened'. He closed his article claiming that 'talk of a "Western bloc" ... is too narrow a scheme. Nothing less than Europe and Europeanism will generate the vital force to survive'.[23] In Zurich and on the pages of *Collier's Weekly*, Churchill firmly attached his flag to the mast of European unity.

***

Ernest Bevin owed a great deal to Winston Churchill. Not only had the former Prime Minister brought him into government with an appointment to the Cabinet in 1940 and found him a safe seat in Parliament to support his ministerial career, he had also proved far more responsive to the role of organised labour in Britain than had Neville Chamberlain or Stanley Baldwin before him. This was perhaps surprising given the known distrust of and animosity towards Churchill from the working classes dating back to his time as Home Secretary in 1910, when he had allowed soldiers to support the local constabulary against coal miners in South Wales during the Tonypandy Riots. Nevertheless, as Attlee put it, Chamberlain 'always treated us like dirt' and at least Churchill was unfailingly courteous.[24] Besides, Churchill seemed to put the national interest above mere pride and prejudice. Upon his appointment as Prime Minister in 1940, he had selected the Labour Leader as his Deputy, telling him that 'it was vitally important that organised labour in industry should be represented' and asking whom he ought to appoint as Minister of Labour and National Service.[25] Attlee immediately pointed to Bevin, who became one of Churchill's most ardent supporters in the Labour Party throughout the war years.[26]

Yet Churchill did not seem to understand the complexities of the post-war world. His greatest strength during the war had been his single-minded devotion to the cause, his unshakeable faith in the rightness of British action and his resolve to mobilise all elements of society in the service of a single purpose. But what was the aim in foreign policy now that the war was over? The pre-war expectations of a British Empire that would 'last a thousand years' and the black and white wartime world of Allied versus Axis had evaporated into a greyness of uncertainty in the Empire, in a devastated Europe and with the Soviet Union. This did not mean that Bevin failed to hold strong convictions about foreign affairs; he did, on many issues with as much if not more passion than Churchill himself. Through his work in the international trade union movements he had come to detest Communism and all it stood for and had criticised Churchill following the Yalta Conference of February 1945 for being too 'soft' on the Soviet Union.[27] He was an avid supporter of the British Empire, which he regarded as 'the greatest collection of free nations' the world had ever seen, and, on arriving in Potsdam as the new Foreign Secretary in July 1945, he had thrilled British officials there with his belief that of the Big Three, 'we were still the biggest'.[28] Yet given the fragility of the peace, the immediate post-war period was a time not for bold visions and sweeping statements but for hard negotiation, close attention to immediate problems and, above all else, a pragmatic, rational approach to what could actually be achieved.

Of all the areas in which Churchill's post-war behaviour was most unhelpful to Bevin, the situation in Europe surely took the prize. What was particularly galling were Churchill's repeated assertions that the Labour government – and the Foreign Secretary in particular – were in some way blocking the road to a free, prosperous and united Europe which under a Churchill government would have been achieved already. His Zurich speech seemed to suggest as much, with its call for action. Yet as far as Bevin was concerned, nothing could be further from the truth. Although Bevin had been forced to abandon his 'grand design' for Europe in the face of the collapse of Lend-Lease, he had held his first official meeting with French Foreign Minister Georges Bidault and French Ambassador René Massigli at Chequers, the Prime Minister's country estate, in early September 1945. He had assured Bidault that the British government wished to 'return to the traditional basis of friendship with France', one of imperial kinship where the two countries would 'present a common front in the Middle East' and other areas of colonial responsibility.[29] From that time forward, Bevin worked to realise Duff Cooper's dream of a close Anglo–French alliance and, in the summer of 1946, instructed the Foreign Office to prepare a paper exploring 'the possible need for close economic cooperation with Western Europe' as a whole, 'in case the policy [has] to be put into operation at short notice'.[30]

On 5 September 1946 – almost two weeks before Churchill's Zurich speech – Sir Edmund Hall-Patch of the Foreign Office submitted the draft paper, arguing that the British government should 'expect not only that the Eastern half of Europe will be excluded altogether from the general free expansion of trade, but also that the U.S.S.R. will seek to expand its political and economic influence into Western Europe'. The only way to prevent this, Hall-Patch argued, was for the British government to pursue 'measures which, involving close economic ties, would bind Western European countries politically more closely to ourselves'. At the heart of this 'Western solidarity' must be 'firm economic ties between the U.K. and France'.[31] A month later, Bevin told Bidault that the British government had decided that 'the time had now come when the tourist traffic to England should be encouraged'; consequently, he wished to offer the French government an arrangement for the 'mutual abolition of visas'. Bidault readily agreed, and the two foreign secretaries prepared a statement to be issued to the Press on 12 October confirming their decision.[32] Winston Churchill could proclaim dramatic constitutional change to his heart's delight, but Bevin knew that real change only occurred through small steps and allowances that incrementally led to something much greater over time.

At their meeting, Bidault also raised the issue of coal supplies. He explained that, since the end of the war, France had been required to buy coal from the United States, paying in gold at twice the cost of production. The Communists in France were arguing that coal from Poland would make far more sense. De Gaulle was further stirring the pot by claiming that all coal for France should be taken from occupied Germany. The political pressure on the French government was enormous, and Bidault feared a backlash from the public. He pleaded with Bevin for any relief on the coal front; imports from Great Britain or the British Zone in Germany would be far more palatable, politically speaking, than from the United States, and would undermine the Communists' argument that coal should be imported from Poland. Bevin sympathised with Bidault but explained that Britain was facing its own coal shortages. In Germany, the British were doing all they could to increase production in their zone, but, ultimately, any progress was at the whim of German cooperation. Bidault then turned to their North American allies, arguing that 'France and Great Britain must not allow themselves to be led by the United States'. He claimed that the American approach to foreign affairs was too 'light-hearted', and if there was another war, there was no guarantee the United States would again come to the aid of Europe. France was ready to 'go along alone' with Great Britain. Bevin did not contradict him, instead suggesting that they talk about the matter privately.[33] Whilst no record exists of their private talks, following their conversation, Bevin instructed the Foreign Office to take an ever more active role in exploring Anglo–French cooperation.

This did not mean, however, that Bevin was abandoning the British commitment to its empire. On the contrary, the closeness he felt for France stemmed in large part from its position as a fellow *imperial* power. On 18 January 1947, the British Embassy in Washington DC sent to the Foreign Office a summary of a speech given by John Foster Dulles on foreign policy at the National Publishers Association dinner. Dulles had informed his audience that, given the increasingly hostile attitude of the Soviet Union, the United States must begin to think of Germany 'more in terms of the economic unity of Europe and less in terms of the Potsdam dictum that Germany shall be a single economic unit'. In this speech, he quoted Clement Attlee's pre-war statement that 'Europe must federate or perish'. The *New York Times* opined that Great Britain's attitude towards European integration would 'depend on its decision whether it was an Empire or a continental power'.[34]

At Bevin's instruction, officials at the Foreign Office returned guidance notes to the British Embassy, stating '[T]here is no question of this country having to decide between being an imperial power or a continental power, since it is perfectly possible for it both to be a full partner in the Commonwealth and to play its part in Europe. A choice of this kind has never presented itself to us and there is no reason why it should do so now'.[35]

In Bevin's mind, that Britain and France were imperial powers did not preclude them from moving towards closer cooperation in Europe. It was precisely *because* both Britain and France were imperial powers that they could integrate so well. They held similar worldviews and had a shared commitment to their overseas possessions and territories. Indeed, it was their empires that gave them strength in Europe. He was not the only member of the Labour government to feel this way. On 17 August 1946, the cabinet approved a statement by Herbert Morrison, the Deputy Prime Minister, for distribution to all overseas departments, the Central Office of Information, the British Council and all diplomatic posts, including those in Western Europe. After proclaiming the many virtues of the British way of life,[36] the statement declared that Britain was 'the centre of a world-wide association of peoples', one of the 'major world powers', and 'particularly fitted to take a leading part in international affairs'. This worldwide association of peoples was the British Commonwealth, and, under the Labour government, the United Kingdom would continue to 'push forward with schemes for the enlightenment and welfare of the Colonial peoples and for giving them an ever-increasing measure of self-government'.[37] In 1946, it was impossible for the Foreign Secretary, the Deputy Prime Minister and the Labour government as a whole to envision a leading world role for Britain without the British Empire. It was equally difficult for Bevin to contemplate a future in which the United Kingdom would not be one of the world's great powers – and a great *European* power at that. On this point, at least, Bevin was in complete agreement with Churchill.

* * *

The response to Churchill's Zurich speech was immediate. *The Daily Mail* opined that Churchill, demonstrating 'the supreme attribute of statesmanship', had spoken 'wise and true'. *The Times* reported that he was 'not afraid to startle the world with new and even, as many must find them, outrageous propositions' and found his inclusion of

Germany in this imagined United States of Europe particularly 'challenging'.[38] The provincial press also took note; Devon's *Western Morning News* reported that his appeal was 'one of the most important and necessary that could be launched at this moment', although, like *The Times*, was troubled by Churchill's vision for Germany.[39] Leo Amery had no such reservations, telling Churchill that he had 'lit a torch to give its message of hope to shattered Europe'. He continued: 'The French are startled, as they were bound to be, but the idea will sink in all the same. As for the Germans your speech may have been just in time to save them from going Bolshevist. You have done few bigger things, even in the great years behind us'.[40] Amery also wrote to Duncan Sandys, Churchill's son-in-law, saying that 'Winston has indeed done the big thing in a big way'. He was excited at the prospect of linking the British Empire and Commonwealth with a European Commonwealth and suggested that the upcoming Conservative Party conference in Blackpool would be the ideal platform to launch his vision in the United Kingdom. He was sure the party was 'in the mood for responding to a vision and a positive policy, whether in foreign affairs or otherwise ... Zurich as seen from the Empire angle would have a great and lasting reception'.[41]

Sandys had already been in conversation with Churchill about the United States of Europe. Shortly after his Zurich speech, Churchill tasked him with establishing an interparty group that could promote his idea both in Britain and on the European continent.[42] On 11 October 1946, Sandys presented Churchill with his first draft of the statement of aims for the 'European Union (British Branch)', an organisation he hoped to spread throughout the continent with separate national branches all working towards the same general aim. His statement read: 'Our first loyalty in this country is to the British Empire and Commonwealth, but we are convinced that the freedom and welfare of its people are intimately bound up with the freedom and welfare of the peoples of Europe'. The aim, he wrote, was to 'unite all Europe from the Atlantic to the Black Sea', 'neither dependent on, nor opposed to, the Soviet Union or the U.S.A.'. If the countries of Eastern Europe were unable to join at this time, then 'the countries of Western Europe should make a start on their own, always leaving it open to the other states to join later as and when they can'. With its 'associated Dominions and Dependencies', the European Union would command resources every bit as great as the United States of America and Soviet Union. Britain's 'sacrifices give us the right, our victory imposes on us the duty and our interests confirm the wisdom of giving a lead to the European nations and assuring them of our fullest support in whatever effort they are willing to make towards a United Europe'.[43] He informed Churchill that the British Branch would hold its first meeting on 3 December, for which he had already received acceptances to attend from Leo Amery, Robert Boothby, Ernest Brown, George Gibson, Victor Gollancz, Commander King-Hall, Sir Walter Layton, Sir David Maxwell-Fyfe and Lady Rys-Williams, with Oliver Stanley sending his regrets for the December meeting but pledging his future support to the cause.[44]

Churchill's only response was to bring the meeting forward from 3 December to 17 October. On that day, the newly formed committee – with Churchill in the chair and Sandys acting as its General Secretary – voted to adopt Sandys' statement of aims, pledging to 'form an international movement with sections in every European country'.[45] Each committee member agreed to do his or her utmost to promote the idea and to reach out across party lines. On 20 October, Churchill wrote to National Coal Board member and Labour Peer Lord Citrine encouraging him to join the movement, explaining that 'Without the resurrection and reconciliation of Europe there is no hope for the world', and, on 9 November, he wrote to the Viscount Camrose, the Trade Unionist George Gibson and Labour Member of Parliament George Hicks asking if each would join the committee and if the former would serve as its honorary treasurer.[46] Whilst the Conservative Peer Lord Camrose immediately agreed, Viscount Citrine declined, claiming it would conflict with his activities on the coal board, and George Hicks – after taking 'a few soundings' – likewise turned down Churchill's offer. Consequently, Churchill wrote to Prime Minister Clement Attlee, angrily telling him that participation in the United Europe Committee was not 'contrary to Party interests of any kind' and expressing his hope that 'no general directions will be given preventing any Members of the [Labour] Parliamentary Party from taking part in it'.[47]

Whilst Churchill waited for a reply from Attlee, he received a note from Sandys summarising his conversation of 28 November with French General Charles de Gaulle, still a prominent public figure in France despite having resigned as Prime Minister in January 1946. The General was optimistic about the idea of greater European unity and 'undoubtedly believes firmly in this project'. However, he was sceptical of Churchill's emphasis on Franco–German reconciliation, which 'all Frenchmen were violently opposed to' and feared 'would become nothing else than an enlarged Germany'. De Gaulle wanted France to 'come in as a founder partner with Britain' but would only agree to do so if the British government first agreed to 'a permanent allocation of coal from the Ruhr; consent[ed] to the continuance of French military occupation in Germany over a long period and possibly the incorporation of the Northern Rhineland in the French Zone; [allowed] the establishment of a regime of international control of the Ruhr industries satisfactory to France; [gave] fuller recognition of French interests in Syria; [and reached] an Anglo–French agreement to adopt a common line towards the Arab countries'.

Sandys' general impression of de Gaulle was that he was 'fully convinced of the desirability of European Union and would from time to time, when he thought fit, express his qualified agreement with the idea' but that he was 'far too much of an individualist to consider working together with any group of people, either in France or abroad, on any project which he had not himself initiated'. De Gaulle's suggestion of a joint Anglo–French approach, followed by his lengthy list of prerequisite demands, was his attempt to take control of the process and manipulate it to serve French interests. Sandys had informed de Gaulle that 'it would be most unfortunate if France's support for the cause of close European co-operation were to be made dependent upon the settlement of all kinds of extraneous issues', to which de Gaulle had 'stuck to his point', saying 'Voilà mes conditions'.[48] De Gaulle's attitude made the British approach to European unity more difficult. A greater feeling of 'European-ness' could not be built on a foundation of unbridled national interest.

Nevertheless, Churchill and Sandys remained encouraged, and, on 30 November, Lord Moran, Churchill's personal physician, noted in his diary that 'In the past twelve months his [Churchill's] spirits have risen and his vigour has come back. He has put vain regrets away; once more there is a purpose in life'.[49] Meanwhile, Leo Amery wrote in the *Sunday Times* that the only hope for the future peace of the world and British prosperity lay in the creation of a United Europe rather than British alignment with either the Soviet Union or the United States. Britons were 'all with America in her love of freedom' but could not 'subscribe to her doctrine of an uncontrolled world economy'. Amery argued that Britain should not 'sacrifice our own trade and employment at home or the strength and unity of the Empire in order to promote American economic imperialism', but should instead provide leadership in Europe, using its own Commonwealth as a model 'more suited to European conditions than the rigid federal system of the United States or of the Soviet Union, with its partial surrender of sovereignty'. In perhaps his most striking line, Amery wrote: 'We owe it to ourselves as well as to Europe to give a lead on this issue'.[50]

Duncan Sandys congratulated him on the piece, but warned against dismissing a federal solution in public. He noted that, from his talks with 'various Left-Wing peoples', the committee would 'obtain more ready support from the Labour and Liberal Parties if our manifesto contains some general reference to the ultimate desirability of world federation'.[51] Amery believed that 'all organisations of a worldwide character [were] mischievous and calculated to lead to war'. Nevertheless, he subordinated his principles to the wider goal of European unity: '[A]s long as world government is definitely relegated to a remote future I do not feel that I can seriously object to your modifying the wording if it is regarded as essential to bring people together'.[52] At a speech in Hull later that month, he told his audience that 'European unity was an aim well worth striving for. A united Europe was a valuable complement to a united Empire'.[53]

By the end of the year, Churchill's European vision was widely known. Summarising it, Harold Macmillan wrote that 'Britain could in his [Churchill's] view play a full role in Europe without loss or disloyalty to the traditions of her Empire and Commonwealth'.[54] There was no question of deciding between the two, nor of Britain simply standing on the sidelines of continental Europe to cheer her on. On 28 December 1946, Churchill wrote to the Archbishop of Canterbury, Geoffrey Fisher, inviting him to join the movement, saying, 'The impact of this initiative on public opinion will largely depend on the representative character of those who sponsor it. The sentiments to which we must appeal and the forces which we seek to stir are rooted in the spiritual depths of our fellow men and women. It is therefore essential that from the outset we should have the support of the Churches throughout Europe'.[55] He included with his letter the Statement of Aims, where he had written, 'If Europe is to survive, it must unite.... The aim must be to unite all the peoples of Europe and give expression to their sense of being Europeans while preserving their own traditions and identity'. The United Kingdom's role in all this was clear: 'Britain has special obligations and spiritual ties which link her with the other nations of the British Commonwealth. Nevertheless, Britain is an integral part of Europe and must be prepared to make her full contribution to European unity'.[56] Britain was the head of a great empire. But Britons were also European. And, as the year 1947 dawned, Churchill and his followers were convinced that the United Kingdom had to be at the heart of both.

* * *

When the British United Europe Committee held its official launch on 16 January 1947, twenty-one members sat on its steering committee. Although the Archbishop of Canterbury was not amongst them, he had spoken with Leo Amery and told him that he was 'most sympathetic to our general idea'; the only reason he had not joined himself was for the fear that it be construed as him 'commit[ting] the Church as a whole to the project'. He did, however, recommend the Dean of St Paul's to join the committee 'as an indication of Church support' and said he would also prompt the Bishop of York to do likewise.[57] With Winston Churchill in the chair and Duncan Sandys its secretary, the committee included the Liberal Nationalist MP Ernest Brown and the Labour MP Evelyn King; the self-described Christian Socialist and co-founder of the Left Book Club Victor Gollancz; the Secretary of the Congregational Union of England and Wales the Rev Dr Sidney Berry; the Welsh Congregationalist Minister and Labour MP the Rev Gordon Lang; the chairman of the *Economist* newspaper group Sir Walter Layton; the academics Lionel Curtis, Gilbert Murray and Bertrand Russell; and the Master of Balliol College, Oxford, and Labour Peer Lord Lindsay of Birker, in addition to the Conservatives Robert Boothby, Sir David Maxwell-Fyfe, Oliver Stanley and Lady Rhys-Williams.[58] The composition of the committee was exactly as Churchill had hoped, with strong cross-party participation and representatives from the political, spiritual and academic worlds.

Its formation made an immediate stir across the country. Newspapers as diverse as the Aberdeen-based *Press and Journal* and the *Yorkshire Post* gave full front-page spreads to the formation of the committee, and, from Devon to Dundee, the news was prominently reported.[59] In response, one reader from Leeds enthusiastically wrote that it was 'the happiest augury yet to emerge for the future of not only our race but all the peoples of the earth'.[60] Nevertheless, the political divisions inherent on the committee soon began to rear their ugly heads. In a meeting open to the general public on 22 January, Lionel Curtis encouraged the committee to look beyond Europe, arguing that 'In a world divided into fifty or sixty states, world war is absolutely inevitable. Nothing can prevent repeated world wars and the utter destruction of civilisation until states learn to fuse their sovereignty into an entity so strong that no aggressor is going to attack them'. The European Union, he hoped, would in time lead to 'a world government', a concept that Leo Amery indicated was unacceptable. Curtis also suggested that, as greater world unity would take time, the committee should support as a temporary measure Churchill's concept of first bringing together the willing governments of Western Europe, after which the Eastern European countries could join if and when circumstances allowed. J. L. Gibson objected to this, arguing that an attempt only to unite Western Europe would be read by the Soviet Union as designed 'not against a vacuum, but against Russia'. Ian MacTaggart suggested that, on the contrary, a 'Federation of Europe' was the best way to *prevent* war with Russia because the latter had fought hard since the end of the war to retain its 'imperialistic conquests'. Craven Ellis added that unless Britain strove for a United States of Europe, with or without the Eastern countries, it would 'have war in the '50s'. Russia had to be deterred.

Seeing that the committee was descending into bickering, Lady Rhys-Williams intervened, arguing that 'the danger of war comes from weakness and disunity'. European unity was essential, but 'France and the other nations fear Germany so much that they may resist the idea of European unity because of the enormous power of Germany'. Britain's role, therefore, was to be a 'balancing factor', a role it had played throughout its history. Britain and France working together at the heart of a United States of Europe would give the other European countries 'more confidence' and would therefore allow Germany to be brought back into the fold. It was in Britain's 'essential' interests to be part of European integration, the first practical steps of which would be 'the linking up of transport, the abolition of visas, and the development of facilities of all sorts, quite apart from weapons, economic or military'. A Mr Cameron agreed, arguing that a united Europe would 'provide a common currency and remove the obsolete idea of export for its own sake'. He added that within the union, 'Sovereignty must be merged and not surrendered'.[61] The meeting ended without resolution but was an early indicator to Churchill that developing a consensus in the United Kingdom around a single vision of a United States of Europe was not going to be easy.

Churchill's committee received a further setback when the National Executive Committee of the Labour Party sent a letter to all its members stating that although the Labour Party found it 'desirable to encourage maximum co-operation between the nations of Europe', Churchill's United Europe Committee was 'not likely to stimulate such co-operation at the present time'. It argued instead that the future of Europe was dependent on the 'strengthening of friendly collaboration between Russia, America, and Britain' and accused Churchill of explicitly excluding the Soviet Union from Europe in accordance with 'his personal record and his known opinions'. For this reason, the National Executive Committee advised all Labour members – both parliamentary and otherwise – to withhold their support from the United Europe Committee.[62] This letter placed those Labour members who had already joined the committee in a difficult position. Lord Lindsay of Birker wrote to Churchill on 5 February explaining that he had discussed the matter with Gilbert Murray, and they had called a meeting with all those committee members in the Labour Party to 'consider our position'. He added that, regardless of the outcome of the meeting, both he and Murray believed that Britain had an integral role to play in European affairs but must do so without prejudicing its leadership of the Empire and Commonwealth or its relationship with the United States of America.[63]

Whilst the Labour members considered their options, Count Richard Coudenhove-Kalargi – the Austrian author of the 1923 book *Pan Europa* and one of the earliest advocates of European integration – followed Churchill's calls for a United States of Europe with interest. He was encouraged by Churchill's speech in Zurich, and, in early spring 1947, began to drum up support for the idea in the United States, where he had lived and worked as a professor at Columbia University since 1940. On 24 March, he wrote to Duncan Sandys to inform him that he had persuaded American Senators J. William Fulbright and Elbert Thomas to put before the US Congress a resolution in support of a United States of Europe. Representative Hale Boggs had agreed to champion the resolution within the House of Representatives. Coudenhove-Kalargi believed that this was 'the best thing that could happen here. It will have great repercussions in Europe, because only

American support can counterbalance the Russia opposition to our plans'.[64] He also wrote to Churchill, telling him that 'we Europeans should not leave the initiative to the Congress of the United States'. Rather, 'European parliaments ought immediately [to] vote similar resolutions'. In particular, he urged Churchill to 'take the initiative to submit together with a group of Laborites and Liberals such a resolution to the British Parliament and have it adopted with a strong majority'.[65] The Count, however, was unaware of the letter sent from Labour's National Executive Committee to its members. Without the support of the Prime Minister, Foreign Secretary and Labour's rank and file, such a parliamentary resolution would go nowhere.

Given Labour's parliamentary opposition, Churchill decided that the United Europe Committee would have to operate in an extra-parliamentary manner. The best way to do this, he concluded, was to officially launch the campaign for a United Europe with a public rally at the Royal Albert Hall in London, changing the name of his group from the United Europe Committee to the United Europe Movement. This he scheduled for 14 May 1947, when he planned to put forward a Resolution in favour of a United States of Europe similar to that introduced to the American Congress by Senator Fulbright, placing it before the court of public opinion rather than a parliamentary chamber.[66] In a remarkable coup for his movement, Churchill asked the Archbishop of Canterbury to chair the meeting who, despite his earlier reservations, happily agreed.[67]

When Churchill rose to speak at the Albert Hall, he left his audience in no doubt of his convictions: 'It has been finely said by a young English writer, Mr Sewell, that the real demarcation between Europe and Asia is no chain of mountains, no natural frontier, but a system of beliefs and ideas which we call Western Civilisation.... These are not my words, but they are my faith; and we are here to proclaim our resolve that the spiritual conception of Europe shall not die'. Europe, he said, was now a 'rubble-heap, a charnel-house, a breeding-ground of pestilence and hate' but with its 'tropical and colonial dependencies', its 'long-created trading connections' and its 'modern production and transportation', it could 'restore itself to greatness'. Turning to specifics, Churchill first addressed France, which must 'go forward hand in hand' with Britain and 'must in fact be founder-partners in this movement'. Yet an Anglo–French alliance was not enough; without the involvement of Germany, there could be no

European unity: '[O]n the wider stage of a United Europe German industry and German genius would be able to find constructive and peaceful outlets. . . . It is for France and Britain to take the lead. Together they must, in a friendly manner, bring the German people back into the European circle'.

And what of the British Empire and Commonwealth? To this question, Churchill had his reply: 'We are the centre and summit of a world-wide commonwealth of nations. It is necessary that any policy this island may adopt towards Europe and in Europe should enjoy the full sympathy and approval of the peoples of the Dominions. But why should we suppose that they will not be with us in this cause? They feel with us that Britain is geographically and historically a part of Europe, and that they also have their inheritance in Europe. If Europe united is to be a living force, Britain will have to play her full part as a member of the European family'. Gone was the earlier ambivalence of Churchill's pre-war speeches and articles. The United Kingdom was 'profoundly blended' with Europe – was, indeed, European – and it would be a 'prime mover' in the cause of a United Europe.[68]

Churchill's speech was met with enthusiastic press coverage across the country, the *Western Morning News*, for example, calling the meeting a 'great gathering' and declaring that Churchill's case was 'a strong one'.[69] Not all Conservatives saw Europe in the same light as Churchill, however. Harold Macmillan, who had supported his leader's views from the beginning, wrote that 'a considerable portion of the Conservative Party were doubtful and even anxious about this new movement. They feared . . . that in one way or another, both on the political and on the economic side, Britain's position as head of the Empire and Commonwealth might be prejudiced'.[70] Leo Amery also encountered this. In the movement's defence, he explained to Sir Herbert Williams that European unity was important both as a 'friendly neutral buffer strong enough to hold its own' between the United Kingdom and the Soviet Union and because 'Europe lies athwart our air and sea communications with all the Empire except Canada and the West Indies'. It was better for Britain to play its full part and seek to lead a United Europe from within than to remain outside.[71]

Churchill's calls for a United Europe received an enormous boost in June 1947 when the American Secretary of State George Marshall delivered an address at Harvard University announcing plans for American aid to Europe, which would eventually become known as the Marshall Plan. Speaking on 5 June, Marshall declared that 'Europe's requirements for the next three or four years of foreign food and other essential products – principally from America – are so much greater than her present ability to pay that she must have substantial additional help, or face economic, social and political deterioration of a very grave character'. Such deterioration would have great negative effects on the American economy, and thus the US government would do 'whatever it is able to do to assist in the return of normal economic health'. It would only do so, however, when there was 'some agreement among the countries of Europe as to the requirements of the situation and the part those countries themselves will take'. Marshall's aid program must be 'the business of Europeans', must 'come from Europe' and must be 'a joint one, agreed to by a number, if not all European nations'.[72]

Churchill seized upon Marshall's words as ammunition to support his push for further European integration, drafting a statement for approval by the United Europe Movement: 'The implications of the Harvard speech are far reaching and magnanimous. It would be a betrayal of the cause of Christian and democratic civilisation if no adequate reply were to be made. It is the inescapable duty of the British and French governments to summon at once a conference of all the nations of Europe – from both sides of the Iron Curtain – to consider how they can best co-operate with the United States in saving something from the wreck of our shattered continent'.[73] Duncan Sandys shared Churchill's enthusiasm, recommending only that he remove the phrase 'the Iron Curtain' as it had an 'anti-Russian ring'.[74]

The former Conservative Foreign Secretary Anthony Eden had doubts, however. Unlike the Conservatives Leo Amery, Robert Boothby and Lady Rhys-Williams, Eden had not joined the movement at its outset, Churchill having to prompt him to do so in April 1947.[75] Eden agreed to have his name associated with the movement and even forwarded to Churchill a message to be read out at the Albert Hall, but its tone was somewhat distant: 'I am so sorry not to be able to be with you to-night, but I want to send you this cordial message of good wishes for the success of the Meeting. . . . All success to your endeavours'.[76] He did not himself go to the rally. Following Marshall's speech, Eden asked if he might discuss Churchill's statement with him before it was issued, preferably at a meeting of the Shadow Cabinet. He feared that any statements issued by Churchill might be read as Conservative Party policy rather than the views of a private individual and wondered 'whether it is wise to tell various Governments how they act ("It is the inescapable duty of the British and French Governments...")'. Eden also worried, given the centrality of France to any European scheme, whether the French government 'might be hurt at your coming out with definite suggestions or instructions at this moment', prior to preliminary talks with other European governments.[77] In the Shadow Cabinet, Churchill dismissed Eden's fears and released the statement with only the changes suggested by Sandys. Whilst it was indeed only read as the work of the United Europe Movement and thus did not in fact reflect on the Conservative Party as a whole, Churchill's behaviour made Eden only more suspicious of the movement, and he became increasingly wary of Churchill's European scheme and its effect on Conservative policy.[78]

Meanwhile, Leo Amery continued to work loyally for the movement. In July, he corresponded with Richard Merton, a German industrialist who had fled the Nazis in 1939 to make his home in England. Merton had returned to Germany for the first time in 1947 and, at Amery's request, investigated the attitude of the German people towards Churchill's ideas. He reported to Amery, 'I found that not only among the intelligentsia but among all classes the idea of creating some kind of a European collaboration or economic and lastly political confederation has been taken up with great interest'. However, his visit confirmed that France and Britain must take the lead: 'A great number of personalities who would be really qualified to take a lead in a movement to further the European idea do not want to be mixed up with anything which looks like politics and my impression is that so far there is no qualified driving power behind the European idea in this country'.[79] Amery agreed that whilst Germans 'should look to European unity as the one way of restoring Germany to an equal position in the family of European nations, they would be wise to avoid anything looking like an attempt to take the lead in the movement in Germany's immediate interests'.[80] Germany had to be involved in future schemes to unite the European continent, but memories of the war were still too fresh in the minds of many Europeans to allow full German participation. Germany could not be seen to be rising too quickly.

In addition to promoting the idea of European unity in Germany, Amery was tasked by Sandys with 'the planning of the

Empire side of our campaign'.[81] He had already corresponded in May with New Zealand Prime Minister Peter Fraser, who told him that the 'idea of a closer integration of Europe, and especially of Western Europe, is one which must command great sympathy in many quarters'. Fraser regretted that New Zealand would 'inevitably and to our great loss be excluded' but recognised that geography ensured that his country would not be part of a United Europe. Nevertheless, he affirmed that the New Zealand government would always welcome 'practical proposals to secure the preservation of European civilisation, from which, indeed, our own is derived', and he asked Amery to send him a manifesto which would show 'the immediate practical tasks which you envisage a United Europe Regional Group' adopting.[82]

Amery did as Fraser asked and also contacted Sir Shuldham Redfern, the former Principal Private Secretary to successive Governor Generals of Canada, for advice. Redfern encouraged him to continue seeking the cooperation of the Dominions, telling him, 'Canada is not only a working model of what Europe should become; her people are for the most part of European origin. Canada is thus a living proof that a federation is within the realm of practical politics. Indeed Canada might well feel that a divided Europe is an anachronism which the rest of the world tolerates at its peril'.[83] Amery took this message to heart, working harder than ever to ensure that in future the Empire and Commonwealth would have a larger role in any schemes for European Unity. His efforts bore fruit in March 1948 when the Economic Sub-Committee of the United Europe movement published a memorandum on the economic aspects of European unity and expressly addressed the Commonwealth, writing: 'Great Britain has an important role to play as a member of the European Union; she has another role as a member of the British Commonwealth. There is nothing inconsistent or incongruous in this. The Commonwealth and the Western European Union have complementary needs, and in close co-operation of Commonwealth and Union Britain would be a vital hinge'. It continued: 'Britain is not faced with a choice of Commonwealth or European Union; Britain needs both'.[84]

Meanwhile, Churchill continued to illicit the greatest possible number of supporters outside Parliament in favour of a United States of Europe. In his party conference speech in Brighton on 4 October 1947, he was 'convinced, and I do not speak without some knowledge of both Europe and of the United States, that it is possible to reconcile our position as the centre of the British Empire with full development of close economic relations with all the friendly countries of Europe'. He continued: 'For my own part I will be content with nothing less. I strive for all three great systems – the British Commonwealth of Nations, the European Union and the fraternal association with the United States. I believe ... this island will become the vital link between them all'.[85] Outside the United Kingdom, the broader movement for a United Europe was also gathering steam. Since the formation of Churchill's United Europe Committee in January 1947, many other European countries had followed suit. In Belgium in March 1947, the former premier Paul van Zeeland established the *Ligue Indépendante de Coopération Européenne*; on 5 July, Coudenhove-Kalergi formed the European Parliamentary Union composed of ex-ministers and heads of parties from across the European continent; and on 16 July in France, the French ex-premier Edouard Herriot formed the *Conceil français pour l'Europe unie*.[86] Shortly thereafter, Sandys led a British delegation from the United Europe Movement to meet with Herriot's *Conceil français* in Paris, and, on 19 July 1947, the two organisations agreed that 'the British United Europe Movement and the *Comité [sic] Français pour l'Europe Unie* should regard one another as sister movements and as far as possible conduct a joint campaign'.[87] The following day, Sandys met with leaders from the other European organisations and agreed to form the International Committee of the Movements for European Unity, an umbrella body that would synthesise the work of the various national organisations on a continental basis.[88]

By March 1948, the International Committee had met on several occasions and had decided that, in May 1948, they would hold a Congress of Europe at the Hague, the Netherlands, to publicise their aims and vision.[89] On 3 March, the Executive Committee of Churchill's United Europe Movement hosted a luncheon at the Savoy Hotel for Senator Pieter Kerstens (former Minister of Commerce in the Netherlands), Monsieur Andre Noel (a French Deputy and member of the French Committee for United Europe) and Monsieur Rebattet (Head of the Paris Secretariat of the International Committee of the Movements for European Unity).[90] There they considered a memorandum by Conservative MP Robert Boothby, which proclaimed, 'Events are now moving with such rapidity as to impose on those movements and organisations which advocate the ideal of European unity the necessity of giving more concrete form to their proposals'. Boothby argued that Europe was moving backwards rather than forwards and in consequence political and economic power had 'passed to the U.S.A. and the U.S.S.R.'. Yet, he said, there were '250 million of the most civilised and intelligent people in the world in the sixteen "Marshall" countries alone, with a productive potential as great as that of the United States'. He concluded: 'Unless this potential is brought within striking distance of realisation, there can be no hope of preventing the total collapse of Western Europe, of arresting the Communist advance, or of restoring any kind of equilibrium between the New World and the Old'. It was now time, he suggested, to institute the Council of Europe that Churchill had called for more than a year before.[91]

The Executive Committee voted to accept Boothby's recommendations and, on 6 March, presented them to the Joint International Committee of the Movements for European Unity. Following discussions in Paris on 12 March, the Joint International Committee officially adopted Boothby's document and published a list of General Principles, pledging any future European Union to free and democratic governance, acknowledging that the Union would begin with the nations of Western Europe and confirming that 'No scheme for European union would have any practical value without the full participation of Great Britain. The United Kingdom is an integral part of Europe'. In time, it hoped that the Council of Europe would evolve towards ever greater steps of integration, including the publication of a Declaration of Rights, the establishment of a European Court, the creation of a European Deliberative Assembly and a common citizenship, combined European Defence Force and an elected European Parliament with legislative capabilities.[92]

However, a Council of Europe at the ministerial level would require the support of the government, which at that time was not forthcoming in the United Kingdom. For that reason, the various European Movements placed their immediate focus on preparing for their Congress of Europe at the Hague in May. In hopes of garnering the most possible attention, the International Committee invited Churchill to serve as the Congress's Honorary President. His acceptance caused an immediate stir, both within the United Kingdom and on the Continent. The Labour Party announced that it would send no representatives to the Congress, repeating its claims that the movement was being used by Churchill for party political reasons. Emanuel Shinwell, the Secretary of

State for War, wrote to Churchill explaining that 'It is felt that the subject of European unity is much too important to be entrusted to unrepresentative interests'.[93] Across the channel, writing in the French newspaper *Le Populaire* (and reprinted in the *Glasgow Herald*), the former French Premier Léon Blum went further, stating that the Labour Party would inevitably avoid any schemes associated with Churchill because the former Prime Minister 'has a character too original and too powerful for him not to leave his mark on everything he touches'. What could at first be read as complementary soon turned otherwise: 'The stamp of his approval brought with it the danger that the European federation would have a character too narrowly Churchillian. Thus is explained the embarrassment, circumspection, and hesitation of the Labour Party, and in consequence, of international Socialism'.[94]

Churchill would not back down. Instead, he sent a lengthy 'open letter' to Blum, forwarding it to many leading dignitaries and statesmen in the United Kingdom and across Europe. He claimed that when he had given his speech in Zurich in September 1946, he had 'no idea it would become a Party question. I thought it would become a movement and an inspiration on a level far above Party politics in any country'. He pointed out that Blum himself had supported the movement 'until you became aware of the adverse decision of Mr Shinwell and the Executive of the British Socialist Party', and explained that when his movement decided to stage a Congress of Europe in the Hague, 'it was the best step open to private people to further the cause'. He hoped, therefore, that 'the French Socialist Party will allow full freedom to its own members; for I am sure that all who fall out of the line in these grave and melancholy times will expose themselves to the reproach of history'.[95]

When the Congress of Europe gathered on 7 May 1948, Winston Churchill sat proudly as its Honorary President. Members of the French Socialist Party were also in attendance, including Léon Blum, and, following pressure from across the Continent, so too were members of Britain's Labour Party. The Executive Committee of the British delegation included Members of Parliament, Lords and Ladies, trade unionists, academics and clergymen of all political and religious persuasions.[96] Harold Macmillan found it a remarkable affair, not only bringing together Europeans of all stripes but also Britons of all sorts, too: 'There were churchman of all denominations, industrialists, trade unionists, administrators, economists, professors, scientists, poets, artists.... [A] great proconsul and administrator like Sir John Anderson [was] seen side by side with John Masefield, the Poet Laureate, and Charles Morgan, the famous novelist. Catholic bishops, leading Anglicans, nonconformist ministers, [and] Fellows of the Royal Society were present. The great chemical industry was represented by Lord McGowan and Paul Chambers, and the Chemical Workers' Union by its General Secretary, Bob Edwards. Among the many economists were Arthur Salter and Roy Harrod'.[97] There had never been a gathering quite like it. For many, it was the first time they had come face to face with European leaders such as Jean Monnet, Paul Reynaud, Paul-Henri Spaak and Paul van Zeeland.[98] At the conclusion of the Congress, Churchill wrote to the Liberal Peer Lord Layton telling him that it would be 'a memorable event in the Movement for European Unity' and that 'The unanimous conclusions arrived at by this influential and representative gathering will give a powerful new impetus to the campaign in all countries'.[99]

In less than two years, Churchill had brought to life the vision he had articulated in his Zurich speech. He had spread his message across the European continent and had placed such moral pressure on the British government that it had been forced to relent and allow Labour members to attend the Congress. If there had been any doubt at the end of the war whether Great Britain would be part of a United Europe, no such question remained by May 1948. The United Kingdom and its Empire and Commonwealth were integral to the whole project. Mr Churchill had much to be proud of when he surveyed the movement for European unity in the aftermath of the Congress of Europe. But Prime Minister Clement Attlee and in particular his Foreign Secretary Ernest Bevin were not pleased. For them, the struggle for Britain's place within Europe (and the world) was just beginning.

3 MR BEVIN'S RESPONSE

The Foreign Secretary Ernest Bevin was sceptical of Churchill's calls for a United States of Europe. He was not the only one. Throughout the Foreign Office as a whole, there was deep unease at Churchill's campaign. On 29 January 1947, just weeks after Sandys formed the British United Europe Committee, Gladwyn Jebb (Assistant Under Secretary of State for Foreign Affairs) sent a note to Sir Oliver Harvey (Deputy Under Secretary of State for Foreign Affairs) suggesting that the idea of a United States of Europe was 'surely a very dangerous thing for us to encourage'. He gave four reasons: first, the original 'Paneuropa' idea presented by Coudenhove-Kalergi envisioned a European Parliament elected by proportional representation, which would give the Germans and Italians a combined 35 per cent of the seats, a frightening concept less than two years after the war's end; second, all member-states would be bound by the decisions of the European Parliament, leading to a distinct loss of sovereignty; third, the creation of a United States of Europe would accomplish what Hitler had failed – binding together all European nations into a single bloc – and would have only one result, 'namely a new war against Russia'; and, finally, the success of such a scheme would put the British people 'completely at the mercy of the Germans' – 'after all, the Count is half German and half Japanese and must therefore be assumed to have the interests of the Axis at heart'.[1] Jebb assumed in his memorandum that 'the U.K. and U.S.S.R. would be excluded' from a United States of Europe. When he was informed, 'No. The advisors of the present movement envisage the inclusion of at any rate the U.K.', his position against it hardened further.[2]

On 3 February, the Foreign Office distributed a statement of official policy: 'His Majesty's Government are definitely opposed to this movement for a United States of Europe.... A United States of Europe would be an artificial grouping which would *ex hypothesi* not include, and thereby would inevitably be regarded as being directed against, Soviet Russia. It would accordingly weaken the United Nations idea which it is the cardinal policy of His Majesty's Government to support, and which itself depends for success upon the fullest co-operation between the Great Powers which grew out of the wartime alliance'.[3] It would, however, support a Western European regional bloc intended to restrain Germany. In contrast to Churchill, who sought to draw Germany into a United Europe and in so doing bring reconciliation to Europe as a whole, the Foreign Office envisioned a Western European regional bloc whose very purpose was to *exclude* Germany.[4]

In addition to the statement of policy, Bevin sent to all British diplomats in Europe a circular which argued that 'Whatever may be the professed intentions of the sponsors of United Europe', a United States of Europe would inevitably come to be seen as 'directed against the Soviet Union'. British governmental approval would therefore give rise to the suspicion that the United Kingdom was 'taking the lead in forming an anti-Soviet coalition'. Furthermore, Bevin was convinced that within a United States of Europe the 'centre of gravity' would naturally migrate to 'the Reich', given that Germany would inevitably be 'admitted on equal terms to an eventual European Federation'. Beyond the obvious threat that this presented, a Europe that was fully integrated in an economic sense would undermine Britain's overseas commitments to the Empire and Commonwealth. The British government could therefore never contemplate full membership of such a federation. The best it could hope for was to be 'loosely associated'. However, this would strip Britain of any potential claims to leadership within Europe. These were consequences that Churchill had evidently not considered: '[T]he prospect of Germany establishing control over the Continent [cannot] be lightly dismissed; and if this were to come about it would obviously constitute a menace to the security both of these islands and of the Soviet Union'. Churchill's United Europe schemes, rather than leading to a more peaceful world, would in fact make the prospects of a third world war far more likely. They were dangerous schemes.

Bevin assured his diplomats, however, that this did not mean that the Labour government dismissed further integration with Europe out of hand. He had been working closely with the French government on a number of measures to promote cooperation, and there were two new lines of development that he was particularly interested in. The first was a 'regional grouping of Western European States for the purpose of general co-operation – social, political, economic, and even military – to guard against Germany again becoming a threat to peace'. The second was 'the formation of the Economic Commission for Europe', whose purpose was to 'facilitate concerted action for the economic reconstruction of Europe and to initiate and participate in the measures necessary for the expansion of European economic activity'. In each of these developments, the United Kingdom was happily playing its full part as a member of Europe.[5] In the winter and spring of 1947, the chief threat envisioned by the Foreign Office still emanated from Germany. The path to peace therefore lay in good relations between the Big Three of the United States, the Soviet Union and Great Britain, a combination that had defeated Germany twice before and could do so again if necessary. In this context, Anglo–French cooperation was essential, possibly to an extent unlike anything ever seen before in their shared history. But that was quite different from an integrated European Union including both the United Kingdom and Germany, as envisioned by Churchill. That vision belied the realities on the ground across Europe.

Nevertheless, it was not always easy to work with the French. In March 1947, Hector McNeil, the Minister of State for Foreign Affairs, wrote to Bevin about a rumour he had 'learned privately' which claimed that the French were going to offer the Foreign Secretary 'a bargain whereby they would support certain United States and United Kingdom proposals regarding Germany in exchange for a guarantee of specific quantities of Ruhr coal'.[6] Bevin confirmed that this information was 'correct'. When the French Foreign Minister Georges Bidault had visited him that week, he had 'told me in so many words that the general French attitude at the [upcoming] Conference [of Foreign Ministers] would be affected by what we could do for them over coal'. Bevin was 'resolutely opposed to these blackmailing tactics' and intended to hold his line that the British government could be of no help to the French on the issue of coal.[7]

The Soviet Union, likewise, presented a challenge to Bevin. In April, he told the French President Vincent Auriol that he had attempted over the previous three years to pursue a 'tolerant and understanding policy towards Russia', even in the face of mounting pressure from the United States and the Conservative Party to take a harder line. Auriol asked if Bevin might be willing to make a declaration to Moscow 'offering a basis of future peace and cooperation'. The Foreign Secretary admitted that he had been contemplating 'the possibility of saying something either to the Labour Party Conference or at a debate in the House of Commons early in May', hoping that the British government could 'make peace with Russia'.[8] Even so, it was difficult for Bevin to hold this line. In February 1946, the Soviets had encouraged the formation of the Socialist Unity Party in their zone in Germany, leading Bevin to accept the advice of his officials at the Foreign Office to adopt a policy of forming a Western Bloc in a divided Germany rather than seeking a unified Germany working under American, British, French and Soviet cooperation.[9] At the Council of Foreign Ministers meeting in July 1946, the Soviets had insisted on their full payment of reparations in addition to a voice in running the Ruhr; in response, Bevin had announced that the British zone would operate independently, without consultation with the Soviets.[10] By January 1947, Bevin was sufficiently uneasy about the Soviet Union to defy the Prime Minister in cabinet when Attlee argued for a reorientation of British policy to minimise provoking the USSR. Bevin had suggested that, on the contrary, if Britain were to remain a world power it could not afford to seem weak in the face of Soviet pressure.[11]

The Soviet question was also becoming inseparable from the situation in Germany. It was easy for a politician like Churchill, without responsibility, to play the magnanimous statesman and publicly call for rapprochement with Germany. However, the realities on the ground were far more complicated. In the spring of 1947, the Nuremburg trials were fresh in many people's minds, having only ended the previous October, when the full extent of the Nazis' atrocities had been laid bare for all to see. And if Britain was still feeling the economic pinch from the war, France was even more so; less than three years after their liberation, few Frenchmen or -women were eager to turn the other cheek. As Duff Cooper wrote to Churchill in September 1946, a Franco–German alliance was impossible, the partnership of 'the wolf and the lamb' being an uneasy one to bear for all those who had just suffered through six years of war and occupation.[12] Nevertheless, the increasingly heavy hand of Soviet occupation in the eastern part of Germany placed the British and Americans in a difficult position. Whilst Bevin continued to believe that a revived Germany posed the greatest threat to British interests, should that situation change and the Soviet Union become its chief rival, the western part of Germany would necessarily form an essential strategic bulwark against further Soviet expansion. When Bevin travelled to Moscow for the fourth meeting of the Council of Foreign Ministers in March and April 1947, it became evident that, in the Soviet mind, Europe was already divided between East and West.[13]

Beyond facing pressures from the French in Europe and an increasingly hostile Soviet Union in Europe, the cabinet also had to contend with an empire that seemed on the brink of collapse. In February 1947 – after three years of insurgency – the British government decided to wash its hands of Palestine and turn it over to the United Nations. Bevin had taken the lead on the Palestine question, despite the territory officially falling under the remit of the Colonial Secretary. He had held conference after conference with both Arab and Jew and sent countless telegrams to the United States, but all seemed to be for naught. President Truman failed utterly to grasp the difficulty the British faced in Palestine, particularly the effect that any concessions to the Zionists would have on Muslims throughout the British Empire. Despite Bevin's attempts at a fair settlement, he was branded an anti-Semite in the American press. Given his belief in the centrality of the Middle East to the future security of the British Empire, it was with a heavy heart that Bevin recommended to the cabinet that the United Nations rather than the British government determine the future of the territory.[14]

More difficult still, that month, the cabinet announced that India, too, would be relinquished. Bevin was deeply opposed to this policy. In January, he wrote to Attlee of the 'defeatist attitude adopted both by the Cabinet and by F[ield] M[arshal] Wavell'. He continued: 'I would impress you with this fact. I can offer nothing to any foreign country, neither credit nor coal nor goods – I am expected to make bricks without straw. And on top of this, in the British Empire, we knuckle under at the first blow and we are expected to preserve the position. It cannot be done'. He closed with a stark warning to Attlee: 'We appear to be trying nothing except to scuttle out of it, without dignity or plan, and I am convinced that if you do that, our Party, as a leading party in this new world settlement, will lose irrevocably'.[15] His pleading did little good. On February 18, the cabinet authorised the Secretary of State for India to issue a statement pledging an end to British rule in India by June 1948 at the latest.[16] Two days later, Attlee proclaimed that 'on behalf of the people of this country [the British government express] their goodwill and good wishes towards the people of India as they go forward to this final stage in their achievement of self-government'.[17] The Foreign Secretary was dismayed. If there were those within the Labour government who believed that Britain's future did not lie in the British Empire, Bevin was not amongst them, and he bitterly regretted the loss of both Palestine and India.

Despite all this, Bevin persevered with his plans for increased cooperation between the Western European governments. This culminated on 4 March 1947 with the signing of the Anglo–French Treaty of Dunkirk and the subsequent agreement of the French and Benelux leaders to enter into a Five Power Conference with Britain. The Dunkirk Treaty promised a fifty-year Anglo–French alliance against German aggression, the first explicit long-term security guarantee the British government had ever given to a continental country.[18] Bevin hoped that the Five Power Conference would expand this treaty in time to cover all Western European countries whilst also providing a venue for ministers from the five countries to discuss issues they held in common. Like the treaty, the conference was again an alignment with the European continent unprecedented in British history. In his conversations with Auriol that April, Bevin confessed that he wanted to further develop his 'policy of Western Union' to include 'the possibility of [a] Western Union bank and currency and of other economic arrangements designed to make the group more independent of the United States'.[19]

Bevin was moving towards some measure of European integration at a steady pace, yet it was not fast enough for some Labour MPs who, like their Conservative colleagues, believed that Britain should be taking a more aggressive stance in favour of European unity. In May 1947, the *New Statesman* published a pamphlet by Labour MPs Richard Crossman, Michael Foot and Ian Mikardo and signed by a further twelve MPs titled *Keep Left*. Whilst addressing some domestic concerns, its primary focus was on foreign affairs, where it claimed that 'Britain had been driven into a dangerous dependence on the U.S.A.'.

It did not, however, suggest that Britain turn instead to the Soviet Union, as some Labour MPs contended. Rather, it argued that the United Kingdom should establish a 'Third Force' with France: '[W]orking together, we are still strong enough to hold the balance of world power, to halt the division into a Western and Eastern bloc and so to make the United Nations a reality'. However, in contrast with Bevin, the Foreign Office officials and members of the Conservative Party, who all fervently believed in the continued maintenance of the British Empire, *Keep Left* also called for a British withdrawal from the Middle East and for the Suez Canal to be internationalised.[20] If Bevin believed that Churchill's United Europe Movement was impractical with its calls for British sovereignty to be subsumed into a United States of Europe, *Keep Left*'s rejection of the British Empire was equally so. In the post-war world, Britain would need both its empire and a closer integration with the European continent if it were to remain a leading world power.

When, the following month, US Secretary of State George Marshall announced at Harvard his plans for American aid to Europe, Bevin was every bit as convinced of the possibilities inherent in it as were Churchill, Sandys and their United Europe Movement. In a telegram to Duff Cooper at the British Embassy in Paris, Bevin described its 'momentous character' and asked Cooper to convey to the French Foreign Minister Georges Bidault and French Prime Minister Paul Ramadier that the British government was 'anxious to co-operate with them at the earliest possible date'. He believed that they should institute immediate discussions between French and British ministers, which could then be expanded to include the Benelux countries and eventually all European countries, East and West.[21] He wrote again to Cooper on 14 June proposing to visit Paris the following week.[22] Before he left, Bevin made his position clear speaking to the Foreign Press Association: 'We are more than ever linked with the destinies of Europe. We are in fact, whether we like it or not, a European nation and must act as such ... [as] a link and bridge between Europe and the rest of the world'.[23]

In Paris, Bevin and Bidault agreed to form an *ad hoc* steering committee to begin talks before the end of June, with Bevin suggesting that Britain, France, Poland, Czechoslovakia, Belgium or Holland and Denmark be invited to join. Bidault agreed on the condition that the Soviet Union also be invited. Neither man made mention of any representatives from the occupied zones of Germany. On 22 June, they received word that the Soviets would participate in an initial tripartite conference with Britain, France and themselves, but not in a larger European grouping. Bevin and Bidault consented and the conference began in Paris on the twenty-seventh of that month.[24] However, the growing chasm between East and West became clear when Soviet Foreign Minister Vyacheslav Molotov suggested that Marshall's offer would 'violate national sovereignties and enable the United States to influence the international affairs of other nations'. The Soviet Union, he said, could only be involved if the United States first announced the exact dollar amount of its aid and agreed to its distribution with no strings attached, after which European nations could then discuss their needs without American influence. Bevin declared that this amounted to asking the United States for a 'blank cheque' which would not be given; consequently, he and Bidault rejected the Soviet approach and Molotov walked out of the talks.[25] Just before he left, Bevin whispered to Sir Pierson Dixon, his Principal Private Secretary, 'This really is the birth of the Western bloc'.[26]

Following the Soviet departure, Bevin and Bidault worked well together, quickly agreeing to the terms of a note to send to twenty-two other European countries inviting them to join a conference, including Turkey and the Eastern European countries but excluding Russia. When the Conference of European Reconstruction opened in Paris on 12 July, it did so with representatives from sixteen countries. The eight invited parties who refused to attend all fell within the Soviet sphere of influence, and, from that point forward, Western and Eastern Europe would follow very different paths in the post-war world. Given this split, Bevin believed that it was his job to ensure that, in the Western sphere, the European nations were led by Britain and were not overly hostile to the United States of America. At the conference, the representatives decided to form the Committee of European Economic Co-operation (CEEC) with an executive committee consisting of the British, French, Italian, Dutch and Norwegian foreign ministers and subcommittees sitting for Food and Agriculture, Energy and Power, Iron and Steel and Transport. They pledged to prepare a report for the US government laying out a plan for European reconstruction no later than 1 September.[27] By the time the report was finished, the Executive Committee had decided to make their organisation permanent, renaming it in April 1948 the Organisation for European Economic Cooperation (OEEC).[28] It would remain in place until 1961, when it was superseded by the Organisation for Economic Cooperation and Development (OECD), a worldwide grouping including the United States and Canada.

Meanwhile, Bevin began to explore the possibilities for expanding European economic cooperation into an actual Customs Union. Hall-Patch warned that there was 'a well-established prejudice in Whitehall against a European Customs Union. It goes back a long way and is rooted in the old days of free trade'. However, he added that this view was a 'relic of a world which has disappeared probably never to return' and did not discourage Bevin from pursuing the idea.[29] The Foreign Secretary had first raised the concept of a Western European Customs Union in late 1946, urging the cabinet to launch an inquiry into its advantages and disadvantages to Britain.[30] The Treasury and Board of Trade, led by Hugh Dalton and Sir Stafford Cripps, respectively, were immediately opposed to the idea, arguing that a European Customs Union would inevitably mean an end to Britain's system of imperial preference and colonial market regulations, which would be detrimental both to British manufacturers and to British leadership in the Commonwealth.[31] Bevin persevered, however, and in January 1947, the cabinet agreed to appoint a committee of experts to examine the issue.[32] This committee reported in June that whilst a European Customs Union would not be the best possible economic outcome for the United Kingdom, should one form on the European continent, British participation would carry some economic advantages whilst a British exclusion would 'be harmful to British interests'.[33] If there was to be a European Customs Union, Britain ought to be part of it.

Although the thrust of the report was that 'a continental customs union had little economically in its favour other than the damage which would be caused by being excluded from it',[34] Bevin grasped at its positive elements, arguing in cabinet that the recent formation of the CEEC provided the perfect vehicle for in-depth discussions of a Customs Union with other European powers. When the CEEC met for the first time later that month, thirteen of the sixteen governments represented (all but Sweden, Norway and Switzerland) agreed to form an International Customs Union Study Group. Cripps remained concerned about the impact of a European Union on the Commonwealth, but he recognised that, with the Marshall offer and the formation of the International Study Group, some element of European economic integration was inevitable. Given that, it was better for Britain to be on the inside than on the outside. It was now only a question of how such integration should take place.

On 3 September 1947, Bevin made his argument again in a speech to the Trades Union Congress, claiming that the only way to restore Britain's leadership in the world was through a Customs Union that could make the United Kingdom independent of the United States. Two days later, he wrote to Attlee proposing that the cabinet form study groups to investigate five possible scenarios: first, a Customs Union for the Empire; second, a Customs Union for the Commonwealth; third, a combined Empire and Commonwealth Customs Union; fourth, a European Customs Union; and finally, the relationship that an Empire/Commonwealth Customs Union could have with a European Customs Union if Britain were a member of each. Attlee put the proposal before the cabinet, which agreed without opposition, Cripps now satisfied that the Commonwealth perspective was being fully considered.[35] Bevin was tasked with exploring further the possibilities of a European Customs Union, whilst Cripps, working with a young Harold Wilson (serving in his first ministerial role as Secretary for Overseas Trade), concentrated on the Empire and Commonwealth.

Bevin wrote to Attlee again on 16 September indicating that a European Customs Union was essential as 'we must free ourselves of financial dependence on the United States of America as soon as possible. We shall never be able to pull our full weight in foreign affairs until we do so. Nor can we rely, in future, on assistance from the United States'. Yet Bevin did not dismiss Cripps' consideration of the Empire and Commonwealth and believed that a European Customs Union must be formed simultaneously 'not only [with] closer trade relations with the Commonwealth and Empire but also of an intensified effort for development within them'.[36] Ironically, when Cripps reported to Attlee in early October, he also concluded that since his question was 'inter-related with that of a possible Customs Union or Unions in Europe', his Study Group would also address them as a single problem, examining the effects of UK participation in a European Union on the Commonwealth, how a Commonwealth Customs Union could be merged with a European Customs Union and how the resources of a European Customs Union could be used to 'promote development of the resources of the Colonial Empire and of the Commonwealth generally'.[37] Neither Bevin nor Cripps could view Europe and the

Empire and Commonwealth as separate entities, and each argued that the two had to be treated as a single, integrated problem.

Cripps and Wilson discovered quickly that theirs was not a simple question. In contrast to the messages Leo Amery had received from the Commonwealth, Wilson found the Australian government to be 'suspicious and unenthusiastic' and reported that the Canadian government might consider a Customs Union with Great Britain, but not with the other Dominions.[38] On 27 October, the Dominions Office sent a telegram to all Commonwealth countries outlining the formation of the International Study Group, promising that 'Commonwealth consultations on [the] issues involved ... should take place as soon as possible'.[39] Meanwhile, Bevin met with French Prime Minister Paul Ramadier, telling him that if the resources of their two empires were combined they would easily match those of the two superpowers, allowing Europe to take an independent course from either the United States or the Soviet Union.[40] Bevin's Minister of State, Hector McNeil, held his own discussions with the French Foreign Minister Georges Bidault and explained to Bevin that Bidault had now 'completely burnt his boats as regards the Russians' yet was equally unwilling to march under the colours of the United States. He was 'profoundly pessimistic' about the future of the United Nations but recognised that France was not strong enough to act alone. Having spurned the Soviet Union and ruled out the United States and United Nations, McNeil was certain that there was now nowhere left for the French to turn than to closer unity with the United Kingdom.[41]

Bidault himself confirmed as much at a private dinner with Bevin during the Council of Foreign Ministers in London that November, telling him that the two men needed to 'come closer together in the face of a situation which menaces all of us'. Bidault feared that France might be invaded 'a second time' and confessed that he did not want to find himself once again a 'leader of the resistance movement'. Bevin, spotting his opportunity, 'drew attention to the great resources of Western Europe, both in Europe and in their African colonies', and laid out his vision for Bidault: 'If properly developed these resources amounted to more than either the Soviet Union or the United States could muster, and should enable Western European Powers to be independent of either. Between us we [have] many raw materials in Africa which [are] deficient in the United States'. The British government was 'already in contact with the Portuguese Government on this and other colonial problems and, indeed, found that their attitude towards Western Europe and Africa was very similar to our own'. Bevin predicted it would take Great Britain another four or five years to fully develop its African resources but was certain that by 1951 or 1952 the government would be ready to enter into a deeper economic relationship with France which would unite the colonial empires of the Western European powers. Bidault agreed that their two countries should 'embark on an intensive programme of co-operation in the economic and military sphere'.[42]

Following the close of the Council of Foreign Ministers on 17 December, Bevin and Bidault again met privately. Throughout the council, the two Europeans had found the American delegation in a 'state of great uncertainty' and American Secretary of State George Marshall in particular to be 'very much afraid of Soviet Propaganda'. The council, however, seemed to have disabused the Americans of any lingering hope they had of breaking the impasse with the Soviet Union. Given that, Marshall now encouraged Bevin and Bidault to establish some form of Anglo–French Committee which would 'help to prevent the Soviet Union attacking the French and ourselves [the British]'. Both men agreed that this was their best option, and Bevin made his fullest comments yet to Bidault of his vision for the future. Europe, he said, 'was now divided from Greece to the Baltic and from the Oder to Trieste'. This line had become impenetrable; Eastern Europe was out of reach. Churchill's iron curtain had become a reality. 'Our task', he continued, '[is] to save Western civilisation'. He believed they would 'have to come to some sort of federation in Western Europe whether of a formal or informal character'. As 'an Englishman', he 'hoped it would not be necessary to have formal constitutions'; any federation could instead have an in-built flexibility to make allowances for different national traditions, preferably modelled on the time-tested example of the British Commonwealth. Regardless, the two countries needed to 'act quickly'.[43]

Beyond Bevin's meetings with Ramadier and Bidault, work continued apace on his concept of a Western European Customs Union. In November, the first meeting of the International Customs Union Study Group gathered in Brussels, with representatives from Austria, Belgium, Denmark, France, Greece, the Netherlands, Iceland, Ireland, Italy, Luxembourg, Portugal, Switzerland, Turkey and the United Kingdom. The governments of Norway and Sweden sent 'observers' but did not directly take part in the talks, and, at the insistence of the British government, the Commonwealth countries of Australia, Canada, India, New Zealand and South Africa also sent observers.[44] In the New Year, Gladwyn Jebb suggested to the Foreign Secretary that he should begin to consider not only an economic customs union but a political union also, so that Britain would not be forced in the future 'to make the dismal choice between becoming a satellite state or the poor dependent of an American plutocracy'.[45] It was a remarkable about-face for the man who just one year earlier had argued against any British participation in schemes for European integration.

Mirroring the language Churchill had used before him, Bevin wrote to the cabinet on 4 January 1948, telling them, 'the Soviet Government has formed a solid political and economic block behind a line running from the Baltic along the Oder, through Trieste to the Black Sea. There is no prospect in the immediate future that we shall be able to re-establish and maintain normal relations with European countries behind that line'. He argued that it was 'not enough to reinforce the physical barriers which still guard our Western civilisation. We must also organise and consolidate the ethical and spiritual forces inherent in this Western civilisation of which we are the chief protagonists'. The only way to do this, he claimed, was 'by creating some form of union in Western Europe, whether of a formal or informal character, backed by the Americas and the Dominions'. This union should at first include Great Britain, Scandinavia, the Low Countries, France, Portugal, Italy and Greece, and in time also welcome into its arms Spain and Germany, 'without whom no Western system can be complete'. He acknowledged that this idea 'may seem a somewhat fanciful conception' but believed that 'events are moving fast and a common danger drives countries to welcome to-morrow solutions which appear unpractical and unacceptable to-day'. He reminded the cabinet that 'We in Britain can no longer stand outside Europe and insist that our problems and position are quite separate from those of our European neighbours', and he concluded: 'Material aid will have to come principally from the United States, but the countries of Western Europe which despise the spiritual values of America will look to us for political and moral guidance and for assistance in building up a counter attraction to the baleful tenets of communism within their borders. . . . We have the material resources in the Colonial Empire, if we develop them, and by giving a spiritual lead now we should be able to carry out our task in a way which will show clearly that we are not subservient to the United States of America or to the Soviet Union'.[46]

Four days later, the cabinet agreed to several conclusions on British foreign policy within Europe, focussing in particular on its effects on the Empire and Commonwealth. Bevin began by stating that the breakdown of the recent Council of Foreign Ministers and the increasingly belligerent attitude of the Soviet Union made it essential for the Western European countries to draw closer. It would also be 'necessary to mobilise the resources of Africa in support of any Western European union; and, if some such union could be created, including not only the countries of Western Europe but also their Colonial possessions in Africa and the East, this would form a *bloc* which ... could stand on an equality with the western hemisphere and Soviet *blocs*'. The cabinet in general agreed with this principle, and Arthur Creech Jones, the Colonial Secretary, emphasised that 'Much progress had already been made in securing the co-operation of Western European countries in colonial matters'. The cabinet also agreed that the 'Dominion Governments should be fully consulted and kept in touch as the proposals for closer union in Western Europe were developed'.[47] If there was to be a European Union, it would be an imperial one, drawing on the resources of the colonies and forged in full consultation with the Dominions.

Bevin made this policy public on 22 January 1948, when he issued a call in the House of Commons for the formation of a Western Union. Echoing the words he had used with both Bidault and the British cabinet only weeks before, he explained to his parliamentary colleagues that his aim was to ensure British independence from the United States. 'As soon as we can afford to develop Africa', he said, 'we can cut loose from [the] US'. For this reason, he believed that Portugal as well as France must be part of the scheme, so that all European colonial empires could be used to Britain's advantage.[48] Concrete evidence of such cooperation was seen at the Anglo–French colonial talks held the following month. In a summary of the meetings, Sir Sydney Caine of the Colonial Office wrote that 'We and the French Colonial authorities are inspired by the common objectives of developing the resources of our respective dependencies for the benefit of their inhabitants, whose standard of living will thereby be increased, and the rest of the world which may hope to secure by such development increased supplies of scare commodities'. Officials also discussed 'the general movement towards a Western Union' and concluded that 'the development of the Colonial dependencies can contribute to the establishment of Western European equilibrium and international trade'. Finally, Caine noted that 'Although the talks were confined to British and French representatives, it was fully recognised on both sides that similar close cooperation is needed between both countries and other powers having Colonies in Africa and indeed elsewhere'.[49] These talks represented the epitome of Bevin's vision for an integrated Europe, with officials and ministers from European countries working together in a practical way to further their positions in the world and to develop their empires.

Over the following months, Bevin worked hard both with his cabinet colleagues and with ministers on the European continent to further his policy. On the home front, he told the cabinet on 3 March that continued Soviet expansion was a 'threat to western civilisation' which could only be met by greater integration in Western Europe. He argued that the British government should 'pursue on as broad a basis as possible in co-operation with our French allies, the conclusions of a treaty or treaties with the Benelux countries' and should 'proceed at once' with 'the whole problem of the co-ordination of efforts for the cultural, social, economic and financial revival and development of the West and for the defence of western civilisation'. Although a Western European Union must be the heart of this defence, it could only be fully accomplished with 'the Commonwealth and the Americas, and eventually every country outside the Soviet group'. The cabinet authorised him to pursue discussions with Commonwealth and European leaders for this end.[50] In culmination of these talks, on 17 March 1948, France and Britain signed with Belgian, Luxembourg and the Netherlands the Treaty of Brussels, which expanded the earlier Treaty of Dunkirk from an Anglo–French defence alliance into a Western European defence alliance. Significantly, in contrast to Dunkirk, the Treaty of Brussels did not specify Germany as the potential threat but provided a fifty-year defence alliance against *all* threats.[51]

Throughout these months, polling suggested that the British public was in favour of Bevin's general stance on Europe, no doubt helped by the positive attitude also shown towards Europe by Winston Churchill and the Conservatives. A survey conducted by Mark Abrams' respected Research Services Limited between 8 February and 8 March 1948 found that 80 per cent of the middle classes and

42 per cent of the working classes were aware of Bevin's plans for 'some kind of a Union of Western European countries'. Of those who were aware, 66 per cent were in favour, 21 per cent had still to make up their minds and only 10 per cent were opposed. The pollsters also asked all respondents – not only those who had heard of the schemes – specific questions about various aspects of a potential European Union. When surveyed about a Customs Union, where 'Our products could go to every country in the Union without paying duty and the products of other countries in the Union could come in here without paying duty', 76 per cent were favourable whilst only 14 per cent were against. Likewise, when asked about the free movement of European peoples, where 'People could travel freely from country to country, so that they could go and work wherever they liked, and people who wanted to, could come here and work', 66 per cent were in favour and 27 per cent against.

It was only once the pollsters began to ask questions on issues that might directly impinge upon British sovereignty that they received a more negative response. When asked their opinion of a Western European Union that 'might mean that all the countries would have the same currency so that your money would be backed by the Union and not by the Bank of England', only 42 per cent were in favour with 39 per cent against and 19 per cent yet to make up their mind. When surveyed about a common European army where 'our men would serve under a commander who might or might not be British', 53 per cent were opposed and only 35 per cent supportive.[52] By May, the number of people aware of Bevin's ideas for a Western European Union had risen dramatically to near unanimity; of those surveyed, 38 per cent were strongly favourable and 24 per cent were favourable, with only 7 per cent either disapproving or strongly disapproving.[53] Polling suggested that, in 1948, so long as Bevin did not pursue European integration by adopting a single currency or subsuming the British Army into a European Army, the British people were generally in favour.

This did not mean that all was smooth sailing for Bevin, however. The closer he worked with his European colleagues, the more apparent it became that there were some differences of opinion in how they approached the European question. In February 1948, the *Economist* reported that the British delegation to the International Customs Union Study Group was having difficulties reconciling the UK's current system of imperial preference with a potential European

Customs Union, despite Bevin's assurances that any union would necessarily have to include the empires of the European countries involved. Furthermore, the Dominion observers were increasingly uncomfortable about the lack of consultation between the British government and themselves over the issue.[54] It was not only the Commonwealth countries that were growing frustrated with Britain's negotiating strategies. Other European powers, particularly Belgium, believed that the United Kingdom was giving the French far too much attention to the exclusion of others, to the extent that, on 18 February 1948, Bevin wrote to Paul-Henri Spaak, the Belgian Prime Minister, to explain the British position: '[W]e must carry the French along with us wholeheartedly. I know that there are practical and psychological difficulties but we must never lose sight of the fact that France's participation is essential'. He continued: '[T]he greatest tact and understanding is required in our dealings with the French. I ask you therefore not to take it amiss if I seem to hesitate to move except in step with them'.[55] As Bevin put it privately to his Minister of State, Hector McNeil, 'It is not always easy to deal with the French but the role which they will have to play in Western Union is an essential one and regard must be paid to their susceptibilities'.[56]

Despite these difficulties, the Western European governments continued to grow ever closer throughout the spring of 1948. At the meeting of the Five Powers following the signing of the Treaty of Brussels in March, the representatives spoke of their desire for further integration. Baron van Boetzelaar, the Dutch Foreign Minister, suggested that their foremost priority should be to establish a Consultative Council in which foreign ministers could meet 'from time to time' and their deputies at least once a month to coordinate policy on economic, military and social issues. Bevin agreed, especially keen to see that the proposed Consultative Council European ministers should aim at 'harmonising and developing our respective social services'. Bidault was also 'in favour of [the Consultative Council] considering all such questions which contribute to bringing the five countries closer together' and hoped to see the finance ministers of the signatories brought into the council as well as the foreign ministers, an idea which Bevin seconded. Bidault closed by urging those present to 'move very fast', a point upon which all agreed.[57]

In June 1948, the Colonial Office published a memorandum outlining European cooperation on colonial affairs since the end of the war, noting that talks 'on technical matters of common concern' were held with the French in November 1945, with the Belgians in June 1946 and with the French and Belgians together in January 1947. These talks culminated in a tripartite Anglo–French–Belgian conference in May 1947, 'where a programme of technical conferences was agreed upon designed to take us up to 1950'. Beyond these talks in Europe, a medical conference had been held in Accra in 1946, attended by representatives from the British and French colonies in West Africa; a veterinary conference was held in Dakar that same year attended by representatives from British and French West Africa; and a communications conference was held in Dakar in May 1947. In the Caribbean, a 'more formal system of collaboration [was] established between the countries with responsibilities for non-self-governing territories in that area', and, in the South Pacific a regional commission was founded in May 1948 with a membership of Great Britain, France, the Netherlands, Australia, New Zealand and the United States.[58]

In a summary of the International Study Conference on Overseas Territories of Western Europe, held in Amsterdam in June 1948, Bevin found it 'noteworthy that in all fields of general colonial policy, both short-term and long-term, there was a considerable measure of agreement between the delegations of the five powers represented'.[59] Arthur Creech Jones, the Colonial Secretary, even sent to all British West African governors a memorandum in August noting that 'The programme of collaboration with the French has made great progress during the past three years. Close contact both in London and Paris and in West Africa has been established in all the more important technical fields. This contact has now been extended to the economic field. Finally in the discussions held in Paris during June agreement has been reached for the exchange of information in the political and constitutional fields'.[60] As in economic policy, in colonial policy the Western European powers were collaborating more closely than they had ever done before.

It was against this backdrop of increasingly close ties between the European governments – with Bevin often taking the lead in pushing for specific, practical steps that could strengthen their relationships – that Churchill's United Europe Movement proposed its Congress of Europe in the Hague. Given all the events of the previous three years, Churchill's claims that the British government was doing nothing to encourage closer integration between the United Kingdom and the European continent was, to Bevin's mind, ludicrous. The Foreign

Secretary had been instrumental in drafting the Anglo–French Treaty of Dunkirk and later the Treaty of Brussels – the first British long-term security guarantees to the European continent in its history – and in bringing together the Five Power Conference. At the Council of Foreign Ministers, he had consistently worked with Georges Bidault to form a common Western European policy. He had led the way in forming the OEEC, an even larger grouping of sixteen European countries, and had pushed hard within the cabinet for his colleagues to consider a Western European Customs Union. He had stood up for British interests, making it clear that he favoured European integration on a flexible model, without the need for a formal constitution or the loss of individual national sovereignties. He had, he believed, done more for the cause of European integration than any previous Foreign Secretary and had established better relations with his fellow Western European foreign ministers than at any time in British history. Under Bevin, Britain had led in Europe.

    The Foreign Secretary was not anti-European, just as the Labour government as a whole was not anti-imperial, despite its relinquishing of Palestine and India. But the government was facing a world situation the complexity of which had never been seen before. Gone were the moral and political certainties that had seemed so self-evident prior to and during the Second World War. With their departure, gone, too, was a place for the sweeping rhetoric and grand gestures of a pre-war political class that had been unchallenged on the world stage. Churchill's notion of a reconciled France and Germany at the heart of a new polity, the United States of Europe, was not only idealistic to the point of foolishness but was also pragmatically unfeasible. Europe in the summer of 1948 was no place for grandiose schemes and visions. To Bevin, this much was clear. Why Churchill, Sandys, Amery and their allies in the Conservative Party could not see this was baffling to the Foreign Secretary. The world had changed. The old ways of doing things had to change too.[61]

4 THE GERMAN PROBLEM

With hindsight, the path that led to the twenty-fourth of June 1948 can easily be traced. On that date, the Russian government severed all land and water communications between the Western zones of Germany and Berlin, in the heart of the Soviet zone but itself divided into four. It also halted all rail and canal traffic into and out of the city and required all road traffic to take a twenty-three kilometre detour.[1] The Foreign Secretary Ernest Bevin had been worried by the steadily hardening position of the Soviets towards Germany ever since the Potsdam Conference of July 1945 but had held out hope that a reconciliation was possible. However, relations between Eastern and Western Europe rapidly deteriorated after American Secretary of State George Marshall's offer of aid to Europe and the Soviet refusal to participate in the summer of 1947. Following Russian intransigence at the Council of Foreign Ministers in November and December 1947, Marshall feared that the USSR was shaping Eastern Germany into a totalitarian state akin to others in Eastern Europe, and he wrote that the 'desire for an undivided Germany cannot be made an excuse for inaction in Western Germany, detrimental to [the] recovery of Western Europe as a whole'.[2]

Consequently, on 23 February 1948, American and French delegations travelled to London at Bevin's invitation to begin a tripartite conference on the future of Western Germany. They were later joined by delegations from Holland, Belgium and Luxembourg, and, on 6 June 1948, released a joint communiqué announcing the merger of the three Western zones of Germany into a single economic unit with a single currency, the 'West mark', to begin circulating on 20 June.³ The Soviet authorities responded by stopping traffic on the autobahn into Berlin and delaying train services with lengthy inspections. On 21 June, they halted a US military supply train and prevented it from reaching Berlin. Finally, on 22 June, Marshal Vasily Sokolovsky, the head of the Soviet Military Administration in East Germany, announced that the Soviet Union would introduce with immediate effect an East German currency, which would become the only legal tender throughout Berlin, including in the Western zones. The United States and Great Britain responded by flooding Berlin with West marks printed with a special 'B' for Berlin, soon to become known as B-marks. It was following the release of these B-marks that on 24 June the Soviet government began its blockade of Berlin, cutting the city off from the Western zones of Germany by all routes other than the air.⁴

The Berlin Blockade provoked a distinct shift in Bevin's thinking about Western Europe and, in particular, Germany. As soon as the Soviets placed the blockade, Bevin warned the cabinet that a 'very serious situation' was developing and ordered the British Deputy Military Governor in Germany, General Nevil Brownjohn, to return to London on 25 June to explain how the British could continue supplying Berlin.⁵ When Brownjohn suggested that the British could not bring in freight trains by force, that to open the roads would require a 'major military operation' and that supplying Berlin by air might prove impossible, Bevin snapped that this was simply not good enough and ordered him to procure 'technical advice' on the matter. He also persuaded the cabinet to form a small group of ministers known as the Berlin Committee to coordinate the British response.⁶

Following the cabinet meeting, Bevin summoned the American Ambassador Lewis Douglas to the Foreign Office, where he recommended that the US government appoint a representative in London 'with the necessary authority' to take decisions on the Berlin crisis without constant recourse to Washington. He also suggested that the American Chiefs of Staff immediately make an appreciation of the situation from a military standpoint; that the Americans and British together 'put into service as many transport aircraft as possible, in order to maintain the morale of the Germans in Berlin'; that the United States Air Force (USAF) place a bomber squadron in Europe to 'persuade the Russians that we meant business'; and, finally, that the British and American governments carefully monitor all Soviet statements to ensure that the Russians did not turn the blockade to their political advantage. Bevin was particularly concerned lest the Russians decided to feed the whole population of Berlin, in the Western zones as well as the East. When Douglas countered that the Western allies should 'presumably be content with that' as it would relieve the need for an air supply, the Foreign Secretary was incredulous. He asked sarcastically why they should not then simply evacuate all Berlin and leave it to the Soviets, allowing the Russians to invade the rest of Germany whilst they were at it. The meeting broke up shortly thereafter.[7]

Bevin's meeting with Douglas was notable for several reasons. Most importantly, it occurred before any similar meetings with the ambassadors or foreign ministers of Britain's European allies. Despite Bevin's calls over the previous three years for the Europeans to build a 'third force' that could stand independently of the United States, when faced with his first major challenge in foreign affairs Bevin's instinct was to turn to the American government. Partly, this was a pragmatic decision. The French and Benelux countries simply did not have the resources of the Americans and would not have been able to protect Berlin without the United States played a leading role. Yet it was also ideological. Unlike Churchill, Bevin had never viewed European integration as an end in itself; he did not believe that a European Union would be a panacea to bring world peace. His primary interest had always been to maintain Britain's position in the world and secure the future of its empire and Commonwealth. In the immediate aftermath of the war, Bevin felt that the political and economic might of the United States undermined the British Empire. Only an alliance of the British and European empires could compete on equal terms with American power. He also feared that a European Union with a Franco–German partnership at its heart might lead to a renewal of German belligerence on the continent. Britain had to form a strong partnership with France whilst Germany was still weak, essentially instituting a British-led Western Europe against a potentially hostile Central Europe.

The Soviet blockade of Berlin demonstrated that Russia and the United States were not equal threats to British prominence, however. The very survival of Western civilisation was now at stake. Given that, an imperial Europe acting alone was insufficient. The issues at play were now larger than Europe. Britain instead needed an Atlantic alliance that would protect the Western world against the Soviet Communist threat. The countries of Western Europe would of course be an essential part of this Atlantic alliance, but at its heart there needed to be a strong partnership between the United States and Great Britain. This would, necessarily, replace the Foreign Office's previous emphasis on an Anglo–French alliance. The Berlin blockade also softened Bevin's stance on Germany. Western Germany was now an essential element of the front against Communism, and it was vital for Britain and the United States to protect Western Germany from Soviet influence. The blockade of Berlin did more to bring Germany back into the fold of Western Europe than any number of speeches by Winston Churchill.

On 26 June – two days after the blockade began – Sir Brian Robertson, the British Military Governor in Germany, provided Lucius Clay, the American Military Governor, with a summary of Bevin's meeting with Douglas. Clay met the following day with Curtis LeMay, the commander of the USAF Europe, who agreed that moving a bomber group to Europe would send the right message to the Soviets. That same day, at the Pentagon in Washington DC, American Defence Secretary James Forrestal suggested that two B-29 bomber groups be moved to England, a request that President Truman granted on 28 June. The British cabinet approved the move on 13 July, and the first US bomber arrived on British soil on 17 July. Initially billed as only a thirty-day 'temporary duty', the squadron's tour was extended first to sixty days and then to ninety. On 13 November 1948, the British Air Ministry informed the Pentagon that the 'long-term' use of RAF bases by the USAF was 'assumed'.[8] An American air force presence has remained in the United Kingdom ever since, ensuring a continued transatlantic commitment that others on the European continent have not always shared.

Meanwhile, on 28 June, Sir Ivone Kirkpatrick, soon to become Permanent Under-Secretary for the German Section in the Foreign Office, sent a telegram to Sir Oliver Harvey, who had recently succeeded Duff Cooper as British Ambassador to France. He explained that Bevin was holding firm to the view that 'a retreat [in Berlin] would be disastrous'. He continued: 'The abandonment of the many Germans who have stood by us in Berlin would cause such lack of confidence in the Western Zone that we should find it almost impossible to maintain our position there. With the loss of Western Germany we should face not only the collapse of our whole Western system, but the complete domination of Europe by Russia reinforced by a Communist controlled Germany'. The threat from Russia was now Bevin's primary concern, far overshadowing any potential challenge from a revived Germany or any sense of British power being undermined by the United States. Kirkpatrick told Harvey that 'we and the Americans contemplate a vast air operation', that the Russians were attempting to 'attain their political ends by starving the Berlin population of our sectors' and that Bevin was 'resolved to do everything in his power to prevent it'. He hoped that Harvey would do all he could to 'infuse courage into the French and to convince them that we have both the will and the ability to carry this thing through'.[9]

The Berlin blockade shifted Bevin's thinking on the Soviet Union, the United States and Germany. For Winston Churchill, likewise, it confirmed all the fears he had voiced in Fulton, Missouri, more than two years earlier. Publicly, he pledged his full support to Bevin and stated that the Foreign Secretary was 'right to speak for a united Britain'. Privately, however, he was plagued by fears of war with the Soviet Union, a war that threatened to destroy his hopes for a united Europe and, ultimately, world peace. On 21 July, he wrote to Attlee about his 'anxiety about the state of our defences and resources' and, on 27 July, he confessed to the American General Dwight D. Eisenhower that he was 'deeply distressed by what we see now'. Yet if Bevin believed that the Western allies should give no accommodation to Soviet demands, standing firm in the face of their belligerency even if that meant war, Churchill took the opposite view, telling Eisenhower: 'I feel there should be a settlement with Soviet Russia as a result of which they would retire to their own country and dwell there, I trust, in contentment'.[10] When it became clear that the Soviets would not retire in contentment, Churchill nevertheless held that delay was preferable to immediate confrontation. He wrote to Anthony Eden, '[I]t must be borne in mind that the American Air Force will be nearly double as strong this time next year as today, that the United States will have a third more atomic bombs and better, and far more effective means of delivery.... Therefore while we should not surrender to Soviet aggression or quit Berlin, it may well be that we and the Americans will be much stronger this time next year'.[11]

Churchill was also unconvinced that a strong Anglo–American partnership necessarily undermined British leadership in Europe, having never envisioned the two communities as mutually exclusive in the same way that Bevin had. On 17 June, just days before the crisis in Berlin began, he led a deputation of the British Section of the International Committee of the Movements for European Unity to meet with Attlee and Bevin in 10 Downing Street. Prior to the meeting, Captain Stephen King-Hall warned Churchill that he had it 'on authority I can hardly doubt' that the government was going to 'turn down the idea' to participate in a European Consultative Assembly, which other Western European leaders had already committed to. King-Hall told Churchill this would be a 'fearful shock to the French and Belgians and like a slap across the face with a wet fish; and a blow to the common man all over W. Europe'.[12]

At his meeting with Attlee and Bevin, Churchill insisted that the May Congress of Europe could 'claim to speak on behalf of all the free peoples of Europe' who had made clear their desire for a united Europe. Attlee agreed that it was important to promote 'a sense of European unity' but suggested that the British government had to take 'special care to ensure that, in growing towards Western Europe, the United Kingdom did not move away from the self-governing countries of the Commonwealth'. Bevin, too, expressed his desire to 'see the creation of a European Union', but he insisted that it must also include the 'development of Africa, South-East Asia and India' and consider 'our affiliations with Middle Eastern countries'. If Britain could fuse its European interests with its imperial responsibilities, it 'had an opportunity to consolidate a strong position in the middle of the world'. But British participation in a European Union could not include 'the surrender of sovereign rights'. Churchill agreed that he preferred to instead 'speak in terms of countries acquiring an enlarged or enriched sovereignty through membership of a European Union'. Bevin and Attlee were unconvinced and said they could not commit outright to a European Assembly without first ensuring that it did not prejudice Britain's links with the Commonwealth.[13]

Less than a week after this meeting, the Soviet Union closed its grip around Berlin, and Bevin's attention was wrested from future considerations of an integrated Europe to the very real situation in Germany. Churchill's cause suffered a further blow in mid-July when the French government of Robert Schuman fell, to be replaced by that of André Marie of the Radical Socialist Party. Although Marie remained in office for only a month before being succeeded by Schuman once more, Marie's time at the head of the French government corresponded with the first meeting of the European Consultative Committee established under the Treaty of Brussels (not to be confused with the more far-reaching Consultative Assembly envisioned by Churchill). Bevin opened the meeting with an update on the situation in Berlin, assuring the gathered foreign ministers of France, Belgian, Luxembourg and the Netherlands that the British and Americans were committed to protecting Berlin in the face of the Soviet onslaught and were undergoing an airlift that had reached 4,000–5,000 tons each day. He also informed them that a squadron of American B-29s would shortly be arriving in the United Kingdom to further convince the Soviets of the support the Western governments gave to Berlin.[14] In their first major disagreement of the post-war years, Georges Bidault sounded alarm at the arrival of the B-29s, expressed scepticism of American assurances of support and asked what the American government would do if its actions caused war in Europe with the Soviet Union. Would they again come to the aid of France? When Bevin asked if Bidault would rather negotiate with the Soviets 'at all costs without conditions', he confirmed that war must be avoided 'at all costs'.[15]

At the next meeting of the Consultative Committee, Bevin encouraged his colleagues to consider an Atlantic Pact between the Western European powers and the United States, but Bidault again resisted, arguing that the Europeans should work alone.[16] To Bevin, this was no longer feasible, given events in Berlin. When Bidault then proposed the formation of a European Assembly as a first step towards European integration, Bevin blanched, fearful that to do so would separate Britain from the United States at the most perilous time since the end of the war.[17] Furthermore, Bevin had always been clear that European unity must enhance rather than detract from existing European empires. Now, Bidault seemed to be suggesting that Britain and the Continent cut themselves off from the outside world, including the Commonwealth, just as they most needed its support. When Robert Schuman replaced Bidault as French Foreign Minister midway through the conference, Bevin's position was not improved, as Schuman pushed aggressively for a preparatory five-power conference to immediately consider the establishment of a European Parliament, a request the Foreign Secretary rejected.[18]

When Churchill heard that the government had thwarted plans for a European Assembly, he was furious. The British All-Party Group for a European Parliamentary Union in the House of Commons had as early as March 1948 tabled a motion to establish a European Assembly, which had gained the support of sixty-eight Labour MPs, fifty Conservatives and five Liberals.[19] Whilst far from a majority in the

Commons, the motion demonstrated the depth of cross-party support for European integration, quite apart from Churchill's own European Movement. On 27 July, Churchill had written to Attlee, enthusiastically telling him that the creation of a European Assembly would 'represent an important practical step in the advance towards a United Europe and would greatly help to create a sense of solidarity among the European peoples in the face of the increasing dangers which beset them'. He had added, 'In this the lead should be taken by Britain'.[20] Attlee had given him reason to hope, suggesting that he was 'in sympathy with the basic idea'.[21] Yet at the Consultative Committee of European Foreign Ministers, when other European governments were indeed seeking to establish such an assembly, it was the British government that had stood in its way.

Attlee wrote to Churchill on 21 August urging calm, explaining that Bevin 'could not for the time being commit himself' at a time of international crisis. Churchill would hear nothing of it, telling the Prime Minister, 'I venture to hope that His Majesty's Government will find it possible to place themselves more in line with Western European opinion upon an issue which they themselves have already done so much to promote'.[22] As far as Bevin was concerned, however, the European political climate had changed dramatically that summer. The French government was showing increasing signs of instability, whilst the Americans had once again proved their worth. There was also the larger question of Germany to consider, beyond the immediacy of the Berlin Crisis. In the immediate aftermath of the war, Bevin, like many Europeans, had believed that the greatest threat to the future peace of Europe would come from the revival of a strong Germany. Post-war British policy had been predicated upon ensuring that Germany would never again be able to wage war against its European neighbours. This policy was shaped not only by the recent experience of two world wars but by the ingrained British belief in a 'deep-seated flaw in the German "national character"; the inherent bellicosity of Germans through the ages, the teutonic lust for conquest and domination'.[23] It was for precisely this reason that Bevin shared Duff Cooper's enthusiasm for an Anglo–French alliance; he had signed the Dunkirk Treaty of 1947 specifically with the German threat in mind.[24]

However, even as the ink was drying on that treaty opinion was changing in the Foreign Office and across the British government. In early 1946, the Soviet government began to place increased pressure on German parties in the Soviet zone, leading to the merger of the Social Democrats with the German Communist Party to form the Socialist Unity Party in February. An internal minute in the Foreign Office remarked that this spelled the end of democracy 'for what is practically half of pre-war Germany.... A German puppet regime for the Soviet Union will soon be an accomplished fact'.[25] By July of that year, Bevin began to reference a more permanent split in Germany, which seemed to take a step closer to reality with the merger of the British and American zones into a Bi-Zone later that year.[26] George Marshall's offer of aid to Europe in June 1947 and the Soviet refusal to accept it led to further demarcation between East and West, and the collapse of the fifth Council of Foreign Ministers in London in December 1947 signalled the crossing of the bridge 'from wartime alliance [to] Cold War confrontation'.[27] When the Allied Control Council collapsed in March 1948, officially bringing an end to four-power control of Germany, it surprised nobody.[28] The beginning of the Berlin Blockade three months later was the culmination of a process that had begun a long time before.

With the Soviet Union now looming as the greatest threat to the maintenance of post-war peace, the position of Germany was transformed. Bevin firmly believed that the best way to combat communism was to bring economic prosperity and security to vulnerable states; now that Germany stood as an essential bulwark against Soviet influence, it was essential that the West German economy be revived and democratic institutions established. The British government had to do all it could to facilitate this.[29] Consequently, on 6 July 1948, the Foreign Secretary welcomed to his offices the first German delegation to come to the United Kingdom since the end of the war. Bevin told them that the British government sought to 'promote co-operation and not division both in Germany and in Europe', a policy that 'depended upon the Germans as well as the rest of Europe'. The British Labour Party believed in 'democracy, not Communists', and they would 'stand up to dictatorship'. Bevin's preference was for a united Germany, but, given recent events, the British government felt that it now had no choice but to concentrate on Western Germany. Bevin encouraged his visitors to 'move quickly so that some organisation on a political basis could be made to work.... It was up to the Germans to see how fast progress could be'.[30]

Bevin sent a summary of his meeting to William Strang, requesting advice on how the Berlin blockade affected British policy in Germany. Strang replied on 8 July with a seven-page memorandum. He began by asserting that the 'Russians are attempting to drive us out of Berlin by measures short of war' for two reasons: first, a Western withdrawal from Berlin would be a 'resounding political success' for the Soviets, not only in Germany but 'in Europe as a whole'; and second, the Western presence in Berlin was a 'political and economic embarrassment' to the Soviets, which prevented them from fully consolidating their purported sphere of influence. Berlin was, as Strang put it, 'an island of liberty...in a sea of growing totalitarianism'. He therefore recommended that 'In this conflict of wills we ought not to yield.... [W]e should maintain our publicly-stated policy that we are in Berlin as of right and intend to stay there, whatever the inconvenience'. Strang predicted that the Soviets would set up an independent Eastern German government with strong Soviet ties, similar in character to Poland or Czechoslovakia. This, he believed, would be 'advantageous' to the British government since it would 'convince the Germans in the West that the present division of Germany cannot be swiftly healed either by doing nothing in the West or by facile methods of negotiation. They would see that their only hope for the future would be to establish the West on a sound economic and political basis'. British policy should therefore be: '(1) Stay in Berlin. (2) Develop an air lift to the maximum. (3) Choose the right moment to reinforce our air forces, if necessary. [and] (4) Proceed with our political plans for Western Germany'.[31] Strang's memorandum confirmed Bevin's instinct and made him all the more determined to stick to his guns in Berlin, no matter how long it might take. The following day, he recommended to the Chiefs of Staff Committee that it 'would be prudent to plan on the assumption that there might be war, as...we could not withdraw from Berlin without making the most strenuous efforts to stay there'.[32]

None of this was possible, however, without major American support, and, in securing this, Bevin continued to clash with US Ambassador Douglas Lewis, who told him that the American government wished to approach Stalin in person to see if agreement might be reached for relaxing the Soviet blockade. Bevin objected strongly, arguing that to do so would be to 'build up his [Stalin's] position in Europe'. Besides, when dealing with an autocratic regime it was essential to negotiate with an institution rather than the dictator himself so as not to reinforce its totalitarian nature. Bevin thus 'wished to approach the Soviet Government and not to approach a man'. The correct protocol for doing so would be to contact the Soviet Foreign Minister, Vyacheslav Molotov. Douglas responded by arguing that the Western governments had just three alternatives if direct negotiations did not take place. The first was to abandon Berlin to the Soviet government, which would be 'a calamity'. The second was to withdraw from Berlin on a temporary basis but then form a 'regional pact' between the United States and Western European countries, reinforce Europe 'from a military point of view' and put pressure on the Soviet government to reopen Berlin to the West. This was likely to fail. The third option was to lobby for the United Nations to reaffirm British and American rights in Berlin, after which the Western governments would have more moral authority to employ force to protect Berlin if necessary. In reality, this meant war. Given that nobody wanted a war, a direct approach to Stalin was the only path forward.

Bevin told Douglas that he was placing him 'in great difficulty' because the other Western European governments had already committed to sending a written note to Molotov. Douglas, however, continued to argue for an approach to Stalin directly. At this, Bevin became exasperated, telling him he was 'at a loss to know how to reach agreement with the Americans'. He thought their approach was 'a weak way of doing things' but was willing to consider an oral rather than a written approach 'if that was what the Americans wanted'. However, he would not direct that oral protest to Stalin: 'I begged him [Douglas] to consider the European position, which people in Washington did not seem to understand. Why should we go hat in hand to Stalin and help to reinforce communism in Europe?' Douglas then asked if the American ambassador in Moscow could approach Stalin 'in the name of all three Governments [Britain, France and the United States]'. To Bevin, this was 'a position which I could certainly not accept. I could not commit our case to the representative of another Power'. Douglas' suggestion was an insult to Bevin's conviction that Britain was still one of the 'Big Three' in the world, and he closed the meeting shortly thereafter.[33]

When Bevin saw the ambassador again four days later, he had softened his stance somewhat. Douglas explained that his government still preferred an oral approach rather than a written note, since it was 'impossible to draft a note which was neither too hard on the one hand nor too conciliatory on the other'. Bevin acknowledged his concerns, said that he was still 'opposed to the approach to Stalin', but that 'in view of the strong views held by the United States Government and of the importance of carrying United States public opinion with us', he was 'prepared to recommend to my colleagues that we should agree to an approach to Stalin'. He was convinced that if the Western powers 'left Berlin now the Slavs would settle on the Rhine, and that would be the end of Western Europe'.[34] For the sake of preserving European security, Bevin therefore bowed to the wishes of the US government. However, in doing so, he directly reneged on the guarantees he had given his fellow European foreign ministers less than a week before at the Hague when he had promised that the Allies would make no direct approach to Stalin. Bevin believed he was acting in the best interests of Europe. To other Europeans, however, it seemed as though he had thrown in his lot with the Americans. He would never again hold the trust of his French and Benelux colleagues as he had prior to the summer of 1948. The Berlin Air Lift, more than any other event in the immediate postwar period, tied the British government closely to the Americans, restoring the wartime partnership the two had shared. In doing so, however, it isolated the government from its neighbours on the continent, in many ways unravelling the work Bevin had done with the French and Benelux leaders over the previous three years.

To make matters worse, in many of his objections to the American ambassador, Bevin – conveying the voice of Europe – was proved right. Representatives from the British, American and French governments met with Stalin in early August 1948. The Soviet leader immediately insisted that following the end of four-power control in Germany, the Western countries had lost any right to remain in Berlin and thus the Soviet government had the right to enact their blockade. So tense did talks become that, on 9 August, Bevin instructed Sir Oliver Franks, British Ambassador in Washington DC, to consult with Marshall to find out how much support the British might expect from the United States if they were to go to war with the Soviet Union.[35] By 11 August, it seemed likely that the talks would fail, and the French representatives began talking of withdrawal from Berlin without conditions. Bevin insisted that in no circumstances must the West leave Berlin, further solidifying his partnership with the Americans at the expense of the French.[36] Whilst the talks did not in fact break down, the conditions put before the Western allies by the Soviet Union were less than ideal: they would lift the blockade, but only if the Western powers withdrew the Western mark from Berlin by 7 September and permitted Soviet currency to be the only legal tender in all four sectors of the city.[37]

There were further complications. In late August, whilst the Four-Power talks were ongoing, the Soviet-supported Socialist Unity Party in Germany began a campaign of intimidation against the Western-supporting population of Berlin, besieging City Hall and occupying the Assembly Chamber. Shortly thereafter, Sokolovsky announced that the Soviet Air Force would begin manoeuvres on 6 September – manoeuvres that just so happened to utilise the same air space as the ongoing Western Allies' airlift.[38] The American government was incensed and immediately threatened to send a written note to the Soviet government protesting the actions of the Socialist Unity Party and breaking off all talks until the intimidation ceased. Bevin, however, counselled caution, telling Douglas that as frustrating as the disorders were, they were nevertheless 'in the nature of a side issue'. Furthermore, the Soviet government would be 'only too glad to see us offer battle on this ground'. He recommended that instead British and American representatives in Moscow speak in person to the Soviets about the issue.[39] Separately, Bevin wrote to the British Ambassador in Washington DC, telling him that the cabinet was 'gravely disturbed' by the American approach and asked him to 'see Marshall personally from me'.[40] In the face of pressure from both Bevin (through Douglas) and Sir Oliver Franks, Marshall agreed on 11 September that, for the sake of unity, he would follow the British approach.[41]

Despite this minor British diplomatic victory, the whole incident caused Frank Roberts, Bevin's private secretary, to rethink the British position. He wrote to Strang that the 'Russians are going to do everything in their power, short of war, to make our position in Berlin untenable' and wondered if 'resolute measures on our part in Western Germany should ensure that, even if we cease to be able to exercise any effective influence in Berlin the shock, great though it will no doubt be, need only be a passing one'. He believed that now the British had accepted the existence of 'two worlds', they could 'never expect to be allowed to maintain indefinitely and with no counter-advantage a footing within the Soviet camp' and thought that the 'real danger would only come... if the Russians advanced beyond the line then reached [in 1945] by the Red Army, which they at present show no intention or capacity of doing'. He recognised that there were 'sentimental feelings about the population of Berlin' and that it would be 'much nicer to be able to stand by them successfully until the bitter end' but reminded Strang that 'it is only three years since we were bombing Berlin to smithereens'. He argued that the 'safety and reorganisation of the whole of Western Europe, including Western Germany, is surely too important to be jeopardised by any sentimental feelings in regard to the Berliners'. This led him to consider if it wasn't time to negotiate a withdrawal from Berlin by the Western Allies in exchange for some guarantees about the permanency of an independent Western German state.[42]

Bevin would have none of it, particularly after the airlift delivered a record 7,000 tons of cargo in a single day on 18 September.[43] The Western strategy was working, and the Foreign Secretary would not abandon Berlin. In a cabinet meeting later that week, Bevin reported that George Marshall shared his commitment and that the Americans had guaranteed the resources to maintain the airlift throughout the winter. He reminded his colleagues that 'Since 1945 it ha[s] repeatedly been shown that any concessions to the Soviet Union [will] be exploited to the detriment of the Western Powers and, unless a firm stand [is] made now, our position in Europe [will] be hopeless'.[44] General Sir Brian Robertson, the British military governor in Germany, also supported Bevin's stance, writing that 'Berlin is but the epitome of the German situation as a whole. We are asking Berlin to hold out unarmed against communist aggression relying on Western support because it is in their interests as well as ours. We are asking Western Germany to do exactly the same'. Robertson argued that the Berliners' determination 'stems from the feeling that they are not alone in this struggle and that their stand has rehabilitated them in the eyes of the civilised world'. He warned, however, that the British government was following two contradictory policies in Germany: 'In the first place, we want her to resist communism and to serve as a buffer against the deadly menace which threatens us from the East. On the other hand we persist in treating her as the big sinner of Europe who must be made to pay retribution for past sins and be prevented at all costs from committing fresh ones'. These policies, he argued, were 'not compatible.... [T]he time has come to choose between them'. In his view, the British government must choose the latter: 'I believe we are committed to war with the Russians eventually. We cannot be choosers in such a conflict when it comes to Allies. The Germans, the best fighters in Europe apart from ourselves, are basically anti-Russian and anti-Communist in consequence. They are indeed I should say more reliable from this point of view than any other continental country'.[45]

Ivone Kirkpatrick, writing on behalf of the Foreign Office, assured Robertson it agreed with his 'general thesis that the situation requires a reorientation of our attitude towards the Germans. Indeed this has been in our minds for some time'. However, he added a caveat: 'It appears to me that what we should seek to achieve is to make the Germans believe that we sincerely welcome them into the European family of nations, but not that we regard them as an essential and indispensable ingredient. Once a German believes that he is indispensable to you, he believes that he holds all the trumps. And when he holds the trumps he becomes impossible to deal with'.[46] Western Germany was an essential buffer against the Soviet Union. Consequently, the German people had to be welcomed back into the European fold sooner rather than later. Nevertheless, it had only been three years since Britain was at war with Germany, when many of the same Berliners now being saved were committed to spreading the scourge of National Socialism throughout Europe. If there were sentimental reasons for standing by Berlin in the face of the blockade, there were equally strong ones for approaching the Germans with an abundance of caution. Where Robertson saw contradiction, Kirkpatrick saw only sound policy.

Meanwhile, from 21 September until 12 November 1948, the third General Assembly of the United Nations met in Paris, providing Britain, France and the United States yet more time to meet with representatives from the Soviet Union. In early October, the Security Council introduced a resolution calling for an immediate end to the blockade. In return, it suggested that a round of talks be held among the four military governors in Germany, who would negotiate a single currency for Berlin. The British, American and French governments accepted the resolution but the Soviets vetoed it, placing them at odds with the majority of the Security Council.[47] Nothing more came of the General Assembly, but with the airlift showing no signs of weakening and world public opinion turning against him, it was becoming apparent to Stalin that his plan had failed. In mid-December, he advised Eastern German communist leaders to stop any anti-Western activities. The following month, he told Kingsbury Smith, the European director of the American International News Service, that he would lift the blockade in exchange for a Western promise not to establish a West German state, along with a guarantee to begin talks for a Soviet–US nonaggression pact. He had abandoned altogether his demand of the previous September that the West withdraw its own currency from Berlin.[48]

Stalin's overtures were too little too late, however. By February 1949, the Western allies had reached their target of 5,620 tons of cargo per day in the airlift and believed it was possible to maintain this quantity indefinitely. Furthermore, 'with a stronger organisation and better maintenance of aircraft', they predicted they could transport an additional 1,000 tons daily.[49] In an appreciation for the cabinet on 4 February, Bevin told his colleagues, 'Thanks to the skill and determination with which the airlift has been maintained, the courage of the Berliners, the mildness of the winter and the general policy of not yielding an inch to the Soviet Government in Berlin, the general position in Berlin is now better than we had anticipated'. He concluded that Britain's 'immediate aim is the incorporation of Western Germany as soon as possible in our Western European system'. The French had now 'been brought to accept this policy in respect of a Federal Western German Government controlled by the Western Powers through the Occupation Statute'. The division of Germany, Bevin told the cabinet, was now 'essential to our plans'.[50]

To assist in better representing the British point of view in West Germany, Bevin arranged for officers from both the Education Branch and the Cultural Relations Branch of the British High Commissioner in Germany to be seconded to the British Council, a governmental organisation founded in 1934 to enhance what today would be called 'cultural relations' and what in the immediate post-war period was still openly described as propaganda. In a report written in early 1949, the British Council suggested that 'culture and politics have been combined in the British zone of Germany'; moving forward, it would be impossible to facilitate the spread of one without the other. It therefore argued that 'there would be more than a symbolic value in the Council proving itself from the very outset to be no more than another limb of the British Foreign Office'.[51] What the British government sought to embark upon in West Germany was nothing less than an imperial mission in the truest sense of the word, pitting British politics, economics and culture against Soviet communism. Although in this instance the battleground had moved from the colonies back to the European heartland, British foreign policy continued in the same vein as it had for many decades before.

Beyond Bevin's new-found conviction that West Germany must rejoin Europe, the Berlin Blockade convinced him that a European Western Union was insufficient to guarantee European security; only the United States, working in partnership with the Western Europeans, could do that. For this reason, an Atlantic rather than simply a European alliance was necessary. The Foreign Secretary first began to talk of expanding his idea of Western Union to include the United States and Canada in December 1947, following the breakdown of the Council of Foreign Ministers, when he had told both French Foreign Minister Georges Bidault and American Secretary of State George Marshall that an 'association of Western democratic countries' was necessary to combat Soviet communism: 'This would not be a formal alliance, but an understanding backed by power, money and resolute action'.[52] Bevin laid out his ideas in an aide-memoire to Marshall in March 1948, following which there were two weeks of secret talks in Washington among British, American and Canadian representatives.[53] The start of the Berlin Blockade just six months later only strengthened Bevin's conviction, and, at the meeting of the Brussels Powers foreign ministers in October 1948, he argued that the group of five European powers should be expanded to include also the United States and Canada.[54]

After receiving general assent from his European colleagues, Bevin put forward a proposal for a North Atlantic Treaty to the cabinet on 4 November, and the following day American President Truman gave his backing for a conference that might lead to a North Atlantic Pact.[55] On 14 January 1949, talks began in Washington DC.[56] The United Kingdom was represented by its ambassador, Sir Oliver Franks, who got on well with the new American Secretary of State Dean Acheson, who succeeded George Marshall on 21 January 1949.[57] However, their friendship once again came at the expense of European unity, and Franks and Acheson ran into resistance from the French ambassador Henri Bonnet, who would only agree to the inclusion of Norway if Italy and Algeria were also included. This, the British, Americans, Canadians and Benelux all opposed. Acheson proposed a compromise, whereby France's Algerian departments would be recognised and Italy invited to participate in return for the inclusion of Norway, Iceland and Denmark. Sweden was also invited to participate but declined. Ireland insisted that the ending of the partition between Northern Ireland and the Irish Free State was a precondition for their joining and thus they were left out. Portugal was likewise invited but not Spain, and all agreed to exclude Greece and Turkey.

When the conference convened, therefore, North America was represented by the United States and Canada and Europe by the United Kingdom, France, the Benelux countries, the Scandinavian countries (minus Sweden), Portugal and Italy. After eight separate meetings and a total of eighteen sessions, on 15 March 1949, a draft treaty was completed, to be signed on 4 April. On that date, the North Atlantic Treaty Organisation (NATO) was born.[58] It had come about largely on the initiative of Bevin, with his ambassador Sir Oliver Franks playing a leading role in the drafting of the treaty.[59] Its delivery, however, ended any chance of a European 'third force' standing independently between the United States and the Soviet Union. NATO ensured that Europe would 'hitch its military machine to the American juggernaut' and further tied Britain to an Atlantic rather than a purely European alliance.[60]

Meanwhile, on 5 March, Stalin replaced his foreign minister Vyacheslav Molotov with Andrey Vishinsky, a man known to hold a more favourable opinion of the West. Within three weeks of his appointment, the Soviets had dropped their demand that the Western powers not establish a West German state, requesting only that a Council of Foreign Ministers be convened where all parties could discuss the future of Germany. Bevin met with Acheson on 1 April, and the latter suggested that the Western Allies send a note to the Soviet government offering a conference immediately if the blockade was lifted. Bevin, however, argued that there was no need to rush. He told Acheson that they should 'insist on discussing not only Berlin and Germany, but Austria, Trieste, Greece, our rights in the Balkan satellite countries and indeed Europe as a whole'. As far as Bevin was concerned, the Russians were beat; why negotiate on a limited matter when the big issues could be resolved?[61]

Attlee agreed with Bevin. A Council of Foreign Ministers held in April 1949 would hold 'inherent dangers', namely that the British government 'should be put in the position of either having to reject apparently reasonable Russian proposals for the re-unification of Germany and the withdrawal of occupation forces, thus making ourselves appear unreasonable, or we should have to accept such proposals, which might lead to the swift establishment of a Central German Government in Berlin, which would have great dangers for all of us'.

Now that the Soviet government was in a position of weakness, the Western allies needed to use the strength of their airlift to redesign a new West German government in their own image, without communist influence. Only once Britain, the United States and France had carried out their own plans for West Germany's government should they meet with the Soviet government to discuss 'the whole German problem', by which time it would be clear that a partition was unavoidable and – from the British perspective – advantageous.[62]

The American government took some persuading of this view.[63] American policy still favoured a united Germany,[64] and Bevin told Franks that he was 'disquieted and uneasy at some aspects of the way things are going'. He warned him that 'It is going to be no easy, and certainly no short, matter for the western Powers to reach agreement on satisfactory terms for Germany with the Russians. Their ideas and objects are exactly opposed to ours'. He feared that there was 'too much readiness in some quarters to believe that merely because the Russians have shown some readiness to raise the blockade the rest will be plain-sailing. On the contrary, in spite of the advantages which we at present hold, I think that if we are to avoid serious danger we shall have to exercise the greatest caution and foresight during the coming weeks'. He asked that Franks express his concerns directly to Acheson.[65] As was so often the case, Bevin got his way. Franks reported on 2 May that he had shared Bevin's message and that Acheson had 'agreed with all of it'. His only worry was that they could not be seen to be 'holding conversations and arriving at conclusions which the French could think were to be imposed upon them'. He therefore suggested that tri-partite talks among the American, British and French foreign ministers take place in Paris before any Council of Foreign Ministers, during which time policy could be 'jointly worked out and agreed' and thus a 'common front' could be presented to the Soviets. Any Council should be preceded by a guarantee for a 'permanent' lifting of the blockade. He also agreed with Bevin that the point had now been reached where the Soviets' vision of Germany and the Western Allies' vision were so different as to be fundamentally incompatible, and thus the British, French and Americans should 'go on with our policies and plans for Western Germany'.[66]

With an understanding between Bevin and Acheson in place by 4 May, the Western Allies offered the Soviets a Council of Foreign Relations meeting contingent on a permanent end to the blockade of

Berlin. One week later – on 12 May 1949 – the Soviet Union agreed and lifted its blockade.[67] The airlift continued whilst ground transportation systems slowly resumed to normal; on 31 August, the Royal Air Force flew its last mission to Berlin and on 30 September, the last American plane landed with a cargo-hold full of coal, the final official drop of the airlift.[68] In all, British and American planes had delivered 2,325,510 tons of cargo to Berlin, whilst bringing out 81,731 tons and transporting in and out of Berlin 227,655 passengers. Of the 277,569 flights to go to and from Berlin, the Royal Air Force had flown 87,606.[69] It had not been an easy fifteen months – the British had suffered thirty-nine fatalities and lost forty-six aircraft – but they had triumphed in the end.[70] However, the Europe of August 1949 was fundamentally different from that of June 1948. This was a reality that those in favour of a European Union would have to contend with.

5 A DISUNITED EUROPE?

Winston Churchill was not immune to the effects of the Berlin crisis on his calls for European unity. Yet nor did he think it in any way undermined the underlying principles he had championed since the end of the war; after all, he had been one of the first to warn of the Soviet threat and the first to suggest that Germany needed to feel the welcoming embrace of the West sooner rather than later. In late July 1948, shortly after the crisis in Berlin began, he dispatched Anthony Eden to West Germany to report first-hand on the situation there. In almost all respects, Eden found it 'far better than it was a year ago'. The Germans had now 'passed out of the stage of apathy which characterised the first two years of the post-war period', and the British and American authorities were 'enjoying considerably more friendly support than they had hitherto'. In Berlin, there was even a 'wave of enthusiasm for the Western Allies', which Eden found quite remarkable given that not three years had passed since they were at war. Nevertheless, he was disturbed by the 'fundamental lack of understanding among almost all classes and ages of the meaning of the word "democracy"', and he found that although the Germans had 'largely discarded Nazism as such, ... nothing has taken its place'.[1] The time was ripe for the British to fill the void with their own ideologies.

Churchill's position was strengthened by a public opinion poll published in the *Daily Express* on 8 September 1948, which suggested that the 'Government are not carrying their own people with them in their policy' of only gradual moves towards European Union.[2] Starting with the premise that the French cabinet had now publicly voiced its support for a European Assembly and a Western Union that would 'embrace Great Britain, France, the Netherlands, Belgium and Luxembourg', the poll found that 65 per cent of the British public favoured an 'economic union...with common Customs' (with just 13 per cent opposed), 68 per cent supported a 'military union' where all countries would 'give and receive armed assistance to any member of the Western Union if attacked' (with 16 per cent opposed) and 58 per cent wanted a 'political union providing for a European Supreme Court with power to impose sanctions' (with, again, 16 per cent opposed). Furthermore, the poll found broad support across party lines: of those interviewed, 41 per cent were Conservatives, 34 per cent Socialists (Labour), 5 per cent Liberals and 2 per cent Other. Whilst Conservatives tended to be keener on European integration than Liberals or Labour (e.g., 73 per cent of Conservatives supported economic union, but just 62 per cent of Labour; 66 per cent of Conservatives favoured political union against 54 per cent of Labour supporters), all three parties showed majority support for economic, political and military union. Of those opposed to all three forms of union, the most common reasons given were that 'Britain should not become entangled with Europe' and that 'Britain should rely more on her Empire'.[3]

The United Europe Movement was well aware that the greatest opposition to British integration with the European continent came from those who feared it would undermine Britain's imperial mission, and it actively sought to counter this concern. In a booklet of 'Speakers' Notes' circulated to its committee on 9 August 1948, the movement suggested that 'the most far-sighted imperialists inside and outside Great Britain are throwing their weight behind the United Europe Movement' and cited the support of the Canadians William MacKenzie King (the longest-serving Prime Minister in Canadian history) and Louis St. Laurent (who was to succeed MacKenzie King in November 1948). It claimed that the 'whole-hearted support given by these Empire and world statesmen' proved that there was nothing 'incompatible between the objectives of Imperial development and the hope of European survival'.[4] Leo Amery also continued to spread this message, writing on 8 October that 'The two conceptions [of European unity and the British Commonwealth] need not be in any sense mutually exclusive. On the contrary, as Mr. [Robert] Menzies [the Australian wartime Prime Minister] has recently pointed out, they are essentially complementary'.[5]

Only days later, Duncan Sandys wrote a long letter to *The Times* asking, '(1) Can Britain, as a member of a world-wide Empire, at the same time become a member of a European Union? (2) What should be the constitutional structure of a united Europe? [and] (3) What is the next practical step to be taken?' He argued that a European Union would be 'nothing but an illusion unless it obtains the effective participation of Great Britain', yet the United Kingdom could not enter 'any continental system which tended to separate her from her partners in the Commonwealth'. For that reason, the task at hand for the British government was to 'devise arrangements for the integration of western Europe of such a nature as will enable Britain to participate effectively without prejudice to the maintenance and further consolidation of her Imperial connexions'. He pointed out that the Brussels Treaty had already joined together European countries with the Commonwealth in the defence sphere and that the Marshall Plan had brought them closer in economic affairs. The path forward was one of many small steps rather than 'one giant stride', but already remarkable progress had been made. He concluded that the best way to 'give new hope and encouragement to all, on both sides of the Iron Curtain', was to 'look to the creation of a "United Europe" as the next essential step towards the creation of a free and united world'.[6] Such a united Europe would necessarily include Britain and its Commonwealth.

The Labour Party, too, sought to dispel speculation that a closer partnership with Europe would undermine the Commonwealth. On 27 July 1948, Sir Stafford Cripps, the Chancellor of the Exchequer, wrote in the *Financial Times* that 'we [the government] feel that there is no conflict [between cooperation with Western Europe and the British Commonwealth]'. He explained that 'by developing production of new resources in the Commonwealth in the field of raw materials, we are creating sources from which we and the other European countries can draw, and thus reduce our dependence upon dollar supplies. ... Our purposes in co-operating with the O.E.E.C. countries and in co-operating with the Commonwealth are complementary, and thus there can be no conflict between them'.[7] The government expanded its thinking further in March 1949, when the Colonial Office circulated a memorandum to assist Labour MPs in promoting the government's colonial policy. In an annex to the main report, it noted that 'British colonial policy is often misrepresented and attacked both in this country and in foreign countries'. Its aims, however, were simple and commendable, namely 'to produce adequate conditions of life for mankind, ... a task which others have been attempting in their own countries, often with indifferent success, for hundreds of years'. The fundamental aim of the British government was 'to guide the colonial territories to responsible self-government within the British Commonwealth, in conditions that ensure to their peoples fair standards of living and freedom of oppression from any quarter'. It was for the purpose of achieving this that the United Kingdom so often collaborated with its European neighbours in 'regular conferences and exchange of information', so that they could together 'secure for [the] colonial territories all the help which can be offered'. An integrated Europe working together could better the lives and futures of colonial peoples across the globe; its intent was certainly not to undermine the Empire and Commonwealth.[8]

Meanwhile, the European Movement took a further step forward on 25 October 1948, when the Belgian Prime Minister Paul-Henri Spaak, the Italian Prime Minister Alcide de Gasperi, the former French Prime Minister Léon Blum and Winston Churchill announced that they would become Presidents of Honour of the European Movement, which from that date forward would be constituted as a single, multinational organisation.[9] Sandys, speaking on Churchill's behalf, said that the 'next urgent step in the building of this new Europe is, we believe, the convening of a deliberative European Assembly, whose task it will be to create a European public opinion and a sense of solidarity among the peoples of our continent'.[10] There was, however, a significant anomaly in this announcement. Whilst Belgium and Italy were represented by their heads of government, the British and French governments sent no official representation. The meeting took place whilst Foreign Secretaries Bevin and Schuman were in the midst of the third UN General Assembly in Paris, trying desperately to place pressure on the Soviet government to lift its blockade of Berlin. Under such circumstances, even the French government recognised that cooperation with the United States was in Europe's more immediate interests than the establishment of a European Assembly. For the first time since 1946, Churchill's efforts seemed less visionary and more out of touch with reality.

Consequently, as the aeroplanes continued to fly to Berlin, members of the European Movement sought to refine its mission.

Speaking to the Anglo–American Press Association in Paris on 1 December 1948, Sandys called for the creation of a European Charter of Human Rights and a European Supreme Court to police any infringements, the rulings of which would be binding on member-states.[11] A week later, he argued at the Paris meeting of the Five-Power Committee on European Unity that a Supreme Court and Charter of Human Rights could only work in the context of a European Assembly. This assembly should initially be open only to the five signatories of the Brussels Treaty but could in time be expanded to include representatives from 'any other of the free countries of Europe, such as Italy, whose governments are willing to participate'.[12] The United Europe movement, however, continued to run on a parallel track to government initiatives at the United Nations and elsewhere, with the two tracks never meeting. Increasingly, members of the movement became frustrated with the Labour government, a frustration shared by Conservatives in the House of Commons. In the New Year, Harold Macmillan lamented that the government had 'neither united Europe nor united the Empire', expressing the growing fear amongst the opposition that Attlee and Bevin were squandering Britain's leadership not only on the continent but also in the wider world.[13]

The British branch of the European Movement was particularly concerned that the United Kingdom was yielding ground to the French on continental plans whilst distracted by the Americans and the Berlin airlift. On 22 April 1949, Count Coudenhove-Kalergi wrote to Churchill, warning him that 'the brilliant progress of our movement for European unity ... is running into a dangerous impasse, since Britain and France have very different views on this issue'. He explained: 'While Britain aims at a European Commonwealth with a consultative Assembly and an international Council, France wishes a genuine Federation under a Federal Constitution and a Federal Government'. There was also the ever-present question of Germany to consider. Coudenhove-Kalergi shared Churchill's enthusiasm for welcoming West Germany back into the European fold, but the French argued that 'no reconciliation with Germany is possible, except within a European Federation'. Only under an arrangement where France could control Germany would the French government be willing to consider expanding European integration to include the Germans. Yet the British government had already ruled out a federation. There was, however, a possible solution, revealed by the Berlin Crisis. The British government could step away from the continent, so that it would 'become, together with the U.S.A., a sponsor and partner rather than a member of a European Federation – in the spirit and framework of the Atlantic Pact'. There would therefore be a triple-Atlantic alliance: the USA, the Commonwealth, and the United States of Europe. This would lead to the realisation of greater European integration, would solve the problem of Germany and would allow Britain to remain close to the United States.[14] It would also, of course, place France rather than Britain in the commanding position in Europe.

Duncan Sandys saw through this letter immediately, angrily telling Churchill that Coudenhove-Kalergi wished to undermine the European Movement in favour of the Count's Pan-European Movement, and he warned that Coudenhove-Kalergi was 'going about abusing the European Movement and, in a more veiled way, abusing you as its leader'.[15] Churchill, too, understood that Coudenhove-Kalergi was seeking to undermine British leadership in Europe, particularly at a time when the British government itself was clashing with other governments on the continent, yet he sought to resolve the matter in a more diplomatic way than Sandys. He replied to Coudenhove-Kalergi on 8 May, thanking him for his letter, agreeing that the European Movement had 'made remarkable progress', but politely disagreeing that it was 'running into a dangerous impasse'. On the contrary, he believed that with 'a little patience' any obstacles between the various European countries could be successfully tackled, and concluded: 'You should certainly not imagine that Britain will not be willing and able to play a full and worthy part in bringing the great conception of United Europe to fruition'.[16] Churchill had refused to take the bait, but the matter did not end there. Coudenhove-Kalergi wrote to him again, saying that 'The impression is growing throughout the Continent that it [Great Britain] wishes to promote Union, but to prevent Federation' and warning that 'nothing short of federation can reconcile France and Germany and thus assure peace and liberty for us all'.[17] Coudenhove-Kalergi's letter confirmed for Churchill the urgency with which Bevin had to take a lead on the continent before it was too late – before the French government redefined the question of European unity in favour of a federal solution that would be in its own best interests but would be detrimental to Britain's.

On the continent, however, Bevin was having his own problems with his European colleagues. He had been meeting throughout the year with Paul-Henri Spaak (the Belgian Prime Minister), Paul van Zeeland (the Belgian Foreign Minister), Édouard Herriot (the President of the French Chamber of Deputies), Robert Schuman (the French Foreign Minister), Dirk Stikker (the Dutch Minister of Foreign Affairs) and Joseph Bech (the Luxembourg Foreign Minister) to discuss issues of common concern in Europe. In October 1948, rumours began to circulate that Spaak might resign as Belgian Prime Minister to instead lead the Organisation of European Economic Cooperation (OEEC) on a full-time basis. Bevin sought confirmation of this from the United Kingdom's delegation to the OEEC in Paris, which informed him that the idea had 'not originated' with Spaak but rather had been put forward by Schuman. Spaak was a firm ally of Bevin's in most discussions of European integration and fully understood Britain's position with the Empire and Commonwealth. Bevin therefore feared that if Spaak were to play a more administrative role in the OEEC, rather than being a direct participant in the talks, Schuman's advocacy for a full federation of Europe would be strengthened, further isolating Bevin. He therefore gave instructions to the UK delegation that 'no (repeat no) pressure should be put on Spaak to leave the Belgian cabinet'[18] and wrote directly to him, saying, 'I look upon you as a great helpmate in building Western Union. . . . I fear that you might not be able to exercise the same influence and authority in the O.E.E.C. For myself, I should greatly miss your support and wise advice in the Councils of the Western Union'.[19]

Bevin also tasked Hector McNeil, his minister of state, to speak directly with Spaak at the UN General Assembly in Paris. McNeil reported that he had told Spaak he was Bevin's 'main hope and confidante in [our] plans for the defence and development of Western Europe' and that Bevin was 'perplexed and distressed to think that he, Paul Spaak, would leave Brussels for Paris'. Spaak, however, replied that whilst he was 'very flattered' by Bevin's comments, he thought he might be of more use in Paris. The OEEC 'badly needed a Director General of stature and energy', someone whose 'reputation and ability [are such] that he could approach as an equal the Ministers of any one of the participating Governments', and one who would be 'respected by the Government of the United States . . . [and] known to the American public'. The OEEC had not yet caught the public imagination, and this was essential if Marshall Aid was to succeed. Consequently, although Spaak was a loyal Belgian and proud to be its Prime Minister, he was also a committed European and would be 'anxious to take the post'.[20] Given these sentiments, it came as a surprise to Bevin when he turned down the position at the OEEC later that month to instead remain Prime Minister of Belgian. Bevin's relief did not last long, however, as he continued to find himself at odds with his fellow Europeans, in great contrast to his ever-closer relationship with the Americans over the issue of Berlin.

At the meeting of the Consultative Council of the Five-Powers in late October 1948, the French and Belgian governments suggested that it was time for the question of European integration to 'no longer be studied on a private level but on a Governmental level', a premise that Bevin thoroughly agreed with, hoping that by doing so he could take the wind out of Churchill's United Europe Movement. However, speaking on behalf of France, Robert Schuman again put forward the proposal for a European Assembly, this time as a Franco–Belgian plan intended to integrate the European countries into an economic federation. Taken aback by the proposal given previous Belgian support for the British position, Bevin said he 'did not see clearly what France and Belgium proposed to do. Did they want to fuse the five countries into one? Did they wish to create a kind of organisation of the United European Nations?' Were they, in other words, looking to create a new European state or simply a regional bloc within the United Nations? He reminded the foreign ministers that 'Great Britain [is] at the centre of a Commonwealth of 400 million inhabitants, which did not seek to consolidate its bonds by means of a constitution, but which formed a voluntary association of nations provided with a spirit of co-operation'. The British Commonwealth worked well and was an excellent model for European countries to consider as they moved towards ever greater union. The Franco–Belgian plan seemed to be something entirely different. Bevin said that if Schuman was seeking 'a new constitution for the countries of Western Europe, it would be better to say so', as Britons had an inherent scepticism of written constitutions. They did not have one at home and had never felt the need to create one for their Empire and Commonwealth.

Bevin was also having trouble envisioning how a European Assembly would work. Was it, in essence, a European Parliament? If so, would its decisions be binding on the national parliaments of its member-states? How could democracy be ensured under such conditions? What would happen if the decision of the European

Parliament clashed with the wishes of a democratically elected national parliament? Which political mandate would take precedent, the European or the national? How would a European Assembly affect national sovereignties? There was also the question of how representatives for a European Parliament would be selected, both in terms of how many from each nation and how their elections would be held within each nation. The British government favoured a first-past-the-post system, in which parliamentary representatives were firmly tied to a political constituency. On the continent, most governments favoured a proportional representation system, whereby the people voted for a party, and representatives were selected from a party list. How could the British public accept the decisions of European parliamentarians who had been elected under a system that most Britons considered undemocratic, particularly when such decisions might overturn legislation passed by Britain's own Parliament? There were too many unanswered questions for Bevin to seriously commit to participation in a European Assembly.

Schuman countered that a European Assembly would be a 'great attraction for Germany'. Given that the UK was Germany's strongest advocate on the European continent, the proposal ought therefore to be favoured by the British government. Bevin replied that the government was quite happy to work with Germany in the context of a European Union following a Commonwealth model, without the need for federation. The ministers' time would be far better spent forming a committee to 'study together all the questions of common interest, with a view to a progressive evolution towards European unity', rather than debating a possible European Assembly. Why busy themselves with the creation of formal institutions and constitutions when they could instead directly address the issues of the day, in partnership and with a spirit of cooperation? Dirk Stikker, the Dutch Foreign Minister, agreed with Bevin. The Netherlands had put on record that it was 'in favour of all efforts which might be made to develop European co-operation in all fields' but was 'not convinced' that a formal constitution and the creation of a European Assembly was the best way forward. Like Bevin, Stikker preferred a 'pragmatic' union with government ministers cooperating as appropriate to coordinate a common European policy. Joseph Bech of Luxembourg likewise supported efforts to coordinate European-wide policy but 'would have grave hesitations if it were a matter of having an assembly'.

The European ministers were thus at an impasse, with the French and Belgians arguing that it was essential to create a constitution and institutions for a European federation, and the British, Dutch and Luxembourg ministers preferring to instead follow a more pragmatic approach addressing specific issues, without need for a loss of national sovereignty or the creation of new institutions. Paul-Henri Spaak, alarmed that divisions were appearing, suggested that he had 'never thought of a constitution, rather of a federation'. 'Not being English', he was 'not perhaps used to showing the same caution as Mr. Bevin in matters of constitution', but he believed their positions were closer than the meeting had allowed. He would therefore support the creation of a committee, which could discuss what form, if any, a European Assembly might take. Schuman, recognising that numbers were against him, agreed to move forward with the committee, and the Council decided that the committee would consist of five representatives from Great Britain, five from France, three from Belgium, three from the Netherlands and two from Luxembourg. In addition to supporting the work of the committee, Schuman promised to drop for the time being any further discussion of a European Assembly.[21]

Although he had secured another British victory, Bevin had further isolated himself from the French, and, although the Benelux countries had supported his vision rather than Schuman's, the Conservative Party at home was only too willing to paint him as obstructing plans for European unity. Indeed, so negative was the coverage by some of the British press, both Conservative and far left, that the Foreign Office drew up guidance notes on how to combat the critical attitude of British newspapers towards the government's policy in Europe. In particular, it was concerned that articles in the usually supportive *Nation* and the *New Statesman* had suggested that 'the United Kingdom in company with the United States of America' wished to 'whittle away' plans for European Union. The Foreign Office believed it was now time to 'counter through the means of [all] publicity open to His Majesty's Government the accusations that we are out to sabotage ... Europe'.[22]

Bevin's position in Europe did not improve. When, at the Fourth Meeting of the Consultative Council in London in January 1949, Schuman again put forward a report 'attempting to set up a Council of Europe and an Assembly of a parliamentary character', Bevin countered with his own report that 'envisaged a purely governmental body consisting of Government delegates'. Paul-Henri Spaak favoured Schuman's report, claiming it was 'what the public were calling for'. Bevin replied that he was 'as keen as any Minister present to get the right approach to European Unity and to make us all feel Europeans' but could honestly not see how the creation of a formal European Assembly was in any way an improvement over the close cooperation through specific organisations that had already been established. He concluded that 'In his Trade Union experience he had found that there was always a difference of approach between different countries, reflecting the differences of their individual constitutional experience. The British and the Scandinavian Unions usually follow the same rule, whereas the French and Belgians had others, and the old German Unions a third. The job was to harmonise'. He was, however, willing to offer a compromise. He would support the creation of a Council of Europe made up of government representatives if the other ministers would postpone a decision on the European Assembly. This Spaak and Schuman agreed to, and, on 28 January 1949, the five governments issued a joint statement announcing that they had agreed to establish a 'Council of Europe, consisting of a ministerial committee meeting in private and a consultative body meeting in public'. This Council would consist not only of the Five Powers but would welcome any free European governments that wished to take part.[23] For the immediate future, Bevin had once again stopped the creation of a European Assembly. It soon became clear, however, that if he envisioned the Council of Europe as a final step in European integration, the French and Belgian ministers saw it as only the beginning.

There were problems, too, on the colonial front. On 2 March 1949, A. B. Cohen of the Colonial Office penned a minute arguing that the British government could not 'go on in West Africa with programmes of constitutional development which ignore the great differences between ourselves and the French'. Since 1945, the government's policy had been to seek ever closer cooperation with the French in the colonial world, an acknowledgement that as imperial powers they would need to work together in the face of a growing anti-colonial consensus led by the United States. However, in forging such cooperation, it had become clear that British colonialism was very different to French; the fact that both were condemned by the United States did not necessarily mean they could easily coordinate their policies. Still, Cohen was not entirely pessimistic. He recognised that 'the policy of Western

Union demands parallel action in Africa' and even suggested that should bilateral talks with the French fail to reach a consensus, the government could attempt 'to work out a policy of closer African union through the machinery set up for Western Union'. Cohen also drew attention to the increasing criticism of British colonialism in the United Nations, which had 'compelled us to adopt a largely negative approach in our international colonial policy'. He suggested that 'The best counterweight to this would be a constructive policy of closer co-operation between our [British and French] colonial territories, particularly in Africa'.[24] There were certainly problems with collaborating with the French, but in the face of general American opposition to colonialism, European solidarity was still the best option available to the British government.

When the Council of Europe met for the first time at Strasbourg in August 1949, it did so with representatives from twelve European countries: France, Belgium, Luxembourg, the Netherlands, Great Britain, Ireland, Italy, Norway, Sweden, Denmark, Greece and Turkey. Within a year, Iceland and West Germany would also join. At Schuman's insistence, the Five-Power Consultative Council did not hold its scheduled meeting that August because the French Foreign Minister felt that the Five Powers 'must not give the others the impression that they were trying to create a *bloc* or adopt a united front'.[25] Harold Macmillan, one of the Conservative Party delegates to the Council, remembered that 'we met in a real atmosphere of spiritual excitement. We really felt convinced that we could found a new order in the Old World – democratic, free, progressive, destined to restore prosperity and preserve peace'. For Macmillan, Britain's goals were clear: 'While nearly all of us [in the British delegation] were averse to the federal concept which a few extremists enthusiastically promoted, we accepted that sincere partnership in the common task of rebuilding Europe must involve some surrender of sovereignty and the creation of some form of political organisation'.[26] In that regard, Macmillan's views did not differ significantly from Bevin's.

Nevertheless, at the Council, there was tension between the ministerial committee (composed only of those parties in power) and the consultative body, which Schuman had succeeded in renaming 'the assembly' (composed of cross-party delegates and other national notables). Bevin told Paul van Zeeland, the Belgian Foreign Minister, that he thought this tension was 'artificial' and had largely 'been developed by Mr. Churchill and his friends with the aid of Duncan Sandys and the

European Movement'. He reminded van Zeeland that, unlike in France and the Benelux countries, which had experienced frequent elections and changes of government since the war, 'in Great Britain this [European] problem had never been put to the test of the electorate'. It was therefore in the best interests of the Conservative Party to turn the government's European policy into a party-political issue and try to undermine Bevin's position. The structure of the assembly made this possible, providing a platform for opposition Conservative politicians that the British people had denied them.[27]

Yet Bevin was perhaps blinded by his partisan concerns over Churchill, all evidence suggesting that the United Europe Movement was in fact genuine in its desire for European integration. Indeed, throughout its history, it had desperately hoped that the Labour Party would join with its efforts. Robert Boothby, one of the five British delegates from the Conservative Party in Strasbourg, had travelled by train to the conference with Churchill. He pressed the former Prime Minister on what exactly he had in mind for Europe. Churchill replied, 'We are not making a machine, we are growing a living plant.... We have lit a fire which will either blaze or go out; or perhaps the embers will die down and then, after a while, begin to glow again'.[28] At the Assembly, Boothby delivered a speech (with Churchill in attendance) calling for all European countries, including the United Kingdom, to 'co-ordinate our monetary and fiscal policies. We must plan investment in our basic industries on a European scale, and encourage specialization. We must also negotiate reciprocal trade and payment agreements on a preferential basis'. He claimed that 'State sovereignty was one of the principal causes of evil in the modern world, and that the only solution to this problem lay in some merging or pooling of national sovereignty', and he suggested that 'in the Assembly and the Committee of Ministers, we had the instruments with which an organic European union could be forged'.[29] There is no reason to believe that Boothby was insincere in his words, and Churchill did not offer a dissenting position. For the European Movement, the issue was larger than party politics. That Conservatives were in general more willing to integrate than the government occurred by chance, not by design. In any case, Bevin's true adversary continued to be Robert Schuman, the French Foreign Minister, who was unable to work with Bevin as closely as Bidault had before him.

When Bevin travelled to the United States in September 1949, he was in a buoyant mood and reminded the gathered press at the New York docks 'what had been done in the past 18-months: the Brussels Pact, OEEC and the ERP, the remodelling of the British Commonwealth with independence for India, Pakistan and Ceylon; the Atlantic Pact; the Council of Europe, the establishment of a democratic government in Western Germany'.[30] He gushed, 'I doubt whether so many impressive and far-reaching political advances have been made in any other eighteen months of the world's history'. And in Bevin's mind, he had been at the centre of it all, many of the things he listed coming by his initiative.[31] Yet by 15 September, following a week of bilateral talks with the Americans, his confidence was knocked. Over the course of the week, it became clear that the US State Department, under the influence of George Kennan, no longer believed in British leadership of Europe but rather in two separate Western blocs, one containing the United States, Canada, Great Britain, the Scandinavian countries and Britain's traditional ally Portugal, and the other France, West Germany and the smaller European countries. The first would be 'maritime, and extra-European in interests and mentality; the second, relatively land-bound and Continental'.[32] Whilst Bevin was certainly not opposed to closer British ties with the United States and Scandinavia, he would not accept a junior role for the United Kingdom in an American-led coalition, distinct from the other Western European countries; his vision was that Britain would lead both Europe and the Commonwealth whilst also providing sage guidance to the United States.

Nevertheless, Bevin's position was further undermined when the French, represented by Schuman, joined his meetings at the State Department for a second week of talks. Here, the focus shifted to the German question. Now that the West German state had been established, Bevin was 'anxious to bring the Germans into the Western European orbit'. He particularly wanted to capitalise on the close relations that had been formed during the Berlin airlift and the good opinion that the German people now held for the Western governments. He argued that the Allies should stop dismantling the German steel plants, which they had been doing punitively since the end of the war, and should instead 'take greater risks on industry'. Schuman, however, countered that it was first important to 'see how the German Government behaved'. Dean Acheson remarked that 'there was a good deal of agitation in the United States, in Congress and elsewhere, in favour of a revision of Allied policy on dismantling', but Schuman stood firm. He appreciated the 'difficulties' of American public opinion but insisted that 'the French Government had also to consider their own people, whose minds were always directed to the problem of security'. For Schuman, the Soviet blockade of Berlin and the subsequent airlift meant very little. Germany had to be subdued; it could not again be allowed to dominate the European continent.[33]

Anglo–French relations soured further the following week when the British government devalued sterling by 30.5 per cent from $4.03 to $2.80. It transpired almost immediately that the American government had known about the devaluation for many weeks, even advising the British Treasury on how far sterling should fall. The French, however, had not been warned, even though they had sat for a week with the British and Americans in private consultation in Washington.[34] The French government immediately issued a formal *démarche* to protest, yet the situation only worsened further when the new West German government followed the British lead by devaluing the mark by 25 per cent against the dollar. This heightened French fears of a possible Anglo–German alliance and further undermined their confidence that the British government sought to act in the interests of Europe as a whole.[35]

Even so, the American State Department continued to show a new-found reticence about a British role in continental Europe. During his talks with Bevin, George Kennan suggested that it would 'be better if the UK were not too closely tied politically and economically to Western Europe, but rather that it should be aligned with the U.S.A. and Canada'.[36] Following the conference, an internal State Department memorandum concluded: 'An attempt should be made to link the U.K. more closely to the U.S.A. and Canada and to get the U.K. to disengage itself as much as possible from Continental European problems. It should assume more nearly the role of adviser to Western Europe and its problems, and less the role of active participant'.[37] Acheson likewise told Schuman privately that the State Department now believed that 'The best chance and hope [for Europe] seems to us to be under French leadership'. He suggested that it was up to the French rather than the British to 'integrate the German Federal Republic promptly and decisively into Western Europe' because Britain's interests were more fundamentally linked to North America than to continental Europe.[38]

The French position in Washington forced the Foreign Office to pay more attention to the United Europe Movement, Bevin finally recognising that Churchill's vision of an integrated Europe united with the British Empire and Commonwealth was far closer to his own than Schuman's federalist plans, which he believed were intended more to restrain a revival of Germany than to promote European unity for its own sake. A minute dated 6 October 1949 noted that 'We originally in the Foreign Office rather disliked the European Movement and tended to boycott their operations. The Labour Party made an attempt to do the same by indicating that it would be *mal vu* for members of the Labour Party to join the Movement'. Since then, however, many members of the Labour Party had disregarded the National Executive Committee's guidance and joined anyway, and the Foreign Office had found that the European Movement 'played a useful part' demonstrating British good faith on European integration. The Foreign Office therefore decided to adopt an attitude of 'benevolent neutrality' to the European Movement.[39]

This was especially the case *vis á vis* strengthening Bevin's hand in tying the interests of the Commonwealth to those of Europe, given that the European Movement had always envisioned the future of Europe as an imperial one. Leo Amery and Duncan Sandys continued to argue for a link between the Commonwealth and Europe, the latter encouraging Churchill to pursue an economic policy of extending 'the Empire system to include other Western European nations and their overseas associates and dependencies'. Sandys wrote: 'Britain, even with such advantages as the devalued pound may offer, does not and never will constitute such an area [that can compete with the United States]. Even the resources of the British Empire taken as a whole are insufficient. On the other hand, Britain and the Sterling Area together with the nations of Europe ... are capable of forming an economic unit, which has undeveloped potentialities of men and materials fully equal to those of the United States and certainly much greater than those of the Soviet Union'.[40] This was the argument that Bevin had been making since August 1945.

The Foreign Secretary crystallised his thinking in a memorandum to the cabinet on 18 October 1949, writing that, until the end of 1947, 'it was assumed, with decreasing confidence, that the general structure of peace would be based essentially on co-operation between the United States, the Soviet Union and the

United Kingdom.... The breakdown on the question of Germany, however, destroyed this conception, perhaps temporarily, perhaps for ever'. Although the Brussels Treaty and NATO had provided a 'military alliance of those free democracies of the West', some (including himself) had 'suggested that this should be a temporary phase, and that the real object should be to organise Western Europe into a "Middle Power," co-equal with and independent of the United States and the Soviet Union alike'. This 'Middle Power' would have as its aim the 'creation of a system which would enable Western Europe, plus the bulk of the African continent, and in some form of loose association with other members of the Commonwealth, to run an independent policy in world affairs'. Such a policy had appealed to 'those who find American capitalism little more attractive than Soviet Communism', as well as those who 'feel a natural dislike of seeing this country in a dependent position'.

However, since 1947, Bevin had come to the conclusion that there were only three possibilities for a Middle Power: the Commonwealth united but acting alone, a Western European grouping (including the United Kingdom) or a combined Western European–Commonwealth *bloc*. Bevin dismissed the first option out of hand, arguing that there were 'no political tendencies in the Commonwealth to-day which suggest that it could successfully be consolidated as a single unit'. Likewise, a Western European grouping would not be strong enough economically or militarily to stand without aid from the United States, as the Berlin crisis had proved. This left only a Western European–Commonwealth grouping, but here, too, Bevin found difficulties because 'Political cohesion of the Commonwealth countries with Western Europe is even less likely than with the United Kingdom'. Bevin therefore recommended that, despite his earlier advocacy of a Third Power, 'the closest association with the United States [was now] essential, not only for the purpose of standing up to Soviet aggression but also in the interests of Commonwealth solidarity and of European unity'. The Berlin airlift had fundamentally changed the European equation and brought into stark light the necessity of a close alliance with the United States. As much as Bevin might prefer a Third Power grouping of Western Europe and the Commonwealth, he had reluctantly to conclude that it was in the best interests of all concerned to create a 'consolidated West' rather than simply a united Europe.[41]

In preparation for the Council of Europe meeting that November, Bevin therefore informed the cabinet that Britain could not 'agree to any proposals which mean our getting involved in the economic affairs of Europe beyond the point at which we could, if we wished, disengage ourselves'. He emphasised that although Britain fully supported the Council of Europe and the OEEC, there existed 'a potential conflict between a policy of full participation in the Council of Europe and the wider interests which His Majesty's Government are always obliged to keep in mind'. He continued: 'Our relationship with the rest of the Commonwealth and, almost equally important, our new relationship with the United States ensure that we must remain, as we have always been in the past, different in character from other European nations and fundamentally incapable of wholehearted integration with them'. He concluded: 'It should, in my view, be our object to postpone [for] as long as possible being faced with a choice between, on the one hand, overstepping the limits of safety in integration with Europe and, on the other, appearing to abandon the ideas of the Council of Europe'.[42]

Bevin's recommendations in November 1949 represented a distinct shift in his thinking on Europe. Whereas in the years 1945–48 he had been convinced that Britain should be at the heart of a united Europe and equally convinced that this united Europe should be closely integrated with the Commonwealth as a Third Force standing between the United States and Soviet Union, he now believed that the United Kingdom, acting on behalf of the Empire and Commonwealth, should ally itself closely with the United States in opposition to the Soviet Union. Its relationships with the other countries of Western Europe still held an important place in Britain's foreign policy, but they were no longer central. Bevin was once again thinking of Britain in global terms rather than simply European, and on the world stage it was the emerging Cold War with the Soviet Union that was dominating his attention.

* * *

Churchill's United Europe Movement had not reached this same conclusion. In November 1949, Sandys invited Paul-Henri Spaak as the keynote speaker at the European Movement's annual meeting. Spaak confessed that in Europe, there was 'a certain feeling of uneasiness. Continental Europeans are very much afraid that Great Britain might abandon their cause and seek her salvation elsewhere than as part of an organised Europe'. Without Great Britain, however, Europe would be 'nothing but a laughable caricature'. Spaak assured his audience that nobody on the continent wished to 'confront Great Britain with a dilemma consisting of a choice between Europe and the Commonwealth. ... We know, and this is very important, when we on the Continent think of Great Britain, that the Great Britain of which we think is Great Britain with all her greatness and all her power, and we know that one of the principal aspects of this grandeur and this power is precisely the fact that Great Britain is the principal partner in the Anglo-Saxon world'.[43] It was Britain's place in the world and its global responsibilities that made it so important to the credibility of a united Europe.

Churchill thanked Spaak for his words, telling the audience that 'We recognise in this island that we have become an integral part of Europe and we mean to play our part in the revival of the prosperity and the greatness of the Continent'. He also confirmed Spaak's sentiments, saying, 'We cannot be thought of as a single state. Britain is the founder and the centre of a world-wide Empire and Commonwealth. We never shall do anything which would weaken the ties of blood, sentiment and tradition, common interest and sympathy, which unite us with the other members of the British family of nations. [But] Nobody is asking us to do such a thing'.[44] The choice between empire and Europe was a false one. Britain could have both. Speaker after speaker confirmed this view. Harold Macmillan warned his audience against a 'revival of isolationism, masquerading as imperialism', stating that it was 'because Great Britain is so closely allied by blood and tradition with the three groups which constitute to-day the free world – America, the British Commonwealth and Europe – it is because of this historic and providential working out of events, that Great Britain has to-day at once so great an opportunity and so great a responsibility'.[45] Lord Layton, the Liberal Peer, also saw a link between Europe and the Commonwealth, saying, 'The dominions and colonies, not only of Great Britain, but of France, Holland and Belgium, have a great part to play in [the] organisation of a United Europe. I will go further and say that there is little prospect for the success of [the] reorganisation of Europe without them. An attempt is being made to persuade the people of this country that they must choose between the Commonwealth and European union. There is no such choice open to us. We must have both'.[46] If it was not clear before, it was now. The United Europe Movement envisioned Europe's future as an imperial one. And in that, the British Empire would play a central role.

For perhaps the first time, the Foreign Office agreed with the rhetoric of the United Europe Movement. Only that month, Bevin had told Schuman that, despite their differences over the exact form European integration would take, he had 'worked very hard for Europe' and wished to maintain 'our connexion with Europe and with the Commonwealth'. Schuman had confirmed that 'there need be no contradiction between our policy towards Europe and our Commonwealth countries'. France also had 'overseas interests which were of great importance to her'. Schuman gave Bevin his assurance that 'France would remain faithful to our common policy and he would do his best to combat all those who appeared to be trying to upset our relations'.[47] The Commonwealth Relations Office in Whitehall confirmed that 'the Government here [has] made it quite clear that there [is] nothing incompatible between our connexions with the rest of the Commonwealth and our support of closer association with Europe'.[48] The problem, of course, came with what each man viewed as something that could 'upset' European relations. Schuman believed that the American government fell firmly into that category and that any attempts by the British government to move closer to the United States necessarily dragged it away from Europe. In contrast, Bevin was convinced that American involvement was central to Europe's future.

As 1950 dawned, Europe as a concept had become defined in the minds of many Britons. The views of Ernest Bevin had become sufficiently close to those of Winston Churchill to allow the two men to present a largely united front on European policy. They were supported in this endeavour by prominent Conservatives such as Leo Amery, Harold Macmillan and Robert Boothby and by those in the Labour government like Sir Stafford Cripps, the Chancellor of the Exchequer. These men, all supporters of the British Empire and Commonwealth, believed that the United Kingdom was a European country and had a leading role to play in developing closer European integration. They shared a common conviction that an Anglo–French alliance was necessary at the heart of this European Union. However, they also believed that it was essential for West Germany to be brought in and were convinced that the future of Europe was inextricably tied to that of the United States. They saw no need for a written constitution or formal federal institutions, instead believing that ever closer union would develop over time through pragmatic steps and close cooperation.

Polling suggested that the British public by and large supported this view; a majority favoured a European customs union, a defence alliance and some form of political integration. Polling on the European continent showed that other Europeans also welcomed British participation. A survey in the spring of 1950 conducted in Norway, Holland, France, Italy and West Germany found that 82 per cent of Norwegians supported British membership in a European Union (with just 4 per cent opposed), 81 per cent of French were in favour (with just 6 per cent opposed), 71 per cent of Germans were supportive (with 11 per cent against) and 70 per cent of Dutch favoured it (with 9 per cent opposed). Only in Italy did a majority of the population fail to support British participation, with only 40 per cent certain that Britain should be a member.[49] Overall, Britons wished to play a role in Europe, and Europeans on the continent wanted them to do so.

And as the first signs of spring began to appear in 1950, there was yet more evidence of a growing understanding between the British government and its European neighbours. Since the end of the war, European countries (including the United Kingdom) had struggled with a monetary disequilibrium and balance of payments problem; namely that their currencies were being used to purchase much-needed imports without being replaced because of difficulties in the export market. Greece, Italy, France and Belgium chose to tackle this problem through inflationary increases in their own money supply, which led to price increases; the United Kingdom, the Netherlands and the Scandinavian countries followed the opposite approach, bringing in tighter controls to prevent inflation and price increases. In 1949, recession hit the United States, resulting in further decline of demand for imports from Europe whilst the US government increased its own export capabilities in order to jump-start the American economy, thus leading to a greater payment imbalance with Europe. It was for this reason that the United Kingdom devalued the pound sterling against the dollar in September 1949, followed by devaluations in Ireland, Norway, Sweden, Denmark, Portugal, the Netherlands, Iceland, France, Belgium, Greece and West Germany within the space of eleven days.[50]

In November 1949, countries within the OEEC began to discuss the need for 'complete freedom of transactions' and 'the transferability of currencies' between member nations.[51] They decided to create an organisation that would stabilise the European currency markets by removing trade barriers and regularising exchange rates. Their idea was that participating countries would agree to accept the currency of any other member country in payment for exports, thereby removing the uncertainty inherent in currency exchange. This 'payments union', operating very much like the International Monetary Fund, would provide countries in deficit with credit to finance temporary trade imbalances, thus allowing them to continue to import necessary goods without financial penalty. A thriving import market in one country would necessarily create a thriving export market in other countries, leading to higher employment and growth across the continent.[52] Although the British government made it clear that 'a payments union ... should, in its view, act as a lender of last resort only', it was nevertheless willing to enter into talks with other European governments to discuss the creation of what eventually became the European Payments Union.[53]

Sir Stafford Cripps, the Chancellor of the Exchequer, tasked Hugh Gaitskell, the Minister of State for Economic Affairs, to take the lead for the government in the negotiations. Throughout the spring of 1950, Gaitskell participated in tense talks in Paris, reaching the conclusion that it would be difficult to connect sterling with the European Payments Union.[54] In March, he therefore proposed that the United Kingdom could participate in the lending activities of the union but not the borrowing. This was rejected by other potential member-states, however, who claimed that it would create a special category for the British, in which they would be one-foot-in, one-foot-out of the union.[55] Negotiations continued into the summer, and, from July onwards, Gaitskell found himself both the UK delegate to the European Payments Union and also Chairman of the Executive Committee of the OEEC. In these positions, he experienced closer harmony with the American delegates than the European. Writing in his diary on 11 August, he commented, 'I think the explanation is that most of them had fundamentally the same outlook as I had. They were and are economist new-dealer types, and anxious to get the same kind of payment system going as we were ourselves.... In contrast to the Anglo–American economists, with whom we might associate the

Scandinavians, we had the Belgian, French and to some extent Swiss banker outlook, who invariably took the side of the creditor and wanted a much tighter system of credit'. The main line of division lay between what Gaitskell called an Anglo–American democratic socialist perspective and a continental European capitalist outlook. In particular, he found it 'an extraordinary situation that the bankers should have so much power. They virtually control the financial system of Belgium and have a considerable influence on that of France'.[56]

Nevertheless, despite his mistrust of continental bankers, it was Hubert Ansiaux of the Belgian National Bank (who also sat as the Belgian representative on the OEEC Payments Committee) who helped Gaitskell overcome the most serious objections of the British government. Ansiaux suggested that there was no reason why creditor countries in the union could not hold the credit portion of their union surpluses in pound sterling and then use these surpluses to provide credit to indebted member-states rather than drawing on the Sterling Area itself, thus protecting its sanctity. Furthermore, if the United Kingdom faced any gold losses from the use of sterling in the union, the British government could be reimbursed the value by the union. In combination, these two measures would protect sterling's special position as a world reserve currency, whilst allowing it still to be used in a European Payments Union.[57]

Over the course of the negotiations, Gaitskell came to recognise that the differences between the British and the continental European governments came less from any insurmountable philosophical divergence than from the recent historical experiences of each: 'We are much more frightened of deflation and unemployment and are quite prepared to impose controls to prevent inflation. They are much more frightened of inflation than they are of deflation and unemployment and are unwilling or unable to impose controls. Hence their insistence on keeping the volume of credit down'.[58] Once he had determined that the impasse was more of an emotional nature than a concrete ideological difference, he concluded there was no fundamental reason why the United Kingdom could not enter a European Payments Union. An agreement was finalised and announced in Paris on 7 July, the OEEC adopted the Code of the Liberalisation of Trade on 16 August, and on 19 September 1950, the European Payments Union was signed into law.[59] In his diary, Gaitskell noted that he found it 'rather fun' to have participated in the creation of 'a new economic system which is definitely going to make some difference. . . . It will be very interesting to see how it all works out and I shall watch the figures of our balances with the E.P.U. from month to month with great interest'.[60]

There is no sense in his diaries that Hugh Gaitskell believed the United Kingdom sat outside the European pale. On the contrary, it is clear that he shared Ernest Bevin's belief in a Britain that could foster closer ties with both Europe and the United States whilst still leading the Empire and Commonwealth. Although the Labour government had not gone as far as Churchill's United Europe movement in its rhetoric, making clear its opposition to any European federation that would require the surrender of sovereignty, it nevertheless believed that a pragmatic, issue-by-issue approach towards integration could be adopted in Europe. However, if Gaitskell (soon to be promoted Labour's Chancellor of the Exchequer) was optimistic about Britain's place in Europe, some on the European continent were less so. And, in May 1950, a continental surprise offered the British government a fundamental challenge to its place in Europe.

6 THE CONTINENTAL SURPRISE AND THE FALL OF THE LABOUR GOVERNMENT

Ernest Bevin was in a meeting with Dean Acheson when, on 9 May 1950, a civil servant brought him a note from the French ambassador René Massigli requesting an urgent meeting that afternoon. Bevin agreed immediately and noticed that Acheson was visibly affected by the interruption. Acheson was in London for the upcoming tripartite conference with the British and the French, and Bevin had the distinct impression that the American Secretary of State had foreknowledge of the French ambassador's request. When Bevin hosted Massigli that afternoon, the ambassador informed him that only hours before the French cabinet had voted in favour of a proposal to create a supranational authority in Western Europe that would control all steel and coal production. Although it would have no ownership rights, it would have controlling power. The French cabinet, Massigli told Bevin, believed it was 'the first concrete proposal to bring about the unity of Western Europe'. Bevin, shocked by this unexpected news, thanked the ambassador for his time but said he could make no comment until he had seen the plan in full. He would not have to wait long, Massigli replied. The proposal would be published in the French press that evening and officially submitted to the tripartite conference for consideration later that week.[1]

When Bevin read the newspapers – seeing the proposal for the first time, as with millions of other Frenchmen and -women, Germans, Britons and other Europeans – his alarm only grew. It claimed that 'for more than twenty years', France had taken 'upon herself... the role of champion of a united Europe'. It denied economic motive, claiming that its essential aim was only 'the service of peace'. It then stated that at the heart of a united Europe must be a strong Franco–German partnership, completely reversing the French opposition over the past four years to British plans to bring West Germany back into the mainstream of European politics. The French government proposed 'to take action immediately on one limited but decisive point' by placing Franco–German production of coal and steel under a common higher authority 'within the framework of an organisation open to the participation of other countries of Europe'. The United Kingdom could certainly join, as well as Belgium, the Netherlands, Italy and Luxembourg, but it would not be at its centre. This pooling of coal and steel, the statement continued, would be the 'first step in the federation of Europe' and would 'lay a true foundation for [its] economic unification'.[2]

The Schuman Plan, as it came to be known, was made public before any consultation with the British government and only hours after Bevin had first been informed of its existence. It also seemed to contradict everything the Foreign Secretary had worked for over the previous five years. First with Bidault and then with Schuman, Bevin had advocated a strong Anglo–French partnership at the heart of a united Europe, an idea also favoured by Duff Cooper and Winston Churchill. He and Bidault had held more bilateral meetings than any other two European foreign ministers and had largely acted with one voice at the various gatherings of European and world leaders. Although his relationship with Schuman had been more strained, the two had nevertheless agreed that Britain and France shared a special relationship within Europe; the upcoming tripartite conference with the United States seemed to confirm that both Britain and France acknowledged their unique position above other smaller European nations. In Syria, Algeria, West Africa and elsewhere, the British and French governments had reached agreement that their colonial responsibilities provided a commonality that could not be understood by nonimperial powers and which necessitated that they stand side by side within Europe. Even on the question of federation – now boldly advocated by the French in their statement – Schuman had claimed time and time again to understand and respect the British position and had explicitly promised that it need not be a stumbling block to further integration.

Only on the question of Germany had the British and French positions been increasingly at odds. Whilst Bevin had come to believe that the German people had to be reincorporated into European life sooner rather than later, that West Germany was an essential strategic bulwark against the growing power of the Soviet Union and that the new government of the Federal German Republic should be encouraged to engage with the West to the greatest extent possible, both economically and politically, the French government had remained resistant. Indeed, its chief concerns seemed to be ensuring that France remained superior to Germany economically, that the West German government not regain a strong position politically and that the French government have cheap access to German resources, particularly coal. On this latter point, both Bidault and Schuman had been quite insistent that Germany be made to compensate France for its wartime suffering by readily making available German coal resources. That the French foreign minister was now welcoming West Germany with open arms, purportedly for the purpose of peace but with a plan that would give the French government partial control over German coal and steel resources, seemed to Bevin suspicious at the very least. He could not believe that other European leaders would fall for it.

The Frenchman Jean Monnet was behind the Schuman Plan. Long an advocate of French economic interests, Monnet had been one of the first Europeans to pursue plans for European integration, advocating an Anglo–French economic union as early as 1939. In the aftermath of the Second World War, Monnet proposed what became known as the Monnet Plan to revive the dilapidated French economy; the plan intended to secure coal and steel supplies from the German Ruhr and Saar in order to promote France as a strong industrial power that could trade with Britain.[3] Following George Marshall's offer of aid to Europe, Monnet soon become disillusioned with the Organisation of European Economic Cooperation (OEEC), which he felt was a weak institution. In his mind, there had to be a more permanent pooling of European resources. In the spring of 1949, Monnet therefore initiated a series of meetings at the British Treasury with Sir Stafford Cripps, the Chancellor of the Exchequer, and Sir Edwin Plowden, Cripps' undersecretary. He contended that Western Europe was 'a vacuum, on either side of which were the two great dynamic forces of communism and American capitalism'. This vacuum would be filled by one of these undesirable alternatives unless the governments of Europe developed a distinctly 'Western European way of life'. Monnet believed that 'the only dynamic force in Western Europe was in the United Kingdom'. Britain and France should therefore 'consider their problems together as if they were one nation'. He requested that the government initiate a series of meetings to discuss how his vision might be brought to fruition, a request Cripps accepted.[4]

In planning for the talks, Plowden suggested that the British position should be predicated on two central assumptions: first, that 'the recovery of France's economy is of importance to the U.K.', and second, that the 'time has come for the U.K. to define more clearly its attitude to Western Germany'. If the government could limit its discussions to a restoration of the Anglo–French relationship and the reincorporation of Western Germany into the European family of nations, then he would be pleased with the outcome.[5] Other Treasury officials held this view.[6] When Cripps met with Monnet, however, he found that the Frenchman's ideas went far further than improving relations. Instead, Monnet argued for 'a truly joint planning operation'. He also seemed to envision something beyond economics, suggesting that it was essential for Europe to develop an ideology that could 'form a rallying ground for the countries concerned'. Discussions of complementary trade practices by technocratic experts would not be sufficient.[7] Whilst agreeing with Monnet in general terms, Cripps and Plowden refused to be drawn into more specific discussions, and the talks went nowhere.[8]

Whilst the Treasury grappled with Monnet, the British government as a whole was growing ever closer to the United States, particularly under Acheson's leadership at the State Department. Given that Bevin's relationships with Schuman were not as strong as they had been with Bidault, Monnet began to fear that the United Kingdom was turning its back on European unity. Matters were not helped when Harold Macmillan visited Paris in December 1949 to speak to the Comite Parlementaire Francais du Commerce on the question of 'What the English think of European Union'. Macmillan, as a rising star of the Conservative Party and a leading figure in Churchill's United Europe Movement, at first did not disappoint. Speaking 'amusingly and effectively' in fluent French, he boasted that the European Movement had persuaded the Conservative Party 'in favour of union with Europe' and had revived 'the internationalist feeling which had been traditional in the Labour Party'. However, as Sir Oliver Harvey, the British Ambassador to France, explained to Gladwyn Jebb, Macmillan 'could not resist the temptation to make a little party capital', and he told his audience that the Labour government had been 'interested in schemes of European union when Socialist ideas seemed to be winning' but were now 'afraid to match their controlled economy with the liberal ideas prevailing outside the United Kingdom'. Macmillan 'wound up by saying that the British had a fundamental mistrust of written constitutions, and it was therefore useless trying to bring them into a federal union of Europe'. Harvey feared that Macmillan had done much 'harm to the cause in which he appears to believe by undermining their belief in our trustworthiness'.[9]

The decision in February 1950 to call a British General Election only complicated things. The Labour Party placed its campaign emphasis on the domestic economy, particularly the effects of the recent devaluation of the pound. Europe was therefore of little concern. The Conservative Party focussed on the loss of India, Ceylon, Burma and Palestine on Labour's watch, together with the continuing insurgency in Malaya, which had been raging since June 1948. Its election rhetoric therefore centred on the defence of the British Empire rather than a commitment to Europe. Macmillan and Eden hardly mentioned Europe, and the young Margaret Roberts (later Thatcher), contesting her first parliamentary seat, argued that 'Britain's reputation in the world had fallen low under Labour from its great height in 1945'. She made no mention of Europe throughout the campaign.[10] Even Leo Amery – one of the European Movement's earliest supporters – spoke of 'concentrating *first* on the development of our vast common heritage in the Empire, then upon the development of that Europe whose inheritance we also shared, and then making our contribution to the development of the world as a whole'. There was a clear hierarchy in his speeches.[11] This, the first General Election held in Great Britain since July 1945, painted a contrasting picture with the numerous elections held across the European continent, all of which had focussed heavily on the question of European unity.

When the election dawned on 23 February, there was an 84 per cent turnout, the highest in British history.[12] The Labour government's lead was slashed from 146 seats to just eight, and when the cabinet met that evening Hugh Dalton argued that it was 'the worst possible situation'. With so few seats separating the parties and the momentum clearly moving towards the Conservatives, he thought it would have been better to be in opposition than government.[13] Others in the cabinet agreed and, on 25 February, the ministers decided that 'there could be no question of attempting to carry through any of the controversial legislation which had been promised in the Party's

Election Manifesto'.[14] There was simply no mandate to do so. In every other Western European country, including the newly formed Federal Republic of Germany, voters had gone to the polls with the question of European integration before them, and all had voted in its favour. Yet in Britain's first post-war election, neither the Labour government nor the Conservative opposition placed Europe at the heart of its campaign; consequently, the government was no clearer on the public's view of Europe after the election than it had been before it, and neither party had put the principle of a European Union to its voters. In the February 1950 General Election, Britain seemed disengaged with the world. Sir Cuthbert Headlam, the Conservative MP for Newcastle North, captured the views of many when he wrote in his diary, 'it is very painful ... to have lived to see the end of an epoch when England meant so much to the rest of the world and when one had such pride in being an Englishman'.[15]

This British ambivalence did not go unnoticed on the continent. Following the election, Monnet lost confidence in the whole concept of an Anglo–French partnership at the heart of a united Europe, a partnership which would have had the economic, political and moral suasion to compel the German government to offer favourable terms to France on coal and steel. Once he had arrived at this conclusion, he took just three weeks in April to draft a proposal for Schuman 'which would enable France to take the initiative in regard to both Europe and Germany at the May talks in London'.[16] He passed the plan to the French Foreign Minister on 28 April. Schuman decided to adopt it as his own and raised it with the French cabinet on 3 May.[17] He discussed the plan with Dean Acheson on 8 May, although swore him to secrecy, and, on the morning of 9 May, sent a private emissary to Konrad Adenauer, the chancellor of the new West German state, to seek his approval. Adenauer immediately gave his consent. With this reply in hand, Schuman formally put the plan before the French cabinet, which quickly voted in its favour.[18]

Throughout this time, British ministers and officials were meeting closely with French leaders yet the latter gave no hint of what was afoot. Bevin, despite a recurrent illness, visited Paris and Strasbourg in early April, and, on 15 April, his Minister of State, Kenneth Younger, travelled to Brussels as part of the British delegation to the Consultative Council of the Brussels Treaty. There he met both with the French Defence Minister (soon to be Prime Minister) René Pleven and with

Schuman.[19] Yet still the French gave no indication of what was to come. As Jean Monnet's biographer has written, 'The whole operation was conducted with a secrecy and speed totally foreign to the Fourth Republic'.[20] It was less than six weeks from when Monnet concluded that an Anglo–French partnership had to be replaced by a Franco–German partnership to when he drafted a proposal, had it accepted by Schuman and had Schuman solicit the approval of the French cabinet, the West German chancellor and the American Secretary of State. Throughout those six weeks, neither Bevin nor anyone else in the British government had any inkling that the French had developed a new plan. Yet those six weeks would fundamentally change Britain's place within Europe and would challenge all that the British government had believed about how post-war Europe should look.

With Monnet's hastily constructed ideas officially put forward as the Schuman Plan on 9 May, it was the responsibility of the Labour government to craft a British response. Bevin knew from Acheson's initial reaction that the American government had prior knowledge of the French plan, and he was furious that the American Secretary of State had given him no warning.[21] He requested an urgent meeting with Acheson and Schuman on 11 May at which he protested the 'form and timing of the announcement'. He said it had embarrassed him not be told at the same time as the Americans, as it was widely assumed in the House of Commons that he must have known. He now had to face the taunts of the opposition and the doubts of his own backbenchers about his lack of knowledge. He was also dismayed on a more pragmatic level, given that 'all three Governments [Great Britain, France and the United States] were administering Germany and he had thought that the principle of consultation had been established'. This was not only a personal slight but also what Bevin considered to be a breach of diplomatic protocol.

Schuman dismissed his concerns, saying that the French government itself had only known about the plan for less than a week, that they hoped not only for a Franco–German partnership but for a 'European organisation' and that the plan was 'no fait accompli'. The French government needed 'to produce a psychological shock both on the European and on the German plane', and for this reason secrecy had been of the utmost importance until the plan was made public.[22] For his part, Dean Acheson showed little desire to intervene on Britain's behalf because the French proposal was 'manna from heaven', and he sat largely silent throughout the meeting. He had been 'urging the Europeans – and especially the French – to take the initiative all along', and now he found himself 'awed and puzzled by Monnet's brilliant, inchoate plan'.[23] The British government had well and truly lost the initiative in Europe, and its Foreign Secretary was left dazed and confused.

Bevin was unable to make a convincing argument in part because he was still struck with illness. He had been released from hospital only days before Acheson arrived in London and continued to be bedridden for large parts of the day. As George Younger wrote in his diary at the time, 'At the talks themselves [both individually with Acheson and then with Acheson and Schuman] he has been far from his best form. He said himself that he is "only half alive". The doctors give him so many drugs that he often had difficulty in staying awake and in taking a proper grip of the meetings, of which he has been chairman'.[24] Younger did not personally blame Bevin, as one does not choose illness, but did think it 'something of a scandal that the P.M. has allowed the situation to develop'. In his view, Attlee should have replaced Bevin as Foreign Secretary as soon as his illnesses became recurrent and incapacitating.[25] When Bevin met again with Acheson and Schuman on 14 May, he was 'pretty sick at the morning meetings', although revived for the afternoon.[26] Bevin tried to get a more detailed understanding of the Schuman Plan but failed. Younger explained that the British government would 'clearly have to be associated with it in some way' but believed that it was 'too soon to make up one's mind. The French themselves have clearly not thought the scheme out, let alone explained it to anyone else'.[27]

Bevin's position was further complicated on two fronts. First, Churchill's United Europe movement released a statement on 15 May 'warmly welcoming' Schuman's proposal and urging 'His Majesty's Government to announce immediately that it is prepared to play its full part with the Governments of other European countries in working out methods for the practical implementation of the proposals'.[28] Other members of the Conservative Party also spoke in its favour, Macmillan saying on 17 May that he hoped Bevin's delay in responding 'does not mean that the British government intend to keep out of the plan themselves, or still worse – to kill it in committee'. He described the proposals as 'an act of high courage and of imaginative statesmanship' and hoped that 'British statesmanship will at least be equal to this new responsibility and this new opportunity'.[29] The second complication Bevin had to grapple with came from the US government, which stood squarely behind the plan. Sir Oliver Franks, Britain's ambassador to the United States, advised Bevin that the proposal had 'struck the American imagination and is widely regarded as the most hopeful development in the direction of European cooperation'.[30] Whatever the realities of the economic motivation behind the French plan, the American people had bought into its rhetoric of peace and European unity. Any hesitation by the British government would be portrayed as petulance and crudely nationalistic.

British reaction beyond the government also greeted the plan with more optimism. Writing in a front page splash on 11 May, the right-of-centre *Daily Mail* chastised the government for being 'noticeably chilly to all suggestions of a United Europe unless every other country affected the same brand of Socialism as themselves' and lamented that the Labour government was 'not likely [to] welcome a scheme which would place their socialised industries on the same plane as others run by private enterprise'.[31] The *Times*, likewise, was 'cautiously supportive' of the Schuman Plan. It did not condemn the British government for failing to take the lead, however, saying, 'Neither Britain nor the United States could have suggested it without French approval and a German proposal on these lines could not easily have been accepted by the French. It was for France and France alone to take the step'.[32] The *Manchester Guardian* and *Financial Times* remained ambivalent in their 11 May coverage, concerned only that the plan economically benefit Britain.[33] Only Lord Beaverbrook's *Daily Express* was unequivocal in its opposition. Schuman's proposal, it wrote, 'if accepted, will end British independence.... No country which loses national control of coal and steel can retain national freedom. This threat to our national sovereignty is not accidental.... It is part of a deliberate and concerted attempt to force Britain into a United Europe'. It concluded: 'The way to peace [for Britain] lies not in an uneasy union with the Continent of Europe. It lies instead in strengthening our comradeship with the Commonwealth and Empire'.[34]

Lord Beaverbrook and his *Daily Express* notwithstanding, the bulk of press opinion in Britain favoured engaging with the French on Schuman's plan, if not an immediate commitment to join the proposed community. On 12 May, the *Times* reminded its readers that a plan very much resembling Schuman's had first been put forward by Anthony

Eden in 1948, and, on 15 May, both the *Times* and the *Manchester Guardian* condemned the government for not committing to the issue.[35] On 20 May, the *Economist* opined that 'For economic reasons as well as political, Britain should participate in the scheme'. It argued that the comparative strength of Britain's coal and steel industries would make it a national leader within an integrated Coal and Steel Community and that this leadership could then extend to other areas of Britain's relationship with the European continent. 'Cautious hesitation', it concluded, 'has become too invariable a factor in the formulation of British policy. On this occasion, at least, no ground should be given for any accusation of "dragging the feet"'.[36] Given the overwhelming and increasingly favourable attitude of the press to the plan, Bevin sought a new approach, sending Schuman a message on 25 May welcoming the proposal and suggesting that 'no time should be lost in following it up'. He then proposed a series of 'direct conversations' among the British, French and German governments, with the hope that the community could be enacted in such a way that would allow the British government to 'join the scheme'.[37]

However, Schuman replied that if concrete results were to be achieved, it was 'necessary that the Governments should be in agreement from the beginning on the principles and the essential undertakings defined in the French Government's document'. For this reason, Schuman had drafted a communique of principles that Adenauer had already signed. If the British government wished to enter the talks (as the French government was 'anxious' that it do), it would first have to agree to the communique. The communique read: 'The Governments of [enter signatories] are resolved to carry out a common action aiming at peace, European solidarity and economic and social progress by pooling their coal and steel production and by the institution of a new higher authority whose decisions will bind [enter signatories] and the countries which may adhere in the future'.[38]

Bevin explained to Schuman that the British government could not possibly accept any principles *before* entering discussions since it was only right and proper that the principles be arrived at collectively *during* discussions, lest the British sign a document which, after its details were finalised, they could not possibly implement. The British government was keen to engage with other European countries on questions of economic integration and desired to 'participate in any discussions which take place'. However, 'if the French Government intend to insist on a commitment to pool resources and set up an authority with certain sovereign powers as a prior condition to joining in the talks, His Majesty's Government would reluctantly be unable to accept such a condition'.[39] Schuman confirmed that this was indeed what the French government intended to do.[40] Bevin tried again, explaining that the British government was ready to 'participate in the proposed conversation in a constructive spirit and in the hope that, as a result of the discussions, there will emerge a scheme which they will be able to join. But they cannot at this stage enter into any more precise commitment'.[41] For Bevin, his position was crystal clear, and he could not understand why the French were proving so difficult. How could the British government possibly agree in writing to accept the pooling of coal and steel without first seeing exactly how this would be accomplished? It would be the equivalent of writing a political blank cheque to the French government.

In the face of Schuman's demand and Bevin's steadfast response, the Foreign Secretary began to win back the support of some elements of the British press, the *Manchester Guardian* concluding that 'There is no doubt now that the declaration which the French required of us was an impossible one'.[42] However, Robert Schuman was equally clear that only those who agreed in principle to the pooling of coal and steel ought to be allowed to enter discussions, lest the proposal be stripped of its fundamental character. On 1 June, he submitted a revised communique to the British government, which read: 'The Governments of [insert signatories] in their determination to pursue a common action for peace, European solidarity and economic and social progress have assigned to themselves as their immediate objective the pooling of coal and steel production and the institution of a new high authority that will bind [insert signatories]'.[43] Schuman gave the British government a 24-hour deadline to decide on participation: should he hear nothing by its expiration, talks would proceed without the United Kingdom, with the option still available to join at a later date.[44] Bevin remained cautious, arguing that 'there is still a difference of approach between the two Governments as to the basis on which the negotiations should be opened. If His Majesty's Government accepted the revised wording they would feel committed in principle to pool their coal and steel resources and to set up a new high authority, whose decisions would bind the Governments concerned'. This he could not do.[45]

The following day, a hastily convened cabinet met to discuss the French proposal. Bevin took no part in it as he was again hospitalised for illness, an absence that doctors estimated would last at least six weeks, if not two months. Kenneth Younger wrote that it was 'rather a disgrace to have allowed our foreign policy to be run so long by a man who is not in a fit state to do a full job. I think it probable that opportunities of all kinds have been missed all along the way'.[46] Attlee and Cripps were likewise absent from the meeting, away on holiday (each, ironically, in France!), leaving Herbert Morrison – the Deputy Prime Minister – to chair the cabinet.[47] Whilst Bevin and perhaps even Attlee and Cripps might have sought a way forward, Morrison was adamant that the government could not countenance the plan, saying, 'it's no good. We can't do it. The Durham miners will never wear it'.[48] In this, Morrison was perhaps correct. The continental European markets accounted for just 5 per cent of all British coal exports, and the British coal and steel industry alone produced half the coal and one-third of the steel of the other six Western European countries combined. Economically, it made little sense to pool resources under a European High Authority with countries that produced so much less than Britain. Furthermore, a European Coal and Steel Community (ECSC) would inevitably place tariffs on all nations outside its boundaries, which would necessarily interfere with Britain's economic relations with the Commonwealth and its system of Imperial Trade Preferences. Politically, the nationalisation of the coal industry was at the heart of the Labour Party's post-war vision of a socialist society, and the government had only just survived a tough parliamentary fight to nationalise the steel industry also. It could hardly be expected to give up such gains so quickly, all for the sake of European unity.[49]

Nevertheless, the whole affair left a bitter taste in the mouths of the British government, the junior Treasury minister Douglas Jay believing that France had deliberately 'excluded' Britain from the Schuman Plan in order to 'steal the leadership of Europe'.[50] Sir William Strang countered that 'the whole thing [is] nonsense & was a French attempt to evade realities', and Sir Roger Makins felt that 'we should not get committed, that the Franco–German talks would inevitably break down sooner or later, and that we would then have a chance of coming in as *deus ex machina* with a solution of our own'.[51] Only Kenneth Younger, the Minister of State for Foreign Affairs, felt that Britain ought to find a way to enter the talks, but he received no backing. He was disappointed at the cabinet attitude, writing, 'it is unfortunate that we appear to be "out on a limb" as usual, and no doubt we shall come in for a good many kicks as a result. What is more important is that no one has yet produced...any alternative proposal for eventually bringing Germany safely into the community of W[estern] Europe & the Atlantic'. He concluded: '[T]his French initiative, even if it was a bit haywire, offered & perhaps still offers a possible solution if only we can get it on a workable basis'.[52]

It was not to be. On 3 June, the European governments issued three communiques. The first, written jointly by the French, West German, Belgian, Luxembourg, Italian and Dutch governments, stated that 'in their determination to pursue a common action for peace and European solidarity, and economic and social progress [they had] assigned to themselves as their immediate objective the pooling of the production of coal and steel and the institution of a new high authority whose decisions will bind France, Germany, Belgium, Italy, Luxembourg, the Netherlands, and other countries which may adhere to it in the future'.[53] The second, issued by the British government, claimed that it had 'from the outset welcomed the French initiative of 9th May and have been fully alive to its bold character and far-reaching importance', 'earnestly hope[ing] that the international discussions upon it may lead to a new era in Franco–German relations, with beneficial effects for Western Europe as a whole'. It was 'most anxious to be associated with these discussions'. However, it was unable to 'accept in advance' nor 'reject in advance' the 'principles underlying the French proposal'. Consequently, it found it 'impossible in view of [its] responsibility to Parliament and people to associate [itself] with the negotiation on the terms proposed by the French Government'.[54] Finally, the French government issued its own communique, stating that it would 'at all times keep in mind the need to carry out exchanges of views with the British Government' and would 'take into account to the greatest possible extent the point of view of the British Government'.[55] Nevertheless, it was clear that, for the first time since the end of the Second World War, the United Kingdom was standing on the fringes of Europe rather than at its heart.

* * *

On 13 June 1950, the Labour Party's National Executive Committee (NEC) issued a statement on European Unity. The party's 'attitude towards the problem of European unity', it claimed, was 'determined by the principles of democratic Socialism and by the interests of the British people as members of the Commonwealth'. Britain, it said, was 'not just a small crowded island off the Western coast of Continental Europe' but the 'nerve of a world-wide Commonwealth which extends into every continent'. 'In every respect', it continued, 'we in Britain are closer to our kinsmen in Australia and New Zealand on the far side of the world, than we are to Europe. We are closer in language and origins, in social habits and institutions, in political outlook and in economic interest'. Britons would never be *just* Europeans. Furthermore, within Europe itself, 'the Labour Party's socialist principles demand that the movement towards European unity should be such as to permit the continuation of full employment and social justice in Britain'; a united Europe could not be one based on laissez-faire economics. The NEC therefore ruled that a 'complete economic Union of Western Europe must therefore be excluded, since it would demand an unattainable degree of uniformity in the internal policies of the member states'. It also ruled out a 'complete political Union', concluding that: 'No Socialist Party with the prospect of forming a government could accept a system by which important fields of national policy were surrendered to a supranational European representative authority, since such an authority would have a permanent anti-Socialist majority and would arouse the hostility of European workers'.[56]

Ironically, the NEC's statement had been drafted long before Schuman made public his proposal for the pooling of French and German coal and steel, but the timing of its release gave the impression that the Labour government was opposing the French plans for party-political reasons whilst other Britons – including much of the press – were fully in support of European initiatives. France had put forward a plan couched in the language of peace; the Labour Party had responded that they could only consent if it guaranteed a socialist future. This did not look good on the world stage. The *Manchester Guardian*, usually supportive of the Labour Party, opined that 'The document is much weakened by this assumption of superior virtue over the benighted Europeans of the Continent ... the Labour Party is all for union if everybody will be like the British!'[57] The *Daily Express* also mockingly noted that the government could not 'join with non-Socialist Governments. No Schuman Plan until Schuman becomes a Socialist!'[58]

If the left-of-centre press found things to critique in the government's handling of the Schuman Plan, the Conservative Party was aghast at the way events transpired. Writing in 1960, Anthony Nutting – first elected to Parliament in 1945 and later Parliamentary Under-Secretary and Minister of State for Foreign Affairs – claimed that the government acted 'with indecent haste and evident relief', 'looking for a way out' rather than 'a way in'.[59] He remembered 'staying with Anthony Eden at his Sussex home.... [H]e was deeply distressed by the Government's rejection of the Schuman Plan. As we paced up and down the garden, he kept repeating, "This folly will divide us deeply from our friends. Twice before in my lifetime we turned our backs on Europe and look what happened – two world wars. I hoped we had learnt our lesson"'.[60] Eden was particularly aggrieved because the French Ambassador, René Massigli, had indicated to him on 23 June that 'had we come into the discussions we could have moulded events the way we wished'.[61]

Eden was not the only Conservative concerned at the government's swift rejection of the French plan. In a speech delivered in his constituency, Harold Macmillan was scathing: 'This has been a black week for Britain; for the Empire; for Europe; and for the peace of the world'. The political importance of the Schuman Plan, he said, 'far outweighs its economic or industrial aspects. Its purpose is the unity of France and Germany. With British participation, this will secure peace'. Without British participation, however, Franco–German unity could 'be a source not of security but danger. In the not too distant future, we may have to pay a terrible price for the isolationist policy which British Socialism has long practised and now openly dares to preach'.[62] In the United States, Sir Oliver Franks wrote to Sir Roger Makins, arguing that the government 'should not be trying to water down the plan but, rather, seeing how they could ally or associate themselves with it'. It was a 'major political question' rather than strictly an economic one and could possibly lead to an 'anchorman over 90 million Europeans'. This was surely a development in which the British government should want to play a leading role.[63]

Under pressure from the Conservative Party, the government scheduled a debate on the Schuman Plan for 25 June. However, the day before it was due to begin, events conspired across the world to wrest the minds of many parliamentarians away from Europe. On 24 June 1950, the communist army of North Korea crossed the 38th Parallel to invade

South Korea, sparking an international crisis that demanded a British response. The Korean War ensured that the parliamentary debate on Europe was once again overshadowed by more pressing international concerns. As Kenneth Younger wrote on 6 July, 'The Korean situation has now knocked Schuman right into the background of public consciousness. It is a fortnight since the invasion, and we are only at the very beginning of what promises to be a difficult business'.[64]

Events in Korea also served to further undermine the government's projection of confidence in foreign affairs. As had happened with the Schuman Plan, Bevin was left in the dark on Korea by Acheson. Immediately upon North Korea's invasion, the American government signalled its support for South Korea, President Truman ordering the US Air Force and Navy to South Korea on 25 June and allowing his forces to engage with the North Koreans on 26 June. Four days later, American ground forces followed the air force and navy onto the Korean peninsula.[65] Yet it was not until 27 June, four days after the invasion, that Acheson first contacted Bevin. Apologising for the delay, Acheson did not seek a British partnership but instead informed Bevin that the American government had been tasked to lead the United Nations effort in Korea and asked if the British could commit any forces to its cause.[66] Any hint of a joint Anglo–American approach was missing. This was to be an American affair, with help from whomever was willing to provide it.[67]

The parliamentary debate over European integration and the Schuman Plan coincided with the outbreak of the Korean Crisis. Throughout the debate, Churchill and Eden lambasted the government for its handling of the French initiative. They argued that Franco–German rapprochement was essential for the future peace and security of Europe, that British absence from the talks strengthened the position of the Soviet Union on the continent and that the Labour government was ceding the leadership of Europe to the French. They deplored the way the French government had sprung the proposal onto Bevin and objected to the preconditions placed upon the talks, but laid the blame for this at the feet of the Labour Party. Had it not been for Labour's known opposition to Churchill's United Europe Movement and the NEC's recent statement on European Unity, no preconditions would be necessary. As it was, Schuman's stance could hardly come as a surprise. Given the necessity for continued British world leadership, both on the European continent and in the Commonwealth, the government now had a responsibility to enter the talks. Churchill and Eden were supported in their arguments by a robust maiden speech delivered by the newly elected Conservative MP Edward Heath, who spoke out passionately in favour of a united Europe. The Conservative argument did little good, however. In a parliamentary split which largely mirrored the political parties, the Commons voted by 309 votes to 289 against participation in the proposed ECSC.[68]

Still, the cabinet could not ignore the implications of Schuman's proposals. It requested from the Colonial Office a memorandum on the effects an ECSC would have on the Commonwealth. The Colonial Office replied that the 'whole nexus of our relations with European countries in recent years – in the Brussels Treaty, O.E.E.C., the Council of Europe and, to some extent, the Atlantic Treaty Organisation – has inevitably brought into question the United Kingdom's relation to the rest of the Commonwealth'. Throughout, the government had had before it two central considerations: '(a) the need to play our full part – and, indeed, to take the lead – in revivifying Europe, while at the same time – (b) not engaging ourselves in anything which was likely to do damage to our relationship with other Commonwealth countries'. Thus far, the Commonwealth countries had largely supported the government's efforts to pursue closer integration with Europe, recognising that it was in their best interests as well as Britain's. However, 'the Commonwealth countries would look askance at any departure from our present policy of combining our responsibilities as a Member of the Commonwealth with support for the development of European unity, and would probably react sharply to any "integration" of our economy into that of Europe in any manner which they regarded as prejudicing their vital interests'. As Schuman was unwilling to consider British concerns in this area, the government was right to refuse entry.[69]

The cabinet also considered its economic implications. In mid-July, the Treasury circulated a memorandum arguing that, in light of the Schuman Plan, the government needed to 'settle in broad outline' its attitude towards European plans for integration. It continued: 'The problem is in essence a simple one. ... Is His Majesty's Government prepared to allow Western Europe full rein to organise itself on a federal or quasi-federal lines without the participation of the United Kingdom ... or are the risks of such a "hands off" policy so great that it is necessary to try to intervene to arrest this process?' Britain would not participate in the Schuman Plan because the government could not consent to a scheme 'for a supra-national authority with power to bind governments'. However, it would be 'a heavy political responsibility for the United Kingdom to seek to prevent forms of closer association which were generally desired by other Western European countries, simply on the grounds that we ourselves, in view of our world obligations and responsibilities, could not participate in them'. Given this, the United Kingdom ought to 'find a means of associating ourselves with whatever organisations may emerge' without either joining or sabotaging the work of other Europeans. 'While we should prefer that European co-operation continued to be built up on the inter-governmental system in which we can participate fully', the Treasury concluded, 'we should not follow a policy of hostility towards, or seek to prevent the realization of, a scheme of European integration or political federation'.[70]

The Conservative opposition was not satisfied with this conclusion. On 2 August 1950, Churchill wrote to Attlee accusing him of short-termism and arguing that 'A three year or long-term plan for Western Europe is as necessary as it was two years ago'. The time had now passed when the government could enter the ECSC, but Britain could nevertheless still lead in Europe. If this was no longer possible in the economic sphere, the government should turn instead to questions of defence, particularly in light of the outbreak of hostilities on the Korean peninsula. Churchill therefore advocated the creation of a European Army 'of at least thirty five divisions' with France providing fifteen divisions, the British six (bearing in mind their simultaneous military commitments in the Empire and Commonwealth), the Benelux countries three each, and, in a departure from post-war disarmament policy, the Germans five. These member countries should 'be of equal status [within the European Army] and equally armed and have a proportionate share in the command'.[71] The government, however, refused to see a connection between the ongoing crisis in Korea and the Cold War frontier in Europe.

Churchill's Conservatives were not deterred. As early as 20 June, Harold Macmillan argued that 'The situation created by M. Schuman may well be a major turning-point in European history. It is certainly a turning-point in the fortunes of the Tory Party. This issue affords us the last, and perhaps only, chance of regaining the initiative'. He suggested to Churchill that there was actually 'no Schuman Plan in existence. . . . There is a plan to have a plan. But this is the very reason why Britain should be in from the start. Then we can mould the plan to our pattern'. He concluded: '[Y]ou must give the lead for which *Britain, the Empire, Europe* and *the world* have been waiting. Everyone looks to you. They feel entitled to look to you.... You started United Europe. Without you, there would be no Council of Europe, no Committee of Ministers, no Consultative Assembly, no Strasbourg. This is the first and supreme test. You cannot let down all Europe'.[72] In Macmillan's mind, European unity was as much the brainchild of Britain as of any other country. It was only right and proper that Britain remain in the lead.

In mid-August, Churchill advised Eden, Macmillan and David Eccles to launch a '*Schuman sans larmes*' or a '*Schuman sans dents*' at the Council of Europe's Consultative Assembly in Strasbourg; essentially, he was advocating an economic arrangement to pool industrial resources that would lack the supra-national binding power of Schuman's High Authority, thereby opening the way for British participation in the scheme.[73] Macmillan immediately agreed, concerned that 'Bevin's refusal to meet the French initiative would mark a turning-point for the worse in the fortunes of United Europe'.[74] Popularly known as the 'Macmillan-Eccles Plan', Macmillan put Churchill's proposal before the Assembly on 15 August, claiming that it would 'meet British apprehensions without injury to the main feature of the [Schuman] plan'.[75] It consisted of three main clauses: first, the European experts coordinating the coal and steel industries would be accountable to a Committee of Ministers rather than an independent High Authority; second, the 'basic social, economic and strategic interests of each country [would be] safeguarded from encroachment by the experts'; and, finally, 'Any member can withdraw on giving 12 months' notice; and any member can be expelled by the others'.[76] Schuman immediately rejected the plan, arguing that six European nations were already committed to pooling some sovereignty under a High Authority and that the Conservative plan was 'quite incompatible with the political aims of the Schuman Plan'.[77] Following this snub, Eden advised Churchill to avoid any 'further initiative which can only court a rebuff'. Continued rejection by Schuman would only weaken the Conservative position and strengthen the Labour government's argument that the continental European powers were acting in an unreasonable way towards Britain.[78]

Churchill followed Eden's advice, recommending that the Conservative Party drop its advocacy of British association with the Schuman Plan and instead concentrate on his idea for a European Army.

This he raised in his own speech to the Strasbourg Assembly on 11 August when he introduced a resolution in favour of a European Army. After only a very brief debate, the Assembly carried his resolution by a majority of 89 to 5, calling for 'the immediate creation of a unified European army, under the authority of a European Minister of Defence, subject to proper European democratic control and acting in full co-operation with the United States and Canada'.[79] Churchill wrote to the American President Harry S Truman two days later, telling him that the resolution was 'the fruition of what I have laboured for ever since my speech at Zurich four years ago'. He also encouraged Truman to support German participation in a European Army, arguing that 'if the Germans threw in their lot with us, we should hold their safety and freedom as sacred as our own'.[80] As he had since 1946, Churchill believed it was essential for Germany to be fully integrated into Western Europe, not only through a limited coal and steel community but in military affairs also.

Churchill, however, was not leading the British government, and Attlee, Bevin and Cripps were sceptical of a European Army. When Churchill requested a special session of the House of Commons to debate his successful Strasbourg resolution, the government turned him down. As Hugh Dalton (now Minister of Town and Country Planning) put it to Bevin, Churchill had 'made a splash and flown away [from Strasbourg]. If he gets a chance to make a speech in Parliament next week or at any time while the Consultative Assembly here [in Strasbourg] is still sitting, he will fly back and try to make another splash. He will say either that he has won a great victory for European defence or alternatively that His Majesty's Government are sabotaging European survival. Neither of these statements would be true or helpful'.[81] Nevertheless, Churchill's Strasbourg resolution placed the government in a difficult position, once again forcing their hand and making it appear that they were not giving European questions their full due, in contrast to a Conservative opposition that was openly advocating British participation in a United Europe.

In August, the government came under further pressure when Kenneth Lindsay (a former Labour MP, now independent, who had lost his seat at the 1950 General Election) and Edward Heath formed a cross-party group to advocate for European integration under British leadership to be fused with an Atlantic alliance, perhaps even becoming a formal Atlantic Union.[82] Meanwhile, Churchill's European

Movement continued to advocate for British participation in schemes for European Union. In October, it confirmed that its objective was 'the creation of a United Europe', which would necessarily involve 'the institution of a European political authority with limited functions but real powers'.[83] The month before, it had commissioned a poll on how British attitudes towards European unity compared with those on the continent. Releasing its results on 22 September, it found that 'the volume of support for the general idea of European union was very little below the average for the twelve countries [Norway, Holland, France, Italy, Western Germany, Sweden, Denmark, Belgium, Luxembourg, Switzerland and Austria] as a whole'. In particular, 51 per cent of Britons favoured 'the idea of a Western European Union', with just 9 per cent opposed (40 per cent were still undecided). Asked if they would support a 'European Union [which] meant that people could travel freely and that workers from other European countries could come and seek employment in your country', 61 per cent of Britons were in favour, with 24 per cent opposed and 14 per cent undecided. On the question of a European customs union, 66 per cent of Britons supported it and 12 per cent opposed.[84] Although the poll demonstrated that on all questions Britons were marginally less supportive than those on the continent, the European Movement put this down to a lack of leadership from the British government. Had Attlee, Bevin, Cripps and Dalton spoken as favourably on questions of European unity as Schuman, Spaak and Adenauer, then surely the British people would have followed their lead, just as the French, Belgian and German peoples had followed their own leaders.

Bevin had his doubts, which were confirmed by a visit on October 31 from Guy Mollet, the leader of the French Socialist Party and Minister for European Affairs in René Plevan's coalition government. Mollet revealed that the French government was not as united around Schuman's plans as he led the world to believe, with many French Socialists sharing Bevin's conviction that a European federation would be harmful to socialist interests, leading to a free market economy dominated by West Germany. Like Bevin, Mollet thought that Europe should be arranged on a 'functional basis' rather than federal. Under such an arrangement, Britain could play its full role. As a member of the French government and the man primarily responsible for promoting France's European policy, Mollet could not make these views public, but he urged Bevin to 'stand in the way' of federation wherever possible. He also suggested that Schuman had never intended Britain to enter the ECSC and that the way in which Schuman had presented the plan and the preconditions he had attached to it had been designed 'to make it impossible for us to come in'. Whether the British government had been led by the Labour or Conservative Party, Schuman's intent had been to prevent the participation of the United Kingdom in his scheme.[85] This confirmed for Bevin that the British government had dodged a bullet by not agreeing to the Schuman Plan. In time, other European countries would conclude likewise, and Britain would be restored to its rightful place as leader of Europe. Now was not the moment for rash behaviour, but a time for patience.

* * *

As the winter of 1950–51 approached, the Labour government's attention was once again distracted from questions of Europe. In Korea, on 19 October 1950, the Chinese government officially entered the war, flooding North Korea with 260,000 Chinese soldiers and launching its first offensive on the twenty-sixth of that month.[86] Kenneth Younger wrote in his diary that the situation was 'very tense'.[87] Elsewhere, things were no better. In Malaya, which had been under Emergency regulations since June 1948, the struggle had descended into a quagmire. In November, Sir Harold Briggs, the British Director of Operations there, informed the cabinet's Chiefs of Staff Committee that 'Progress of the [counter-insurgency] plan has not been as quick as was hoped and is already seriously behind schedule'. He warned that 'unless the [Malayan] Federal Government is placed on a war footing and the gravity of the local situation in its relation to the present world situation is realised by H.M. Government, no quicker progress can be made and a still graver emergency will arise'.[88]

When Briggs reported that British efforts in Malaya had fallen 'far short of requirements',[89] the committee hastily arranged a meeting at 10 Downing Street attended by Sir Henry Gurney (the British High Commissioner in Malaya), Ernest Bevin, James Griffiths (the Colonial Secretary), John Stratchey (the War Secretary), Emmanuel Shinwell (the Minister of Defence) and Clement Attlee. At this meeting, the cabinet approved Briggs' plan to place the Malayan administration on a 'war footing', with 'full executive and financial control of Emergency matters' given to a Federal War Council which would take 'ruthless action against the Malayan Communists'.[90] It is perhaps no wonder that Bevin was less engaged with Europe than his colleagues on the Continent. In both Malaya and Korea, the threat of communism seemed far more real and immediate than in Western Europe, and the performance of the British armed forces in Asia was of far greater consequence than the creation of a new army in Europe. Throughout the British world, the government was facing crises, and its Foreign Secretary was struggling to cope. Kenneth Younger ended the year writing in his diary entry, 'I saw Ernie B[evin] a couple of times [during the Christmas holidays] & thought him unwell, discouraged & without ideas. Very depressing'.[91] His demeanour was quite the contrast to Robert Schuman's, who had been energised by international developments affecting France.

It was not only in foreign affairs that the Labour government came under pressure that winter. As the days grew shorter and the nights colder, Britain faced an unprecedented coal shortage, leading the government to issue advice on 1 January 1951 to 'Use Less Coal' whilst encouraging the miners to work a bit harder.[92] In February, the National Union of Railwaymen threatened to strike unless they were given an immediate 7.5 per cent pay raise, a figure the government simply could not afford. When a compromise offer of 5 per cent was rejected, the government withdrew its objections and granted the full 7.5 per cent anyway.[93] This about-face undermined confidence in the Labour Party's ability to govern, and, in an opinion poll of voting intentions taken that month, the Conservative Party led by 13 per cent.[94] The Conservatives, recognising that the government was beginning to implode, embarked on a political strategy intended to undermine the government at every turn. This was begun unofficially in December 1950 when Julian Amery attacked Ernest Bevin in a debate in a more personal manner than had ever happened before. When questioned by Eden about his harsh tone, Amery explained: 'I agree that – his wretched health apart – he [Bevin] is probably the soundest man the Government has got.... I can't help feeling, however, ... that Bevin, thanks to his personal honesty and patriotism, gets away with mistakes and general incapacity in a way in which no other man possibly could. Indeed, without Bevin, I think the Government would find it very hard to conceal from the public the weakness of their Foreign Policy and the hesitation of their backbenchers'.[95] It was therefore essential to undermine Bevin for if he fell, then so too would the government.

At the time, Eden – with Churchill's backing – instructed Amery to tone down his attacks on the government.[96] In March 1951, however, the Conservative Party launched a tactic best expressed by Robert Boothby, who said 'We shall harry the life out of them. ... We shall make them sit up day and night, and grind away until they get absolutely hysterical, and say "We can't stand it anymore"'.[97] These tactics quickly took their toll. In October 1950, Sir Stafford Cripps had resigned as Chancellor of the Exchequer due to ill health, and on 10 March Bevin was likewise forced to resign as Foreign Secretary because of illness. In April, Clement Attlee had to stand down for several weeks for treatment of a duodenal ulcer.[98] Finally, on the fourteenth of that month Bevin died in bed whilst reading his official papers, 'the key to his red box still clutched in his hand'.[99] Just four days after his death, the official signing ceremony to institute the ECSC took place in Brussels, uniting Belgium, France, Western Germany, Italy, Luxembourg and the Netherlands into an integrated European economic community, albeit on a limited basis.[100] It is perhaps ironic that the demise of Ernest Bevin, a man who had done so much for the cause of European unity and was so keen to see strong British leadership in Europe, corresponded with the birth of a European organisation in which Britain would play no part.

Bevin's passing was a significant event for the post-war Labour government. Kenneth Younger wrote in his diary that 'Poor old Ernie's death ... marked the end of a stage in the history of the party & the government'.[101] Attlee replaced him at the Foreign Office with Herbert Morrison, but Morrison failed to make the same impact. Younger found him 'more ignorant of foreign affairs than any other member of the Cabinet', a man who was 'basically ... a little Englander who suspects everyone who is foreign'.[102] His appointment did not hold much hope for further British integration with Europe. There were other problems. With Bevin on his deathbed and Attlee in hospital, the new Chancellor of the Exchequer, Hugh Gaitskell, presented his first budget in the Commons on 10 April. Facing escalating costs in the newly formed National Health Service (NHS), he proposed that patients pay for half the cost of their spectacles and dentures. Aneurin 'Nye' Bevan, who as Minister of Health had largely founded the NHS and was now Minister of Labour, immediately resigned from the cabinet in protest, as did Harold Wilson (President of the Board of Trade) and John Freeman (Parliamentary Secretary at the Minister of Supply). Coming in combination with Bevin's death, these resignations rapidly depleted Attlee's frontbench team and furthered the sense of a government in crisis.[103]

Meanwhile, in January, the French government sent out invitations to all European members of NATO inviting them to a conference in Paris on 6 February to discuss the formation of a European Army. The United States and Canada were also invited, although as observers rather than participants. The previous October, the French Prime Minister René Pleven had proposed to the French National Assembly the creation of a European Defence Community along the lines of the European Army proposed by Winston Churchill at Strasbourg. The French Assembly voted in its favour by 349 to 235. In November, the Consultative Assembly of the Council of Europe reintroduced Churchill's resolution, this time enunciating the principle of German participation on an equal basis, which was again passed by 83 votes to 7.[104] However, that same month, the British Cabinet Defence Committee ruled that the United Kingdom would not participate in either a European Army or a broader European Defence Community because it was committed first and foremost to the Atlantic Alliance and NATO, of which Europe was already a part. A European Army would therefore be redundant. Consequently, upon receipt of the French invitation in January, officials advised Attlee that 'Since it is not our present intention to join the European Army, and rest of the world know this, we cannot very well agree to be a full member of the conference'. The government therefore requested that they attend the conference as an observer rather than participant, placing them in the same position as Canada and the United States, but separated from the other European countries of NATO.[105]

The growing distance between the United Kingdom and the continental European powers worried Guy Mollet. Although he had previously encouraged Bevin to discourage plans for a European federation, events on the continent were moving rapidly. He now feared that Britain had isolated itself from other European powers on both the economic and military fronts and that their growing rapport with the United States (strengthened by their joint participation in the Korean War) was a greater threat to socialism than a United Europe heavily influenced by Germany. In March 1951, he therefore suggested to Herbert Morrison that the British government 'find a way to show its interest [in Europe] by taking initiative in some field'. Morrison, however, in his job at the Foreign Office for less than a week, was noncommittal, vaguely suggesting that Britain could perhaps propose the establishment of 'some European body charged with a special responsibility, such as coordination of European science'. He also emphasised that there were 'difficulties that existed in British minds, particularly Labour Party circles', in giving economic power to European bodies that did not share the British government's policies of full employment. The United Kingdom, Morrison claimed, could only enter a united Europe that shared Britain's socialist principles.[106]

Even within the United Kingdom, those socialist principles were coming under increasing pressure, though, with Mollet's message corresponding with the start of the Conservative campaign to explicitly undermine the government at every turn. Polling continued to suggest that political support was swinging rapidly from the Labour Party to the Tories, on economic issues as well as foreign affairs. Within the Labour Party itself, doubts about the leadership were also seeping in. In late March 1951, Kenneth Younger offered a harsh assessment of his colleagues in the cabinet: 'Clem Attlee is practical & sensible, but doesn't really make the grade as P.M. . . . Shinwell is terrible, Jowitt & Dalton incalculable & several, such as George Tomlinson, Tom Williams & Chuter [Ede], more or less out of their depth. . . . Jim Griffiths, whom I like very much, is a bit disappointing. . . . All in all, it is not a very impressive group & it has little internal cohesion'.[107] Overall, the cabinet showed 'a lack of understanding of the art of leadership which is a bit shocking'.[108] Sensing a rapidly changing mood, Attlee decided on an October General Election to secure another five years of Labour government before it was too late. Hugh Dalton encouraged him in this decision, as did other members of the cabinet, and, at the September party conference, Attlee announced that the General Election would be held on 25 October 1951.[109]

In the run-up to the election, the Consultative Assembly of the Council of Europe met at Strasbourg, and Churchill was once again determined to make a splash, this time by inviting members of the Commonwealth countries to attend in order to demonstrate the important links between Europe and the Commonwealth. Throughout the summer, members of the Conservative Party had lobbied these Commonwealth statesmen to attend. On 24 June, for example, Churchill sent a telegram to all Commonwealth Prime Ministers insisting that 'it is of the greatest importance to British leadership in

Europe... to ensure that developments towards European unity should be in fullest harmony with broad Commonwealth interests',[110] and, on 26 June, Harold Macmillan repeated the message, writing, 'It has long been our British theme that the interests of the Commonwealth and the movement towards greater unity in Europe are complementary and not competitive'.[111] In July, Leo Amery published an article in the *European Review* arguing for 'a considerable interlocking or partial integration between Europe and Commonwealth, to the benefit of all concerned, without facing the United Kingdom with the alternative of going in with Europe or staying with the Commonwealth'.[112]

In contrast to his idea for a European Army, however, Churchill's efforts to bring the Commonwealth leaders into the European sphere bore little fruit. Louis St. Laurent, the Canadian Prime Minister, told Macmillan that he agreed that it was 'very important that the kind of unity which is achieved in Europe should in no way be inimical to the true interest of our Commonwealth association' but did not think this was best achieved 'by having representatives of non-European Commonwealth nations brought into the deliberations of European Councils and Assemblies'.[113] Sidney Holland, the New Zealand Prime Minister, likewise wrote that he was unable to send any representatives to Strasbourg. Robert Menzies, the Australian Prime Minister, said that all his parliamentarians would be 'extremely busy [in September] and most reluctant to leave the country'.[114] Sir Frank Keith Officer, the Australian Ambassador to France, apologised to Julian Amery for his government's response, saying that his personal view was that the United Kingdom 'has to be both a member of the Council of Europe and the cornerstone of the British Commonwealth'. Nevertheless, he also recognised that Australia had 'special difficulties: we are away in the Pacific, engrossed all too much no doubt with the problems in that area'.[115] Britain was a European country. The Commonwealth nations were not.

Despite these initial responses, Macmillan did not give up. He wrote again to Menzies in early September, asking him to send government officials if he could not send parliamentary representatives, saying 'how anxious we are to see Britain play a proper role both as an Imperial and as a European power'.[116] Again, though, Menzies rebuffed him, sending only his 'very best wishes to you in your coming venture'.[117] Macmillan had no better luck with the Canadians or New Zealanders, and his correspondence suggests that whilst the Conservative Party in

Britain was keen to see British leadership of both the Commonwealth and Europe as an integrated whole, those in the Commonwealth were far less interested in Europe. This was a significant development. For Churchill, Macmillan, Amery, Sandys and other pro-European Conservatives, the question of Europe had never been separate from the question of the Empire and Commonwealth. Their concept of British leadership in Europe was predicated on British leadership of the Commonwealth; it necessarily implied (and often explicitly stated) Commonwealth participation in any schemes for European integration. For the Commonwealth leaders themselves to shy away from a role in Europe undermined the very foundations of Conservative thought on Britain's place in Europe.

On the continent, too, there was noticeably less interest in British involvement in European affairs following the government's refusal to discuss the Schuman Plan. On 12 July 1951, Sir Oliver Harvey, the British Ambassador to France, wrote to Morrison, saying that he was 'rather concerned at the position we seem to be getting into over the various schemes for European integration'. He continued: 'We seem to be in some danger of finding ourselves in isolation from our principal Allies over these questions. Most of the schemes in question were started by the French. They seem to be receiving more and more enthusiastic backing from the Americans, while our own attitude appears aloof and disinterested'. Macmillan's correspondence with the Dominions revealed an independence of mind in the Commonwealth countries that had not been present only a few years earlier. Now, Harvey seemed to be suggesting that the British were also becoming isolated from both France and the United States.

Few in the government took much notice, however. Only days before Macmillan received his final snub from the Australian Prime Minister, Geoffrey Alchin, the British Ambassador to Luxembourg, wrote to Evelyn Shuckburgh, Morrison's private secretary, that 'we should in no circumstances be carried away by the current talk of surrender of sovereignty.... Many respected people, including some of our own, say that integration and even federation of Europe "must come" but I do not think that they have ever said why'. He continued: 'There seems really to be nothing sound in this talk of a United Europe. Even if something came of it, it would not be likely to last'. He concluded, 'When the balance of power in Europe is disturbed, the Continent tends to fall to the aggressor. Behind the moat of the

Channel we marshal our strength (now with powerful aid from the West) and restore the balance. But this could not come about and we could not serve even as an "aircraft carrier" if, through some European integration folly, we had entered into free trade or pooling agreements with the Continent'.[118] For Alchin, Britain's future lay in the Empire and Commonwealth, now allied with the United States. His new master in the Foreign Office, Herbert Morrison, was no more inclined than he to look to Europe. With Bevin gone, there were few men remaining in the Labour Party to advocate a strong British presence in Europe.

Sir Roger Makins, Deputy Under-Secretary at the Foreign Office, reached a similar conclusion. On 11 August 1951, he wrote a memorandum on British foreign policy, arguing that its strategy should be fourfold: '(a) to maintain the maximum cohesion in the Commonwealth and Empire, and to hold the sterling area together; (b) to maintain a partner relationship with the United States; (c) to promote the cohesion of Western Europe; [and] (d) to strive for the fullest measure of economic independence and strength for the United Kingdom'. On Western Europe, he wrote, 'Our policy is, very broadly speaking, to support and co-operate with the Western European countries to the fullest extent possible short of entering into an organic relationship with all or any of them'. This, he confessed, was 'the most difficult of the three facets of our policy, since we are of, not in, Europe. The Europeans are conscious of their own weakness and are trying to pull us in, and some Americans are sometimes trying to push us in'. The British government must resist this: 'We want Europe to be strong, but if we were classed as just a European Power and bound in an organic relationship to a predominantly Latin and Catholic grouping, we should soon lose our world position and a great deal of our liberty of action without strengthening either Europe or ourselves'.[119] The Empire had to come first.

Makins offered a stark warning, one which betrayed a sentiment held by many throughout the British Isles. Following the death of Bevin and the troubles in the Empire, there was an increasing feeling that Britain was losing its place in the world. This message was hammered home by the Conservative Party throughout the General Election campaign in September and October, arguing that, in Europe, the Empire and Commonwealth, Korea and throughout the wider world, the Labour Party had lost the plot. When in late October the British electorate went to the polls, they restored the Conservative Party to governance with a majority of 321 seats to Labour's 295.[120] On 26 October 1951, Clement Attlee travelled the short distance from 10 Downing Street to Buckingham Palace to offer his resignation to King George VI, who immediately invited Winston Churchill to form a new government as Prime Minister.[121] Within days, Churchill's cabinet emerged as a veritable who's who list from the European Movement: Anthony Eden as Foreign Secretary, Harold Macmillan as Minister of Housing and Local Government, Duncan Sandys as Minister of Supply, Peter Thorneycroft as President of the Board of Trade, Edward Heath as Lord of the Treasury and Sir David Maxwell-Fyfe as Home Secretary, supported from the backbenches by MPs such as Julian Amery, Robert Boothby, David Eccles and Raymond Gower. It is unlikely that a more pro-European government could be found in British history, and its members were eager to restore the United Kingdom to what they believed was its rightful place leading both Europe and the Commonwealth.

Shortly after the election, Amery wrote to Macmillan, telling him that 'Churchill's return has, certainly, created the psychological background for us to take up the leadership of Europe and the present state of the Schuman and Plevan Plans seems to offer a practical opportunity to take the initiative'. He continued: 'The Schuman Plan and Plevan Plan are groggy. We could still save them. It is a question of going in and making them work'.[122] The Conservative Party of October 1951 still believed in a Britain that could lead both Europe and the Commonwealth. With a workable majority in the House of Commons, a cabinet with deep experience of international affairs and a leader who was still revered at home and abroad, it was time to put into practice in government what the Tories had been preaching for the past six years in opposition.

7 THE REALITIES OF GOVERNMENT

The Prime Minister finalised his cabinet in the late hours of 30 October 1951. At its first meeting that day, he made no mention of either the Commonwealth or Europe, instead appointing a committee to begin an 'urgent' investigation into how to reverse the Labour government's Iron and Steel Act, which had nationalised the steel industry. He also announced that all ministers would take a reduced salary for three years and suggested that Britain should support Israel in its ongoing dispute with Egypt, the latter having blocked the passage of oil tankers bound for Haifa through the Suez Canal. When the new Foreign Secretary Anthony Eden spoke against this, arguing that it was more important to avoid creating resentment in Egypt and other Arab states than to support Israel, Churchill deferred to his judgment and so the status quo remained in the Middle East. Beyond this brief discussion, there was no further mention of foreign or imperial affairs.[1]

When the cabinet met for the second time, on 1 November, there was again no consideration of Europe or the Commonwealth, its members instead examining the recommendation by the new Chancellor of the Exchequer, R. A. Butler, for a drastic reduction in government expenditure.[2] That evening, when speaking in the House of Commons for the first time as newly re-elected Prime Minister, Churchill called for 'several years of quiet, steady administration, if only to allow Socialist legislation to reach its full fruition',[3] and, at the cabinet meeting of 7 November, his only reference to the Empire was to ask Oliver Lyttelton, the new Colonial Secretary, to investigate ways to reduce the cost of the ongoing counter-insurgency operations in

Malaya.[4] It was clear that the new government's focus would be on economics rather than foreign policy and that its priority would be to reduce public spending. For a party that, in opposition, had spoken with sweeping rhetoric of grand visions for the world, the first days in government for the Conservatives were marked by a distinct and unambitious pragmatism.

Yet if in his initial weeks as Prime Minister Churchill had been more concerned with reducing the cost of peacetime governance than with foreign policy, for others in the government and civil service Europe, the Empire-Commonwealth and Britain's place in the world more generally were at the forefront of their deliberations. The immediate concern of Pierson Dixon, Deputy Under-Secretary of State at the Foreign Office, was the upcoming talks with the French government in Paris, which had been planned long before the results of the General Election were known. In an internal minute summarising the new government's policy on European integration, Dixon wrote that the United Kingdom was 'ready to play an active part in all plans for integration on an inter-governmental basis'. It wished to encourage those countries in Europe that hoped to federate and would support them 'short of actual membership'. It would also continue to play a leading role in the Council of Europe. European integration, the new government believed, offered 'the only way of resolving the traditional Franco–German conflict, and of successfully associating Germany in the Western democratic world for all purposes including that of common defence, an aim to which we attach the highest importance'. The government could not 'subordinate ourselves and our control of policy to any European supranational authority'.[5] Although this policy differed little from the Labour government's before it, the Conservatives hoped to demonstrate a shift in tone that might generate significant amounts of goodwill on the European continent. The new government would work as closely as possible with the European Coal and Steel Community (ECSC), would continue to play its full part in the Council of Europe and would support the creation of a European Army, which had, after all, first been proposed by the new Prime Minister Winston Churchill.

However, when Churchill first raised the question of Europe with the cabinet in a memorandum on 29 November, his rhetoric was distinctly different from his words spoken in opposition. Acknowledging that he had provided the initial spark for the

European Movement with his Zurich speech in 1946, he drew back from the effusive support for European integration he had given prior to the General Election, suggesting that 'As year by year the project advanced, the Federal Movement in many European countries who participated [in the European Movement] became prominent'. This, he claimed, was never part of his original conception, and he 'never thought that Britain or the British Commonwealth should, either individually or collectively, become an integral part of a European Federation'. As far as the European Army was concerned, his idea was that it would exist 'inside the N.A.T.O. Army' with 'national characteristics . . . preserved up to the divisional level'; it was not intended to be its own entity. Finally, he 'welcomed the Schuman Coal and Steel Plan as a step in the reconciliation of France and Germany' but said that he had 'never contemplated Britain joining in this plan on the same terms as Continental partners'. In general, when examining questions of European policy, 'We help, we dedicate, we play a part, but we are not merged and do not forfeit our insular or Commonwealth-wide character'. The first priority of the British government was the 'unity and the consolidation of the British Commonwealths [sic] and what is left of the former British Empire', followed by 'the "fraternal association" of the English-speaking world'. Only once these were assured could the government turn to 'United Europe, to which we are a separate, closely- and specially-related ally and friend'.[6]

If this sudden about-face came as a shock to those in the cabinet who had campaigned with Churchill for a British role at the heart of a United Europe, his Foreign Secretary Anthony Eden could not have been more pleased with the memorandum. Eden had never embraced Europe to the same extent as Churchill, Sandys, the two Amerys and Macmillan. As he once said to Robert Boothby, 'The difference between us is that you are a European animal, whereas I am an Atlantic animal'.[7] Writing long after Eden had left Parliament, Harold Macmillan regretted that 'Anthony Eden stood aloof. . . . I felt then, and still more later, how much we had lost'.[8] Whilst in opposition, Eden had been happy to toe the party line and support Churchill in his European dreams, but as Foreign Secretary Eden's attitude shifted abruptly. In part, he was encouraged by other European leaders in this evolution. In late November, H. Hayat, a member of the Belgian Chamber of Representatives in Brussels, informed him that 'The number is growing here of those who realise that it would be wrong to become tied hand

and foot to the Continent, while our relationship to Great Britain remained of a much looser kind'. Hayat continued: 'Let the three great continental powers [France, West Germany and Italy] federate on their own if they wish to do so, but I can see no point in dragging into the process – without their full and free consent – three small countries whose interests lie as much in close association with the Anglo Saxon world as with their neighbours on the mainland'.[9] Eden was also encouraged by a voluminous correspondence from the United States insisting that now the Conservatives were back in power, the British government ought to reassert its position as one of the three Great Powers, the American D. Fairbanks (for example) telling him that it was 'so revivifying to the spirit to see Britain once again taking hold of her fate and acting with decision'.[10]

Eden's first real test came shortly after the General Election, when the European Consultative Assembly at Strasbourg hosted a debate between members of the Assembly and a delegation from the US Senate. Churchill chose Robert Boothby to represent the Conservative Party – and by extension, the government – in this debate. Boothby found the Americans to be 'strongly in favour of European unity', although he sensed that many of the European delegates were beginning to become disillusioned by the lack of power held by the Assembly. He wrote to Eden that he was 'disturbed and depressed' by what he saw. He continued: 'In politics you can play with people's careers and even their lives; but you cannot, with impunity, play with their faiths. Today the youth of many continental countries in Europe believe, passionately, in the ideal of European union. That is their faith; and many of them have no other. I fear the consequence of disillusionment'. He urged Eden to consider how the Consultative Assembly could be 'given something to do' that would revitalise Europe.[11] Julian Amery, likewise, felt that the time was right for Britain to retake the leadership of Europe, telling Macmillan that 'our continental colleagues were naturally much encouraged by the change of Government at home'. Amery was particularly encouraged by Guy Mollet, who 'went so far as to say that he would be quite prepared to see the different countries of the Continent become Dominions of the Commonwealth, if that would make things easier for us'.[12]

The British delegation's position was strengthened when the new Home Secretary, Sir David Maxwell-Fyfe, flew to Strasbourg for a plenary session to summarise the new government's policy on the proposed European Defence Community. He said that although he could not 'promise that our eventual association with the European Defence Community would amount to final and unconditional participation', he could nevertheless assure the Assembly that the government held a 'determination that no genuine method shall fail for lack of thorough examination which one gives to the needs of trusted comrades'. When asked for clarification later that evening, he said in a press conference, 'It is quite wrong to suggest that what I said was any closing of the door by Britain. . . . I made it plain that there is no refusal on the part of Britain'.[13] At Strasbourg, the tone taken by Conservative ministers and backbenchers was entirely different to the previous government's. It was open and welcoming, and their fellow Europeans responded warmly, sensing that a page had been turned in Britain's relationship with the European continent.

That same evening, however, Eden also gave a press conference – his in Rome – and offered a conflicting message. He declared that although Britain would support a European Defence Community, under no circumstances would it actually join one. When Maxwell-Fyfe received news of this statement at dinner, he was 'on the brink of resignation'.[14] Eden's announcement, in direct contradiction to the government policy announced by Maxwell-Fyfe earlier that day at Strasbourg and a clear departure from the views Churchill had promulgated throughout his time in opposition, caused an immediate stir on the European continent, completely overshadowing the earlier remarks by the Home Secretary. Julian Amery told Macmillan that their European colleagues 'felt, not unnaturally, that we had let them down'. Spaak immediately resigned the Presidency of the Consultative Assembly in protest at what he believed to be a deliberate sabotaging of the Council of Europe by the British government.[15] Amery was not surprised by this overly emotional reaction but warned Macmillan that 'if we miss this opportunity, it may be a case of "*le bonheur qui passe*"'. He complained that when Sir James Salter, the Minister of Economic Affairs, had arrived from London, he had brought with him instructions from the Foreign Secretary that 'we are opposed even to the merger of the cultural and social functions of the Brussels Pact with the Council of Europe!' This left the British delegation with no ability to 'really defend ourselves very effectively as none of us know what are the reasons for our apparently negative policy towards the Council of Europe'.[16] Indeed,

Eden's tone was as much a shock to his own cabinet as it was to his European colleagues.

On 3 December, Boothby angrily wrote to Churchill in a letter signed by all other members of the Conservative delegation in Strasbourg. 'A week ago', he said, 'events appeared to be moving in a manner favourable to British interests'. Eden's speech had changed all that, however: 'It is no exaggeration to say that the unexplained and unqualified refusal of Great Britain to participate in a European Army, announced by the Foreign Secretary in Rome, came as a shattering blow to most members of the Assembly. Had the Home Secretary been anyone other than Sir David Maxwell-Fyfe, few could have been persuaded that he was unaware of the decision when he spoke'. Boothby ended with a plea for Churchill to 'take some positive action designed to restore British prestige in the Consultative Assembly, and to show that His Majesty's Government mean[s] to play their part in the military defence and economic development of a united Europe'.[17] Yet the Prime Minister made no reply, and, in a single press statement, Eden served to undermine all the goodwill that Churchill and the European Movement had so painstakingly developed for the Conservative Party since his 1946 speech in Zurich.

It was not only Boothby and Maxwell-Fyfe who were angered by the Foreign Secretary's new tone on Europe. Richard Crossman, a backbench Labour MP, noted in his diary on 6 December that 'in Washington, Paris and Strasbourg (where the Council of Europe is sitting) the whole world is up in arms and incensed by Mr Churchill's cool writing-off of British participation in European Army, which he himself proposed at Strasbourg last year'.[18] On 8 December, Dwight D. Eisenhower, the Supreme Commander of Allied Forces in Europe, wrote to Eden, wondering 'whether all of you, on that side of the Channel, realize how hungrily many Europeans look to Britain for political guidance. They read with real concern every British pronouncement, or even opinion, when such pronouncement or opinion affects continental Europe'. He warned that 'many Europeans believe that the British Government really opposes a unity of European nations or the formation of a united defense force'. Although Eisenhower had himself 'pointed out [to European governments] the great benefit to all of us of Great Britain's continuing to carry out her world-wide responsibilities', the Europeans with whom he had spoken were having none of it. He found that 'the apparent emphasis in some British statements on the negative attitude toward participation has obscured the approval of these ideas so far as the Western Continental countries are themselves concerned' and hoped that 'authoritative statements would emphasize Britain's approval of these projects, its readiness to associate on a cooperative basis with European organisms so as to advance the development of collective security'.[19]

Eden chose to ignore Eisenhower's warnings, further undermining the government's position, both in Europe and with the United States. Four days after Eisenhower penned his letter, Boothby wrote again to the Prime Minister, telling him, 'The anxieties expressed in my letter to you from Strasbourg have been justified by events. We seem now to be moving into a position of some isolation; and I believe that this could have been avoided'. He warned that the Conservative delegation in Strasbourg had been 'placed in a position of considerable difficulty. We felt ourselves circumscribed by the negative Ministerial briefs of our successive "leaders"; and were unable to speak frankly, for fear of apparent disloyalty'. He reminded Churchill that 'In the early days of our movement you told me that the idea would either catch on, or it would not; and that, if it caught on, nothing – in the long run – could stop it. I believe this to be profoundly true. There can no longer be any doubt that, in continental Europe, it has caught on'. The only question remaining was whether the United Kingdom would lead or be left behind. Boothby urged British leadership, saying, 'We have made a bit of a mess of this; but I have no doubt that you could restore the whole position, and with it our prestige in a single speech delivered at the appropriate time'.[20] The Conservative Party had been in power for less than six weeks and it was not too late to correct its course. Yet any further delay could set it on a very dangerous path indeed.

Churchill was quite taken by Boothby's argument, telling Eden that it was 'a good and carefully thought out letter' and that he was 'naturally distressed at the way things have gone at Strasbourg'. The Prime Minister took 'the full blame because I did not feel able either to go there myself or to send a message'.[21] Eden was less impressed, however. Boothby 'mentions, and by implication supports, "the creation of an organic union of Europe under British leadership." This sounds all right but what does it mean?' It was a rhetorical question: 'It can only mean that we are being asked to merge ourselves in a European federation. But as you yourself said in the Defence Debate we cannot merge ourselves in schemes like the Plevan Plan for a European Defence Community. We can only associate ourselves with them as closely as possible'. The Foreign Secretary stood fast to the position he had articulated at Rome, saying, 'The trouble at Strasbourg was that we were being urged to come right in to European federative schemes. To my mind we must stoutly refuse to do anything of the sort, however severe the criticisms from Spaak, Reynaud, and the rest at Strasbourg'.[22] Although many in the cabinet disagreed with Eden's approach, it was the Foreign Secretary who represented Britain on European affairs. And on the question of British involvement in European integration Eden had never shared the enthusiasm of some of his colleagues. For the time being at least, Churchill was happy to leave matters to his Foreign Secretary, even if that meant a contradiction of much of what he had pronounced over the past six years.

* * *

It was not only on domestic European policy that the Conservative government immediately clashed with its European neighbours. In colonial policy, too, the new government took a more aggressive stance, particularly towards the French. Immediately after the General Election, the Quai d'Orsay invited the British Colonial Office to official talks to discuss West Africa, which it hoped would take place around Christmas. The new Colonial Secretary, Oliver Lyttelton, agreed, but his hands were full with the ongoing insurgency in Malaya. He therefore tasked his Minister of State, Alan Lennox-Boyd, to lead the British team. He also requested that the Foreign Office join the Colonial Office in the talks because colonial concerns in Africa were inseparable from the government's bilateral relations with the French, which fell under the portfolio of the Foreign Secretary.

In preparation for the talks, C. P. Hope of the Foreign Office noted that 'Our colonial policies are fundamentally different [from the French]'. In particular, the French government opposed 'the speed of development in the Gold Coast' and wanted the British government to 'restrain Nkrumah, the present Prime Minister of the Gold Coast'. Meeting with other officials from the Foreign and Colonial Offices, Hope suggested that any discussion with the French 'would inevitably show that present British policies in West Africa could not be changed. They might therefore leave the impression that French policies in the area were not only inconsistent with present day conditions but that, if they were to be acceptable to the indigenous inhabitants, they would need amending to bring them more into line with British policies'. Once again, the government would be faced with the prospect of telling the French that they must change to cooperate. They therefore decided to 'offer [something] to the French to sweeten this unpalatable pill'.[23]

A. B. Cohen, head of the Africa Division in the Colonial Office, agreed that there was a significant difference between French and British colonial policy in West Africa. British policy was to 'build up each of the West African territories as a country with its own political institutions, the aim being self-government within the British Commonwealth'. British reforms in Africa were based on the premise that 'a sense of responsibility can only be created by giving responsibility; that no constitution which did not provide for full participation by Africans would have any chance of success under present conditions in West Africa; and that such a constitution provides the best defence against Communism in West Africa, the only chance of friendly co-operation between this country and the West African territories and the best chance when the time comes of securing a favourable decision by the Gold Coast and Nigeria to stay within the British Commonwealth'. The British government of the early 1950s recognised that the Empire could no longer survive as it once had. Its aim now was to devolve power to the indigenous peoples in such a way that, upon independence, former colonies would remain within the Commonwealth and thus within the British sphere of influence during the Cold War.

The French government, in contrast, believed that British policy was 'moving too fast'. More fundamentally, whereas the British government aimed 'at developing political institutions in colonial territories and gradually handing over power to them', French policy sought 'to link these territories constitutionally to France itself through the Union Française'. This meant that 'Control over finance, administrative action and legislation is to a great degree concentrated in Paris'. Britain's policy 'in the constitutional sphere is to devolve; theirs is to centralise'. The French government feared that British moves towards self-government in its West African colonies would inevitably encourage French West African colonies to also seek self-government and eventual independence, thus undermining the very foundations of French colonial policy. Cohen concluded, 'It may seem arrogant to suggest that British policy is right and French wrong ... [but] the French themselves will sooner or later realise that their own policy must be modified'.[24] The British government was happy to meet with the French on colonial matters whenever the French desired, but there was no question of the British adapting in any way its own colonial policy. Should the French seek closer integration in the colonial field, it was they who would have to change their policy, not the British.

The proposed meeting between the French Quai d'Orsay and the British Foreign and Colonial Offices was delayed several times due to crises in the French cabinet, eventually taking place in London on 31 March 1952 rather than in Paris at Christmastime. Throughout the intervening months, British politics was largely overshadowed by the death of King George VI on 6 February and the subsequent ascension of the young Queen Elizabeth II.[25] By late March, however, 'business as usual' had returned to London and parliamentary affairs were 'curiously flat'.[26] In talks chaired by Oliver Lyttelton rather than Lennox-Boyd, British and French ministers agreed to establish a joint consultative machinery in West Africa to allow communication, if not coordination, on Anglo–French colonial policy.[27] Little came of the machinery, however, and although further Anglo–French colonial talks were held in May 1953, January 1954 and March 1954, the French argued that they were 'too short and too infrequent to be of much value'.[28] Indeed, H. T. Bourdillon, the Assistant Under-Secretary of State at the Colonial Office, privately wrote that 'the whole idea of ... forming a defensive alliance with other Colonial powers is repugnant to us – and this goes for the Foreign Office as much as for the Colonial Office'. The British should of course 'show as much readiness as possible to give the French full *information* about important developments in our own territories' but not discuss any concrete forms of collaboration between the two powers.[29] Much had changed in the five years since Bevin and Bidault had dreamed of a shared Anglo–French empire standing independently of the United States. European colonialism, which at one time was presumed to share so much in common, had unveiled a fundamental philosophical difference as decolonisation began. If European unity was to develop, it would not – as had once been expected – do so in the colonial world.

* * *

If the Conservative government's policy in the colonial field was to distance the French from British action, to inform but not collaborate, then closer to home the government increasingly sought to assert British leadership on the European continent. Churchill instructed that Eden send a memorandum to the British Embassy in Paris, the British delegation to the Organisation of European Economic Cooperation (OEEC) and the British delegation at the United Nations General Assembly in mid-December 1951 clarifying the government's position and casting a more positive light on its approach towards Europe. Eden backtracked on his earlier scepticism, writing that 'Much of the criticism of our policy stems from a failure to distinguish between co-operation in Europe and the federation of Europe'. He therefore offered a clarification: 'His Majesty's Government are willing and anxious to play their full part in the former. We want a united Europe because the security and prosperity of Europe can only be achieved by united efforts. We are playing and will continue to play our full part in plans for uniting national efforts on an intergovernmental basis. It is only when plans for uniting Europe take a federal form that we cannot ourselves take part, because we cannot subordinate ourselves or the control of British policy to federal authorities'. It was government policy to 'reconcile our worldwide commitments with our responsibilities towards Europe and the Commonwealth'. The best way to do this was through the Council of Europe, where the government was 'determined to play our full part as active members'. He also promised to 'carefully consider all plans for European integration put forward there to see whether it is possible for us to participate or associate ourselves with them'.[30] There was, however, no question of a full embrace of Europe. Given the Conservative Party's critiques when in opposition, it was astounding how similar its European policy was to Ernest Bevin's. The new government was showing consistency with the old to a fault.

Following delivery of Eden's memorandum, Churchill travelled to Paris himself. Ahead of his visit to the United States, Churchill thought it necessary to demonstrate to governments on the European continent that although the United Kingdom sought closer ties with the United States, it was doing so as a European power for the good of all Europe. He therefore intended to make a very public show of consultation with his European allies before taking their message to the American government. Nevertheless, Sir Evelyn Shuckburgh noted in his diary that it was 'not an easy visit for A[nthony] E[den]', coming so soon after his press conference in Rome.[31] Ironically, the one area upon which Churchill and Eden did reach agreement during their Paris visit was on Egypt. Late one evening, Eden broached with Churchill the growing problems he was having with the Egyptian government, and, somewhat prophetically, 'the old man advanced on Anthony with clenched fists, saying with the inimitable Churchill growl, "Tell them that if we have any more of their cheek we will set the Jews on them and drive them into the gutter, from which they should never have emerged"'.[32] Neither Churchill nor Eden had much time for the growing nationalism in Egypt.

On Europe, however, Churchill took a calmer approach and Eden followed his lead. When he arrived home from Paris, the Foreign Secretary wrote to Harold Macmillan, telling him that 'far from wishing to prevent others [on the Continent] from going ahead with such federal plans we have given them what encouragement we could'. He added, 'It is absurd to say that simply because we decline to federate, we are, therefore, abandoning Europe. On the contrary, we shall continue our present policy of positive and active co-operation'.[33] Whatever had driven the Foreign Secretary's sharp tone towards European integration in November had softened by mid-December, and, by the end of the month, even the pro-European Harold Macmillan was congratulating him on 'the change of climate that has followed your return to the Foreign Office. It is a triumph for you'.[34] Macmillan only hoped that Eden's embrace of Europe had not come too late.

In the New Year, Churchill and Eden travelled to the United States, where they argued that Britain still held leadership ambitions in Europe, despite failing to join the ECSC or enter negotiations for a European Defence Community. In a speech delivered at Columbia University in New York, the Foreign Secretary claimed that, despite Britain's limited resources, the country still had an important role to play in world affairs, for 'in a matter like this it is not only physical resources which count. Prestige, political experience, technical skill, a reputation for fair dealing, and above all national will are vital assets in calculating a country's influence in world affairs'. The United Kingdom was also 'not an isolated unit'. It was 'the focal point of a wider group of states and peoples: the British Commonwealth and Empire, which together make up a family bound by ties of sentiment and common interest'. Beyond the Commonwealth, the British people also had 'our own particular interest in Europe, where for centuries we have played a leading role. . . . We want a United Europe because security and prosperity can only be achieved by united efforts'. Although Eden confirmed that the government could not participate in any schemes for a *federal* Europe, it would 'merge [itself] whole-heartedly in associations for common purposes among the European Governments, when control remains in the hands of Governments'.[35]

Whilst Churchill and Eden travelled to the United States and France, Macmillan worked on the home front to persuade his cabinet colleagues to pay more attention to Europe. On 16 January 1952, he circulated a memorandum arguing that although Britain could not join a federal Europe, 'Federation is not the only form of constitutional association between states. The British peoples have themselves devised another – the Commonwealth relationship. Britain, with the full support of the Commonwealth, might join with a European Union or Confederation organised on similar lines'. He continued: 'With the Commonwealth behind us and holding, as we should, a balance between France and Germany, Britain would be the unchallenged leader of the European Confederation. This, in itself, would further strengthen our position within the Commonwealth. As the leaders, moreover, of both the Commonwealth and Europe we should be able to establish a more equal partnership with the United States both in the immediate task of containing Russia and in the longer term'. The 'negative attitude of the Labour Government' had made Britain's position in Europe more difficult, but Macmillan was certain that the Dutch and Belgian governments 'would prefer a loose European Union including Britain' and so, 'in all probability, would a majority of the French Parliament, as well as important elements in the German Parliament'. The problem Britain faced was not that continental Europeans disagreed with their position. It was that they had never been offered a choice. 'It should', Macmillan wrote, 'be British policy to announce the kind of European Union which we should be prepared to join. It would then be for the Continental nations to choose between such a Union and a Federation without Britain'.[36] Britain should not be content just to join or remain outside the type of Europe proposed by the French. It should instead offer an alternative.

Julian Amery agreed with Macmillan, writing to the newly elected MP Robert Carr that 'Anthony is quite right to say that Britain can never join a European Federation. But it is not enough to leave the matter there'. Repeating Macmillan's words, he argued that 'we ought to come out with a constructive alternative, and define the kind of Europe which we could join as full members. This, in my view, should be a Europe organised on Commonwealth lines'. France and West Germany would be unlikely to support this approach, but the government ought nevertheless to 'make the offer as the alternative possibilities are not very attractive. Frankly, they are black'.[37] Not all in the cabinet agreed, however. Robert Boothby felt that Macmillan's words were 'like a Papal Bull, but even more magisterial'. He satirised them, writing to Amery, '"All right, you funny little European boys", you say: "Play away with federation, if you like. And, when you have burnt your fingers, this is what the great and glorious and most high and mighty British Commonwealth and Empire, by the Grace of God Defender of the Faith, might conceivably do"'. Boothby didn't like Macmillan's tone and felt certain that the government couldn't 'possibly issue a statement of any kind now'.[38]

Boothby need not have worried. Before Macmillan could receive cabinet assent to issue his statement, the government faced its first serious financial crisis since the General Election. Following his visits to the United States and France, Anthony Eden travelled to Lisbon for a meeting of the NATO Council. Whilst there, Eric Berthoud, Assistant Under-Secretary in the Foreign Office, delivered a message from London stating that the government was facing an urgent balance of payments crisis and that the Bank of England had produced a 'really alarming plan' to resolve it, which the Chancellor of the Exchequer R. A. Butler had apparently accepted. Churchill, Berthoud told Eden, supported the plan and had sent a letter containing instructions for Eden.[39] When Eden opened it, he read that there was a 'new financial super-crisis which Rab [R. A. Butler] opened on us under the influence of the Governor [of the Bank of England].... I gather it spells the doom of the E.P.U. [European Payments Union] and you should bear in mind in all your negotiations the danger of the other powers complaining later that you knew all this and did not tell them. Yet you cannot tell them'.[40] Berthoud, however, suggested that Churchill and Butler (along with officials from the Treasury) were isolated in their support of the plan and that Lord Cherwell, Lord Swinton, Robert Hall and Lionel Robins had all spoken in opposition to it. Sir Evelyn Shuckburgh, who was with Eden in Lisbon, noted in his diary that 'It was clear that it was a bankers' plan: logically unassailable, but open to the gravest political objections'.[41]

The plan, code-named Operation Robot, was prompted by a drain on Britain's gold reserves, which had led to a loss for the British Treasury of $297 million in January 1952 and a further loss of $224 million in the first three weeks of February alone. The government's reserves had now fallen to $1,800 million (£650 million at the current exchange rate), which was equivalent to only three and a half weeks' turnover of the Sterling Area's transactions with the rest of the world. Butler warned that although the losses ought to lessen over the next few months, unless the government took 'drastic action' the reserves would fall 'to a point at which we can no longer be in effective control of the situation'. This crisis matched – and was perhaps worse than – every crisis faced by the previous Labour government, and Butler felt obliged to 'disclose the January and February losses in my Budget speech', scheduled to be given in March. In order to prevent adverse effects from the disclosure, he wanted to simultaneously announce a number of measures to restore the economy to a stable level. It was these measures that constituted Operation Robot.

Arguing that Britain's choice was between 'bad and less bad' and that the worst option of all would be 'to let things drift', Butler put forth his proposal in four parts. First, the government should 'allow the exchange rate to float, and find its own level as determined by the London Foreign Exchange Market'. Second, all 'foreigners' sterling balances [sh]ould be blocked (except for the American and Canadian Accounts, which are already convertible into dollars)', with 10 per cent of these immediately released as 'overseas sterling' that would be convertible to gold or any other currency at the ruling market rate. Third, 'the present structure of the sterling area would be maintained; the U.K. and other sterling area countries would retain full exchange control'. And, finally, not less than 80 per cent of sterling balances held by the Central Banks of independent Sterling Area countries should be funded, providing an instant buffer. Butler acknowledged that this would be 'a complete reversal of the policies of the last twelve years'. The Bank of England would no longer be able to provide foreign currency at a fixed rate; instead, Sterling Area citizens authorised to obtain foreign exchange and those outside the Sterling Area holding 'overseas sterling' would have to buy it on the market at the prevailing rate. There was inherent risk in this, and the policy had 'considerable uncertainty as to the outcome'. However, Butler predicted that under these circumstances, the 'drain on the gold reserves would...automatically cease, and we should lose gold from the reserves only if a decision was taken to intervene in the market to prevent the rate from falling too far'.[42]

Butler wrote to Eden on 22 February, the day after the Foreign Secretary had received Berthoud's visit. He told Eden that he was 'sympathetic [to] the anxiety which might be caused [in] Europe' but felt that 'the European economy, which is strained and in flux, may out of this build a better and less artificial future'.[43] The Chancellor of the Exchequer was the only cabinet member to offer Eden a positive explanation. Edward Plowden, who was with Eden in Lisbon, doubted 'whether the situation really warranted such drastic measures and he thought it looked as if the Chancellor had allowed himself to be rattled by the Bank of England'.[44] Eden sent a note to Churchill suggesting that 'a good deal more careful thought should be given to it' before any announcement was made.[45] When he arrived back in the United Kingdom on 27 February, a letter was awaiting him from Lord Cherwell, the Paymaster General, who argued that the plan would 'do more harm than good economically and... will cause a considerable rise in prices and unemployment; moreover it will certainly do immense damage to our relations with Europe, the U.S. and probably many of the Commonwealth countries'.[46] When the cabinet met later that week to discuss Butler's plan, Eden found it sharply divided, with the eventual outcome hinging on where the Foreign Secretary placed his vote. Having decided before he left Lisbon that 'the plan was premature', Eden 'went into the fray to kill the plan'. As Shuckburgh recorded in his diary, 'After a series of evidently very stormy meetings, the Cabinet rejected the plan. It was impossible not to be sorry for Rab Butler, but Whitehall as a whole was profoundly relieved. In the event, the Budget was remarkably well received in the country and abroad, and the position of sterling dramatically strengthened.... A[nthony] E[den] rightly takes credit for these developments. It has, however, left a scar on his relations with the Chancellor'.[47]

The schism between Eden and Butler – and between the Foreign Office and the Treasury – continued to grow. In the meantime, Eden received a boost of confidence from the support he had in the cabinet and saw in stark light how perilously close the British economy had come to complete ruin. His earlier visit to the United States had convinced him that the Americans believed they had provided enough economic support to the United Kingdom. This left only Europe and the Commonwealth to turn to for salvation. When Eden travelled to Paris for the Committee of Ministers of the Council of Europe in March 1952, he was determined to rectify the bad impression he had left the previous November. He did this by proposing that the Council of Europe 'provide the political institutions for the E[uropean]

D[efence] C[ommunity] and the Schuman Plan', ensuring that although the United Kingdom was not part of those communities, it would nevertheless take responsibility for them. Shuckburgh reported that this plan was 'extremely well received, and for the first time at a meeting of the Council in my experience the United Kingdom was not "dragging its feet"'.[48]

Over the next two months, Eden adopted the role of pulling together the European Defence Community, acting as ringmaster for a show in which the British would never participate. First proposed by Churchill in August 1950 and introduced to the French parliament as the Pleven Plan that October, the European Defence Community was the most ambitious scheme for European unity since Schuman's plan to pool French and German coal and steel under a supranational High Authority. It was intended to allow German rearmament – crucial for Europe's defence during the Cold War – without actually creating a German Army that could threaten other European countries.[49] The Labour government's policy had been to associate itself with a European Army but not to join it, and it had refused to participate in talks aimed at its foundation. At the time, the Conservative opposition had implied that it would have supported British membership, an assumption that the Home Secretary David Maxwell-Fyfe, Julian Amery, Harold Macmillan and Robert Boothby were clearly operating under when they attended the Strasbourg Consultative Assembly in November 1951. Yet Eden's speech in Rome that same week had suggested that the new Conservative government would instead follow the same policy as the Labour government before it. With the Foreign Secretary's words, the suspicion held by continental European governments that Britain was untrustworthy on the question of Europe seemed to be confirmed.

It was not until the spring of 1952 that Eden concluded it was in Britain's best interests to become involved in the formation of what was by then known as the European Defence Community (EDC). By that point, a conference had been held in Paris between those who wished to join the EDC. It had proposed that the community be composed of fourteen *groupements* of between 12,600 and 13,000 men each from France, twelve from West Germany and Italy, and five and three-quarters each from the Benelux countries. Yet when this conference closed in December 1951, the French were unhappy that they contributed just two more groupements than the West Germans, concerned also that the German contribution would be close to one-third of the entire EDC (almost half, when combined with the Italians). The Benelux countries, likewise, were suspicious of the derogation of their sovereign powers in military affairs to a European High Authority which would undoubtedly be dominated by the French and Germans. The Netherlands and Belgium were particularly concerned that Great Britain would not be involved, given that the British had traditionally guaranteed their security against France and Germany.[50]

When the Paris Conference reconvened in January 1952, its delegates quickly reached a compromise whereby the EDC would be controlled by a Board of Commissioners, numbering nine members with no more than two from any single state, thus ensuring that France and West Germany would have no more control than the Benelux countries, despite their larger contributions. This Board of Commissioners would then appoint the High Authority, which would ultimately manage the budget. Nevertheless, there was still disagreement, particularly between the French and Germans. First, Adenauer asked how the EDC could be associated institutionally with NATO when West Germany was the only member of the EDC that had no formal voice in NATO. This would put Germany at a distinct disadvantage. The EDC either needed to be completely separate from NATO (which neither the Americans nor the British supported) or West Germany needed to be brought into NATO (which the French objected to). Second, the French representatives raised without warning the issue of the Saar region, which had been granted a position of political autonomy but was temporarily in economic union with France. The French government wished to have its position resolved, preferably with the Saar becoming permanently annexed by France, before it would enter into a defence agreement with Germany. This, however, was unacceptable to the Germans.[51]

It was with this impasse in Paris that Eden spotted his opportunity. He proposed talks in London from 13 to 19 February among himself, Robert Schuman and the American Secretary of State Dean Acheson, with Adenauer joining them later in the week. At these talks, Eden and Acheson persuaded Schuman to treat the Saar issue as separate from the EDC and allayed Adenauer's fears about a possible conflict of interest with NATO, describing West German participation in the EDC as the first step towards full NATO membership rather than as an alternative. Following the conference, Eden told the House of Commons that 'The European atmosphere, heavily charged a fortnight ago, has been lightened, and the way is clear for concrete agreements'.[52]

Negotiations continued in Paris without British involvement throughout March 1952, but again became deadlocked over a West German proposal for an automatic defence guarantee, whereby if one member of the EDC was attacked all members would join in its defence. It was the Dutch who raised the first objection, refusing to enter into any form of collective defence unless the British were members also. The conference therefore proposed to the British government that it sign a treaty with the EDC for collective security, which would extend the guarantees given to France and the Benelux countries under the Brussels Treaty to West Germany and Italy. Eden informed the cabinet that 'the EDC is not likely to be established unless we respond to this latest proposal' and warned that a failure to establish the EDC would be blamed on the British, both by the continental European governments and by the United States. Consequently, on 4 April, the cabinet agreed to accept 'an obligation to provide military assistance in the event of an attack on any party to the EDC or the European Defence Forces'.[53] The British government was unwilling to enter the EDC because of its supranational nature, but it would nevertheless fight alongside it in the event of war.

The creation of a permanent alliance between the EDC and Great Britain eased any fears the Benelux countries had. Furthermore, the West German government was satisfied that the EDC provided its best route to full NATO membership, and the French were content that, at least in the short term, the Saar region remained in their hands. The final weekend of talks took place in Bonn from 24–26 May 1952 and was tense, particularly between the French and Germans. For the first time, the British participated fully in the talks, and Sir Evelyn Shuckburgh had 'never seen Schuman so obstinate and unreasonable, putting himself into the worst light before Adenauer'. In his opinion, the French could not 'make up their minds...to have the slightest confidence in the Germans, to whom at the same time they are offering this long-term unity and merging of sovereignty'. At one point, Schuman 'even refused to agree to the abandonment of the principle of taking reparations out of current production' until pressured to do so by Eden.[54] Over the course of the weekend, however, the differences dissipated, and, on 26 May, the British, American and French governments signed what were known as the Bonn Conventions, allowing the

Germans to rearm and thus paving the way for the EDC.[55] The following day, the foreign ministers of France, Belgium, West Germany, the Netherlands, Italy and Luxembourg travelled to Paris to sign the European Defence Community Treaty.[56] With their signatures, the Anglo–EDC Treaty also came into force, binding Great Britain to the continental European nations.[57]

In Bonn, there was 'a great scrimmage with cameras and newspapermen breathing down our necks and burning us with arc lamps', but in France the 'ceremony appeared to attract no interest from the Paris population. There was not a soul at the gates'.[58] This surprised both Shuckburgh and Eden, who suspected that French disappointment at Britain playing the leading role in the final negotiations had soured any sense of satisfaction they might have felt otherwise. Regardless, it was a good outcome for the British government, and, on 4 June, Eden wrote to Sir Ivone Kirkpatrick, the British High Commissioner for Germany, telling him, 'Your task has been arduous and complicated. You have had to deal not only with the Germans but also with your United States and French colleagues in forging a common policy acceptable to all. Whatever may come in the future, you will have the satisfaction of knowing that you have performed a great service in bringing matters to their present stage'.[59]

* * *

It was not only in the discussion surrounding the formation of the European Defence Community that Anthony Eden began to project leadership in Europe. In June 1952, he also took the chairmanship of the OEEC. On the sixteenth of that month, he received a letter from Edward Beddington-Behrens, who informed him that he had just returned from a meeting of the European League for Economic Co-operation (ELEC), a 'purely voluntary organisation ... which submitted the first draft of what was eventually the E[uropean] P[ayments] U[nion] scheme'. At its most recent meeting, ELEC had discussed evolving the EPU into a 'longer term organisation which we might call E.M.U. (European Monetary Union), comprising the present E.P.U. countries'. This would involve 'the closest monetary co-operation between the Sterling Area and other Western European countries'. However, it was actively opposed by the Western Germans, the French, the Italians and the Belgians, who hoped instead for 'close economic and monetary union of the six Schuman Plan countries ... to the exclusion of the rest of the world, including Great Britain'. In contrast, the Netherlands and Luxembourg, despite being members of the ECSC, supported ELEC's proposal, having never been convinced of the wisdom of excluding Great Britain. The European countries outside the Schuman Six (particularly the Scandinavian countries and Portugal) all favoured the plan. Beddington-Behrens therefore urged Eden to meet with the ELEC and consider putting forward a British plan for a broad-based European Monetary Union that would pre-empt French and German plans for a more exclusive European grouping.[60] Above all else, Eden had to make the case to the world that Europe was larger than France and Germany.

With Beddington-Behrens' letter in hand, Eden presented a memorandum to the cabinet on 18 June 1952 detailing Britain's overseas obligations. He argued that British foreign policy was determined by three fundamental factors: '(a) The United Kingdom has world responsibilities inherited from several hundred years as a great power. (b) The United Kingdom is not a self-sufficient economic unit. [And] (c) No world security system exists, and the United Kingdom with the rest of the non-Communist world, is faced with an external threat'. He argued that the 'essence of a sound foreign policy is to ensure that a country's strength is equal to its obligations'. Where this was not the case, 'either the obligations must be reduced to the level at which resources are available to maintain them, or a greater share of the country's resources must be devoted to their support'. Given the United Kingdom's continuing financial problems, Eden could reach only one conclusion: '[R]igorous maintenance of the presently-accepted policies of Her Majesty's Government at home and abroad is placing a burden on the country's economy which it is beyond the resources of the country to meet'. Something had to give. In the short-term, Eden could see 'few ways to effect any reductions in our overseas commitments which would provide immediate relief to our economic difficulties'. In the long-term, however, 'the maintenance of the present scale of overseas commitments [would] permanently overstrain our economy'. The United Kingdom was 'over-committed' and had to 'reduce the commitment'.

Eden argued that there were two major obligations where Britain might draw back: first, in the defence of the Middle East, 'for which at present we bear the responsibility alone'; and second, in the defence of South-East Asia, 'where we share responsibility with the

French'. The only way to relieve these burdens was to create an international defence organisation in which both the United States and the Commonwealth countries could participate. 'Our aim', he wrote, 'should be to persuade the United States to assume the real burdens in such organisations, while retaining for ourselves as much political control – and hence prestige and world influence – as we can'. Eden did not ignore Western Europe in his memorandum, noting that 'Western Europe is, within the Atlantic Pact, the heart of the defence of the British Isles and the nucleus of any Western system of defence.... Broadly speaking, our obligations here must have the first priority'.[61] In the Middle East and South-East Asia, the government could contemplate some form of withdrawal; in Western Europe, there could be no let-up of British engagement.

In response to Eden's report, the Overseas Information Services (OIS) tasked a Committee of Enquiry to investigate how best to promote British aims in foreign affairs. The committee reported that, in the United States, the OIS ought to 'maintain and enhance the United States public's confidence in the value of the United Kingdom as its best ally in the "cold war"'; in the Soviet and Chinese spheres, it ought to 'maintain the faith of non-Communists in Western democracy, ideals and policies (short of arousing hopes of early liberation) and to sow doubts of ultimate success at home or abroad in Communist minds'; and in Western Europe, it ought to 'maintain and enhance the popular will to resist communist, accept the cost of rearmament and trust in the determination and capacity of the United Kingdom and United States to defend Europe'.[62] The committee viewed Britain's place in the world through the prism of the Cold War and perceived both the United States and Western Europe as strategic necessities in that context, nothing more, nothing less.

On the European continent, the governments thought very differently. On 26 June 1952, Robert Boothby wrote to Brian Goddard, secretary of the United Europe Movement, informing him that 'the French Government is giving serious consideration to a proposal to elect a European Constituent Assembly, charged with the task of creating a political structure corresponding to the proposed military [European Defence Community] and economic [ECSC] structures'. If that happened, Boothby warned, 'not only the United Europe Movement but H.M.G. will be faced with a difficult decision. It will mean, in effect, the victory of Pleven-Monnet-Spaak over Eden'. This would be an unfortunate victory for the French government. It would also halt the progress of European integration on a popular level because 'the proposal for a European Federation which excluded Britain would almost certainly be rejected [by the public] in France, Holland and Belgium, where the politicians do not reflect the opinion of the majority'.[63]

Indeed, the more Eden dealt with the French and Belgian governments, the more he became convinced that British leadership of Europe could not be gained simply by joining the six Schuman Plan countries and trying to insert its influence. The British government could only regain the initiative in Europe by redefining the continent as something larger than the ECSC. Following visits to Strasbourg and Yugoslavia in September 1952, Schuckburgh noted in his diary, '[I]n Strasbourg... we were depressed by the defeatism of Guy Mollet and the other professional Europeans. Great contrast to arrive in Belgrade, where the people seem confident, energetic and boastful'.[64] The fourteen-day trip convinced the Foreign Secretary that plans to create a federation in Western Europe would ultimately subdue European ingenuity, enterprise and culture. Indeed, he began to envision a larger European free trade area that would remain part of a broader Atlantic Community, having the economic strength to stand shoulder to shoulder with the United States rather than one step behind it. In any case, he felt that a limited Common Market of a handful of European countries would come to nothing and was not something the British government should tie itself to.

Shortly after his trip to Yugoslavia, Eden travelled to Paris for a meeting of the OEEC, which he was chairing. He again sought to play ringmaster to the circus of Western Europe and 'all but succeeded in bringing the French and Germans together in a solution of the Saar problem', as well as 'persuading the Europeans of the United Kingdom's interest on the economic side [of European integration]'. However, just as Eden was becoming more convinced of the need for a British role in Europe, his Prime Minister Winston Churchill was losing interest. The Foreign Secretary found it 'very galling' when he returned to London that 'all Winston had to say was, "What have you done about getting the Duke of Windsor invited to the Embassy in Paris?"'[65] Schuckburgh reported that 'This sort of comment, which is constant, and the irrational interference in all sorts of small matters, ... is making A[nthony] E[den]'s position most difficult and irritating for him'.[66]

Eden was not the only cabinet member growing frustrated with Churchill's erratic behaviour, and, by the autumn of 1952, the Foreign Secretary's colleagues in cabinet were increasingly looking to him rather than the Prime Minister for direction and leadership.

Others beyond Churchill's cabinet were also experiencing doubts that autumn. On 30 October, Edward Beddington-Behrens complained he would be 'the only English member' at the upcoming Executive Committee meeting of the European Movement. This was because the committee had 'changed the date of [the] meeting this week, probably with a view to making it difficult for the English members to attend!' He added that it would 'probably be my last attendance, as with the emphasis now on the "little Europe", I find myself out of harmony with my Continental colleagues'.[67] Beddington-Behrens sensed that a distinct shift had taken place within the European Movement. It had evolved from a more organic, visionary organisation to something legalistic and rules-based, focussing entirely on securing measures of European Federation. Its once big tent had shrunk considerably.

Beddington-Behrens clarified his thoughts the following week in a letter to the Belgian Baron Rene Boel, explaining that when he attended the meeting he 'gained the impression that under its present direction it is solely concerned with pushing the "Little Europe" idea, which is quite different from our original conception of a movement propagating the idea of the unity of Europe'. He continued: 'The British never at any time said that they would enter a Federal Union; and now that the British Government is moving much more actively in the direction of European unity, the tendency seems to be for it to be cold shouldered by the supporters of the "Little Europe.... This makes the task of your British friends on United Europe much more difficult". He added that 'as an Englishman, I do not feel at all ashamed of our contribution and assistance towards Western Europe. We certainly played our very full part in the war. We poured immense sums into Germany afterwards, to prevent distress and starvation. We are maintaining a larger effective army and air force in Western Europe than all the Western Powers put together, and this is no small contribution in terms of money and sacrifice'. The United Kingdom, Beddington-Behrens believed, had done more for the security and future of Europe than any other European country, and he was dismayed that now simply because six of the many European countries were moving towards closer federation, Britons were being treated as 'bad' Europeans. Their views on Europe certainly differed from those of the French, Belgians and West Germans, yet were similar to those of the Dutch, Portuguese and Scandinavian countries. Furthermore, British views were closer to the original conception of the United Europe Movement. It was the French who had evolved their views on Europe, not the British. Beddington-Behrens warned Boel that 'if the whole activities of the European Movement are now to be developed solely in furthering a "Little Europe" idea, to the total exclusion of the wider conception, it may no longer serve a useful purpose for a person like myself'.[68]

When the European Movement again called a meeting with a week's notice, Beddington-Behrens and Robert Boothby refused to attend. The former wrote to R. A. Butler, the Chancellor of the Exchequer, explaining that British involvement in the European Movement was now at its end and that the British delegation would instead focus on participation in the ELEC. Joined by Leo Amery, Lady Rhys-Williams, Sir Cecil Kisch and Bob Edwards, Beddington-Behrens put before ELEC a proposal for a 'Commonwealth Scandinavian Movement for European Unity, as a counterpart to the narrow Little Europe policy of the European Movement'.[69] The European Movement, founded by Winston Churchill, Duncan Sandys and other British Conservatives, no longer had any place for Britons within its rank.

The resignation from the European Movement of Beddington-Behrens and Robert Boothby – two of the earliest post-war advocates of European unity – marked the closure of an important chapter in Britain's history with the European continent. If the British were to again lead Europe, they would have to do so in another manner. And it was not only in Europe that Britain's prospects were looking dim. In his first diary entry of 1953, Sir Evelyn Shuckburgh wrote: 'I ended today extremely gloomy about British prospects everywhere. In Kenya: the Mau Mau. In Egypt and Persia: the Americans refusing to support us. Even Iceland in process of destroying our deep-sea fishing industry. I see no reason why there should be any end to the surrenders demanded of us. International law and the temper of international opinion is all set against the things which made us a great nation, i.e. our activities outside our own territory. Bit by bit we shall be driven back into our island where we shall starve'.[70] It was a gloomy assessment to begin the New Year. It was one that Shuckburgh's boss – Anthony Eden – would have to grapple with, both in Europe and in the Empire and Commonwealth.

8 PERFIDIOUS GAUL

Six months after the Treaty for a European Defence Community (EDC) was signed in Paris, none of the national parliaments of the six signatories had yet ratified it. As Eden explained to Churchill in early January 1953, the West Germans were concerned that the EDC Treaty conflicted with German Basic Law, which made no allowance for rearmament. The treaty would therefore need a two-thirds majority in the Bundestag to pass rather than a simple majority. However, the German Chancellor Konrad Adenauer had only the support of just over half of German parliamentarians – far short of the necessary two-thirds. The German Constitutional Court was examining the issue, and Adenauer was 'determined to secure German ratification as soon as this is politically and constitutionally practicable'. In doing so, however, he faced a political risk: the German people were by no means united around his policies of greater integration with other European countries, and a narrow victory in the Bundestag could undermine his support in the long run.[1]

In France, the problem was even greater. Antoine Pinay's government had been defeated in the recent election, leading to the rise of René Mayer. It was the eighteenth change of power in France since the end of the war, and Mayer was the twelfth man to lead the French government in eight years. He immediately attempted to renegotiate the Treaty, linking its ratification to the drafting of some additional protocols, a definition of the European status of the Saar region and closer British association with the EDC. Bidault, replacing Schuman as French Foreign Minister for the third time, assured the British government that there was 'no question of modifying the main principles of the E.D.C. and that the new protocols are intended to clarify and reassure French opinion'. Nevertheless, he had yet to make their wording public, which had 'perturbed' Adenauer. The British Ambassador in Paris, Sir Oliver Harvey, had patiently explained to Bidault the reasons why it was impossible for the United Kingdom to become a member of the EDC, but his position had been undermined by Field Marshal Montgomery, who had publicly urged British Members of Parliament visiting the headquarters of the Supreme Headquarters Allied Powers Europe (SHAPE) to reconsider their position and accept British membership of the EDC.[2] This had greatly confused Britain's European allies, who largely considered Montgomery a member of the government, and Beddington-Behrens wrote to Julian Amery from Paris, saying, 'Britain is having rather a bad press on the Continent just now'.[3]

The United States, too, was complicating the situation. In the presidential election of 1952, Dwight D. Eisenhower – the Republican candidate – had swept to victory, bringing with him as Secretary of State John Foster Dulles, a man who made the British government nervous. Furthermore, shortly after the presidential inauguration in January 1953, Senator Alexander Wiley, the Chairman of the Senate Foreign Relations Committee, gave a speech that was 'somewhat threatening in tone', warning EDC countries that 'the new United States Administration is unlikely to tolerate indefinite delay'. Eisenhower had also made clear the US government's 'desire to see early ratification' and had written personally to Adenauer about it. Whilst the West German chancellor was receptive to American intervention, the tone of Senator Wiley served only to aggravate the French and caused them to delay further, out of principle if nothing else.[4] This concerned many in Britain, and, on 12 January, Lady Rhys-Williams wrote to Macmillan, asking, 'Is it possible that America is really contemplating that, if the E.D.C. is not signed immediately, she will think herself free to pull-out of Europe?' She warned Macmillan that she had seen 'real fear in old Motz's face [Roger Motz, President of the Belgian League for European Cooperation] when he heard that Adenauer had failed to get through the E.D.C. on account of legal difficulties. He seemed to believe that the Americans would use this as an excuse to pull out of Europe, and he said – and he meant it – that everyone in Europe would have to look after themselves and make terms with the Communists'.[5]

For Rhys-Williams and Macmillan, it was only common sense that America's best interests were served by Europe succeeding. The United Kingdom was America's closest ally in that endeavour. But many in the United States did not share this analysis. Although the British government viewed the delay in the EDC's ratification as entirely the fault of France and, to a lesser extent, West Germany, in the United States, the media blamed Great Britain for any and all delays to further integration in Europe. Sir Roger Makins wrote to Eden on 27 January 1953, warning him that there had been 'a recrudescence of criticism of ourselves in the press and radio for alleged foot-dragging and even sabotage of European unity'. He cited a recent piece in the *New York Times*, which was 'not an isolated article' but rather was evidence of a trend that was 'endemic'. He intended to counter the criticism when he gave a speech at the Press Club, but recommended that the Foreign Secretary address the issue directly with Dulles, who was certain to receive some 'high powered indoctrination...on his arrival in Paris'.[6]

Dulles was travelling to France in late January, his first overseas trip as American Secretary of State, and Eden arranged to meet him there for talks. Despite the ongoing war in Korea, the need for continued American financial assistance in the United Kingdom and the general British desire to maintain a strong and 'special' Anglo–American relationship, Eden had just one topic on his agenda for this first meeting: the British approach to European unity. When he sat down with Dulles, he explained that, since the end of the Second World War, a 'major objective of British post-war policy has been to promote the recovery and unity of Western Europe'. He pointed to the Dunkirk and Brussels Treaties that Bevin had negotiated, to British leadership at the founding of the Organisation of European Economic Cooperation, to the establishment of the Council of Europe at Churchill's urging and to continued British military and economic involvement in Europe in the face of the Soviet threat.

Eden explained, however, that unlike France, West Germany, Italy and the Benelux countries, the United Kingdom could not join 'federal or supranational institutions' where national sovereignty was pooled. The reasons for this were clear: '(i) our position as the leading member of the British Commonwealth and banker of the Sterling area; [and] (ii) our world-wide interests and commitments'. This did not mean that the British government did not perceive a British leadership role in Europe. On the contrary, the United Kingdom had to 'preserve our individuality and freedom of action in order to serve as a bridge between Europe and the rest of the free world'. Britain was both a European nation and a Great Power with extra-European responsibilities. The government hoped to reconcile its 'responsibilities to the Commonwealth and Western Europe and the special relationship we hope to maintain with the United States' through the framework of the Atlantic Alliance. He did not rule out some European countries forming a closer federation within that framework. The policy of the government was: '(i) to encourage the Six in their plans for closer integration; (ii) to establish the closest possible association with the European institutions, in the hope that our support will give them extra strength and stability and that by close contact we can influence their policies in desirable directions; [and] (iii) to ensure that the new federal developments do not run counter to the wider unity of Free Europe as a whole, nor weaken the Atlantic Alliance'. Eden stressed to Dulles that there was 'no real difference of view between the Americans and ourselves on this issue', but indicated that Europe was far larger than just the six countries of the European Coal and Steel Community (ECSC). It was this larger Europe, Free Europe as a whole, that Britain sought to lead.[7]

Nevertheless, the fact that the EDC Treaty had not yet been ratified by a single European country concerned Eden, and he began to worry that after all his hard work carefully managing the negotiations, the concept might still collapse. Whilst he did not doubt the commitment of Adenauer to the project – or, indeed, that of the Benelux governments – the Foreign Secretary was increasingly sceptical of French motivations and even began to wonder if the Pleven Plan was simply a French ruse calculated to delay the rearmament of Germany. Despite French accusations that the United Kingdom was putting its own self-interest above the greater good of European unity, Eden was convinced that, throughout the post-war period, French schemes for European integration had been motivated as much by their desire to contain West Germany as by the nobler notions of human peace and understanding. Indeed, the imperialistic impulses of the French government were every bit as strong as the British, and some historians have argued that it was the French colonial mindset more than anything else that encouraged the French government to seek greater integration in Europe. In much the same way as the post-war Labour government recognised that its only hope of standing up to American anti-imperialism was to join forces with other European colonial powers, so the French government saw in European unity the salvation of its own empire.[8]

As 1953 dawned, the British government was faced with the very real prospect that the EDC might collapse before its first uniforms were tailored. On 26 February, Churchill suggested in cabinet that, in the event of its failure, Britain might seek a 'looser arrangement with a German national Army, as an alternative to the E.D.C. scheme'.[9] Eden wrote to him that afternoon, arguing that his suggestion was problematic as Adenauer faced a General Election that upcoming September: 'His whole foreign policy is based upon the concept of Franco–German reconciliation and cooperation through such organisations as the Coal and Steel Community (Schuman Plan) and the European Defence Community. In particular he does not think that German democracy is yet stable enough to be trusted with a national Army. He thinks Germany should at least serve a period of apprenticeship within an international organisation like the E.D.C.'. In contrast, his 'Socialist opponents and even some of his right-wing coalition colleagues' were opposed to the EDC precisely *because* they wished to see the formation of a German Army with no strings attached and without any form of international oversight. If the EDC collapsed, it would heighten Franco–German antagonism and thus place great strain on the ECSC. If that, too, were to collapse, it 'might well result in his defeat at the elections'. Adenauer recognised that West Germany had a special place in Europe due to its wartime transgressions. This was not the case with some of those who wished to replace him, individuals who Eden believed were bent on a restoration of Germany to its full glory. It was therefore essential that the EDC be saved, 'with all its shortcomings', if for no other reason than to contain West Germany under the leadership of its moderate chancellor.[10]

If this logic was clear to Anthony Eden, it was not so to the French, who were content to 'dilly dally and make further demands upon us'.[11] Bidault in particular seemed determined to delay implementation of the EDC by creating additional hurdles before ratification could take place. He had always shared Bevin's view that European integration should come through intergovernmental agreements and was wary of Schuman's vision of a federated Europe. Following his demand for additional treaty protocols in January, in February, he informed Eden that the French parliament would only ratify the treaty if Britain and the EDC adopted 'a relationship of organic co-operation going further than mere association'.[12] Although Eden did not 'feel like being blackmailed by the new French Government into any more concessions', on 24 February he recommended to the cabinet that it formalise official consultations between the British government and the EDC on British troop numbers on the European continent if 'that would help the French to secure ratification of the Treaty'.[13] As Eden suspected, however, as soon as he made this concession to the French, their government only found other reasons to delay putting ratification to a vote, much to the frustration of the other signatories of the Treaty who were unwilling to consider ratification themselves until the French had voted, fearful that, if they did they might be forced to make significant changes after ratification.

Other European leaders recognised the French tactic. When Eden flew to Paris in late March, he was surprised by an abrupt change in tone, whereby the 'Europeans were highly pleased with our statements' and the 'French were left in the dog house'.[14] Despite remaining outside the EDC, through their support, the British had been welcomed back into the European fold and it was now the French who were being portrayed as the roadblocks on the way to further European integration. Indeed, the European attitude became so positive by the late spring of 1953 that Julian Amery suggested it might 'still [be] possible for us to remodel the High Authority into something we could join, something, perhaps, along the lines of the so-called Macmillan-Eccles proposals on Coal and Steel which we put forward at Strasbourg in 1950'. Although the 'ball [still] doesn't seem to be in our court', the field of play in Europe was shifting in favour of the British.[15] Sir Cecil Weir, the British Ambassador to Luxembourg, agreed, noting that the United Kingdom ought to 'exercise a strong degree of leadership without surrendering the sovereignty which we are unwilling to surrender'.[16] He added that, regardless of eventual British participation in the ECSC, 'it would be a disaster for all the free countries, including ourselves, if attempts to bring nations and peoples, who have so often been at war with one another, into indissoluble association were to fail, unless they should of their own free will accept some other satisfactory and dependable means of partnership'.[17]

Weir's was a message that would not reach the highest levels of government, however – not, at least, for several months to come. On 12 April, Eden underwent routine surgery that was terribly bungled by the operating doctor, leading to a further two surgeries and six months of convalescence before he could return to the cabinet table; he never recovered fully from the surgery, and its lingering effects would force his resignation as Prime Minister three and a half years later.[18] With Eden leaving the care of the National Health Service for private facilities in Boston, Massachusetts, Churchill took direct control of the Foreign Office. As Eden was undergoing this third surgery on 23 June, Churchill's personal physician Lord Moran noticed that Churchill's 'speech was slurred and a little indistinct'.[19] Just after midnight, 10 Downing Street contacted him to ask if he could see the Prime Minister at nine o'clock that morning. When he arrived, he was informed that the previous evening Churchill had collapsed, unable to stand, with his speech inarticulate. Upon examining him, Moran noticed immediately that 'the left side of his mouth sagged'. Churchill had suffered a major stroke.[20]

Had it not been for Eden's incapacity, the Prime Minister would have resigned there and then, but he felt that there were too many people to whom he was still responsible, and he did not trust anyone but Eden to take his place. As he confessed to Moran on 26 June, 'I'm not afraid of death, but it would be very inconvenient to a lot of people. Rab [Butler] is very efficient to a point, but he is narrow and doesn't see beyond his nose. If Anthony [Eden] were standing by the door there, and I was here, and a telegram was given to him involving a decision, well, in nine cases out of ten we should agree'.[21] But Eden was not there, so Churchill determined to carry on as Prime Minister. This he did largely *in absentia*, and throughout the rest of the summer Butler chaired no fewer than sixteen cabinet meetings whilst the Prime Minister rested at Chartwell.[22] Throughout those long months, Britain's ship of state was largely adrift.

* * *

Anthony Eden returned to the cabinet more quickly than Churchill. He had arrived back from the United States in early August and, with no EDC ratification in sight, composed from his recovery bed a memorandum of 'Reflections' for the cabinet's consideration. In it, he merged his thinking on Europe and on Britain's relationship with the United States. The Western Alliance, he wrote, 'creaks', but its 'defensive power in Europe is growing'. He was convinced that 'A German contribution to western defence is indispensable....

E.D.C. is [the] best instrument available to give it effect'. The Soviets wished to 'disrupt [the] western alliance' and prevent the EDC from coming into force, and, in that regard, the French were playing right into their hands. The United Kingdom's chief concern was therefore for 'early operation of [the] E.D.C.'. Given French intransigence, this would require 'some plain and private speech to the French by Britain and the United States'. Such cooperation was not always easy, however, as Anglo–American relations were at a difficult stage in their existence. The Americans were 'at present more friendly to [the] British than [the] British [are] to [the] Americans'. This benevolent American attitude would not last long, and he warned the cabinet that 'The smaller, poorer and more experienced partner is easily resentful. We have to beware of encouraging anti-American prejudice. "We will go it alone" cries can be dangerous in either country'. It was of the utmost importance for Europe that the United States and Great Britain remained close partners, and it was essential for the Western strategy in the Cold War that West Germany developed a defensive capability. The best way to achieve that was through the EDC, and thus it was in Britain's interests to ensure that the treaty was ratified.[23]

    Eden shared his memorandum with Churchill before presenting it to the cabinet as a whole. The Prime Minister, still convalescing at Chartwell, found his Foreign Secretary's conclusions 'depressing', failing to grasp why German rearmament and British support of an EDC was so important. He also expressed disbelief that Anglo–American relations were in any way strained.[24] Macmillan, too, was sceptical. Although a passionate advocate of European unity and one of the most ardent supporters of Churchill's European Movement throughout the 1940s, he was more fearful than some of his cabinet colleagues of West Germany's growing power. He asked, 'Are we really sure that we want to see a six-power Federal Europe, with a common army, a common Iron-Steel industry (Schuman Plan), ending in a common currency and monetary policy? … Will not Germany ultimately control this state, and may we not have created the very situation in Europe to prevent which, in every century since the Elizabethan age, we have fought long and bitter wars?' He wondered if the EDC was in Britain's long-term interests 'as an island or as an imperial power', and he argued that the government should 'let events take their course, and bring no further pressure on the French. If E.D.C. falls down, then will be the opportunity for us [to take the lead in Europe], should we wish to seize it'.[25]

Churchill and Macmillan were the only cabinet members to show such hesitancy, however. The others welcomed Eden's memorandum. Prior to the Foreign Secretary's 'Reflections', Selwyn Lloyd had written privately to the Prime Minister, telling him that 'Germany is the key to the peace of Europe'.[26] This view was also shared by American President Eisenhower, who told Churchill in July 1953 that 'only closer union among the nations of Western Europe, including Western Germany, can produce a political, economic and military climate in which the common security can be assured'. Eisenhower warned that should France reject the EDC Treaty, the results would be 'catastrophic for us all'. After years of providing aid to Europe with little to show for it, the American Congress and its public would 'return, no matter how reluctantly, to a policy of almost complete isolationism, or at the very least, to a "Western hemisphere only" philosophy of security and interest'. If that happened, then 'Heaven help us all'.[27] Churchill might prefer to focus on the Anglo–American 'special relationship' at the expense of continental Europe, but the American government had a clear need for Britain to become more involved in Europe.

Shortly after circulating his 'Reflections' memorandum, Eden left the United Kingdom for yet more recovery, this time in the Mediterranean, to return only in early October. On the third of that month, the cabinet met with both Churchill and Eden in attendance for the first time since June.[28] The Prime Minister's attention was focussed on the Soviet Union, but his Foreign Secretary argued that not until the question of German rearmament was settled could they turn to Russia. Macmillan, too, had become convinced of the necessity of supporting German rearmament in the context of the EDC. He had corresponded with Lady Rhys-Williams who, on meeting Sir Pierson Dixon at the Foreign Office, had been shocked to find there were '*no* plans for cooperation between Britain and Europe'. In a stinging critique, she told Macmillan that 'Beaverbrook seems to have won hands down all round' and warned him that if further delays in European unity continued 'for very much longer' there would be 'a serious increase in Communism in France and Italy, heavy loss of prestige by the Conservative Party in Britain and a serious increase in the chances of war!'[29]

In November, the French Senate passed 'a vague resolution asking the [French] Government to ensure before ratification that French interests and the integrity of the French Union were safeguarded and that a proper European balance of power should be constituted with the aid of the United Kingdom'. Eden reminded Churchill that 'the great merit of this [EDC] scheme from our own and from the French point of view is that it will impose definite controls and limitations upon German rearmament, and more especially upon armaments production. . . . If we were now to move away from the E.D.C. towards a "Grand Alliance", we should have to start all over again and open new negotiations to obtain Germany as an ally and a Germany army'. An independent German Army would necessarily provide Germany with greater strength and sway within Europe and would not solve the problem of French intransigence: 'We could not leave the French out of these negotiations and they would be just as difficult, if not more difficult, than they have been up to date'. It was far better for the EDC Treaty to be ratified, with close British support and a defence alliance between the United Kingdom and the EDC, than for it to fail, with all the consequences that such failure would entail.[30]

Eden had further opportunity to press his case when he travelled with the Prime Minister to Bermuda for an Anglo–American–Franco Summit, intended to define a Cold War strategy for the Western Allies. The previous August, the Soviet Union had announced that it had exploded a hydrogen bomb, thus sharpening the minds of those in the West and bringing the question of German rearmament and the EDC into full focus. In November, clearly feeling that its new munitions technology had levelled the playing field with the West, the Soviet government produced what were, in Macmillan's words, 'eighteen pages of "dismal and turgid smog" . . . [proposing] a series of impossible conditions for the solution of the German problem'.[31] When the three Western governments travelled to Bermuda on 4 December 1953, they had before them a new Soviet Note published on 27 November, softer in tone than the previous communications but requesting that the British proposal for a Four-Power Conference with the United States, Great Britain and France become instead a Five-Power Conference with China added to its number.[32]

Prior to leaving London, Eden briefed the cabinet on British aims for the Bermuda Conference. These included showing 'Anglo–United States–French solidarity in support of the N.A.T.O. defence effort' without 'hamper[ing] or [embarrass]ing the French government in securing ratification of the E.D.C. early in the New Year' and issuing 'some restatement of the peaceful purposes of the three Governments and the defensive character of the Western Alliance'. In particular, Eden hoped that the conference would 'assure Western public opinion and the U.S.S.R. that a rearmed Western Germany will not be used as a springboard for attack on Eastern Europe and will not seek the revision of Germany's eastern frontiers by force'. He added that it would be 'most unwise to discuss any possible alternatives to the E.D.C., in the event of its non-ratification. This would only jeopardise an early decision in Paris and would also make it more difficult for Dr. Adenauer to prevent German public opinion from becoming impatient and restive'.[33] Eden wanted the French to understand that there was no Plan B if the EDC were to fail.

Upon arrival in Bermuda, all of the Foreign Secretary's best-laid plans were cast asunder by Eisenhower. The American President began the talks with discussion of Korea and China rather than the Soviet Union, making it clear that the American government would 'hit back with full force' in the event of a 'Communist breach of the Korean truce and appear[ing] to imply that they would use atomic weapons'.[34] Although Eisenhower had assured Churchill at lunch that the American Air Force would spare 'the centres of population' when 'go-[ing] for China with all the weapons at her command', such talk alarmed Eden, who told Churchill that it went 'far beyond anything we have hitherto agreed'. He protested that 'we have never given, or been asked to give, approval to widespread bombing of China proper nor, of course, to the use of atom bombs', and he reminded the Prime Minister that the main American nuclear deterrent was based in East Anglia, which would bear the brunt of any retaliation, including by nuclear weapons.[35] Over lunch with Churchill again on 6 December, Eisenhower confirmed that although it would be most unusual for the United States to resort to nuclear weapons, he would not rule out their use, to which Eden insisted, 'The minimum requirement is that the United Nations should be consulted before steps are taken which could result in retaliation on East Anglia or unleash a third world war'.[36] The President, however, would make no promises.

Eisenhower also pulled no punches in his displeasure at the British proposal to meet with the Soviet Union in four-power talks, telling Eden that it was a 'trap' set by Russia to delay implementation of the EDC, a trap into which both the British and French had walked. The President threatened 'grave consequences' if anything were allowed to derail ratification of the EDC. Neither Eden nor Churchill liked to think they had walked into a trap, and Churchill took his anger out on French Foreign Minister Georges Bidault, going into an 'emotional attack on the French for not ratifying E.D.C., during which he said that if it is not through in 6 to 8 weeks there would have to be a German army'.[37] Churchill had expected Eisenhower to support him in this tirade, but he was disappointed. The President turned to Bidault and asked him 'what "we" could do to help', a question which Sir Evelyn Shuckburgh – ever present at Eden's side – thought 'had obviously been cooked up with the French when they [Eisenhower and Bidault] lunched together and gave Bidault a golden opportunity to put all the blame on the British'. This placed additional pressure on Eden to offer more concessions to the French over British support for the EDC, which Shuckburgh suspected was the American intent all along: 'We are obviously for it. We walk into every trap and ambush with flags flying, drums beating and the goat marching in front'.[38]

However, when Churchill again attacked Bidault the following day, Eisenhower's tone had shifted, and he warned Bidault that 'the U.S. may change their whole policy towards Europe if E.D.C. is not ratified'. This time the French were 'in the dock', and Shuckburgh realised that Eisenhower would lash out at any- and everyone whom he thought threatened ratification. When on 7 December Bidault refused to include in the Conference closing statement any reference to 'European unity', both Eisenhower and Churchill exploded, the former leaving the conference table in anger, telling his Secretary of State John Foster Dulles that 'Never again will I come to one of these, unless it is all prepared and agreed beforehand'. Churchill was equally angry and said in front of Bidault, 'The E.D.C. is dead. We want a German army'. When Eisenhower returned to the table, 'Everybody [was] very angry . . . [and] Bidault looks like a dying man'. At one o'clock in the morning, a statement was finally agreed, although it had to be approved by the French Prime Minister Joseph Laniel, who had been incapacitated by illness throughout the conference. When Bidault failed to gain such approval, Eden himself went into Laniel's bedroom and, after half an hour, 'succeeded in his mission and came down with the text agreed. Everyone worn out and bad-tempered'.[39]

Little came of the Bermuda Conference beyond demonstrating to the French the seriousness with which the American government held EDC ratification, and Shuckburgh wondered if this had been worth the cost of angering the Americans. When he flew to Paris on 13 December and dined with Adenauer, he began to think more seriously about a defence agreement with West Germany outside the EDC: 'Extraordinary how the Germans should have so far calmed down as to have a Chancellor like this. "I want England to come as close as possible to E.D.C. in order that France may not fear Germany". He wants "British experience, character and way of life" to play a dominant part in Europe'.[40] Adenauer was far more reasonable than the French had been in Bermuda, and, on 16 December, Shuckburgh discussed with Eden, Lord Ismay (the Secretary-General of NATO) and Sir Oliver Henry (the British Ambassador in France) alternatives lest the French fail to ratify the EDC Treaty. There were, he believed, three options. First, the British could 'take the lead and run Europe as the French want. But we must eliminate the federal elements in E.D.C. and Schuman Plan if we are to do this'. Second, the government could '[t]ry to persuade the Americans to take over' so Britain could withdraw from the continent altogether. Finally, the British could 'rescue what we can by gathering Norway, Denmark, [and the] Low Countries to our side'. Each of these alternatives was, however, a '[b]leak prospect'.[41] Despite British frustration with the French, it was still in everyone's best interest for the EDC Treaty to be ratified.

The New Year brought little change. Those in Britain continued to argue for a broader understanding of European unity, beyond the federal structures of the ECSC and the EDC. At the Conference of the European League of Economic Cooperation (ELEC), held at Westminster in early January 1954, Leo and Julian Amery issued a joint memorandum arguing that a 'United Europe' could still mean 'all the nations of Western Europe in close connection with their overseas associates (especially the Commonwealth and the French Union)', a union which would be based on economic cooperation 'between the different European governments' rather than federal supranational institutions. They argued, rather optimistically, that 'The fact that the Commonwealth already interlocks with the Dollar system through Canada and that Europe may come to interlock with the Soviet system through Eastern Europe may well foreshadow a wider unity between these main groups in a remoter future'.[42] The Amerys, father and son, still envisioned an imperial Europe that would work in concert with the United States and the Soviet Union to achieve world peace. Lady Rhys-Williams, likewise, suggested to Duncan Sandys that 'before long there will be a big glut of steel and coal both here and in Europe unless we can find a way to open up new markets by developing Africa, the Colonies, South East Asia and elsewhere'. This, she told Sandys, would be 'too big a job' to do alone, 'but in partnership with Europe it could be done and with profit to all'.[43]

Yet if those outside government still believed in sweeping visions of a European empire, those walking its corridors had long abandoned the sweeping rhetoric of the European Movement, facing instead hard questions of economics and defence. In particular, the cabinet had before it the Four-Power Talks among Britain, France, the United States and the Soviet Union, scheduled to begin in Berlin on 6 February 1954. British policy for the conference was to 'give way over trifles' but 'show every sign of firmness on essentials, e.g., free elections in Germany before any peace treaty'. The government was not, however, willing to let the talks drag on as they had in London under Bevin and was determined to 'either get results or break off in a matter of three or four weeks, for after that every day spent undecided will obstruct the passage of the E.D.C. and of American Congressional votes for defence aid to Europe'.[44] When the talks got under way, the government found that the presence of the Soviet Union drew Britain, France and the United States closer together, removing the animosity that had been present in Bermuda. Eden wrote to Selwyn Lloyd, his Minister of State for Foreign Affairs, that although things were 'very difficult with the Bear', they were 'on the whole quite smooth with the Allies.... Both Bidault and Dulles and their delegations have been steady and helpful. I don't think that Molotov has enjoyed the conference, and I have felt almost sorry for him sometimes!' He added, 'If we can go away with the front of the three Western Powers unbroken, and international tension not increased, I shall not be entirely dissatisfied'.[45]

In the end, the conference came to very little, but many within the government considered Eden's handling of the meetings to have been 'brilliant', and his international reputation (and that of Britain's) was greatly enhanced.[46] Having suffered no damage from the Soviet Union, Eden turned his attention back to persuading the French to ratify the EDC Treaty. He calculated that the fiftieth anniversary of the Entente Cordiale on 8 April 1954 would be an excellent opportunity to 'demonstrate the value which we have attached and still attach to Anglo–French friendship'. As a concrete example of this friendship, he suggested to Churchill that the government propose new measures to the French for closer British association with the EDC, measures which could be announced in a joint press conference with the French on the anniversary and could pave the way to speedy French ratification.[47] Given that Eden had made what he believed to be a generous gesture to the French government, he was furious when Bidault sent back a curt note refusing a joint press conference and asking that the British government not announce any closer British association with the EDC. The Foreign Secretary 'kept saying [to Sir Evelyn Shuckburgh] they are such a miserable contemptible Government they cannot even say "yes" when we offer to help', and he asked his private secretary to make a note that 'never in all my experience have I known such conduct'.[48]

The passage of time did little to heal his wounds and Sir Roger Makins, the British Ambassador in Washington DC, threw salt in them when he told Eden on 21 May that the American government was growing closer to the French whilst simultaneously distancing itself from the British. This split hinged around the question of South-East Asia. The United States had determined that 'further Communist expansion in Asia must be stopped' and had 'assumed British partnership' in this effort, particularly considering Britain's robust counter-insurgency campaign against the Communists in Malaya. The American Secretary of State John Foster Dulles believed he had secured from Eden 'agreement in principle to a policy of collective security in South-East Asia' when the two had met in London on 19 April. However, when the French sought air intervention from the British government in Dien Bien Phu and the British refused, Dulles took this as a 'retreat from what the Americans regarded as the basic understanding in London'. This provoked a reaction from Dulles. 'The first American instinct was to turn to us', Makins wrote, 'and having been, in their judgement, repulsed, they reached still further into their subconscious and turned to France'.

On the surface, this shift seemed irrational. In 1954, the 'two main planks of [American] foreign policy, namely the E.D.C. and security in South-East Asia, [were] threatened simultaneously by the weakness of the French Government'. Nevertheless, the White House had become 'disposed to try and strengthen the French hand as far as they could', even if that came at the expense of Anglo–American relations.

Makins had 'the impression that the American people are moving slowly to a historic decision to accept far reaching commitments on the mainland of Asia which carry with them risk of involvement in another war'. He was worried about the effect on Anglo–American relations if, 'at the time of such a fundamental decision, the British were standing aloof or were opposed to the American policy'. Although the British government could not make policy based purely on American interests, Makins wanted Eden to be aware of the consequences of a rift with the Americans on South-East Asia, a rift that could strengthen the Franco–American relationship and, in so doing, undermine the British position in Europe. Above all else, he thought the government should prioritise mending 'broken fences' with the Americans.[49]

At Eden's prompting, Makins wrote to him again on 18 June providing further detail on the American mindset towards the British, the French and Europe in general. Dulles had told a select group of American journalists that 'the differences between us [the United States and Great Britain] were much deeper and more serious than was generally realised; indeed, there were more differences than points of agreement between the two countries'. This was most evident on the question of South-East Asia, but there was also 'Egypt, there was Saudi Arabia, there was colonialism'. Dulles believed 'the United States had weakened her relationship and her mission in the world by supporting, or appearing to support, British and French policies in the Middle East and North Africa, thus incurring the charge of being an imperialist power'. Any benefit derived from the American relationship with Britain and France had not been worth the cost, and Dulles wanted to 're-establish the American moral position on the issue of colonialism'. Makins thought this outburst was probably a consequence of Dulles' vanity and his ambition 'to go down in history as one of the great American Secretaries of State. In his soul-searching he finds himself deeply troubled by the accusations that he, who should be advocating the American mission of freedom for all peoples, should, in his desire to work with Allies, who (he thinks) have let him down, be branded a supporter of colonialism'. In his private conversations with the American press, Dulles was likely doing no more than trying to restore his pride. Nevertheless, Makins warned Eden that 'on your visit [to Washington DC], the Prime Minister and yourself will be confronted not only with intractable political questions, but with a complicated personal and psychological question as well'.[50]

When Churchill and Eden travelled to the United States the following week, they found Dulles somewhat calmer than Makins had suggested, and, after extensive talks on 25 June, Eisenhower and Churchill issued a joint press statement agreeing that 'the German Federal Republic should take its place as an equal partner in the community of Western nations'. They noted that the 'European Defence Community Treaty has been ratified by four of the six signatory nations' and encouraged the French government to do so also without further delay. They praised the French for inspiring 'the program for European unity' and assured them of American and British 'firm support', but also made clear their displeasure at French delay.[51] The visit demonstrated once again that whenever Anglo–American relations became frayed, the two countries could always find common cause against the French government and thus restore their friendship; yet by doing so, they further encouraged French obstinacy and strengthened the view of certain French politicians that the United Kingdom, with its heart so closely tied to the United States, could never be fully 'European'.

In August 1954, the French government released yet more amendments to the EDC, claiming that their passage was necessary before it could consider ratification. Macmillan suspected that the amendments would not satisfy anybody and wrote to Eden that 'The general situation in Europe looks very bad'.[52] Churchill, too, was concerned about the worsening French attitude, telling Eden that he 'grieve[d] for the much maltreated famous Benelux as well as for faithful Adenauer'. He hinted that the time might have come to begin planning an alternative alliance with Germany should the French fail to ratify the EDC.[53] Eden agreed and thought that a first step would be to bring West Germany into NATO as soon as possible. He therefore proposed to visit Brussels (for the three Benelux countries), Bonn, Rome and Paris to 'establish contact in each of the capitals with men whom I know' and to begin laying the ground for his argument. He planned to visit France last so that he would have 'a formidable body of opinion behind me, supposing we were all agreed upon the general line for handling this problem, i.e., that Germany must be brought along into the NATO family'.[54] Britain was no longer the outlier in Europe as it had been throughout the final years of the Labour government. That role had now fallen to France, and Eden was convinced that it was the responsibility of the British government to lead the other European powers in coalition against France for the benefit of Europe as a whole.

Little did Churchill and Eden know how little time they would have. On the evening Eden wrote to the Prime Minister, Pierre Mendès-France (who had succeeded Lanier as French Prime Minister in June) at last put the EDC Treaty before the French National Assembly for ratification. Long known as a French nationalist who did not conflate the interests of France with those of Europe, Mendès-France and his ministers abstained from the vote. Without leadership from their premier, the National Assembly put forward a motion not to put the Treaty to a vote, which passed by 319 votes to 264, essentially killing ratification.[55] Macmillan wrote immediately to Eden, telling him that 'Like poor Mrs. Disraeli, who never could remember which came first, the Greeks or the Romans, the poor French cannot make up their minds of which they are most afraid, the Russians or the Germans'. The Germans, in contrast, were 'not at all alarmed by the French' but feared both the Russians and themselves: 'that is, a revival of Prussianism, militarism, Nazism – call it what you will'. Macmillan reminded Eden of the two great post-war defence pacts, the Brussels Pact (once known as Western Union), which had been designed for protection '*against* the revival of German militarism' and was entirely European, and NATO, which had in mind protection against the Soviet Union.

He then made an audacious suggestion: 'Would it be possible to revive Western Union, instead of E.D.C.? Germany could join it, as a sort of solemn declaration against the wrong Germany. Italy could join it. So could Norway, etc. It would be a *European*, and not an *Atlantic* organisation'. Its 'economic, social and cultural' functions could be managed by the European Consultative Assembly at Strasbourg, which could also form a formal association with the ECSC. Its military functions could be managed under the umbrella of NATO, but with 'regular meetings of their Ministers of Defence and Commanders on a European basis'. The great advantage of his plan, Macmillan thought, was that it would be intentionally European rather than Atlanticist and thus would appeal to the French, but it would also bring West Germany into NATO, albeit through the back door. It would place the Schuman Plan under the supervision of a larger community of European nations in the Consultative Assembly and would restore British leadership to the movement for European unity.

Best of all, it would do so on a pragmatic basis and would avoid any supranational or federal organisations.[56]

Macmillan placed his idea before the cabinet as a whole shortly after writing to Eden, telling them that the collapse of the EDC was a blessing in disguise: 'If we now come out with any plan to save something of the European conception no one can accuse us of sabotage. It will be a rescue operation'. Whilst for some in the cabinet – and certainly for the American government – the failure of the French Assembly to ratify the treaty was a matter of grave concern, for Macmillan it was a rare opportunity. The British had been unstinting in their support of the EDC. It had collapsed, and only the French could be blamed. The British government could now step into the breach with no accusations of opportunism. He argued that at the upcoming meeting of European Foreign Ministers Eden should say that the 'death of E.D.C. does not mean the death of the European idea' and should announce plans to reinvigorate the Western Union. In Strasbourg, the British government would speak 'as Europeans, and not merely as Anglo-Saxons' and could use that moment to present a plan to reincorporate West Germany into European defence plans without creating an organisation that Germany could dominate. After all, 'German idealism must look somewhere. Europeanism is better for their souls than nationalism'.[57]

Eden was immediately taken by Macmillan's idea and began to plant its seeds in the minds of other European leaders during his tour of the four capitals. Then, beginning on 28 September, he hosted a nine-power conference in London, with the United Kingdom, France, West Germany, Italy, the Benelux countries and the United States participating.[58] Speaking to a crowded room of foreign ministers, many of whom were deeply depressed by the collapse of the EDC, he proposed that West Germany be immediately recognised as a sovereign state and permitted 'limited and controlled' rearmament; that West Germany and Italy be allowed to join the 1948 Brussels Pact, which would be renamed the Western European Union (WEU); and that, in return, the United Kingdom would maintain its current army and Royal Air Force numbers on the European continent. The council and secretariat of the WEU would be based in London, its Parliamentary Assembly (composed of national parliamentary representatives) would meet at the same time as the Council of Europe's Consultative Assembly and its military functions would exist within NATO ('a European box inside an Atlantic box', as Macmillan put it) for as long as NATO was primarily responsible for the defence of the West.[59]

The response to Eden's proposal was immediate. Other European foreign ministers greeted the proposal eagerly, and even the French seemed pleased. Macmillan congratulated him, telling him that when he dined at the French Embassy in London on the day after the announcement, the French were 'in a most elated mood'.[60] Gladwyn Jebb in the British Embassy, Paris, was even more effusive in his praise: 'We live in an ancient society which tends to resist new ideas and bold initiatives. How you managed to overcome the doubts, hesitations, fears, forebodings, and suspicions which stood in the way of yesterday's splendid offer I simply do not know. What I do say is, thank God that we have a man with the intelligence to perceive the truth and the guts to apply it'.[61] Little did Jebb know that the idea was entirely Macmillan's; on this occasion, Eden was simply the messenger. The Foreign Secretary certainly benefited from being such. Sir Victor Mallet, who had recently returned to London after six years as Britain's ambassador to Italy, described Eden's actions as 'a real triumph for your diplomacy...the whole civilised world owes you its gratitude';[62] Ashley Clarke (Mallet's successor as Ambassador to Italy) told him that his diplomatic successes had 'sent our prestige up in all the countries of Europe and in none more than in Italy';[63] and Edward Beddington-Behrens, writing on behalf of the European League for Economic Cooperation, expressed his 'profound satisfaction' for Eden's 'brilliant leadership'.[64] The British Consul-General in Marseille told Sir Anthony Rumbold (Eden's Principle Private Secretary) that after 'an extensive tour of my district ranging from Corsica to Andorra', 'all the Prefets and other officials whom I met paid spontaneous and enthusiastic tribute to the Secretary of State whenever foreign policy was mentioned'.[65]

If Eden received most of the public praise for the Western European Union, Macmillan was not without recompense. His reward was to be promoted by Winston Churchill from the Department for Housing and Local Government to the Ministry of Defence. In the former role, he had brought an important domestic victory to the Conservative Party, delivering on its Manifesto promise to build 300,000 houses per year. As Minister of Defence, he could finally turn to the subjects that had always most animated him. On 29 December 1954, in his first substantial memorandum to the cabinet as Minister of Defence, Macmillan sought to bring together his recent advocacy for a prominent British role in Western Europe with his continuing belief in the importance of the British Empire and Commonwealth. He argued that over the 'next few years our Colonial Empire in its varying stages of development is likely to be a vital "cold war" battleground. If we are defeated here much of our effort in Western Europe will be wasted'. He argued that 'Our objective must be to prevent trouble arising. It will pay us to spend some money if we can achieve this end', and he suggested that the government needed 'good security intelligence, efficient and well-trained police forces and properly organised Colonial armed forces'.[66] As Ernest Bevin had argued from 1946 onwards, the security needs of Europe and the Empire could not be viewed in isolation. They were both integral for the maintenance of Britain's place in the world.

Macmillan's vision hinged on the establishment of the Western European Union, however, and British officials and ministers waited with nervous anticipation to see if the French Assembly would pass it. In contrast to the EDC, the WEU would not collapse following a potential French rejection, instead continuing with Britain and West Germany at its heart. Nobody but the French government could be blamed for a French failure to enter the Union. Nevertheless, for the general cause of European unity and the smooth running of NATO, it was far preferable that France be in the Union than outside it. Furthermore, the agreements had stipulated that ratification be completed by 15 March 1955; time was of the essence.[67] The British government therefore worked diligently to put pressure on the French government, both Eden and Churchill writing directly to Mendès-France, and Gladwyn Jebb using any influence he had as British Ambassador on the French Deputies.[68]

On 24 December 1954, the French Assembly voted on ratification, and it was defeated by 280 votes to 258. According to Anthony Nutting, the Minister of State for Foreign Affairs, Churchill was 'more angry' than he had ever before seen him.[69] Eden was also furious and wrote angrily to Mendés-France. He then issued a public statement, claiming that if the French government did not reconsider its position, he would withdraw the entire British security commitment from the European continent.[70] Gladwyn Jebb reported that his statement had 'done good' and that the Deputies would vote again on ratification before the end of the month.[71] Whilst he was awaiting the result of this second vote, Eden sought agreement from American President Eisenhower to issue a joint Anglo–American statement should the

French again refuse to ratify the agreements. On 29 December 1954 – the eve of the crucial second French vote in the Assembly – Eisenhower informed the British government that he would rather issue 'a personal statement' in the event of French rejection, so as to avoid any accusation of Anglo–American alliance against France.[72] It was with enormous relief, therefore, that the British government learned that the French Assembly had changed its mind and voted in favour of ratifying the agreements.[73]

Formal ratification still required approval by the French Council of the Republic, and Churchill confessed to Eisenhower that the 'French obstructers' could 'spread the whole process out for four or five months', which would only waste 'the ever-shortening interval of time before the Soviets have developed their nuclear strength ... to what is called "saturation point," namely the power to inflict mortal injury upon the civilized structure of the free world'. It was essential that Europe's future defence prospects were secured, sooner rather than later.[74] Eisenhower agreed, replying to Churchill that he 'bitterly regret-[ed] that all of us did not put our shoulders to the wheel some three years ago when the prospects for the approval of the EDC looked bright. All the free world could breathe easier today had that venture been a success'.[75]

As the clock continued to tick, Churchill recognised that his time as Prime Minister was growing ever shorter. He had celebrated his eightieth birthday on 30 November 1954, and there was growing impatience amongst the Conservative ranks for him to give way, particularly from Anthony Eden and his supporters who felt he should have been handed the keys to 10 Downing Street years earlier. Sir Evelyn Shuckburgh, Eden's principal private secretary from 1951 until June 1954, noted as early as 3 November 1952 that Churchill was beginning to lose his grip on governance, and from November 1952 onwards his leadership was under growing pressure.[76] The Labour backbenches delighted in this distraction to the Conservative Party, Richard Crossman noting in his dairy that 'the myth of Churchill is completely dissipated, even in Tory circles. But the worse the press, the more obstinate I guess Churchill will be and I still feel sure he will hold on till after the Coronation and delight in frustrating the competing plans of Eden and Butler for shoving him out'. He added, 'He [Churchill] really hates the Conservatives'.[77] By January 1954, cabinet ministers were privately talking about resigning unless Churchill would go, and, on 11 March 1954, the Prime Minister summoned Eden to 10 Downing Street to discuss 'the future of the Government', where he told him that he would resign in May.[78] Yet the summer came and went and still Eden remained Foreign Secretary, with Churchill becoming ever less capable and his cabinet growing more concerned with each passing day. It took many by surprise when, after his eightieth birthday in November, Churchill indicated that he hoped to remain Prime Minister until the summer of 1955.[79]

In Churchill's correspondence with Eisenhower in January and February 1955, there was little indication that he had changed his mind, and Eden continued to play the role of Foreign Secretary – a position he had first held twenty years before in 1935. Eden's primary focus remained on the French Council of the Republic, which had yet to provide the final ratification for the WEU. When this had still not been accomplished by March, Dulles suggested that Eisenhower make a personal visit to Paris to be present at the ratification, as a way to focus the minds of the French Senators.[80] Eden dismissed this suggestion, however, fearing that it would have the opposite effect: 'The Senators have their attention fixed on their own forthcoming elections and many of them are reluctant to run the risk of being presented as voting for German Rearmament under American pressure. If it were made known that the President had promised to come to Paris in person, as a kind of reward for their good behaviour, the effect would be more likely to increase than diminish their reluctance to ratify'.[81] Churchill disagreed, telling Eden that it would be 'wrong to assume that the French Senators or the French people would be disdainful of a procedure which would accord to France the leading position in Europe'.[82]

In the end, a compromise was reached, and Eden wrote to Sir Roger Makins on 15 March informing him that the British government would 'warmly welcome' a visit by the American President to Europe but was 'not convinced that it would be wise to link the proposed meeting directly with French ratification. There is the risk that it might be interpreted by the opponents of the Treaty as interference in French politics'.[83] Eden's judgment proved to be correct. Without any American intervention, the French Council of the Republic ratified the agreements for the WEU on 29 March 1955, becoming the last country to do so. Sir Frank Hoyer Millar, the British Ambassador to West Germany, immediately passed a message from Adenauer to Eden. It read: 'If today we have reached this important stage on the road to the unity of the Free Peoples of Europe, we owe it above all, my dear Sir Anthony, to your great initiative in September of last year'.[84] Because Europe had come together under British leadership, Anthony Eden was the hero of the hour.

French ratification of the WEU was an important milestone on the road to European unity, but Eden would soon confront a far greater one in his own political journey. On 30 March 1955, the day after the French Council of the Republic finally assented to the WEU, Churchill summoned Eden and R. A. Butler to the Cabinet Room and informed them that it was his intention to relinquish the premiership. Less than a week later, on 5 April, he travelled to Buckingham Palace and offered Queen Elizabeth II his resignation. The following day, the monarch summoned Anthony Eden and asked him to form her next government. After many years in waiting, Britain's long-standing Foreign Secretary finally walked through the door to 10 Downing Street as Prime Minister.

9 THE DECLINE AND FALL OF THE IMPERIAL EUROPEANS

When Anthony Eden entered the House of Commons as Prime Minister on 6 April 1955, he was greeted with a standing ovation. Although this was a parliamentary tradition for any new premier, it was perhaps just a little bit more satisfying for Eden. He had, after all, been waiting a long time for this moment; thirteen years earlier, Churchill had even written to George VI telling him that should he (Churchill) die in the course of carrying out his wartime duties, the King should 'entrust the formation of a new Government to Mr. Anthony Eden, the Secretary of State for Foreign Affairs, who is in my mind the outstanding Minister in the largest political party in the House of Commons and in the National Government over which I have the honour to preside'.[1] As Sir Evelyn Shuckburgh noted in his diary, 'It is a relief that one can now revert to admiring W[inston] for what he has done and been, and not worry about what he is doing or will do.... The "myth" will now take over, and none will want to listen to the carping voice or the awkward derogatory fact.... The great thing is that he has gone from the active scene and can be a great man again without damage'.[2]

Eden's ascent of the greasy pole brought few changes to the government. He moved Macmillan from the Ministry of Defence to the Foreign Office and promoted Selwyn Lloyd from the Ministry of Supply to Defence, but he left Butler as Chancellor of the Exchequer, Lloyd George as Home Secretary, Lennox-Boyd as Colonial Secretary, Thorneycroft as President of the Board of Trade and Duncan Sandys as Minister of Housing. It was the leader of the government rather than his cabinet that had been replaced, and Eden's ministry would be one of continuity rather than change.[3]

Nevertheless, the emergence of a fresh leader at the head of the party provided an immediate up-tick in Conservative fortunes. Given that the last General Election was held in October 1951, Eden was not required to request a dissolution of Parliament until October 1956, but he decided to go to the country earlier rather than later, setting the date at 26 May 1955.[4] The Labour Party was in a buoyant mood, and a Gallup Poll in early May suggested that it was in a strong position to regain control of the government.[5] At the Council Elections on 12 May, however, the Conservative Party swept to a landslide victory, regaining three-fifths of the seats it had lost in 1951 and securing a net increase of 311 council seats. When the General Election occurred two weeks later, the results mirrored this swing, with the Conservative Party increasing its seats from 319 to 345. Although fewer votes were cast across the country as a whole, the Conservative Party lost only 500,000 voters to a Labour loss of 1.5 million, and thus the government's mandate was strengthened.[6]

In the midst of the General Election campaign, the new Foreign Secretary Harold Macmillan travelled to Paris to take part in the 'solemn and moving scene' of West Germany joining NATO, a ceremony that was held on the tenth anniversary of VE Day. It was remarkable that just one decade after the war ended, a rearmed Germany could join with France, Britain and the United States in a ceremony demonstrating international solidarity. Macmillan went from Paris directly to Vienna to witness the signing of the Austrian Treaty granting Austria its full independence for the first time since the German Anschluss of 1938 and beginning the withdrawal of the 60,000 Soviet troops who had occupied the territory for the past decade. Thus, in the space of a week, the Foreign Secretary had been part of two of the most remarkable events in post-war Europe. The news that his parliamentary majority had been increased by 1,000 votes in the General Election only confirmed what had been a highly successful month. Reflecting on the victory, Macmillan wrote, 'if Anthony's government lasts five years, I'll be 65 or so and I will have had five years at the Foreign Office. Then I shall retire. That will be enough'. Macmillan had reached, he believed, the pinnacle of his career, and he looked forward to spending his final years in Parliament at the Foreign Office.[7]

It was not to be. On 21 December 1955, Eden reshuffled the cabinet, moving Butler from the Treasury, replacing Macmillan at the Foreign Office with Selwyn Lloyd and 'promoting' Macmillan to become Chancellor of the Exchequer. Although he now held the keys to 11 Downing Street and was quite literally within shouting distance of the Prime Minister, Macmillan found the reshuffle a 'shattering blow'.[8] In the months leading up to it, his focus as Foreign Secretary had been almost entirely on the European continent. Although the Western European Union was a diplomatic triumph by providing a way to resolve the question of German rearmament and West German membership in NATO, it did not provide a strong foundation to pursue further integration, as the planned European Defence Community would have done. For this reason, in June 1955, the six countries of the European Coal and Steel Community (ECSC) met in Messina, Italy, to discuss further measures of economic integration, in particular the creation of a European Common Market.[9]

The group invited the British government to participate in the Messina Conference, but Eden snubbed the offer, sending instead only an 'observer' who was himself withdrawn in November.[10] Eden's refusal to participate, whilst no doubt influenced by his own reticence to involve the United Kingdom in European affairs, was also a reflection of the general British belief that talks to form a Common Market would fail. Sir Ivone Kirkpatrick, the Permanent Under-Secretary at the Foreign Office, wrote in a memorandum on 25 November that 'Messina is a doubtful, if not actual wrong approach, and OEEC is a better one', and Gladwyn Jebb suggested that the British government's approach to the Messina talks should be to 'embrace destructively'.[11] Even Macmillan, one of the cabinet's leading Europeans, wrote in his diary on 14 December that 'The French will never go into the "common market" – the German industrialists and economists equally dislike it'.[12] In the Foreign Secretary's explanation to 'the Six' (as the Messina countries were now known) he stated bluntly, 'There are, as you are no doubt aware, special difficulties for this country in any proposal for a "European Common Market"', but the British government would be 'happy to examine, without prior commitment and on their merits, the many problems likely to emerge from these studies'.[13]

Macmillan no less than Eden was certain that, given time, the furore over Messina would simply blow over. His judgment was in part encouraged by the British Ambassador to Italy, Sir Ashley Clarke, who wrote to him in early June, saying, 'The Messina conference did not arouse much enthusiasm in the Italian Press, which was fully occupied with the Sicilian election campaign. According to my Dutch colleague it was not intended to achieve anything, but all the Foreign Ministers enjoyed their holiday at Taormina'.[14] Even Jean Monnet described the Messina Conference as 'an important but somewhat timid step, towards the making of Europe'.[15] It certainly did not demand the reams of papers that British ministers and officials had written five years earlier when Schuman unveiled his plan for the ECSC, nor did it capture the imagination or attention of the press or public, either in Great Britain or on the European continent. At the time, there was no sense that a dramatic step had been taken on the path towards European unification.

In any case, the Foreign Secretary had far larger issues to contend with. On 1 April 1955, the Cypriot group EOKA had launched a terrorist campaign against the British administration there, hoping to bring about *Enosis* (or the incorporation of Cyprus as a Greek island). Furthermore, the insurgency in Malaya (raging since 1948) was still ongoing, and a fresh outbreak of violence had erupted in Kenya in October 1952, in the form of the Mau Mau insurgency. Although the crises in Malaya, Kenya and Cyprus rightly fell under the portfolio of the Colonial rather than the Foreign Secretary, as Minister of Defence, Macmillan had taken a special interest in colonial defence, warning Churchill as early as November 1954 that something was brewing in Cyprus. In December 1954, he had recommended that General Sir Gerald Templer (recently stepped down as Director of Operations in Malaya) be tasked with leading a wide-ranging investigation into 'the intelligence, security, police and armed forces of the Colonial Empire, with a view to the Cold War struggle and to preventing such breakdowns as have led to the necessity for large-scale armed intervention as in Kenya and Malaya'.[16] For Macmillan, colonial security was as much of an obsession as the unity of Europe.

Promoted Foreign Secretary just seven days after the outbreak of terrorist violence in Cyprus, Macmillan did not easily relinquish his interest in the Empire. He persuaded the Colonial Secretary Alan Lennox-Boyd that since the Cyprus question also involved Greece and Turkey, it was best tackled jointly by the Foreign and Colonial Offices. Lennox-Boyd agreed, and they collaborated on a report for the cabinet in late June – just as the Messina Conference was coming to a close on the European continent. They began by describing the United Kingdom as a 'world power with primary responsibility for the defence of the Middle East' and as a 'Colonial power with a reputation for sagacious and disinterested administration'. Britain's interests in Cyprus were to 'Secure bases for the deployment and supply of troops in the Middle East', to maintain 'a physical symbol of British power in the Eastern Mediterranean and Middle East', to preserve 'good relations with Greece and Turkey' and to 'maintain order and good government in Cyprus itself'. Their recommendation was that the government call a Tripartite Conference among the United Kingdom, Greece and Turkey, at which they would offer Greek and Turkish association with the Cyprus Government in the administering of the island and the 'immediate introduction of a liberal constitution for Cyprus' whilst keeping sovereignty 'indefinitely maintained by Her Majesty's Government'. Macmillan felt certain that Greece and Turkey would reject this offer, at which point the government would have a free hand to unilaterally determine the best future for Cyprus.[17] At the conference that August, Macmillan, not Lennox-Boyd, took the lead. It opened in violence when EOKA murdered a Greek police constable in Nicosia, casting an immediate shadow over its deliberations.[18] Macmillan recommended to Eden that seven senior British police officers from Malaya and Kenya be sent to Cyprus to act as counter-insurgency advisors, and, on 7 September, the conference collapsed without resolution, just as the British government had expected it would.[19] The troubles in Cyprus would continue to plague the British government for another four years.

It was not only the colonial insurgencies in Malaya, Kenya and Cyprus that demanded Macmillan's time. In July, he led a British delegation to Geneva for the Four-Power Summit on German reunification which, given the strong Soviet presence, was unable to reach a successful conclusion.[20] By far the greatest amount of Macmillan's time, however, was spent on the Middle East. In November 1954, General Gamal Abdel Nasser had ousted the Egyptian ruler Muhammad Neguib and immediately began advocating pan-Arab nationalism, turning to the Soviet Union and Czechoslovakia for arms.[21] Given that British troops remained in Egypt to protect the Suez Canal and that British investors were the majority shareholders in the Suez Canal Company, Macmillan found this a 'new and sinister' development.[22] Throughout 1955, he feared that the Soviets were moving 'into a field from which hitherto they [have] kept studiously aloof'.[23] That November, Macmillan confessed to Churchill that 'there is a certain unreality about our arguments on Europe when so much of our thoughts are on the Middle East'.[24] As Foreign Secretary, Macmillan was no less of a European than he had always been, but he was also deeply committed to the British Empire and Commonwealth and to Britain's role in the wider world. In November 1955, the extra-European problems facing the United Kingdom made questions of a purely European dimension pale in comparison.

As Chancellor of the Exchequer from late December 1955 onwards, Macmillan had less reason to concern himself with foreign affairs, including Europe. Eden, likewise, was too focussed on Anglo–American relations, the deteriorating situation in Egypt and his desire to pursue rapprochement with the Soviet Union to pay much attention to the European continent. In April 1956, he invited the new Soviet leader Nikolai Bulganin and his foreign minister Nikita Khrushchev to Britain. Robert Boothby praised Eden for his courage in hosting the Russian leaders, writing to him: 'Three years ago you told me, in a restaurant car from Aberdeen to Edinburgh, that the only thing that kept you in public life was the feeling that you might help to save the world from final catastrophe. And that is precisely what you are now doing'.[25] However, the visit did not go as well as planned. Cultural misunderstandings plagued the trip. Khrushchev could not understand why in Britain people protested his visit rather than praising it; at the Prime Minister's country house at Chequers, the Russians insisted on keeping security guards outside their bedroom doors; and the Soviet foreign minister mistook the senior members of the General Assembly at the Church of Scotland as peasants who were being looked after in their dotage at Britain's equivalent of Siberia – Holyrood House in Edinburgh![26] More seriously, the Soviet representatives engaged in a heated debate during a Labour Party dinner when it became clear that British socialism was quite different from Soviet communism. The visit finally ended with a scandal over spying.[27]

Following Eden's failure to recalibrate relations with the Soviet Union, the government reappraised Britain's place in the world. At the request of the Prime Minister, in early June 1956, officials from the Treasury, Foreign Office and Ministry of Defence co-authored a memorandum for the cabinet policy review committee addressing the future of the United Kingdom in world affairs. It began with two central premises. First, 'The external situation confronting us has changed. The hydrogen bomb has transformed the military situation. It has made full-scale war with Russia and China unlikely. And conventional forces, though still of great importance in some situations, have become a relatively less important factor in world affairs'. Second, 'It is clear that ever since the end of the war we have tried to do too much – with the result that we have only rarely been free from the danger of economic crisis. This provides no stable basis for policy in any field. Unless we make substantial reductions in the Government's claims on the national economy we shall endanger our capacity to play an effective role in world affairs. We must therefore concentrate on essentials and reduce other commitments'.

These essential objectives were '(a) to avoid global war; [and] (b) to protect our vital interests overseas, particularly access to oil'. They could only be achieved if the government could 'maintain North American involvement in Europe', 'maintain a large measure of identity between the interests of America and Canada and our own and develop closer co-operation with those countries' and 'maintain the cohesion of the Commonwealth'. The report did not reach a happy conclusion: 'The United States and Russia already far outstrip us in population and material wealth, and both have untapped resources. Canada, India and China, to name only three, are at the beginning of their development and in time will certainly outstrip us. Nearer home, Germany has re-established her economic position and currently has gold and dollar reserves 50 per cent greater than the central reserves of the whole sterling area.... Thus we cannot hope that, on the basis of material strength alone, we shall be able to play a major or dominant role in world affairs. We shall always be competing with countries whose population or wealth or command of essential food and raw materials is much greater than ours. Even our present material strength – in fact our whole livelihood – is at risk, because among our raw materials one, namely oil, *which is absolutely vital to us*, already comes largely, and in the future will have to come still more, from the Middle East'.[28] The report made alarming reading for the members of the committee and illustrated a Britain that was in a very different place in the world than even a decade before.

On 15 June 1956, Eden repeated for the cabinet the main findings of the memorandum, including a word-for-word reading of the political and military objectives. He then informed his colleagues that, in future, all policy planning must take into consideration that 'The main threat to our position and influence in the world is now political and economic rather than military: and our policies should be adapted to meet that changed situation'. He added that 'The period of foreign aid is ending and we must now cut our coat according to our cloth. There is not much cloth'. Finally, he concluded: 'In our defence programmes generally we are doing too much to guard against the least likely risk, viz., the risk of major war; and we are spending too much on forces of types which are no longer of primary importance'.[29] The whole ethos of British governance needed to change. It was no longer the Empire it had once been.

Things looked no better in the Commonwealth. Working under the assumption that Germany and the Soviet Union would be the 'dominating powers inside Europe', with 'German military resurgence... counterbalanced by the Soviet [Union]' and 'France increasingly in decline', the Commonwealth Relations Office produced a paper for the cabinet assessing the probable development of the Commonwealth over the next ten to fifteen years (in other words, until 1966–71). Within the Commonwealth, it stated, the United Kingdom would continue to be the 'keystone', without which the Commonwealth would 'disintegrate'. The Commonwealth was held together by 'sentiment', 'tradition' and 'interest'. Sentiment was most important to the 'old' Commonwealth of Canada, Australia and New Zealand. Tradition was 'of great importance in all cases'. The 'new' dominions had been 'shaped by British political thought. They have inherited, to a greater degree than they realise, British cultural and governmental standards'. And for the entire Commonwealth, old and new, 'interest' would increasingly become 'the decisive link'. Yet this 'interest' would not always coincide with the interests of the British government. The Commonwealth would expand 'at the expense of the Colonial Empire', leading to a lessening of direct British control and, potentially, prestige. This expanded Commonwealth would be 'increasingly non-European and tropical'. Constitutionally, many of its new members might 'incline to a Republic status', reducing the role of the British monarch as the glue that holds the Commonwealth together. The United Kingdom would become 'progressively less a dominating feature in the *Commonwealth* as the "old" Commonwealth countries expand industrially and in population'. The report's conclusions were not encouraging: 'While it [the Commonwealth] does so remain, the United Kingdom as its oldest member, occupies a world position far more important than she could claim solely in her own right; though that will increasingly cease to be the case as the major elements in the Colonial Empire become self-governing. Were the United Kingdom to stand by herself, her importance would still be great, but immensely less than it is while she remains the centre of the Commonwealth'.[30]

Britain's place in the world stemmed from its leadership of the Commonwealth, just as British greatness from the eighteenth century onwards had always been connected to its empire. Yet that Commonwealth role was quickly abating and, within a decade, could be gone. How the United Kingdom would position itself in a post-imperial world was a question the report could not answer.

* * *

It was in the midst of these challenging debates on Britain's place in the world that the government returned to the question of Europe. At Macmillan's request, officials from the Treasury produced a memorandum outlining ways Britain could better integrate itself with the European continent. They also sent it to Selwyn Lloyd at the Foreign Office and Peter Thorneycroft at the Board of Trade.[31] The memorandum listed six potential options: first, to deepen cooperation with the Organisation of European Economic Cooperation (OEEC); second, to formally link the OEEC with the Council of Europe; third, to begin tariff negotiations with 'the Six' on European goods entering the UK and vice versa; fourth, to discuss with 'the Six' linking the ECSC with a wider free trade area in European (including British) steel; fifth, to expand this conversation into advocacy for a European free trade area in general; and, finally, to propose a trade preference scheme linking Europe with the Commonwealth.[32]

Lloyd replied immediately that it was 'a major Foreign Office interest to prevent the disruption of Europe threatened by the continuing deterioration of France and the growing strength and independence of Germany'. He argued that 'If we are to bind Germany to the West, we must associate ourselves more closely with Europe'. Therefore 'all the projects listed in this report are to be welcomed'.[33] Thorneycroft went even further, writing his own paper in reply, titled 'Initiative in Europe'. He said that the 'most tempting course of all, namely to do nothing', was no longer acceptable and may indeed 'prove to be the most difficult and dangerous of the lot'. The key to Macmillan's suggestions, he said, was 'to find a method of taking the lead in Europe and securing the advantage of the fullest possible commercial opportunities in that Continent, while holding the maximum we can of our [Commonwealth] preferential system and carrying public opinion with us at home'. He argued that, of Macmillan's six proposals, the best option was a free trade area with continental Europe. However, it would need to exclude from the outset the whole of agriculture and horticulture, given the fundamentally different approach Britain took to the continent on those issues.[34] As Macmillan had lettered his six proposals 'a' through 'f', Thorneycroft's amended proposal soon became known as 'Plan G'.

Macmillan was thrilled at the response of Thorneycroft and Selwyn Lloyd, and he immediately proposed to the cabinet the creation of a Working Group on the United Kingdom Initiative in Europe. For the first time in Britain's post-war history, the Treasury, Foreign Office and Board of Trade were equally committed to a European vision. The group held its first meeting on 21 June, with Macmillan in the chair and Thorneycroft sitting at his right-hand side.[35] To mark the meeting, the two ministers sent a joint statement to the Commonwealth Prime Ministers. It read: 'If closer economic integration in Europe developed without us, both our political and our economic position there might suffer. If we made counter suggestions on the lines of the thinking of the Messina Powers, some quite considerable adjustments in our own tariffs and trading arrangements might well be involved'. No matter how the British government chose to deal with the proposals of the Messina Conference, the Commonwealth would be affected. There were no easy answers. It was for this reason that the cabinet was now exploring the best path forward, both for Britain and for its Empire and Commonwealth.[36]

After a month of talks, Macmillan and Thorneycroft sent to the cabinet a report on the 'United Kingdom initiative in Europe, Plan G', noting that the cabinet would have to move fast due to the 'current proposal to create a Common Market in Europe and from the difficulties into which we are running on Imperial Preference with Australia'. Under the auspices of their Working Group, Macmillan and Thorneycroft had asked officials from the Foreign Office, Treasury, Board of Trade, Ministry of Agriculture, Commonwealth Relations Office, Colonial Office, Board of Customs and Excise and Bank of England to work cooperatively to create a plan for the future. 'Plan G' was the resulting paper, and it was this that Macmillan and

Thorneycroft were now circulating for the first time.[37] Plan G intended to associate the United Kingdom with a potential Common Market of the six Messina Powers by creating a European Free Trade Area (FTA) between the Messina Six and the other members of the OEEC. This FTA would 'extend to all goods except agricultural produce... and would not prejudice our freedom in regard to revenue duties'. Within this system, 'all tariffs would be progressively reduced by all members of the Free Trade Area, and would be eliminated within, say, ten years'. In time, the countries involved could also discuss 'the possibility of reducing barriers to trade in agricultural products'. Finally, the United Kingdom would 'retain freedom to continue free entry for Commonwealth goods, and preferences for Commonwealth agricultural products'. In essence, Plan G sought to create a European-wide FTA (including the six Messina Powers) that would prevent the United Kingdom from being negatively affected by the establishment of a European Common Market. Plan G would require no surrender of national sovereignty, involved no supranational political organisations and allowed the United Kingdom to retain its system of Imperial Preferences.[38] Under its terms, the British government could have its cake and eat it, too, aligning itself with its European neighbours without in any way distracting from its Commonwealth relations.

Little more was said of Plan G over the summer, but, beginning in September, the question of Europe once again came to the fore. On the third of that month, Lord Home, the Commonwealth Secretary, sent to Macmillan his views on the proposed FTA. He acknowledged that, over the next few years, the government would need to negotiate 'some modification of our Ottawa preferences with a number of the Commonwealth countries, as we are doing at present with Australia' but did not think that these modifications needed to be 'fundamental'. In the long run, he argued, the 'rapidly expanding populations of Canada, Australia and New Zealand and the increasing sophistication of African and Asian markets' were a far safer bet for British trade than the European continent. Beyond these trade considerations, Home argued, 'Where our trade goes, there will go our capital investment, which has been one of the main bonds of the Commonwealth; and there also our political interests will tend to lean'. A greater British interest in Europe would inevitably lead to a lesser interest in the Commonwealth and 'in due course a position would arise in which we could not hope for the same assistance in times of trouble as we have had in the past from Commonwealth countries in military and economic matters'. The 'alignment of their foreign policies with ours would be more difficult to secure', and, in general, a European FTA would 'permanently loosen the bonds of the Commonwealth'. Plan G would be an abandonment of a tried and tested past in favour of an uncertain future. For Home, the risks outweighed the purported benefits.[39]

However, the Commonwealth Secretary was the only minister to express misgivings to Macmillan, and, on 11 September, he again raised the issue with the cabinet as a whole, asking two central questions: first, 'is this a good plan for the British economy? Will it bring us strength in the long run, even though the risks may be great in the short run?'; and second, '[i]s this politically sound? Can we retain the leadership of the Commonwealth world and at the same time seize the leadership of Europe? Would it help us to create a new period of British strength and power, or should we be foolishly throwing away what we have?' Politically, Macmillan wondered if 'our Party [will] accept it both in the House of Commons and in the country' and if the government could 'swing from the old policy of insular protection to the new policy of wider free trade areas'. Finally, he asked, 'Can we combine in a common policy the Commonwealth wing and the European wing?' It was the same question that both Labour and Conservative governments had been asking since the end of the Second World War. For Macmillan, the answer was a resounding 'yes', as it had always been. Yet it could not be achieved 'only on a material and economic basis. It will require an emotional and idealistic theme'.[40] Only once the British people began to feel 'European' could any progress on European integration be made. According to Macmillan, the time was ripe to begin such a campaign. Lord Home wrote a counter-memorandum, arguing that should the government adopt Plan G, Commonwealth countries would 'interpret the plan as meaning that the United Kingdom had decided to identity her fortunes more closely with Europe'. He warned that 'Plan G could lead to a permanent loosening of the Commonwealth bonds and through that to a weakening of the United Kingdom as a world power'.[41]

The cabinet met to discuss the two memoranda on 14 September. Thorneycroft opened the discussion, arguing that although it had been the aim of Britain's post-war commercial policy to 'secure the advantages of liberal trade practices in the world at large while retaining the benefit of the preferences system within the Commonwealth', this policy was 'under pressure and we could no longer expect to continue to enjoy the best of both worlds'. The question, then, was not how to integrate Commonwealth and European policy into a single whole, but rather which in the long-run would better serve Britain's commercial interests. It was time for the government to decide into which basket it would place its eggs. After some debate, the cabinet was 'impressed by the arguments in support of a new economic initiative on these lines [Plan G], and conscious of the limited scope for an alternative policy which would offer the prospect of economic security in the longer term'. The reasoning was clear, if negative in character: 'Although a commercial policy based on the Commonwealth connection would be much to be preferred, the conditions for such a policy no longer existed. ... The United Kingdom had now become too small an economic unit and if we did not attach ourselves to Europe we should be drawn inevitably, as a minor partner, into the sphere of influence of the United States'.[42] It is notable that, for perhaps the first time, the cabinet no longer talked of 'leading' a new Europe, but rather of being 'attached' to something that already existed.

Only Lord Home remained unhappy, warning that 'as the United Kingdom turned to Europe, Canada, Australia and New Zealand – with whom we [have] had the firmest bonds – must be expected to turn increasingly towards the United States'.[43] He argued that 'although the United Kingdom might not be pursuing irreconcilable objectives in attempting to assume leadership in Europe while remaining the centre of a powerful Commonwealth, the prospects of success in such a venture were at best speculative, and we might find that in concentrating our efforts on advantages in Europe which might not accrue we lost the most tangible benefits of the Commonwealth countries'. Europe was a risk; the Commonwealth was a reality. Why gamble the good that Britain already had in the hopes of something whose benefit was as yet unclear? Macmillan countered that 'the fact must be faced that the United Kingdom had declined in relative economic power in comparison with the other large economic units now dominating the world'. The Commonwealth was not the solution to that problem; Europe might be. Eden summed up the dilemma facing the cabinet: 'An economic plan based on the Commonwealth connection would no doubt be preferable. ... But there was little prospect of devising [such] a policy. ... Unless, therefore, we were capable, acting alone, of meeting formidable European competition in overseas markets, there seemed no alternative but to base our policy on the proposed plan for closer association with Europe'.[44]

The Prime Minister, one of the more sceptical members of the Conservative Party and a man who, as Foreign Secretary, had sought to undermine the government's European policy upon taking office in 1951, had, by 1956, reached the same conclusion as his Chancellor of the Exchequer: Europe offered Britain's only salvation. He therefore instructed the Foreign Office to prepare a summary of Plan G to circulate to all government departments, which it did on 21 September, explaining that 'The United Kingdom would enter a partial free trade area with the Customs Union of the Messina Six (Benelux, France, Germany, Italy) and all other O.E.E.C. countries that wish to join (probably Norway, Sweden, Denmark, Switzerland, Austria)'. It added that the FTA would not include Britain's dependent territories or the Commonwealth countries, but instead limit itself solely to European countries.[45] Plan G, in contrast to previous British schemes for Europe, was not one intended to enhance its imperial and colonial interests.

As the cabinet debated Plan G, the French Prime Minister Guy Mollet raised with Eden the 'possibility of a reversion to Sir Winston Churchill's offer in 1940 of a union between the United Kingdom and France'. The cabinet met to discuss his suggestion on 24 September, but concluded that, in 1956, there was 'no analogy with 1940; our offer then was an attempt to keep the French Union in the war, and in fact to merge the only two great Powers who were then fighting against Hitler'. In 1956, an Anglo–French Union would no longer be appropriate because there were 'basic differences of racial origin, language, religion and outlook; we should be likely to be weakened economically and financially; the move would be unwelcome to the Commonwealth (particularly to the new and emergent members); our cooperation with the U.S.A. in defence, intelligence and atomic matters would be immediately prejudiced; [and] the formation of exclusive ties with France would weaken our wider association with Europe in military and economic matters'. Although the cabinet took it as a positive sign that the French government was proposing the closest cooperation with Great Britain, Britain was now looking for an association with Europe as a whole. Eden planned therefore to brief the French premier on Plan G when he visited Paris on 27 September.[46]

When the two leaders met at the Hotel Matignon, Eden told Mollet that the British government would 'like to draw close to Europe, but we must contrive to do so without losing the Commonwealth'. Mollet agreed that this was of the utmost importance, said that there was 'immense hope' in France that the United Kingdom would 'take her place in Europe and indeed lead the movement towards closer European unity' and suggested that the French government would even be willing to join the Commonwealth if it should make Britain's position in Europe easier. Eden replied that whilst French membership of the Commonwealth would be difficult to achieve pragmatically, the British government hoped for 'co-operation on a broader basis' in Europe. He then revealed to Mollet Macmillan's Plan G.[47] Without encountering any objections from the Frenchman, Eden returned to London, where he informed the cabinet that it could proceed with Plan G without any serious opposition in France.[48]

Consequently, Macmillan and Thorneycroft held a joint press conference to brief the media on 3 October. In its aftermath, they reported to the cabinet that 'public opinion in this country has been fully as favourable as we had hoped. A satisfactory body of support has emerged in the Press and among all sections of political opinion. The views of industry are, and will no doubt remain, divided; but there is support even in industries likely to suffer, and over industry as a whole it seems likely that the weight of opinion will be in favour'. Overseas, too, the opinion was largely favourable. In continental Europe, there had been 'a considerable welcome', although 'they are not yet certain whether we are flying a kite or whether we mean business'. In the United States, Eisenhower had spoken 'with warmth of this "challenging idea"'. Canada was 'unlikely to oppose the Plan in principle', and Australia and New Zealand had 'expressed appreciation of the considerations that commend the Plan to the United Kingdom'. South Africa would not dissent, India had 'expressed general support' and Pakistan and Ceylon were indifferent, not appearing to 'consider themselves greatly affected'. Macmillan and Thorneycroft concluded that 'the reception of the Plan, both at home and by the Governments concerned, has been favourable enough to justify a further step forward; and that step should be taken now'.[49] Less than two weeks later, on 12 October, Macmillan announced at the Conservative Party Conference in Llandudno that Plan G was now official government policy.[50]

* * *

What Macmillan had not counted on, however, was the adverse reaction to the government's autumn adventure in Egypt, which was rapidly gathering steam and threatened to derail everything in its path by October. The British economy had been linked with Egypt since 1815, when Manchester's textile industry demanded large quantities of raw cotton and the American markets were temporarily lost following the War of 1812. Although officially part of the Ottoman Empire, Britain compelled the Egyptian government to adopt a system of free trade in 1838, and, by 1880, 80 per cent of Egypt's exports went directly to Britain, which in turn supplied 40 per cent of Egypt's imports. With foreign investment in mind, the Egyptian khedive began raising state bonds to fund a canal in 1862; by 1873, British investors held more than half of this Egyptian public debt. The Suez Canal itself was completed in 1869, and, in 1875, the British government became a part-owner, when the khedive put up his shares for sale to pay off substantial personal debt. After the Egyptian government went bankrupt the following year, the British government and British investors stood to lose the most financially, so British Prime Minister Benjamin Disraeli negotiated joint Anglo–French control over all Egyptian finances. Under the direction of British banker George Goschen, Egypt entered a period of austerity, which led to popular protest and the deposing of the khedive in 1880. In 1881, the Egyptian nationalist leader Ahmed 'Urabi led protests against foreign control of Egypt's finances, and, in July 1882, riots erupted in the city of Alexandria. Consequently, the British government – now under the premiership of William Gladstone – ordered the Royal Navy to bombard the city and Royal Marines to invade it. From that time forward, British forces occupied Egypt, which held the unique position of being part of the Ottoman Empire and a British protectorate.[51]

The British continued to formally occupy Egypt until 1936, when Anthony Eden – then Foreign Secretary in the Chamberlain government – negotiated the Anglo–Egyptian Treaty, which granted Egypt full independence. Nevertheless, British investors remained the majority shareholders in the Suez Canal Company and British forces remained in Egypt to properly safeguard the canal. At the close of the Second World War, some 80,000 British troops were still stationed in the Canal Zone. In July 1952, Egyptian Colonel Abdel Nasser seized power from the Egyptian King Farouk I in the first Arab nationalist coup of its kind. For the next four years, a tense situation existed between the British government and Nasser, the latter insisting that Britain withdraw all its forces from Egypt.[52] On 26 July 1956 – the day before Macmillan and Thorneycroft first proposed Plan G to the cabinet – Nasser announced the nationalisation of the Suez Canal Company, claiming that the canal was 'one of the façades of oppression, extortion and humiliation'.[53] Within two days of his announcement, Eden had written to the Prime Ministers of Canada, Australia, New Zealand and South Africa to warn that the British government would use all means in its power to protect British interests in the Canal.[54]

Despite Eden's initial instinct to brief the Commonwealth, it was not to the Commonwealth but to Europe that the government eventually turned for support, and to France in particular. Eden first met with representatives of the French and Israeli governments on 1 August – five days after Nasser's announcement to nationalise the canal. Discussions continued throughout August, September and October, and, on the twenty-fourth of that month, the three governments signed the secret Protocol of Sèvres, pledging them to take immediate action against Egypt. They devised a plan whereby Israeli forces would invade Sinai, after which the British and French governments would launch a joint Anglo–French 'intervention', purportedly to separate the warring Egyptian and Israeli armies and to protect the Suez Canal. Once this intervention had taken place, British and French forces would remain, creating an International Zone around the Suez Canal.

On 29 October – just five days after Selwyn Lloyd had returned from France having negotiated the Protocol – an Israeli parachute battalion dropped onto the Sinai Peninsula, followed by a ground invasion of two Israeli infantry brigades. The British and French governments immediately issued a joint statement, threatening that if Egyptian and Israeli forces did not disengage within twelve hours they would be forced to 'intervene in whatever strength may be necessary to secure compliance' and protect the Suez Canal.[55] When the twelve-hour ultimatum expired on the morning of 31 October, Eden ordered Operation Musketeer, beginning with an RAF air offensive that evening followed by a ground invasion on 5 November.[56] Although British forces achieved their objectives in a military sense by the morning of November 6, politically and economically the campaign was in crisis.[57]

On 1 November, New Zealand withdrew its support for the operation, and, the following day, the governments of Canada and

Australia each condemned British action. In the Westminster Parliament, the legislation authorising force had only passed by 270 to 218 votes (the Labour and Liberal parties united in opposition). With criticism coming from the Commonwealth governments, those opposed in Parliament began to protest more loudly. Elsewhere, at Oxford University, 335 members of the Senior Common Rooms, including ten college masters and presidents, issued a statement condemning the action, and newspaper editorials began to question its wisdom. On 2 November, Saudi Arabia closed its oil supplies to Great Britain, and, on 5 November, the United States announced its own oil embargo, followed shortly thereafter by other NATO countries collectively pledging not to sell any oil to the United Kingdom that had first come from either the United States or the Middle East.[58]

When the cabinet met on the afternoon of 6 November, Plan G and European integration were far from Macmillan's mind. Instead, he informed his colleagues that the Sterling Area's currency was 'haemorrhaging', with reserves falling by £20.3 million in September, £30 million in October and £100 million more in the first five days of November alone. He warned that without access to the International Monetary Fund (largely controlled by the United States) and with no possibility of a direct loan from America, the cabinet faced the death of sterling itself.[59] Despite its military victory, under immense economic pressure, the cabinet had little choice but to declare a ceasefire in the Canal Zone and order a withdrawal of all British forces. Following the cabinet meeting, Eden telephoned American President Dwight Eisenhower to inform him of the British decision. The president, delighted, withdrew all economic sanctions, and Anglo–American relations were restored.[60] In doing so, however, the British government had abandoned its French allies who, without British support, were forced to issue their own ceasefire. The ill-fated Suez adventure would be the last act of Anglo–French cooperation in the colonial sphere.

Two decisions were taken by the British government in the autumn of 1956. The first was to move forward with Plan G, an attempt to draw together European countries into an FTA and restore (at least in part) British leadership in Europe. The second, to abandon its mission in Egypt, had the opposite effect, isolating the United Kingdom from France whilst doing very little to restore its damaged relationships with the Commonwealth countries and the United States. In

November 1956, Britain's place in the world – under threat since the end of the Second World War – seemed to come unstuck entirely.

The Suez Crisis spelled the end of Anthony Eden's premiership. On 23 November, he left Britain for Jamaica to take a holiday on doctor's orders. The following day, the United Nations General Assembly passed by 63 votes to 5 a resolution censuring Britain and France for their actions in Egypt. For the Conservative Party, Eden's departure signalled that the time was ripe for a change in leadership, Viscount Montgomery writing to Churchill that 'In all my military experience I have never known anything to have been so "bungled" as the Suez affair. You would not have handled it that way. Nor would you have gone off to Jamaica. Under such conditions the captain of the ship does not go sea-bathing – he dies on the bridge'.[61] When Eden arrived back in London on 14 December, his reception at 10 Downing Street was cold and his greeting in the House of Commons colder still. Sensing that the writing was on the wall, Harold Macmillan and R. A. Butler began to jockey for position as the next party leader, and Anthony Eden fell ill. Consequently, on 8 January 1957, Eden informed the cabinet that he was tendering his resignation due to poor health. Nine days later, he boarded a steamer for New Zealand and did not return to the United Kingdom for four months.[62] Following his resignation, the Queen sought advice from Churchill whom to choose. Without hesitation, Churchill advised her to pick Macmillan, who was duly invited to Buckingham Palace and asked to form Her Majesty's next government.[63]

Following the fiasco in Suez, the government entered a period of soul-searching. On 22 November, the Treasury sent to the Foreign Office a memorandum summarising Britain's difficult position: 'We in this island are founder members of a great community with which we all feel the strongest of ties [the Commonwealth]. . . . Secondly, we are Europeans, geographically and culturally. . . . And thirdly, we are members of a great alliance [NATO] and our relations with the leading members of that alliance, the United States, are of utmost importance to us'. To balance these three competing interests was 'not easy'.[64] Churchill himself wrote to Eisenhower, lamenting that 'There seems to be growing misunderstanding and frustration on both sides of the Atlantic'.[65] Reports from British officials in the Netherlands and West Germany noted that there was increasing scepticism towards Plan G,[66] and, on 5 December, Sir Evelyn Shuckburgh commented that everyone had become 'suddenly very gloomy and all the Services feel they have been betrayed, and that we will never be able to show any independence as a nation again'.[67]

But then, on 5 January 1957 – in the dying days of the Eden administration – the Foreign Secretary Selwyn Lloyd put before the cabinet what he called 'The grand design'. His grand design, he said, was 'co-operation with Western Europe'. If Britain was to again become a 'first-class Power', he wrote, 'it can only be done in association with other countries. Britain and the other six Western European Union (W.E.U.) Powers have a combined population of over 210 millions, together with very considerable industrial capacity, resources and skill. If these were pooled, the resultant association could afford to possess full thermo-nuclear capacity. It could be the third great Power'. This force would not stand alone between the United States and Soviet Union, as Bevin had once envisioned, but would instead operate within NATO 'almost as powerful as America and perhaps in friendly rivalry with her'. Its military associations would 'in practice entail a closer political association', although Lloyd denied that a 'supranational machinery not responsible to Government' would be necessary. Beyond the military sphere, Lloyd's 'grand design' included an economic component, whereby the OEEC would be the driving factor, merged with a European-wide FTA. The ECSC need not be dissolved, but would work 'within the framework of the O.E.E.C'. Finally, his grand design called for 'a General Assembly for Europe which would replace the separate assemblies which have been or are liable to be set up for each organisation, e.g. Council of Europe, W.E.U., EURATOM, N.A.T.O. This General Assembly could divide its work as is done in the United Nations Assembly between Committees, each discussing a different category of subjects'. He concluded with a consideration of North America: 'We should at all stages emphasize to the Americans and the Canadians that our ideas were within the ambit of the Atlantic Alliance and designed to strengthen it. We should also make it clear that we relied on their encouragement and regarded their continued co-operation as essential'. Britain needed Europe, but it could not afford to upset the Americans.[68]

In his memorandum, Selwyn Lloyd made no mention of the Empire or Commonwealth. He did not talk of a European association that was backed by colonial dependencies. In many respects, his words mirrored those of Ernest Bevin ten years earlier, but much had changed in a decade. Whilst Bevin spoke with certainty of the future of the British Empire and Commonwealth and with a belief that Britain would always be a great power, leading both Empire and Europe, Selwyn Lloyd wrote from a position of weakness. The Empire was crumbling, Britain's place in the Commonwealth was being reduced day by day and any claims of British world leadership now seemed disingenuous at best. In the years after the Second World War, Britons – both Conservative and Labour – had acted as imperial Europeans, confident in their place in the world and convinced that their empire gave them the right and the responsibility to reorganise Europe and lead it to greatness. In the aftermath of the Suez Crisis, the government's only certainty was that the place Britain held in the world was no longer what it once was. In January 1957, the government turned to Europe not out of a presumptuous arrogance of a right to lead; it turned to Europe because it had nowhere else to go.

PART 2
POST-IMPERIAL EUROSCEPTICS

10 AT SIXES AND SEVENS

Eden sought continuity in his cabinet following his ascent to the premiership, intentionally demonstrating a unity of purpose with the Churchill government. Macmillan tacked a different course, promoting Peter Thorneycroft as Chancellor of the Exchequer and moving Duncan Sandys to the Ministry of Defence. The press immediately noticed that the new Prime Minister had brought two of Parliament's most ardent Europeans into the inner cabinet, the Labour MP Richard Crossman opining in the *Daily Mirror* that Macmillan's reshuffle revealed 'a lot about the policy he intends to follow'. In particular, his aim in foreign policy would be 'a European Third Force, led by Britain and backed by the United States'. Crossman disapproved, but felt sure that Britain's North American allies would be satisfied: 'The Americans have always believed in the United States of Europe and blamed us British for dragging our feet.... If Mr. Macmillan can get together with the French and Germans and create a Third Force which can stand on its own feet without dollar assistance, no one will be happier than the Americans'.[1]

If Crossman was hostile to Macmillan's European turn, those on the continent were more receptive. The Foreign Secretary Selwyn Lloyd reported from Rome on 18 January 1957 that the Italian government was 'most friendly' towards the British position and wanted to further discuss Lloyd's 'grand design' for Europe. In particular, the Italians had welcomed his call for a wider European Free Trade Area (FTA), including and closely associated with the organisations of 'the Six', which would 'lead the way to cooperation between us and Europe'.[2] Consequently, and with Italian support, the British government submitted a memorandum to the Organisation of European Economic Cooperation (OEEC) outlining UK plans for a European FTA in early February.[3] The French Ambassador René Massigli commended it and suggested to Macmillan that the British government 'hurry with our plans for European unity'.[4] It was, as one historian has written, 'European policy *par excellence*.... [I]t was extremely clever in both conception and design. From a British point of view, moreover, it promised neatly to defuse the European problem ... without compromising either Britain's Commonwealth ties or, still more vital for the Treasury, the world-wide role for sterling'.[5]

All did not go as smoothly as the Italians had led them to believe, however. At the OEEC Council meeting on 12 February, other European leaders were less receptive to British plans. In its aftermath, Macmillan suggested to Thorneycroft that it might be better to assemble a committee of representatives from only those governments interested in the FTA idea, which could meet outside the formal OEEC setting, as 'the present practice of doing everything through [the] O.E.E.C. may prove a handicap'.[6] At home, the *Sunday Express* launched a 'bitter personal attack' on Macmillan and his European policy, which Macmillan ascribed to Lord Beaverbrook's 'fanatical hatred' of a possible European FTA.[7]

The Empire and Commonwealth offered little more support, with the Canadians giving only a lukewarm acceptance of the Prime Minister's ideas and the governments of Bermuda, Gibraltar, Tanganyika, Uganda, Antigua, Cyprus, Zanzibar, Sierra Leone, Nigeria and the Western Pacific expressing concerns at a series of meetings held on closer British economic association with Europe from 27 March through 2 April. In particular, Tanganyika protested that the present system of imperial preferences was essential for the maintenance of its coffee, lead concentrates, beans and peas agriculture; Antigua claimed that its sugar and cotton industries needed protection; Cyprus feared that a European FTA would negatively affect its trade with other areas of the Empire and Commonwealth; Zanzibar worried about its coffee and cocoa industry, which would be 'especially hard hit'; Nigeria was concerned about groundnut oil, palm oil and hardwood; and Bermuda stated bluntly that it 'does not wish to be associated with any European Customs Union or Free Trade Area'.[8] Furthermore, in separate telegrams, the government of Kenya argued that Britain could only join a European FTA if 'the Six' would 'allow tropical foodstuffs from British Colonies to enter the Customs Union Countries in Europe on the same terms as those from the Colonies of Messina Powers', and the Hong Kong government recommended that the government 'proceed with the free trade area proposals only if adequate compensation can be secured for Hong Kong or... if Hong Kong is admitted to the free trade area'.[9] The view of Britain's dependent territories was quite clear. Selwyn Lloyd's 'grand design' for Europe could only proceed if colonial interests were borne in mind, with Great Britain, its Empire and the Commonwealth treated as a single entity, either all coming into the FTA or all remaining beyond its borders.

The signature of the Treaty of Rome by the six Messina powers giving birth to the European Economic Community (EEC, or 'Common Market', in British parlance) only heightened Macmillan's determination to secure a European FTA with Britain at its heart. On 18 April, he wrote that the government needed to avoid 'at all costs' the 'Common Market coming into being and the Free Trade Area never following'. If this were to happen, 'the Germans would dominate the six countries and in a short time put us in a very bad position'.[10] He was surprised that the French government failed to see the potential danger in this situation, and he confessed to Lord Layton that throughout British negotiations for a FTA the French had been 'our main difficulty'.[11]

Given French obstinacy, Macmillan decided that the best path forward was to approach the Germans directly, making it clear that 'a customs union excluding the possibility of an industrial free trade area along the lines of the U.K. suggestion [would] lead to the disintegration of the U.K.'s European policy and the collapse of NATO'. Should the OEEC fail to accommodate the British government's economic plans for Europe, British military support for the continent would become similarly imperilled, leaving West Germany to face the Soviet Union alone, without the British Army of the Rhine.[12] Macmillan dispatched Selwyn Lloyd to Bonn to deliver his message on 6 May, following himself for direct talks with Adenauer two days later. Lloyd reported that although the German Foreign Minister Walter Hallstein had emphasised the importance of 'supra-national institutions as an essential element in the development of European unity', he had nevertheless offered 'wholehearted support' to the FTA idea. However, the German government was unwilling to do anything which would bring it into open disagreement with the French until the latter had ratified the Treaty of Rome: 'Hallstein stated that in his view the French had made great concessions in agreeing to the common market and he doubted whether it was realistic to expect them to make many more in the context of the free trade area'.[13] Adenauer repeated the same message, telling Macmillan that the German government was 'on our side' but could not 'raise controversial subjects with the French until the Treaty of Rome is safely ratified'.[14] Macmillan noted in his diary that it was clear that the Germans 'still have grave suspicions of the French. They fear that it will be the EDC [European Defence Community] story all over again'.[15]

The main French criticism of the British proposal was that it was insincere; that the British government had little interest in actually implementing its policy, but was using it as an instrument to delay and ultimately sabotage the ratification process for the EEC. Some in the United States had also raised this concern, including with the ambassador, and British protestations to the contrary had been undermined by the constant stream of negativity from the Commonwealth. For that reason, in late May, the Commonwealth Relations Office sent to the UK High Commissioners in Canada, Australia, New Zealand, South Africa, India, Pakistan, Ceylon, Ghana and the Federation of Rhodesia a telegraph saying 'We are disturbed by [the] signs of failure of Commonwealth Governments to appreciate [the] vital importance of securing [an] industrial Free Trade Area now that [the] Treaty establishing [the] European Economic Community has been signed'. It chastised the Commonwealth countries for fuelling rumours of indifference and stated that 'It cannot be emphasised too strongly that, far from being indifferent to a Free Trade Area, we are convinced that [the] existence of [the] Customs Union without a Free Trade Area would represent a grave threat to [the] interests not only of [the] United Kingdom but also of [the] rest of [the] Commonwealth and indeed [the] free world'.[16] The international community was no longer one in which the Commonwealth could stand alone; British engagement with the European continent was the best hope for the continuation of the Commonwealth.

The government's telegram did little to quell the public airing of Commonwealth fears, and continental suspicion of the British plan continued to rise. Macmillan feared that the government was 'not making the progress we ought to be making about Europe, either in the political or the economic field',[17] and, in June, he decided that the Commonwealth Prime Ministers' Conference that month would be devoted to the subject of Europe. The *Daily Mail* found it 'strange' that Commonwealth Prime Ministers should be coming to London to talk about Europe but nevertheless urged the Commonwealth leaders to support the British government in its European endeavours: 'Some people believe the Commonwealth would suffer a mortal blow if Britain joined. If we had to choose between Empire and Europe there could be but one verdict. The Empire every time. But are these two conceptions mutually hostile? We do not think so. We believe they have much to give each other'. It concluded: 'The Commonwealth needs a strong Britain – and Britain would be tremendously strengthened by the industrial surge forward which should develop from FTA membership. The Commonwealth, in turn, would give substance and ballast to Europe'. The proprietor of the *Daily Express*, Lord Beaverbrook, saw Britain's imperial interests and closer association with Europe as mutually exclusive, but the *Daily Mail* clung to an earlier vision of an imperial Europe led by Britain, first articulated by Ernest Bevin. Its editors concluded, 'A Europe buttressed by overseas territories and strong enough to stand as an equal with the Big Boys of East and West would make for a better balanced and saner world'.[18]

Macmillan's vision was that of the *Mail* rather than the *Express*. Speaking to the United Kingdom Council of the European Movement on 9 July, he said, 'There are some who believe that there is an inherent contradiction between our links with the Commonwealth and our aims in Europe. If I believed that I should not be here'. The Commonwealth, he said, was a 'living force which we in Britain understand and cherish'. It stretched 'to all corners of the earth, is based upon sentiment and understanding', and had a unity that was 'symbolised in the Crown', a 'living thing, all the time growing and changing'. It was Britain's successful experience with the Commonwealth, the most diverse community on earth, that had convinced Macmillan that a united Europe was possible and could work best without the formal federal structures and rules favoured by the French. And it was not only in the example of its constitutional form that the Commonwealth had much to offer Europe. The United Kingdom's trade relations with the Commonwealth were largely agricultural in nature – 'Indeed, 90 per cent of Britain's purchases from the Commonwealth fall into this category' – whereas British trade with the European continent was largely industrial. For that reason, there was no contradiction 'between our determination that inter-Commonwealth trade should grow and our proposal for a freer flow of industrial production throughout Europe'.[19] The Commonwealth and Europe were complementary, not contradictory.

Shortly after addressing the European Movement, Macmillan told Thorneycroft that although Great Britain was unable to join the EEC in an economic sense because of its supra-national nature, it could nevertheless show the other European countries that 'we are prepared for a close political association' short of federation.[20] Given that many on the European continent were still sceptical of the government's plans for a European FTA, Macmillan suggested that the cabinet appoint a minister to be responsible for European affairs, one who would be 'charged with collecting all the material, guiding all the studies, and being answerable to a group of Ministers consisting of myself, the Foreign Secretary, the President of the Board of Trade and yourself [the Chancellor of the Exchequer]'. The Colonial and Commonwealth Secretaries would also be consulted on 'major decisions', although the new European Minister would not report to them on a regular basis. Macmillan concluded, 'It would be very important to travel both among the Six [the EEC] and among the Eleven [the OEEC]. On the whole, it is as important to hold firm the Eleven as it is to break into the Six. He should therefore be something of a St. Paul: not merely the Jews but the Gentiles should be his care'.[21] Thorneycroft agreed and, on 7 August 1957, Macmillan announced that Reginald Maudling, the Paymaster-General, would become the government's first Minister for European Affairs.[22]

The Prime Minister's advice for Maudling was blunt. He would be unlikely to convince the French of the merits of the British proposal and should therefore work to 'get the Germans on our side'.[23] British plans hinged not on overcoming French opposition, but on convincing the Germans to come out in support of the proposal. Throughout the remainder of the summer of 1957 and into the autumn, Maudling travelled across the European continent, expressing the seriousness of British intent and arguing that a European FTA was in the best interests of *all* European countries, including those within the EEC. On 7 October, he briefed the cabinet on his findings. Within 'the Six', the only country to express serious disagreement was France; West Germany, Italy, Belgium and the Netherlands had all given strong support. Beyond the Six, Scandinavia, Switzerland, Austria and Portugal were committed to the British proposal. Denmark was supportive so long as special arrangements could be negotiated for its agricultural produce. Ireland, Iceland, Greece and Turkey favoured a European FTA *en principe*, but could not fully commit until they had seen the fine print. No European country, with the exception of France, was completely opposed.[24] Macmillan described Maudling's efforts as 'quite admirable'.[25] When the Council of the OEEC met on 16 October, it declared its determination to 'promote the establishment of a European Free Trade Area',[26] and, with the Treaty of Rome now fully ratified and coming into force on 1 January 1958, even the West German leaders were ready and willing to publicly express their support for the creation of a European FTA.[27] By the late autumn of 1957, Macmillan's European policy seemed to be falling into place.

Yet if eleven out of the twelve countries of the OEEC were in favour of a European FTA, the one outlier still had enormous potential to cause damage. Furthermore, although the American government fully understood the political significance of the EEC and used its full weight to ensure ratification of the Treaty of Rome, it failed to see the import of the FTA. When Selwyn Lloyd travelled to the United States with Macmillan in late October, John Foster Dulles, the American Secretary of State, told him that the Common Market was 'a political aim and the Free Trade Area [was] just an economic benefit'. British officials later commented that the American government had 'no conception of the divisive effects which a high tariff Common Market might have upon the political and military set-up in Europe'.[28]

In an attempt to pacify American hostility, officials at the Foreign Office drafted a memorandum for Dulles outlining the British position. It stated that although the British government had concluded that it could not participate in a European Common Market, as this would 'substantially weaken the Commonwealth relationship', it was 'in no way hostile to the plans for the Six'. Nevertheless, a European Common Market existing outside a larger European FTA would 'divide Free Europe politically between the Six on one side and on the other the United Kingdom and those other European countries who, for political or economic reasons, could not join the Six'. For that reason, in 1956, the government introduced the option of an FTA including (but wider than) the EEC, a proposal that the British Parliament endorsed in November 1956 and which the government officially submitted to the OEEC Council in February 1957. When the OEEC meeting agreed in October 1957 to support the establishment of a European FTA, the government considered the outcome its greatest achievement of 1957.

The memorandum concluded: 'The Free Trade Area is as complementary to the political aspirations of the European Economic Community as to their economic aims. Without a Free Trade Area H.M. Government do not see how it would be possible to preserve that special relationship between the United Kingdom and the Continent of Europe which is not only to their mutual benefit but, they believe, to the benefit of the Free World'.[29] If the United States supported the EEC, it ought for the same reasons to support the European FTA.

The French government did not see the situation in the same light. On 13 January 1958 – less than two weeks after the EEC came into being – Hugh Ellis-Rees of the UK Delegation to the OEEC warned Sir John Coulson, the ambassador's right-hand man at the British Embassy in Washington DC, that the French press had adopted an 'increasingly negative attitude' towards the FTA that consistently portrayed it as a 'British plot to overthrow the Common Market'. Ellis-Rees was convinced that these attacks emanated from the French administration.[30] His suspicions were confirmed three days later, when the French government announced that it was preparing its own plan for an FTA. Although no details of the proposal were forthcoming, it was clear from the French announcement that it was designed to further the interests of the EEC and ensure that any future plans for European integration were centred on the Six rather than on a larger grouping of European countries in the OEEC.[31]

In announcing its plan, the French government was banking on the support of West Germany; although Macmillan had once believed the Germans would support the British in their endeavours, he now feared that they would once again line up with their neighbours on the continent. In mid-December 1957, he had met privately with the aging Adenauer, who had expressed his concerns about the future of Germany once he left office. Macmillan noted in his diary: 'He would like to see W[est] Germany definitely bound up with the West – through NATO or other means. That is why he was so keen on EDC, the European Army, the 6 Power Common Market plan, the Free Trade Area – in a word, everything which w[oul]d range Germany in the ranks of the civilised countries'. By January 1958, however, Adenauer feared that once he was dead, the German people would turn East rather than West, accepting a unified but neutral Germany in favour of a divided country. For this reason, he felt compelled to do all he could to tie West Germany strongly to the Western countries whilst he was still alive. Although ideologically he preferred British plans, formal federal union with the French was a better guarantee of that than informal and pragmatic cooperation with the British. For this reason, Adenauer felt compelled to side with French government plans for an FTA of the Six rather than British plans for a larger grouping, despite his personal sympathies lying with the British.[32]

In an attempt to counter the negative attitude of the French press, on 17 January the British Embassy arranged for six of France's leading journalists to have lunch with Reginald Maudling, the new British Minister for European Affairs, who could put the British position to them directly.[33] The meeting did little good, however, and the attacks on Britain's proposal continued unabated. Meanwhile, on 8 January, Macmillan embarked upon a five-week tour of the Commonwealth, the first such visit by a British prime minister in the twentieth century. For the first three weeks of his tour, he visited the 'new' Commonwealth countries, where Britain's European policy was of little interest. Upon arrival in New Zealand, however, Macmillan was greeted with a barrage of sceptical questioning from both the media and politicians. He explained to the Kiwis that it was precisely *because* of the British government's high regard for Commonwealth interests that the United Kingdom had refused to enter the Common Market, but that an industrial free trade area including the EEC would preserve imperial preference whilst enlarging the market for Commonwealth goods.[34] He convinced no-one.

When the Prime Minister travelled to Australia two days later, he again had to defend British policy, explaining that the *industrial* free trade area would allow complete free trade in industrial goods between its member nations, thereby enhancing the British (and therefore the Commonwealth) market whilst allowing its members to maintain their own tariffs or give concessions on nonindustrial trade (e.g., by imperial preference). It would, he argued, have no affect whatsoever on the existing trade relations between Britain and the Commonwealth but would provide the Commonwealth as a whole with more clout by maintaining Britain's world leadership in the economic sphere.[35] As in New Zealand, Macmillan's audience was unmoved and when he met with the Australian Prime Minister John McEwan on 11 February, McEwan bluntly informed him that the Australian government did not believe that the UK would be able to 'maintain her stand against including agricultural products'. McEwan suspected that the governments of the Six, particularly the French, intended to 'use the U.K.'s attitude as an excuse to wreck F.T.A. proposals'. Consequently, rather than enhancing Britain's position in the world, Macmillan's negotiations would in fact lead to its further decline.[36]

McEwan's gloomy assessment was borne out as winter turned to spring. Macmillan informed the cabinet on 21 February that the French were 'being very difficult and the Germans less helpful than they might have been', and, on 17 March, he speculated that the French were 'determined to wreck it [the FTA]'.[37] The resignation of Felix Gaillard as French Prime Minister in April (who himself had only been Prime Minister since February) did little to change the situation because the new French government was distracted by the deteriorating situation in Algeria. In early May, the French military command there set up a 'Committee of Public Safety' and French parliamentarians feared that it might lead to a *coup d'état* in Paris itself.[38] Pierre Pflimlin was appointed Prime Minister on 14 May (the fourth prime minister in a year), but he did not last long. On 21 May, Macmillan wrote in his diary: 'The French situation is still obscure. The P.M. (Pflimlin) seems to be putting up quite a fight. But de Gaulle has taken up a pretty good strategic position'.[39] A week later, the situation had not improved, and Pflimlin resigned after only two weeks in power. 'The French crisis is still unresolved', Macmillan wrote. 'The army are in virtual command of Algeria and now of Corsica. They threaten to seize different areas of France and perhaps to attack Paris by parachute troops.... [French] President [René] Coty is consulting the various party leaders'.[40] Removing the reference to paratroopers, Macmillan's words were reminiscent of some that could have been written in 1815.

Throughout the month of May 1958, the British government was unsure whether French democracy would survive the month, an uncertainty that only heightened British instincts against entering any federal institutions with the French. When on 1 June the French General Charles de Gaulle secured enough votes in the National Assembly to become Prime Minister through constitutional means, leaders across Europe breathed a sigh of relief.[41] Nevertheless, as they were soon to discover, de Gaulle had a very different way of working with his European colleagues than his predecessors. 'Gaullism', as it would soon be known, had far more in common with the philosophies of Napoleon Bonaparte than Robert Schuman or Jean Monnet.

* * *

De Gaulle's first act as French Prime Minister was to fly to Algiers to reassure the European population there that French *gloire* would be restored in Africa and throughout the world. Whilst committed to a continued French role in the EEC, de Gaulle's vision of European unity was distinctly different from his predecessors in the Prime Minister's office.[42] He had opposed the EDC and been critical of the Treaty of Rome. When his proposals for a three-power (France, Britain and the United States) directorate to lead NATO were spurned by the British government, his suspicions of an Anglo–American vendetta against France were confirmed.[43] Upon taking power, de Gaulle gave every indication that he would continue French opposition to British plans for a European FTA and, at a cabinet meeting on 23 June, Macmillan asked his colleagues 'what (if anything) can be done to save the European Free Trade area project, which is being strangled by the French'. He authorised Maudling to 'tell the Germans that we [are] almost at the end of our patience. But if this fails, it means (in my view) the end of much more than trade cooperation in Europe. I don't see how NATO could survive'.[44]

Macmillan also spoke privately with Selwyn Lloyd ahead of his first meeting with the new French Prime Minister, suggesting that a change in tactics might be necessary. Wondering if 'our difficulties with our friends abroad result from our national good manners and reticence', he thought that in order to avoid the accusation of perfidy the British government needed to be more forceful in future: '[W]e ought to make it quite clear to our European friends that if Little Europe is formed without a parallel development of a Free Trade Area we shall have to reconsider the whole of our political and economic attitude towards Europe'. The British would not, he said, 'allow ourselves to be destroyed little by little. We would fight back with every weapon in our armoury. We would take our troops out of Europe. We would withdraw from NATO. We would adopt a policy of isolationism. We would surround ourselves with rockets and we would say to the Germans, the French and all the rest of them: "look after yourselves with your own forces. Look after yourselves when the Russians overrun your countries"'.[45] In one of the angriest memoranda Macmillan wrote as Prime Minister, he made clear that his patience for European resistance to the Free Trade idea had reached its limit.

When Macmillan travelled to Paris five days later, his mood had not improved and on the eve before his departure he confessed to Lady

Rhys-Williams that he was 'not at all confident about the Free Trade Area'.[46] He also sent to de Gaulle a letter prior to their meeting warning that if the French government continued to thwart British plans, his government would be forced to 'bring to an end all that progress towards general European co-operation to which I personally attach so much importance'. Pleading with the new French Prime Minister, he wrote, 'I do not see how one can divorce economic and political grouping. Europe is already tragically divided from Stettin to Trieste and I am very anxious to avoid any further division'.[47]

His words fell on deaf ears, meeting first ambivalence and then hostility. When the two men met, the general was 'neither interested nor unimpressed' with Macmillan's plans for a FTA.[48] Although the Prime Minister wrote in his memoirs that 'Outwardly everything seemed friendly and the omens hopeful', it was not to last.[49] Macmillan tried to persuade de Gaulle of the political and economic good sense of a European FTA including the EEC but, facing the general's resistance, predicted that 'the whole of this great effort will break down, foiled by the selfishness and insularity of the French'.[50] On 5 July, de Gaulle brought their discussions to a close, writing: 'France is not at all unfavourable, quite the contrary, to an enlargement of economic cooperation in Europe, in which Great Britain is naturally included.... But we must find means of arriving there without destroying the equilibrium of France's economy ... and without putting at issue the agreements existing between the six member countries of the European Common Market'.[51] The French government would not consider an FTA that did not include agricultural produce. However, the British government could not agree to this because of its Commonwealth interests. The British and French visions for European economic cooperation simply did not mesh.

On 11 September 1958, Macmillan confirmed for the cabinet that the French government would only entertain further negotiations about an industrial FTA if Britain would simultaneously discuss agricultural trade. Since any arrangements for agriculture would only be acceptable to the British government if they 'did not conflict with our commitments to the Commonwealth and home farmers', the outlook was 'not good'.[52] A visit to West Germany in October did little to ease the situation, and Macmillan informed Selwyn Lloyd that his meeting with Adenauer on 9 October had revealed signs of a 'growing Franco–German rapprochement' since de Gaulle took office.[53]

German officials in particular were convinced that it was 'the British who [were] being obstructive' in Europe, a message they were repeatedly feeding Adenauer.[54] Macmillan wrote to the Foreign Secretary a week later, asking if he and the Chancellor of the Exchequer Heathcoat Amory would 'consider what we are to do if the negotiations for the European Free Trade Area break down completely'. 'Fortress Britain', Macmillan suggested, 'might be our right reply'.[55]

By the end of the month, Macmillan had concluded that the French were 'just wasting time' and that Britain should look for alternatives to a Europe-wide FTA.[56] The French, he found, were 'determined to exclude [the] U.K.' and de Gaulle was 'bidding high for the hegemony of Europe'.[57] He informed the cabinet on 4 November that 'if, by the end of November, it has become clear that the French are unwilling to make any genuine progress, we should ourselves break off the negotiations'.[58] On 6 November, he visited the French Foreign Minister Maurice Couve de Murville in person to press his case and make clear the seriousness of British intent.[59] His meeting was unsuccessful ('a painful discussion, esp[ecially] with an old friend'[60]), and the following day he wrote to de Gaulle that he was 'deeply disturbed at the position we have reached in our negotiations for a Free Trade Area'. He purported 'great shock' to learn from Couve de Murville that France was 'not after all aiming at the same objective'. The French Foreign Minister had 'insisted not only that France is not prepared to stand a regime of free trade in Europe (in spite of the safeguards we are all prepared to consider) but that such a regime must inevitably destroy the objectives of the Common Market'. Macmillan disputed this conclusion, claiming that 'Nobody has striven harder than I to put Europe in its rightful place in the world. Nobody has made greater efforts to find the means whereby Britain can be brought closer to Europe'. Nevertheless, there was only so much Macmillan could do. If France would not cooperate, the British government would be forced to withdraw from the negotiations.[61] Significantly, in contrast to his earlier writings and speeches (and those of Britons such as Ernest Bevin, Duncan Sandys, Sir Stafford Cripps and the two Amerys), Macmillan no longer referred to a singular Europe inclusive of the United Kingdom but spoke instead of British relations with an external Europe, as if Britain was not truly part of 'Europe'. In this regard, Macmillan had already lost an important semantic battle with 'the Six', ceding to them the definition of what was or was not 'Europe'.

Following Macmillan's letter to de Gaulle, British and French ministers spoke no more on the European FTA proposal and the General pre-empted the British Prime Minister by announcing on 14 November that it was 'not possible to create a Free Trade Area as wished by the British – that is, with free trade between the Common Market and the rest of the O.E.E.C. but without a single external tariff barrier round the 17 countries, and without the harmonisation in the economic and social spheres'.[62] Macmillan had threatened de Gaulle that if the French did not agree to British plans by the end of the month the government of the United Kingdom would withdraw from negotiations. De Gaulle beat him to the punchline, announcing that, on behalf of Europe (and against the wishes of many of its governments), the French government could not accept the British vision for Europe. Three days later, Reginald Maudling – Britain's first Minister for European Affairs – delivered a statement in the House of Commons: 'The unanimous determination of all Governments to secure the establishment of a Free Trade Area seems to have been brought into question. H.M.G. will enter as soon as possible into consultations with all Governments concerned in order to clarify the resulting situation'.[63] *The Times* declared on its front page that France was 'the wrecker' and predicted a trade war in Western Europe; the British public, likewise, perceived France as the chief roadblock to British plans in Europe.[64]

Maudling's statement suggested some ambivalence on the part of the government about the status of negotiations, but behind closed doors all knew the exact consequence of the French announcement. Selwyn Lloyd's 'grand design' for Europe – a design Macmillan had heartily embraced and campaigned for throughout the continent – had failed. If Britain were to move forward with an economic FTA within Europe, it would be without the six nations of the EEC and would thus have lost its *raison d'être* before it had even begun. Writing in his diary on 17 November, Macmillan lamented that the collapse of the European FTA discussions 'must mean the disintegration of [the] OEEC and other European institutions'.[65] All that he had believed in and worked for in Europe since the end of the Second World War seemed to be imperilled.

* * *

The proposal for a smaller FTA excluding the Six came not from the British but from Sweden. The British government had long been considering the idea, having established a committee in December 1958 under the chairmanship of Sir Roger Makins to explore alternatives to a Europe-wide FTA. When Makins reported to the cabinet in February 1959, he recommended that the government pursue negotiations for a European FTA of those countries excluded from the EEC. His committee stressed that this was time-sensitive given that trade discrimination by the Six against the United Kingdom and the other eleven countries of the OEEC had come into force on 1 January 1959.[66] However, before the government could act on this recommendation, it received an invitation from the Swedish Foreign Minister Hubert de Besche to attend talks in Oslo on 21 February with ministers from Norway, Denmark, Austria, Switzerland and Portugal (who, along with Britain and Sweden, would soon become known as 'the Seven').[67] These talks were aimed at establishing a European FTA to rival the EEC.

Following successful talks in Oslo, a second round followed in Stockholm in March, after which de Besche travelled to each of the capital cities of the Seven to negotiate with governments on a bilateral basis.[68] His vision was for an industrial free trade area that would encourage closer economic ties but remain politically neutral. Although the United Kingdom would receive few economic benefits from this arrangement, the government believed that being part of a distinct group of seven European countries would give it greater leverage when negotiating with the Six. Macmillan noted in his diary on 6 May that the proposed grouping was 'obviously in our interests, industrially and commercially', although he recognised that there would be 'Commonwealth objections'.[69] Such objections were far outweighed by British interests in Europe, however, and on 7 May the cabinet approved formal British entry into talks to create such a group.[70] The following month, British officials travelled to Sweden for the Stockholm Convention. Macmillan noted that 'The stakes in this affair are very high – no less than the survival of the industrial life and strength of Britain'. He continued: 'if we cannot successfully organise the opposition group – Scandinavia; Denmark; Switzerland; Austria etc – then we shall undoubtedly be eaten up, one by one, by the 6'. He was convinced that 'American factories' that had been planning to open in Scotland, Northern Ireland and other areas 'of unemployment in England' had already been cancelled, drawn instead to France and Germany by the 'pull of the Common Market'. Only by coming together as the Seven could Britain secure its economic future alongside the Six.[71] The convention ended on 23 July 1959, with each government pledging to create a European Free Trade Association of the seven European countries.[72]

Before the ink was dry on the page, however, problems arose. On 9 August, David Eccles, President of the Board of Trade, wrote to Macmillan with alarming news from his 'Italian friends'. The Italians, who had always claimed to be Britain's strongest supporters in the EEC, now believed that the Commonwealth had become a stumbling block to closer British relations with the European continent; only by choosing Europe over the Commonwealth could the British truly be accepted as 'Europeans'. Eccles had pointed out to his friends that the Commonwealth had not prevented the British from 'going in with the Seven', but they had replied, 'Yes, but you did not have to make the political concessions to the Seven which the French will insist on'. The conclusion Eccles drew was that there were 'a number of formidable opponents to an association between the Six and the Seven'. These included 'our own farmers and Commonwealth farmers', the 'internationalist disciples of Jean Monnet', the 'nationalist party in France who do not want their country's renaissance to be harassed by British competition either in exports or in politics' and 'the rising self-confidence of many Europeans who believe they can outstrip us in economic and political power'.[73] The Italians, so long supporters of Britain in Europe, now had to be included in this latter group.

Macmillan had other problems. American President Eisenhower was due to visit France on 20 August 1959, and Macmillan was travelling to Paris to dine with him and de Gaulle. Since the Suez fiasco of November 1956, Macmillan had worked hard to restore the battered Anglo–American 'special relationship', with some success.[74] Yet this very success presented problems to the French government, which had become jealous 'of the special position which we appear to have built up for ourselves with the Americans and which they regard as Anglo-Saxon dominance'. British officials feared that de Gaulle, already angered by the failure of his proposed tripartite directorate for NATO, might use the occasion to try to drive a wedge between the British and Americans, thus enhancing France's own position. He was particularly keen to have a greater say in the Western nuclear strategy and was hinting that France might withdraw from NATO if he did not get his way. A Foreign Office brief warned

Macmillan that, in his meetings, he must not 'prejudice our special ties with the Americans' or 'appear to be taking the side of the French or even acting as mediator in any Franco–American argument'. Furthermore, the British could not 'compromise any fundamental interest whether in defence or other matters in order to meet French susceptibilities'. Yet Macmillan could not entirely dismiss the French either, as 'we are much more dependent on good relations with our nearest neighbour than are the Americans who could in the last resort suffice independently of any European countries'.[75] The British needed the Americans, yet they could not entirely divorce themselves from the French.

The Prime Minister had little time to ruminate on Anglo–American–Franco relations, however, as in late August he requested that Queen Elizabeth II dissolve Parliament and call a General Election for 8 October 1959, the first to be held since the events in Suez, Anthony Eden's resignation and Macmillan's ascent to the premiership.[76] Capitalising on the recent economic upturn, the Conservatives campaigned on the slogan of, 'Life is better with the Conservatives, don't let Labour ruin it', Macmillan claiming that Britons had 'never had it so good'. Despite Labour's best efforts, the election was centred on the economy and neither the Suez fiasco; the ongoing counter-insurgencies in Malaya, Kenya and Cyprus; nor the government's failure to create a European FTA encompassing the EEC were majors points of contention. When the votes were counted, the Conservative Party increased its majority in the House of Commons to 107 – its strongest showing since the war. Jubilant in his triumph, Macmillan boasted to his diary that 'Altogether, the result is remarkable. I don't think any Party has won three times running, increasing its majority each time'.[77] One of those newly elected MPs who entered Parliament on 9 October 1959 was a young Margaret Thatcher, taking her place in the Commons for the first time as the new Member for Finchley.[78]

The General Election shored up Macmillan's position in Parliament and gave him a wide personal mandate. However, it did little to change the dynamics of Britain's position within the European continent. On 22 October, just three weeks after the election, Selwyn Lloyd wrote to Macmillan, arguing that 'one of the most important tasks of the next five years will be to organise the relations of the United Kingdom with Europe'. He suggested that for the 'first time since the

Napoleonic era', the major continental powers were united in a political and economic grouping which, whilst not specifically directed at Britain, might nevertheless 'have the effect of excluding us both from European markets and from consultation in European policy'. The establishment of 'the Seven' represented the 'first line of defence in the economic field' against the EEC, but it was a 'rather tender plant'. Furthermore, the emerging European FTA was only a temporary fix; the future of Europe lay in the Common Market. Consequently, whilst the British government should continue to facilitate the growth of the Seven, it should also explore 'the sort of price it would be worth paying in order to be economically associated with [the EEC] (something more in fact than just the concept of the Free Trade Area)'. The Foreign Secretary concluded: 'Since the French are fundamentally in a very strong position politically, I believe that we shall not succeed in bullying them into accepting us as a partner in Europe; we shall have to coax them.... The Germans, however, are not in a strong political position, and I would have thought that there was some chance of bullying them'.[79]

Selwyn Lloyd's memorandum was followed by a note from Philip de Zulueta, Macmillan's private secretary, who included a memorandum from the Foreign Office Planning section. De Zulueta prefaced the memo suggesting that the central question faced by the British government was 'how to persuade the French to *want* us to take some part in Europe', a question which really had only two answers: '(a) to persuade the French that our presence in Europe in some form of association with or even membership of the European Economic Community would be a positive advantage to them; or (b) to persuade the French that our absence will either fatally divide the E.E.C. or reduce its effectiveness'.[80] The Foreign Office memorandum reached a similar conclusion, one that is worth quoting at length: 'After ten years waiting we can now see that the essential core of Western Europe – that is to say, a combination which includes both France and Western Germany – has grouped itself together and already laid the ground-work of a viable, integrated entity. There is a profound and widespread desire in the countries of the Six to enjoy a larger degree of political and economic unity.... The move towards a genuine community is gathering momentum'. The British government, the report concluded, could not 'afford to be isolated from a more integrated Western Europe'.[81]

When the British Chancellor of the Exchequer Heathcoat Amory travelled with Reginald Maudling to Stockholm on

20 November 1959 to sign the final agreement establishing the European Free Trade Association, the British government had already decided that its future lay not with the Scandinavian countries but with France and Germany.[82] This sudden muddle of British European policy was noted in the press. Macmillan told his Foreign Secretary on 22 November that he had 'read the week-end press carefully and it is obvious that there is a good deal of confusion'. He himself was unclear how best to present the events in Stockholm: 'Are we to represent the Seven as a thing in itself, or merely as a bridge? Is this country to take the lead?'[83] For perhaps the first time in his career, Macmillan was uncertain how best to proceed in Europe or what Britain's role there should be, and, on 29 November, he retired to the prime ministerial country house Chequers with the Foreign Secretary, Chancellor of the Exchequer, Sir Norman Brook, Sir Roger Makins and Sir Frederick Robert Hoyer Millar to have a full and frank discussion about 'Europe and the world'.[84]

The American government continued to cause Macmillan more concern, showing 'increasing anxiety...over these developments in Europe'.[85] In early December, C. Douglas Dillon, the American Under-Secretary of State, told British ministers that 'the United States would back the Six rather than the Seven', a statement that was widely reported in the British press. Macmillan was not surprised by Dillon's attitude, given that he had served as American Ambassador to France from 1953 to 1957, but nevertheless regarded his statement as 'a considerable setback to our policy', as it was 'the first time (I believe) that their [the American government's] position has been made public in such explicit and unfavourable terms'.[86] When the cabinet met two days later, Macmillan asked his colleagues to consider 'the value of our "special relationship" with the U.S.A. if they prefer the Six as their major ally?' What were the economic and political considerations of this preference? Would it develop into an 'economic threat'? Would it affect NATO and the whole 'question of defence'? The British government had assumed it would always be America's closest ally in the post-war world, but now the American government was favouring a European organisation that excluded Britain. Could the Anglo–American 'special relationship' survive whilst Britain remained outside the EEC? These were questions Macmillan could not answer.[87]

Selwyn Lloyd took a stab at them, writing to the Prime Minister on 13 December with his 'tentative answers (prepared rather hastily)'.

The British government should support 'the Six' for a variety of reasons. If it were to oppose it, 'they will grow together just the same, and perhaps, feeding on hostility to us, faster'. It was better 'if we are felt to be specially close to it'. This would 'stop a special relationship growing up between the Six and the United States, exclusive of us', would make it 'easier for the Dutch [whom were now considered Britain's closest ally in the EEC] to influence the Six' and might allow Britain to bring about a reconciliation between de Gaulle and the American administration, thus strengthening Anglo–French relations. Whilst stopping short of recommending British entry into the EEC, Selwyn Lloyd made clear that Britain's European future lay with the Six rather than the Seven.

He also addressed the 'special relationship' with the United States. This, he assured Macmillan, did exist: 'It means preferential treatment for us in discussion and in certain types of knowledge (nuclear, intelligence, etc.). It gives us considerable influence on United States policy'. Now more than ever, it was essential not to undermine this relationship, given Britain's weakened position in the world: 'We ceased to be on an equal basis with the United States and U.S.S.R. when we gave up the Indian Empire. We have been in retreat since. We have or have had a number of albatrosses about us. By albatrosses, I mean the Iraqi Alliance, Cyprus, the disputes with Argentina and Chile over the Antarctic, Buraimi, Malta, Gibraltar, the financial settlement with Egypt, race relations in the Federation and Kenya, etc., etc.'. Britain's post-war history was not one resplendent with political victories, and the Anglo–American 'special relationship' was essential to Britain's future position in the world. This did not mean, however, that Europe could be ignored. If the United Kingdom were to once again become a significant power 'we need to play in the game both as pro-Europeans and pro-Atlantic Community'.[88]

The day after Selwyn Lloyd wrote to Macmillan, the House of Commons voted by 183 to 3 to accept a resolution 'welcoming the European Free Trade Association'.[89] This did little to cheer Macmillan, however. As he later wrote, 'Although efforts continued to be made throughout the year to bridge the gap between the two groups, the Common Market and EFTA, in spite of much good will little progress was made. If ever European unity was to be achieved, a bolder initiative would be needed'.[90] Before he could attempt such an initiative, he first had to turn back to the Empire and Commonwealth, bringing to a final close one era of Britain's world leadership before another could begin.

* * *

Harold Macmillan stood before the South African Parliament in Cape Town on 3 February 1960 as his month-long tour of Africa came to a close. Notwithstanding the Prime Minister's focus on Europe, the 1950s had been an important decade for the British Empire, following on from the trials of the 1940s which had seen the loss of India (partitioned into India, Pakistan and – later – Bangladesh), Palestine (newly renamed Israel), Burma and Sri Lanka. By 1960, the insurgency that had raged in Malaya from 1948 onwards had largely come to a close, the Federation granted independence in 1957 (although British troops remained for the following three years to extinguish the final embers of the Communist uprising). In Kenya, too, Mau Mau violence that had begun in 1952 was largely quelled by 1960 and the British governor lifted the State of Emergency on 12 January that year. After a gruelling counter-insurgency campaign, the British defeated the EOKA terrorist group in Cyprus, the Zurich agreement ending the conflict there in February 1959. Under more pacific circumstances, in January 1956, the British government granted Sudan independence, and, in March 1957, the Gold Coast also declared independence from Great Britain, renaming itself Ghana. And then, of course, there was the Suez fiasco of 1956, whose shadow seemed to linger over all other elements of British foreign policy. The speed with which the Empire was crumbling was enough to make the head of even the most demure colonial administrator spin.

Nevertheless, each of these former colonies (with the exception of the new state of Israel) chose to remain within the Commonwealth upon independence, suggesting to Macmillan that although the form of British power was changing, its sphere of world influence might still remain.[91] The key for Macmillan was to convince those who sought independence to do so in a 'civilised' and ordered manner and to convince the British public and sceptical members of the Conservative Party that this was not a failure of British imperialism, but rather the culmination of the British imperial mission. Those subjects who had fallen under British control were not rebelling against the British ideal; they had now, under British guidance, become worthy of their own self-governance in the British mould. The story of decolonisation was thus one of success rather than catastrophe.[92] Consequently, on 5 January 1960, Macmillan embarked upon a six-week tour of Africa to spread his message, travelling first through Ghana, Nigeria and the Central African Federation (with stops in Southern Rhodesia, Northern Rhodesia and Nyasaland) before arriving in South Africa to address both Houses of the South African Parliament in early February.[93] Standing before an all-white audience and seeking to distance himself and the British government from South Africa's racist policies of apartheid, Macmillan delivered what some historians have called 'one of the most iconic speeches in the history of the British empire'.[94]

'The wind of change is blowing through this continent', he told his audience, 'and, whether we like it or not, this growth of national consciousness is a political fact. We must all accept it as a fact, and our national policies must take account of it'.[95] His words had been a long time coming; he had first used the phrase 'the wind of change' earlier on his African tour in Ghana (although with much less impact). Since becoming Prime Minister, Macmillan's approach to the Empire had been characterised by 'hard-headed pragmatism rather than sentiment'.[96] In his memoirs, Macmillan writes that upon taking the premiership, he had asked himself the question, 'Was I destined to be the remodeller or the liquidator of Empire?'[97] However he chose to answer that question, what was certain was that change was coming, much to the chagrin of many of his Conservative colleagues in Parliament. Lord Salisbury, Macmillan's Leader of the House of Lords and previously Commonwealth Secretary, even resigned in protest from the government in March 1957 when Macmillan chose to release from detention the Cypriot Archbishop Makarios III.[98] There was little such resignations could do to slow the pace of inevitable change, however.

When, two years later, Macmillan initiated a 'significant acceleration' of British decolonisation policy, the long-standing Colonial Secretary Alan Lennox-Boyd also tendered his resignation, although he agreed not to make it public until after the October 1959 General Election. In the cabinet reshuffle that followed, Macmillan replaced Lennox-Boyd with Ian Macleod, a man who described himself as 'Macmillan's chosen instrument for decolonisation' and who, by the end of the year, had 'announced the end of the Kenyan emergency; overturned the Conservatives' policy of "multi-racialism" in favour of a transition to African majority rule in east Africa; and initiated Tanganyika's progress towards independence'.[99] Strengthened by an intake of fresh, young Conservative MPs who had little experience in imperial affairs, were instinctively pro-European and held personal loyalty to Macmillan, the Prime Minister determined that it was in Britain's best interests to transfer power to local elites in Africa as quickly as possible and to restore the focus of his government to economic affairs, particularly in Europe.[100]

The 'Wind of Change' speech made an immediate political splash, both at home and around the Empire and Commonwealth. Amongst the white settler population in British Africa, there was a widespread feeling that Macmillan's words signalled the end of British support for their position there, with Roy Welensky of the Federation of Rhodesia and Nyasaland describing it to Anthony Eden as the 'last act of betrayal', to Alan Lennox-Boyd as 'wrecking' all that 'we started out to achieve', and to Lord Salisbury as a policy to 'liquidate what is left of the British Empire as quickly as possible'.[101] The Australian Prime Minister Robert Menzies told Welensky, 'Our real trouble is that now that the "winds of change" have blown us into the new Commonwealth, we are...rather at the mercy of the new members', and in New Zealand the British High Commissioner in Wellington Sir Ian McLeannan was 'alarmed at the extent of public support' for the white settler communities in Africa, particularly in Rhodesia.[102] It was not long before New Zealanders, like the white populations in Australia, Rhodesia, South Africa and Kenya, perceived Macmillan's speech as heralding the end of Britain's worldwide role. Within a decade, the New Zealand newspaper *The Dominion* led with the headline 'The Day Britain Let Us Down', commenting, 'The Commonwealth has become a shadow without the substance of trust. Can we trust Britain again?'[103] Throughout the 1960s and across the white dominions, the answer seemed to be a resounding and final 'no'.

At home, the reaction was more mixed. Many Conservatives of the older generation were aghast, feeling commonality with the white populations of the Empire and fearing that Macmillan's words would usher in change that would lead to an irreversible decline of Britain's place in the world. Even Churchill expressed dissent, albeit behind closed doors, asking the cabinet secretary Sir Norman Brooks, 'Why go and pick a quarrel with those chaps [the Afrikaners]?'[104] Yet for many others, Macmillan's speech was nothing more than a reflection of the reality that now faced all Britons, at home and around the world.

Most of the British public received the speech with 'general satisfaction', and American President Eisenhower wrote that the Cape Town speech was 'masterful'.[105] By February 1960, it had become clear that Britain's future no longer lay with the Empire and Commonwealth, but rather in a Cold War alliance with the United States and an economic partnership with continental Europe. As the Conservative Party Manifesto said in 1959, British foreign policy was no longer predicated on invasive colonialism but rather on helping countries 'to nationhood within the British Commonwealth'.[106] Once Britain's colonies had reached this 'nationhood', they would very much be left to their own devices. And with the children grown and departed, the parents had the luxury of turning their hand to other endeavours. Chief amongst these, for Macmillan's government, was Europe.

11 TOWARDS THE COMMON MARKET

'No matter how much this fact may shock you, our future is in Europe not in the Commonwealth'. So opined the *Daily Mail* on Friday, 16 June 1961. George Murray, the lead writer, gently informed his readers that Britain's imperial past was now over and that its present (as well as its future) lay with the European continent: 'The British Empire, like all others, was built by power and sustained by power. When that power was removed the edifice began to crumble'. Over the past decade, this loss of power had become plain for all to see. When the British government tried to 'assert...her rights at Suez in 1956', the United States government showed the world that Britain could no longer act in a unilateral way. Would Britannia, Murray asked, 'have allowed the Royal Navy to sink to the position of a bad third if she could have prevented it? Or the R.A.F., which saved freedom in 1940, [to become] so small compared with the U.S. bomber fleet? Or... Britain [to] consent to be defended by American missiles based on her own soil?' These were the facts, Murray insisted, but not ones that should bring shame on the country: 'On the contrary, this is the price Britain has paid for her lone stand in 1940 and 1941'. And what of the Commonwealth, if the Empire had now gone? It was a 'noble experiment in multi-racial relations' which had been held together 'partly by sentiment and tradition, and partly by economic ties'. Both of these had now 'lost a great deal of their force'. As the march of time continued, Britain's ties with the Commonwealth would become only looser; it was certainly no guarantee of a future world role for the United Kingdom.

This, then, left only Europe as the vehicle in which Britain's future greatness could be driven, and it was right and proper that this be the case: 'Britain is essentially a European country. She has derived her strength from Europe, and the Empire was built up through her assertion of power on the Continent'. It was from European ground that the fountain of empire had sprung, and once the river which flowed from that fountain ran dry, the European ground below would remain – eroded, perhaps, but still viable. In seeking a place in Europe, the United Kingdom would not be tacking a new course through rough seas but would instead be returning to the safe harbour where it had always sought shelter in difficult times. George Murray, writing on behalf of the *Daily Mail*, had no doubt. It was time for the British government to join the European Economic Community (EEC).[1] If this argument might have shocked his readers in 1959 or early 1960, by June 1961 Murray was far from the first to proffer this suggestion. The following month, the British government itself officially applied to join the Common Market, hoping that the Six would agree to become Seven.

In some ways, the government's decision to enter the EEC had been made long before. Once it decided that Britain's future lay in Europe and not with the Empire or Commonwealth, it was only a matter of time before the economic strength of the Six would dictate that those within the Seven seek to join it. If Britain's future was to lie within the European continent, it only made sense to plan it in alliance with the continent's biggest states, France and Germany. Consequently, even as they negotiated with the Scandinavian countries for an alternative European Free Trade Area (EFTA), British ministers and officials had only ever envisioned the EFTA as a stepping stone policy to enable their government to gain better leverage with the Six. Indeed, as the historian Thomas Raineau has shown, in the years after the Suez Crisis officials throughout the British government had adopted a new ethos that was decidedly friendlier towards European integration. Following a rash of retirements and new recruitment, by 1960, the civil service was 'producing officials who were, if not Europhiles, at least convinced of the necessity for Britain to join the Common Market'.[2] Upon his return from Africa in February 1960, Macmillan turned immediately to his European policy. In this endeavour, he continued to run into problems with the French General Charles de Gaulle.[3]

If 1959 was an important political year for the British Prime Minister – increasing his Conservative majority in the House of Commons and stewarding an upturn of the British economy – it was an even better year for de Gaulle. Since his resignation as French Prime Minister in 1946, de Gaulle had suffered through what one historian has called his 'desert years'.[4] Yet this description is perhaps not quite apt. Whilst it is certainly true that de Gaulle spent much of 1946 brooding over his own loss of power, in April 1947 he relaunched his political career with the creation of the Rassemblement du Peuple Français, the Rally of the People of France (RPF). By May of that year, more than 800,000 Frenchmen and -women had joined his movement, and 'Gaullism' soon became an integral component of French politics, often to the dismay of those in government.

Gaullism was predicated on the notion of French greatness; of a strong France, standing as an autonomous nation-state in the league of great powers. It envisioned a France that was beholden neither to the United States nor to the Soviet Union, and one that was stronger than its allies on the European continent, particularly Germany. Above all else, it sought a France that was 'independent'. It was suspicious of international organisations such as NATO, the World Bank and the International Monetary Fund (IMF) (which it perceived as tools of the American government) and was the very antithesis of the movements for European unity and integration that had emerged in the post-war world. De Gaulle and his followers had been opposed to the creation of the European Coal and Steel Community (ECSC), had argued against the European Defence Community and viewed the newly created EEC cautiously, believing each undermined the destiny of France. As de Gaulle wrote on the first page of his war memoirs, 'All my life I have thought of France in a certain way.... The emotional side of me tends to imagine France, like the princess in the fairy stories or the Madonna in the frescoes, as dedicated to an exalted and exceptional destiny.... But the positive side of my mind also assures me that France is not really herself unless in the front rank.... In short, to my mind, France cannot be France without greatness'.[5]

In the years 1947 to 1956, although de Gaulle's ideology reached a ready audience throughout France, it was nevertheless overshadowed by the creation of the ECSC, the initial talks for the creation of the EEC and the general 'mood' in favour of supranational institutions, federalism and European unity. Paul Reynaud, the former premier of France, lampooned de Gaulle's ideas, writing, 'Naturally every patriot wants France to be a leader among nations.... But she is no longer the France of Louis XIV or of Napoleon'.[6] However, following French failures in Indo-China (soon to be called Vietnam), the disastrous campaign in Suez (an event every bit as traumatic for the French consciousness as for Britain) and the continuing insurgency in Algeria, de Gaulle's message of a greater France leading a Europe of strong nation-states in defiance of the United States struck a chord with the French people. His calls for a new constitution which would replace the primacy of the parliamentary system with strong presidential power were also immensely compelling given that France had seen seventeen Prime Ministers representing twenty-four separate governments over the past twelve years.[7]

Upon coming to power in June 1958, de Gaulle addressed the National Assembly, stepping foot inside the building for the first time since January 1946. He told them in no uncertain terms that he expected them to grant him full powers, which he would use to submit a new Constitution to the country for a referendum. Until such time as the referendum could take place, the assemblies would be prorogued. This he was granted immediately, and, as the sun set on 1 June 1958, the French parliament dissolved itself, bringing to an end the French Fourth Republic.[8] The new constitution that emerged heralded the beginning of the French Fifth Republic, strengthening the President at the expense of the Prime Minister and carving out for him a role that made him 'all-important'.[9] When this constitution was put to the French people in a referendum on 28 September 1958, they voted in its favour in overwhelming numbers, by 17,666,828 (79 per cent) to 4,624,475 (21 per cent).[10] At the first General Election of the new Fifth Republic, de Gaulle's party the Union de la Nouvelle République (the Union for the New Republic, or UNR) secured 206 of 576 seats, far more than any other party. Under the constitution, some 70,000 French notables, including all French deputies, senators, department councillors, mayors and municipal councillors, then elected a president as head of state. Standing for election for the first time in his illustrious career, de Gaulle easily won with 78 per cent of the vote. He was officially installed as President of the French Fifth Republic on 8 January 1959.[11]

Throughout 1959, de Gaulle proved to be a thorn in the side of the British government. He did all he could to thwart first the creation of an EFTA that would include the EEC and then the establishment of a group of seven outside it. Nevertheless, de Gaulle's position on European unity was ambivalent, and Macmillan sensed that his philosophy of a Europe made up of strong nation-states might have more in common with British policy than the views of previous French presidents and prime ministers. As de Gaulle later wrote in his memoirs, 'It was my belief that a united Europe could not today, any more than in previous times, be a fusion of its peoples, but that it could and should result from a systematic *rapprochement*.... My policy therefore aimed at the setting up of a concert of European States which in developing all sorts of ties between them would increase their interdependence and solidarity'.[12] These were words that could have been written by Ernest Bevin fifteen years earlier and were a far cry from the musings of Monnet, Schuman and Spaak. They betrayed a sentiment that Macmillan hoped he could manipulate to the benefit of Britain.

Consequently, in preparation for Macmillan's meeting with de Gaulle on 12 March 1960, Philip de Zulueta, Macmillan's private secretary, composed some speaking points for him to use. He noted that it was 'still not clear exactly how President de Gaulle sees the future of Europe and indeed the future of NATO'. Did he, for example, think that 'by means of the Six he can dominate Europe (the Louis XIV plan) or would he be inclined towards an Anglo–French alliance which would control Europe with American assistance?' Did he actually believe that France could 'by herself build up again into a world power or is he merely anxious to secure the best possible position for France within the Alliance?'[13] De Gaulle was as sceptical as Britain's officials about supranational institutions and federalism, yet throughout Whitehall there was uncertainty about whether his views on Europe would benefit the United Kingdom or France alone. It was this important question that de Zulueta hoped Macmillan would pose to de Gaulle during their meeting.

Macmillan did not receive an immediate answer. On the one hand, the French President told him that the 'E.E.C. is purely a commercial arrangement, and a treaty should be possible between [the] E.E.C. and [the] E.F.T.A.'. On the other, however, he refused to elaborate on that possibility. After the meeting, Macmillan noted that there was 'just a chance that I can get him to act in this dreadful Six-Seven economic situation which – if it is allowed to develop – may become really serious'.[14] He later wrote that de Gaulle believed the EEC should be 'rated with that class of affairs which are looked after by the supply and commissariat departments and scarcely worth the notice of the high command'.[15] Partly because of this dismissive attitude, when communicating with de Gaulle about Europe, Macmillan faced an up-hill battle. The French President would later describe his diplomacy with the British as an adversarial game, as a 'match' that had to be won, and he was absolutely convinced that the British government could never enter the Common Market: 'It was not surprising that Great Britain should be radically opposed to the whole venture [the EEC], since by virtue of her geography and therefore her policy, she has never been willing to see the Continent united or to merge with it herself. In a sense it might almost be said that therein lay the whole history of Europe for the past eight hundred years'.[16] De Gaulle held a distinct view of himself as an historical figure, and he perceived it his great destiny to rescue Europe from the entrapments and false promises of the British.

By early 1960, Macmillan had become concerned about de Gaulle's position and so tried to impress upon the American government the gravity of the separation of Europe, appealing for it to avoid 'encourag[ing] [the] economic division of Europe' by providing 'wholehearted support to the EEC at the expense of the EFTA'.[17] When he met with C. Douglas Dillon, the American Treasury Secretary, and Christian Herter, who had succeeded John Foster Dulles as American Secretary of State, Macmillan took a firm line. After the meeting, he reported that the Americans 'seemed rather taken aback by my vehemence', and details of their conversation were soon leaked to the American, German and French presses.[18] Sir Christopher Steel, the British Ambassador to West Germany, wrote that the German newspapers were reporting that Macmillan had 'warned' the United States that there would be 'serious economic and political consequences' if the American government continued to support the EEC, that it was Britain's 'historic role to prevent Napoleon's planned economic integration of Europe'. He also added that the newspapers claimed that Macmillan had said, 'Adenauer was reliable, but after him would come the danger of a Nazi revival'. The headlines spoke of Britain 'torpedoing' the EEC, and the newspaper commentaries took the line that 'Britain's real motives towards Europe – hostility to European integration – are now unmasked'.[19]

In Paris, the British Ambassador Sir Gladwyn Jebb had likewise seen similar news coverage and hoped that 'the Prime Minister would take an early opportunity of publicly repudiating the sentiments attributed to him'.[20] From Germany, Steel sent a second telegram suggesting that 'a mere statement that the leaks are unauthorised and inaccurate will [not] do much good.... In my view what is needed is a definite statement in the House of Commons that we have confidence in all our European allies, including Germany, and intend to proceed on this basis'.[21] Macmillan was unmoved. Contrary to his ambassadors, he *did* think that there would be grave economic and political consequences if the EEC were allowed to grow unchecked, he *had* always conceived of Britain as a moderating influence in Europe and he did indeed worry what would happen when Adenauer departed because he was the glue that held a moderate Germany together. Just fifteen years after the end of the Second World War, Macmillan firmly believed that it was impossible to predict how long West Germany's democratic stability would last. The leaks to the press were not 'inaccurate', as Steel had suggested. They captured Macmillan's message to Herter perfectly.

It was against the backdrop of these leaks and their continuing controversy that de Gaulle arrived in Britain on a state visit. At their first meeting on 5 April, Macmillan tried to persuade the general that the continuing division of the Six and the Seven was 'splitting Europe', but de Gaulle 'affect[ed] not to understand', a tactic he would use throughout the coming decade when communicating with the British government.[22] Sir Frank Lee, Permanent Secretary to the Treasury, wrote to the Earl of Cromer, the UK Executive Director of the IMF and World Bank and soon to be appointed Governor of the Bank of England, immediately after de Gaulle's visit, suggesting that it was now 'clear that we have consistently tended to under-estimate the force of the political factors which have helped to bring about the formation of the Common Market'. These political factors included, above all else, a desire to create a 'federal European state'. Any attempt to 'dilute or delay' the implementation of the Treaty of Rome was considered a sabotaging of that ultimate goal. 'Thus there has been a sort of double misunderstanding', Lee wrote, 'the failure on our part to appreciate that our efforts to secure a free trade area inevitably cut across the political aims of the Six, and a failure on the part of the Six to understand that, in however illogical a way, we sincerely believed (and believe) that the political objectives of the Six would be compatible with, and could be achieved alongside, a European Free Trade Area'. Lee could not say how de Gaulle's attitude would change; the French leader certainly did not share the goal of other European leaders for a federal European super-state. Lee was certain, however, that the American government would continue to encourage deeper integration of the Six, as it had 'never accepted the U.K. view... that economic division in Europe will lead sooner or later to political division and a weakening of the cohesion of the West'. Consequently, Lee did not believe that Britain could have both a 'special relationship' with the United States and remain detached from the EEC. The Common Market now provided Britain's best channel to American support.[23]

In public, Macmillan continued to argue to the contrary, calling for the EEC to join with the Seven in a larger European-wide Free Trade Area. He urged de Gaulle to reconsider deepening the economic integration of the Six, telling the French premier, 'I beg you to believe my anxiety in this matter is because I know that the unity of Western Europe is absolutely essential and that the close friendship of France and England is the first condition of this unity'.[24] Behind closed doors, however, he was less sure, and, on 22 April 1960, he informed Selwyn Lloyd that 'it would be a fine thing if we reconsider the case for the United Kingdom joining the European Coal and Steel Community and Euratom [the European Atomic Energy Community, which came into being with the Treaty of Rome]'.[25] He also instructed all cabinet members to explore with their departments the advantages and disadvantages of British membership of the ECSC and Euratom, asking only that 'no approach should encourage the idea that this is a surrender on [the] U.K.'s part'.[26] Whilst Macmillan stopped short of calling for British entry into the EEC, if the government chose to pursue membership of the ECSC and Euratom, eventual entry into the Common Market could only be a matter of time.

Over the course of the spring, Macmillan's convictions about Europe only hardened. On 1 May, he wrote to Paul Einzig, who had served as political and lobby correspondent for the *Financial Times* from 1939 to 1956, telling him that the French 'seem to see the Six developing into a sort of Holy Roman Empire with the addition of and dominated by France'. Whilst the Dutch liked this politically, both they and the Germans disliked the economic implications of it, particularly because they feared that the Seven might be 'driven into a closer association for trade with the iron curtain countries'. The Germans in particular feared that this would 'deprive them forever of their Eastern markets'. The British government would certainly not turn to Soviet markets under Macmillan's watch, but the wider concerns of the

Germans and Dutch were very real. Macmillan suggested that, in order to prevent a 'Holy Roman Empire' forming in opposition to the United Kingdom, the British government could play on these fears to perhaps enter and dominate the EEC on its own terms.[27] This was the first time Macmillan committed to paper his desire to join the EEC. A week later, he wrote to Selwyn Lloyd, saying, 'I think both you and I feel that it would be a good thing for us to join, if there are no obvious objections on technical grounds'.[28]

On 23 May, Macmillan called a full meeting of the cabinet to discuss the United Kingdom's relationship with Europe and, in particular, to examine a paper produced by Sir Frank Lee's Economic Steering (Europe) Committee. In this paper, Lee argued that 'even discounting political factors, we must on economic grounds maintain the broad objective of having the United Kingdom form part of a single European market'. He added that this 'could not be achieved without payment in political terms or in terms inconvenient for or damaging to such interests as the Commonwealth, domestic agriculture and our tariff policy'. Despite these political costs, Lee recommended that Britain seek 'near identification' with the Common Market, which would be 'an arrangement between the Six and the Seven going as far as possible towards acceptance by the Seven of most of the essential features of the Common Market without the formal absorption within it'.[29] Sir Roger Jackling, Assistant Under-Secretary at the Foreign Office, wished to go further, doubting whether 'anything short of an offer to join the Common Market, subject to reasonable safeguards for the Commonwealth and the working out of appropriate arrangements for those of the Seven (e.g. Austria) who could not become members, would achieve the necessary effect'.[30]

Lee's report, along with Jackling's amendment to it, caused the cabinet to seriously debate British entry into the EEC for the first time. As the historian Peter Hennessy has written, 'Lee more than any other civil servant was responsible for the decisive shift of opinion in Whitehall in favour of the Common Market'.[31] On 2 June, British officials hinted at a meeting of the Western European Union that the government might seek to join the ECSC and Euratom,[32] and, on 12 June, Macmillan confessed to Lady Rhys-Williams that 'the question of the so-called "Sixes and Sevens"' concerned him more than anything else. The 'usual defeatist quarters' of the *Times* and the *Observer* were beginning to suggest that Britain 'should surrender to the Six and, incidentally, abandon our honourable commitments to our friends in the Seven'.[33] Macmillan was still unconvinced that entry into the Common Market was the *only* way to ensure a British voice within Europe, but his doubts were rising. On 9 July, he asked his cabinet colleagues, 'Must we abandon the Seven, and British Agriculture and the Commonwealth and try and join the E.E.C., because if we don't we shall be caught between America on the one hand and Europe on the other?'[34]

To help him think through this problem, Macmillan reshuffled the cabinet on 27 July, promoting Edward Heath to become Lord Privy Seal and Foreign Minister with a special responsibility for European Affairs. Heath, a man who had given his parliamentary maiden speech in favour of British entry into the ECSC in 1950, was known to be one of the most ardent 'Europeans' in the Conservative Party.[35] Although just two days earlier Selwyn Lloyd had announced in Parliament that the government 'did not believe that the time was ripe for negotiations with the Six', this was largely interpreted to be a statement on procedure rather than eventual intent; it was evident that the European question was not being put to bed.[36] By promoting Heath to the cabinet and giving him special responsibility for Europe, Macmillan succeeded in wresting control of the European question from the more sceptical Treasury to the Foreign Office. From that moment on, it was Heath as the Lord Privy Seal rather than the Chancellor of the Exchequer who answered parliamentary questions on Europe in the House of Commons.[37]

In the same reshuffle, Macmillan moved Selwyn Lloyd from the Foreign Office to become Chancellor of the Exchequer, transferred Alec Douglas-Home from the Commonwealth Office to the Foreign Office, promoted Duncan Sandys (another leading 'European' in the Conservative Party) to become Commonwealth Secretary, made Christopher Soames (who was later to become the first British vice-president of the European Commission) Secretary of State for Agriculture and Peter Thorneycroft Aviation Secretary, surrounding himself with those in favour of British integration with Europe.[38] As historian Jacqueline Tratt has written, 'Although evidently not contrived solely for the purpose of facilitating a more easy passage for "Europeanist" ideas, the timing and nature of these cabinet changes certainly did no harm to the cause of those who advocated a radical change of direction for Britain'.[39] She adds, 'There is some irony in the fact that, in the same week that parliament was told of the reasons why Britain could not apply for membership of the EEC, a cabinet reshuffle took place, which was to make realizable the adoption of just such a policy'.[40]

Europe was now front and centre. Only days after the reshuffle, Macmillan wrote, 'The great threat to the U.K. is not nuclear war; not tariff barriers; but a weight of American capital investment in the Six. Somehow we must do a deal with the French'.[41] His mind was made up. On 1 August, in his first note to Duncan Sandys as Commonwealth Secretary, he asked him to study 'the problem of the Commonwealth in relation to Europe'. He wrote: 'At present, as you know, very few imports from Commonwealth countries pay duty in coming into the United Kingdom. If we are in the Common Market they would be hit this way. Then of course there is the question of preference. If we went into the Common Market we should give up the preferences and all that that implies. Finally, there is the question that we would really be discriminating *against* the Commonwealth'. Having outlined the problem, he gave Sandys' his charge: 'I know how keen you are on the European Movement, as I have always been. I am not satisfied that there is not a way to be found [of] getting over the Commonwealth difficulty. If you could put your acute and active mind to the study of this you would be doing a great service. It is perhaps the most urgent problem in the Free World today'.[42] Macmillan's letter to Sandys marks an important stage in the development of his thinking. For perhaps the first time, he acknowledged that it was his preference for Britain to enter the EEC. If Commonwealth interests could be protected – which he believed possible – the Six could become the Seven. If not, then it might still be necessary for Britain to join regardless.

* * *

The British government had largely been concerned with French intransigence throughout its efforts to secure a European Free Trade Area. Nevertheless, its relationship with the West German state and its Chancellor Konrad Adenauer did not go unaffected. Whilst both Anthony Eden and Churchill before him had maintained close relationships with Adenauer, the same could not be said of Macmillan. Sir Frank Roberts, Britain's permanent representative to NATO from 1957 until 1960 and then the British Ambassador in Moscow until 1962, noted that 'Macmillan was, to put it bluntly, anti-German and certainly anti-

Adenauer, while Adenauer was immensely suspicious of him and of what Macmillan was going to do, all the time'.[43] Their relationship did not improve when, in November 1958, the Soviet leader Nikita Khrushchev delivered a speech at the Polish Embassy in Moscow demanding that the Western allies remove all troops from West Berlin and cede all occupation rights, reigniting the Berlin crisis of nine years earlier. Khrushchev followed this speech with a diplomatic note to the Western Allies demanding that negotiations for the future of Berlin commence within six months.[44]

Whilst the American and French reaction to Khrushchev's note was distinctly cool and Adenauer demanded an immediate response to what he considered Soviet aggression towards the German people, the British position was more ambivalent. On 18 November – just one week after Khrushchev's speech at the Polish embassy – Selwyn Lloyd advised the cabinet that the UK government had three possibilities: first, it could abandon Berlin; second, it could institute an airlift on par with that of 1948–49; and finally, it could come to some arrangement with the authorities of the German Democratic Republic (East Germany). Lloyd recommended the third choice, as it was 'the most realistic'.[45] Khrushchev's diplomatic note did little to change this analysis. Throughout these weeks, Adenauer fell into a state of 'acute anxiety', and, on 6 December, he requested an 'urgent meeting' with Macmillan. When Macmillan gave only a 'cool response', he cancelled the meeting and instead turned to de Gaulle.[46] The following week, Adenauer withdrew German support for a wider EFTA, causing Macmillan to scribble, 'Adenauer has betrayed me'.[47]

Whilst the French and German leaders discussed the developing crisis, Macmillan embarked on an official visit to the Soviet Union, hoping to defuse the situation diplomatically. He succeeded in persuading Khrushchev to abandon his six-month deadline and instead attend a meeting of Foreign Ministers in Geneva in the late spring and summer of 1959 but only by agreeing to discuss possible Western recognition of East Germany as a permanent state at this meeting. Adenauer immediately accused Macmillan of failing to protect the interests of West Germany, and even a visit by the Prime Minister to Bonn could not assuage the Germany Chancellor's fears. Macmillan's Russia trip 'marked the start of an unchecked decline in Anglo–German relations', a decline which perhaps inevitably strengthened the relationship between Adenauer and de Gaulle.[48] As far as Macmillan was concerned, the collapse of Anglo–German relations was the price he had to pay to secure peace with the Soviet Union. Sir Bernard Ledwidge, who from 1956 to 1961 was the Foreign Office political advisor in Berlin, remembered that Macmillan was 'constantly saying during the [Berlin] crisis, everything could easily be settled if only we didn't have to pay so much attention to Adenauer and the Federal Germans'.[49] His disregard for West Germany only further isolated Britain from its continental neighbours.

Furthermore, little came of the meeting of Foreign Ministers in Geneva beyond the continued cooling of Anglo–German relations. Selwyn Lloyd reported to Macmillan in May 1959 that 'The German Government is in a curious situation: Adenauer is still Chancellor, though he is soon to become President. He has become – like many very old men – vain, suspicious, and grasping. . . . [He] has been carrying on a great campaign of vilification of Her Majesty's Government and especially of me. I am Neville Chamberlain reincarnate, and so on'.[50] The German government could see only danger in a dialogue with the Soviet Union, but Macmillan still spotted opportunity. In any case, Adenauer's presence would continue in the German government. Within days of Selwyn Lloyd's memorandum, Adenauer announced that he would in fact not be standing for the Presidency but would instead remain Chancellor, citing the 'international danger' which had come about 'due to British weakness towards Russia'.[51] When the meeting of Foreign Ministers finally dissolved in August, little had been accomplished, and only after a personal visit from Khrushchev to the United States did American President Eisenhower announce that he had agreed to a Summit in Paris with the American, British, French and Soviet governments, to be held in May 1960, with the West German government invited as observers.[52] This was an American initiative, however. Macmillan's diplomacy had few results to show.

In preparation for this summit, Selwyn Lloyd travelled to France in November 1959, where he found de Gaulle 'affable and relaxed'.[53] The following week, Adenauer visited London for talks with Macmillan which, after a luncheon at the German Embassy, continued at Chequers. Although it was clear that Adenauer 'had been told by his advisers to make an effort to be polite',[54] Macmillan reproached him 'for his attacks on HMG and spoke very strongly'.[55] Adenauer was initially 'startled and angry' by Macmillan's tone, but, over the course of the conversation, his position softened. Following the meeting, Macmillan wrote that '[O]n the whole, the visit has done good. The Germans are pleased – although they fear that the old man [Adenauer] will probably have another relapse into his suspicions and fears. The trouble is that they are all afraid of him'.[56]

Beyond his problems with Adenauer, Macmillan had another reason to pay close attention to West Germany. He had noticed a rise in anti-German feeling in Britain over the course of the previous few years which threatened to derail any remaining plans for closer cooperation with the European continent. He wrote to Selwyn Lloyd that 'Apart from the papers which specialise in working up anti-German feeling (chiefly Beaverbrook, etc.) there is I think a genuine apprehension'. This stemmed both from an instinctive jealousy at the economic rise of West Germany so soon after the war and from a feeling that nobody could be certain 'how many ex-Nazis are in fact employed either in the Army, Civil Service or judiciary'. Britain may have won the war, but its people were unconvinced that they were winning the peace. Macmillan hoped to 'have a word' with his Foreign Secretary about 'how to deal with it'.[57]

The Paris Summit in May 1960 did little to ease British tensions with either France or Germany. It did, however, end any hopes Macmillan harboured of a rapprochement with the Soviet Union. The reason for this was that, on 5 May, only days before the conference was due to begin, Khrushchev announced that an American U-2 spy plane had been shot down over Russian territory. Although the conference went ahead as scheduled, it was completely overshadowed by the controversy and achieved nothing. Macmillan later wrote, 'Before the third week of May had reached its close the grand edifice which I had worked so long and so painfully to build seemed totally and finally destroyed'.[58] It soon became clear that there was little hope of resurrecting that edifice. On 20 May, Khrushchev announced that he would have no further discussions over Berlin until a new American President was chosen in November 1960.[59]

The election of John F. Kennedy and his inauguration in January 1961 promised to provide a break in the deadlock. In his inauguration speech, Kennedy made no mention of Berlin or the Soviet Union, and his approach seemed to share more in common with Macmillan than Adenauer, de Gaulle or Eisenhower. Whereas Eisenhower had 'really gone over to the idea of his own military, that the nuclear bomb was the only weapon which could defend Berlin', Kennedy took a more nuanced approach, prompting both de Gaulle and

Adenauer to accuse him of weakness – an accusation they also levelled at Macmillan.[60] By April 1961, however, the position of the new American administration hardened, particularly after Khrushchev issued a new ultimatum on Berlin.[61] Kennedy appointed Dean Acheson, the former American Secretary of State, to write a report on Berlin. Acheson informed the American National Security Council (NSC) that confrontation with the Soviet Union over the city was likely in 1961. Furthermore, he argued that American force could be justified to achieve three basic objectives: '(i) [to secure] the freedom of the people of West Berlin to choose their own system; (ii) [to protect] the presence of Western troops so long as the people required and desired them; and (iii) [to maintain] unimpeded access from the West to the city'.[62] Acheson also met with Macmillan and Alec Douglas-Home, who had replaced Selwyn Lloyd as Foreign Secretary the previous July. In what was described by Macmillan as a 'blood-curdling' presentation, Acheson outlined which military actions needed to be taken in Berlin, including sending tanks down the autobahn into West Berlin. Macmillan argued that the crisis could still be resolved diplomatically, but Acheson's mind was made up.

Macmillan's faith in the new American administration was further undermined on 17 April when the United States launched the ill-fated Bay of Pigs landing in Cuba, a military operation that Macmillan had no prior knowledge of.[63] In June, Kennedy met with Khrushchev in Vienna but undercut his own negotiating position when he acquiesced that a permanent division of Berlin might indeed be necessary. Meanwhile, the East German President Walter Ulbricht protested to Khrushchev that he was facing a crisis in the German Democratic Republic, with approximately 3.5 million East Germans (20 per cent of the total population) having fled to the West through Berlin since the end of the war.[64] With the flood of refugees from East Germany reaching 3,000 per day by August 1961, on the thirteenth of that month Khrushchev gave permission to Ulbricht to build the Berlin Wall, physically separating East Berlin from the West on a permanent basis and demonstrating in a highly visible manner the division of Europe.[65]

It is perhaps ironic that it was against the backdrop of this physical separation of Berlin, with relations between the West and the Soviet Union falling to a new low and deep divisions opening up between the British, Americans, French and West Germans, that the British government decided to do something that only months before had seemed so impossible. The cabinet concluded that it was time for Britain to join 'Europe', as the six countries of the Common Market had now almost universally become known.

* * *

On 27 February 1961, just days after Khrushchev issued his second ultimatum to the West, Edward Heath – Lord Privy Seal and Minister of State for Foreign Affairs, with special responsibility for European Affairs – stood before the Western European Union Council of Ministers and announced that Britain was prepared to contemplate 'a fundamental change of principle' in its approach to the EEC. The British government was now ready to adopt a 'common tariff' and to 'participate in the political consultation of the Six if unanimously invited to do so'.[66] In essence, Heath had announced that the British government wished to join the Common Market. It had only to be asked.

Heath's announcement came after six months of intense debate by ministers, officials and the press within Britain.[67] In August 1960, Macmillan set in train a series of discussions to examine British entry into the EEC, asking the new Commonwealth Secretary, Duncan Sandys, to study how to 'reconcile Commonwealth interests with our being in the Common Market'; forming a cabinet committee on 12 August to investigate the various paths the British government could follow to join the EEC; and, at the Commonwealth Finance Ministers meeting on 20–21 September, informing those present that the United Kingdom intended to move closer to the Common Market, if not to join it fully. In December, following the November election of John F. Kennedy, the British government received information from its embassies in the United States and West Germany that the president-elect had requested papers on European integration, and a source in Sweden suggested that Kennedy's chief advisor was a 'pro-Six man'.[68] The Earl of Cromer, the economic minister at the Washington Embassy (and soon to be appointed Governor of the Bank of England), suggested that the new administration would not 'want to carry on just the same way as their predecessors'.[69] British influence with the new American government could only be strengthened with closer ties to the EEC.

Towards the end of that month, the Foreign Office requested further information from the British ambassador in Washington Sir Harold Caccia, telling him that the government was 'waiting with great interest to see what policy the new Administration will follow on the Six/Seven issue'.[70] Caccia confirmed that Kennedy was unlikely to do anything that would disrupt the Common Market and advised that it was 'essential to bring the two European economic groups together if the Western world is to present a properly organised and united front in the cold war'. He added that it was important for the British government to 'move as rapidly as we can towards an economic system embracing the North American countries as well as the rest of Europe'.[71] It could only do this, he advised, if the new administration fully understood the British position. Consequently, in the New Year, the Foreign Office composed a memorandum for selected members of the new US administration. It explained that it was the 'policy of the United Kingdom Government ... to work for a united Europe – politically, economically, and commercially'. The government had joined the Seven, it claimed, as a 'means to [an] end', the end being a 'wider European arrangement which would include both the Six and the Seven'. It had never intended Europe to be divided into two rival trading blocs. Its objective now was to 'promote the closest possible unity between Western European countries without damaging the integrity of the E.E.C.' whilst also taking into account its 'relations with the Commonwealth' and 'the differences between the system of agricultural support in force in the United Kingdom and that envisaged in the common agricultural policy now under discussion by the Six'. The British government no longer ruled out joining the Common Market and, contingent on appropriate arrangements being made for Commonwealth trade and British agriculture, was willing to enter negotiations to that end.[72]

Only days after providing this policy memorandum to the Kennedy administration, Heath wrote to Macmillan to inform him that he had met with the Dutch ambassador who advised him that the Dutch government would raise the question of British EEC membership at the meeting of the Foreign Ministers of the Six, due to take place on 31 January.[73] Macmillan received Heath's telegram in Paris, where he had travelled on 27 January for talks with de Gaulle. On the day he arrived, the *Daily Mail* opined that 'Britain has not known since the war what she wanted'. The government had also never 'fully faced' the fact that Britain, 'though still a very great nation, is no longer a first-ranking Great Power'. It explained: 'At any time in the post-war decade Britain could have had the leadership of Europe for the asking. She rejected it, because she continued to regard herself as an imperial and oceanic power. Now, the Empire has almost gone and Britain is one among a number of equal, sovereign Commonwealth states. In the meantime Europe has forged ahead'. It was the British government's continued allusions of grandeur that had kept it from fully embracing Europe. Now the era of British imperial greatness was over. The *Daily Mail* concluded: 'The danger is that a lack of aim and direction will induce a "couldn't care less" frame of mind in the population at large. This nation possesses great qualities of heart and mind and huge reserves of talent, energy, and "know-how". But if these are to be used to the full, one thing more is needed. A sense of purpose'.[74] Whilst the *Daily Mail* did not spell out what that sense of purpose should be, it strongly hinted that it lay in Europe rather than with what was left of the Empire and Commonwealth.

Whether or not Macmillan read the newspapers that morning, when meeting de Gaulle he pitched the idea that 'Europe should be united, politically and economically; but France and Great Britain [should] be something more than European Powers and be so recognised by the U.S.A.'.[75] De Gaulle, he noted in his diary, 'seemed genuinely attracted by my themes'.[76] Whilst in Paris, Macmillan also received a telegram from Adenauer, informing him that although the Western countries were, 'perhaps inevitably, less united in their policies [than the Soviet bloc]', Western statesmen had nevertheless to 'do their best to achieve a greater Western unity'.[77] Macmillan agreed, although in the secrecy of his diary was less gracious: 'the large economic issues wh[ich] face the world they [the Germans] affect not to understand. In other words, they are rich and selfish – and German'.[78] Nevertheless, Heath's telegram detailing the Dutch attitude, Adenauer's on Germany, and his own conversations with de Gaulle convinced Macmillan that the tide was turning in Britain's favour, and, on 7 February 1961, he informed the French President that the United Kingdom was 'not opposed to joining in political consultations with the Six'.[79]

Macmillan could not entirely rely on the continent, however. He recognised that if the British government was to be successful in its negotiations with the Six, particularly in securing concessions for the Commonwealth, it would need the support of the United States. Beyond the necessity of using some British territories to further its aims in the Cold War, however, the American government had always been lukewarm about British imperial concerns and thus was unlikely to have much sympathy for Commonwealth concerns. Consequently, the Prime

Minister tasked Caccia to explain to Dean Rusk, the new American Secretary of State, both the necessity of the Commonwealth to British interests and Britain's policy towards Western Europe. Turning first to the Commonwealth, Caccia told Rusk that over the past thirteen years – since 1948 – the Commonwealth had undergone a dramatic change, evolving from a 'tightly knit association of predominantly Anglo-Saxon States, with their overwhelmingly white population of some 70 millions', to a 'multi-racial society of close to 700 million, some 80% of whom are of Asian or African descent'. The four original dominions (Canada, Australia, New Zealand and South Africa) had now 'fully achieved their own entirely international personalities', although were still 'firmly in the Western camp'. The new Commonwealth countries, however, presented 'major problems' as well as 'a major challenge and opportunity'. The opportunity lay in Britain's ability to 'exert wide influence through her Commonwealth partners, who straddle the world and most of whom occupy important positions in their own regions'. In the context of the Cold War, this gave the West an enormous strategic advantage. It was therefore in the best interests of the United States to support Britain's endeavours in the Commonwealth.[80]

Caccia next turned to Europe. It was, he said, 'the firm conviction of the United Kingdom Government that their close and special relations with the Commonwealth, the United States and Western Europe are not incompatible one with the other'. Nevertheless, British participation in the EEC would 'inevitably place some strain on our relations with the Commonwealth', as was made evident at the Commonwealth Finance Ministers meeting the previous September, when both Canada and New Zealand expressed considerable opposition to Britain forging closer links with the Common Market. The British sympathised with the old dominions, as the economic consequences of Britain joining the EEC would 'to some extent be bound to damage particular Commonwealth interests'. It was for this reason that the government had to tread carefully in Europe, negotiating an entry that would safeguard Commonwealth interests to the greatest extent. If it did not do so, instead jumping in with two feet the consequences be damned, there could be 'damage to the rest of the Commonwealth to a degree which could not fail to weaken seriously the structure of the Commonwealth as a whole'. Because it was essential that the Commonwealth remained oriented towards the West as a vital buffer against the spread of communism, the British government had to carefully balance its own economic interests in joining the EEC with its prior commitments to the Commonwealth. Caccia hoped that Rusk would see the importance of both. For the sake of the Western position in the Cold War, the British government could not afford to isolate the Commonwealth. The American government should therefore support the UK in its negotiations to join the Common Market and allow it the space and patience to do so properly.[81]

It was following Caccia's meeting with Rusk – and after assurances from the French, West German and Dutch leaders – that on 27 February Heath announced publicly at the WEU Council of Ministers that the United Kingdom wished to enter political consultations with the ECC. This did not mean that all would be smooth sailing, however, and the British government immediately faced a backlash from the Commonwealth, particularly from the Australian and New Zealand governments. In early April, the Prime Minister travelled to the United States, where he met Kennedy alone for forty-five minutes, with no advisors or staff members present. The President seemed to 'understand and sympathise' with most of Britain's plans for entry into the EEC but was unsure 'how far he [would] be able to go with de Gaulle to help me'. Kennedy was travelling to Paris in late May and would do his best to promote the British position, but he could make no promises.[82]

On 15 April, Macmillan attempted to persuade leading members of the Commonwealth that Britain's position was right, explaining to Robert Menzies (the Australian Prime Minister) and Keith Holyoake (the New Zealand Prime Minister) that the US administration 'believed it would be better if the United Kingdom were to join the political associations of the Six, where they would provide an element of stability'. He had already explained this to John Diefenbaker, the Canadian Prime Minister, two days earlier during a visit to Ottawa. Macmillan promised to 'not overlook the interests of other Commonwealth countries' and hoped that the Six would 'recognise the need to make special provision in favour of Commonwealth trade'. Nevertheless, he admitted to Menzies and Holyoake that there would be 'some economic disadvantage' both to the UK and to the rest of the Commonwealth. This was perhaps inevitable: '[T]he real choice may well be between maintaining a system of Commonwealth preferences with a United Kingdom of declining economic strength and surrendering some of the advantages of the preferential system in return for a stronger United Kingdom and a wider European market'.[83] Macmillan was convinced that the latter path was the wisest route to go.

Holyoake disagreed, telling Macmillan that 'while important political advantages would accrue in the case of the United Kingdom they would notwithstanding our common political interests have no such direct significance to New Zealand'. For this reason, his government was 'more alert to the direct economic consequences of an association between the Six and the United Kingdom'. He was 'deeply concerned lest the achievement of European unity should result in restriction in market outlets for our products'. He also corrected Macmillan on his assumptions: 'For New Zealand the real choice is not one of maintaining a system of Commonwealth preferences with a United Kingdom of declining economic strength or of surrendering some advantages of preferential system in return for a stronger United Kingdom and a wider European market. Preferences are important to us but not vital.... What is vital to us, however, is the maintenance of unrestricted duty and duty free entry to the United Kingdom which our products at present enjoy'. Without this, Holyoake could see 'no prospect' of the New Zealand government ever supporting British entry into the EEC.[84]

In the grand scheme of things, Holyoake's support counted for very little, however. In the United Kingdom itself, most members of Macmillan's cabinet – like the Prime Minister – were now more concerned with securing Britain's economic future than protecting its sentimental past through its Commonwealth ties. At a meeting on 20 April 1961, Reginald Maudling, the President of the Board of Trade, suggested that Britain would suffer economically in the long run if it did not soon enter the EEC and argued that British industry was becoming 'aware of the advantages' of belonging to 'one of the largest and most dynamic markets in the world'. Duncan Sandys, the Commonwealth Secretary, likewise thought it worthwhile to enter negotiations for entry to see 'whether terms could be arranged to safeguard Commonwealth interests'. Christopher Soames, the Minister of Agriculture, thought that the long-term damage of staying out would be greater than the short-term damage of going in. In his view, 'the sooner we could join the Six the better so that we could influence the remaining stages of the developing agricultural policy'. With both the Commonwealth and Agriculture ministers in favour of British entry, it was unlikely that the opposing arguments of Commonwealth prime ministers and British farmers would hold much sway. As a whole, the cabinet concluded that '[i]ndustrially, the case for joining was overwhelming', and although farmers would be opposed, 'British agriculture was quite efficient enough to hold its own against European competition'. In general, 'the degree of surrender of national sovereignty involved was acceptable'.[85]

The following week, the cabinet continued its discussion, Macmillan unveiling what he called 'The Grand Design' (borrowing the phrase from Selwyn Lloyd's plan of four years earlier, who had himself taken the phrase from Ernest Bevin's 1946 plan for Europe). Meeting from half past ten in the morning until after one o'clock in the afternoon, the cabinet had an 'excellent discussion on Europe', and Macmillan was very pleased with the 'intellectual power of the discussion, as well as the high sense of drama and responsibility'.[86] Although Rab Butler, the Home Secretary, was 'dubious' about the loss of sovereignty and the short-term damage entry would do to particular parts of British agriculture, both the Minister of Agriculture and the Minister of Labour assured him that, in the long-term, Britain would lose more than it would gain from remaining outside the Common Market. The most delicate part of the discussion concerned the relationship between Britain and the Commonwealth, but even here Sandys was confident that Commonwealth interests could be protected in the negotiations. Overall, the cabinet was united in wishing to see British entry.[87]

Nevertheless, by mid-May 1961 the outcome remained 'very delicate'. Although in April there had been early indications that agricultural and Commonwealth interests could be protected, by 17 May the situation had changed, Macmillan noting in his diary that 'The Commonwealth and Agricultural interests are anxious, even alarmed. The French seem more flexible'. Even Duncan Sandys – the leading light of the European Movement and its first secretary – began to have doubts, joining Rab Butler in raising concerns that the Commonwealth may not be protected after all. Sandys vision for Britain and Europe had always been one of Europe and the Commonwealth co-existing, perhaps even of a joint European Commonwealth. Now that entry into the EEC implied injury to the Commonwealth and perhaps a lessening of Commonwealth ties, he was becoming far less enthusiastic.[88]

It was not only Sandys whose pro-European sentiments were challenged by possible entry into the Common Market. On 19 May,

Christopher Soames spoke to the Conservative Party's 1922 Committee (made up of all backbench Conservative MPs) about the government's plans but 'was *not* very successful'. The Press was divided, too, with Lord Beaverbrook's newspapers – the *Daily Express*, the *Sunday Express* and the *Evening Standard* – all 'already hysterical in opposition', and the *Times*, the *Daily Telegraph*, the *Daily Mail* and the *Daily Mirror* broadly sympathetic. Such sympathy did little to overcome Conservative fears about the effects of EEC membership on the Commonwealth, however. Macmillan acknowledged that 'there are many very *anxious* Conservatives' and feared that it was 'getting terribly like 1846', when the young Benjamin Disraeli denounced the then Conservative Prime Minister Sir Robert Peel's decision to repeal the Corn Laws, leading to a schism within the Conservative Party that took more than a generation to heal.[89] That Macmillan chose to describe the debates over British entry into the EEC in such terms showed how much Conservative sentiment to Europe had hardened in less than a decade, in large part due to the dawning realisation that European integration would more closely resemble continental federal ideas than the British vision of a Europe of closely cooperating but independent nation-states.

The Prime Minister's suspicions were confirmed on 22 May, when the *Sunday Express* ran a leading article demanding a General Election before the government decided the European issue, placing its commitment to join the EEC at the heart of its election manifesto for the British public to judge. It claimed that the Home Secretary R. A. Butler had now 'definitely decided to play the role of Disraeli – break the Government and lead the orthodox "Country Party" to the defence of British Agriculture and the Commonwealth'. Macmillan was unconvinced this was true, but feared that Beaverbrook's commentaries would create a narrative of a Tory party at war with itself over Europe, thus casting doubt upon the government's policy and raising suspicions within the general public.[90]

To counter this shift in public opinion, at the end of May, the cabinet agreed that Macmillan should send a telegram to the Commonwealth Prime Ministers; that Sandys would visit Australia, New Zealand and Canada in person to explain the government's position; and that other ministers would visit the newer areas of the Commonwealth.[91] It was later decided that Heath would go to Cyprus; Lord Perth to the West Indies; Thorneycroft to India, Pakistan, Malaya and Ceylon; and John Hare to the African continent, including Ghana, Nigeria, Sierra Leone and Kenya. These tours began in late June and lasted until the middle of July. They represented a remarkable expenditure for the government, one aimed not directly at the British public but rather to sell their European policy in person to the Commonwealth leaders and provide a counterargument to that put forward in the Beaverbrook press. If they could win over the Commonwealth, ministers were sure they could gain back the support of the vast majority of the Conservative Party.[92] Those tasked to go overseas met with the Prime Minister at Chequers on 18 June and agreed to take the line that the government would be unable to 'make an assessment of the conditions [of entry] which would meet our own requirements and those of the Commonwealth' without first entering negotiations. The government would therefore apply to accede, at which point they would discover the attitude of the Six towards the Commonwealth. Under no circumstances would they allow negotiations to continue at the expense of the Commonwealth, and therefore there was no risk in beginning negotiations immediately.[93]

Beaverbook was unconvinced by the government's arguments, the *Daily Express* headlining on 5 June that the choice was now 'the Empire OR Europe: It cannot be both'. The *Express* provided its own explanation for the sudden turn in public opinion: 'People are waking up now because they have suddenly begun to fear that talk may give way to action; and that the Government may actually be thinking of going in'.[94] Two days later, it warned that, should the government succeed in its aims, 'Britain would be separated from her Empire trading partners and eventually would have to give up part of her political sovereignty'.[95] If the Empire and Commonwealth were once seen as providing the strength and stability that allowed the United Kingdom to lead Europe from within, the Beaverbook press now claimed that Europe and the Empire were fundamentally incompatible. A British decision to enter the EEC would spell an end to the Commonwealth and thus bring to a close 300 years of a glorious imperial past.

In the face of this press onslaught, on 8 June Macmillan was presented with an honorary degree from Cambridge University. That same day, Jean Monnet also received an honorary Cambridge degree, and the two were able to meet informally and in congenial circumstances. Although the latter's degree was completely unrelated to Macmillan's (his having nothing to do with European affairs), the Prime Minister nevertheless took this as a 'happy omen for European unity'.[96] It was not to be. On 15 June, Labour backbench MPs in the House of Commons pressed Macmillan to produce a White Paper 'setting out the obligations which membership of the Common Market would entail'. He feared such a White Paper would make the Treaty of Rome seem necessarily more onerous than it would turn out to be in practice and therefore asked Philip de Zulueta, his private secretary, to begin work on a 'rather long and complicated document giving an analysis of the Treaty of Rome, perhaps paragraph by paragraph', which would bore rather than enlighten its readers.[97] De Zulueta did as asked, and, on 13 July, Her Majesty's Stationary Office published a thirty-one-page document of dense, technical prose that only those having the greatest will would be able to decipher.[98] On the day of its publication, Macmillan addressed the Conservative Party's 1922 Committee of backbenchers – the first time he had personally done so on the European issue – and was 'rather nervous about it, having heard talk about great discontent in the Party'. However, the White Paper seemed to have done the trick, and the questions he faced were 'not hostile'. Overall, he received a strong reception from his backbenchers, leading him to believe that the hostility to Europe might be more in the imaginings of Lord Beaverbook and the *Daily Express* than in the Conservative Party at large.[99]

Meanwhile, ministers travelled throughout the Commonwealth seeking support for the government's European policy. They had with them a brief prepared by the Cabinet Office laying out the government's view. The EEC, it claimed, was 'developing into a really effective political and economic force' which had 'acquired a dynamic of its own'. It was likely to become a 'dominating influence' in Western Europe and might even develop into a bloc to rival both the United States and the Soviet Union. If Britain failed to enter the Common Market, its influence in Europe would decrease and its 'special relationship' with the United States would be placed in jeopardy, as the latter would 'inevitably tend to attach increasing weight to the views and interests of the Six'. If the United Kingdom lost its influence both in Europe and with the United States, it would cease to be a world power. This would 'gravely impair our usefulness to the Commonwealth. As a result the part which the Commonwealth as a whole could play in world affairs might be seriously affected'. Only by Britain joining 'Europe' could the Commonwealth have any hope of being an influential organisation in the world. The briefing paper concluded, '[I]t is as the centre of the

Commonwealth that we shall be able to play a leading part in an enlarged E.E.C. ... [W]e shall only be able to retain this leading role if we keep our links with the Commonwealth strong'. The Commonwealth, it argued, had nothing to fear from British entry into the Common Market. It had everything to gain.[100]

The Commonwealth leaders still did not see it this way. Although Lee Kuan Yew, the Prime Minister of Singapore, indicated to Thorneycroft that he was quite happy for Britain to enter the Common Market, other Commonwealth leaders were less keen.[101] Sandys found the New Zealand press 'distinctly hostile', and 'Holyoake and his colleagues were jumpy and on the defensive'.[102] In Australia, Sandys encountered an even tenser climate, the Commonwealth Secretary engaging in a 'most difficult meeting'. The Australian ministers insisted that 'British membership of [the] E.E.C. would inevitably weaken [the] political ties of [the] Commonwealth' and stated that 'whether we negotiate or not is our business and that they therefore have no right to object, implying clearly that they do in fact object'.[103] In Ottawa, Sandys experienced 'the same anxieties...about the possible political consequences on Commonwealth relations if we join the Common Market',[104] and from India Thorneycroft reported that Indian ministers 'evinced a number of real anxieties on both the political and economic front. They have an ideological dislike of a rather intangible kind of what seems to them likely to turn into a getting together of the industrial countries at the expense of the developing countries'.[105] Macmillan had hoped that the visits of ministers in person would persuade the Commonwealth leaders to support Britain's European policy, but in this regard the mission failed. Sandys reported on 15 July that most Commonwealth Prime Ministers had conceded that if Britain did join the EEC, they would 'not wish to behave in a resentful way. They would do their best to maintain the Commonwealth relationship unimpaired and so prevent their fears being realised'.[106] That was hardly the ringing endorsement for British policy that Macmillan had hoped for, however.

Throughout these weeks, the *Daily Express* continued to stir up anti-European sentiment, telling its readers on 19 July that 'Mr. Macmillan – if he is determined on a link-up with the Six – cannot join the Common Market except at the expense of a Commonwealth sell-out'.[107] It also linked its defence of the Commonwealth in the face of the European 'threat' with a revival of anti-German sentiment and an explicit attempt to link the EEC with Germany's war aims of the 1940s, claiming that Walter Hallstein, the first President of the European Commission, '[a]lthough no Nazi himself, . . . succeeded in holding university posts undisturbed under Hitler. . . . Diplomats who knew him say he was doctrinaire, almost without humour, but with a highly developed political sense. All his life, work has been his only hobby. He is still unmarried. Friends say he has never had time for courtship. The union of Europe must seem a satisfying substitute as he surveys the Continent from his big office in Brussels'. The article concluded: 'Only the growing opposition inside this country stands between Walter Hallstein and his next aim – to rope in Britain on Hallstein's terms'.[108] It was a deeply personal attack, and one that was quite shameless in linking the Common Market with Germany's National Socialist past, pitted against a Commonwealth standing independently of continental Europe. UK entry into the EEC would not be Britain's finest hour, but an act of surrender.

The cabinet took no notice. On 21 July 1961, at a fully attended meeting (with the exception of Selwyn Lloyd, now the Chancellor of the Exchequer), ministers unanimously agreed that Macmillan should announce the following Monday that the government would apply for entry into the EEC.[109] The day before, the Conservative MP Edward Boyle wrote to Macmillan, telling him that the 'anti-Europeans' were '*organised* – in the Press, in the House, and to some extent in the country generally; they consist in considerable measure of militant politicians (of both parties) who know just what they are *against* – though it is not easy to discern with any precision what they are really *for*'. The position of the pro-Europeans was just the reverse: 'They are not organised, either in the House or outside; they are not, for the most part, tremendously strong party politicians; but they are all of them – I believe – trying conscientiously to work out a sensible interpretation of Britain's position in the world of the 1960's'. Macmillan's job, Boyle contended, was to organise the pro-Europeans to as great an extent as the anti-Europeans, although he could not see 'how the Conservative Party can avoid some sort of split on this issue'.[110] It would certainly be the campaign of his life if he was able to pull it off.

With the cabinet standing behind him and with Boyle's warning still ringing in his ears, the Prime Minister knew it would be a long road ahead. On 31 July, he announced in the House of Commons that the government had decided to seek entry into the EEC, a decision which he wrote in his memoirs could be regarded 'as a turning-point in our history'.[111] There followed on the third and fourth of August a debate in the Commons on the motion that 'this House supports the decision of Her Majesty's Government to make formal application under Article 237 of the Treaty of Rome in order to initiate negotiations to see if satisfactory arrangements can be made to meet the special interests of the United Kingdom, of the Commonwealth and of the European Free Trade Association'.[112] When it came time for a division, the Labour opposition abstained, with the exception of four who voted against the motion. On the government's benches, twenty-two abstained and only one voted against. The motion therefore passed by 313 votes to 5, although it was an entirely partisan affair. The Labour opposition would not vote against the motion, but nor did they wish their names to be associated with the decision to enter the EEC.[113]

After the great debate in the House of Commons, Macmillan sat down before a BBC television camera to address the nation. 'I know that some people think if we were in the Common Market, the Commonwealth family would never be quite the same again', he said. 'And I can understand that feeling, although I do not believe it to be true. But the Commonwealth depends, of course, on sentiment and memories of the past. But important as these are, it must look to the future. And the future of the Commonwealth depends upon whether Britain has the will and the strength to lead'. He concluded, 'I believe that if we can get these arrangements with Europe, Britain will be a better and stronger member of the Commonwealth'.[114] The decision was made, the die had been cast. The United Kingdom was placing its bets on Europe. On 10 August 1961, the British government submitted its application to join the EEC.[115]

12 THE RISE OF THE ANTI-MARKETEERS

A week before the House of Commons' vote authorising negotiations for entry into the Common Market, Sir Derek Walker-Smith (Minister of Health from 1957 to 1960), Robert Turton (Minister of Health from 1955 to 1957) and Hamar Nicholls (Parliamentary Secretary at the Ministry of Agriculture from 1955 to 1957), supported by the Conservatives Lord Hinchingbrooke, John Biggs-Davidson and Anthony Fell, tabled a motion in the House expressing their 'fear' that British sovereignty would be imperilled by an entry into the European Economic Community (EEC). In all, forty-nine Conservatives signed the motion. Although many of these were unwilling to defy the government in the debate that followed, Fell did vote in opposition and a further twenty Conservative MPs abstained.[1] This motion and the subsequent abstentions signalled the first organised attempt in the House of Commons to oppose the government's European policy. Ironically, it came from the Conservative rather than the Labour benches.

It was not only in the House of Commons that rumblings were stirring. On the day of the vote, Anthony Montague Browne sent to Philip de Zuleuta a copy of a letter delivered to Winston Churchill, which Browne claimed was 'typical of many being addressed to Sir Winston'.[2] The letter-writer purported to be 'worried to death lest we join the Common Market', which she thought 'inevitably means the end of the Commonwealth which is dreadful to contemplate'. She continued, 'Is Mr. Macmillan out of his mind and has he no feeling for our country, sovereign rights and world prestige? . . . I feel it will be nothing less than a tragedy to upset Canada, Australia, New Zealand and other countries linked with us'.[3] Churchill himself was doing little to dissuade those who wrote to him, telling the chairman of the Woodford Division Conservative Association that although Britain 'might well play a great part in these developments [on the continent] to the profit not only of ourselves, but of our European friends also', Britain nevertheless had 'another role which we cannot abdicate: that of leader of the British Commonwealth'. Churchill's vision of Europe, he said, 'had never contemplated the diminution of the Commonwealth', instead favouring a united European Commonwealth. If Britain's European policy were to come into conflict with its support for the Commonwealth, Churchill would choose the Empire and Commonwealth over Europe every time.[4]

Macmillan himself admitted to Queen Elizabeth II that 'sentiment and tradition made many Conservatives unwilling to associate themselves more closely with Europe'. Nevertheless, he was convinced that British entry into the EEC was the only way to make Britain a 'strong, active, and well-balanced country economically', and this in itself would make the United Kingdom 'a better member of the Commonwealth and more fit to lead it'. Over time, the Conservative Party would recognise this and become more 'fluid, ready to move with the times, and, especially among the younger men, anxious to seize new opportunities'.[5] Opposition within the party to closer relations with Europe was a generational issue, which would pass with time. It was understandable that those who had served in the Empire or governed on its behalf were reticent to contemplate a lessening of Commonwealth ties in favour of greater integration with Europe. Yet amongst the younger generation, there was a growing recognition that the wind of change was indeed blowing through the Empire and that if Britain was to secure its future, it could only do so anchored in Europe. It was this forward-thinking attitude, Macmillan believed, rather than any nostalgia for a rapidly disintegrating glorious past that would carry the day.

Even so, on a day-to-day basis, it was not always easy to maintain the faith, particularly in the face of an increasingly vocal minority in the party who were adamantly opposed to 'Europe'. Joining the Commons' 'anti-marketeers', in the House of Lords the Marquess of Salisbury wrote to Lord Plowden on 9 August to express how 'unhappy' he was about Britain's entering the Common Market, particularly the effect it would have on British sovereignty and its Empire and Commonwealth.[6] Plowden provided in response a lengthy explanation of how he had evolved from opposing British entry into the EEC to now believing that it was absolutely essential to the future of the country. Although it had been the economic argument that finally won him over, he did not believe 'one can separate it from the political'. The reality was, he wrote, that the United Kingdom could no longer, 'on its own, support all the things it is trying to do in the political and military field'. Whatever he and Salisbury might think about giving up the Empire, it was now an 'established fact'. Personally, Plowden thought that 'the policy of successive Governments in freeing black men in Africa has been irresponsible', but it was the policy nevertheless and by 1961 had largely been accomplished. The Indian Army and the colonial forces were now gone and the Dominions offered little support. Yet the government was 'still trying to maintain world-wide forces, give money away to former Colonies, and provide free access of their goods and people to this country'. It simply couldn't be done any longer.

The solution, Plowden believed, was either 'to look outwards, which must mean some change, or to look inwards, think about our glorious past and decline not only materially and politically but in our whole moral fibre'. He desperately wished 'we could become as we were, or even stay as we are' but thought this impossible. Instead, he had decided to embrace the EEC in the hope that 'we will find an out-let for our undoubted political talents in building up some kind of unity in the free world, first through Europe and then through a wider Atlantic community'. The government still had a responsibility to 'do our best to hold the Commonwealth together, at least the white part', but entry into the Common Market had to come first.[7] For Plowden, it was less a choice between Empire and Europe than an unhappy realisation that Europe was the only option remaining.

If Plowden had evolved from being sceptical about European integration to becoming a committed 'European', Duncan Sandys travelled in the opposite direction. He told the Commonwealth Parliamentary Conference in late September that 'If we are faced with the necessity of choosing between the Commonwealth and Europe we should unquestionably choose the Commonwealth'.[8] Like his father-in-law Winston Churchill, since the end of the war, Sandys had always believed that no such choice was necessary; the Empire and greater integration with Europe were fully compatible. However, the looming negotiations with the Six had forced the Colonial Secretary to have second thoughts and re-evaluate his priorities. It was easy to be pro-European and advocate European integration when that unity would enhance Britain's position in the world and strengthen its empire, perhaps even linking together the colonial territories of Britain, France and Belgium into a greater European Commonwealth to compete with the Soviet Union and the United States. It was far harder to muster enthusiasm for British integration with Europe when it meant entering a closed club dominated by the French and Germans, without an imperial connection and with a loosening of Britain's economic ties with the Commonwealth.

The Prime Minister was sympathetic to the views of Churchill, Salisbury and Sandys, but rejected their growing belief that British entry into the Common Market would undermine its commitment to the Commonwealth. He would have been a fool to ignore them altogether, though, and he fully recognised that the key to British success in the negotiations was securing an economic arrangement for the Commonwealth which would be acceptable both to Commonwealth leaders and to those within Great Britain who cherished the continuation of Commonwealth ties. On 6 October 1961, therefore, he lunched with Jean Monnet to discuss his concerns. Monnet was 'full of vigour' and 'very hopeful about the Common Market negotiations', believing that de Gaulle's view on British entry had softened and that, in France, the 'mood has changed'. Macmillan was encouraged by the French attitude but warned Monnet that if things were becoming easier on the continent, the opposite was true in Britain: 'I had to tell Monnet that I thought the difficulties here were growing – pressure from Canada and Australia; anxiety of farmers; Trade Union fear of "competition" etc etc'. A quick negotiation would therefore be preferable, Macmillan argued, so that the government could pass legislation through Parliament with haste; if there was a delay, 'opposition and pressure groups w[oul]d grow in strength'.[9]

Macmillan need not have worried. At the Party Conference in Brighton, the motion to join the Common Market received 'overwhelming support', with fewer than forty delegates voting against it out of an assembly of more than four thousand.[10] The following day, the Prime Minister noted that the Beaverbook press seemed 'subdued', the *Guardian* – 'with typical Liberal meanness' – seemed 'chagrined at the disappearance of Colonel Blimp', the *Mirror* was 'very good, praising HMG and the Conservative Party about the Common Market' and the *Daily Telegraph* was 'for once ... fairly polite to the Govt'.[11] This was helped no doubt by the efforts of Lord Gladwyn, who in May 1961 had formed the Common Market Campaign, a committee established at Macmillan's urging to solicit full support for British entry into the EEC, both from other European leaders and amongst the British public. In its founding statement, Gladwyn wrote, 'No-one can doubt the force and momentum of the European Economic Community. Its policy is proving more liberal, both politically and economically, than originally seemed likely, which makes it easier for Britain to join.... We therefore believe that Her Majesty's Government, after the necessary consultation with the Commonwealth and the European Free Trade Association, should formally and explicitly declare their readiness in principle to join the European Economic Community.... Only thus can the Commonwealth, of which the United Kingdom would remain the senior partner, be associated with a vast, new, outward-looking political organisation, capable of accumulating and deploying the necessary capital for the development of the less fortunate nations of the world'.[12]

By the time of the Conservative Party Conference in October, Gladwyn had secured more than 200 signatories for the statement, including such academic luminaries as Professor Sir Isaiah Berlin, Sir Kenneth Clark, T. S. Elliot, Michael Howard and Professor Hugh Trevor-Roper; civil servants such as Sir Orme Sargent; and the military leaders Field Marshal Sir Claude Auchinleck and Captain Basil Liddell Hart.[13] As he wrote to Jean Monnet and other European leaders on 13 October, 'To us, the idea that the United Kingdom will have to "choose" between Europe and the Commonwealth seems fundamentally false.... [I]t seems to us that the result would be to place the Commonwealth, of which the United Kingdom would continue to be the leader, firmly behind a united Western Europe and thus increase the chances of political stability, the accumulation of capital for investment in the underdeveloped countries, and, in general, of the successful development of international trade'.[14] The old European dream of Ernest Bevin was still alive and well within most parts of the Conservative Party, even if the beliefs of some of the original members of the European Movement were challenged by the Common Market.

That same October, Heath issued a statement in Paris to the governments of the Six, formally launching Britain's negotiations to join the EEC. The success or failure of the negotiations, he said, would 'determine the future shape of Europe. They will affect profoundly the way of life, the political thought and even the character of each one of our peoples'. The British government and its public, he continued, had been through a 'searching debate' about its place in Europe and had concluded that membership of the Common Market offered the brightest future. This judgment was 'a great decision, a turning point in our history, and we take it in all seriousness'. He concluded: '[W]e desire to become full, wholehearted and active members of the European Community in its widest sense and to go forward with you in the building of a new Europe'.[15]

Individual statesmen, including de Gaulle, welcomed Heath's statement, but the official response of the Community – drafted at the EEC's ministerial meeting of 8–9 November – was cooler. It recognised Britain's unique circumstances and problems in joining the Common Market (Heath had raised in his statement the question of the Commonwealth and British agriculture) but ruled that any additional protocols added to the Treaty of Rome 'must not be allowed to modify the tenor and the spirit of the Treaty and must essentially concern transitional arrangements'. It clarified: '[H]owever grave and important the problems facing the United Kingdom may be – and we are willing to recognise that they are in many cases grave and important – they need to be settled without exceptions becoming the rule and vice versa. Exceptions must not be of such scope and duration as to call into question the rules themselves or impair the possibilities of applying these rules within the Community'.[16] The Six would do all they could to assist Britain's transition to membership, but British entry could not change the EEC. The fundamental character, goals and future aspirations of the EEC were already set. To use a metaphor common at the time, Britain was welcome to purchase a ticket and board the train at any station, but it had to recognise that the destination had already been mapped. Britain would be a passenger, not the driver.

The Dutch, Germans, Italians and Belgians were delighted at the British application, despite the problems it raised. The same could not be said of the French, whose leader's kind words did little to hide his true hostility. Macmillan knew that if he was to succeed in bringing the United Kingdom into the EEC, he would first have to persuade de Gaulle that it was the right thing to do. For that reason, he invited the French President to his Sussex home at Birch Grove on 25 November for some intimate talks. He began optimistically, telling de Gaulle that what was at stake was European civilisation, which was being menaced 'from all quarters, by Africans, Asians and Communists and, in a quite different way, even by our Atlantic friends such as the North Americans, and New

Zealanders and Australians'. Only 'real political unity in Europe' could save it, a 'united Europe based not on integrationist ideas but on confederal ideals'. Macmillan pointed out that this was very close to de Gaulle's vision. Yet trade *within* Europe was not enough. The members of the EEC had to 'look outwards towards their old empires and aim to become the most powerful trading body in the world'. It was here that Britain's greatest advantage lay. The British government could harness its leadership of and ties to the Commonwealth to the service of Europe.

Describing himself, de Gaulle and Adenauer as 'men of destiny', he warned that if Britain's application was rejected, his government would be 'forced to set out on another course, which would mean turning away from Europe'. This would include withdrawing all British troops from continental Europe, leaving NATO, and in effect 'shattering the organisation of the defence of Europe', as the British public would be unable to understand 'why it was necessary for Britain to abandon her commitments all over the world in the defence of Europe if the Europeans did not want her in Europe'. The Western European Union would collapse and in doing might unleash Germany, which throughout the 1950s and early 1960s had been held in check by being subsumed within a larger defence agreement. A rejection of the British application would mean the end of Anglo–French leadership of Europe and would cut short the restoration of the continent that had been ongoing since 1945: 'History would regard it as a repetition of the story of the city states of Greece which could not unite or could unite only occasionally as at Marathon'. The British government was willing to weaken some of its Commonwealth ties to preserve European civilisation, but only if Europe was willing to welcome it into European arms in a spirit of cooperation and without onerous preconditions.

De Gaulle agreed that there was 'no point, politically speaking, in living in a world where only the United States and U.S.S.R. remained'. He supported Macmillan's contention that Europe 'must be made to live' and that its rich civilisation must be preserved. However, he was concerned about what British entry might do to the EEC, particularly in the political realm, where the Commonwealth had to be considered. The populations of Canada, Australia and New Zealand might once have been Europeans but they were 'no longer Europeans in the same sense as the British'. The Indian and African countries had 'no part in Europe'. For this reason, whilst the French welcomed with open arms the United Kingdom, they 'did not want to change the character of their

Europe, and therefore did not want the British to bring their great escort in with them'. Any attempts to associate the Commonwealth with Europe would 'inevitably weaken the spirit of Europe' and was unacceptable to the French. As this was non-negotiable, the two men were at an impasse, Macmillan confirming that the United Kingdom 'could not enter Europe if it involved abandoning the Commonwealth'. The meeting broke up without resolution, de Gaulle saying only that 'more thought' was needed.[17]

The meeting left Macmillan exasperated. In a lengthy diary entry he wrote that the 'tragedy of it all is that we agree with de G on almost everything. We like the political Europe (*union de patries* or *union d'Etats*) that de G likes. We are anti-federalists; so is he. We are pragmatists in our economic planning; so is he. We fear a German revival and have no desire to see a reunited Germany. These are de G's thoughts too'. It was, Macmillan believed, not a question of policy but one of raw emotion that was preventing de Gaulle from embracing British entry: 'We agree; but his pride, his inherited hatred of England (since Joan of Arc), his bitter memories of the last war; above all, his intense "vanity" for France – she must dominate – make him half welcome, half repel us, with a strange "love-hate" complex'. The resulting ambivalence was maddening to Macmillan and other members of the British government and civil service. Set against all objective criteria, a strong Anglo–French partnership should have been at the heart of Europe, with Macmillan and de Gaulle working in close cooperation. Yet even when Macmillan met de Gaulle in person and seemed to make progress, as soon as the French premier returned to France he went 'back to his distrust and dislike, like a dog to his vomit'.[18] De Gaulle's attitude made a successful outcome to the negotiations near impossible because there was no way to predict how he might act. It also confirmed the worst suspicions of the British public against continental politicians, suspicions that were being stirred up by the Beaverbrook press and were undermining Macmillan's position, feeding the stirrings of anti-European sentiment in the British public at large.

The Prime Minister took out some of his anger on Lord Gladwyn, the former British ambassador in Paris who was now chairing the Common Market Campaign, After one such outburst, Gladwyn had to be reassured by Philip de Zulueta that he might have got 'the wrong impression.... Of course the Prime Minister does not think you are doing badly'.[19] Tensions also continued to rise between Macmillan and the British press, especially Lord Beaverbrook's *Daily Express*. Following a particularly unfair article in March 1962, Macmillan complained to Beaverbrook that 'the paragraph is false. The headline is absurd. The inference is ridiculous, as well as prejudiced'.[20] In a rare moment of contrition, Beaverbrook insisted that the journalist in question print an apology,[21] and he wrote to Macmillan that he was 'ashamed of the *Daily Express* organisation', his newspapers having 'every intention to support you in everything but that blasted Common Market, which is an American device to put us alongside Germany'. On the issue that mattered most to Macmillan, however, he could expect no backing, as Beaverbrook wished him 'out of the Common Market'. He explained to the Prime Minister, 'As our power was broken and lost by two German wars, it is very hard on us now to be asked to align ourselves with those villans [sic]'.[22] When the British public examined the issue more closely, Beaverbrook was convinced that they, too, would become as anti-Common Market as the *Daily Express*.

Ironically, the increasing support from the European continent for British EEC entry (with the notable exception of de Gaulle) only furthered the suspicions of Beaverbrook and the other anti-marketeers, confirming in their mind that the application represented a fundamental political and constitutional shift upon which they had not been consulted. For example, speaking in London on 1 May 1962, Jean Monnet proclaimed that 'the prospect of Britain's entry into the European Community has not only an economic significance but is a historic political event'. He continued: 'We are used to thinking that major changes in the traditional relations between countries only take place violently, through conquest or revolution. We are so accustomed to this that we find it hard to appreciate those that are taking place in Europe.... We can see the Communist revolution, because it has been violent and because we have been living with it for nearly fifty years. We can see the revolution in the ex-colonial areas because power is plainly changing hands. But we tend to miss the magnitude of the change in Europe'. Such talk flew in the face of British ministers' claims that the Common Market was primarily a trading agreement. Yet Monnet did not finish there. He told his audience that Britain's application was 'changing the tradition of centuries', that it represented a 'way out of the conflicts to which the 19th Century power philosophy gave rise'. He concluded: 'European unity is the most important event in the West since the war, not because it is a new great power, but because the new institutional method it introduces is permanently modifying relations between nations and men'.[23] These were hardly words of comfort to a nation that still saw itself as a Great Power and which had, since the end of the Second World War, sought unity in Europe in order to assert itself as a Great Power against both the United States and Soviet Union. It had no desire to become part of a post-Great Power new world environment.

Monnet's speech was particularly uncomfortable for British ministers precisely because they knew he was right. Despite their many public pronouncements emphasising the economic basis of the Community, ministers were well aware of its political implications. As Heath told the Western European Union's ministerial meeting in April 1962, 'We are looking forward to joining you as soon as possible in constructing a Europe *politically* as well as economically'.[24] Throughout May 1962, the government turned its attention to planning for the talks that were to take place between Macmillan and de Gaulle in Paris in early June, talks that it believed would 'represent the last opportunity of convincing the General that it is *politically* desirable for France to assist the United Kingdom to join the European Economic Community on reasonable terms'.[25] Macmillan knew that, in the abstract, it was not a hard sell, but he recognised that there was a 'strange ... paradox' that 'de Gaulle wants the kind of Europe that we w[oul]d be able readily to join, but he doesn't want us in it'.[26] Sir Pierson Dixon, the British Ambassador in Paris (whom Macmillan described as 'the most subtle mind in Whitehall') was convinced that de Gaulle had already decided to exclude the British from the EEC, but Macmillan hoped that his objections might still be overcome, being as they were 'torn between emotion and reason'.[27]

In mid-May, Macmillan invited the Foreign Secretary Alec Douglas-Home and Ted Heath to Chequers for the weekend to discuss the strategy for his upcoming meetings. Heath warned him that, based on the negotiations over the previous seven months, de Gaulle would claim that 'the present Community was an organic whole and the countries were complementary to each other. There was therefore a natural unity, particularly in economic matters'. The entry of the United Kingdom would unbalance this natural dynamic. Furthermore, de Gaulle would argue that 'the Six had a greater chance of achieving a close political unity than with an enlarged body'. Finally, he would attempt to turn the tables on the British, suggesting that 'British membership would weaken the Commonwealth' and was thus not in the interests either of Britain or the wider Western world. However, each of these excuses, Heath alleged, was a smokescreen. The real reason for French opposition was that 'Basically President de Gaulle hated the United States and disliked the U.K. He believed that the U.K. was subservient to the United States and therefore feared the role which the British might play in the Six. We seemed to him a Trojan Horse'. Whilst the Community was small, de Gaulle could 'hope to dominate it'. He could therefore 'achieve the conquest of Germany which Louis XIV and Richelieu had never got'. If the UK entered the Community, this 'dream of French domination would disappear because at least the smaller countries and probably Germany would prefer some degree of British leadership to French domination'.[28] If Heath was right, the foremost obstacle between Britain and entry to the EEC was the vanity of de Gaulle. In his meetings with the French president, Macmillan would have to tread very carefully indeed.

When the Prime Minister met de Gaulle at the Château des Champs in early June, the two men had a spirited debate. Macmillan explained that the British government was negotiating 'in good faith' and that the general public were receptive to their efforts. He was, he said, 'convinced that Britain was ready for the change on the political plane'. The younger generation, he insisted, 'felt much more European than the older people who had been brought up in the days of Kipling with the idea that their work in the world lay inside the British Empire'. With the collapse of that empire, 'the European idea gave the young people an ideal to work for'. Indeed, European unity had replaced the British Empire as the vehicle for the aspirations of young Britons. This he emphasised more than once to the French President: 'Now that the Colonial Empire in Asia and Africa had disappeared the young people in Britain felt that they needed something else to believe in. Britain had a great friendship for the United States but in 20 years Britain would be relatively weaker even than she was now by comparison with the United States. National pride was not sufficient'. The British people *needed* Europe.[29]

De Gaulle was unmoved. There were, he argued, two primary factors that mitigated against British entry. First, it would '*alter the character* of the Community, both in the economic and political field'. Second, the British government was and would remain 'too intimately tied up with the Americans' regardless of Macmillan's claims to the contrary. And as for the Commonwealth, Macmillan had repeatedly said that he would always choose it over Europe. On those terms, no compromise seemed possible.[30] For perhaps the first time, Macmillan began to have serious doubts about whether he could persuade the French government – and de Gaulle in particular – to overcome its suspicions and support British EEC entry. His predecessor Lord Avon (Anthony Eden) shared these doubts, telling Philip de Zulueta that the ongoing Brussels negotiations 'resembled a good deal the E.D.C. The only thing to do was to go on quietly until they broke down'. Once that happened, something else 'might present itself'. Avon therefore advised the government to 'cast round in our minds very discreetly for what possible alternatives there might be, so as to have some idea ready if a crisis occurred'.[31] Avon had waged his own battles with the French a decade earlier; he had no confidence that Macmillan would succeed where he had failed.

De Gaulle's fear that Britain in Europe would be little more than a Trojan Horse for the United States was not calmed by the actions of the American government itself, which had begun to campaign prominently for British entry into the EEC. Since coming to office in January 1961, President Kennedy had instinctively understood better than Eisenhower the necessity of bringing together the Six and the Seven and of supporting Britain's attempt to join the Common Market.[32] Shortly after entering the White House, he had told Macmillan how 'anxious' he was for Britain to join the Six, arguing that it would mean 'better tariff bargaining' and that 'if we [the UK] were in the Six, we should be able to steer them, and influence them, whatever might be the political personalities'.[33] Jean Monnet also viewed the Anglo–American attachment as essential for the future of Europe, telling Macmillan that once the United Kingdom was within the Common Market, 'the field will be open to us for a real partnership with the United States and conditions will then be created that should enable us to transform the constant conflict between East and West into some kind of peace'.[34] Contrary to de Gaulle, Monnet perceived Britain's close relationship with the United States as one of the most appealing aspects of the British application to entry.

Nevertheless, Macmillan realised that the American intervention was unhelpful when it came to de Gaulle, and when he met with Dean Rusk in late June 1962 he told him 'what terrible damage the

Americans are doing in every field in Europe'. In particular, the American government was doing 'great harm' to Britain's attempts to join the Common Market precisely *because* they were advocating in favour of it: 'The more they tell the Germans, French etc that they (U.S.A.) want Britain to be in, the more they incline these countries to keep us out'. Macmillan continued to press his case to the American administration – and to both Kennedy and Rusk directly – throughout the summer but to no avail, and he noted in his diary (somewhat condescendingly) that it was 'rather sad' as 'the Americans (who are naïve and inexperienced) are up against centuries of diplomatic skill and finesse [in Europe]'.[35]

That the American government was drawing more attention to Britain's negotiations further inflamed the Beaverbrook press, and, on 7 July, the *Daily Express* again called for a General Election before any final British agreement to enter the EEC. Yet it was not only Beaverbrook and the *Daily Express* putting pressure on the Prime Minister. That July, his old friend Lady Rhys-Williams also wrote to him in opposition to the Common Market, arguing that her previous support for and involvement with the European Movement had never envisioned Britain entering a federal structure. Macmillan replied on 2 August, telling her that 'the prospect if we cannot accede to the Treaty of Rome is rather gloomy'. He explained: 'I do not mean gloomy particularly for me personally, nor for the Conservative Party, nor even for the country in the short term, but in the long run I believe that power will pass from us to the large European group. American policy will follow power and so in the end will the Commonwealth'. These facts would not be 'palatable' to Lady Rhys-Williams, but as Prime Minister he nevertheless had a responsibility to face them.[36]

Lady Rhys-William's letter surprised Macmillan, and he was 'saddened' that some of his old colleagues from the European Movement were turning against the government's attempts to enter the EEC, with Roy Harrod joining Lady Rhys-Williams ('dear, trusted, loyal friends') to become 'violent opponents'.[37] Anthony Eden, likewise, was becoming more vocal in his opposition to a British role in the Common Market. Whilst never a 'pro-European' in the sense that Macmillan, Harrod and Rhys-Williams had been, Eden had always stressed that his ultimate goal was to see Britain within rather than without Europe. By 1962, however, having recently been elevated to the House of Lords, the tone of Lord Avon had changed, the former

Prime Minister stressing that 'the British people should know where they are going before they wake up and find themselves where they do not want to be'.[38] The rationale behind this change of heart was much the same as other pro-European Conservatives who were now sceptical of British engagement with the Common Market. They had hoped to see Britain leading a united Europe founded on the model of the British Commonwealth, a Europe that was intimately connected to Britain's imperial mission in the world. British entry into an already-existing European organisation with a federal structure was not what their vision of 'Europe' had been, a vision that they now struggled to articulate following the collapse of the British Empire.

Throughout this time, a small core of Conservative MPs continued to raise objections to the government's policy. In March 1962, thirty backbenchers put down a motion in demanding that the government confirm that without 'special arrangements for the Commonwealth' Britain would not join the EEC, and thirty-six MPs put forward a similar motion in July. Each was defeated by the far larger pro-European Conservative majority, and the Labour opposition abstained on both votes rather than commit itself to a European position.[39] Nevertheless, there was a clear energy and momentum in this small grouping. Robert Turton, one of the leading 'anti-Marketeers' (as opponents to EEC entry were now being called across the political spectrum), wrote to Lord Avon in July claiming that Conservatives across the party were 'deeply worried' and that only fear of reprisals from Macmillan following the recent 'Night of the Long Knives' was 'keeping them from signing'.[40]

The 'Night of the Long Knives' was Macmillan's cabinet reshuffle of 12 July 1962, when the Prime Minister promoted those who had shown great personal loyalty and whose commitment to his European vision was absolute. Selwyn Lloyd was sacked from the Treasury, Harold Watkinson was removed from the Ministry of Defence and David Eccles (a one-time European, now hostile to British entry) was asked to resign as Minister of Education. Reginald Maudling became the new Chancellor of the Exchequer, Rab Butler was promoted Deputy Prime Minister, Henry Brooke was moved from a junior position in the Treasury to replace Butler as Home Secretary, Sir Edward Boyle went to the Department of Education to take Eccles' position, Peter Thorneycroft was promoted Minister of Defence and Julian Amery became Minister of Aviation.[41] Nevertheless, even after this reshuffle, word reached Macmillan that if the negotiations were successful, Rab Butler would 'lead a revolt'. If they failed, Macmillan might 'have to resign', leaving him between a rock and a hard place within the Conservative Party.[42] Only on 21 August did Butler confirm to Macmillan that he would support the government's pro-Market stance, 'in spite of agriculture, Commonwealth and the possible destruction of the Conservative Party'.[43]

So great was the pressure upon Macmillan that, in early August, he wrote to the Queen, reassuring her that whilst it was 'very disagreeable having to seem at variance with Commonwealth countries', it was nevertheless in the Commonwealth's long-term interests that Britain should enter the EEC: 'This market of fifty million people cannot be expanded unless we join one the great groups. These are Russia, which is out of the question, America, which is too distant and too large and in which we would be swamped, or Europe, where with skill and management once we are in we will be able to dominate or at any rate lead'.[44] Europe was Britain's only option, even if it did make the Conservative anti-Marketeers uncomfortable. In this regard, Macmillan received some comfort from Jean Monnet, who told Lord Gladwyn in early September that he was 'sure that Britain will soon be a member of the Common Market and Europe'.[45] Coming from a man largely hailed as the 'founder' of 'Europe' there could be no better appraisal, and Macmillan was confident when he opened the Commonwealth Conference in September, telling the Commonwealth heads of government that 'Britain has always been part of Europe'.[46]

In the United Kingdom, however, the picture grew only more complicated. In September, the Labour Party under Hugh Gaitskell chose to move decisively against British entry into the EEC, turning European policy into a party-political issue, with a united Labour Party in opposition and a Conservative Party ostensibly in favour, although experiencing deep unease within its ranks. Until September 1962, Gaitskell had claimed to be in favour of the principle of membership but insisted that entry could only occur under the correct conditions and with sufficient safeguards for the Commonwealth and British agriculture. When Harold Wilson, the Shadow Foreign Secretary, presented to the House of Commons a challenging list of conditions that the government would have to meet before the Labour Party could support negotiations, Roy Jenkins resigned from the shadow cabinet in disgust, believing that Britain's future lay in Europe and that British leadership of an Empire-Commonwealth had become an anachronism.[47] He went on to chair the Labour Common Market Committee, a party organisation formed in January 1962 that was committed to promoting Britain's entry into the EEC. He was unable to secure the support of more than thirty-three Labour MPs, however, scarcely more than the number of Conservative rebels who were actively campaigning against entry.[48]

The vast majority of the Labour Party was anti-EEC, believing that it was a capitalist conspiracy that would undermine Britain's control of its own industry. In this regard, James Callaghan, the Shadow Chancellor of the Exchequer, was more representative of Labour thought than Jenkins, telling the annual dinner of the Edmonton Labour Party on 15 September that the 'Common Market is a bad bargain for all the Commonwealth countries'. He rejected the view that British trade would suffer if the government remained outside the EEC, arguing instead that British trade with Europe had expanded over the past few years and would continue to do so. Finally, he said that he did not 'wish to sink the identity of the British people in a federal Europe.... We must...face the fact that if we join Europe we cut ourselves adrift from much of the Commonwealth by the very act of accepting the Treaty of Rome'.[49] It was under the influence of leading anti-Market Labour MPs such as Callaghan and Douglas Jay that Gaitskell delivered a political broadcast on 21 September 1962, positioning the Labour Party decisively against British entry into the EEC. He argued that what was really needed was 'building a bridge between the Commonwealth and Europe; and we cannot do that if we destroy the Commonwealth by our entry'. He continued: 'And if by our entry we are committed to European Federation or anything of that kind, we do destroy the Commonwealth. And if by our entry the economic damage to the Commonwealth countries is so serious the links are all broken, and the Commonwealth fades out, we cannot do it either'.[50]

Gaitskell's position was clear. If British entry in any way damaged the economic interests of the Commonwealth, the Labour Party would oppose it. On 29 September, the National Executive Committee (NEC) of the Labour Party supported their leader's stance, publishing a statement that insisted that Britain's 'connections and interests, both political and economic, lie as much outside Europe as with in'. It continued, 'Unlike the Six, Britain is the centre and founder member of a much larger and still more important group, the Commonwealth. As such we have access to the largest single trading area in the world; and political influence within a world-wide, multi-racial association of 700 million people'. There could be no abandoning that community. The NEC's conclusion is worth quoting at length:

> If we look to the future, we can get our priorities right. The real dangers that confront us are not the old rivalries of France, Germany and other Western European powers but those that arise from the continuing hostilities of the Communist and non-Communist world and from the terrible inequalities that separate the developed and the underdeveloped nations, the white and the coloured races. Britain by herself cannot, of course, solve these problems, but more than any other advanced country of the West, we have the greatest opportunity and the greatest incentive to tackle them. For the 700 million people of the Commonwealth, with whom history has linked us, form a truly international society, cutting across the deep and dangerous divisions of the modern world. By its very nature the Commonwealth must think of global not regional problems; of the interest of all races, not just of one; of the problems of age-old poverty as well as those of new-found affluence; of non-commitment as well as of cold war. If we are ever to win peace and prosperity for mankind, then the world community that must emerge will be comprised of precisely such diverse elements as exist in the Commonwealth today – pledged, as we are, to friendship and mutual aid. This is our vision of Britain's future and of the world's future – and it must not be allowed to fade.[51]

By the time the Labour Party Conference met in Brighton, the party's position was clear. Gaitskell rose to address the delegates at ten o'clock in the morning on 3 October and spoke with a clear anti-Common Market message. Britain's entry into the EEC, he claimed, meant 'the end of Britain as an independent European state.... It means the end of a thousand years of history.... And it does mean the end of the Commonwealth'.[52] There could be no stronger statement of opposition, and the Labour MPs and delegates were – with very few exceptions – delighted.

Leading Conservatives were alarmed by Gaitskell's speech, fearing that it might resonate with members of the Conservative Party. After Gaitskell's first 'anti' speech on the twenty-first, Lord Balfour had written to Home, telling him that although he remained 'a critic of the proposed terms', he had been careful to steer clear of the 'anti-movements' and felt strongly that 'when we sign up – and on assumption we have got all we can – then I feel we must close our ranks and be united for the fight against the Socialists. Unity in the future should replace division in the past'.[53] Home agreed, replying to Balfour that 'We are apt to take our eye off the main purpose which is to keep the Socialists out. When they may come sneaking in by the back door this is particularly important'.[54] Now that the Labour Party had committed to an anti-Common Market stance, it was essential that Conservative Party leadership prevent its own anti-Marketeers from joining forces with the opposition and providing the Labour Party with an electoral victory by default. Party loyalty had to come before all else.

Conservative fears were only heightened by a public opinion poll published in September which focussed on the 'target' voters who were neither consistent Conservative nor Labour voters and were therefore likely to 'swing' the issue. It found that the number who disapproved moderately of British entry into the EEC had risen from 9 to 12 per cent, and those who disapproved strongly had increased from 19 per cent to an alarming 30 per cent, suggesting that opposition was close to 50 per cent amongst 'swing voters'.[55] With the Labour Party now united in opposition, there was little room for dissent within Conservative ranks if the government was to maintain support for the issue.

On 4 October, the day after Gaitskell's conference speech, Lord Chandos (Oliver Lyttelton before his elevation to the House of Lords) and Alan Lennox-Boyd warned Macmillan that the 'sovereignty argument was going to cause [trouble] in the Party'. They also warned him that a rumour was circulating, particularly outside Parliament, that Macmillan was 'determined to abandon the Queen and promote a federal Europe at the expense of the national identity'. This Macmillan found 'absurd', but he recognised that such sentiment might be 'dangerous' if not quelled.[56] At the end of September, Chandos lunched with Avon and both expressed their concerns over the new Conservative policy. Writing after their lunch, Chandos told Avon that 'The more I think of it, the more certain I am that the country must be told about the possibility of federalism quite openly and secondly I am equally sure that they would reject it'.[57] Having served as Colonial Secretary from 1951 to 1954 and after that as a prominent business leader, Chando's was not a voice Macmillan could afford to ignore.

Nevertheless, if trouble was rumbling below the surface of the Conservative Party, it did not show itself at the Conservative Party conference later that month. In the run-up to the conference, Macmillan published through the Conservative Central Office a pamphlet – partly in response Labour's NEC statement – summarising his position on the relationship among Britain, the Commonwealth and Europe. He stated that in applying to join the EEC, the Conservative government had 'taken what is perhaps the most fateful and forward-looking policy decision in our peacetime history'. In doing so, it was not breaking from Britain's past: 'We in Britain are Europeans. That has always been true, but it has now become a reality which we cannot ignore. . . . We have to consider the state of the world as it is today and will be tomorrow, and not in outdated terms of a vanished past'. The Empire was, to all intents and purposes, gone and the Commonwealth was not (and never would be) strong enough to stand alone against the United States and Soviet Union. He concluded, 'To many of us, and to our younger generation in particular, the time is past for harping on old disputes and nursing obsolete conceptions. We want to see Britain taking the lead in building a new future and working towards that unity of the world which is the ultimate vision of mankind. The European Community is a signpost to that future and we must play our part'.[58]

When the Prime Minister rose to speak at the Conservative Party Conference in Llandudno exactly ten days after Gaitskell had given his conference speech, he offered a counterargument to the Labour leader every bit as heart-felt: 'Britain in Europe will have a double influence, both as a European country and one of world-wide interests. Britain's power and value to the other Commonwealth countries, old and new, will be greatly enhanced. And we can hope that our European associates will share with us that outward-looking attitude by which alone the prosperity and so the peace of the world can be secured'.[59] British entry into the Common Market did not mean the end of the Commonwealth; it spelled the salvation of the Commonwealth and of Britain with it.

The Conservative Party delegates greeted Macmillan's speech with the same level of enthusiasm as the Labour Party delegates had Gaitskell's. Walker-Smith was one of only a handful of Conservatives who spoke against the government's motion to enter the Common Market, warning that, in Europe, 'Little by little the political cat has eased his way out of the economic bag. He is not just a soft, fluffy, friendly little kitten; he is a full-grown political cat with his complement of claws'.[60] Walker-Smith was only able to muster forty votes in opposition to British entry into the EEC, however, from amongst the more than 4,000 delegates in the hall, many of whom wore badges proclaiming the single word 'yes'.[61] On the morning following the conference, *The Times* wrote that it was 'as though the Common Market controversy inside the Conservative Party had moved peacefully but decisively towards its close'.[62] Lord Casey – soon to become Governor-General of Australia – wrote to Macmillan on 17 October confirming this, telling him that he had 'admired your fortitude and decision on the matter of Britain joining the European Common Market – as we believe the great majority of thinking people in this country do also'.[63] It was not, Casey said, a matter of choice between the EEC or the Commonwealth, but 'rather a question of both or nothing'. For Macmillan, Casey's words were music to his ear.

The Conservative Party Conference was the calm before the storm, however. On 22 November, five by-elections were held across the United Kingdom, all of them 'safe' Conservative seats. The party held three of them, although with reduced majorities in every case. Of those that were lost, both went to Labour. Somewhat alarmingly, the reason for this loss in South Dorset was that an anti-Market independent Conservative candidate, campaigning on the single issue of opposition to the EEC, had taken 5,000 votes off the official Conservative candidate, allowing the Labour candidate (who was himself anti-Common Market) to sneak in.[64] If these results were replicated across the country at a General Election, it would be Harold Wilson rather than Harold Macmillan who was forming the next government. British entry into the EEC might well be in the best interests of the country, but it was also becoming an electoral liability to the Conservative Party and costing Macmillan the support of some of his closest friends, many of whom had previously worked alongside him in the European Movement.

On 1 December, Ted Heath briefed Macmillan in person about the negotiations with the Six, which were running into difficulties. The French had opposed British efforts 'by every means, fair and foul' and were being 'absolutely ruthless'. They 'terrify the Six – by their intellectual superiority, spiritual arrogance, and shameless disregard of truth and honour'. He expected that the 'crunch' would come in January or February 1963, at which point the British government would know better whether their bid for entry had been successful. Macmillan warned Heath that these final weeks would be a 'trial of nerve and will' and that the British negotiating team should not be afraid to 'show up the French before the world'.[65] The Labour Party reached a very different conclusion, producing an internal memorandum that same month arguing that as 'the odds are increasing that the negotiations will fail', the party ought to provide some serious alternatives to Common Market membership. The EEC was a capitalist institution that was 'prepared to have us in only on terms that are damaging to our interests and still more to those of the Commonwealth'. The answer to Britain's post-war economic woes lay not in a European Common Market predicated on free trade principles, but rather 'in more, not less, government intervention'.[66] This could only be achieved with absolute economic independence. It was this that the Labour Party would be campaigning for.

The French and the Labour Party were not Macmillan's only burdens. On 5 December, the former American Secretary of State Dean Acheson delivered a keynote address at the United States Military Academy, West Point, on US foreign affairs and, in particular, on the 'Atlantic Community'. The majority of his speech focussed on strengthening NATO and was without controversy. However, midway through he offered a small detour and pointed the finger at Great Britain for impeding Atlantic progress, saying, 'Great Britain has lost an empire and has not yet found a role. The attempt to play a separate power role – that is, a role apart from Europe, a role based on a "special relationship" with the United States, a role based on being the head of a "Commonwealth" which has no political structure, or unity, or strength, and enjoys a fragile and precarious economic relationship by means of the Sterling area and preferences in the British market – this role is about played out'.[67] In a single sentence, Acheson had rubbished the entirety of post-war British foreign policy as advanced by both the Labour and Conservative parties.

After hearing of Acheson's speech, Macmillan pretended indifference, claiming that Acheson was 'always a conceited ass, but I don't really think he meant to be offensive'. Nevertheless, public opinion in Britain was 'upset' and Acheson's words confirmed for many that the United Kingdom was losing influence in the world day by day.[68] In the Sunday newspapers, many leading editorials directly linked Britain's negotiations for entry into the EEC with its imperial decline, becoming 'hysterical about Europe'.[69] *The Daily Express* claimed that Acheson had offered a 'stab in the back' to Britain, the *Sunday Times* criticised his 'tackless commentary' and *The Daily Telegraph* scoffed that Acheson was 'more immaculate in dress than in judgment'.[70] Macmillan noted in his diary that he could not remember a time when 'there [were] so many difficult problems to resolve and awkward decisions to be made'.[71] He therefore decided that a response was necessary, publishing a letter to the British public in all the leading newspapers that rebuked Acheson for making 'an error which has been made by quite a lot of people in the course of the last four hundred years, including Philip of Spain, Louis XIV, Napoleon, the Kaiser, and Hitler'.[72] Britain's power was not on the wane, he assured the British public, and its entry into Europe would prove that point, not diminish it.

Yet it was not to be. On 27 December, Macmillan travelled to Rambouillet for a final round of talks with de Gaulle. Julian Amery, who accompanied Macmillan, sent a summary of the talks to Heath, writing that the 'most striking things about the talks are the General's apparent disillusionment with the idea of a political union of Europe and his almost open opposition to the idea of Britain joining the Common Market'. De Gaulle was particularly insistent that 'Britain will have to choose between America and Europe' and was sceptical that the British government would ever commit to Europe over the United States.[73] After the meeting, Macmillan was despondent about Britain's hopes of joining the Common Market. Although de Gaulle cited Britain's Commonwealth interests, its agriculture and its relationship with the United States as reasons for opposition to Britain's application, Macmillan believed that 'jealousy of Britain is an even stronger motive. The French (or rather de G. and his friends) want the Six dominated by France. They do *not* want a Europe of 8, 9, or 10 states, with an equilibrium of power'. Macmillan's only glimmer of hope was that the French might be unwilling to 'be held up to all the world as having openly wrecked our entry and having never really tried to negotiate seriously'. His long talks with de Gaulle, Pompidou (the French Prime Minister) and Couve de Murville (the French Foreign Minister) did not suggest this to be the case, however.[74]

Writing in his diary on the first day of the New Year, Macmillan reflected that 1962 had been 'a *bad* year, both in Home and Foreign politics. The Govt's position is weak and there is a general view that the

Socialists will win the General Election. The country is in a dissatisfied and petulant mood. My own popularity has gone down a lot. There is a wave of anti-European, *and* anti-American feeling'.[75] His mood did not improve when, on 11 January 1963, the British ambassador in Paris reported that 'so long as de Gaulle sees a prospect of being leader of the Six he will oppose [the] UK'.[76] His words were prescient. Three days later, de Gaulle gave a press conference denouncing Britain and opposing on principle its entry into the Common Market. Speaking to the gathered journalists at the Elysée, de Gaulle described Britain as 'insular and maritime, linked by her trade, her markets and her food supplies to diverse and often far-flung countries'. Its economy was largely industrial and commercial rather than agricultural, and Britain had, 'in all her patterns of work, habits and traditions which are highly distinctive and original'. He concluded: 'In short, the nature, structure, the economic situation, that characterise England, differ profoundly from the Continent. How then could England, as she lives, as she produces, as she trades, be incorporated into the Common Market as it was conceived and as it works?'[77]

Couve de Murville immediately went to Brussels to demand an end to the negotiations, which were now futile without the possibility of French agreement. Macmillan noted in his diary that 'De Gaulle is trying to *dominate* Europe. His idea is not a partnership, but a Napoleonic or a Louis XIV hegemony'.[78] De Gaulle's Europe was not the united Europe which Macmillan had always believed in and which he had devoted himself to through Churchill's European Movement. Nor was it the Europe envisioned by Monnet, Schuman, Spaak and the other post-war European federalists. De Gaulle's Europe was one of individual national interests, a Europe that more properly belonged in the nineteenth century than the post-war world of the twentieth. However, all hope was not entirely lost. Spaak, Schröder and Luns immediately issued statements contesting de Gaulle's view, and the European Commission rejected Couve de Murville's call for an end to negotiations. After a further four days of intense negotiations, the five other powers of the EEC turned against the French, and, on 18 January, Couve de Murville requested a ten-day postponement so that the French government could re-evaluate its position.[79] The French, it seemed, were having second thoughts.

This news was greeted with profound relief on the European continent. It was completely overshadowed in Britain, however, for on that same day the long-serving Labour leader Hugh Gaitskell died after an illness that had first emerged in June 1962 and had kept him hospitalised since the New Year. Macmillan immediately moved the adjournment of Parliament, the first time in history this had happened at the death of a party leader who had not been Prime Minister.[80] After a quick leadership battle among Harold Wilson, George Brown and James Callaghan, Wilson won the first round by 115 votes to 88 and 41, respectively, and then in the second round defeated Brown by 144 votes to 100, becoming leader of the Labour Party and of Her Majesty's Official Opposition on 14 February 1961.[81]

As he did so, he met a Conservative government in crisis. On 29 January, the negotiations for British entry into the EEC collapsed only one day after recommencing. Macmillan, distraught, scribbled, 'All our policies at home and abroad are in ruins. ... We have lost everything, except our courage and determination'.[82] The French were entirely to blame. As Spaak said: 'Today five delegations of the Six consider that these negotiations, although they have been long and sometimes difficult, have not reached an impasse, and that the wise policy would be to continue them in the spirit of cooperation and honesty'. He added, 'if the Treaty of Rome is not rent asunder as a result of what is taking place, the Community spirit will nonetheless be gravely and I fear mortally wounded for a long time. For the moment when, in a Community, one of the partners alone tries to compel all the others to take decisions which are of capital importance for the Community's life, the Community spirit no longer exists'.[83] Schröder also voiced his 'deep disappointment', and Colombo expressed his 'sincere regret'.[84] There was nothing they could do, however. In January 1963, five members of the EEC had said 'yes' to the United Kingdom entering the Common Market as a full partner. But the French had said 'non'.

13 EMPIRE ECLIPSED, EUROPE EMBRACED, BRITAIN REJECTED

When Harold Wilson walked through the polished black door of 10 Downing Street on 16 October 1964, he was very much a 'Commonwealth man', keenly supporting the 'multiracial grouping of nations with Britain as its leader'. He intended to 'develop British links with the Commonwealth by extending Commonwealth preferences in new commodities and matching Britain's plans for national economic development with specific needs in the Commonwealth'.[1] For Wilson, the Commonwealth was the key to future British economic success, looming far larger than either Europe or the United States. He had supported Hugh Gaitskell's opposition to British entry into the European Economic Community (EEC) in 1962–63, and he was as ambivalent about American power as Ernest Bevin had been two decades earlier. His analysis of Britain's place in the world economy differed sharply from Macmillan's, Eden's or Churchill's before him, all of whom had recognised (at least to some extent) that the Commonwealth would play an increasingly small role in British economic life. As the Labour Party manifesto stated before the 1964 General Election, 'Although we shall seek to achieve close links with our European neighbours, the Labour Party is convinced that the first responsibility of a British government is to the Commonwealth'.[2]

Much had happened over the months leading up to the election, from the French veto in January 1963 to October 1964. Immediately after the veto, the *Daily Mirror* opined that 'the world now knows' what Britain had always suspected, that General de Gaulle would forever 'sabotage Britain's efforts to join the European Common Market'.

The newspaper was not despondent, however, as Britain's course was clear: 'She is forced to mark time in her attempt to join the Common Market as it now stands. But she must not turn her back on Europe. This government (and the next) must continue to strive for a wider European unity.... This is the real European ideal'.[3] The French newspaper *Le Monde* also blamed de Gaulle, lamenting that 'A single man in the name of his own idea of Europe and the world, has vetoed the entry into the Common Market of a country whose application had the sympathy of all our allies'. It wondered how 'after such a display of bad faith, can one be believed when one repeats that the door remains open to England'.[4]

Others on the European continent agreed. The Vice President of the European Commission, the Dutchman Sicco Mansholt, gave a press conference on 1 February 1963 claiming that de Gaulle's actions had 'caused a crisis in Europe' and that the Community could not and would not accept the French veto. He also added that, contrary to de Gaulle's hopes, the Community 'could not be neutralist and must stand loyally by the Atlantic Alliance'. Europe's future, he said, was inextricably linked with the United States. Great Britain could help with this essential relationship.[5] Five days after Mansholt's conference, the European Parliament debated the collapse of the negotiations. Led by European President Walter Hallstein, it concluded that the chances of a successful outcome to the negotiations had been 'good enough to justify continuation', that the Community had now suffered its 'first serious crisis of confidence' and that the Community was 'not a third force but a part of the free world'. Most importantly, it confirmed that it would 'not turn its back on Britain'.[6] Sir Arthur Tandy, the British government's envoy to the Common Market, wrote from Strasbourg that Hallstein's speech was 'an unequivocal indictment of [the] French violation of the Treaty's basic principles and has made a deep impression here'.[7] Contrary to the earlier accusations of the *Daily Express*, Hallstein would continue to be one of Britain's strongest advocates on the continent.

Nevertheless, the French veto in January 1963 changed the dynamics in Europe. Writing in early February, Edward Heath – still holding the office of Lord Privy Seal and Minister of State for European Affairs – noted that despite the opposition of the Five to French actions, their 'economic interest, ... their loyalty to the Community idea and their lack of will to sustain a long struggle will cause them gradually to succumb to General de Gaulle unless we do something about it'. De Gaulle's policies represented a 'major challenge to his partners in the

Common Market, to Britain and to the Western Alliance', and Heath warned that the government now faced what was 'likely to be our last chance of securing the sort of Europe we want'.[8] Philip de Zulueta explained to the Prime Minister that Britain could still achieve the Europe it wanted by, on the one hand, 'prevent[ing] the consolidation, still more the expansion, of de Gaulle's Europe' whilst on the other continuing to 'unite a wider Europe'. He estimated that the government had 'about two months in which to do this', after which time 'de Gaulle's band wagon is likely to be joined by a lot more people'. The way to succeed, pragmatically speaking, was to 'always try to leave him [de Gaulle] a line of retreat' and to 'take the line with any Frenchmen we can who are near to the General that the breakdown in Anglo–French co-operation is a tragedy because it will inevitably allow Europe to fall apart to the profit of the Russians or Americans or both'.[9] The government had to at once distance itself from the American government, convincing de Gaulle that a collapse in Anglo–French relations would lead to a strengthening of an American hegemony in the West, whilst at the same time drawing the French government into a stronger alliance with the United States. It was not going to be an easy path to travel.

Before the month was out, the Foreign Office contacted the American State Department, explaining that when, over the next few months, the British government tried to establish even closer relations with its allies on the European continent, it was not intended 'in any way to undermine N.A.T.O.'. On the contrary, the government's aim was to 'show the Europeans that there are genuine alternatives to General de Gaulle's idea of Europe within the Atlantic Alliance'. By taking the lead in Europe and 'appearing sometimes to act in the name of the Europeans', the government was in fact 'acting in the best interests of the United States and the Alliance'.[10] It was also, it believed, acting in the best interests of British business. In a survey of the views of Britain's leading chairmen and managing directors in May 1963, polling found that 73 per cent believed that the development of trade with the Common Market was 'very important' and 20 per cent 'fairly important'. In contrast, only 71 per cent held trade with the Commonwealth to be 'very important', 60 per cent trade with the United States, and just 59 per cent trade with the European Free Trade Area (EFTA).[11] As far as Britain's firms and companies were concerned, the United Kingdom's trading interests lay primarily in the EEC.

Despite this, many of those outside the business community were still committed to the Commonwealth above all else. In a survey carried out for *The Times* in the autumn of 1963, pollsters asked 'every other name in the *Who's Who* how valuable they saw various international groups with which Britain interacted. Overwhelming, these men and women supported the Commonwealth, with 69 per cent viewing it as "highly valuable" and 25 per cent as "fairly valuable". Next came NATO (with 63 per cent seeing it as "highly valuable"), the "Special Relationship" with the United States (53 per cent as "highly valuable") and the United Nations (44 per cent "highly valuable). Just 42 per cent believed that Britain's relationship with the EEC was "highly valuable"'. As the survey concluded, 'commitment to the Commonwealth and to NATO is particularly strong'.[12] Those in trade and manufacturing saw reason to support Britain's European policy, but other movers and shakers in British society were far less convinced.

Such views belied reality. Although in September 1963 the Colonial Office noted that there were still forty British dependent territories, how long these territories would remain useful to the United Kingdom was doubtful. The Colonial Office wrote that 'Our colonial relationship with them is becoming outdated; it affects adversely our position in the United Nations and our relations with other countries'. Twenty-four of the forty would gain independence by 1965. For those that remained, the time had come to 'devise new "post-colonial" forms of association which will honour our obligations to their peoples and preserve our interests, while gaining general acceptance both in Britain and among our friends abroad'. Britain's colonial policy was: '(a) to bring to independence as soon as possible all territories capable of it . . . (b) to bring into "free association" as many as possible of those for which this seems the final destiny . . .; [and] (c) to make whatever changes in form we can which will help to avoid criticism'. It concluded: 'The Colonial Office will cease to exist in 1965. The word Colony might go too and remaining places be known as "associated states" or some such word'.[13] The Colonial Office memorandum was quite clear. The era of British imperialism was over.

It was not only Britain's empire that was crumbling in 1963. The turbulent waters of politics battered the Macmillan government like never before and 'Super-Mac' began to lose his aura of invincibility. The Prime Minister was already reeling after the French veto when the Profumo Affair erupted. John Profumo, the Secretary of State for War, had an affair with Christine Keeler, a model who was also liaising with the Soviet naval attaché at the London embassy. This affair first became public in July 1962 but gathered little attention. However, the story broke again in March 1963, and, on the twenty-first of that month, the Labour MPs Barbara Castle, Richard Crossman and Michael Foot all mentioned it during a parliamentary debate. Macmillan informed Profumo that he must either issue a statement denying the allegations or resign immediately. Profumo chose to lie to his Prime Minister and to Parliament. The *Daily Herald*, *The Times* and *Private Eye* immediately cast doubt on his denial. By 1 April, the French *Paris Match* and the Italian *Tempo Illustrato* were also carrying the story. Keeler confessed to the police on 5 April that she had indeed been Profumo's mistress. The British Security Service (MI5) was soon brought into the mix when rumours circulated that Keeler's other lover, the osteopath Stephen Ward, had asked Keeler to learn nuclear secrets from Profumo. By June, the story could no longer be contained, and, on the fourth of that month, Profumo resigned from the cabinet.[14]

Much of the blame for the Profumo Affair fell not on Profumo himself but on Macmillan, whom many judged should have resolved the crisis when the accusations first came to light in 1962. The Conservative-leaning *Daily Telegraph* opined that 'the Conservative Party is a shambles', and *The Times* commented that it was 'strange that not a single member of the Government resigned when the affair broke in March ... There is no hiding place from the tidal overthrow and disaster'.[15] More damaging, perhaps, was the announcement by the Conservative MP Donald Johnson that he would be unable to fight his seat at the next General Election if the party was still led by Macmillan, a man he said had been brought into 'widespread ridicule'.[16] Following a debate in the House of Commons during which Harold Wilson repeatedly pressed Macmillan on the affair, *The Times* declared that Macmillan was 'unlikely to be leader in the next Election'. By the end of June, both the *Daily Telegraph* and the *Economist* were openly discussing who would succeed Macmillan as Conservative Party leader.[17]

In the end, it was not the scandal that ended Macmillan's career but illness. On the night of 7 October 1963 – on the eve of the Conservative Party conference – Macmillan was struck by prostate trouble and immediately taken to the King Edward VII Hospital for surgery to remove his prostate gland. On 9 October, it fell to his Foreign

Secretary Alec Douglas-Home to inform the Conservatives gathered in Blackpool that Macmillan could no longer continue as Prime Minister. Coming as it did amidst the Party Conference, the announcement ensured that there would be a scramble for the leadership. As Macmillan wrote in his memoirs, 'Political death is always uncomfortable; but in my case it could not have been more untimely'.[18] There followed a battle of wills and wits, but, in the end, it was Lord Home who travelled to the Palace on 18 October, where he was asked by Queen Elizabeth II to form her next government.[19]

The Queen wrote to Macmillan shortly thereafter, telling him that whilst she had the 'greatest confidence in Alec Home' and had not the 'least doubt that as the fourth Prime Minister of my reign he will lead my Government and our country with an equally firm and sure hand', she nevertheless regretted Macmillan's departure: 'There is ... no question of your successor, however admirable he may be, being able to perform exactly those services which you have given so generously and for which I am so deeply grateful. During these years you have had to unravel a succession of major and intricate problems affecting the peace of the world and the very existence of Britain and the Commonwealth. History will witness to the masterly skills with which you have handled them'.[20] It was a fitting tribute to the man who had continuously held the office of Prime Minister for longer than any other in the twentieth century to that point. His was always going to be a difficult act for Lord Home to follow, and, as it turned out, his successor was to last just one year in 10 Downing Street before suffering a General Election loss at the hands of Harold Wilson's Labour Party. There was little Home could point to in the way of achievement, and, for the first time in thirteen years, it became the responsibility of the Labour Party to manage Britain's place in the world.

* * *

Less than twenty-four hours after completing his audience with the Queen, the new Prime Minister Harold Wilson met with his Chancellor of the Exchequer James Callaghan and the Secretary of State for Economic Affairs George Brown to discuss a memorandum left on their desks by Treasury officials. The memorandum showed that for the year 1964, the British economy was facing a balance of payments deficit of £800 million, more than twice the amount Wilson had suggested during the election campaign. This figure stunned the new

Labour government; as Wilson wrote in his memoirs, 'It was this inheritance which was to dominate almost every action of the Government for five years of the five years, eight months we were in office'.[21]

The three men briefly discussed an immediate devaluation of the pound to stabilise the losses but determined that the international ripples would be too great, especially as the world did not yet know the extent of Britain's deficit. They also rejected quotas on imports, recognising that they would necessarily inflict damage on industrial production. This left only a temporary surcharge on imports. They feared this would mean running afoul of both the General Agreement on Tariffs and Trade (GATT) and the European Free Trade Agreement and were convinced it would antagonise the Commonwealth and the United States. This could not be helped. The new government had to act. On 17 October, therefore, before the full cabinet was even chosen, Wilson instructed the relevant departments to begin drafting details to impose an import surcharge of 15 per cent on all imports except food, tobacco and 'basic raw materials'.[22] When the cabinet met for the first time on 19 October, Wilson briefed them on the economic situation. In addition to the £800 million balance of payments deficit, the government faced a domestic economy that was succumbing to ever-increasing prices and a desperate need for revenue which existing rates of taxation could not meet. They agreed to issue a statement announcing the import surcharges in addition to an export rebate scheme, the establishment of a Commonwealth Exports Council and the creation of a Price Review Body for industry. There was no discussion whatsoever of Europe; the effects of the government's new economy policy were debated solely in the context of the Commonwealth and the United States.[23]

Since becoming Labour Party leader after Hugh Gaitskell's untimely death in January 1963, Wilson had continued to steer the party along a decidedly anti-European path. He was instrumental in developing Labour's five 'essential' conditions that they would demand be met before supporting British entry into the EEC. These included the 'right to plan our own economy', 'freedom to pursue our own foreign policy', 'binding safeguards for the trade and other interests of the Commonwealth countries', 'guarantees to safeguard British agriculture', and the fulfilment of the government's pledges to the countries of the EFTA.[24] Throughout 1963 and 1964, Wilson repeatedly restated these conditions, and his Shadow Foreign Secretary and Deputy Leader of the Opposition George Brown suggested in public that the British government could best spend its time considering what options were available for 'fruitful co-operation between us and members of the Six' and between the EFTA and the Six rather than actually seeking to join the EEC.[25]

Now that Wilson was sitting at the head of the cabinet table with real economic problems to contend with, his stance towards the EEC did not change. 'Europe' was an inconvenience that would eventually have to be managed; it did not occupy a central place in the government's thinking. For the first time since the end of the Second World War, British European policy was relegated to a distinct second tier of priorities. Wilson immediately wrote to the American President Lyndon Johnson – himself within ten days of his own presidential election – to explain his decision on the economy, telling him that 'We knew, while in opposition, that the [economic] position was deteriorating; but we deliberately refrained from turning it into a major election issue in order not to undermine confidence. Now that we have examined all the facts I find the situation is even worse than we had supposed'. He explained that the United Kingdom was facing a 'probable deficit on external account for this year which may be as high as £800 million'. The new Labour government had no choice but to take 'firm remedial measures'.[26] This would, unfortunately, have an effect on Britain's position in the world and on its relationship with the United States, Europe and the Commonwealth.

Wilson wrote again on 19 November 1964, warning Johnson that the British government was 'facing a serious situation on sterling'. If the run on sterling continued, he feared that the UK would 'exhaust the credit facilities at present available to us in a matter of weeks'.[27] It was a line the American government had heard time and time again since the end of the war, and the President replied with the vague platitudes of his predecessors: 'Thank you for your frank exposition of the problems you are facing with sterling. You can be sure of our deep interest in your efforts to maintain its integrity'.[28] Johnson went beyond Kennedy, however, and, on 25 November, agreed to a $1 billion short-term loan from the American Export-Import Bank and the Federal Reserve, providing confidence to European central banks to provide an additional $2 billion. Although Europeans had provided the bulk of the loan, Wilson felt the greatest debt of gratitude to the Americans, claiming that the financial crisis had 'made clear' who Britain's friends were.[29]

Beyond the economy, Wilson's main efforts were focussed on preserving the Commonwealth. Writing to Johnson after the Commonwealth Prime Minister's meeting in July 1964 (whilst still leader of the opposition), he had enthused that he was 'convinced that the new Commonwealth has taken shape and will have a major role to play in the future as we turn our minds to the problems of the next decades'. In particular, he hoped that as Britain was so gracious in granting colonies independence during decolonisation, these former colonies might 'in the future help up to take the sting out of the worlds [sic] racial problems'.[30] Wilson continued to press his case for the Commonwealth upon entering 10 Downing Street, informing Johnson in late December 1964 that Britain had a 'complementary' role to play to the United States, 'exploiting our particular advantage as the centre of the Commonwealth and as a member of all three regional alliances and the fact of the British presence from Gibraltar to Singapore, no longer for imperial purposes but simply to keep the peace, to promote a stable and just order and to be ready to respond to United Nations calls'.[31] He made no mention of the Common Market or, indeed, of the European continent in general. For Wilson much more so than for previous Conservative and Labour governments, Britain was simply not a European country.

Nevertheless, the Prime Minister quickly discovered that Europe was the one topic he could not avoid. In early February 1965, Lord Gladwyn wrote to Wilson following a conversation with the French deputy Jacqueline Thome-Patenôtre. Thome-Patenôtre had heard that Wilson had informed de Gaulle that Britain was 'not yet ripe' ('*pas encore mure*') for a European solution, implying that it may well be ripe in the near future. This implication was in stark contrast to any of Wilson's previous public statements, which gave no hint of possible entry under a Labour government. Gladwyn suggested that de Gaulle might even 'be prepared to make some advances towards you when you meet next month'.[32] Wilson soon quelled the rumour, however. He replied that he had not mentioned a 'European solution' to the General, saying only that he saw 'no reason why Britain and France should not try to develop warmer political and closer economic relations', particularly in the industrial field and advanced aviation.[33] The Labour government's approach towards Europe would continue to be one of pragmatic cooperation when it was in the interests of Britain and the Commonwealth. It was not one of grandiose visions of European unity.

Lord Gladwyn was not the only individual to press the Prime Minister on Europe. On 12 February (the day before Wilson replied to Gladwyn), Oliver Wright, Wilson's private secretary, wrote to him arguing that the Labour government had to recognise that 'Geographically, we exist in Europe; and increasingly, I suspect, industrially and commercially we shall have to earn our living in Europe'. Since the end of the Second World War, he said, British foreign policy had always rested on a 'four-legged chair', with the Commonwealth, the United Nations, the Atlantic Alliance and Europe forming the four legs. However, the Commonwealth leg was growing ever shorter, the United Nations leg had found itself hamstrung by the Soviet Union and President Johnson seemed far less committed to the leg of the Atlantic Alliance than Kennedy had been before him. For this reason, the British government had to turn to Europe, the only leg left standing, where the problem was 'what sort of Europe can Britain best live with'. The answer, Wright suggested, was 'a Europe of the whole of Europe, not a Europe divided three ways between the Six and the Seven and the Soviet satellites'. This could best be achieved by appeasing de Gaulle, reuniting Germany and reaching détente with the Soviet Union. Britain's policy under Labour should be 'to modify the nature of the Six, to create the sort of Europe we could live with and be a part of, to de-fuse the German problem and to re-make Britain a key power in the jigsaw. At the end, the situation would be: – An All-Europe des Patries, led by Britain and France; Germany reunified; Détente with the East'. Neither the Commonwealth nor the United States lay in Britain's future.[34]

Wright's contention was shared by Gladwyn. He wrote to Jo Grimond, the leader of the Liberal Party, informing him that the Dutch Ambassador had told him that, according to the French Ambassador, Wilson had told de Gaulle that he 'never resented the General's veto: on the contrary, he had positively welcomed it, since he believed that the Conservative Government had been on the point of taking the nation into the Common Market without regard to our own interests or those of the Commonwealth'. Wilson had added that, in the short-term at least, there was little reason for Britain to enter 'Europe'. It would be far better to 'think of "common projects" on which your two countries [said the Dutch ambassador] might embark and in general see what the possibilities were of cooperation'. Finally, Wilson had reportedly said that his own preference within Europe was for 'something even looser than de Gaulle's idea of a "Europe des Etats"'.[35] Although the Dutch ambassador's information was largely second-hand rumour, it seemed to mesh with Wilson's reply to Gladwyn about Thome-Patenôtre's assertions. Gladwyn therefore encouraged Grimond to ask Wilson at Prime Minister's Questions if 'Her Majesty's Government's conception of an eventual Western European Association was something even looser than General de Gaulle's own conception of a "Europe of States"'?[36]

When the House of Commons met the following day, Wilson was indeed questioned on the European Economic Community, although Grimond was beaten to the chase by the Conservative MP and long-time supporter of the European Movement Raymond Gower, who asked the Prime Minister to make a statement on the Common Market. When Wilson replied that there was 'no reason to suppose that the circumstances which led to the breakdown of the Brussels negotiations have changed' and that the government's policy was to 'do all we can to build a bridge between EFTA and the EEC', Gower suggested that Wilson's answer 'hardly creates the impression of an adventurous, forward-looking Administration ready to contemplate change but rather an inward-looking, old-fashioned, tired Administration'. Wilson, however, swept Gower aside, painting the Labour government as one of pragmatists as opposed to those across the aisle who had 'sulk[ed] in [their] tents after the last breakdown ... cancelling Royal visits to Paris and [making] peevish and pettish remarks from this Box'. When the Labour MP Trevor Park asked the Prime Minister to confirm that 'the primary responsibility of the British Government is not to the European Economic Community, but to the Commonwealth', Wilson was only too happy to oblige: 'We want the best possible relations we can get with Europe. ... However, I am perfectly certain that the House would agree that if we were faced with terms of entry in which we had to choose between accepting entry and the interests of our trading and other relationships with the Commonwealth, as we were faced in November 1962, we would be right to reject those terms'. Following Wilson's response, the Speaker finally called on Grimond, who put to the Prime Minister Gladwyn's question. Wilson again swatted aside the potential criticism, saying that if by calling for European 'political unity' Grimond was 'suggesting our entering some supranational organisation where vital questions of foreign policy going far beyond Europe – and we have very vital interests far beyond Europe – or of defence were to be decided by some system of majority voting, I am sure that the whole House would unite in saying that that would not be possible for this country'.[37] Wilson was a Commonwealth man, and, in February 1965, there was little either the Liberals or the Conservatives could say to make him change his mind.

* * *

The Commonwealth, however, was not what it once was, and its relevance to the future of the United Kingdom was increasingly cast into doubt. In early March 1965, the Conservative MP Richard Hornby, who had served as Parliamentary Under-Secretary of State for the Colonies when Duncan Sandys was Colonial Secretary, sent to his former boss a paper titled 'A Changing Commonwealth in a Divided World'. In words that left little to the imagination, Hornby wrote that 'Few institutions have suffered so much from the language of make-believe. Again and again in speeches and writings the Commonwealth has been given a political cohesion and an economic unity which it plainly does not possess'. Britain, he said, needed a reality-check: 'Within a generation [the Commonwealth] has changed from the closely-knit group of Britain and the white dominions and become instead an association of twenty-one independent nations, of whom nine are in Africa, comprising some 750 million people, the majority of whom are Asian'. For each of these new countries, the 'immediate and understandable instinct has been to show proof of their sovereignty'. This had necessarily meant a certain distancing from Great Britain. The consequence had been to leave the United Kingdom as a 'country of 50 million peoples...dwarfed by the new giants of America and Russia and China'. For Hornby – a man who knew the Commonwealth as well as any other in the British government – there was only one solution: 'By geographical position Britain is a part of Europe. It is right, and important, that she should play her part in Europe's political affairs.... Economically too Britain needs to associate with Europe'. Only by 'joining Europe' could the British government once again make itself relevant to the Commonwealth. In so doing, it would make the Commonwealth 'an example of understanding and breaking down the barriers of geography, colour and race and an instrument of efficient mutual assistance, for which a divided world as a whole could be grateful'.[38]

The influential Conservative Research Department agreed, writing that same month that 'The Commonwealth is not a centre of power and, therefore, it does not offer Britain the means of strengthening herself economically and military against the harsh realities of a competitive world. ... British membership of E.E.C. could achieve both these requirements'.[39] Harold Wilson and the Labour government remained committed to the Commonwealth. The opposition Conservative Party no longer shared their allegiance. Its members had once believed it was possible to lead both the British Empire and Commonwealth and a united Europe. Now they just desperately hoped that a Europe-already formed would accept Britain into its ranks. For the Conservatives, it was no longer a question of leadership but of national survival at the political and economic levels.

There was also a rigorous debate amongst officials in Whitehall over how Britain's Commonwealth membership affected its policies towards Europe. L. B. Walsh Atkins, Assistant Under-Secretary of State at the Commonwealth Relations Office, wrote to his boss Sir Neil Pritchard (Deputy Under-Secretary of State) on 15 April, arguing that if the British government wished to reduce its forces on the European continent (particularly in Germany) at any point in the future, it would be easier to do so if Britain were already part of the 'European political community'. He quoted from a Foreign Office memorandum, which read: 'British membership of a European community is not an incompatible alternative to maintaining the Commonwealth connexion, nor to active policy East of Suez, nor to wider European unity including members of E.F.T.A., nor to a continuing relationship with the United States as partners of the Atlantic tandem. Indeed, if we remain outside [the] European community, all these policies may be eroded'. Atkins recognised that the memorandum was in part an attempt by the Foreign Office to plug its well-known 'closer to Europe' policy. Nevertheless, he found that there was 'a good deal to be said for it'.[40]

Pritchard also heard from Sir Algernon Rumbold, his colleague at the Commonwealth Relations Office, who shared Atkins' suspicions that 'the Foreign Office are taking one more opportunity to root for Europe'. Unlike Atkins, however, he was unconvinced that there was a 'good deal to be said' for this position, as in his view the Foreign Office tended to 'confuse the issues by muddling up the question of our joining the European Economic Community with other ways of getting closer to Europe'. He was very happy to support any Foreign Office attempts to engage in greater political consultation in Europe and to assist government efforts to work out pragmatic cooperation on an issue-by-issue basis, but when it came to the desirability of the United Kingdom one day entering the EEC, he believed that the Commonwealth Relations Office was 'in a different country' from the Foreign Office. British entry into the Common Market would 'be the end of the Commonwealth trading system: Commonwealth exports to the United Kingdom would rapidly decline and as a consequence our exports to the Commonwealth would decline. In due course that would bring an end to the Commonwealth in any sense that we now use that word'.[41] Perhaps unsurprisingly, the views of the Commonwealth Relations Office were closer to Labour Party ministers than the more pro-European Foreign Office officials. Nevertheless, most civil servants in Whitehall took their lead from the Foreign Office, believing that the Commonwealth had already come to an end in any meaningful sense of the word, even if their elected leaders in the Labour Party had not yet reached this conclusion.

In May 1965, the Conservative Party put further pressure on the government over Europe, publicly restating its policy of 'secur[ing] Britain's entry into the European Economic Community, in order to obtain the commercial benefits of the Common Market, and the opportunity to influence the future economic policies, both internal and external, of the Community; and (b) [of] secur[ing] for Britain a full say in whatever decisions may be taken to establish closer European unity in the political and defence sphere'.[42] Lord Gladwyn also decided to launch a multi-party organisation called Britain in Europe, hoping that Conservatives and Liberals working together would be able to draw more Labour supporters to their cause. He began this campaign on 20 May 1965, circulating a draft declaration to close associates that argued 'Membership of the European Community should...be the policy of the British Government'. The reasons, it said, were clear: 'Economically, there is the large market and the stimulus of competition. Politically, there is the influence borne by [being] a member of a closely united Europe; and the satisfaction of participating in a far-reaching experiment in international government where decisions in certain defined spheres are taken in common'.[43]

Gladwyn explained to Kenneth Keith, an influential merchant banker, that the goal for his campaign was that it 'should *not* be construed as an attack on Her Majesty's Government; that it should always be emphasized that the whole thing was tripartisan; that at the same time it should be recognized that both on the Tory and on the Labour side it consisted of people who were probably in advance of the general thinking of their own party; and that the principal object of the campaign would really be one of enlightenment'. For this reason, although he (as a Liberal) would be chairing the organisation, he had persuaded the Labour MP Geoffrey de Freitas (who at that time was the principal Labour spokesman in the Council of Europe and the Western European Union) and the Conservative David Ormsby-Gore (recently elevated to the House of Lords as Lord Harlech, following four years in the United States as British Ambassador) to serve as vice-chairmen. To make his lobbying run more smoothly, he hoped to hire a 'paid Director who preferably should have Labour sympathies, even if he were not necessarily an active member of the Labour Party'.[44] Keith agreed to participate, and, in July 1965, Gladwyn officially launched Britain in Europe.[45]

Not all pro-Europeans were in sympathy with Gladwyn's efforts, however. Sir Edward Beddington-Behrens wrote to him on 29 July claiming that his new organisation 'merely duplicate[s] some of the work of [the European Movement] Council'. He pointed out that Gladwyn himself sat on the European Movement Council and was thus 'at a loss to understand the need for your break away organisation'.[46] Gladwyn replied that he was 'rather surprised' by Beddington-Behrens' letter, as he had hoped the two organisations could work together. He had no intention of resigning from the Council, but 'quite seriously believe[d] that Britain in Europe can go further in supporting the idea that we should join a supra-national political European community than the Council can'.[47] For Gladwyn, the key consideration was not about drawing dividing lines between the various organisations in favour of British integration and staking out political territory. It was instead about working together when possible and separately when necessary to persuade both those within and those outside Parliament that Britain's future lay in Europe. The Conservative Party, at least, needed no such persuasion. On 28 July, its parliamentary members elected as their party leader Edward Heath, a man who, more so than any other in Parliament, believed in British EEC entry. Under Heath, the

Conservative Party would turn to Europe without equivocation. It was now up to Harold Wilson's Labour Party to determine *its* position.

* * *

Following a meeting with EFTA Prime Ministers in May 1965, Wilson launched a new European policy that he called 'bridge-building'. It was intended to bring together the EEC and the EFTA in a scheme that, in its tone and structure, differed very little from Macmillan's 'grand design' for Europe in 1961.[48] In contrast to Macmillan, however, Wilson dismissed the idea that this 'bridge' would ever lead to Britain joining the EEC. Even when launching this new European policy, he emphasised that the Commonwealth would remain the United Kingdom's economic priority. Perhaps unsurprisingly, the response of the Six to his '"trawling operation" to find areas for bridge building was lukewarm'.[49]

Wilson's attitude was challenged in late June, however, when the EEC member-states reached deadlock over agricultural financing arrangements and de Gaulle withdrew French participation from the Community, leaving an 'empty chair'. The Five (the Six minus France) immediately turned to the UK for assistance. Sir Con O'Neill, head of the Foreign Office's European Economic Organisations Department, argued that this presented a unique opportunity for the British government, opening up the possibility of its joining the EEC without French obstruction, perhaps even replacing France to become the sixth member. He wrote to John Barnes, head of the Western Organisations Department, saying, 'If I were able to push France out of the Community it is a responsibility I would willingly accept. If ... we stiffen the Five and help them to resist French terms to the point where France might fail to get her way and so encourage the Five to turn to us, we could hardly be said to have been responsible for pushing her out'.[50] The Foreign Secretary Michael Stewart agreed, fearing that if Britain did not fill the vacuum created by the absence of France, either the Five would bend to de Gaulle's will to make him re-engage, or Germany would come to dominate the EEC and, by extension, continental Europe. Neither scenario was attractive to the British government. Stewart wrote to Wilson, saying, 'It is a turning point: we must do what we can to make a French victory less likely'.[51] Nevertheless, Wilson was still hesitant to fully embrace British entry, fearing that it would do untold damage to British agriculture and, more importantly, could sever Britain's relationships with the Commonwealth. His delay represented another lost opportunity, and, as expected, the French eventually re-engaged with de Gaulle's position strengthened.

By the end of 1965, however, even Wilson had to admit that his vision of the Commonwealth as Britain's primary economic partner had run aground, the Commonwealth leaders themselves rejecting it in favour of a wider trading base, often with either the United States or the Soviet Union as their primary partner. Britain's former colonies had turned to the future, uninterested in returning to the ties that had once bound them.[52] On the home front, the Conservative opposition continued to ratchet up the pressure, with party chairman Edward du Cann proclaiming that 'we must go into Europe'. At his first party conference as leader in September 1965, Edward Heath declared that the Conservative Party was the 'European' party. As *The Times* reported that month, Conservative policy and rhetoric under Heath had 'confirmed the belief that the Common Market, combined with close Commonwealth links, would provide the wider market that Britain needs for survival and stimulate industry to modernize and keep down costs'.[53]

Indeed, so great did the pressure become that the Labour Party Chief Whip Edward Short informed Wilson on 16 December 1965 that the Labour MP Geoffrey de Freitas had already secured the support of 'a fair number of Ministers' in his campaign to get Labour MPs to join the United Kingdom Council of the European Movement whilst simultaneously encouraging their participation in Gladwyn's 'Britain in Europe' organisation. Short reminded Wilson that 'When the Common Market controversy was raging [in 1962–63], the Party became rather badly polarized'. That was no longer the case, and there had been 'a considerable change of opinion in the Party on the question of Europe'. In previous years, it might have been advisable for the Prime Minister to discipline those Labour MPs who became involved in the European Movement or Britain in Europe. Now, Short did 'not think there is any need to ask the Ministers who have joined this Council to withdraw from it'.[54] It was no longer good politics – and perhaps not good policy, either – for the Labour Party to be as adamant in its opposition to British entry into the EEC as it once had been.

* * *

In late February 1966, Wilson advised the Queen to dissolve Parliament, triggering an immediate General Election. He wrote to the American

President Lyndon Johnson, warning that the *Sunday Express* was calling on electors to vote Conservative to avoid a descent towards 'satellite status' of the United States. The Prime Minister joked that if he 'took this particular threat seriously, I might suggest to you that we should have a row in order to help me, but quite honestly I cannot think of anything to have a row about. Should you think of a suitable subject you will no doubt let me know'. Joking aside, Wilson still told Johnson he still had to keep in mind the British electorate, and the best way to deflect anti-American criticism was to accentuate another foil. He was, therefore, prepared to take a 'slightly anti-German line. If I have to employ xenophobia, which I hope will not be necessary, I would rather it be of that variety than the Tory anti-Americanism'.[55] Despite the urgings of his Chief Whip to rethink Britain's relationship with the EEC, for Wilson, Europe was still his least important ally. If he had to choose between isolating Europe and isolating the United States, he would spurn Europe every time.[56]

Still, an alliance with the United States alone was insufficient, particularly when the official policy of the American government was to encourage the United Kingdom to enter the EEC. For this reason, when the March General Election successfully returned Labour to power with a greatly increased majority, Wilson finally consented to the establishment of a Cabinet committee to explore British membership of the Common Market. Many had already begun to suspect that the Labour position towards Europe was softening. In contrast to the 1964 election, in 1966, the Common Market had become a major issue, in large part driven by Ted Heath's insistence. Despite his pre-election comments to Johnson, Wilson decided to neutralise Conservative critiques, announcing in a speech, 'Given a fair wind, we will negotiate our way into the Common Market.... We believe that given the right conditions it would be possible and right to join [the] EEC as an economic community'.[57] The Common Market was no longer a party-political issue, and, consequently, much of Heath's general election campaign fell flat.

The Commonwealth countries noticed this policy shift. It immediately aggravated them for, despite their autonomy and distance from Great Britain, they nonetheless wished to be seen as the United Kingdom's foremost priority. On 1 February 1966, Sir Laurence Lindo, the High Commissioner for Jamaica, wrote to Arthur Bottomley, Labour's Commonwealth Secretary, reminding him that, after the collapse of the last negotiations in 1963, the government had 'given members of the Commonwealth an assurance that in the event of Britain's accession to the Treaty of Rome the opportunity for association would be made available to them'. Lindo wished to confirm, on behalf of the Jamaican government, that this policy would remain in effect after the General Election.[58] The Commonwealth Relations Office sought clarification from the Foreign Office,[59] after which Bottomley replied to Lindo that the government was 'not at present negotiating for Britain's entry into the European Economic Community and you will understand that it is accordingly not possible for me to say just what arrangements we should aim to secure under various heads in the hypothetical event of our entering into negotiations'.[60] It was the classical political stall.

The government also heard from Ian Maclennan, the British High Commissioner in New Zealand, who told the Commonwealth Office that 'both the Government and the people in New Zealand still have a nagging worry about the damage which our entry might do in New Zealand's economy'. Although most New Zealanders had by and large 'begun to live with the idea that at some stage we shall "go into Europe"', they nevertheless still viewed this as a distant prospect, and 'an announcement that negotiations were reopened with the Six would still come as a shock, particularly to the farming community'. To the New Zealander, 'whether Minister or man in the street, it is not just a matter of economics but of the basic traditional relationship between our two countries. If we were thought to have accepted, or even to be ready to accept, abandonment of New Zealand's interests as the price for our own entry into the Common Market there would be great resentment'.[61] The views of the Australians and Canadians, as well as other Commonwealth governments in the Caribbean and sub-Saharan Africa, were no different.[62] Any hint that the government was willing to reconsider British entry into the European Common Market would be met with suspicion throughout the Commonwealth. The General Election campaign did nothing to calm their fears.

It was within this context that Wilson authorised the Cabinet to establish its committee exploring British entry into the EEC. After the announcement, Maclennan wrote to him again. He acknowledged that New Zealanders understood the reasons that Britain was exploring EEC entry, but reminded him that, in the previous negotiations, the British government had insisted that 'special arrangements would have to be made to cover New Zealand's special position'. The New Zealand economy, he wrote, was 'heavily dependent on the export of [its] foodstuffs to Britain', and New Zealand had 'always valued its close trading relations with Britain'. Because of this, the New Zealand government and people had 'drawn confidence from past assurances that Britain would not feel able to join the Community unless arrangements which protected New Zealand's vital economic interests had been secured'. He hoped that the government would renew its pledge; the 'reiteration of those assurances at the present time would undoubtedly contribute to maintaining that confidence'.[63]

The New Zealanders would have an uphill battle. There was increasing sentiment in Britain for a re-engagement with the European continent, and it was British public opinion rather than that of New Zealand that was Wilson's primary concern. In early May, a group from the Royal Institute of International Affairs at Chatham House and the Franco–British Society travelled to Paris to meet with French politicians, businessmen and journalists at the Centre d'Etudes de Politique Entrangere. They found that the 'British conversion to European ideals has not yet come to be fully accepted by a number of informed French Anglophiles'. It was also 'hard to envisage French acceptance of Britain's entry into [the] E.E.C. in the near future', largely due to the fact that de Gaulle's beliefs were 'shared by substantial sections of French opinion'. Despite this, the British contingent was optimistic that British political will was now 'directed both to joining and supporting a Europe conceived on the lines of the Rome Treaty and to supporting a NATO alliance'. Furthermore, they felt certain that if de Gaulle were 'to depart from the scene, it seems unlikely that his stance could be maintained unchanged for long'. It was only a matter of time before Britain's efforts to join the Common Market would be accepted by the French.[64]

This conclusion was reached not only by those at Chatham House but also by an increasing number of British MPs. On 28 June, Lord Gladwyn officially launched his Campaign for a European Political Community, noting that 150 Members of Parliament from all parties had signed a declaration supporting British entry into a united Europe. Beyond the hallowed corridors of Westminster, his declaration was also signed by the Masters or Wardens of St Catherine's College Oxford, Churchill College Cambridge, New College Oxford, All Souls College Oxford and Marlborough College; the vice-chancellor of the University of Sussex; the chairmen of such firms as John Lewis, Boots,

Rolls-Royce, Shell and the Wellcome Foundation; the director of Barclays Bank; the managing director of the *Financial Times*, the chairman of the *Economist*, the editor of the *Sun*, and the deputy editors of the *Sunday Times* and *Sunday Telegraph*; and the General Secretaries of the Transport and Salaried Staffs Association, the Amalgamated Engineering Union, the National Union of General and Municipal Workers, and the Chemical Workers Union; as well as leading clerics and servicemen. Across British society, culture and politics, there was an increasing recognition that Britain was a European country and that its future lay in a united Europe. As Gladwyn said in his speech, 'from today onwards one thing is certain. No longer can it be asserted that Britain is "an island" above all intent on maintaining her links with a Commonwealth, which, however valuable, has no longer the same economic, still less the same political significance, or an unreal "special relationship" with the United States'.[65] The United Kingdom was now a European nation.

British MPs and the movers and shakers across British society were joined in repeating this message by Britain's allies in the United States. On 11 July, the British Ambassador Sir Patrick Dean wrote to Sir Burke Trend, the Cabinet Secretary, informing him that George Ball of the American State Department had insisted that 'our economic survival could only be assured if we joined the E.E.C.'. Britain should therefore 'sign the Treaty of Rome as soon as possible, or at least announce our willingness to do so, and count on sorting out the problems of application after we had signed up'. When Dean explained to Ball that the British government's approach was the opposite – that the technical questions had to be settled *before* Britain could apply for membership – he was chastised: '[Ball] considered that our position as supplicant was much weaker and that our bargaining position would be much enhanced once we were inside the organisation. If we pursued our present tactics we could be sure that the French would obstruct us all the way down the line'. Ball informed Dean that 'For all its goodwill and the efforts made, the U.K. was only able to contribute to the problems of free-world defence outside the Atlantic area by providing small numbers of troops scattered around the world. The rest of Europe contributed almost nothing at all'. The 'only chance' he saw for Britain and Western Europe to 'play the part which they should on the international scene' was for Britain to 'join the Community and lead Western Europe towards the assumption of a more meaningful outward-looking worldwide role'.[66] In Ball's view, Britain should become exactly the Atlanticist Trojan Horse within Europe that de Gaulle most feared.

Henry Kissinger – soon to be National Security Adviser and Secretary of State under President Richard Nixon, but in 1966 still a faculty member at Harvard University – shared Ball's appraisal, writing to Gladwyn in early August that 'Britain ought to seek its future in Europe instead of the Himalayas'. This, he thought, was only prevented 'by the inability of the present government to establish the right priorities (or any for that matter)'.[67] The sense of drift that Kissinger described was heightened by a renewed economic crisis that summer and autumn (the third since the government took office in 1964), when confidence in sterling collapsed and the government was forced to increase the bank rate from 6 to 7 per cent, place travel restrictions on government employees, impose a six-month freeze of wage and price increases and introduce cuts in public expenditure. When these measures failed to quell the crisis, the United States, Canada and several Western European countries put together an aid package totalling $400 million, to supplement a previous aid package from September 1965 of $925 million.[68] Lord Plowden explained to American Senator Lee Metcalf that 'Each time the Government has been faced with a run on sterling it seems always to have done too little too late, and even then to have presented its measures in public that this is not really going to hurt. At the present time, if they carry out all the things they say they are going to do, there is no doubt we have a quite exceptional squeeze on the economy. I would expect there to be quite a recession in the early part of next year'.[69]

The British economy was broken, and neither the Commonwealth nor the close relationship with the United States offered a long-term solution to fix it. In the face of the third sterling crisis in just two years, Wilson began to recognise what many had been telling him since he became Prime Minister: Europe offered Britain's only economic salvation. In October 1966, therefore, Wilson told the cabinet that he intended to 'embark on a "probe" of the countries of the Six to see if the conditions existed for membership'.[70] Following his announcement, the Prime Minister wrote to the American President to explain his decision. He had never been, he insisted, 'one of the little band of so-called "Europeans"' and still disagreed with the way the Conservative Party had approached Common Market membership in the years 1961–63. At that time, he had doubted whether the

Six would ever develop into a community 'dedicated to a concept of ever-widening and freer trade', believing instead that they would turn towards 'a tight little inward-looking group of countries concerned essentially with their own affairs'. Now, however, the situation was quite different. Europe had 'changed pretty fundamentally since 1962', and Wilson believed that 'the prospects of building a new and wider community including, as well as ourselves, a number of if not all of our EFTA partners, are now much more promising than they were'. He was certain that such an expanded community would 'greatly strengthen not only Britain and Europe, but the West as a whole'. He claimed his was a vision of an 'outward looking European Community, designed to play the constructive role in world affairs that each of us individually is now finding too difficult'. Above all else, he wished to assure Johnson that his cabinet colleagues and he held a 'firm determination... that there shall be no change in the fundamental relationship between our two countries and in our own basic loyalty to and belief in the Atlantic concept'. British membership of the EEC would strengthen the Anglo–American relationship, not detract from it.[71]

Johnson replied that he was 'immensely heartened by your courageous announcement', the outcome of which would 'strengthen and unify the West'. He had no objection to Britain 'joining Europe'.[72] Sir Patrick Dean confirmed the American position in a December memorandum, writing to Sir Con O'Neill that the United States government 'believe firmly in the progressive unification of Europe for political and strategic reasons', so much so that it was 'prepared to put up with some economic disadvantage, by way, for example, of discrimination against American trade'. American thinking was that if the United Kingdom entered the Community, any short-term economic disadvantage would be mitigated by long-term British encouragement of free trade in Europe, thus opening up the EEC market to American goods and services. The American government supported a united Europe as a point of principle, with or without the United Kingdom; pragmatically, however, it would be far preferable for a united Europe to have Britain at its heart championing a strong Atlantic political and economic alliance.[73]

Even so, Britain's continued objection to the Vietnam War placed strains on the Anglo–American 'special relationship', and, as the sun set on 1966, the commonality that had lingered since the Second World

War came under almost constant pressure.[74] As Britain lost both its Empire and Commonwealth and its close Atlantic Alliance, the role of Europe in its foreign policy loomed ever larger.[75] When the American Ambassador David Bruce met with Wilson on the morning of 10 January 1967, the Prime Minister advised him that the best American policy concerning British entry into Europe would be for the Americans to 'keep their heads down'. If the United States government came out too strongly in favour of British entry, it would only inflame de Gaulle and potentially isolate Willy Brandt, the leader of the German Social Democratic Party, who was already outspoken in his support of American policies. Should the United Kingdom choose to enter the EEC, it would have to be seen as a British decision, not merely answering the call of the Americans.[76]

The American Embassy in London took this message to heart, conveying it to the State Department in Washington DC. On 8 February, the American Minister for Economic Affairs at the Embassy arranged a meeting with Sir Con O'Neill at the Foreign Office, where he provided him with a copy of the 'Summary of Guidance to United States Diplomatic Posts Abroad on the Attitude of the Administration towards the British approach to the E.E.C.', a telegram that had been sent from Washington to all American diplomatic posts, including those throughout Western Europe. He gave it to O'Neill as proof of American good faith, who in turn forwarded to A. M. Pallister, the Permanent Under-Secretary at 10 Downing Street. The guidance confirmed that the United States government wished to see UK membership of the EEC in order to 'advance the process of political unification in Europe' and to create 'a more open Community with closer ties with the United States'. However, the American government agreed that 'further public statements of United States support for British membership would not at this time be helpful. They would risk giving ammunition to opponents of British membership in Europe'.[77]

The American telegram gave the British government the space it needed to develop a European policy that could not be accused of being a mere extension of the Atlantic Alliance. In doing so, it had the support of the British public, at least as demonstrated by opinion polling. On 17 February 1967, Duncan Sandys received copies of two polls, one from the *Daily Telegraph* and the second from the *Daily Mail*, both of which had taken their samples in the closing days of the previous year. The former found that 67 per cent of the population approved of the

British government joining the Common Market if 'Britain's best interests would be served', compared to just 17 per cent who were opposed. Significantly, when asked to choose between the Common Market or closer association with the United States, 56 per cent chose the EEC, with only 24 per cent favouring the 'special relationship'. The *Daily Mail*'s survey found similar results, with 58 per cent responding that the British government 'should try to join the Common Market' and only 17 per cent opposed.[78] This conclusion was supported by business interests across the United Kingdom, with the Confederation of British Industry (CBI) reporting that 'virtually everyone in the City was in favour' of British entry into the EEC.[79]

The Conservative Party took advantage of this favourable public opinion, launching its own probe into British policy towards Europe to mirror that of Wilson's.[80] Heath delivered the results on 4 March, concluding that 'the Government ought now to accept the Treaty of Rome, and the structure of the European Community which has been built upon the foundation of that treaty'. The time had come to stop haggling over membership conditions and calling for special provisions. Instead, the British government had to accept that the Six were 'moving towards a European view on international finance, on defence, on the political development of Europe'. The government had to 'show that we too want to see a European view emerge on these matters'. If the government was serious about Europe, the European view would necessarily dictate government policy over the whole spectrum of issues: 'Ministers have sometimes tried to put these subjects [finance and defence] on one side. They say that there is nothing in the Treaty of Rome about sterling or reserve currencies, nothing about defence. This is to misunderstand what the Community is all about. The fact is that if we believe, as I do firmly, that our future lies within the Community, then this belief will colour and influence our major problems. This is true whether we talk about defence or disarmament or sterling, or about home policies of taxation or agricultural support'.[81] It was the Conservative belief that Europe must permeate all areas of British policy. The United Kingdom must become, without caveat, a European country.

Shortly after the Conservatives published the results of their probe into Europe, the Labour government announced its findings. Since November 1966, Harold Wilson and his Foreign Secretary George Brown had toured European capitals to see if the ground was now ripe for Britain to renew its bid for EEC membership.[82] In mid-March 1967, they composed a joint memorandum for the cabinet on the government's approach to Europe, providing a summary of their visits. The Italian government had been 'entirely favourable towards British entry to the Community, and would do all they could to facilitate it'; in Brussels, Belgian ministers had 'reaffirmed their full support for British entry' saying that 'Britain needed Europe and Europe needed Britain'; the Dutch government, which had always been 'the principal supporters of British entry', repeated their 'enthusiasm for British entry'; and in Luxembourg, ministers assured Wilson and Brown that 'their positive attitude towards British membership of the Community had not changed over the years since the question was first discussed'.

Only in West Germany and France did the duo run into trouble. In Bonn, although the German government professed support for British entry 'for political and economic reasons', the German press commentary was less positive, both before and after the visit. And in Paris, de Gaulle remained noncommittal, reminding British ministers that 'the question of British entry raised the problem of a change in the fundamental character of the Community', a change de Gaulle was hesitant to accept. Wilson and Brown concluded that 'there can be no doubt whatsoever that, with the exception of the French, all members of the Community retain a strong interest in and desire for British membership'. There was 'a clear recognition that, with the entry of Britain, they will be taking into partnership a major European Power, with the economic and technological capacity, the political will and the kind of associates to ensure that the enlarged Community will at last have the strength and the balance to play the role in the world which the importance of Europe warrants'.[83]

On the day that Wilson and Brown presented their findings to the cabinet – 16 March 1967 – the Action Committee for the United States of Europe published a call for Britain to join the Common Market 'as it is today'. The committee, with a membership of forty-four European notables including the West German Foreign Minister Willy Brandt and the French Socialist leader Guy Mollet, represented all continental European political parties except de Gaulle's UNR Party. Its statement claimed that British entry would create an EEC of '240,000,000 Europeans matching the scale of the modern world'.[84] In response to its call, Wilson announced that he would hold three special meetings of the Parliamentary Labour Party to allow them to air their views on joining the Common Market.[85] Three weeks later, George Brown addressed the Parliamentary Party at the last of these meetings, reminding them of their 1966 General Election Manifesto pledge to be 'ready to enter the European Economic Community, provided essential British and Commonwealth interests are safeguarded'. The government had no intention to renege on that pledge. The time had now come to explore the potential for moving forward: 'We need the strength that comes from economic and political unity. We need a strong place in a strong continent if we are to play a world-wide role'. There was only one continent to which Britain could look: 'We must join up with the others in Europe so that together we create the resources and the scale we need'.[86] It was a simple matter of economics. Britain needed Europe. From that day forth, it became the Labour government's policy to actively seek membership in the EEC.

* * *

The biggest roadblock to this new policy, as it had been in 1962 and 1963, was the French government of General de Gaulle. On 26 April, the British Embassy in Paris confirmed that 'the personal reactions of General de Gaulle will determine those of the French Government'. Unfortunately, there was no reason to believe that de Gaulle had changed his mind about British entry. The challenge, therefore, was to 'convince the General that he is wrong in thinking that, however strong British feelings towards "Europe" may now be, permanent forces ("necessities") will always make her turn towards "le Grand Large": away from Europe and towards America'.[87]

The Foreign Office recommended that the government do all it could to emphasise to de Gaulle 'a real and growing parallelism... between French and UK interests'. It should also point out to de Gaulle that 'if Britain were excluded [from the EEC] she would *de facto* become comparatively more aligned with the United States'. De Gaulle could not, on the one hand, continue to reject British membership of 'Europe' whilst on the other accuse the British government of moving from Europe to become closer with the United States. He could not have it both ways. The Foreign Office memorandum ended with a warning to the French: 'If Britain's exclusion proved permanent, this would immeasurably strengthen the world role of the United States. It might result in a new political association embracing the United

States, Britain, Canada, Australia and New Zealand, with perhaps the additional or associate membership of some present EFTA countries. If British entry to the Community appeared as something of a risk to de Gaulle, the long-term risk to France of such "liaisons" surely was greater and more dangerous?'[88]

On 28 April 1967, the member countries of the EFTA issued a communique stating that free trade within the EFTA had become so established that a concurrent British application to join the EEC would not violate the original Stockholm Convention, thus opening up for the government the possibility of simultaneously being a member of both the EEC and the EFTA.[89] This was all the encouragement it needed. On 2 May, Harold Wilson rose from the green benches of the House of Commons to announce that 'Her Majesty's Government have today decided to make an application under Article 237 of the Treaty of Rome for Membership of the European Economic Community and parallel applications for Membership of the European Coal and Steel Community and Euratom'.[90] De Gaulle's response came within days. On 16 May, he issued what the British press at the time called the 'velvet veto',[91] arguing that Britain's balance of payments emphasised its extra-European role in the world: 'Britain was an island, with ties of the Commonwealth and to the US, unable to participate in Six-wide interests such as monetary solidarity.... Britain remained insufficiently "European" to take on the obligations of membership'.[92] It was as good as a French promise to reject the British application, no matter how well it was put together.

De Gaulle's press conference shocked many on the European continent. The German MP Dr Kurt Birrenbach lamented to Lord Gladwyn that 'almost nobody in Europe stands up to answer this man. If we miss this opportunity to get you in, this would mean a tragedy for Europe'.[93] George Brown sought to counter the French criticism, speaking to the Council of the Western European Union in early July. The British, he said, were 'conscious that this is a decisive moment in our history. The issue will shape our future for generations to come'. He insisted that the government no longer viewed joining the EEC as merely an economic question, but rather that 'the most decisive considerations for us have been political. Together we have the possibility of gradually building up between us a true unity of purpose and action'. He closed in gushing tones, which deserve to be quoted at length:

> The history and culture of our continent is the birthright of us all. We have all contributed to it and we all share in it. Our application flows from the historical development of our continent, from the sentiments, which, as Europeans, we all share and from the idea we all have of the part our continent should play in the world. Today the European spirit flows strongly in the movement towards a greater unity. Surely it is in the interests of all our countries that Britain should make her full contribution to this unity.[94]

The Five were immediately impressed, Willie Brandt commenting afterwards that 'A milestone on the road to a united Europe had been reached'.[95]

As the summer of 1967 progressed, however, the French government remained resistant to any UK entry. Without its support, there was little the British could do. As early as June 1966, Olivier Wormser (head of the Direction des Affaires Economiques et Financières in the Quai d'Orsay since 1954) had opined that 'To be tolerable, a regional organisation must not be too large'.[96] The entry of Britain and other European countries would threaten the internal stability of the Community and thereby lessen its voice in world affairs. Beyond that, there were economic reasons to deny Britain entry, particularly after the third Sterling Crisis. De Gaulle himself said in October 1967, 'The fact is that England is in no state to enter. England herself doesn't deny this, but she has successfully performed a conjuror's trick, creating the illusion that she can'.[97] An internal French memorandum noted, 'From the English point of view, belonging to the Common Market has stopped being principally a manoeuvre to get back a lost supremacy; that decision (to join) now appears to be the only means to avoid an industrial and commercial decline which will be irreversible in ten years' time'.[98] The French certainly had no interest in being the nurse to Europe's new 'sick man'.

Yet, as with French opposition to Macmillan's application, the greatest objections came again from de Gaulle's political sensibilities and his insistence that France remain the foremost power within the EEC and Europe more generally. Following French withdrawal from NATO in 1966, de Gaulle became fixated on achieving détente with the Soviet Union through a 'European Europe', distinct from the United States and repelling its power. By 1967, he had come to believe even more strongly than in 1963 that Great Britain was an Atlanticist Trojan

Horse which would tilt the Common Market irreversibly to North America, thus thwarting French relations with the USSR.[99] By the time Wilson travelled to meet de Gaulle at Trianon on 19 June 1967, the General had already made up his mind. Despite Wilson's pleading, his response was cold: 'If we play this game, perhaps there will not be an end to it and the Atlantic idea will submerge us and the whole world. In this case, there will not be a Europe, still less a European Europe; of course there will be Europeans but they would be placed in a hole where they would have lost their character and their personality. We do not want this'.[100] Britons, rather than being true Europeans, existed outside Europe. Their very presence in the Community would pollute its pure European air.

De Gaulle's tone concerned those in other European countries. On 27 July, Signor Bottati, an Italian diplomat working at the embassy in London, indicated privately to the British government that the view of the Italian Minister of the Treasury, Emilio Colombo, was that 'de Gaulle was showing increasing signs of madness'. European leaders could not 'allow 1963 to be repeated with the same resignation on the part of everyone'. Indeed, Colombo was of the view that 'If de Gaulle were to issue a veto, we should all of us consider seriously refusing to acknowledge that it existed'.[101] Although it was unlikely that the Italian government could persuade the Dutch, Germans and Belgians to support such an extreme position, the evidence was growing that the governments of the Five were at odds with de Gaulle's hostility towards British membership. Consequently, on 16 August, the Foreign Office drafted a memorandum exploring what actions the British government could realistically expect the Five to take in the event of a second French veto. It concluded: 'Our response to the French "veto" should be to refuse to accept it as such. We should get the Five to continue to discuss our application in the Council of Ministers. We should issue, with them and other Europeans, a solemn declaration'.[102] If diplomatic pressure would not work, then the British government – in concert with the governments of the Five – could turn to the theatre of public opinion to gain their approval, an audience that it hoped would be able to influence de Gaulle and cause him to have second thoughts.

The government faced this scenario sooner than it had imagined. On 27 November 1967, de Gaulle issued a statement to the press. He said that the Common Market was 'incompatible with the economy as it exists at present of Britain', was 'incompatible with the manner in which the British provision themselves', was 'incompatible with the restrictions laid down by the British concerning the transfer of capital which, by contrast, circulates freely between the Six', and was 'incompatible with the state of sterling'. British entry would lead to 'the virtual destruction of an edifice which has been built at the price of so many difficulties and amidst so much hope'. Only if the British government was willing to change its entire political, economic and agricultural structure could it join the Six: '[F]or the British Isles really to moor themselves alongside the Continent, a very vast and very deep transformation is still required. Everything depends therefore not on a negotiation which would for the Six be a renunciation tolling the knell of their Community, but on the will and action of the great English people who would make of themselves one of the pillars of European Europe'.[103] And with that, the bid of the Labour government to join the EEC was over. Once again, the French had rejected Britain, and there was little the rest of Europe could do about it.

14 ENTERING THE PROMISED LAND? BRITAIN JOINS 'EUROPE'

The French rejection of Britain's application to join the European Economic Community (EEC) was not the only shock to rock British politics that November. On the eighteenth of the month, Wilson was forced to devalue the pound by 14.3 per cent to just $2.40.[1] His actions confirmed publicly what many had already known in private: the government was no longer able to manage the sterling crisis without drastic intervention, despite having received more than $4,370 million from the International Monetary Fund (IMF) and other central banks since 1964.[2] The November crisis was 'shorter in duration and – until the last hours – less intense than those which sterling had weathered in the three preceding years', but Wilson was under no illusions about its seriousness. In his memoirs, he wrote ominously, 'this time it was lethal'.[3]

American President Johnson applauded Wilson's courage in devaluing the pound but could not hide his dismay at the hard times upon which the United Kingdom had fallen. Commenting that it was 'somehow just wrong for Britain to be off balance this way', he promised that Wilson would have his support at the IMF, adding that his 'faith' was 'deep that the British people have the will and the means both to pay their way and to continue to play the part they must in the world'.[4] The Conservative opposition and British press were less kind. Ted Heath seized upon Wilson's words that the 'pound in the pocket' would not be effected by devaluation, and, from that point until the 1970 General Election, a centre-piece of Conservative rhetoric was that Wilson had lied. The conservative newspapers – particularly the *Daily Express* and *Daily Mail* – spent countless columns highlighting the effects of devaluation on everyday price increases, and even de Gaulle's infamous 'non' to British EEC membership ten days later did little to draw attention from the failing British economy. As Wilson later wrote, British politics at that time became 'totally dominated by devaluation'.[5]

The UK's economic crisis not only affected the value of sterling but also its worldwide commitments. In the summer of 1967, the cabinet concluded that it needed to reduce its military commitments in order to find economic efficiencies, particularly in the area east of Suez. It therefore determined that, by the end of fiscal year 1970–71, British forces in Singapore and Malaysia would be reduced by half and the government would pull out entirely from mainland South-East Asia by the mid-1970s. In July, Wilson explained to Johnson that Britain would be unable to play 'any effective part in world affairs' unless the government got its 'economy straight now: and to do this we have no option but to bring our defence spending into line with our resources'.[6] Following the devaluation of sterling, the financial situation became far graver. On 4 January 1968, Roy Jenkins, the new Chancellor of the Exchequer, showed the cabinet the savings the government could achieve from an even hastier withdrawal from the area east of Suez. The government, he said, needed to find £1,000 million in either spending cuts or tax increases. After hearing this dire finding, the cabinet concluded that they needed 'substantial reductions in our programmes of expenditure both at home and overseas, including defence expenditure'. The best way to do this was for the government to 'withdraw from its political and defence responsibilities in the area East of Suez by the end of the financial year 1970–71, instead of by the mid-70's'. This far-reaching and final contraction of British world power included withdrawing all forces from Malaysia, Singapore and the Persian Gulf by the end of 1971.[7]

The British Foreign Secretary George Brown broke the news to American Secretary of State Dean Rusk on the morning of 11 January 1968. He explained that the government considered these steps 'essential to help achieve $1 billion in overall budget savings which will also involve heavy cuts in social welfare expenditures and steep tax increases'.[8] Over lunch later that day, Brown confessed to Walt Rostow and Bob McNamara that these were 'the saddest days of his life'.[9] Rostow was sympathetic but advised Johnson that this was 'the tragic fate of nations which increase their wages faster than their productivity'. He added that he hoped American 'industrial and labor leadership learn the lesson before we go this way'.[10] Johnson wrote to Wilson recognising what 'soul-searching' the Prime Minister and his cabinet colleagues had been through 'in trying to find the means for restoring the health of the British economy'. Nevertheless, he could not 'conceal [from him his] deep dismay upon learning this profoundly discouraging news'. He warned that 'If these steps are taken, they will be tantamount to British withdrawal from world affairs, with all that means for the future safety and health of the free world. The structure of peace-keeping will be shaken to its foundations. Our own capability and political will could be gravely weakened if we have to man the ramparts all alone'. He pleaded with Wilson 'once more to review the alternatives before you take these irrevocable steps', arguing that 'Even a prolongation of your presence in the Far East and the Persian Gulf until other stable arrangements can be put in place would be of help at this very difficult time for all of us'.[11]

The following day, Brown met again with Rusk for a 'bloody unpleasant meeting in Washington'. Rusk told him in no uncertain terms that the United Kingdom's decision to withdraw from the area east of Suez would 'have a profound influence on the total world situation'. He dismissed it as 'an illusion' that British forces in Europe could have 'some general capability' and warned Britain against withdrawing 'into a sort of "little England" ... pending [its] entry into the EEC'. He argued that 'If the teacher was now leaving the pupil Americans would be deeply affected', adding that they would 'ask why they should be interested in the peace of the world if the British were opting out'. Finally, in a last cutting barb, he found it 'embarrassing to say to his British colleague quote for God's sake be Britain unquote'.[12]

Wilson was unmoved. He sent his reply on 15 January, telling Johnson 'how profoundly my colleagues and I regret the necessity for our decisions'. They were 'bitter decisions for us to have to make: and only our conviction that they are vital in the long-term interests of Britain, and that the British people will accept them as such, has made it possible to stomach them'. 'The heavy sacrifices at home', he said, 'would have been pointless without drastic retrenchment abroad', and he told Johnson that 'the British people were sick and tired of being thought willing to eke out a comfortable existence on borrowed money'. Finally, he rejected the label of 'Little England', disputing that the United Kingdom would no longer have a role to play in the world: '[T]he spirit that has been running through this nation in recent weeks is not that of quote Little England unquote. I believe it to be a blend of exasperation at our inability to weather the successive economic storms of the past 20 years and determination, once and for all, to hew out a new role for Britain in the world at once commensurate with her real resources yet worthy of her past. There is at last a nationwide realisation that this cannot be done on borrowed time and borrowed money'. He closed, writing, '[T]he decisions we are having to take now have been the most difficult and the heaviest of any that I, and I think all my colleagues, can remember in our public life.... We are taking them because we are convinced that, in the longer term, only thus can Britain find the new place on the world stage that I firmly believe the British people ardently desire'.[13] The matter was closed. From 1 January 1972, the United Kingdom would no longer have a world role to play beyond Europe.

On 4 March 1968, Sir Patrick Dean, Britain's ambassador to the United States, wrote a lengthy memorandum to the Foreign Secretary detailing the effect on the American administration of the British decision. His despatch was one without optimism. The President, he said, had taken the decision 'hard' and the British government could 'not assume that the Anglo–American relationship has emerged unscathed'. Once the withdrawal took place, the British government would have 'no claim to special military partnership, except insofar as we may still be the only friendly nuclear power'. The best it could hope for in the short term was to be 'treated with the consideration due to a distinguished footballer who can still play a useful game and has a rich fund of experience to be drawn on, but who can no longer turn out in all weathers and whose retirement is not far off'. Britain's only hope lay in Europe, upon which the Americans had always 'set great store'. If Britain could show itself to be a great European power – perhaps the 'leading European military power' – with an ability to sway those countries on the continent in favour of American policies, 'it will do much to compensate in the American mind for the disappointment they feel about our withdrawal from a global defence role'.[14]

The Americans, however, were less certain. In a June 1968 memorandum, the State Department concluded that Britain's future was 'at best, a middle-sized European power, albeit one with a nuclear capability, a residual sense of extra-European responsibility and a continuing, if diminished, status as a favoured partner of the US'.[15] Of Winston Churchill's three great circles of empire, the Anglo–American relationship and Europe, the British government had abandoned the first and risked losing the second. If it was to belie American expectations and continue to play a world role, it could do so only in the third. It had to turn unequivocally towards Europe.

* * *

Whilst Wilson and Brown concentrated on strategic withdrawal from the area east of Suez, other officials in the British government focussed on Europe, arguing vigorously that despite de Gaulle's second veto the government had to keep alive its hope of joining the EEC. The decision to withdraw from the area east of Suez only accentuated the importance of this. As one historian has written, 'If East of Suez was to go, the British had no choice but to turn to the EEC if they wished to retain a role upon the international stage'.[16] In January 1968, Sir Paul Gore-Booth, Permanent Under-Secretary of State at the Foreign Office, directed his staff to prepare a memorandum explaining how British public opinion could be 'kept up to the mark' on Europe.[17] The Foreign Office was particularly concerned that 'if interest in a genuine European policy is not kept alive, the game may be handed to those who believe in partial solutions or who are actively opposed to our going into Europe'.[18] George Thomson, the Secretary of State for Commonwealth Affairs (a new office created in 1966 by the merger of the Colonial Office and Commonwealth Relations Office), likewise felt that the 'longer-term interests of Britain and of Europe require that we should become a member of the European Communities'. When he visited Malaysia, Singapore, New Zealand and Australia in January 1968, he emphasised that a British entry into the EEC was '[not] inconsistent with our Commonwealth relationships. We have long had arrangements for consultations and cooperation both with Australia/New Zealand/Malaysia/Singapore individually and with other Commonwealth Governments collectively which are as valid as they ever were. We intend to keep those arrangements alive'.[19] Few in the Commonwealth were convinced by these words, however.

Recognising that a cross-party wind was finally blowing in its sails, the European Movement organised a 'Europe Rally' at the Albert Hall in February 1968 to mimic Churchill's rally of two decades before. Chaired by Sir Edward Beddington-Behrens, its speakers included the Foreign Secretary George Brown, the deputy leader of the Conservative Party Reginald Maudling, the leader of the Liberal Party Jo Grimond, the chairman of Imperial Chemical Industries Sir Paul Chambers, the recently knighted Frederick Hayday (former President of the Trade Unions Congress) and Duncan Sandys, the founder of the movement.[20] Although neither Wilson nor Heath could themselves attend, the Conservative leader's support was well-known and reaffirmed by Maudling, and Brown was able to confirm the Labour government's commitment to British EEC entry, despite de Gaulle's veto. The rally demonstrated that the leaders of the Labour, Conservative and Liberal parties, as well as business and trade union leaders, were united behind British entry into the EEC and were willing to stand together in defiance of de Gaulle's veto.

Still, not all was as smooth-sailing as the leadership of the European Movement hoped. In April, the Executive Committee of its British Council acknowledged that two distinct schools of thought had emerged about how Britain's European policy should evolve in the aftermath of the French veto. The first was articulated at the February rally and argued that Britain should 'keeping knocking at the door and wait for de Gaulle to change his mind'. The second, however, concluded that the EEC was growing 'stagnant', that Britain was now 'more European than France', and that the British government should 'take the lead in pursuing "parallel paths to Europe"'. European support for de Gaulle's EEC policies was at an all-time low, which – this school of thought maintained – presented the perfect opportunity to resurrect the old post-war dreams of British leadership of a Europe that was broader that the Common Market.[21]

The Western European Union (WEU) recognised that the British government and its people might drift from their support of the EEC, and, on 7 May, the WEU's rapporteur, Dutchman Max van der Stoel, drafted a report condemning the 'refusal of the French Government to agree to the opening up of negotiations with the Government of the United Kingdom' and warning of the 'serious setback which the efforts to build a larger and stronger European community have suffered'. Writing on behalf of the WEU's Ministerial Council, he urged the EEC governments to 'prevent a widening gap between the EEC and EFTA' and to 'create new forms of co-operation with Britain and other applicant countries in fields not covered by the EEC Treaty'.[22] He was, in essence, calling on the Five to bypass France and establish a European Community in defiance of de Gaulle. The Five, however, were hesitant to act outside the existing boundaries of the EEC, and the

Foreign Office noted that, by July 1968, 'The drive for European unity [had] slowed down badly'.[23] When Wilson met with Jean Monnet on the fifteenth of that month, Monnet admitted that he had previously been 'over-optimistic in his assessment of General de Gaulle's intentions' and therefore 'felt obliged to be cautious in his [new] forecasts'. In particular, he 'now reluctantly concluded that there was no hope of a change of heart by General de Gaulle'. Until the French government received new leadership, Britain's entry prospects were bleak.[24]

This did not mean, however, that Monnet was abandoning his dream for European unity. On the contrary, when meeting with Wilson, he pitched to the Prime Minister his idea that the Labour Party join the Action Committee for the United States of Europe. The Action Committee had been established in 1955 as a way for the political parties of the six Messina countries (as opposed to simply their governments) to cooperate towards the goal of establishing a United States of Europe.[25] By inviting the British parties to join, the political parties of the six EEC countries were sending an explicit message to de Gaulle that they considered Great Britain part of 'their Europe'. Wilson saw the rationale for this as clearly as did Monnet. After speaking with the leaders of the other main British parties, therefore, on 25 October 1968 Monnet announced that the Labour, Conservative and Liberal Parties of Great Britain would be joining the Committee, an organisation that was 'unanimously convinced that Britain must be a full member of the European Community with the same rights and the same obligations as the present six member countries'. He added that 'Although Britain has for the present been prevented from joining the Common Market, the Committee does not intend to take no for an answer'.[26]

Only days earlier, the British government had undergone another reorganisation, merging the newly formed Commonwealth Affairs Office with the Foreign Office to form the Foreign and Commonwealth Office (FCO). In a sign of how far colonial and Commonwealth affairs had fallen in importance, it was the Foreign Secretary Michael Stewart who continued in his role rather than the Commonwealth Secretary, whose job simply disappeared. Significantly, the physical location of the ministry remained in the Foreign Office building rather than the Commonwealth, and the new Secretary of State for Foreign and Commonwealth Affairs continued to be known colloquially as the Foreign Secretary, all mention of the Empire and

Commonwealth now removed from the vernacular of British governance. Despite the semblance of a *merger* between Foreign and Commonwealth affairs, in reality 17 October 1968 – the day the new office of state was created – marked the end of colonial affairs in British governance. From that day forth, Europe would be the central concern of Britain's foreign policy.[27]

When Harold Wilson sat down with Monnet in January 1969, the Frenchman was in a buoyant mood about Britain's prospects in Europe. Ironically, this was because of an increasingly tense situation in France itself, where there was 'a mood of general discontent and a feeling that the country was approaching the end of a period in its history'. There was 'wide-spread dissatisfaction with the Government', 'wide-spread uncertainty about the economic situation of the country' and a growing belief that 'the General had now "gone beyond reason"'. If the French people lost faith in de Gaulle – which was now a distinct possibility – the door would be opened to British membership of the EEC. When Wilson asked Monnet how he should proceed given this information, Monnet recommended that he concentrate on 'improving [his] relations with Germany', which could only strengthen British interests once the French allowed their entry. The Germans would not 'risk ... the relationship with France which they had built up laboriously and were determined to maintain' and 'could not be expected' to enter into 'open conflict' with the French government. However, once de Gaulle left office and the German government was no longer required to choose between France and Britain, Germany would prove a valuable ally within the EEC for the British.[28]

Monnet's analysis, as so often, proved astute. Only days after the two men met in 10 Downing Street, de Gaulle granted an audience to the British Ambassador in Paris Christopher Soames, indicating his willingness to consider British entry into the EEC if the British government would support his quest to transform the Common Market into a 'looser organisation' with no aim of federation. Wilson described the conversation in his memoirs, as it was related to him by Soames via Stewart: 'He [de Gaulle] personally foresaw it [the EEC] changing, and would like to see it change, into a loose form of free trade area with arrangements by each country to exchange agricultural produce. He would be quite prepared to discuss with us what should take the place of the Common Market as an enlarged European Economic Association'. The French President also suggested 'bilateral talks with Britain initially in conditions of great secrecy, on a wide range of economic, monetary, political and defence matters'.[29]

Given de Gaulle's previous treatment of Britain, Wilson was sceptical of his intent and chose to instead follow Monnet's advice to become closer to West Germany. Consequently, on 11 February, he travelled to Bonn to meet with the West German Chancellor Kurt Kiesinger where, with the encouragement of the Foreign Office, he revealed to Kiesinger the content of the Soames–de Gaulle exchange, fearful that had he not, de Gaulle could have used it against him to claim that the British government was not truly interested in a community-wide approach but rather only in the traditional bilateral diplomacy – that Britain was, in some senses, a traitor to the EEC cause.[30] Stewart also sent a summary of the meeting to the British ambassadors in all EEC countries, with instructions to brief their respective foreign secretaries, and to the government of the United States. In several of these subsequent briefings, the British ambassadors informed their European hosts that this conversation revealed that it was de Gaulle rather than the British who had always been hostile to the ideals of the Common Market.[31]

For two weeks, the content of the exchange did not make it into the public sphere, French officials instead trying to clarify with their European counterparts their version of events. However, *Le Figaro* eventually broke the story, reporting that 'inaccurate reports' were circulating about proposals made by de Gaulle to the British Ambassador in Paris. Stewart immediately took the bait and, in an effort to demonstrate the accuracy of the reports, released to the press the full text of Soames' account of his conversation with de Gaulle. As the historian Bernard Ledwidge has written, 'Such treatment of the text of a confidential diplomatic exchange with a foreign Head of State is perhaps without precedent in British history'.[32] The press immediately dubbed the scandal the 'Soames Affairs (or, '*l'Affaire Soames*' in the French press), and de Gaulle remained embittered towards Britain throughout the remainder of his Presidency.[33]

He did not have long to brood, however, for on 19 February the French Council of Ministers set 27 April as the date for a referendum on de Gaulle's plan to reform the French Senate and promote greater regionalisation in government. When the results came through in the early hours of 28 April 1969, 52.41 per cent of the French population voted against de Gaulle's reforms. Having already lost the confidence of the French people on a number of other measures (as Monnet had articulated to Wilson), de Gaulle immediately resigned the Presidency, leaving Paris to return to his country estate, La Boisserie.[34] Eighteen months later, just weeks shy of his eightieth birthday, he died suddenly from a ruptured blood vessel in his neck. His presidential successor, Georges Pompidou, spoke to the nation in a live, televised address, stating simply: 'General de Gaulle is dead. France is a widow'.[35] From the British perspective, she was a widow that was now ready to be courted.

* * *

When Charles de Gaulle died on 9 November 1970, the British Prime Minister conveyed to President Pompidou a message of condolences, as was only right and proper. It was not Harold Wilson who was writing the letter, however, but Edward Heath, who had led the Conservative Party back to governance in the General Election of 18 June 1970. Since the resignation of de Gaulle in April 1969, Wilson had renewed his efforts to lead Britain into the EEC, the Board of Trade having confirmed that the Germans would 'welcome the entry of the United Kingdom into the EEC', now that a strong Franco–German relationship was no longer incompatible with such support.[36] Likewise, John Freeman – the newly appointed British Ambassador to the United States – told the Foreign Secretary Michael Stewart that as it was now likely that the British government would enter into new EEC negotiations 'in the fairly near future', it was essential to 'discuss with the Americans the implications which closer U.K. association with Europe is likely to have for Anglo–American relations'.[37]

Stewart tasked Sir Arthur Snelling, the Deputy Under-Secretary of State at the Foreign Office, to draft a memorandum relaying the advantages the US government would gain from British EEC membership. However, Snelling argued that the greatest advantage came in a field that was particularly inconvenient for Wilson. 'The biggest potential gain to the United States', he wrote, 'would arise from the termination of the Commonwealth preference arrangements which our entry into [the] EEC involves'. He continued: 'The United States would then be trading on a basis of competitive equality with us, the Japanese, the Six, etc., in the Australian, Canadian, etc., market. This could be of very great importance to the U.S.'.[38] Europe now wanted Britain to join the club, and they would have the support of the United States in doing so. But membership would come at the expense of the Commonwealth.

Snelling's conclusion was what the Commonwealth had most feared since Britain's first application to join the Common Market in the early 1960s. As Sir Arthur Galsworthy, the British High Commissioner in New Zealand, wrote to Stewart in late May, 'For some years New Zealand (while greatly concerned) has been tempted to regard our application as posing a potential, rather than an actual, problem simply because few believed that the United Kingdom would gain entry'. Now, however, the situation had changed: 'Britain is still insistent on EEC membership, General de Gaulle is off the stage, and the United Kingdom–New Zealand Trade Agreement is open to renegotiation after the end of 1969'. The New Zealand government faced a unique problem, which was 'how far she should go in fostering her traditional trade with Britain and how far she can and should, instead, actively foster new patterns of trade elsewhere, for the sake of New Zealand exports'.[39] The New Zealand economy was entirely dependent on the Commonwealth trade preferences it received from Great Britain. It now needed to know if Britain intended to turn its back on the Commonwealth and look to Europe. If so, New Zealand needed to make contingency plans. It was a question Galsworthy alone could not answer.

In September 1969, Sir Basil Engholm, Permanent Secretary in the Ministry of Agriculture and Fisheries, travelled to New Zealand to see for himself local opinion on Britain and Europe. He wrote that the country 'still has the outlook of a British colony. Both young and old regard the United Kingdom as the mother country. Although the umbilical cord has been severed, they don't believe that they can yet be expected to fend for themselves, and go out and earn their own living in the cold hard world'. This view, he said, 'colours their attitude to the U.K. going into the Common Market'. The New Zealand government hoped against hope that Britain would not enter the EEC, but increasingly recognised that this was unlikely. Even with this acknowledgement, however, it was convinced that 'because their eyes are still fixed very much on the United Kingdom, and because their export trade is still, and as far as they can see, [is] likely to remain, predominantly, dependent on our markets, they believe that if the United Kingdom joins the Common Market, their interests must, and will, be looked after – not only in the short term but in the long term'. It was 'inconceivable that anything else could happen'. New Zealand considered itself a British nation, and for the United Kingdom to enter the EEC without securing adequate safeguards and special arrangements for its Commonwealth brethren would be viewed as a great betrayal.[40] *The Daily Express* echoed this sentiment, writing that far preferable to joining the EEC would be 'some less formal union of the English speaking peoples, which would embrace New Zealand, Australia, Canada, and others of the Commonwealth and Scandinavian people who were prepared to conduct their affairs in the English language and embrace the spirit of Anglo-Saxon institutions'. Language and common law, it told its readers, drew the United Kingdom far closer to the Commonwealth than to Europe, and closer also to the United States. A broader Atlantic Alliance – incorporating the United States, the English-speaking Commonwealth countries and Scandinavia – served British interests far better than a European Union.[41]

In 1969, however, the views of the *Daily Express* were held by a distinct minority of Britons. As had been made clear in the 1967 bid, the British government was concerned first and foremost with British rather than Commonwealth opinion, and, for most people in the United Kingdom, the resignation of de Gaulle was viewed not as an ominous sign that could allow the break-up of the British world but rather as a great opportunity. On 22 July 1969, the Chairman of the British Council of the European Movement proposed to his Executive Committee that the organisation be merged with Britain in Europe, to create a single pro-Europe campaign.[42] This the committee agreed to and, after securing the support of Britain in Europe, on 25 July, Lord Harlech (before his elevation to the House of Lords, David Ormsby-Gore) announced the merger. The move, he said, would 'create a single unified organisation in Britain to strengthen the campaign for British membership of the Community, and for the development of a politically and economically integrated United Europe'. This would be no easy task. Harlech admitted that the uniting of Europe was a 'complicated business' which would require 'a sustained campaign'. He also recognised that British entry into the EEC would 'change the course of British history' but was convinced that this would be 'a decisive change for the better'. He concluded, saying, 'I have no doubt that the European idea is the most important political idea of this generation. It offers all of us the hope that, after centuries of selfish nationalism which have led us from one terrible war to another and have soaked the Continent's soil in the blood of its youth, we can establish an integrated Europe with a world vision'.[43] Having served as British Ambassador to the United States from 1961 to 1965, these were remarkable words for Harlech to speak, particularly as he was renowned for being a strong supporter of the Anglo–American 'special relationship'.

In September 1969, Michael Stewart recalled Sir Con O'Neill to the Foreign Office following his resignation in 1968. O'Neill had been passed over for the British ambassadorship to West Germany following stints as ambassador to Finland (1961–63), to the European Communities in Brussels (1963–65), and as Deputy Under-Secretary of State (1965–1968) where he managed the bureaucracy of the 1967 EEC application. His expertise and experience was now needed once again.[44] His new task, the Foreign Secretary told him, was to once again head the team which would negotiate Britain's entry into the EEC, only this time without the shadow of de Gaulle and a possible French veto hanging over his head. O'Neill, recognising that effective communication of British policy would be half the battle, immediately established a Common Market Publicity unit.[45] He was supported in this task by George Thomson, whom Wilson had brought into the cabinet as the Chancellor of the Duchy of Lancaster with special ministerial responsibility for the EEC negotiations.[46] Thomson had previously served in this same role, albeit without a seat in the cabinet, from 1966 to 1967, following which he was Secretary of State for Commonwealth Affairs before its merger with the Foreign Office.[47] It is perhaps ironic that Britain's last Commonwealth Secretary returned to the cabinet as Minister of Europe, mirroring in more ways than one Labour's own journey from a 'Commonwealth' to a 'European' government.

Thomson quickly discovered that the post-de Gaulle climate was entirely different from his last stint as 'Minister for Europe'. De Gaulle's successor Georges Pompidou had worked since his election in April 1969 to portray himself as a 'European' president who was in favour of both Community enlargement and a deepening of integration.[48] In this, he was joined by Willy Brandt, elected West German Chancellor on 21 October 1969. Brandt had been a close ally and friend of Harold Wilson's throughout the latter's time in 10 Downing Street, and his ascension to the German Chancellorship ensured that Great Britain and West Germany would have a close working relationship. The Americans, too, sensed that there was a new understanding between the continental European powers and Britain following de Gaulle's resignation and, on 16 December, even suggested that 'the climate in France had now improved sufficiently to make it possible for the U.S. to speak out more openly in favour of enlargement of the Community', something that had been impossible throughout de Gaulle's time in office.[49]

The issue of American support for British entry was far from simple, however. The presumption on the part of American policy-makers was that a Britain within Europe would be able to advocate Atlanticist concerns on behalf of the US government and steer the Common Market along economic and policy lines that would be favourable to American interests. To the American mind, there was little to separate the United States and Britain, and a British seat at the European table would ensure that the Anglo–American voice was heard. However, the Planning Staff of the Foreign and Commonwealth Office, with the approval of George Thomson, sent to Wilson a memorandum at the end of December suggesting that the reality was quite different. There were, it pointed out, 'certain inconsistencies and divergences of interest' between British and American policy that were 'likely to emerge more clearly as we pursue our candidacy and European integration develops'.

Whilst Britain sat outside the EEC, Europe had been 'only one of three intersecting circles of our interests', and there was no reason to preference European concerns over American. If Britain were to join the Common Market, however, it would 'often be compelled to give, and to be seen to be giving, priority to our European interests'. The United Kingdom would no longer be mediating as an outside party among three distinct circles (the Empire/Commonwealth, the United States and Europe); rather, it would be a central part of one of these three circles, placing the interests of that circle above all others. This would inevitably affect the Anglo–American 'special relationship'. As the report concluded, 'If integration proceeds Western Europe will be a considerable power in its own right and the temptation to pursue [a] course independent of the United States will no doubt be stronger'.[50]

As 1970 dawned, there was a sense of European optimism in the British air. That January, the French Foreign Minister Maurice Schuman spoke warmly before the Franco–British Society in London of Anglo–French cooperation during the Second World War, telling his audience of his 'most indestructible memory of a period that was marked by such sacrifice and greatness'. This memory was 'the image of an England that I shall never cease to conjure up to my dying day. . . . An image offered to a group of French officers and men who, towards the end of June 1940, hearing de Gaulle's appeal, flocked to the shores of this besieged island, last resort of hope and refuge of freedom. We could have been greeted merely as friends, who had fled captivity. Instead we were welcomed as the depositories of France, of her soul, her past, her future'. It was Britain, he said, that in 1945 took the initiative of calling Europe to unite. It was Britain who, had its government chosen at that time, could have become 'the nerve centre of a new Community'. He fully understood, as anyone with 'just a little history and a smattering of geography' would, why Britain in 1950 had chosen not to join with the Six to form the European Coal and Steel Community. But now, twenty years later, the conditions within both Britain and Europe had changed. The problem, he said, 'is no longer whether we wish England "in". We do. Nor is the problem to know whether England herself wishes to be "in". She does. The problem is thus to decide what we wish her to enter and what she, herself, wishes to enter'. Schuman could not answer that question for Great Britain, but he could give France's reply: 'We want England to enter into a Community, in fact *the* Community'.[51] France was now saying 'oui'.

Yet it would not be the Labour government that would walk through this door. On 18 May 1970, Wilson informed the cabinet that he had asked the Queen to dissolve Parliament on 29 May, with a General Election on 18 June.[52] Since April, opinion polls had shown a swing in support for the Labour Party, and the Prime Minister took the strategic decision to go to the people whilst the fortunes of his party were looking up.[53] He had already promised other European leaders that negotiations for British entry into the EEC could begin again in June and, as both the Conservative Party and the Liberals supported this position, there was little debate about Europe during the General Election campaign. The Labour Manifesto noted that new negotiations would begin shortly after the election and suggested that these would 'be pressed with determination with the purpose of joining an enlarged Community provided that British and essential Commonwealth interests can be safeguarded'. Perhaps surprisingly, the Conservative Manifesto was more cautious, claiming, 'Our sole commitment is to negotiate; no more, no less'.[54] The Tories did not expect to be given the chance, and, throughout the campaign, polling consistently predicted the return of the Labour government. As the morning of 19 June dawned, however, the British public woke to an upset. The Conservative Party had won a majority of thirty-one seats, and Ted Heath was Britain's new Prime Minister. Having led the negotiations for British entry in 1961–63 and been a consistent supporter of the EEC since his election in 1950, there was little doubt that Britain would now 'join Europe'.[55]

* * *

If for the Conservative Party June 1970 was a very good month, it was less so for the Labour Party, which sought someone or something to blame for its unexpected loss. Its members picked Europe, which – with the benefit of hindsight – they claimed had pulled Labour from its traditional socialist values to instead support the European 'capitalist club'. Support for Europe had cost the Labour Party its soul and therefore the election; only opposition to British entry could redeem the party. That the Tory leader was such an ardent Europeanist only sealed the deal, providing a single figure to oppose, caricature and demonise. In the aftermath of the General Election loss, this sentiment (which many had held privately) became accentuated, as grass roots Labour supporters and MPs alike blamed their party's loss on Wilson's support for the EEC. Opposition to the EEC therefore became 'one of the touchstones of the Left as support for Europe became for the right and centre'.[56] As George Thomson later remembered, the 'mood began to change in the party fairly quickly after Labour lost the election.... Dick Crossman was editing the *New Statesman* at that time. The *New Statesman* within a month or so of the election came out against Britain going into Europe'.[57] The issue of Europe, which had gained a surprising cross-party consensus from 1965 onwards, was once again a partisan battleground following the 1970 General Election.

Yet it was not only those on the Left who were showing signs of discomfort at continued British efforts to join the EEC. The Anti-Common Market League, established in 1961 when Macmillan first sought to steer Britain into the EEC, became highly vocal again after Wilson announced a second British attempt to enter the Community. Its campaign was renewed still further when it became clear that de Gaulle's days as French leader were numbered. Initially a fringe organisation within the Conservative Party (and one that was distinctly out of step with the party's leadership and broader constituencies), by 1969, it was attracting support from both Conservative and Labour members. One of those who flocked to its ranks was the Conservative MP Neil Marten, who – although having served under Macmillan and Douglas-Home as a junior aviation minister – refused to accept ministerial rank when offered it by Heath in June 1970, claiming he would be unable to support the Government's policy on Europe.[58] Although Marten was one of only a few Tory MPs at that time to publicly oppose the Conservative consensus on 'joining Europe', he estimated that there were between seventy and eighty Conservative anti-Marketeers in Parliament who were less vocal, leaving Heath's majority of only thirty quite vulnerable, particularly if the Conservative anti-Marketeers joined forces with an increasingly anti-Europe Labour Party.[59]

Consequently, in contrast to the 1940s, 1950s and early 1960s, there was by no means unanimous support for joining 'Europe' amongst Conservatives, although (as Marten's own estimates showed) those who opposed it were still in a distinct minority. Furthermore, the French veto in 1967 caused far more self-reflection amongst Conservatives than had the 1963 veto, and, in 1968 alone, there were twelve pro-North American Free Trade Agreement resolutions put forward by party members as an explicit alternative to the EEC.[60] In February 1969, the Anti-Common Market League published its first newsletter in more than a year, arguing that although the Labour government was once again renewing its focus on Europe, amongst the British public there was 'a mixture of apathy, boredom and sheer disbelief that there is any danger of Britain ever joining'. It warned of the fight ahead and urged those opposed to Britain entering the Common Market to prepare themselves against the onslaught that was sure to come from the 'merchant bankers and rich vested interests, dedicated politicians, one-sided and slanted press reporting, and the unscrupulous use of official information services for putting the government view'.[61] Following de Gaulle's resignation as French President and the embrace of the British application by the new French leader Pompidou in April, the Anti-Common Market League reminded its supporters of the great efforts it had undertaken in 1962, when it had held 237 meetings, recruited a membership of 30,000 individuals and distributed 31,000 copies of the newsletter each month, as well as 600,000 copies of a leaflet titled 'Commonwealth or Common Market'. That fight would pale in comparison to the one they now had on their hands, and they argued it was the duty and responsibility of every member to redouble his efforts to prevent British entry.[62]

More important than the Anti-Common Market League's newsletters, in March 1969 the Conservative MP Enoch Powell delivered a public statement in opposition to British entry despite having supported it in the Shadow Cabinet, thus opening the floodgates for discontented Conservatives to voice their disapproval.[63] Powell was the first high-profile Conservative to oppose the party consensus on Europe, and his intervention was to be a significant one. Yet he was not the only one. In March 1967, A. P. Herbert (writing in the *Daily Telegraph*) had lamented that 'We are being dragooned into decimals, coaxed into Centigrade. . . . All this is while we are still gabbling and grovelling our way into the Common Market. Once we are in we shall hardly have a habit, a weight or a measure left. We shall drive on the right (we shall be told to) and change all the cars. We shall turn miles into kilometres and change all the maps and sign-boards. The poor inch will go with the mile. A man will be one metre and so many centimetres tall. . . . Deci-this and kilo-that will confront us everywhere. We shall drink in litres instead of pints'.[64] His fears would continue to resonate for decades to come.

On 14 July 1969, Neil Marten tabled a motion in the House of Commons that 'This House believes the Government should not at present pursue its application to join the Common Market'. By the summer recess, it had received the signatures of thirty-eight Labour MPs (in defiance of their Party's official policy), thirty Conservative MPs (the largest number of Conservative anti-Marketeers to publicly oppose 'Europe' since 1945), two Liberals, one Welsh Nationalist and a Scottish Nationalist.[65] And it was not only in Parliament that opposition to the EEC was growing. That summer, the *Daily Telegraph* commissioned a Gallup Poll asking the same questions on Common Market entry in September 1969 as it had in March 1965. When asked, 'If an opportunity occurs for Britain to join the Common Market would you like to see us try or drop the idea altogether?', in 1965, 57 per cent of those asked supported trying, with just 22 per cent opposed. By September 1969, those figures had been reversed, with only 26 per cent supporting trying and 57 per cent hoping that the idea would be dropped entirely. Perhaps more surprising still, 17 per cent of the British public had yet to make up their mind about EEC membership, showing a disengagement with the European question that was unparalleled anywhere on the continent.[66]

When, in January 1970, Wilson indicated that the British government would re-enter negotiations to join the Common Market, those involved with the Anti-Common Market Campaign decided to launch a new organisation, the Common Market Safeguards Campaign, to 'voice the opinion of that large and growing section of the public in all Parties and all walks for life who believe that Britain should not join the Common Market without far more stringent and effective safeguards than the present Government has yet undertaken to secure'. In particular, the Campaign referenced the necessity to 'safeguard Britain's balance of payments and worldwide trading interests and her Commonwealth responsibilities', intentionally renewing the dichotomy of Europe versus the Commonwealth which had always been such a key part of anti-Marketeer rhetoric despite Britain's ever-shrinking Commonwealth role. Led by the historian Sir Arthur Bryant, it included as its Vice Presidents the Labour MP Emmanuel Shinwell and the Conservative MP Robin Turton. Amongst its thirty-nine patrons there were thirteen other MPs, including both the Tory Neil Marten and the future Labour leader Michael Foot.[67] Immediately after its launch, the Anti-Common Market League announced that it would 'co-operate closely with the Common Market Safeguards Campaign'.[68] By June 1970, the Campaign's patrons had risen to ninety-two individuals, including forty-six MPs.[69]

Even so, the forty-six MPs who supported the Common Market Safeguards Campaign, the seventy who had signed Neil Marten's parliamentary motion the previous summer and the handful who were officially members of the Anti-Common Market League still represented a small minority in the House of Commons, and, following the General Election of June 1970, the anti-Marketeers were faced with a new Conservative government that explicitly favoured EEC entry. On 29 June, the Common Market Safeguards Committee released a statement reminding the new government that 'public opinion in Britain is now firmly and over-whelmingly opposed to entry' and demanding a referendum should the government negotiate entry into the EEC. It said, 'Profound constitutional changes of the unprecedented kind involved in the signing of the Rome Treaty, and submerging Britain in a European Federal State, cannot be introduced by Parliament alone'.[70] Despite their efforts, however, within Parliament, their voices were still very much crying out into the wilderness. At the time of the General Election in June 1970, all three main parties supported negotiations for Britain to join the EEC, and both of the main party leaders – Edward Heath and Harold Wilson – had been personally involved in making an application to do so. The anti-Marketeers were a movement without a party.

* * *

Following the Conservative victory in the General Election and the rise of Ted Heath to the Prime Ministership, those who had been campaigning so vigorously for British entry into the EEC sensed that their time had finally come. Coupled with the demise of de Gaulle and new French and German leadership, they were determined not to let the opportunity slip through their fingers. As the historian Catherine Hynes has written, 'as a committed European [Heath's] one clear priority on taking office was to secure Britain's belated accession to the European Community. ... As Heath stepped across the threshold of 10 Downing Street, he was prepared to subordinate whatever was special in London's relationship with Washington to the single-minded pursuit of his European ambitions'.[71]

On 22 July 1970, the European Forum – which had been established to 'bring Conservative Europeans together and further the Party's policy on Europe' – voted to change its name to the Conservative Group in Europe, emphasising its party affiliation. In justifying this change, it pointed to 'the activity of the anti-marketeers within the Party and outside'.[72] As Labour MPs were becoming increasingly anti-European, the Conservative Group believed it was essential to explicitly link Conservative Party ideology with the European cause in an effort to chastise those within the party who challenged its European policy. They hoped a vote against Europe would be seen as a vote against the Conservative Party and thus a vote for Labour. Under such circumstances, only the most committed of Conservative anti-Marketeers would place their hostility towards Europe above the interests of their party.

As expected, Heath showed little hesitation in beginning negotiations to enter the Community. Delivering the Godkin Lectures at Harvard University whilst leader of the opposition in 1967, he had proclaimed that British membership in the EEC was 'in the interests of Europe as well as of Britain'.[73] Now, on 26 June 1970 – only weeks after the General Election – Heath established a Cabinet Ministerial Committee on the Approach to Europe, chaired by his Foreign Secretary Alec Douglas-Home. Four days later, Douglas-Home travelled to Luxembourg to take part in a formal ceremony marking the opening of negotiations for Britain to join the EEC – a date that had been planned by Harold Wilson prior to his calling the General Election.[74] The new Conservative government took as its basis for negotiations the 1967 statement from Labour Foreign Secretary George Brown, intentionally indicating a continuation of European policy between the Labour and Conservative governments, with only de Gaulle's November 1967 veto preventing Britain's accession to the Community several years earlier under a different party.[75]

The main point of contention, as in 1961–63, was the Commonwealth and, in particular, the position of New Zealand. As Sir Con O'Neill wrote in his definitive account of the negotiations, the New Zealand issue 'create[d] an infinity of work and paper almost more than any other subject'.[76] When it became clear that negotiations would begin on 30 June, officials throughout the British government began to prepare. New Zealand loomed large in these preparations, and a civil servant laid out the problem for John Diamond, the Labour Chief Secretary to the Treasury, on 19 May, just prior to the dissolution of Parliament: 'New Zealand remains heavily dependent on her exports of dairy products to the UK market; we take about 90 per cent of her butter exports and 80 per cent of her cheese. At present the Six plus the four applicant countries have a net deficit of about 75,000 tons of butter; with an enlarged Community, the Ten would probably have a net surplus of about twice that amount'. He clarified what this meant for the New Zealand government: 'Without a special arrangement, New Zealand would therefore find herself virtually excluded from the market of the enlarged Community. Outlets elsewhere are and will be minimal. . . . No practical remedies can be looked for by negotiating worldwide agreements on dairy products, nor by institutional arrangements between New Zealand and an enlarged Community. The only feasible approach is to negotiate special arrangements for the two products'.[77]

Such negotiations would be difficult, however. As a cabinet brief pointed out in early June, New Zealand's national income per head was 'higher than any of the Six (and that of the United Kingdom) and not far off double that of Italy. Unemployment is – and has long been – negligible. It is hardly surprising that New Zealand was once referred to by one of its Prime Ministers as "God's own country"'. This lifestyle was, in large part, made possible by its dairy industry, which was propped up by Commonwealth preferences and a guaranteed, secure market in Britain. This meant that, despite its current prosperity, New Zealand had 'too many of its eggs in one basket'. If the basket were to spill, New Zealand's economy would be broken. British entry into the EEC would almost certainly cause such as spill. As the brief pointed out, however, 'the Six are not going to take kindly to the proposition that the EEC should solve New Zealand's inherent economic problem in order to maintain its population in a style which many in the Six would envy'. If Britain had any chance of entering the Common Market, there could be 'no question of an assurance of permanent access to the United Kingdom market'. Before the negotiations had even begun, successive British governments – first Labour, and then Conservative – had decided it was in Britain's best economic interests to choose Europe over Commonwealth. As the cabinet brief concluded, 'The essential need is to provide New Zealand with a breathing space long enough for her to have a reasonable chance to make the necessary painful adjustments to her economy'.[78] It was not to prevent the adjustments being necessary in the first place.

On 8 June – whilst politicians were campaigning to secure their political futures – Sir Con O'Neill held his first meeting with officials from New Zealand. He informed them that, regardless of the General Election result, it was now '99 per cent definitive that our first meeting with the Six [will] be held on 30 June', with further meetings taking place in July. He informed the New Zealand delegation that the British government recognised that its European policy raised 'serious problems' for New Zealand and acknowledged their request to have a special representation at the negotiations. However, although promising that consultation would be 'especially close', he could not agree to a formal New Zealand role: 'This was a battle which the British delegation must fight'. It was not a Commonwealth war.[79] Following the meeting, M. J. Moriarty, the New Zealand Secretary of Industries and Commerce, issued a statement claiming that New Zealand was 'by far the most vulnerable of the developed Commonwealth countries to economic dislocation as a result of British entry into the EEC'. He therefore sought recognition that New Zealand was 'a special case, requiring special measures to accommodate its trading problem – and indeed, its national interest – in the context of the enlargement negotiations'.[80] In public, O'Neill promised Moriarty that 'New Zealand's problem should be treated by the Community as a separate item for negotiations'. He did not inform him, however, that the cabinet had already determined that the most they could seek for New Zealand was short-term comfort rather than a long-term arrangement.[81]

There followed nine days of negotiations, after which Moriarty – on the eve of the British General Election – confessed that 'right from the beginning we were more than a little disappointed'. The British position did not 'strike an acceptable balance between the negotiating difficulties you will undoubtedly face, and the protection of New Zealand's interests about which we have had repeated assurances from British Ministers'. Moriarty was certain that if Britain would just show a 'firm lead', the Six would be willing to concede a 'special arrangement' for New Zealand. As it was, British officials simply insisted that 'Britain must come to terms with the [European] Common Agricultural Policy', which would necessarily negate any special arrangements for New Zealand's dairy products and lamb.[82] Moriarty was no doubt correct that the United Kingdom had a certain amount of political capital to spend in its discussions with the Six, and, if it so chose, it could have used that capital to purchase special arrangements for New Zealand. What Moriarty did not realise was that British officials were already beginning to think like 'Europeans' and that any capital they chose to spend would be used to assure a better position for the UK in Europe's future, not to protect Commonwealth interests from Britain's past.

It was precisely this attitude that began to stir more open anti-Market sentiments within the Labour Party. On 22 September, the Common Market Safeguards Campaign released a statement expressing 'increasing anxiety' by 'all who put faith in the present Government's undertaking to protect essential Commonwealth interests in its negotiations with the Common Market'. Having heard that the government, and in particular Geoffrey Rippon (who had been given ministerial responsibility to negotiate British entry), was 'not even in the case of New Zealand to promise permanent arrangements', the Campaign accused the government of 'failing to carry out undertakings previously given. For it would mean abandoning safeguards for the mainstream of Commonwealth trade and food supplies for this country'. It concluded, 'We do not believe the British public wish to see Australia, New Zealand

and the rest of the Commonwealth thus treated with indifference. For the damage to Britain would be every bit as great as the damage to the Commonwealth'.[83]

In drafting this statement, the Common Market Safeguards Campaign gave the rank-and-file of the Labour Party – as well as many of its former ministers – just the justification they needed to turn away from their previous support for British entry into the EEC. Under Wilson, the government had always maintained (publicly, at least) that no Commonwealth interests would be injured by British entry. Wilson was, after all, a 'Commonwealth man' who – like those in the Conservative and Labour Parties before him – had fervently believed that Britain could lead both Europe and the Commonwealth without contradiction. Now, the Conservative government (to anti-Marketeer eyes, at any rate) was jettisoning the Commonwealth in order to 'join Europe', undermining a central tenet of British ideology towards Europe since the end of the Second World War. That the Labour government itself had overseen a large part of decolonisation and had taken the decision to withdraw from the area east of Suez mattered little; if anything, it made protection of Britain's remaining worldwide interests all the more important. New Zealand and the other 'white settler dominions' were all Britain had left of its old empire. If the government could sacrifice New Zealand on the altar of European unity, it could sacrifice anything. Europe, the anti-Marketeers claimed, was costing Britain its Empire and Commonwealth. To a post-imperial public that was struggling to understand its place in the world after empire, this analysis was compelling.

Less than a week after the Common Market Safeguards Campaign published its statement, the Labour Party held its annual conference in Blackpool. Although the Conservative government had maintained continuing with the previous government's policy on Europe, the party was growing restive, uncomfortable supporting a European policy that had become so closely associated with the Tories. Consequently, at the conference, Wilson faced a resolution from the floor calling for a new policy opposing British entry into the EEC. Although the resolution was (narrowly) defeated, it revealed to the Labour leadership the depth to which anti-European sentiment had developed within the party.[84] After the conference, the Labour MP Tony Benn suggested to Wilson that an easy way for the party to save face was to take the issue out of the hands of the government and give it to the British public in a referendum, thus on the one hand alleviating the need for the Labour leadership to make an apparent U-turn on Europe, whilst on the other allowing its supporters to oppose British entry. The party could then pledge to support the judgment of the British people, no matter which way they voted. Wilson, however, objected, claiming that Britain was not and never would be governed by plebiscite.[85]

Nevertheless, the evidence was increasing that the public at large was uncomfortable with the government's position towards Europe. A national opinion poll taken just after the Labour conference found that 61 per cent of the British people now opposed joining the Common Market, with just 24 per cent in favour. The same poll found that more Britons felt that the United Kingdom's future lay with the Commonwealth than with Europe or the United States, with 32 per cent envisioning a Commonwealth future, 26 per cent a European future and just 8 per cent a future with the United States.[86] Those in favour of British entry were well aware of the significant opposition to the EEC that had developed since de Gaulle's second veto and sought to counter it as best as they could. Lord Harlech, chairman of the British Council of the European Movement, sent a memorandum to Geoffrey Rippon in late August suggesting that a 'vital element' to the success of the negotiations would be 'the build-up and maintenance of a favourable state of public opinion over a period of the next two years'. Only a sustained political campaign with 'mass public meetings, a wide distribution of literature, and at the appropriate time... national advertising on street posters and through the press' would suffice. The European Movement was best placed to lead such a campaign, Harlech argued, but it would be costly. He therefore asked Rippon to seek the Prime Minister's assistance with a private financial appeal directed at fifty leading figures in banking, commerce and industry, who would donate sufficiently for the campaign to reach a goal of £250,000. In return, they would receive an invitation for a private dinner with Heath at 10 Downing Street.[87]

In response to this request, Rippon invited Harlech and other leading members of the European Movement to the Foreign Office, where he agreed that the negotiations should be accompanied by a vigorous public campaign. It was, he said, 'right to appeal to idealism: we were not simply concerned with a trade treaty. The time had now come when we must nail our colours to the mast: we must assume that the Six would offer reasonable terms, and we must stress the mutual advantage and the opportunities instead of the burdens'. They also discussed the issue of sovereignty, which leading anti-marketeers had been using to their advantage. Rippon suggested that they should take the line that 'as a member of the E.E.C. we would be sharing a more important sovereignty than we now had'. Finally, Rippon agreed to assist the British Council in raising funds. He could not promise that the Prime Minister would agree to be used for this purpose, as that was a decision only the Prime Minister could take. In general, however, the European Movement could expect the fullest support from the government in its efforts to publicise the benefits of EEC membership.[88]

Within the Conservative Party itself, the Conservative Research Department (CRD) was working closely with the European Communities Information Unit, which had been established by the Foreign and Commonwealth Office in June to support the work of the government in its negotiations with the Six. On 10 September, the CRD's Michael Niblock sent to the Information Unit a paper laying out six 'Themes for Europe' which the government should 'get established in the public mind if the E.E.C. enterprise is to be accepted by the people in Britain'. First was that, in the Common Market, living standards had improved at a faster rate than in Britain. In 1958, the British had 'enjoyed higher living standards than their counterparts in the E.E.C. Now this gap has been closed. Indeed, there is a reverse gap opening up as living standards in some of the Common Market countries, notably Germany and Benelux, moved ahead of ourselves'. By the end of the 1970s, Niblock predicted, the United Kingdom would 'be well on the way to being one of Europe's poorest countries'. Second, Britain could only improve its living standards if it succeeded in 'producing more and selling more abroad to pay for our increased demands for imports'. The Common Market would 'help us achieve a higher rate of economic expansion'. Tied closely to this, Niblock's third theme was that the EEC would place Britain in a single market of nearly 300 million people (including the other states also applying for membership), compared to its present market of just 55 million. This would provide British manufacturers with a 'home market' five times larger than at present, which could only help stimulate economic growth.

Shifting from economics, Niblock suggested as his fourth theme that by joining the Common Market, Britain would 'become an influential member of an organisation which itself is proving a major influence in world affairs'. Particularly given its imminent withdrawal from the area east of Suez, the United Kingdom needed to carve out a new role for itself. This the EEC could provide. In return, the United Kingdom could share with Europe its 'experience with democratic institutions and in diplomacy, its world-wide contacts and interests and its technological skills'. The EEC would allow Britain to remain a world player whilst Britain's past global responsibilities and experience would provide the EEC with much-needed international gravitas. His fifth theme was that, given the trajectory of Britain's changing (and shrinking) world role, should it decide not to enter the EEC, its 'influence in the world relative to that of continental Europe would certainly be less than it is today'. Finally, Niblock argued that the choice facing the British government was not about trade and economics in the short-term, but 'about the future of Britain in the late twentieth century'. If the government repeated each of these 'themes' to the public time and time again over the next few years, Niblock predicted there would be a rise in support for British membership of the EEC.[89]

The CRD's strategy for winning public support was not one that an increasingly agitated Labour Party was willing to accept. In January 1971, 119 Labour MPs signed an early-day motion opposing British entry 'on terms so far envisaged'.[90] Roy Jenkins, a pro-Europe Labour MP, tried to persuade Michael Foot to support the government in its negotiations. Foot, displaying an attitude characteristic of many in the Labour Party, countered, 'Here we are, confronted by one of our most reactionary governments since Lord Liverpool's day. Here we have an opportunity to defeat it and here you attach more importance to your particular attachment to this little nostrum of Europe than bringing down this foul government, which is desecrating our country'.[91] For Foot, Europe had once again become a party-political issue, support for the EEC being regarded as a Tory concern. It was vital that the Labour Party oppose entry. If the negotiations were to fail, the scandal of such might even be sufficient to bring down the government, particularly as the Prime Minister was so closely and personally associated with the cause of Europe. In the aftermath of the motion, R. C. Beetham from the Foreign Office News Department confessed to Caroline Petrie of the European Communities Information Unit (ECIU) that it had been 'by far the most difficult week with the press, British and overseas, since the negotiations started'. He continued: 'At every single lunch, every single briefing and in every single conversation I have had this week, particularly with the foreign press, I have been – there is no other word for it –

attacked for what is alleged to be the Government's failure to inform or inspire public opinion in favour of entry into the EEC.... There is no doubt that the Motion signed by 108 Labour M.P.'s has inflamed doubt about whether the final terms will be approved in Parliament'.[92]

It was precisely such doubts that Michael Foot wished to sow. In this, he was joined by Jim Callaghan, who became the first of Wilson's former cabinet ministers to speak out in opposition to the current terms for British entry. Although he had voted in 1967 to support the Labour government's application for membership, by February 1971, Callaghan was giving speeches all but opposing British membership under *any* terms.[93] In May, he told an audience that British entry into the EEC 'seems more and more to mean that we must cut adrift from other countries, especially from the Commonwealth, old and new, and the United States. We are told that we must put off old friends in order to put on the new'. This, he argued, was unacceptable: 'We have a deep attachment to the continent of Europe and are part of its ancient civilisation but we are obstinately Atlantic Europeans. The very words "a European Europe" give an aroma of Continental claustrophobia'.[94] In response to his speech, Callaghan received a voluminous correspondence, including from many usually opposed to Labour policies. As one Conservative voter told him, 'like thousands of citizens, I appreciate the value of your Southampton speech in bringing in a measure of moderation and common-sense to counteract the irresponsible optimism of "negotiator" Rippon and the irrational impatience of "Europremier" Heath'.[95]

In an attempt to gain a better sense of the views of the British public, the ECIU, in coordination with the European Movement, launched a study on British attitudes in the spring of 1971. Reporting back to O'Neill on 21 April, it found that although the public was not 'as ignorant of the facts about the EEC and our negotiations for entry as is sometimes believed', only 10 per cent felt they had enough information to themselves make an informed decision or take part in a referendum. Furthermore, although most people believed that in the long-term Britain would benefit by 'becoming more modern and efficient', they also believed that the rich would benefit most from entry ('45 per cent believe *only* the rich'). Finally, and perhaps most alarmingly for the government, the study found that there were 'no grounds for believing that if the British public were given more information about the EEC they would necessarily become more favourable to our entry'. This was because, regardless of 'the facts', there was 'considerable anxiety about impact effects and a certain lack of confidence about Britain's ability to exploit the opportunities'.[96] Polling data seemed to confirm these findings. In a Gallup survey taken between 21 and 23 May 1971, 58 per cent of the British public believed that the negotiations would be successful, with only 19 per cent thinking they would fail. Yet in this same survey, only 27 per cent of the public were either strongly in favour or in favour of joining the EEC. In contrast, 22 per cent were against joining and 36 per cent strongly against.[97] The British public were resigned to the fact that the United Kingdom would enter the EEC; however, they were not happy about it.

This did not stop the government and its supporters from trying their level best to make an argument in favour of entry. Speaking to the Conservative Party Seminar on the Common Market in late April, Duncan Sandys – still an MP and now leading the United Kingdom's delegation to the Council of Europe and the WEU – argued that 'those who warn us of the irrevocable nature of the decision to go into the Common Market should recognise that a decision to stay out would be equally irrevocable. . . . It is said we cannot afford to go in. The truth is we cannot afford to stay out'.[98] The Prime Minister, likewise, refused to be cowed by the increasingly negative attitude of the Labour Party and wider British public. As he told the American President Richard Nixon after meeting with French President Pompidou in late May, 'The prospect which is now before us is both challenging and exciting. Within an enlarged Community I see for the first time, following my meeting with President Pompidou, real possibility of future joint and co-operative action with the French, as with our other friends in Europe, over a wide field. I am confident that the consequences for all of us can be nothing but good'.[99]

Those within the Six shared Heath's optimism. O'Neill noted in his report on the negotiations that the Heath–Pompidou summit was 'by far the most significant meeting that took place in the whole course of the negotiations'. It established 'at the highest level on either side broad understandings about the main outstanding issues of the negotiations in Brussels', 'inaugurated an Anglo–French reconciliation which the events of the previous 10 years had made most necessary and desirable', and 'avoided causing any offence to the other five members of the Community'.[100] On 21 June, William Whitelaw, the Leader of the House of Commons and Lord President of the Privy Council, informed the cabinet that general agreement on the main points of the negotiations would be reached within days and it was now time to 'start preparing the ground in the country for a long and intensive campaign'.[101] In the early hours of 23 June 1971, a deal was reached between Britain and the Six providing guarantees to New Zealand on its butter and cheese markets and a British contribution to the Community of 8.64 per cent of the Community budget in 1973, rising to 18.92 per cent in 1977.[102] The deal was done.

In a front-page splash the next day, the *Daily Mail* announced, 'Now we can lead Europe'. It was effusive in its praise. 'The way is open', it said. 'At last, after ten years of false starts and disappointments, Britain has a genuine opportunity for a great new future inside Europe. The *Daily Mail* believes that the British people will grasp it.... The *Daily Mail* has never wavered. We have always supported the cause of British entry into the Common Market'. The *Mail* also became the first newspaper to directly link British membership of the EEC with a new post-imperial role, writing, 'Nine years ago Dean Acheson, the American statesman, said: "Britain has lost an empire and not yet found a role". At the time his words hurt – because they were true. Now at last we have a role again. A role which can give us back the sense of pride and confidence which alone makes a great nation. Churchill said it. Macmillan said it. Now the six nations of the EEC have said it. And we believe that, when it comes to the choice, the people of this country will say it too: Britain's future lies inside the family of Europe'.[103]

Despite the successful negotiations, however, the battle was just beginning, for the terms that had been accepted by the Conservative government still had to be accepted by Parliament. And, in words mimicking those of General de Gaulle, Jim Callaghan spoke for many Labour MPs (and some Conservative ones, too) when he said, '*Non, merci beaucoup*'.[104]

* * *

On 28 October 1971, after more than 300 hours of debate and 104 voting divisions, the House of Commons passed the European Economic Communities Bill by 356 votes to 244, committing the British government to joining the EEC on 1 January 1973.[105] As the Labour MP Roy Jenkins remembered, 'I certainly felt and I believe a lot of other people did, in the division on 28 October 1971, that people felt they were voting in a division comparable with that on the Great

Reform Bill or the repeal of the Corn Laws, or one of Gladstone's Home Rule Bills, or the Parliament Bill, or the division which brought about the fall of the Chamberlain government. People saw it in the context of great historical divisions'.[106] It had not come without cost, however. The Conservative government suffered its greatest backbench rebellion since May 1940, with fully one-fifth of Conservative MPs voting against the government's policy. It was passed only with the support of a minority of pro-European Labour MPs who defied their own party's three-line whip to vote against it. The majority of Labour MPs, following the Party's official policy, were by now openly against British entry.[107]

Immediately after the publication of the government's White Paper in July 1971 laying out the terms of entry, Harold Wilson had issued an ambivalent statement claiming that the decision before Parliament was 'the most important political choice to come before us in this generation' and, 'if we could get the right terms for entry, it would be good for Britain and for Europe'. However, he added that 'the choice depends on this, whether the terms of entry, the price of admission, are too costly in terms of the advantages we should get'.[108] Publicly, he was in favour of the principle of British entry, but he was leaving the door open for a Labour rejection of the terms as negotiated by the Conservative government once they had been properly examined. In private, he was less ambivalent. When his next-door neighbour, Lord Drogheda, sent him a note urging him 'not [to] repudiate his own policies',[109] Wilson replied that 'the Labour Party, and I myself, find it difficult to support entry into [the] E.E.C. on the terms negotiated'.[110] This was confirmed on 28 July when, after a Special Conference of the Labour Party, the National Executive Committee of the party voted to reject the terms that Heath and Rippon had negotiated.[111] From that day forth, it became official Labour policy to oppose entry.

George Thomson, the former Minister for Europe who had managed the 1967 application, immediately caused a stink in the Labour Party when he appeared on a programme for Thames Television claiming that if he had 'still been the Minister for Europe these were the only terms that were available and I would have recommended the cabinet to accept [them]'. His words completely contradicted the party line that the Conservatives had sold out Britain in a way the Labour Party would never have done.[112] His voice, however, was drowned out by those who smelled Tory blood. In a speech on

8 September, Jim Callaghan promised that 'even if Mr. Heath insists on plunging ahead, it is important that he and his Party should know, and that the Community should know, that a majority of the British people are opposed to him on this issue'. He added that 'even if Mr. Heath has his way about taking us in – nevertheless, when a Labour Government wins the confidence of the people then it should be its intention to re-negotiate, on a Government-to-Government basis, those terms which at the time will have been found objectionable and harmful to the interest of the British people'.[113] On 17 September, Callaghan accused the government of 'concealing' the truth from the British people, and, on 21 September, he gave his strongest speech yet: 'Don't be faint-hearted, down at the mouth and resigned to the obliteration of this country's independent political role.... We do not need to throw our hand in, beset by a false and unworthy despair. We need to believe in ourselves again. We do not need to submerge ourselves in a foreign super-state'.[114]

It was little surprise, then, that at the Labour Party Conference in early October Wilson came out in opposition to British entry into the EEC. Had he not done so, he would almost certainly have faced a leadership challenge from Callaghan.[115] It was also no surprise that, at the end of the month, he imposed upon his own MPs a three-line whip to vote against the government's bill despite it differing little from what could have been achieved by his own government in 1967. That sixty-nine Labour MPs rebelled to vote with the Government in favour of the bill whilst thirty-nine Conservatives voted against did little to change the perception that the Tory Party was the 'party of Europe' and the Labour Party was now the bona fide 'anti-Market' opposition. For arguably the first time in British history, the United Kingdom now had a 'Eurosceptic' party.[116]

For many, the parliamentary vote was a long time coming. As Sir James R. H. Hutchinson penned to Duncan Sandys on 1 November, 'May I just write a line to you of congratulations on the outcome of the Common Market division.... [Y]ou were, in the early days, one of the main impulses which drove the idea to the success it has to-day. I well remember the pathfinder team which, in 1947 was it?, [you] led to France to explore, at Winston's behest, the feeling in France on a United Europe'.[117] Now, almost twenty-five years later, Sandys replied to Hutchinson, 'We have waited long to get into the Club, though it is our own fault since we had the chance to be founder members. Now we must make up for lost time and begin to think seriously about European integration, not only in economic matters but also in the sphere of foreign affairs and defence'.[118] As far as Sandys was concerned, the United Kingdom was now beyond a shadow of doubt a European country.

Following the parliamentary vote in October 1971, there was little that could stop Britain's entry. On 22 January 1972, Britain signed the Treaty of Accession, in February the bill passed through its second reading in Parliament, and that July it was given its third and final reading, after which it was signed into law by Her Majesty Queen Elizabeth II. From 1 January 1973, the United Kingdom would be a member of the EEC.[119] Heath claimed that the world was now 'in a fantastic period of readjustment, in which all relationships have been thrown into the melting pot'. He visibly cringed when American President Richard Nixon described the US–UK relationship as 'special', undermining as it did his contention that Britain was first and foremost a European nation, and its foreign relations were being recalibrated to demonstrate that.[120] As Michael Pallister, who was shortly to become the Permanent Representative to the European Communities, said in an address to the Civil Service College in July 1972, 'Life in the Community is not the lowest common denominator of national interests: it is not even the highest common factor. British national interest will in future be subsumed within the interest of the Community as a whole'. He did not finish there: '[B]ut the converse is just as true. There will be no reality of Community interest that does not take proper account of British interests and those of the other members. This is what integration and interdependence are all about. And it is with the fascinating and challenging task of reconciling these interests that we in Brussels, and, I hope, you in Britain, will be engaged in the years head'.[121]

Britain was finally 'in Europe'. But the British public, no less than some of its politicians, were now less certain Europeans than they had been at any time since the end of the Second World War. As the sun finally set on the British Empire with the withdrawal of Britain's responsibilities from the area east of Suez, so, too, did Britons look to their lost empire for solace in a post-imperial world that was looking ever smaller. As the historian Kenneth Morgan has written, 'The mood when Britain joined was one of wary acceptance, since no obvious alternative could be found. It even appeared a kind of surrender, a recognition that the loss of Empire and the breakdown of an equal partnership with the

Americans had left Britain as an enfeebled and divided offshore island with nowhere else to turn'.[122] In such circumstances, it was perhaps inevitable that many would look to the 'golden age' of Britain's imperial past with longing when faced with the reality of a reluctant European present. In his speech to the Labour Party Conference in October 1972, Callaghan – after speaking of the 'traumatic changes over the last generation in Britain's world role' – publicly renewed his 'faith in a Commonwealth which remains a unique bridge between rich and poor, black and white'. The Conservative Party, he said, had decided that the Commonwealth was 'a gigantic farce', but a new Labour government would 'promot[e] a new pattern of intra-Commonwealth trade and the potential for increased Commonwealth political consultation which could make the Commonwealth an essential part of the nervous system of a new world order'.[123]

The Foreign and Commonwealth Office disagreed. In a memorandum sent to all British heads of mission on 5 December 1972, Sir Denis Greenhill – the Permanent Under-Secretary of State and Head of the Diplomatic Service – called for a 'fresh look at some of our old assumptions and ideas'. His analysis, he said, was 'deliberately radical' but came 'close to the mark'. Focussing entirely on the Commonwealth, he wrote that 'the truth of the matter is that we exercise very little influence over the new members of the Commonwealth and will exercise less. It is almost impossible to reconcile the practices of African dictatorships and one-party states with our own. The Asian members have democratic roots but, with the departure of the officials directly trained under us, they are tending to return to a corrupt form of democracy'. His conclusion was damning to those in the Labour Party, as well as to the anti-Market faction of the Conservative Party who clung to the Commonwealth as a shield against further integration with Europe: '[T]he British posture towards the Commonwealth is primarily a collection of particular policies towards individual members. There is not and cannot be a Commonwealth policy in the sense that there is a Western European policy. There is understandably no Commonwealth equivalent to the Prime Minister's directive of 1971 that all Government Departments must "think European"'.

Some elements of the Commonwealth would remain important to British interests, particularly the existing bilateral relationships with Australia, Canada and New Zealand. In general, however, when playing a hand in the game of international affairs, 'the aces will only appear if we are rich and powerful in our own right and that means giving priority to Europe'.[124] The United Kingdom was now a post-imperial country. It was also a European country. But, for many in Britain, the very loss of the Empire and Commonwealth to which Greenhill referred was the greatest reason to develop a deep Euroscepticism.

15 SEASONS OF DISCONTENT

When it awoke on the morning of 1 January 1973 as a full member of the European Economic Community (EEC), the British public was deeply ambivalent. In a poll taken from 3–7 January 1973, 36 per cent of the public reported being 'quite or very pleased'; 33 per cent were 'quite or very displeased' and an astonishing 20 per cent purported to be 'indifferent' (the remaining 11 per cent were undecided, but not indifferent). Even so, fully 51 per cent believed it would be a good thing for them and 66 per cent felt that it would be good for their children.[1] Overall, Britons were not enthused about joining the EEC, with only a third pleased with the outcome, yet the majority – perhaps grudgingly – recognised that it was probably in the best interests of the country, particularly for its economic future.

The Prime Minister Edward Heath did not share this ambivalence. Claiming in his autobiography that the Conservative victory in the October 1971 debate was his 'greatest success as Prime Minister' and that signing the Treaty of Accession in January 1972 was the 'proudest moment in my life', he later wrote of his 'thrill [that] setting out to establish a peaceful Europe had come to fruition'.[2] He was not the only one to feel a sense of great accomplishment. One member of the cabinet described a 'mood of euphoria in the Establishment'.[3] On the night of the 1971 vote in Parliament, Harold Macmillan lit a bonfire of celebration on the cliffs of Dover,[4] and David Heathcoat-Amery – who was later to become a leading Eurosceptic in the Conservative Party – cracked open a bottle of champagne.[5] Margaret Thatcher, who by this point had experienced a rapid rise through the parliamentary ranks to become Secretary of State for Education, was 'wholeheartedly in favour of British entry', although became somewhat concerned about the 'psychological effect [entry had] on Ted Heath. His enthusiasm for Europe had already developed into a passion. As the years went by it was to become an obsession'.[6]

To celebrate Britain's entry, the government set up the 'Fanfare for Europe', a series of concerts and other events intended to symbolise Britain's new relationship with Europe, beginning with an opening night gala at Covent Garden on 3 January 1973, which was attended by the Queen and included performances from distinguished actors such as Laurence Oliver and Judi Dench and the famed musicians Tito Gobbi, Elisabeth Schwarzkopf, Geraint Evans and Kiri te Kanawa. There followed on 4 January a concert at the Royal Albert Hall with a performance by the Berlin Philharmonic Orchestra and a football match at Wembley Stadium between the Six and the Three (Britain, along with Ireland and Denmark, who had likewise joined on 1 January 1973). Heath recalled that it was 'all an appropriately high-spirited and good-natured introduction to Britain in Europe, and my heart was full of joy'.[7]

Not all saw it in such terms, however. The cost to the taxpayer of the Fanfare for Europe (announced to the public by Secretary of State for Education Margaret Thatcher) was £350,000. The Minister of State for Trade and Consumer Affairs Sir Geoffrey Howe wrote to Douglas Hurd – at that time Heath's political adviser – providing a letter from one of his constituents, which read, 'Surely at a time when our economy is at such a low ebb, there are better and more useful ways of spending taxpayers' money. . . . May I suggest that we erect a block of old peoples' flatlets (so sorely needed) as a monument to this event'.[8] As a direct result of this letter, the government provided £100,000 to establish a 'Europe Chair of Rehabilitation' at Southampton University in recognition that, throughout Europe, there was a 'need to encourage training in, and development of, rehabilitation of sick and disabled people'.[9] This only added to the taxpayer's burden, however, and did little to encourage good feeling towards the European continent.

By August 1973, 52 per cent of those polled believed the government had been 'wrong' to join the Common Market, with only 32 per cent still supportive. Of those surveyed, 48 per cent said they would be 'pleased' if told the Common Market would 'be scrapped tomorrow' (22 per cent were 'indifferent' and only 20 per cent would be 'sorry').[10] It was hardly the embrace of 'Europe' that Heath had dreamed about since first delivering his maiden speech in the House of Commons more than twenty years earlier. This continuing (and increasing) dissatisfaction with Britain's EEC entry was not the only concern facing the government, and Heath was soon pulled from what Thatcher called his 'European fixation'. As the long-time British civil servant Stephen Wall has written, 'A year which started in bright lights was to end in fuel-starved, strike-ridden, three-day-week candle light in Britain and ill-tempered tensions within Europe and between Europe and the United States'.[11]

Even prior to the start of the year, Heath's government had come under increasing criticism for its handling of the economy. By the beginning of 1972, unemployment had reached its highest level since the disastrous winter of 1947 that had caused Clement Attlee's government so many problems. As the figure passed 1 million out-of-work, Heath feared it had become politically unsustainable. This rise in unemployment was compounded by the collapse of the Bretton Woods system of monetary management, forcing Britain to adopt a regime of floating exchange on 23 June 1972.[12] In an attempt to weather these economic storms, the government embarked upon its infamous 'U-turns', undermining its manifesto promise of a turn towards free market economics (or, as Heath put it, 'a new economic order deliberately based on the disciplines of the market economy'[13]) to instead return to the 'corporatist and interventionist ways of the post-war era'.[14] These U-turns included nationalising Rolls Royce after first promising that the government would not 'bail out' so-called 'lame duck companies' and rescuing the Upper Clyde Shipbuilders; passing the 1972 Industry Act to strengthen industry by providing state assistance; the introduction of a compulsory prices and incomes policy in November 1972; and, between July 1971 and March 1973, the adoption of 'classic Keynesian reflationary methods by increasing public expenditure'.[15]

Heath's government was rewarded for its efforts by distrust from the public and increased militancy by the Trade Unions when the National Union of Miners (NUM) called a national strike in January 1972 demanding a 47 per cent pay rise. By the end of that year, 23 million man-days had been lost to strikes, the highest number since the Great Strike of 1926.[16] To compound these industrial problems, a minority of anti-Marketeers in the Conservative Party and an even greater number of Labour Party 'Commonwealth sentimentalists' argued that the government's decision to float the pound in June 1972, essentially dismantling the Sterling Area and with it a large part of the rationale for maintaining close Commonwealth ties, was directly influenced by 'a more compelling doctrinal loyalty to the EEC'.[17] The government had chosen Europe over the Commonwealth and in so doing had placed itself in peril. When the United Kingdom entered the EEC on 1 January 1973, it was arguably in its worst economic position since the immediate aftermath of the Second World War, and there were already those who blamed this economic plight on Heath's European policy.

If 1972 had been a difficult economic year for the government, things were going to get much worse in 1973. Inflation, which had been running at an annual average of 5.2 per cent in the late 1960s, reached 9.3 per cent by 1973 and would soon skyrocket to 27 per cent.[18] Inflation was particularly severe in commodity prices. Between 1 January 1972 and 31 December 1973, 'the price of copper rose by 115 per cent, cotton by 127 per cent, cocoa by 173 per cent and zinc by a massive 308 per cent'. In all during these months, the price of imports into Britain rose by an average of 26 per cent.[19] It was the rising price of food, however, that most caught the public's imagination, because it was fear of such that the Labour opposition had firmly planted in the voter's mind during the negotiation for British EEC entry and which was most closely tied to the question of British membership. When it became clear that the British people were paying a higher price for food – particularly butter – after accession than before, the public became highly critical of the decision to enter, linking in their minds the loss of Commonwealth preference with the steadily worsening economic situation that was haunting much of the West.[20]

Throughout it all, Heath and his government sought desperately to keep the focus on the more positive aspects of Europe and make a success (both politically and otherwise) of Britain's entry into the Common Market. In mid-September 1973, Douglas Hurd held a late-night session with John Harris and Geoffrey Tucker, the latter of whom was Director of Publicity at Conservative Central Office, to discuss Conservative policy on Labour's proposed renegotiation and referendum on British membership. Writing to Heath the following day, Hurd advised that politically the best course of action would be to 'take every opportunity to rub the noses of Labour leaders into their past commitments on Europe'. This could be done in one of two ways. First,

Conservatives could 'claim that behind the verbiage, the Labour Party was trying to get us out of the Community', or, second, they could 'claim that behind the verbiage, the Labour Party would almost certainly keep us in'. Either way, their stated policy of a renegotiation followed by a national referendum was disingenuous, as the party had already determined the desired outcome. The three men agreed that the second option was the best, as it 'caused greater embarrassment to Wilson and [Peter] Shore inside the Party.... It reassured our Continental friends. It also happened to be true'. Hurd was convinced that Wilson's promise of renegotiation and a referendum was a ruse to appease the anti-Marketeer majority within his party; as soon as he was back in power, he would attempt a minimal renegotiation and then go to the people with a referendum, certain that he 'would be supported by the Conservatives and Liberals and would have no trouble'.[21]

Nevertheless, Hurd's recommendations, however right they may have been, had little effect on public opinion, which was quickly souring. On 25 September 1973, the Parliamentary Secretary of the Cabinet Ministerial Committee on Europe noted that, since the first of the year, there had been 'a steady decline in public and political support for the Community'. Increasingly, the public equated the Community with 'rising prices and juggernauts', a mood which had 'been fortified by the continued articulate campaign of anti-Marketeers'. Within Parliament itself, 'both sides of both Houses feel that decisions taken in Brussels are effectively beyond their influence'. Pro-Europeans, both inside and outside Parliament, had 'expected too much from our entry' and were now 'suffering from a sense of anti-climax', providing a distinct opportunity to those who were opposed to British membership.[22] Three days later, an official from the Department of Trade and Industry provided a similar analysis to the Cabinet office. The public 'mood', he said, resembled 'a crowd of holidaymakers who after much doubt and some expense have made a dangerous journey only to find the climate chilly, the hotel not what it was cracked up to be and the food too expensive'. In these circumstances, 'bloodthirsty feelings are mounting not only towards the other nationalities in the hotel but to the courier who got them there'. This spelled great danger to the Heath government, which had staked so much since its election in 1970 on a successful outcome to the 'European question'. There was, the analysis concluded, a 'feeling in general that things nationally are not going well'. In the 'popular mind', this was associated with British entry into the Common Market. This feeling of 'cause and effect' – 'largely divorced though it may be from reality' – would be difficult to eradicate.[23]

Worse was still to come. On 6 October 1973, the Yom Kippur War erupted between Egypt and Israel, disrupting oil supplies from the Middle East and prompting Arab governments to impose restrictions on their oil exports, despite a guarantee by the Organisation of Petroleum Exporting Countries (OPEC) in 1971 to maintain prices for five years. Consequently, British imports of Middle Eastern oil were cut by 15 per cent, and, by the end of October, the price of fuel had risen dramatically, mirroring the inflation in food prices that had already done so much damage to British morale.[24] By the beginning of November, a barrel of crude oil cost more than $5, compared to $2.40 in January.[25] Heath was hosting Willy Brandt at Chequers when they heard the news and, although they 'briefly assessed the crisis', their main concern was that it might affect the prospects of European economic and monetary union.[26]

Consequently, and with reference to the earlier reports from the Cabinet Ministerial Committee on Europe and the Department of Trade and Industry, on 25 October, Heath authorised officials to form a committee to 'deal with the problem of public relations aspects of the European Community'. He believed that if people were only better informed about the EEC and its benefits, they would be less likely to associate the deteriorating situation in Britain with UK entry of the Common Market. It was, as one civil servant described it, a 'comprehensive campaign of enlightenment in the country'.[27] J. A. Robinson of the European Integration Department summarised the situation facing the government, writing, 'The discontent clearly centres on the fact that things are not going well, and that the Government appears incapable of correcting the trend. In former, better, days bad trends were corrected by Governments in London. Something has happened to prevent this Government correcting these bad trends. It must be the fact that we have joined the Community, lost sovereignty and lost the power of independent action'. To combat this 'caricature', Robinson suggested that the government needed to show that, in fact, 'the Government has not lost the power to correct things' and that 'the Government's impetus to correct things has nothing to do with membership of the Community'.[28]

As so often in politics, however, events overtook Heath. On 10 October, the National Coal Board (NCB) offered the NUM an average pay raise of 13 per cent in response to their July demands for increases of up to 50 per cent for some workers. This was the highest the government was willing to go, particularly given the uncertainty of rapidly rising oil prices. The NUM immediately rejected the offer. Heath invited representatives of the miners' union to meet with him personally at 10 Downing Street, but to no avail. On 12 November, the NUM announced that it was banning all overtime for its members, causing coal production to fall rapidly, in what was described as a 'go-slow' tactic that could eventually evolve into another full strike if the miners' demands were not met. Heath immediately declared a state of emergency.[29] Only days earlier, the long-time Cabinet Secretary Burke Trend had retired, to be replaced by John Hunt. When the latter man arrived in his position, he felt as if he was 'boarding a sinking ship'; he later recalled 'a smell of death hanging over the Government with very tired ministers not making the best decisions'.[30]

It seemed incongruous that, in the midst of all this, Heath continued to host musical evenings at Chequers, even noting in his memoirs that on the night of 27 October his event was 'disrupted by affairs in the Middle East' because Pinchas Zukerman refused to play his promised violin duet with Isaac Stern because of the war. Undeterred, Heath invited the Amadeus Quartet to take his place and later provided an account of the performance – complete with details of a broken bow and the 'memorable' final piece (Haydn's String Quartet Opus 54 No 2) – which demanded almost as many words in his autobiography as the entire Yom Kippur War.[31] The music could offer little respite, however, perhaps no more than the band that continued to play on the *Titanic*. In November, the Treasury offered a forecast of a balance-of-payments deficit of £3 billion for 1974 and predicted that the economy would retract by 4.5 per cent.[32] As the news media continued to draw a link between the failing economy and membership of the EEC, the Home Secretary Robert Carr wrote in exasperation to the Conservative Chief Whip Francis Pym, 'I remain thoroughly fussed at our consistent failure apparently even to try to sell Europe and the advantages of our joining a European Community to the British people. I accept it is a most difficult thing to do but one never hears any trumpet blown in its favour except by the Prime Minister from time to time'.[33]

Pym took Carr's concerns to Heath, who, on 27 November, sent to all ministers a minute on the presentation of 'Europe'. There was, he wrote, 'still much public misunderstanding and misrepresentation of our European policies. It is important that we should all play a part in what must be a long and sustained effort to explain the benefits stemming from our membership of the EEC, and to counter criticism of some of the inevitable areas of difficulty'. In particular, he would be 'grateful' if ministers would 'whenever possible in your speeches and briefings, explain the advantages of membership and counter criticisms. Invitations from press, radio and television should whenever appropriate be accepted and encouraged'. He also hoped that ministers would ensure that their 'departments are fully alive to the constant need to publicise or counteract items of EEC news'.[34] In the midst of continuing problems with the miners' union and a declared state of emergency, Heath believed it was even more important that the Common Market not be blamed for the ills besetting Britain's economy.

There was little he could do to improve the public's opinion of the EEC or, for that matter, the government, however. In the face of continuing problems of the supply of both oil and coal, on 13 December 1973 the Prime Minister announced the introduction of the three-day working week to conserve energy beginning in the New Year. This – according to his Education Secretary Margaret Thatcher – 'gave an impression of crisis'.[35] The three-day week was accompanied by a compulsory 50 mph speed limit throughout the country, a maximum heating limit imposed upon all offices and commercial premises and the mandatory closing of television at ten thirty each evening.[36] The government had, quite literally, shut off the lights. It was only a matter of time before they would be forced to call another General Election or else face a vote of no confidence from an ever-vocal Labour opposition. The public perception of an out-of-touch government was not helped when, on 14 December, the Foreign Ministers of the Nine Member-States of the EEC (including Britain's Foreign Secretary Sir Alec Douglas-Home) issued a statement that they had 'decided that the time has come to draw up a document on European identity. This will enable [us] to achieve a better definition of [our] relations with other countries, and of [our] responsibilities and the place which they occupy in world affairs'.[37] For many Britons in December 1973, identity – European or otherwise – was very far from their minds as they shivered before a blank television screen.

* * *

Much had happened in the year that Britain 'joined Europe'. Sir Michael Palliser, the UK's first Permanent Representative to the European Communities and son-in-law of Paul-Henri Spaak, wrote to the Foreign Secretary on 25 January 1974 to provide an overview of 'Year One in the European Communities'. Over the course of the year, he wrote, the 'mood' of the EEC had 'changed from hope to uncertainty'. In 1973, 'fortune was not smiling on the Community or on Britain'. Whilst the Six had only encountered problems after twenty years of progress within 'the charmed circles of the European Communities', for Britain, the difficulties had been more accentuated: 'The fact that the first year of British membership of the Communities coincided with these daunting economic trends was at the root of the growth in disaffection with the Community evident in Britain throughout the year. Opinion in the six original Member States, acclimatised by over a decade of uneven but essentially successful European co-operation, quite rightly saw no reason to blame the Treaty of Rome and all its works.... But in Britain the gathering economic storm has led those with no confidence in the prospects of "fair gain" from European Community membership to take a jaundiced view of the unfolding scene in Brussels, ample confirmation as they saw it of their initial distaste for the whole enterprise'. His prediction for the future of Britain's position in Europe was no more optimistic. The year 1974, he wrote, 'could be the most difficult in the Community's history. And the Community is not in good shape to face difficulty on that scale'.[38]

The Conservative government recognised that it would only be able to tackle such challenging conditions with a fresh mandate from the British people. In a cabinet meeting in early January 1974, Heath floated to his colleagues the possibility of a snap election. Both Willie Whitelaw and Francis Pym spoke in opposition, and the decision was postponed. On 24 January, however, the NUM held a ballot to evolve their 'go slow' tactic to a full strike. When the result was announced on 4 February, more than 80 per cent of its members voted to strike, to begin on 9 February. Heath again consulted his colleagues on the wisdom of an early General Election, and this time there was no dissent. On 6 February 1974, he submitted to the Queen a formal request for the dissolution of Parliament, with a General Election set for the twenty-eighth of that month. At that time on the royal yacht during a tour of Australia, Elizabeth II was forced to cut short her trip to return to the United Kingdom. Calling his manifesto *Firm Action for a Fair Britain*,

Heath decided that the election would be fought on the concept of 'Who Governs Britain?', a direct challenge to the striking miners who had so dogged his time in office.[39]

Despite the significance of the failing economy and the industrial strife, it was the Common Market more than anything else that came to dominate the February 1974 General Election, a topic which gave a distinct advantage to the Labour Party. This was ironic, given that business leaders were convinced that – in the midst of so much other economic trouble – Britain's membership of the EEC was the one bright spot. In a poll published by the *Economist* on 29 December 1973, of the 165 leading British companies 84 per cent believed that 'membership of the Community will help them in the long term' and, 'When asked whether the firms would be harmed if a future Government took Britain out of the Community, 78 per cent said "yes"'. The *Economist* also reported that although 60 per cent of companies said the EEC had had no effect on sales, 38 per cent reported higher sales 'as a result of Community membership', with only 2 per cent showing poorer sales.[40]

This was not the message the British public at large was consuming. The Eurosceptic public found its leader in the Conservative MP Enoch Powell who, starting in June 1973, began to meet informally with Labour leader Harold Wilson, telling him that following the latter's promise to renegotiate the terms of British EEC entry, he would do all he could to see that the Labour Party rather than the Conservatives won the next General Election.[41] On the eighth of that month, he indicated in a speech that he might even 'recommend to his followers to vote Labour in the next Election on the grounds that only the Labour Party would offer an opportunity to the people of this country to vote against the Common Market'.[42] Tony Benn noted in his diary that evening that it had 'created an enormous sensation: Will he be thrown out [of the Conservative Party] and what are his motives'.[43]

Enoch Powell had long been a thorn in the side of the Conservative leadership. An unabashed imperialist in the early stages of his life, in 1946 Powell resigned his army commission to seek a seat in the House of Commons, which he believed was a necessary step to achieve his ultimate ambition: to become viceroy of India.[44] When this goal was thwarted the following year by Indian independence, Powell became viscerally anti-imperialist, convinced that once India had gone the entire British Empire must follow. Elected as a Conservative MP in 1950, he refused to support Churchill's advocacy of British membership of the European Coal and Steel Community, revealing a Euroscepticism that was uncommon in the Conservative Party of that time. In late 1955, Anthony Eden appointed him to his first ministerial position, and, in January 1957, he was promoted financial secretary to the Treasury. It was under Harold Macmillan that Powell became an active opponent of much that the leadership stood for. At the Treasury, he advocated a free market approach when the Keynesian consensus still dominated the economic thinking of both major parties, and, in September 1957, he convinced the Chancellor of the Exchequer Peter Thorneycroft that inflation was a monetary phenomenon and thus the responsibility of the government. At Powell's urging, Thorneycroft increased the bank rate from 5 to 7 per cent to combat inflation. When in January 1958 Macmillan refused to back the Treasury's request for an additional £50 million in spending cuts, both Thorneycroft and Powell resigned in protest.[45]

From the parliamentary backbenches, Powell became an outspoken critic of the Macmillan government, making his most famous intervention in July 1959, when he spoke on the Hola Camp massacre in Kenya, rubbishing the government's colonial policy by saying, 'We cannot say, "We will have African standards in Africa, Asian standards in Asia and perhaps British standards here at home".... We must be consistent with ourselves everywhere. All Government, all influence of man upon man, rests upon opinion.... We cannot, we dare not, in Africa of all places, fall below our own highest standards in the acceptance of responsibility'.[46] Powell's isolation on the backbenches did not last long, however, and, in the remaining years of the Macmillan and Douglas-Home governments, he rapidly advanced. Following the Labour victory in 1964, he sat on the Opposition Front Bench as Transport Spokesman and, in July 1965, ran against Heath and Maudling for the leadership of the party. Although coming a distant third, Heath was kind to Powell, offering him his pick of shadow portfolios. Powell chose defence, although immediately fell into controversy when at the 1965 Party Conference he advocated a British withdrawal from the area east of Suez, which at that time few supported. In the spring of 1968, he placed himself beyond the pale when, in a speech in Birmingham, he opposed Tory support of the government's Race Relations Bill, predicting that if immigration were allowed to continue on its current trajectory there would be a massive 'breakdown in public order'. In what has become known as his 'Rivers of Blood' speech, he told his audience, 'Like the Roman, I seem to see the River Tiber foaming with much blood'.[47] The following day, Heath sacked him from the cabinet; he would never again return to frontbench politics. Recognising that he had now been ostracised by the party elite, Powell determined to play an active role as a critic from the backbenches. On no subject was this truer than the question of Britain's relationship with Europe, upon which he had always vehemently disagreed with Heath.[48]

Powell's motives for opposing British EEC membership were drawn directly from his experience of the collapse of the British Empire, where – beginning in the late 1950s and early 1960s – he had begun to argue that post-imperial Britain was just as much of a new nation as the post-colonial states that empire's collapse had created. Given this new reality, Britain had to find itself again, which it could not do subsumed in a European super-state. As he said on 8 June 1973, 'Independence, the freedom of a self-governing nation, is in my estimation the highest political good, for which any disadvantage, if need be, and any sacrifice are a cheap price. There is not a state in Africa or Asia, hewn out of some administrative unit of Western colonial rule, which would not scorn to bargain away its independence.... It is for us, and us alone, to determine if we will continue to be a free, self-governing people. I refuse to imagine that we shall answer no'.[49] As an imperialist with dreams of becoming Viceroy of India, Powell had assumed it only natural that Britain would be a leader amongst other European empires. With the loss of India and his quickly developing anti-imperialism, however, he determined that Britain first had to discover its true post-imperial self before it could, in his mind, subjugate itself to Europe. For Powell, this imperative was more important than loyalty to party.

Powell was not the only one to think this way. On 27 July, Tony Benn rang his fellow Labour MP Peter Shore following the by-elections at Ripon and the Isle of Ely, which had seen the Labour candidates pushed to third place in both races. Shore predicted 'a massive national crisis coming' and told Benn they should 'politicise it'. He did not only mean to politicise it for party advantage, however: 'He said, "Of course there could be more than one coalition," and he sort of indicated that there might be some Tory anti-Market people who would bring Heath down and we would then find ourselves with two coalitions the Centre-Right European coalition with some Conservative leader other than Heath, and an uneasy correspondence of interests between the Left and the anti-Market right of the Tory Party, Neil Marten [Conservative MP for Banbury] and others, with Powell in the background'.[50] Like Powell, Shore believed that the issue of Europe was so important to Britain's future that it transcended party politics.

On 7 February 1974, the day before the election was announced, Powell indicated in private to Wilson that he would use the Common Market issue to strategically undermine Heath's leadership.[51] The next day, he announced that he would stand down as a Conservative candidate in the forthcoming election, believing the election to be 'a fraud'.[52] As soon as Parliament was dissolved, Powell began to directly attack Heath's role in bringing Britain into the EEC.[53] By the twenty-first of the month – one week before the election – he was opening calling for Tories to vote Labour, so that Britain could withdraw from the Common Market.[54] This culminated in a speech in Birmingham on 23 February, where he used his most forceful language against Heath and the Conservative leadership to date. Consequently, the newspaper coverage in the final week of the General Election was dominated by Powell's defection, divisions within the Tory Party and the British public's growing unease with the EEC.[55] As Tony Benn wrote in his diary, 'The Common Market has come into its own in the last week. It is the big question because it touches at food prices, at Heath's misunderstanding of the character of the British people and also at the basic questions of the freedom of Parliament and the people'.[56] By focussing attention on Heath's support for the EEC, Powell ensured that the election would be won or lost on the issue of the Common Market, not on the threatened miners' strike and industrial relations.[57]

Margaret Thatcher later wrote that she could 'understand the logic of his [Powell's] position, which was that membership of the Common Market had abrogated British sovereignty and that the supreme issue in politics was therefore how to restore it', although confessed that she was 'shocked' by his tactics.[58] Heath was less understanding: 'This champion of the right showed that he would sacrifice all his principles for a remote chance that Labour might take Britain out of Europe'.[59] In this, Heath was quite right. Powell was doing just enough to ensure that the Left would return to power, a Left which was loudly opposing Conservative policy on Europe and stirring up public sentiment against British membership of the EEC. As Jim Callaghan, the Labour Shadow Foreign Secretary, told a crowd on 21 February, 'Whatever Mr. Heath may do, a Labour government will not take its orders from Brussels where vital interests such as the control of rising prices are concerned.... At the end of the day, a Labour Government will decide whether there is or is not an acceptable basis for Britain's continued membership, and we give this pledge – the British people themselves will declare on the final decision'.[60] Heath had asked who governed Britain. The British people increasingly feared that it was bureaucrats in Brussels, not their elected parliamentarians at home.

When the votes were counted on 28 February 1974, the Labour Party received four more seats in Parliament than the Conservatives, although it failed to secure an absolute majority of all constituencies, leading to the first 'hung' Parliament since 1929. Without Powell's 'intervention' on the Common Market, it is difficult to see how Labour would have won those four necessary seats. Heath described it as 'the worst possible result for the country.... The press had portrayed the contest as a trial of strength between the elected government and an extra-parliamentary force [the unions]. Once people began to talk about the question "Who governs Britain?" an indecisive outcome was bound to be a threat to democracy, no matter which party actually formed the next administration'.[61] Heath had put to the nation a question, but the electorate had failed to provide a clear answer. After proving unable to secure a coalition government with the Liberals, the Prime Minister travelled to Buckingham Palace to offer his resignation, after which Harold Wilson was invited once more to form Her Majesty's Government.[62]

* * *

When Wilson returned to 10 Downing Street on 4 March 1974, he was in a more precarious position than during any of his years in the 1960s. Not only was he presiding over a government whose MPs formed only a minority in Parliament, but the economy was in shambles, the Trade Unions had great (and arguably impossible) expectations and, despite the assistance it had given Labour in winning the General Election, the Common Market issue threatened to rip the party apart. Upon entering the great house, the '30 staff [who] lined up in the front hall and along the corridor' gave off a 'feeling of hostility and discomfort. Top civil servants look[ed] very smooth, trying not to show their horror'.[63] It was the worst of all possible outcomes, and it was clear from the outset that Wilson could not sustain his position for long. He later wrote, 'Although Labour's representation in Parliament was

34 less than a putative coalition of all the other parties, I was confident that a Government could be formed, and that on its first major Parliamentary test, the adoption of the Queen's Speech setting out the Government's programme for the coming session, we should be sustained by the vote of the Commons'.[64] Beyond that, he could make no promises. What was a political certainty was that, within a matter of months, another General Election would be necessary to shore up his position in Parliament and his authority throughout Whitehall. The only real question was when.

In the meantime, Wilson and his cabinet colleagues had to govern and, although his immediate priority was to reach a resolution with the miners and get the country back to work, he could not escape the issue of Europe for long, having made such a clear promise in his election manifesto for a renegotiation of Britain's terms of entry followed by a referendum. Those within his party and on the Conservative right who were anti-Marketeers were elated at the Labour victory, however slight it might have been. As the Common Market Safeguard Campaign wrote in a pamphlet published shortly after the election, 'The defeat of Mr. Heath's pro-Market Government...gives Britain the chance of fundamental re-negotiation of his disastrous 1972 Treaty of Accession'. The first year of Common Market membership was 'one of gathering gloom for Britain. Food prices rose faster than ever before in our history – 15 per cent between autumn 1972 and autumn 1973; and by the end of the year were 50 per cent above the level of June 1970, when negotiations to join the Market began'.[65] It was time for change.

In Wilson's choice for Foreign Secretary, the anti-Marketeers received welcome news. Jim Callaghan – one of the most fervent opponents of the Conservative government's EEC negotiations – had been asked to take the reins at the Foreign Office even before the Queen officially invited Wilson to form a government. He set about his task to renegotiate Britain's terms of entry with gusto. Meeting with the American Helmut Sonnefeldt, Counsellor at the US State Department, less than two weeks after the government was formed, Callaghan summarised his position on Europe: 'He himself was an agnostic, neither convinced in the Community's favour nor against it. His position was that of a humble Christian among lions. The Government's position had not yet been worked out and this would take a little time'. Nevertheless, Callaghan was convinced that 'the bargain struck by Britain with the Community was not good...[and] must be re-negotiated subject by subject'. Furthermore, regardless of how the renegotiation went, the government would ensure the results were fully debated in Parliament ('He was not sure how the debate would go') and then 'presented to the British people to make their choice'.[66] The Labour Government would seek to get the best deal they could for Britons but, ultimately, it was up to the electorate to decide whether or not they remained within the Common Market.

Not all shared the public ambivalence of Callaghan (who, in private, was far less convinced of the possible merits of continued membership than he claimed to Sonnefeldt). Lord Gladwyn worried that, in spite of the Foreign Secretary's 'mild tone' on the EEC, 'the situation as regards Britain's participation in the continuing work of the E.E.C., and even of its continuing membership, remains rather disturbing'. He explained that a recent poll showed that only 12 per cent of the electorate 'believed that we had obtained any benefit as a result of membership', which was hardly surprising given that the public had been 'so drenched with anti-market arguments during the last year – often advanced, of course, for political purposes – that [they] may attribute any misfortune, from cholera to the Middle East War, to our present close association with Europe'. Given this public sentiment, the Labour government's policy of offering a referendum on continued membership was a risky one, to say the least, and could only be interpreted as a move on the part of the government to withdraw British participation from the Community.[67]

One of those whose scepticism towards 'Europe' had increased over the past year was Tony Benn, whom Wilson appointed Secretary of State for Industry. On 8 April Benn met with George Thomson, now an EEC Commissioner, and explained his reservations about Britain's position in Europe. In his diary, he summarised his conversation, saying, 'I have never been on an explicitly anti-Market platform in my life but since we had been in the Community, I felt the House of Commons had become a spectator of great events, and that too much power had been drained away to Europe through all the official committees that had been set up'.[68] For Benn, as for so many other Labour MPs, the experience of Europe had been far more disappointing than the promise.

Even so, Callaghan sought to project an attitude of open-mindedness and a genuine desire to remain within the Common Market, if only the right terms could be negotiated. Speaking to the European Communities Council of Ministers in Luxembourg on

1 April, he told his European colleagues that it would 'come as no surprise to you that the Labour Government opposes membership of the Community on the terms that were negotiated at the time of our entry in January 1973'. He promised to negotiate in 'good faith and if we are successful in achieving the right terms we shall put them to our people for approval'. Should the terms not live up to Labour's expectations, however, he would explain 'to the British people the reason why we find the terms unacceptable and consult them on the advisability of negotiating the withdrawal of the United Kingdom from the Community'. He stressed that he did not 'hope for a negotiation about withdrawal. I would prefer a successful renegotiation from which the right terms for continued membership will emerge'. He also made clear that the British government was 'not asking for charity. We seek a fair deal'.[69]

There was good reason for Callaghan to project such studied indifference. Within the Labour Party there was a minority of pro-Europeans to whom 'adherence to the EEC was not so much a policy as a way of life. A good number believed more strongly in British membership than in any other tenet of policy, and would, if the choice had to be made, reject the Party in favour of what was to them the wider aim, Europe'.[70] Given that there were other members who were equally convinced that it was the duty of the party to wrong the rights of the Tory government and withdraw from the EEC, there was no easy solution for the party leadership. As Wilson later wrote in his memoirs, 'In all my thirteen years as Leader of the Party I had no more difficult task than keeping the Party together on this issue'.[71] It was not a problem the Tory Prime Ministers Heath, Douglas-Home, Macmillan, Eden or Churchill had faced before him, but one that would become more familiar to the future Conservative leaders Margaret Thatcher and, especially, John Major. In 1974, though, it was the Labour Party not the Conservatives who were haemorrhaging over the question of Britain's policy towards Europe. The letters to the editor of the *Daily Mail* on 5 April made this divide clear for all to see. One congratulated the Foreign Secretary 'on the way in which he is tackling the EEC negotiations.... It's really astonishing that many newspapers still do not realise the bitter resentment felt by the majority of the electorate at not being consulted on joining the EEC, and at the dictatorial methods that were used to achieve this'. Printed directly beside this, another reader wondered 'whether Mr Callaghan realises the legacy which he will give the young people of today if he negotiates British withdrawal from the European Community. It will be the final relegation of this country into the "third division"'.[72]

The elites of the Conservative Party had no such doubts. In May, Julian Amery – one of the last imperialists in Parliament – wrote to Heath laying out the Opposition view of the necessity for continued EEC membership and the danger of renegotiation: 'Alone among nations we have lived under free institutions and avoided violent revolution for three centuries.... We have been preserved from invasion, partly by geography; partly by naval and air power. We have secured growth partly through technology; partly through Empire.... Empire gave us a much broader and better balanced "home" market than Britain alone could provide. Its resources, added to our own, provided a solid backing for our currency'. Over the past two decades this had all changed, and the 'pillars of our economic growth – security, technology, and Empire – have been eroded'. In a post-imperial world, there was only one solution: 'If, with our partners in the European Community, we could build an effective European Union we could restore the foundations of growth and political freedom'. There was, Amery wrote, 'no valid alternative for Britain to Europe. We cannot find safety or growth on a purely national basis. Neither can we recreate the British Commonwealth.... For Britain it is Europe or stagnation, and stagnation means socialism, mass emigration, and in all probability an authoritarian regime'. Enoch Powell, recognising the reality of a post-imperial Britain, had concluded that the future of the United Kingdom was to be a small but uniquely free country. Membership of a supranational European entity would only complicate this, threatening the one advantage Britons still held: their personal liberties. Amery had likewise recognised the realities of post-imperial Britain, but, in contrast to Powell, saw in Europe not Britain's demise but its salvation. For that reason, Europe was the most important question of the day. 'We have', he concluded, 'to make Europe the central theme of our policy, in much the same way as the Conservative Party made Commonwealth and Empire its central theme from Joe Chamberlain's time to the 1950s. We have to present Europe as the condition of national security, economic growth, political freedom and international influence'.[73] In Amery's mind, the Labour Party's policy of renegotiation and a referendum threatened Britain's very existence.

This was a view held by most, if not all, Conservatives in 1974. Those within the Labour Party remained to be convinced. The cabinet held its first meeting on renegotiating the terms of Britain's entry on 25 April 1974. Callaghan, with a certain amount of resignation, said that the government had to 'face the fact that the EEC exists and is acknowledged to exist by the rest of the world'. Bernard Donoughue, head of the No. 10 Policy Unit, noted in his diary that the anti-Marketeers 'looked stunned [by this statement] – Peter Shore, Judith Hart, Tony Benn and Michael Foot, all sitting together at the far end of the table. Even the PM looked agitated, and he asked Robert Armstrong to open the windows and let in some fresh air'.[74] Michael Foot spoke on the sovereignty issue and its implications for Britain. Roy Jenkins, however, warned that a quick decision to withdraw would be 'very grave' and offered 'a clear warning to the PM that he and his pro-EEC friends would then resign'.[75] Although Wilson shrugged this off, the meeting 'ended very well for the pros, the antis looking grim, and with a timetable [for renegotiation] ahead till the autumn'.[76] From Donoughue's perspective, the Prime Minister appeared to be 'hoping to get the election out of the way before this EEC question comes to a head'.[77] Tony Benn left the meeting with a less favourable opinion: 'There was a great pessimism about the future of Britain. The myth of Empire had been replaced by the myth of Europe'.[78]

That there would have to be an election before the terms could be fully renegotiated and a referendum offered to the people was by now a certainty. Wilson wrote in his memoirs that although Callaghan's statement to the European Council of Ministers was regarded as an 'opening bid' in the renegotiations, it was 'clear that there was little prospect of meaningful negotiations while the Government was in a minority situation in Parliament, with the real prospect of being ousted in the forthcoming General Election'.[79] For the sake of good governance, it was better to have the necessary election sooner rather than later, so that the government could roll up its proverbial sleeves and get to work. Wilson settled on the autumn, and on 20 September requested from the Queen a dissolution of Parliament, with the election set for 10 October. When she assented, she closed the shortest Parliament ('a mere 184 days') since 1681.[80]

In the run-up to the General Election, Heath decided to put British EEC membership at the centre of the Conservative campaign, believing it to be the most significant achievement of the Tory government and the issue upon which there was the greatest difference with the Labour Party. In its manifesto, the Conservative Party reminded the electors that 'Membership of the EEC brings us great economic advantages, but the European Community is not a matter of accountancy. There are two basic ideas behind the formation of the Common Market; first, that having nearly destroyed themselves by two great European civil wars, the European nations should make a similar war impossible in future; and, secondly, that only through unity could the western European nations recover control over their destiny – a control which they had lost after two wars, the division of Europe and the rise of the United States and Soviet Union'.[81] In contrast, the Labour manifesto promised to pursue a fundamental renegotiation of the terms of British entry, followed by a referendum within twelve months of the General Election to determine whether Britain should remain within or withdraw from the EEC.[82] When the election results came in in the early hours of 11 October, the Labour Party had won 319 seats to the Conservatives' 277, providing Wilson with a solid mandate in Parliament to pursue renegotiation.[83]

* * *

With the election out of the way, Wilson could turn more fully to the business of government, which was no small task. As he later wrote, 'The pressure on Government, and on individual ministers, from the October 1974 Election to the Summer Recess, beginning on 7 August 1975, was the most hectic and demanding of any I have known in over thirty years in Parliament'. At the heart of it all was the government's Europe policy, which came to dominate the next eight months. Although many in Labour were dismayed at the prospect of Britain's continued membership of the EEC and hoped that the referendum would fail, Bernard Donoughue reported in his diary that, by 3 December 1974, it was 'absolutely clear to me that he [Harold Wilson] wants the UK to stay in. . . . He said that the only two stick-points [in the renegotiation] were that we must get a concession on *cheap food* – access from the Commonwealth – and we must get some compromise on *parliamentary sovereignty*. He was fairly confident he could do this'. Donoughue added that Wilson was now 'in bubbling form. Obviously he has come to grips with the EEC and now wants to do it all himself'.[84] In a speech to the London Lord Mayors' Association on 7 December,

Wilson gave his most positive assessment yet, saying, 'We will work wholeheartedly for the success of the European venture if we get the terms for which we have asked and the endorsement of the British people'.[85]

Callaghan, too, had come to a similar conclusion. The renegotiation had to work, and the Labour Government had to succeed in persuading the British public to accept its results in the promised referendum. Whilst Wilson was delivering his speech to the Lord Mayors' Association, the Foreign Secretary clipped and kept a publication from the European Movement which read: '[I]n the present era of growing political and economic interdependence, the concept of exclusive national sovereignty is already outdated. ... Britain's very existence depends upon international trade. We cannot feed ourselves, or keep the wheels of industry turning, without importing most of our energy and raw material needs. ... For Britain to stand alone in the name of a mythical national sovereignty would spell certain disaster'.[86] Only together with its European neighbours could Britain succeed in a world without empire. Yet this implied a dependence on others that the British Empire had never required. Such dependence seemed to indicate a loss of national greatness for which Europe was a poor substitute. In a way that was simply not true for the continental European powers, British membership of the Common Market represented a failure to stand alone – a concept which had acquired near religious significance during the Second World War.

On 9–10 December 1974, the nine EEC heads of government met in Paris to discuss the Labour government's demand for renegotiation of Britain's terms of entry. At this meeting, Wilson laid down the seven issues that the government wished to address. First, within the Common Agricultural Programme (CAP), the United Kingdom wanted special arrangements for Commonwealth producers, particularly from New Zealand, Australia and the Caribbean. Second, the government wanted a fairer deal on its contribution to the Community Budget. Third, Wilson wanted to be clear that Economic and Monetary Union, whilst an ultimate goal, was not feasible in the immediate future (his preference would have been to see it taken off the table entirely, although he recognised that it was an important concept for some of his European colleagues). Fourth, he wished to reassert Parliamentary Sovereignty on a national level and, fifth, he raised the issue of capital transfers. His sixth area for renegotiation was the Community's collective approach to developing countries and, finally, his seventh was to formalise the concept that Value Added Tax (VAT) would be determined by politicians rather than bureaucrats.[87]

Wilson's European colleagues were pleasantly surprised by the unobtrusive nature of the Prime Minister's demands, the West German Chancellor Helmut Schmidt commenting that 'Renegotiation had proved a misleading term'.[88] What the British government really wanted was a *reinterpretation* of some aspects of the entry terms, which would require no Treaty revision or amendment of existing statutes. At the Paris summit, the continental European leaders realised what the Conservative Party had long accused the Labour Party of. The Wilson government had no intention of leaving the Community or even of substantially amending its terms. It was simply playing politics with Europe to appease its own sceptical members.

It was not only the European heads of government that recognised how minimal Britain's renegotiation demands were. The anti-Marketeers within the United Kingdom itself were just as surprised. On 17 December, the Common Market Safeguards Committee, Get Britain Out, British Business for World Markets and the Anti-Common Market League launched a joint National Referendum Campaign under the leadership of Conservative MP Neil Marten, with the Labour MP (and former President of the Board of Trade) Douglas Jay and Christopher Frere-Smith (who had stood for Parliament twice as an independent anti-EEC candidate, in 1966 and 1972) serving as Vice-Chairmen. Its aim was to 'restore to the British Parliament the exclusive right to pass laws and impose taxation binding on citizens of the U.K.' and to 're-establish the power of the U.K. to trade freely, particularly in the case of food, with any country in the world'. It was formed upon the recognition that neither the Conservative nor the Labour parties could now be relied upon to successfully take Britain out of the Common Market. It was now a foregone conclusion that the renegotiation would be successful. The only chance of 'freeing' Britain from 'Europe' was for the people to vote to leave the EEC in the promised referendum.[89]

Some in the cabinet were likewise furious at Wilson's stance during the Paris Summit. When he reported back to the cabinet on 12 December, Tony Benn told him, 'I don't accept this, I'm not committed to it, and we must all be free to discuss this'. That evening, Benn wrote in his diary that Wilson's was 'a most unsatisfactory, devious report'.[90] Peter Shore, the Trade Secretary, likewise said he was 'deeply shocked' by what had been agreed in Paris. This angered Wilson, who responded: 'I strongly resent the idea that I was an innocent abroad, that I went there and was just swept along. I've been negotiating since some members of this Cabinet have been at school'.[91] This reaction confirmed for Benn and other cabinet anti-Marketeers that Wilson had now made up his mind to remain within the EEC and there was little they could do at the cabinet level to prevent that. They therefore turned to extraparliamentary methods to press their point.

On 29 December, Benn sent to his constituents a New Year's Message that centred entirely on the upcoming referendum: 'In 1975 you will each have the responsibility of deciding by vote whether the United Kingdom should remain a member of the European Common Market, or whether we should withdraw completely and remain an independent self-governing nation'. He warned that this decision would 'almost certainly be irreversible', and that 'Britain's continuing membership of the Community would mean the end of Britain as a completely self-governing nation and the end of our democratically elected Parliament as the supreme law-making body in the United Kingdom'. Membership of the EEC, he wrote, 'subjects us all to laws and taxes which your Members of Parliament do not enact, such laws and taxes being enacted by Authorities you do not directly elect, and cannot dismiss'. It meant that 'Community laws and taxes cannot be changed or repealed by the British Parliament, but only by Community Authorities not directly elected by the British people'; it required 'British courts to uphold and enforce Community laws that have not been passed by Parliament'; it imposed 'duties and constraints upon British Governments not deriving from the British Parliament'; and, 'by permanently transferring sovereign legislative and financial powers to Community Authorities, who are not directly elected by the British people, [it] also permanently insulates those Authorities from direct control by the British electors who cannot dismiss them'.[92] The European Common Market was an affront to Britain's democratic past and a threat to its future.

For a cabinet minister to release such a statement in contradistinction to his own government's official policy was highly irregular, casting a shadow across the constitutional precept of collective cabinet responsibility. It caused an immediate stir. The BBC radio news reported that 'The Secretary of State of Industry has made an attack upon the Common Market and said the British people would be signing away their democratic rights if we remain in the Common Market',[93] and *The Times* headlined its front page with the statement, 'Mr Benn makes a sweeping attack on the EEC'.[94] His letter was also picked up with glee by the various anti-Marketeer organisations outside Parliament. On 1 January 1975, the Get Britain Out campaign issued a statement mirroring the language Benn had used in his letter. That evening, Benn noted in his diary that 'Get Britain Out is a negative title, but more important is getting the Labour Party to come out against the Market at a special conference'.[95] Given the attitudes of Wilson and Callaghan, it was unlikely to do so, although Benn could count on a large number of Labour members actively campaigning against continued membership of the EEC. This all but guaranteed that no matter which way the referendum went, it would not settle the issue of Britain's place within Europe.

The Conservative MP Neil Marten was likewise heartened by Benn's letter, releasing a public statement from the National Referendum Campaign on 7 January 1975 reiterating that he had 'never regarded the issue of the Common Market as a Party matter; it is essentially a subject which cuts right across Party allegiance'.[96] Privately, he warned his Campaign colleagues that they should 'expect the negotiations to be over by April and be ready for the referendum in June'.[97] Wilson was furious with Benn but decided to 'deal with him in his own way',[98] which in the end amounted to nothing more than 'a schoolboy telling-off'.[99] This emboldened others within the Labour Party to speak out publicly. On 19 January, Peter Shore – the Trade Secretary – gave a speech in Brighton titled 'Worse off in the Common Market', where he asked the gathered audience, 'Has there ever been a time when the British people felt less secure, less confident than they do today as members of the EEC?' He answered his own rhetorical question in no uncertain terms: 'The sense is not one of gain but of loss: of an abrupt severance from the more broadly based English speaking world without the creation of effective new ties with the nations of the EEC. And along with the uncertainty about the future is a new and dangerous weakening of our internal coherence and our common purpose as a people'. Britons no longer knew who they were. The Empire had provided a *raison d'être*. Following its loss, Europe could not provide an alternative. Shore closed, saying, 'The argument about the EEC is indeed about the Treaty of Accession: but it is also and inescapably about our political heritage and our National future'.[100]

As Marten had predicted, on 23 January, Wilson announced in the House of Commons that the negotiations would end by April and, given their likelihood of success, that the new terms would be put to the British people in a referendum that June. Yet Wilson did not stop there. He also revealed that, for the referendum campaign and vote, the doctrine of cabinet collective responsibility would be suspended, allowing cabinet members such as Benn, Shore and Barbara Castle to campaign against the policy of their own government. The *Daily Mail*, at that time an ardently pro-Europe newspaper, was unimpressed. In a front page editorial entitled 'Midsummer Madness', it opined that the Prime Minister had 'dragged the British constitution into a Wilsonian Wonderland over the proposed Common Market ballot. . . . From now on politics – and Britain's economic prospects – face a period of Parliamentary chaos and uncertainty. . . . The situation became curiouser as the Premier, in an incongruously lighthearted mood, explained the "unique" circumstances in which Cabinet Ministers will be freed of the doctrine of collective responsibility and MPs will be under pressure not to "pit their judgement" against the national vote'.[101]

With Wilson's announcement, the referendum became a certainty. Immediately afterwards, the United Ulster Unionists, the Scottish Nationalist Party, the National Council of Anti-Common Market Organisations and Conservatives Against the Treaty of Rome (CATOR) joined with the Anti-Common Market League, the Common Market Safeguards Campaign, the Get Britain Out Referendum Campaign and British Business for World Markets under the umbrella of Neil Marten's National Referendum Campaign.[102] Wilson's announcement also undermined what many Eurosceptics had regarded as a Labour commitment to withdraw from the EEC, leading to an impression of chicanery. The Labour Committee for Europe sought to dispel accusations of duplicity, arguing that the process of renegotiation had 'revealed a degree of flexibility in the way the Community actually operates which was not expected by many people on either side of the EEC debate'. It added that, given the deteriorating world economic situation, it was essential to find 'new ways of international co-operation', particularly 'when so many of our friends in the Commonwealth and the Socialist parties of Europe are suggesting we will do best for ourselves, and for them by staying in'.[103] There was some evidence to suggest that the pro-Europe message was getting through to the British public. A poll published in late February showed a 'remarkable ... surge of support for the Community' with 55.5 per cent of the public now wanting to remain in the Common Market and 44.5 per cent favouring withdraw.[104]

The cabinet met on 17 March 1975 to approve Wilson's renegotiation. The meeting continued throughout the day and into the eighteenth. When the roll was called, the final vote was 16 to 7 in favour of accepting the terms. Michael Foot, Peter Shore, Barbara Castle and Tony Benn all voted against. *The Sun* reported that there was 'a burst of cheers from jubilant pro-Marketeers on both sides of the Commons who felt the country was in Europe for good – bar the shouting'. It claimed that 'This decisive verdict represents a remarkable conversion inside the Cabinet, which a year ago contained a sizeable majority of Common Market opponents'.[105] *The Guardian* was more cautious, describing a 'slightly tattered European ensign over the Labour government'. It continued: 'Mr Wilson's commitment to Europe was matched last night by 118 signatures to a Labour anti-Market motion declaring that it was in the true interests of the British people to withdraw from the EEC'. This number included nineteen ministers, including five of the seven cabinet members who had rebelled, and signalled the 'start of an unprecedented national confrontation over Britain's continued membership of the Common Market'.[106]

For his part, Harold Wilson was elated. On the evening of the eighteenth, Donoughue told him that 'Ted Heath took the British Establishment into the Market. You will take in the British people'.[107] The cabinet vote was only the first battle of a long war ahead, however, and Wilson and Donoughue could be forgiven for not recognising quite how difficult the fight ahead would be and how the referendum – whilst providing the Conservative Party with an issue to rally around – would rip the Labour Party apart. As the Labour MP Ian Mikardo described to diners at the Annual Dinner of the Wythenshawe Constituency Labour Party on 21 March, the Prime Minister had 'two-thirds of the Cabinet; over half of the rest of his Government; about half the back-bench Labour MPs; a large majority of the Conservative MPs, all the Liberal MPs without exception; the Confederation of British Industry, who believe that what's good for General Electric is good for the nation; the City, who don't give a damn for what's good for the nation as long as they get some easy pickings out of it; all the Conservative newspapers and most of the other papers; [and] the vast funds of the European Movement'. This was, he said, a 'pretty motley, multi-coloured army for a Prime Minister'.

Opposing them would be 'the solid heart of the Labour Movement – the two-thirds of the Party's Executive; the bulk of the active members who keep the Party's working going in the constituencies; and an overwhelming majority of the General Council, the Trade Union Congress and the Trade Unions as a whole'. This would be joined by 'the taxpayers who don't like paying out their money to subsidise the sale of Common Market butter to Russia; by the shopkeepers and other traders who are plagued by VAT, which has been forced on us by Brussels; by the housewives out shopping who, for the first time ever, are paying taxes on the food they buy; and by the good democrats who want laws passed and taxes imposed only by representatives whom they elect and whom they have the power to change'. Mikardo had no doubt which army of the two he would rather belong to.[108] What he hadn't realised was how much of a civil war the conflict would turn out to be.

* * *

It was perhaps ironic that as the Conservative Party rallied to support continued British EEC membership in the referendum campaign, it did not do so under the leadership of Ted Heath, the man whose maiden speech in Parliament had urged Britain to join the European Coal and Steel Community, who had led the negotiations for British entry under Macmillan in 1961–63 and who, in 1972, had signed the Treaty that brought the United Kingdom into the Common Market. Instead, the party was led by Margaret Thatcher who, on 11 February 1975, was elected Conservative Party leader against all the odds, soundly defeating Heath in the first round of voting and securing a majority over Willie Whitelaw in the second.[109] The US Embassy in London sent a diplomatic cable to Washington DC shortly after her victory, providing essential background on the new leader: 'Margaret Thatcher has blazed into national prominence almost literally from out of nowhere.... She had never been a member of the inner circle of Tory power brokers, and no politician in modern times has come to the leadership of either major party with such a narrow range of prior experience'. The cable described her as 'an effective and forceful parliamentary performer. She has a quick, if not profound, mind, and works hard to master the most complicated brief. She fights her corner with skill and toughness'.

It added that 'In dealing with the media or with subordinates, she tends to be crisp and a trifle patronizing. With colleagues, she is honest and straight-forward, if not excessively considerate of their vanities. Civil servants at the Ministry of Education found her autocratic'.

The American diplomatic service did not hold out much hope for Thatcher's future, however, writing, 'Unfortunately for her prospects of becoming a national, as distinct from a party, leader, she has over the years acquired a distinctively upper middle class personal image. Her immaculate grooming, her imperious manner, her conventional and somewhat forced charm, and above all her plummy voice stamp her as the quintessential suburban matron, and frightfully English to boot. None of this goes down well with the working class of England (one-third of which used to vote Conservative), to say nothing of all classes in the Celtic fringes of this island'. It concluded: 'If she is ever to become Britain's first woman Prime Minister, she must use that time [in opposition] to humanize her public image and broaden the base of her party's appeal. The odds are against her, but after her stunning organizational *coup d'etat* this past month, few are prepared to say she can't do it'.[110] The EEC Referendum campaign would be Thatcher's first major challenge as party leader, and her first opportunity to narrow the gap of understanding between herself and the general public that the US Embassy perceived.

Many saw Thatcher's victory over Heath as highly significant for Conservative European policy. Although she had always supported the party's line of Europe – refusing to openly rebel as Powell and Marten did – she was decidedly cool on the topic and was believed by many to be sceptical of its merits. James Goldsmith (the Anglo–French billionaire financier who in the 1990s would become a prominent Eurosceptic) wrote personally to Heath after his defeat, saying it was a 'tragic day for you, for Britain, for Europe and for us all'.[111] The more 'European' ministers, such as Peter Walker and Geoffrey Rippon, refused to join Thatcher's shadow cabinet, and Heath was not invited. He later wrote that when Thatcher ascended to the leadership, 'The economy was faltering and Britain's future in the European Community was unpredictable. All of my hard work and achievements were threatened'. He did not trust Thatcher on either the economy or Europe and felt 'both disillusioned towards the party and apprehensive about the future of the country'.[112] Tony Benn noted that '[Francis] Maudling, who is anti-Europe, has been brought into the new Tory

Front Bench (Mrs Thatcher is anti-Europe); Peter Walker who was very pro-Europe has been dropped.... There is now a little group of experienced pro-European Ministers on the Back Benches and the Front Benches are Rag, Tag and Bobtail'.[113] He thought that 'we may be witnessing the break-up of the Tory Party'.[114]

The referendum presented a dilemma for Thatcher. Her instincts were hesitant about the EEC, and she retained a Germanophobia dating from the Second World War that was difficult to shake; put simply, she did not trust the Germans and did not like the French. However, given that the Labour Party was deeply divided on the issue, it was only good politics for the Conservatives to unite in favour of Europe, thus highlighting the divisions besetting the governing Labour party. As Tony Benn remarked, it was 'really rather sad to see the Tories waving their Order Papers and Labour people silent, except for the pro-Market group'.[115] Consequently, Thatcher's approach to the referendum was pragmatic but lacked the passion of Heath. During the leadership campaign, she had already been accused of being 'less enthusiastic' about Europe, a stance which at the time seemed contrary to basic Conservative principles. What enthusiasm she was able to conjure up was for economic affairs rather than political, and she did not 'see the European issue as a touchstone for everything else'. Heath had ordered all government departments to 'think like Europeans'. The new Conservative leader would certainly not do that. For Thatcher, it did not seem that the 'high-flown rhetoric about Britain's European destiny, let alone European identity, was really to the point'.[116] Consequently, Heath remained the public face of the Conservative defence of the EEC, with Willie Whitelaw acting as the Conservative Vice-President of Britain in Europe, the cross-party 'Yes' campaign chaired by Sir Con O'Neill.[117]

It was to be a hard-fought battle. The dissenting cabinet members on the Labour frontbench kicked off their campaign with a joint statement, saying, '25 years ago Britain dismantled a vast empire in the belief that no country has the right – or the wisdom – to govern another. Now we demand for ourselves what we freely conceded to the 32 members of the Commonwealth: the right of self-government'.[118] The Conservative MP Neil Marten proclaimed that 'a lot of today's crisis is due to the Common Market' and warned that it was '9 countries trying to do what only one country can do. So, if it is ever to succeed, it must integrate into one country. This is the real intention behind the Common Market.... Integration would mean the end of Britain as an independent country – not all at once, but ultimately. For that is the true aim of the pro-Marketeers'.[119] Ironically, the Commonwealth itself now fully supported Britain's membership, the heads of government releasing a statement in May that placed on record their 'firm opinion that Commonwealth interests were in no repeat no way prejudiced by such membership'. British membership, they argued, was in fact 'of value in encouraging the Community to be more outward looking towards the rest of the world', which could only help the Commonwealth.[120]

Throughout it all, Thatcher was less conspicuous on the campaign trail than Heath or Whitelaw for the Conservative Party, or Wilson or Callaghan for Labour. On the eve of the poll, she did contribute an article to the *Daily Telegraph* arguing in its favour, as was only right and proper for a party leader advocating a particular position in a referendum, but otherwise she remained in the shadows of the campaign.[121] This disappointed her predecessor, who scathingly described her 'modicum of campaigning up and down the country'.[122] The *Sun* also noticed Thatcher's position playing second fiddle to Heath, which it found unbecoming for a Conservative Leader. In one article, it wrote, 'Missing: one Tory Leader. Answers to the name of Margaret Thatcher. Mysteriously disappeared from the Market Referendum Campaign eleven days ago. Has not been seen since. Will finder kindly wake her up and remind her she is failing the nation in her duty as Leader of the Opposition?'[123]

Whilst such commentary stung Thatcher on a personal level, she understood its utility. She had argued in favour of continued British membership of the Common Market but was seen to be less enthusiastic about European affairs than her predecessor. She therefore survived the campaign without undercutting in any way the pro-Europeans (who were still by far the majority of the party), yet without isolating the Conservative anti-Marketeers. As she wrote in her memoirs, 'I emerged from the campaign as a unifying figure for the Party. The anti-Market Tory MPs felt no bitterness towards me'.[124] The same could not be said of Heath, who has since gone down in the annuls of Conservative Eurosceptic history as the man who betrayed Britain's independence by bringing it into Europe, thus forever diminishing its national greatness.

On the eve of the poll, the dissenting Labour ministers released a statement telling the British people, 'Tomorrow's vote is your chance to get back for yourself and your children three rights. First, your right to obey those laws you yourself have voted for and pay only those taxes agreed by your elected MPs who you yourselves can dismiss. Second, your right to buy in the shops untaxed food from the cheapest markets in the world. Third, your right to a job, in Britain, which can only come from the re-equipment of British industry and from trade with the nations of the world where Britain's goods are needed'.[125] Michael Wolff offered a compelling retort in the *Evening Standard*: 'We *are* in Europe, and have been ever since time began. A mere 5000 years ago or so we were actually physically joined to the continent. A mere 500 years ago or so vast tracts of that continent were under the sovereignty of the King of England. The Anglo-Saxons came from Europe. The Celts came from Europe. Our bishops and our Kings came from Europe. We're here because we're here'. The question, he said, was 'not whether we wish to remain a European nation, but whether we want to act as one – for our own sakes, and for the sake of the rest of Europe'. For Wolff, the answer was clear: 'I do remember Dunkirk – this was our finest hour and all that. But I also remember being hauled out of bed on a December night to hear of Japan's attack on Pearl Harbour and America's long-waited entry into the War. That was *my* finest hour – and that of a lot of others in these islands who breathed a sigh of relief that we were no longer going it alone'. He closed, writing, '[P]eace and stability may not mean much to the generations whose lives have never been touched by war. But they remain good reasons for sticking close to the friends one has. As it is, the winds of economic crisis are blowing chills across the land. It doesn't seem a good moment to leave what shelter we have with our friendship in Europe. Baby, it's cold outside'.[126]

When the final votes were counted on 6 June 1975, the British public voted by 67.2 per cent to 32.8 per cent to remain within the European Community, demonstrating a higher level of support for European integration than at any time since the Second World War.[127] Bernard Donoughue, who listened to the results on his transistor radio whilst sipping Champagne, described it as a 'glorious sunny day – European weather'.[128] Yet this victory had only been achieved with enormous expense and almost constant campaigning. Such pro-Europe sentiment would be much harder to sustain. The new leader of the Conservative Party was still far from convinced of the wisdom of European Union, and Harold Wilson was ambivalent at best.

Writing in his diary on the evening the results were announced, Donoughue noted: 'in my view, H[arold] W[ilson] is still mildly anti-European, in the sense that *personally* he doesn't like Europeans, their style of life or politics. But he decided – probably after October [1974], possibly from long ago – that a "yes" position was in fact best for Britain, most likely to hold the party together (because the pro-marketeers were more passionately pro than the antis were anti and more likely to split the party) and more likely to be a winning position. So he suppressed his prejudices and took a pro-position'.[129] He was less than happy about it, however.

The same could be said of the British public at large. In his diary entry on 6 June, Tony Benn related a conversation he had with Enoch Powell at the National Referendum Campaign Party, a conversation that is worth quoting at length:

> 'Well, Enoch,' I said, 'you certainly got your case across clearly and concisely, and the great merit of it all was that it was good political education.'
> 'The great political education is only just beginning,' he replied.
> 'What do you mean?'
> He told me that he'd just come from the ITN studios in a taxi, and the taxi driver had asked him, 'Are you Mr Powell?'
> 'Yes,' said Enoch.
> 'What attitude are you adopting towards the Common Market, Mr Powell?'
> Enoch was much humbled by this and said to the taxi driver, 'Do you remember I used to be a member of the Conservative Party?'
> 'Yes,' the taxi driver said.
> 'Do you remember why I left the Conservative Party?'
> The taxi driver said no, he had never heard the reason. So Enoch asked how he had voted in the Referendum.
> 'I voted No.'
> 'Oh, did you.' said Enoch. 'Why?'
> 'Well, I heard there was some talk of a European Parliament and I was not prepared to see the British Parliament put under a European Parliament.'
> The point Enoch was making to me was that the campaign had not gone on long enough for people to understand exactly what everybody was saying, but they had picked up the gist of it.[130]

Ted Heath, Harold Wilson and, to a certain extent, even Margaret Thatcher believed that when the British people voted to stay in the EEC on 5 June 1975, the issue had been put to bed once and for all. Yet for the anti-Marketeers, the battles had only just begun. And in their minds, it would be a long-time before the war was over.

16 HALF-HEARTED EUROPEANS

The world that faced Margaret Thatcher on 4 May 1979 was very different from the one she had surveyed when becoming Conservative Party leader four years earlier. As Britain's newly elected Prime Minister, one of the first briefings she received from the Cabinet Secretary that afternoon concerned 'European Issues', and it laid out the great 'challenge and opportunity' in Europe that faced the new government in May 1979. The challenge lay in the 'number of difficult negotiating objectives' left unresolved from the previous Labour government, despite the renegotiation of 1975. The opportunity came from the 'greater commitment to Europe expressed publicly' by the Tory Party, which would 'ensure a more sympathetic hearing' from the other Europeans.[1]

Whilst welcoming the opportunities, Thatcher relished above all else the challenge. When the briefing indicated that 'in the last two or three years, the mood of the Community has changed and there is less emphasis on supranationalism, and a greater readiness to accommodate different national requirements', she scribbled 'good' in the margins. When advised that 'The last thing we should do is to give the impression that the United Kingdom is now a soft touch, or to arouse exaggerated expectations', she wrote 'agreed'.[2] For her first meeting with a foreign head of government, Thatcher hosted Helmut Schmidt, the West German Chancellor. It fell only days after her ascent to the Prime Ministership and had been arranged by the previous Labour government prior to the General Election. Speaking at the dinner in his honour on 10 May 1979, she warned him, 'It has been suggested by some people in this country that I and my Government will be a "soft touch" in the Community. In case such a rumour may have reached your ears, Mr Chancellor, ... it is only fair that I should advise you frankly to dismiss it. ... I intend to be very discriminating in judging what are British interests and I shall be resolute in defending them'.[3] Britain once again had a Conservative government, but it was not the pro-European government of Ted Heath.

In the immediate aftermath of the 1975 referendum, the anti-Marketeers, although bruised and beaten, were undiminished in their conviction that Britain should leave the European Economic Community (EEC). Sir Cyril Black wrote to Neil Marten on 13 June, reassuring him that 'A Referendum in 1938 on the policy of appeasement of Hitler and Mussolini would, I think, undoubtedly have produced a majority of two to one in favour, but the men of Munich are now dishonoured, and Winston Churchill – the outstanding leader of the minority at that time – has been abundantly vindicated'. He predicted that in twenty years (or by 1995), 'the men of Brussels will be regarded as the betrayers of our highest national interests, and those of us who opposed will be seen to have been right'.[4] Marten agreed, but worried how the legacy of the referendum might affect the Conservative Party, as it was now in a 'somewhat difficult position because it was largely responsible for the "yes" vote. Between now and the General Election, I reckon that [the] Common Market is going to be extremely unpopular in this country'.[5] The Tories had defined themselves as the 'European Party'. If the British public soured on the EEC, it would fall to the new leader, Margaret Thatcher, to steady the ship in the face of rough seas.

In their predictions of a shift in public opinion, both Black and Marten were correct, and, over the subsequent years, there was a steady decline in support for British membership of the Common Market. Although more than 67 per cent of the public had voted to stay in the EEC in the June 1975 referendum, by January 1976, the number of respondents to a Gallup poll who felt that membership was a 'good thing' had dropped to 50 per cent, falling still further to just 35 per cent by January 1977. In contrast, the percentage of those who felt it to be a 'bad thing' rose from 24 per cent in January 1976 to 41 per cent by January 1977.[6] Throughout these months, Thatcher had to balance supporting the overwhelming Conservative consensus in favour of a

British Europe whilst introducing a level of caution not seen before by Conservative leaders.

In this task, she faced a new Prime Minister, for on 15 March 1976 Harold Wilson offered his resignation as Prime Minister, having said for some time that he would go before his sixtieth birthday.[7] There was never much doubt that Jim Callaghan, his Foreign Secretary, would succeed him, although Michael Foot (the standard-bearer for the Left of the Party), Roy Jenkins (right-leaning and pro-European), Tony Benn, Tony Crossland and Denis Healy also challenged for the leadership. Benn, Crossland and Jenkins withdrew after the first round, as did Healy after the second. In the third and final ballot, Callaghan defeated Foot by 176 votes to 137, and, on 5 April, he entered 10 Downing Street as Prime Minister.[8] Although Callaghan represented Labour's first change of leader in more than twelve years, his was far from a fresh government. Thatcher wrote in her memoirs that 'Within weeks of Jim Callaghan's becoming Prime Minister, relations between Government and Opposition chilled to freezing point as a result of Labour chicanery on a Bill nationalizing the aircraft and shipbuilding industries'.[9] Over the next three years, there would be no thaw. The one silver lining for Thatcher was that Callaghan's reputation as a more outspoken anti-Marketeer than Wilson allowed her both to criticise his 'U-Turn' on EEC membership (standing firmly on ground that was more pro-European than the Labour party) whilst avoiding Heath's open embrace of Europe.[10]

In a speech in Rome in June 1977, for example, Thatcher reaffirmed that the Conservative Party was 'the European party in the British Parliament and among the British people; and we want to co-operate wholeheartedly with our partners in this joint venture'. However, in a manner that would have been unthinkable for Heath, she also said that it was only 'fair to point out that the C[ommon] A[gricultural] P[olicy] has been administered in a way which for us has produced some damaging results' and promised that CAP reform should be a 'major objective of any British government'. She then laid down a series of principles for the European Community that were by no means shared by the governments of continental Europe: 'economic freedom, because the evidence shows that a free economic system provides the individual and the community with the best hope of that material prosperity which is the legitimate aim of our peoples'; 'a commitment to the family as the natural and fundamental unit of society'; and 'a commitment to the widest possible diffusion of ownership. Every man a capitalist should be our aim'. Finally, she argued that Europe's present integration was a continuation of its imperial past, saying, 'The story of our Continent is of European man, the explorer and the trader, the missionary and the settler, carrying the fruits of his scientific discoveries, of his artistic and cultural achievements, above all of his political values, across every sea and continent. No European need apologise for the accomplishments of our peoples in the wider world'.[11] In contrast to Heath and Macmillan before him, both of whom had perceived Britain's EEC entry as a direct consequence of the *loss* of the British Empire, Thatcher portrayed it as the next stage of British expansion. Hers was a fundamentally different understanding of Britain's place within Europe. It was bound to cause some friction in the Community once she put it to the test.

The first such test came whilst she was still in opposition. In the summer of 1978, West German Chancellor Schmidt and French President Valéry Giscard d'Estaing came together to create a European Monetary System (EMS), which would take effect on 1 January 1979, and which might lead eventually to a European common currency.[12] Neither man was interested in working with the British Labour government as both were suspicious of Callaghan (Schmidt believed that Europe had 'never meant anything to him and that he remained mired in Britain's historical [Commonwealth] role' and Giscard said he was 'too English' with a 'non-continental attitude').[13] They formally proposed the EMS at the conference of European heads of government at Bremen in July, and, although Callaghan initially showed willingness to consider the idea, he received significant push-back from his cabinet colleagues, the Trade Unions and the Labour Party National Executive Committee (NEC).[14] This placed Thatcher in a difficult position. On the one hand, if she came out in support of EMS, she would shore up her credentials as Britain's European leader and would place intolerable pressure on Callaghan. As she later wrote, 'Her Majesty's Opposition under my leadership would have been less than human not to take advantage of this as evidence that sterling was too weak to join as a result of Labour's mismanagement of the economy'.[15] On the other hand, however, Thatcher's instincts told her that the Labour Party at large was right to be suspicious of the EMS and that it was Callaghan's judgment in considering British membership that was flawed. Had she been Prime Minister in 1978, she would not have taken Britain into the EMS.

Others in the shadow cabinet sensed Thatcher's predicament. Shortly after the Bremen conference, John Nott – the Shadow Trade Secretary – warned Thatcher to be 'exceptionally cautious and leave your subordinates to argue this for you – both ways'. The EMS had 'more to offer the Labour Party than the Conservative' as it would 'place yet another massive constraint on the free market.... It is a Socialist solution, and we should move in the opposite direction'. In opposing the scheme, the Labour Party membership was acting against its own economic self-interest, blinded by its strong anti-European ethos. There was a danger the Conservative Party would do the same, to the same effect: 'You will hear strong arguments the other way, not least from those who write your speeches, but they will all come from "Europeans" who tend to abandon economic common sense in this field for their "sense of vision" – the vision of a United Europe'. The best-case scenario was that Callaghan would give in to the NEC and Trade Unions, thus giving the Conservative Opposition the opportunity to accuse his government of economic mismanagement without themselves committing to join the EMS if elected. The further Thatcher could remove herself from the debate, the better.[16]

Adam Ridley of the Conservative Research Department offered similar advice, telling Thatcher that 'we must re-affirm our commitment to some kind of European ideal without falling into the dangerous position that Mr. Callaghan threatens [of actually joining the EMS]'. The Conservative vision, he argued, should be 'a relaxed and pragmatic approach, one which builds on those areas where collaboration is productive, politically realistic and compatible with a political framework in the community which does not involve total and immediate pooling of sovereignty on a scale which none of the populations of the Community's countries will tolerate'.[17] The trick would be to continue to paint the Conservative Party as the pro-European party whilst simultaneously opposing a degree of European integration that the Labour Prime Minister – if not his party – now seemed to be embracing. If at all possible, the Opposition should goad the government into adopting a more extreme anti-Market position so that the Conservatives could move away from Heath's unquestioning embrace of Europeanism without being seen to do so.

Geoffrey Howe disagreed, writing to Thatcher that 'We should pronounce in favour of the EMS – not as the ideal way ahead, but nevertheless to be welcomed for providing greater currency stability and encouraging convergence of economic policies'. The political case, he said, 'is a strong one: the alternative means surrendering the direction of the EEC and its policies to the Franco–German high table'. The Conservative Party ought to 'admit, and possibly stress, that there are dangers in entering EMS as we are, and argue that we should be best placed to enter it once we are committed (as a Conservative Government would be) to tighter monetary and expenditure discipline, and have liberalised exchange controls'. Above all, it should be 'highly critical of Callaghan's mishandling of the issue up to now' as 'Callaghan/Labour are largely responsible for the unpalatable nature of the choice now facing us'. Even with Callaghan's support, it was unlikely that the Labour government would actually join the EMS, and Conservative support for doing so would thus 'maintain our Party's stock of European goodwill, if only to make palatable in Europe the qualifications and transitional provisions that will eventually be necessary if a Conservative Government is ever to be able to get us back to the European high table, probably within something like the present EMS'. By supporting British entry now, when it would almost certainly be prevented by the Labour government, the Conservative Party would gain some political capital to later drive a harder bargain on eventual EMS entry.[18]

Thatcher followed Howe's advice, 'adopt[ing] a positive general approach to the EMS while avoiding making any specific commitments'. This both capitalised on the disunity within the Labour Party and generated goodwill on the European continent, all without committing a future Tory government to the EMS.[19] And Howe's gamble that Callaghan would back down in the face of widespread Labour opposition paid off. Between 2 November and 14 December, the cabinet held no fewer than six meetings on joining the EMS and decided in the final analysis that 'it was too premature to arrive at a view'.[20] A decision was never taken one way or another. Consequently, the EMS was formed with eight of the nine EEC countries, the United Kingdom the only one to remain outside. Thatcher said that it was a 'sad day for Europe' and that the 'failure to join was a sign of Britain's economic weakness and of Labour's divisions'.[21] Despite this, the Labour decision not to join the EMS was highly beneficial for the Tory leadership. Callaghan had played into Thatcher's hands, allowing her to avoid a firm commitment to the EMS whilst still portraying the Labour leader as the true Eurosceptic.[22]

There was a larger problem facing the Callaghan government than simply its internal splits over Europe, however. In July 1978, the government published a White Paper indicating its intention to limit industrial pay settlements to just 5 per cent. The membership of the party rejected the White Paper at its annual conference in September, indicating that in a standoff between the government and the unions, the party would support the unions. This encouraged the workers at Ford to embark upon a nine-week strike. The government relented to their demands and provided a pay rise of 17 per cent, provoking a call from the Transport and General Workers Union (TGWU) for its road haulage drivers to receive a raise of 22 per cent. When the government countered with an offer of 13 per cent in January 1979, its members came out on strike, marking the beginning of what became known as the 'Winter of Discontent'. In a show of solidarity, on 22 January, 1.5 million public service workers went on strike, followed over the subsequent months by a series of rolling strikes that led to school children not being fed, rubbish lining the streets in great piles higher than a person, and, in Lancashire, the dead going unburied.[23] Tony Benn described the press as 'full of crises, anarchy, chaos, disruption – bitterly hostile to the trade union movement'. He had 'never seen anything like it'.[24] Such industrial unrest could not have come at a worse time for the Labour Party as it had no choice but to request from the Queen a dissolution of Parliament and a General Election by October that year. As it turned out, Callaghan's hand was forced long before then when, on 28 March, his government faced and lost a vote of no confidence. Parliament was dissolved immediately and the polling day set for 3 May.[25]

In the midst of this economic chaos, there were signs that the Conservative Party's approach towards Europe was changing. Speaking on 14 March, John Nott announced that whilst personally committed to the 'free trade principles of the Treaty of Rome', the EEC was 'fast becoming the despair of its friends' as '[e]ach meeting of the Council of Ministers and too many acts of the Commission take us ever further from the basic principles which guided the authors of the Treaty'. The British contribution to the Community budget was 'self-evidently far too large' and the Common Agricultural Policy was 'absurd'. The members of the European

Commission were 'drawing huge salaries', and its bureaucracy, which 'may be smaller than the Scottish Office', nevertheless 'intrudes increasingly in areas of personal discretion which are not the concern of the Euro-bureaucrats in Brussels'. A Conservative government, he promised, would fight 'for the liberal policies of the Rome Treaty in place of the creeping dirigisme, the electoral cynicism and the wholly unwarranted destruction of British national interests which is being attempted at this time'.[26] These were not the words of Edward Heath's Tory Party, but they *were* representative of the view of many members of Thatcher's shadow cabinet and an increasingly large proportion of the Conservative Party at large.

The General Election, when it came, paid little attention to Europe. In contrast to 1974, when Heath had wanted the debate to be about industrial strife only to have it overshadowed by the question of EEC membership, in 1979 the 'Winter of Discontent' drowned out everything else. For Thatcher, it began with a personal tragedy when on 30 March the Irish National Liberation Army (INLA) – an offshoot of the IRA – murdered the Conservative MP Airey Neave with a bomb under his car as he left the House of Commons. Neave, a close friend of Thatcher's who had organised her leadership campaign in 1975, was in 1979 Shadow Secretary of Northern Ireland and was targeted by INLA for his belief in moderate integration between Catholics and Protestants in Northern Ireland rather than immediate power-sharing (as was favoured by Heath). A British war hero (he was the first officer to escape from the legendary Colditz Castle in January 1942), his death focussed public attention on the more personal side of Thatcher whilst simultaneously securing her reputation as someone who 'was serious, and stood for something important'.[27]

In the final Conservative election broadcast, Thatcher described Britain as a 'great country gone wrong'.[28] She did not mention the EEC, yet in the mind of the public it was Britain 'joining Europe' that had led to many of the economic ills of the 1970s, from inflation and rising food prices to unemployment, industrial unrest and a sense of detachment from Britain's past. From this perspective, there was little to separate the collapse of the British Empire, UK entry into the EEC and the rise of militant Trade Unionism. They were all symptomatic of a general British malaise, and if Britain was once again to be restored to the greatness of its imperial past, the issues of Europe and industrial unrest would both have to be tackled. It was this public 'mood' that Margaret

Thatcher sensed better than most in the election campaign of May 1979 and what she meant by a 'great country gone wrong'.

When the votes were counted on the morning of 4 May, the Conservatives had secured 339 seats to Labour's 269. The swing from Labour to the Tories was 5.2 per cent, the biggest since 1945, with a 7 per cent gap between the two major parties that had not been seen since the Attlee years.[29] Speaking before the polished black door of 10 Downing Street after being asked by the Queen to form her next government, Thatcher read the prayer of St Francis of Assisi, a choice that was later to be much criticised given her style of government. In her memoirs, Thatcher justified its use: 'St Francis prayed for more than peace; the prayer goes on: "Where there is error, may we bring truth. Where there is doubt, may we bring faith. And where there is despair, may we bring hope". The forces of error, doubt and despair were so firmly entrenched in British society, as the "winter of discontent" had just powerfully illustrated, that overcoming them would not be possible without some measure of discord'.[30] Thatcher was to be a new sort of British Prime Minister, one who placed conviction and ideology over consensus. It was a message that was soon to sink in with the Labour opposition, civil servants in Whitehall and the British public at large. It was also one that did not go unnoticed on the European continent.

* * *

On 7 June 1979, only a month after the General Election, Britain held its first direct elections for the European Parliament. Thatcher had already made clear that her government would not be one of unquestioning Europeans, telling the Foreign Secretary Lord Carrington and the Lord Privy Seal Ian Gilmour on 8 May that the British contribution to the EEC budget was 'unfair, unreasonable and unjust' and that it was 'essential to make progress towards changing it before the European Elections'.[31] Thatcher also used the European election campaign to lay out her goals for Europe over the coming years. On the one hand, she defined Britons as true Europeans sharing a European heritage. On the other, however, she dismissed any attempts to create a single European identity: 'We believe in a free Europe but not a standardised Europe. The intellectual and material richness of Europe lies in its variety. Diminish that variety within the Member States, and you impoverish the whole Community'.[32] In her memoirs, she gave just one paragraph to the elections, stating simply that there had always been 'a contrary tendency in the Community – interventionist, protectionist, and ultimately federalist', a tendency that was 'never far beneath the surface of events' and of which she was 'always aware'.[33]

In Thatcher's mind, the Labour Party epitomised that contrary trend, issuing a statement at the beginning of the campaign that was in marked contrast to the Conservative vision for Europe. The socialist parties of Europe, it said, sought 'more ambitious regional and social policies to reduce inequalities between regions', an 'effective common programme for energy saving' and greater 'industrial democracy'. Above all, the Labour Party would 'co-operate with the other Social Democratic Parties of Europe to help achieve the goals of full employment, stable prices and greater equality throughout the E.E.C'.[34] Such policies were anathema to Thatcher. On 2 June, she called for reform of the Community Budget, where 'the United Kingdom pays more than any other Member Country . . . even though we are the seventh poorest of nine', and suggested the Common Agricultural Policy was 'collapsing under the weight of its own surpluses'. She declared that in Europe, as in Britain, the Conservative Party was 'the Party of conviction'. It would 'insist that the institutions of the European Community are managed so that they increase liberty of the individual throughout our continent. These institutions must not be permitted to dwindle into bureaucracy. Whenever they fail to enlarge freedom the institutions should be criticised and the balance restored'. Finally, she reminded her audience that a directly elected European Parliament would be the 'expression of the [European] voice'. Conservative Members of the European Parliament [MEPs] would 'ensure that the Voice of Freedom speaks with firmness and courage and imagination in a troubled world'.[35]

On the eve of the election, the *Yorkshire Post* published the 'final appeals' of each of the party leaders. Thatcher described the European Community as a 'phoenix which emerged from the ashes of two world wars'. The Conservative Party, she said, would fight to ensure that there was 'a full and competitive free market within the whole of Western Europe in the knowledge that a vigorous free economy is the only sound base for political liberty'. Callaghan, in contrast, accused the Tories of going 'overboard in unquestioning support of the Community's policies in recent years'. The Labour Party was 'committed to protecting the consumer and guaranteeing the right to work, particularly for young people'. It would liaise with other European socialists to 'ensure more financial aid to regions in need and for social policies to reduce unemployment'. Both the Conservative and Labour leaders agreed that this election – the first in which MEPs would be directly chosen by the people – was one for the heart and soul of the future EEC.[36]

Nevertheless, the European elections failed to capture the imagination of the British people. Throughout the rest of the European Community, two-thirds of its eligible 200 million electors cast a vote. In the United Kingdom, only 32 per cent went to the polls, the lowest of any EEC country. Those who did vote cast their ballots overwhelmingly for the Conservative Party, which gained sixty seats against Labour's seventeen, but the level of participation was disappointing. Heath, watching from the parliamentary backbenches, was 'dismayed at the lack of effort in campaigning by all three main political parties'.[37] His angst only increased as, despite the Conservative victory, Thatcher became ever more cautious about the European project. On 8 June, the day after the election, Carrington sent her a memorandum on the Community Budget, writing, 'The European Council recognise[s] that at present the financial consequences of the Community budget create difficulties for certain member states in achieving the Community's aim of convergence in economic performance'. She furiously scribbled at the bottom of his memo, 'This is jabberwocky to me. What is it supposed to mean'.[38] Her words succinctly summed up her attitude towards the EEC, much of which she regarded as jabberwocky.

Following the June elections, Europe loosened its grip on the imaginations of both the public and the political class in Britain, and it was not until October 1979 that Thatcher again spoke on the topic. Delivering the Winston Churchill Memorial Lecture in Luxembourg, she chose as her topic the 'obligations of liberty'. Liberty, she said, rested upon the three pillars of representative democracy, economic freedom and rule of law. It was these principles that had to be at the heart of the EEC. There was a danger in the way the Community had evolved, however, as 'some of the Community's activities ha[d] given rise to resentment and irritation. People are anxious that bureaucracy in Brussels, added to bureaucracy at home, is acting against their true interests'. In the Community, she reminded her audience, 'as at home, less government is good government'. She concluded that the Community, 'like an oak tree, will continue to develop imperceptibly but inexorably.... As it develops the Community must continue to reflect the interests and the aspirations of the democratic nation states which make it up. In its sense of purpose lies its strength; in its variety its richness. Above all the Community must remain true to the principles and to the obligations of liberty'.[39]

This was all well and good, but in the United Kingdom Thatcher was struggling to convince the Opposition, her electorate and even some of her cabinet colleagues of the wisdom of her vision of liberty, which sought to overturn the post-war Keynesian economic consensus and introduce what at the time was considered a radical doctrine of free market *laissez-faire*. Within her cabinet and throughout the Conservative backbenches, those who were sceptical of her policies became derided as 'wets' whilst those who subscribed to them were either 'dries' or, in the words of the Prime Minister, 'on my side' or 'one of us'.[40] This new economic orthodoxy, based on the teachings of the American academic Milton Friedman, held that 'the money supply was the central determinant of inflation and that governments could therefore by controlling it reduce the rate of inflation'.[41] In contrast to Keynesianism, Thatcherite economics preferenced reducing inflation over keeping unemployment at low levels; in this analysis, full employment was not the goal, nor should it be.[42] As the historian Eric Evans has written, 'the thinking behind it was brutally simple: restrict the supply of money and reduce government borrowing needs and you squeeze inflation out of the system'.[43]

Whilst those in economic affairs – such as the Chancellor of the Exchequer Sir Geoffrey Howe, the Secretary of State for Industry Sir Keith Joseph, John Nott at the Ministry of Trade, the Secretary of State for Energy David Howell and the Chief Secretary to the Treasury John Biffen – were all monetarists who favoured Thatcher's approach, the party at large had not yet made a full conversion to Thatcherism, as her policies collectively soon became known. Consequently, her political bench was not yet deep enough to fully stack the cabinet team with 'dries'. Several 'wets' who were uncomfortable with her economic theories received high-profile positions, including the Foreign Secretary Lord Carrington, Francis Pym at the Ministry of Defence, Peter Walker in Agriculture, the Secretary of State for Employment James Prior, Michael Heseltine at Environment and the Lord Privy Seal Ian Gilmour, all of whom were closer to Heath than Thatcher and, indeed, had mostly supported the former in the 1975 leadership ballot.[44] When Howe published his first budget on 12 June 1979, less than a week after the European elections, it was 'more radical than had been expected by many financial experts'.[45] He reduced the top rate of income tax from 83 per cent to 60 per cent and the standard rate from 33 per cent to 30 per cent. To afford this, he doubled Valued Added Tax (VAT) from 8 per cent to 15 per cent. The burden of taxation therefore shifted from what Britons earned to what they spent, in theory reducing the penalty for promotion to higher salaries and providing an incentive to save and invest rather than spend. Howe also raised the interest rate to 14 per cent, increasing it to an unprecedented 17 per cent by the end of the year.[46] Ministers such as Prior, Walker and Gilmour – who only learnt of the details of the budget on the day it was delivered – were 'horrified',[47] and the *Guardian* newspaper described it as 'the richest political and economic gamble in post-war parliamentary history'.[48]

The initial evidence suggested that the gamble failed to pay off. In 1980, manufacturing production fell by 16 per cent, the Retail Price Index (RPI) rose by 20 per cent between May 1979 and May 1980 and unemployment, which had begun to fall in the closing months of the Callaghan administration, rose from 1,288,000 at the General Election to 2 million by November 1980.[49] By the end of 1981, it had reached 2.8 million, having risen faster in a twelve-month period than in any single year since 1930.[50] In May of 1980, inflation reached a post-war peak of 21.9 per cent, a seemingly damning figure given that Thatcher's government had loudly proclaimed that the primary purpose of the 1979 budget was to *reduce* inflation. Now the British people had both inflation *and* unemployment.[51] Furthermore, because of the interest rate rise, in 1980, the value of the pound sterling skyrocketed, having an adverse effect on British exports. Consequently, company profits fell by 20 per cent and manufacturing output by 15 per cent in 1980, only increasing inflationary pressure and unemployment.[52] In the fiscal year 1980–81, Britain's Gross National Product (GNP) contracted by 3.2 per cent, officially dragging the country into the grips of recession.[53]

In February 1980, Angus Maude the Paymaster General asked all Whitehall departments for 'good news' that could be 'used as a quarry for Ministers' speeches', explaining that he was 'concerned that the prevalent gloomy news in the media will affect support for the Government's policies and hopes'.[54] At the October 1980 Conservative Party Conference in Brighton, several cabinet 'wets' offered veiled criticism of her policies, and the media began to speculate that the government might be on the cusp of softening its economic policies.

In response, Thatcher defended the government's record, admitting that unemployment was a 'human tragedy' but claiming that it could not be properly tackled until 'the fight against inflation had been won'. She then uttered her famous words, 'To those waiting with bated breath for that favourite media catchphrase, the "U" turn, I have only one thing to say, "U-Turn if you want to. The lady's not for turning"'.[55] She won a six-minute standing ovation. Five days later, in the face of extreme hostility from left-wing critics, the Labour leader Jim Callaghan resigned to be replaced by Michael Foot, the most radical of the Labour leadership candidates and the most fervently anti-European.[56]

Foot's election isolated the more moderate social democratic wing of his party and provoked even greater disunity, leaving little choice for the British electorate than the current Tory government, despite its many problems. Given the increasing economic hardship many were facing and the heightened levels of dissatisfaction after a decade of apparently failing governance, in April 1981 riots erupted in Brixton in south London, followed by riots on the night of 3 July in Southall (London) and Toxteth (Liverpool). For the first time in British history (excluding Northern Ireland), the police fired CS gas cartridges at rioters, providing sensational television viewing. 'Copy-cat' riots broke out on the Moss Side in Manchester on 8–9 July and, on the weekend of 10–12 July, in Brixton, Birmingham, Blackburn, Derby, Leeds, Leicester and Wolverhampton. Toxteth was again set alight on 28 July, and the rioting only fizzled out in the face of the wedding of Charles the Prince of Wales to Lady Diana Spencer.[57] In his diaries, Tony Benn described it as 'a great contrast – between riches and rioting, privilege and poverty. It's terrifying'.[58] He added, 'The image presented to the rest of the world was of a Britain about as socially advanced as France before the French Revolution! We are slipping back to eighteenth-century politics'.[59]

Yet even the drama of a Royal Wedding could not distract the public for long from the very real problems that were assaulting them throughout the country. The unease that was beginning to spread throughout British society made many within the Conservative Party decidedly queasy. To stamp out dissent, on 14 September 1981, Thatcher reshuffled her cabinet, removing the 'wets' Christopher Soames, Mark Carlisle, Norman St John-Stevas and Ian Gilmour and exiling James Prior from Employment to Northern Ireland. In their place, Nigel Lawson was moved to the Department of Energy,

Norman Tebbit to Employment and Nicholas Ridley to the Financial Secretaryship of the Treasury. Upon his sacking, Gilmour issued a 'furious resignation statement', accusing Thatcher of 'steering the ship of state straight on to the rocks'.[60] He received little sympathy from the press. As Thatcher's official biographer Charles Moore has written, 'the Wets looked much less dignified sacked than they would have looked if they had resigned on principle; and there was something in their sense of affront at being sacked by a woman which was haughty'. Moore continues: 'Mrs Thatcher still did not have a majority of true believers in her Cabinet, but by the addition of Tebbit, Parkinson and Lawson she had installed a new generation of active, clever, enthusiastic supporters. Equally important, she had proved that she could sack the grandees without the heavens falling'.[61]

Although now more in control of her cabinet, Thatcher still had to confront a hostile electorate, which was beginning to wonder if it had made the right decision in May 1979. In the face of this increasing economic dissatisfaction, the one area that Thatcher seemed to be walking in step with the British public was on Europe, where she perceived an opportunity to reassert her credentials as a leader who would stand up for Britain. On 2 June 1979, just days before the European elections, the *Economist* had published a leaked copy of the valedictory despatch of Sir Nicholas Henderson, the British Ambassador to France, which he had sent to the Foreign Office the previous March. Titled 'Britain's Decline: Its causes and its consequences', Henderson's report argued that the United Kingdom had been in decline since the mid-1950s and that 'the prognosis for the future is discouraging'. The facts he provided to support his argument brought the situation into a stark light. Income per head in Great Britain was, he said, 'for the first time for over 300 years, below that in France.... If present trends continue we shall be overtaken in GDP per head by Italy and Spain well before the end of the century'. In 1954, French GDP per head was 22 per cent lower than British; by 1977, it was 34 per cent higher. German GDP, which had been 9 per cent lower, was an astonishing 61 per cent higher.

Yet it was not only in economics that Britain had declined: 'You only have to move about Western Europe nowadays to realise how poor and unproud the British have become in relation to their neighbours. It shows in the look of our towns, in our airports, in our hospitals and in local amenities; it is painfully apparent in much of our railway system, which until a generation ago was superior to the continental one'. The bearing of this 'weakness' upon foreign policy was 'almost too obvious to require analysis'. Nevertheless, he attempted to provide one. In the Far East, the Mediterranean and the Persian Gulf, Britain had lost all influence and, despite the 'Special Relationship', the United States listened to the French as much as it did to the British. In Europe, the situation was likewise bleak. The fact must be faced, Henderson wrote, that 'for the first time for centuries British policy cannot be based upon the prevention of any single power dominating the continent because, out of weakness, we would be unable to do this'. In the immediate aftermath of the Second World War, the British government had refused to join any schemes for European unity because 'we were confident of our superior strength in relation to our European neighbours, and we did not think that anything would succeed without us'. The decline of British power had revealed this premise as a falsehood: 'when the others showed that they were determined to go ahead on their own we found that we were unable to prevent them doing so or to shape what emerged in the way we wanted'.

In this, his last diplomatic telegram, Henderson did not hold back. In the immediate aftermath of the war, he wrote, 'We had every Western European government ready to eat out of our hand.... For several years our prestige and influence were paramount and we could have stamped Europe as we wished'. The government, however, failed to 'respond' to Europe's wish for leadership, and this failure marked a 'turning-point in post-war history'. By clinging to a Commonwealth link that was soon to weaken, the government had lost the opportunity to shape the future of Europe. Britain continued 'for too long to try to play a world role and failed to cut our coat according to our cloth.... In consequence we were over-extended financially and then when the realities of our economic weakness became inescapable we had to draw our horns precipitously'. He concluded: 'Viewed from the Continent our standing at the present time is low'.[62]

Whilst such blunt language from one of Britain's top diplomats was perhaps shocking, it only confirmed what many politicians and a large percentage of the British public already believed. Britain was in decline, a deterioration marked by the multiple post-war economic crises, by the loss of the British Empire and by Britain's inability to stand alone as it had purportedly done throughout most of its proud history. British membership of 'Europe' seemed to symbolise each of these deficits, providing an economic crutch when the United Kingdom could no longer stand on its own two feet and a unifying concept to replace the loss of an imperial identity. Thatcher recognised these thought patterns and, in part playing to public sentiment and in part out of conviction, concluded that only by distancing itself from Europe and clinging to an imperial past could Britain return to the path of greatness.

The Prime Minister decided to draw her battle lines on the British contribution to the EEC Budget as renegotiated by the Wilson government in 1975. Treasury officials estimated that the United Kingdom would make a net contribution of some £1,000 million in 1979, making it the largest EEC contributor despite being one of its poorer members.[63] Shortly after delivering her Churchill lecture in October of that year, Thatcher attended her first EEC Heads of Government summit in Dublin. There, she shocked her European colleagues with her abrasive and hostile demeanour and her demands for a significant budget rebate from Britain's contribution, arguing for a *juste retour* or a 'broad balance' between what Britain put into the Community Budget and what it got in return. When her Community colleagues offered a refund of £350 million, she rejected it, calling it 'a third of a loaf'.[64] In the aftermath of the summit, the Irish premier Jack Lynch described Thatcher as 'adamant, persistent and, may I say, repetitive', and the French Foreign Minister Jean François-Poncet, in rejecting Thatcher's concept of a *juste retour*, said it was 'not a Community idea. ... The British and we are not speaking of the same Community'.[65]

At the Luxembourg Summit in April 1980, Schimdt and Giscard sought to appease Thatcher, offering a substantially greater budget rebate of £760 million. However, although 'virtually everyone on the British side was strongly in favour of accepting it', Thatcher refused and 'the conference broke up in disarray, and the crisis in the Community deepened'.[66] Throughout the preceding months of negotiations, she had become more angered with the EEC and its bureaucrats, telling Howe at one point that 'The more I read the more appalled I become'. On another occasion, she responded – when an official explained how EEC rules on budget rebates worked – 'No – the procedure is ridiculous. Its whole purpose is to demean Britain'.[67] Even when Carrington and Gilmour succeeded in securing a higher £820 million refund the following month, Thatcher was hesitant to accept. Only when Carrington and Gilmour threatened to resign did Thatcher agree.[68] As Gilmour later wrote about his visit to Chequers to present the terms of the rebate, 'Had we been bailiffs arriving to take possession of the furniture, or even Ted Heath paying a social call in the company with Jacques Delors, we would probably have been more cordially received. The Prime Minister was like a firework whose fuse had been already lit; we could almost hear the sizzling'.[69]

Although Thatcher ultimately relented, she was convinced that Carrington and Gilmour had 'let the country down and had behaved as any good Thatcherite expected the Foreign Office to behave, especially when it was headed by two notorious wets'.[70] In her memoirs, Thatcher commented dryly, 'My immediate reaction was far from favourable'.[71] Gilmour could find no rational explanation for her hostility, given that the budget rebate was unprecedented in the history of the Community and more than twice what had originally been offered. Only an underlying distrust of the European project as a whole could justify it.[72] This was confirmed in the aftermath of the Brussels deal, when Trade Secretary John Nott sent her a memorandum opining that the budget negotiations had highlighted 'deep but genuine differences of opinion about the Community among colleagues', an organisation where 'far too much power already resides in the institutions of the Community'.[73] Thatcher showed her approval with multiple underlinings and positive ticks on his paper.[74]

In June 1980, Jim Prior (the Employment Secretary) sent to Carrington a paper written by his special advisor, Rob Shepherd, who had recently published a book titled *Public Opinion and European Integration*. Shepherd wrote that the British were 'the reluctant – even grudging – Europeans. It is hardly surprising that the British do not exhibit the same sense of commitment to the European ideal as the public in the original Six. Basic attitudes in the UK are not predisposed towards the idea of European integration'. The reason for this, he suggested, was that, in the Six, there was 'a strong sense of European identity and strong support for the E.C. – so there is a sense of being European which can be tapped'. In contrast, within the United Kingdom, Britons 'may be "willing" Europeans, but nationalistic sentiments remain strong and they do not take an wholly uncritical view of the EC and its institutions'.[75] The cabinet as a whole received a briefing that month indicating a 'deterioration in UK public attitudes towards Community membership over the last five years'. Indeed, those who believed British membership of the EEC to be a good thing had fallen from 47 per cent in May 1975, to 33 per cent in June 1977, to just 22 per cent in April 1980. In contrast, those believing it to be 'bad' had risen over those same months from 21 per cent, to 42 per cent, to an incredible 57 per cent.[76]

Carrington recognised that this fall in support could place in jeopardy the government's position, given that the Conservatives were still regarded as the 'European Party'. He warned Thatcher that a fall in British support for the EEC could result in 'a very difficult situation at the next election unless the tide of public opinion can be reversed', particularly given 'the trend [towards anti-Common Market sentiments] within the Labour Party'. Consequently, he argued that the government should 'embark on a sustained campaign to increase public support for the Community'.[77] The Prime Minister, however, disagreed. She recognised that 'public attitudes towards Europe in this country have deteriorated and that it would be desirable to halt, and if possible, reverse this trend', but disagreed 'that this is the right time to launch a major campaign on Europe'. It should be left 'to the discretion of Ministers' whether or not they would address Europe in their speeches. As a government, she wanted to focus attention on trying to 'secure progress [in Europe] on practical matters of direct value to the citizen'.[78]

Thatcher had good reason to be cautious. Not only was support for the EEC rapidly deteriorating amongst the general public, but within the Conservative Party also. This mattered because, particularly following Michael Foot's election to the Labour Leadership in October 1980, the Opposition had become fervently and very publicly Eurosceptic. Given the challenging economic climate and the scant evidence of success for the government's monetarist policies, were it also to isolate itself from the public on the question of Europe there was a very real risk of a resurgence of support for the Labour Party. The Conservatives could not be seen to be too close to Europe. This problem only deepened when, in late June 1980, the Labour MP Nigel Spearing launched 'International Project 1980' as part of the Safeguard Britain Campaign, a project that intended to show that 'the EEC as at present constituted in its supra-national and authoritarian form must lead to British withdrawal – with or without economic collapse – and that in any case the Treaty of Rome cannot by its very nature provide the fruits that were popularly supposed'.[79]

Whilst withdrawal was not at that time the official policy of the Labour Party, this was soon to change under Foot's stewardship.

The left wing of the party (the most anti-Common Market throughout the 1960s and '70s) had become strengthened by the woes besetting the Thatcher government, believing that 'the government's policies would be so unpopular that electors would now be more willing to listen to arguments in favour of a "socialist" alternative'.[80] At the 1980 Party Conference – Callaghan's last – the Labour NEC had introduced a resolution to withdraw from the EEC in defiance of its party leader, which passed by 5,042,000 votes to 2,097,000. It was for this reason that Callaghan resigned twelve days later, opening the way for Foot to take the leadership as a left-wing challenger to the more establishment figure of Denis Healey.[81]

Immediately after Foot's election, the Labour Party split, the social democrats believing it to have become unelectable with its new platform. Under Roy Jenkins's leadership, the so-called 'Gang of Four' (Jenkins, along with the former Foreign Secretary David Owen, the former Education Secretary Shirley Williams and the former Transport Minister William Rodgers) decided to form a new centre-left party to oppose Thatcher's conservativism without making the radical lurch to the left that would surely follow Foot's election. In March 1981, they (along with ten other Labour MPs) announced that they were leaving the party to form the Social Democratic Party (SDP). In addition to holding more centrist views, the SDP also represented the pro-European left.[82] By 1983, its numbers had swelled to thirty, twenty-seven of whom had been elected Labour MPs in the 1979 General Election (including the former Foreign Secretary George Brown who had attempted to negotiate British EEC membership under Harold Wilson and had been so disappointed by the opposition Labour had shown to Heath's negotiations).[83] In late 1981, the SDP formed an alliance with the Liberals under David Steel, and, by 1989, they had formally merged to form a new party, the Liberal Democrats.[84] As the Liberals had been since the Second World War, the SDP-Liberal Alliance was throughout the 1980s the most unabashedly pro-European Party in Britain, as the Liberal Democrats would be in the 1990s and beyond.

The defection of the more pro-European, centrist Labour MPs to the SDP allowed the Labour Party under Foot to stake out its territory as an official Eurosceptic party, and local district branches throughout the United Kingdom latched onto 'Europe' as a way of differentiating themselves from both the Tories and the newly formed SDP. In

Glasgow, for example, the local party published a series of pamphlets on the Common Market, with the introduction penned by Foot ('As one who has campaigned for many years against British membership of the Common Market, I warmly welcome the initiative of the Glasgow District Labour Party'). The first pamphlet asked if socialism could be achieved inside the EEC ('No. The Treaty of Rome is a capitalists' charter'.); if withdrawing from the EEC would cost jobs ('No. On the contrary, our trade deficit with the EEC is a major cause of mass unemployment'.); if withdrawal would 'threaten our food supplies' ('No. It will enable us to buy cheaper, untaxed food'.); and if the EEC bureaucracy was 'wasteful and extravagant' ('Yes!').[85] It seemed to capture the mood of the public, which by May 1981 polling indicated would 'now vote to withdraw from the E.E.C.' by a margin of 64 per cent to 36 per cent.[86] At the Labour Party Conference in October 1981, the delegates voted 'by a large majority for British withdrawal from the Common Market', although they decided against again putting the matter to a referendum. As the Safeguard Britain Campaign explained, 'This last decision has been criticised but there is no need for a referendum if the Labour Party wins an election on a manifesto which includes a commitment to withdraw'.[87] From that point forward, withdrawal from the EEC became official Labour policy.

On the European continent, the open disdain of the Labour Party for the EEC and the tough negotiating stance of the Thatcher government threatened to undermine whatever goodwill British governments of the 1970s had attained from their fellow Community members. In early February 1981, Oliver Wright, the outgoing British Ambassador to West Germany, paid his farewell call to Chancellor Helmut Schmidt. Holding little back, Schmidt said that, until the mid-1960s, he had been an Anglophile but had then come to the conclusion that 'Britain was really indifferent to what was happening on the Continent'. This had been true of both Wilson and Callaghan, and now in Margaret Thatcher 'the instinctive reaction was ... to say whatever suited the American Administration'. This meant that 'Britain was no more than a half-hearted member of the European Community and tended to see the world from an Atlantic rather than a European perspective'.[88] In his valedictory despatch ten days later, Wright wrote that 'our European credentials are by no means yet established here. ... [W]e [at the British Embassy] have taken our 10 per cent cut as ordered [but] I have to tell you that our ability to understand the country in which we serve and to transact business with its government have thereby been impaired. I hope that... as our national fortunes revive, my successors will receive the resources to do what the national interest requires'.[89]

Almost a year to the day later, on 15 February 1982, Reginald Hibbert, the British Ambassador to France, likewise sent to the Foreign Office his valedictory despatch, which was no more optimistic about Britain's future in Europe. He warned that 'Although the French have great affection and respect for Britain, this has been tempered in recent years by Community problems and the UK's economic decline'. He closed with some words of advice for his successors: 'Britain is a natural historical rival of France and it seems to suit French Governments to keep the feeling of rivalry with Britain alive. ... Germany is less loved and more feared and does not appear to give the French people the same sense of comprehensive challenge as Britain does. The way to a close and loyal understanding with France is therefore uphill'. It was not, however, an entirely lost cause. In the end, French governments would 'accept partnership with Britain and make it work fruitfully in proportion to Britain's strength. The revival of Britain's economy will make it possible to deal more equally with France. Cool, hard, unsentimental bargaining, with many warm words clothing calculated and often combative gestures, would be the right way to deal with France'.[90]

If the government was to operate on an equal basis with the European continental powers, it could do so only from a position of strength. Both Wright and Hibbert – the two Britons closest to West Germany and France, respectively – confirmed this. Yet, in the spring of 1982, the Thatcher government was struggling, with few signs of an economic revival yet visible and a Labour opposition that tacked closer to the public's preferred course on Europe than did the Conservatives. At the Crosby by-election in late November 1981, the Liberal Shirley Williams took the seat from the Tories with a majority of more than 5,000, and, in December, a group of Conservative backbenchers known as the Gang of Twenty-Five wrote a letter 'expressing anxiety' about the situation facing the government. Michael Jopling, the Conservative Chief Whip, told the Prime Minister it was 'a very serious situation', and Peter Jenkins, writing in the *Guardian* said, 'A brief obituary of Thatcherism is now in order'.[91]

Yet, if perhaps lying in a hospital bed on life support, the Thatcher government was not yet dead. Michael Foot, although in sync with the British public on Europe, had otherwise shown himself incapable of being considered a serious leader. Consequently, although the SDP could provoke some political embarrassment at by-elections, there was no realistic challenge to Conservative rule. And then, on 2 April 1982, Argentine forces invaded the Falkland Islands in the South Atlantic. For the first time since the 1956 Suez Crisis, the House of Commons met on a Saturday, where it debated the invasion for three hours. Tony Benn recorded that the House was 'in the grip of jingoism'.[92] He was convinced that the saga raised 'a complex question about the remnants of empire' and equally convinced that the government should not respond with force because 'it's a colony we grabbed years ago from somebody and we have no right to it'.[93] Benn's opinion counted for very little, however. At 2.30 a.m. in the early morning hours of 4 April, a task force of nine British warships set sail for the South Atlantic, where they were soon joined by two aircraft carriers and twenty Sea Harrier fighter jets. By the end of the month, the task force numbered sixty-five ships with more than 15,000 men, 7,000 of whom were marines and soldiers prepared to launch an invasion to take back the Falkland Islands.[94]

For Thatcher, the war could not have come at a more convenient moment. The Europhile Foreign Secretary Lord Carrington immediately resigned, as did the Foreign Office Ministers Humphrey Atkins and Richard Luce, removing from the cabinet some of the last remaining 'wets'. Thatcher later wrote that 'Peter's [Carrington's] resignation ultimately made it easier to unite the Party and concentrate on recovering the Falklands'.[95] She might also have added that it removed an obstacle to initiating an even tougher approach within the EEC. But beyond the internal politics of the Conservative Party, the Falklands War allowed Thatcher to reinvent herself and her government after what can only be described as a difficult first three years. Speaking in the parliamentary debate on 3 April, Enoch Powell looked directly at Thatcher and said, 'The Prime Minister, shortly after she came into office, received a soubriquet as the "Iron Lady".... In the next week or two this House, the nation and the Right Honourable Lady herself will learn of what metal she is made'.[96] Quite against the odds, Margaret Thatcher had now become a war-time Prime Minister fighting one of Britain's last colonial campaigns. The invasion of the Falkland Islands, quite apart from being a humiliation for the government, proved to be Margaret Thatcher's salvation.

17 MRS THATCHER, JOHN MAJOR AND THE ROAD TO EUROPEAN UNION

On 3 July 1982, Margaret Thatcher spoke to a crowd gathered at Cheltenham. It had been a heady three months for the Prime Minister. Upon announcing the invasion of the Falkland Islands on 3 April, she had been accused by the Labour Party in the House of Commons of abject failure, of bringing a final humiliation to Britain in one of its last colonial possessions. This weighed heavily upon her, already conscious of and sensitive to British decline. In his diary, the Conservative MP and historian Alan Clark described 'how low she held her head, how knotted with pain and apprehension she seemed'.[1] In a second parliamentary debate later that week, her predecessor Jim Callaghan held the Prime Minister personally responsible for the war and lambasted British unpreparedness, saying, 'we are sending an aircraft carrier that has already been sold to meet cash limits, from a port that is to be closed, and with 500 sailors holding redundancy notices in their pockets'.[2] But war transforms a person for better or worse, and this was certainly the case with the British Prime Minister. By the time it was all over, 'All over the world, Margaret Thatcher now became a figure of legend, the embodiment of strong leadership, more famous, perhaps, than any other political leader at the time'.[3]

Addressing the crowd at Cheltenham, she reflected on what the Falklands War had meant for Britain. 'We have ceased', she said, 'to be a nation in retreat. We have instead a newfound confidence – born in the economic battles at home and tested and found true 8,000 miles away. . . . And so today we can rejoice in our success in the Falklands and take pride in the achievement of the men and women of our task force. But we do so, not as at some flickering of a flame which must soon be dead. No – we rejoice that Britain has rekindled that spirit which has fired her for generations past and which today has begun to burn as brightly as before. Britain found herself again in the South Atlantic and will not look back from the victory she has won'.[4] There was no need to ask which 'spirit' had been lost and rekindled, nor in what way Britain had 'found herself again'. Thatcher had been very clear throughout her political career that national decline had accompanied the loss of empire; only an imperial triumph could stem the tide of that decay. On the day the victory was announced, Alan Clark met Ian Gow, Thatcher's parliamentary private secretary, who was 'looking like the cat that has swallowed all the cream'. In a prescient remark, he commented to Gow that 'the Prime Minister has complete freedom of action now. . . . [N]o other Leader has enjoyed such freedom since Churchill, and even with him it did not last very long'.[5] In a matter of eleven weeks, Thatcher's position in the nation had been transformed utterly.

The Falklands War allowed Thatcher to make a decisive break from the Conservative Party's past and to re-evaluate policies and principles across the board. In no area was this truer than with regards to Europe. On 31 December 1982, on the tenth anniversary of British accession to the European Community, she released a statement to mark the occasion. Describing the previous decade as 'ten of the most continuously difficult years Europe – and indeed the world – has known since World War II', she purported to be 'convinced that Britain has weathered the storms of the last decade far better in the Community than we could have done outside it'. Nevertheless, she tempered her praise by noting 'disappointment' that the Community had not reached a common fisheries policy or established a 'fair financial system'. It had 'made progress over the last ten years', but for Thatcher such progress was not enough. Furthermore, the European Economic Community (EEC) was still just one part of Britain's foreign policy; it was not the primary consideration, as Heath had once conceived it to be.[6]

If anything, the Falklands War only strengthened Thatcher's convictions about what Britain's role within Europe should be. When the war began, the majority of EEC members had demonstrated full solidarity with Britain, and Thatcher was pleasantly surprised that the newly elected French socialist leader François Mitterrand was amongst the most supportive. As the war progressed, however, both Ireland and Italy refused to renew sanctions on Argentina, and, during the course of the conflict, the UK government suffered an unprecedented majority vote against blocking agreement on farm prices until the rebate question was settled, which the British government had declared a 'vital interest'.[7] This distraction during a time of war 'raised new doubts not only about the usefulness of the community's political cooperation but also about the future of the EC itself', prompting America's Central Intelligence Agency (CIA) to warn the US government that although French and German support for Britain 'suggest[s] that pressures to hold the community together may be at least as strong as the centrifugal forces', nevertheless 'Those [centrifugal] forces did surface clearly [during the war] and will produce alarms again. Mistrust of the UK's commitment to the community is profound'.[8]

This 'mistrust' flowed in both directions, particularly when, in the aftermath of the war, the French government quickly restored its economic ties with Argentina. These ties had already caused some controversy during the war as it was French-supplied Exocet missiles (fired from French-built Super Étendard aircraft) that had sunk the *HMS Sheffield* and the *Atlantic Conveyer* and badly damaged the *HMS Glamorgan*.[9] During the war, Mitterrand had remained steadfast with Britain, even delaying a French contract to supply Exocets to Peru lest they fall into Argentinian hands before the war's end.[10] Once the Falklands were restored back to British control, however, it was largely business-as-usual as far as the other EEC countries were concerned. Thatcher saw this first-hand at the Paris Summit with Mitterrand in November 1982, when she was briefed to 'thank Mitterrand for his help during the campaign and explore his intentions about arms sales to Argentina now'. She was also advised to turn his attention back to the issue of Britain's contribution to the Community Budget, leaving Mitterrand 'in no doubt that he cannot have good Anglo/French relations while allowing the budget problem to drift on'.[11]

When they met, Mitterrand was evasive, but the matter was soon brought into clear focus by Emmanuel Jacquin de Margerie, the French Ambassador to the UK. Writing to Sir Anthony Meyer, the Chairman of the Franco–British Parliamentary Committee – and speaking as 'a friend of your country who has lived here through the Falklands Crisis' – he explained that 'The delivery to Argentina of military equipment has been provided for in a contract signed well before hostilities broke out in the South Atlantic. . . . When the hostilities broke out, the French Government imposed an immediate arms embargo on Argentina, and was party to the commercial embargo decided by the E.E.C. When the hostilities ceased, the situation was reviewed. The Community lifted its commercial embargo. The French Government lifted its arms embargo on 10th August, and warned the British Government of its decision. ... When the hostilities ceased and our embargo was dropped, the French Government were under legal and binding obligations to fulfil their contract with the Argentinian Government'. Arms sales would resume, notwithstanding Argentina's continued claims over what it called 'las Malvinas'.

If the question of French arms sales to Argentina was difficult, the issue of British contributions to the Community Budget was trickier still. This was complicated further by the election in West Germany of Helmut Kohl as Chancellor in October 1982. When the Socialist François Mitterrand became French President in May 1981, many had expected Anglo–French relations to deteriorate given the obvious ideological differences between the two leaders. Yet, in early 1982, Thatcher's son had become stranded in the Sahara Desert whilst taking part in a motor rally. With 'prompt and adroit courtesy which Mrs Thatcher never forgot, President Mitterrand offered her any military service that might help her find her son'.[12] This cemented a bond between them, however irrational it may have seemed to outsiders, which was only strengthened by Mitterrand's staunch support during the Falklands War.[13] In contrast, Helmut Kohl – who as a Conservative should have been a closer confidant of Thatcher's – never impressed the Prime Minister. Her foreign policy advisor George Urban perceived her long-standing anti-German prejudice as an important factor in her approach towards him: 'She didn't hide her cordial dislike of all things German (forgetting, it seemed, the Teutonic descent of the English nation, of the English language and of the royal family), aggravated by her distaste for the personality of Helmut Kohl, whom she saw not at all as a fellow-Conservative or a Christian Democrat, but as a German deeply mired in provincialism. The contrast between herself as a visionary stateswoman with a world-view, and Kohl the wurst-eating, corpulent, plodding Teuton, has a long history in MT's imagination'.[14] Kohl picked up on her dislike, once remarking that 'Dealing with Margaret Thatcher was like taking hot and cold baths'.[15]

When Thatcher met with Kohl at an Anglo–German Summit in April 1983 – the fourth bilateral meeting they had held since he became Chancellor – she described it publicly as 'a most useful, enjoyable and wide-ranging summit'. However, she also noted that 'Our priority... is to clear out of the way a lasting solution to the Budget problem and agreement on our refunds, pending the eventual solution, for 1983'.[16] Until that was achieved, Thatcher saw little point in discussing further EEC initiatives. As far as her European colleagues were concerned, however, her stance was unreasonable. The British government had agreed to a budget formula in 1972, only to renege and renegotiate in 1975 – a renegotiation that was overwhelmingly approved in a national referendum. It had, once again, sought better terms in 1979, with much more success than the Community had anticipated. The Community had gone out of its way to accommodate the British. It was now irresponsible for the British government to prevent Community business from moving forward until a still more favourable outcome could be negotiated. From their perspective, Thatcher was essentially holding the EEC hostage to British demands. Consequently, Kohl and Mitterrand – despite their opposing ideologies – worked together to thwart Thatcher's goals on the budget, preventing broad agreement from being reached until the Fountainebleau Summit in June 1984.[17]

Before this could happen, Thatcher asked the Queen to dissolve Parliament so that she could go to the country for a new mandate, guaranteeing her at least five more years in power. Since the Falklands War, her fortunes had been restored in more ways than one. Although unemployment would continue to rise until peaking in 1985, by 1983, inflation had fallen from its height in 1981 to just 4.5 per cent, indicating that Thatcher's economic policies – whilst painful – had achieved their central goal of dramatically reducing inflation.[18] Furthermore, the recession had reached its lowest point in 1981, after which economic growth had resumed in 1982 (conveniently corresponding with the Falklands War). By 1983, it was approaching 4 per cent, a far higher growth rate than in any year since the 1960s. The mortgage interest rate had also fallen by 4 per cent in 1983, and, for the 87 per cent of the nation that was in work (unemployment having stabilised at 12–13 per cent) standards of living were better than they had been in a decade.[19] Combined with the 'Falklands Factor', which had seen Thatcher's personal popularity rise above 50 per cent at the end of 1982, the time seemed ripe for an election.

On 9 May 1983, Thatcher announced that she would seek an early dissolution of Parliament and four days later Parliament closed, with a General Election set for 9 June. The 1983 Conservative Manifesto promised a continuation of the government's policies, in foreign affairs committing to a continuation of British membership of the Common Market and maintenance of its independent nuclear deterrent, and at home pledging to reduce taxes, fight inflation, reform the trade unions and privatise much of the publicly owned industries that had been nationalised in the aftermath of the Second World War.[20] The Labour Manifesto offered a radical contrast, promising to withdraw from the EEC, abolish the House of Lords, cancel the Trident Program (thus ending Britain's nuclear deterrent), create a National Investment Bank and re-nationalise the aerospace and ship-building industries whilst preventing further privatisations.[21] As the Labour MP Gerald Kaufman later remarked, it was 'the longest suicide note in history'.[22]

When the votes were counted, the Conservative Party had an overall parliamentary majority of 144, larger than any post-war government since Clement Attlee's. It had secured 397 seats to Labour's 209. The SDP–Liberal Alliance had also picked up twenty-three seats, eating into Labour's share of the vote throughout the country. Indeed, on percentage of votes (as opposed to seats), the Alliance had secured 25.4 per cent to Labour's 27.6 per cent, demonstrating that, despite the imbalance in Parliament, almost as many Britons had voted for the Alliance as for Labour. It was the Labour Party's worst showing since the 1920s, particularly in the south of England where it secured just two seats out of 110 (excluding London).[23] The left-wing MP Tony Benn was one of those cast out of Parliament. He described the 'full scale of the losses' as 'enormous'.[24] On 12 June, Foot resigned as Labour leader, and, two days later, Roy Jenkins did the same as leader of the SDP, the party having expected to see a far greater rise in its number of seats (of the 23 Alliance MPs, only 6 were SDP).[25] Neil Kinnock, a young Labour MP from Wales who had first joined the Shadow Cabinet in 1979, was the immediate favourite for Labour leader. After a long election campaign, his victory was announced on 2 October 1983, he having secured 71 per cent of the vote.[26] His was not an enviable position, however, leading a Labour Party with fewer seats than at any time since 1935 against a leader who, in the minds of much of the public, was the second coming of Churchill.

* * *

Whilst the position of the Labour leader was one to be pitied, the Conservative Prime Minister had received an immeasurable boost from the election. Thatcher used her new mandate to begin mopping up the Conservative floors of the remaining 'wets'. As she wrote of the reshuffle in her memoirs, 'There was a revolution still to be made, but too few revolutionaries'. The new Parliament offered 'a chance to recruit some'.[27] She began by removing Francis Pym from the cabinet, he having replaced Lord Carrington as Foreign Secretary during the Falklands War. Upon his sacking, Pym preferred to return to the backbenches than become Speaker of the House, which Thatcher offered him. She also removed David Howell from the Department of Transport and asked Janet Young to step down as Leader of the Lords to make way for Willie Whitelaw. She chose Leon Brittan to replace Whitelaw at the Home Office, placed Cecil Parkinson into the newly created (by merger) Department of Transport and Industry, moved Geoffrey Howe to the Foreign Office and promoted Nigel Lawson to be Chancellor of the Exchequer.[28] Keith Joseph and Norman Tebbit remained, respectively, at the Departments of Education and Employment,[29] and Thatcher left a young man by the name of John Major as an assistant in the Whips' Office, where he had been since that January.[30] It would be another two years before Major would receive his first ministerial post outside the Whips' Office.

Following the June 1983 reshuffle, Thatcher was surrounded in the cabinet and at the junior ministerial level by 'dries' who thoroughly supported her program of economic and social reforms. There was, however, one area in which she was suffering ever-increasing agitation within the ranks of the party: Britain's European policy. In March 1984, with the issue of Britain's contribution to the Community Budget yet to be resolved, the League of Concerned Conservatives, an anti-EEC group that had been formed to put grassroots pressure on the party leadership, published an 'open letter to European Democrats', asking 'Who are you really?' With an eye to the European elections that would take place that June, it stated that 'The term "Conservative" is well understood in Britain, but not in the E.E.C. A European Democrat, on the other hand, means nothing to the British, but is acceptable in the Euro-Assembly. A Conservative is disposed to maintain existing institutions and to promote individual enterprise; a European Democrat does neither'. The letter condemned the 'chameleon candidates' who stood as Conservatives in the UK European elections but became European Democrats on arrival in Brussels. It argued that the Tory Party, rather than being the self-proclaimed 'Party of Europe', should be far more hesitant in entering European institutions. British Conservatism, it claimed, was unique and did not sit easily with continental politics. It closed by asking, 'Is a European Democrat a Conservative? If so, let him support Conservative principles. If he is not, then he should not claim to be one at the Euro-election in June. Otherwise he can legitimately be accused of deceiving the British on the one hand and the Europeans on the other'.[31]

One Conservative voter, having read the open letter, wrote to Enoch Powell in late April. The letter, he wrote, 'horrifies me'. He had written to his MP Ian Gilmour 'which has proved a waste of time' and now hoped that Powell would lead the campaign in Parliament to 'oppose' any further moves towards European integration.[32] Powell also heard that spring from Jonathan Poulton, vice-chairman of the Bournemouth East Young Conservatives, who described attending a meeting with a Conservative European Parliament candidate and being 'shocked and surprised to learn that he looked forward to a time when all members of the E.E.C. would not only share a common currency and passport but perhaps one day form a United States of Europe'. Poulton 'could not believe this was a Tory speaking' and felt it was time to say 'enough is enough'.[33] Powell sent his reply on 15 May, hoping that the Young Conservatives would 'exercise their influence within the Conservative Party for the re-examining of Britain's political and parliamentary independence'. He added that 'It may be that this is in fact the Prime Minister's object'.[34] Even Powell recognised that Thatcher was not Heath, tacking much closer to the course sailed by previous leaders like Ernest Bevin and Anthony Eden than her immediate Conservative predecessors.

Shortly after Powell's correspondence with Poulton, Thatcher launched the Conservative European Manifesto for the 14 June 1984 election. Writing in its forward, she said that the Conservative aim was to 'develop the full potential of the Community.... It is vital that Britain's voice remains strong in Europe. We do not want to see our accomplishments and our future damaged by those who seek only to destroy what has already been achieved'.[35] She was less confident in private than in public, however. At the March 1984 European Council, she encountered a 'gush of Euro-idealism' that did not sit well with her, from Kohl becoming 'quite lyrical on the subject of getting rid of frontier controls', through Mitterrand urging that 'Europe should not be left behind by the USA in the space race', to the Italian Foreign Minister arguing that Europe should be 'in the vanguard against the "militarization" of space'. Yet when it came to the British contribution to the Community Budget, there was less enthusiasm. Kohl – with the support of Mitterrand – offered Thatcher a five-year budget rebate that was 'much less than I wanted and still only a temporary arrangement'. When she refused to accept the deal, France and Italy 'blocked payment of [Britain's] 1983 refund'.[36] Such behaviour on the part of her European colleagues frustrated Thatcher and only strengthened the hand of the anti-Marketeers within the Conservative Party. Following her refusal to accept Kohl's five-year rebate offer, one parliamentary colleague wrote to her, 'Glory Glory Halleluia [sic] and many congratulations on your courageous and absolutely correct stand at the EEC summit tonight'.[37]

Many other Britons were likewise frustrated by what they perceived as the unreasonable demands of the EEC. In the midst of the European election campaign that summer, one Conservative voter wrote to Enoch Powell asking, 'do you believe that one day the electorate of Great Britain could be persuaded to vote for our leaving the EEC, and to be willing to pay the political and commercial price (in the short term) in order to regain the freedom and self-respect to which I believe this country was once entitled?' He added that personally, he would 'never concede that we should be (or should have become) a member of the EEC, and shall continue to carry a small torch for my version of patriotism'.[38] Powell replied that 'the practical consequences of our membership, which mean the loss of our political independence as a nation, are coming home fast to various sections of the electorate. In due course, if only for electoral reasons, I believe that political parties are likely to listen'.[39]

If Margaret Thatcher – and many Conservative voters – were feeling increasing unease at British membership of the EEC, the new Labour leader Neil Kinnock was moving in the opposite direction, attempting to moderate the fervently anti-European position of his own party. Speaking to the Socialist Group at the European Assembly in September 1983, just before his rise as party leader, he argued that by 1988 Britain would have been in the Common Market for fifteen years, making withdrawal 'a last resort that is considered only if and when the best interests of the British people cannot be feasibly safeguarded by any other means'. There was certainly cause for concern in Europe. He argued that the Common Agricultural Policy (CAP) was 'intolerable' and that EEC trade policy had resulted in a 'continual outflow of investment and employment'. Nevertheless, using words that would have been considered sacrilegious by Foot, he claimed that 'Our future, like our past and our present, lies with Europe for all of the obvious historical and geographical reasons. . . . The inspiration of the EEC as an organisation to bind and stabilise the democracies of Western Europe was – and is – decent and desirable'.[40]

By the time of the European elections in June 1984, Kinnock had steered his party policy from calling for absolute and unconditional withdrawal from the Community, to instead favouring withdraw only if reform of the EEC was unsuccessful, reform that included modification of the CAP, a better budget rebate for Britain and community-wide policies to reduce unemployment throughout the continent (the first two of these were already being pursued by the Conservative government and the latter was supported by Mitterrand and other European socialist leaders).[41] Whilst Kinnock betrayed a greater caution towards Europe than the Conservative Party, he nevertheless softened Labour's approach to the EEC and brought it closer to the guarded optimism that characterised the Tory position at that time. This 'middle ground' seemed to better mirror the ambivalence of the British public, a public that was neither as enthusiastic towards 'Europe' as Heath's government, nor as convinced of the need for an immediate withdrawal as Michael Foot's Labour Party. Consequently, when the public went to the polls on 14 June 1984, the Labour Party gained fifteen seats in the European Parliament and the Tories lost fifteen (although whether this was because of Kinnock's moderating influence or because of the previous and still prevalent Euroscepticism of the Labour Party was unclear).

It was therefore with a smaller contingent of returned Conservative MEPs in the European Parliament that Thatcher travelled to Fontainebleau on 25 June for the European Council. The French Foreign Minister, Claude Cheysson, initially offered Britain a permanent rebate of between 50 and 60 per cent, having previously told the BBC in 1982 that a permanent budget rebate for the UK would be a 'complete deviation of the Community'.[42] Thatcher claimed to be in 'despair' at this offer and told the gathered heads of government that 'if this was the best they had to offer the Fontainebleau Council would be a disaster'. She then said she would accept nothing less than a permanent

70 per cent rebate.[43] At this, Mitterrand suggested they break from the full setting into bilateral meetings. Thatcher met first with the French President, who would not move above 60 per cent, and then with the West German Chancellor, who offered 65 per cent. Bringing the full meeting back together again, Thatcher proposed 66 per cent, or a permanent two-thirds budget rebate. Mitterrand, on hearing what Kohl had offered, supported the German suggestion of 65 per cent but Thatcher repeated that she wanted the full 66 per cent and said it would be 'absurd' if the Council broke down over 1 per cent. Mitterrand smiled and said, 'Of course, Madame Prime Minister, you must have it', and with that the issue was settled.[44] The UK's budget rebate has remained at this level ever since.

During both the General Election and European Election campaigns of 1979, Thatcher promised to seek for Britain a better budget deal within the EEC. She had placed the issue front and centre at each European Council since that time to the point of almost bringing community business to a halt. She eventually got her way, but it was not without cost. In the aftermath of the Fontainebleau Council, the British Embassy in Bonn warned the Foreign Office that the budget battle had brought Mitterrand and Kohl closer together, united in their vision of a federal Europe that was far from Thatcher's concept.[45] The negotiations also took their toll on Thatcher's views of Britain's place within Europe. Stephen Wall, who was present at the Fontainebleau negotiations as a junior diplomat, later wrote, 'Thatcher drew from it the lesson that, on the whole, our partners were not people to be trusted. ... [T]he successful outcome could never have been achieved without the ferocious energy and intransigence with which Margaret Thatcher had pursued her goal. But the success for British diplomacy had been achieved at a heavy cost, especially in terms of Mrs Thatcher's personal relations with the other European leaders. There was plenty of grudging admiration, but she did not have a single friend among them'.[46] She had become, as Wall titled his book, a 'stranger in Europe'.

* * *

Margaret Thatcher stood before the Prime Minister of Belgium; the rector, faculty, staff and students from the College of Europe; members of the general public and various notables from the Brussels diplomatic corps. It was an awkward venue, the audience largely flanking her on either side, and she had to read from paper rather than auto-cue, as would have been her preference. She had been invited to Bruges by the rector, Professor Jerzy Łukaszewski. David Hannay, the UK Permanent Representative to the European Community, recommended that she accept, pointing out that during the previous year – 1987 – French President Mitterrand had done so, and before that so, too, had President Soares of Portugal, Prime Minister Gonzalez of Spain and Chancellor Kresiky of Austria.[47] Her charge was to 'spell out her own vision of the future development of Europe rather than leaving the field clear to others'.[48] As she began her speech, she congratulated Łukaszewski on his 'courage' for inviting her, quipping that 'If you believe some of the things said and written about my views on Europe, it must seem rather like inviting Genghis Khan to speak on the virtues of peaceful coexistence!'[49]

Such had developed the Prime Minister's reputation in Europe. Since the European elections in June 1984, Thatcher's government, backbench Conservatives and an increasingly large segment of the British public had become interestingly disillusioned by the EEC. That autumn, the Anti-Common Market League proclaimed that 'Most Conservatives now agree that times have changed since the days 12 years ago when the then Prime Minister, Edward Heath, took Britain into the Common Market'. It added that Thatcher had 'brought home to us that the E.E.C. operates on principles that are often inconsistent with basic Conservative thinking'.[50] Much of this anti-Market backlash had resulted from the disclosure to the public of the Spinelli Draft Treaty Report for European Union, which passed the EEC Assembly on 14 February 1984. Altiero Spinelli, a member of the European Commission from 1970 to 1976 and of the European Parliament from 1979 onwards, had established the 'Crocodile Club' (named after the Crocodile Restaurant in Strasbourg where it first met) in the early 1980s to further dreams of European unity. In January 1982, its members tabled a motion in the European Parliament to establish the Committee on Institutional Affairs with Spinelli serving as General Rappourteur. Its purpose was to draft a new treaty on European Union. His eventual report recommended that the European Parliament act as a constituent assembly of what would essentially be a European super-state. It was adopted by the European Parliament by 237 votes to 31 (with 43 abstentions), becoming the Draft Treaty Establishing the European Union. The heads of EEC governments (as opposed to the MEPs who had voted for the measure) buried the Draft Treaty, however, preferring to reach a settlement among themselves which would have the support of national politicians and survive the ratification process. Spinelli's work nevertheless caused a stir in the EEC, providing a spark to those who had always favoured a European federation and sending a shiver down the spines of anti-Marketeers. As the Scottish Anti-Common Market Council wrote to Enoch Powell, 'if ratified by Britain and other countries it would have the effect of eliminating the United Kingdom and other members as individual states and transforming them into one centrally controlled (not federal) supra-state with our sovereignty completely gone'.[51]

On 1 January 1985, the Frenchman Jacques Delors became President of the European Commission.[52] The former Minister of Finance, he was a largely unknown quantity to Thatcher, except for his reputation as an 'intelligent and energetic' man who 'rein[ed] back the initial left-wing socialist policies of President Mitterrand's Government'. She was happy to cast her vote in his favour for the Commission presidency.[53] In his first speech as President to the European Parliament on 14 January, however, he shocked Thatcher – and delighted many others – by asking, 'Is it presumptuous to announce, and then to execute, a decision to remove all the borders inside Europe between now and 1992?'[54] This directly contradicted Thatcher's view that the EEC should be nothing more than a large single market. She was further alarmed when, having persuaded the Commission to assign Lord Arthur Cockfield (the former chairman of the Boots pharmacy chain) to draw up a White Paper detailing the complexities of Delors's vision, Cockfield drafted a plan to unify twelve separate markets by eliminating more than 300 physical, technical and fiscal barriers which at that time existed within the Community. The White Paper proposed to achieve this by 1992.[55] Rather than finding holes in Delors's scheme, Cockfield had shown the Commission exactly how to achieve it.

The European heads of government approved the White Paper – which would eventually become the Single European Act of 1986 – at the Luxembourg European Council in early December 1985. At the time, Thatcher accepted it as a way to codify capitalist market principles into the workings of the EEC in the face of what she perceived as a socialist onslaught. She later wrote that 'we were going to get the Community back on course, concentrating on its role as a huge market, with all the opportunities that would bring to our industries'. However, not all saw it in this light, and 'the new powers the Commission received only seemed to whet its appetite'.[56] Chief amongst those who held a different view was Delors. With the support of Cockfield, he managed to link the completion of a single market with new governance procedures within the EEC, extending the powers of the European Parliament and introducing 'qualified majority' voting to most White Paper areas. This meant that 'Henceforth in single market areas member states might very well have to accept legislation they did not desire'.[57] Thatcher later laid all blame on Cockfield, writing, 'Arthur Cockfield was a natural technocrat of great ability and problem-solving outlook. Unfortunately, he tended to disregard the larger questions of politics – constitutional sovereignty, national sentiment and the promptings of liberty. He was a prisoner as well as the master of his subject. It was all too easy for him, therefore, to go native'.[58] Her choice of language was telling. Europe was still 'foreign', 'other', 'exotic' and, ultimately, 'less' than Britain. To become 'European' was to succumb to the temptations of a seductive but ultimately dangerous temptress. It was very much like the imperial adventurer who, after years of living in the bush, married a native and forgot where he was from and to whom he owed his allegiance.

The Conservatives Against the Common Market (CACM) group was unimpressed, writing to Enoch Powell that it had received a 're-assurance from Mr Malcolm Rifkind (Minister of State at the Foreign Office)' that 'Britain can[not] be compelled to join the proposed Euro-megastate against our will'. Rifkind had implied that 'the whole European Parliament do not know what they are talking about'. Given that the Minister of State 'was in short pants' when Spinelli was a 'fully-fledged Common Market Commissioner', the chairman of CACM doubted his sincerity: 'It was the Foreign Office who re-assured Mrs Nichols of Gerrards Cross that the Argentines would not invade the Falklands because we have 25 marines stationed there! As Gertrude Stein might have said, a re-assurance is a re-assurance is a re-assurance. Let us not be caught napping again; when a Foreign Office minister such as Mr. Rifkind gives us a re-assurance it is time to prepare for the worst!'[59]

The Single European Act was signed on 17 February 1986, coming into effect after ratification on 1 July 1987. The anti-Marketeer Labour MP Nigel Spearing described it as attempting to 'transform relations as a whole among [the EEC states] into a European Union', which it would do by 'extending the scope of its legal authority and enlarging the powers and influence of most of its centralised institutions ... at the expense of member states, their Government and Parliaments whose views and will are currently expressed through the European Council'. He warned that the Act would 'have significant effects on the powers of the UK Parliament in respect of UK legislation, supervision and accountability for the policy of the UK Minister of Foreign Affairs, and could have profound constitutional implications for the Crown and Parliament of the United Kingdom, not least in the establishment in UK law of the supremacy of the EEC Parliament'. Put simply, what constitutional purpose would the monarch still serve if legislation that was binding on the British people could be passed that did not require the assent of the Crown? By signing the Single European Act, Spearing believed that Thatcher had in the stroke of a pen accomplished a constitutional revolution which had eluded republicans in the United Kingdom for hundreds of years.[60]

At the time, the Prime Minister gave no hint of hesitation in signing the treaty that brought the Act into being. With hindsight, however, she expressed regret that the Common Market did not provide a single explanation of what the Act actually meant and what its implications would be. Delors described it as 'a compromise of progress', a stepping stone to the much greater integration that he envisioned. The Dutch were disappointed that it had not created a full European federation, leading one Dutch newspaper to lament that 'the ideal of European unity would have to wait until there was a new incumbent in No. 10'. The Germans, as well as the French, saw it as a positive step in the direction of a full European Union. Kohl told the Bundestag that the Council had 'taken the political and institutional development of the Community a decisive step forward'. Only Thatcher perceived it somewhat differently, telling the House of Commons, 'I am constantly saying that I wish that they would talk less about European and political union. The terms are not understood in this country'.[61] In a form reply sent to concerned Tory voters, the Conservative Central Office quoted the Foreign Secretary Sir Geoffrey Howe, who said in April, 'We are not talking about the declaration or proclamation of a United States of Europe or about vague political or legal goals. We are talking about practical steps towards the unity (not union) that is essential if Europe is to maintain and enhance its economic and political position in a harshly competitive world'.[62] Many in the Community begged to differ.

By the time Britain took up the presidency of the European Council in December 1986, Thatcher had soured on Delors, whom she described as a 'Euro-demagogue' who wished to 'belittle' Britain.[63] In her mind, the Europe of Delors's imagination was a project that was doomed to failure, not because of a flaw in the intellectual argument or from a structural problem but because of the varieties of languages and cultures that were present there and which were, in Thatcher's eyes, fundamentally incompatible.[64] This was a long-held idea; indeed, following a visit to Luxembourg to attend the European Assembly in 1975 she had concluded that 'such an Assembly in which people did not speak the same language or share the same traditions illustrated the shortcomings of attempts to create artificial Europe-wide institutions'.[65] The title of the chapter in her memoirs discussing the European Community from 1987 to 1990 is perhaps telling in this regards – she called it 'the Babel Express'.

When, in May 1987, Thatcher once again asked the Queen to dissolve Parliament and call a General Election for 11 June, the Prime Minister's approach to Europe was noticeably different than it had been in 1983. Her only engagement with the subject came at the G7 Summit in Venice, where she stood shoulder to shoulder with American President Ronald Reagan to block Kohl's call for negotiations with the Soviets over the removal of shorter range nuclear weapons from Europe. It hardly presented a picture of European unity.[66] When the votes were counted, Neil Kinnock's Labour Party had made small in-roads, particularly against the Alliance, but it hardly mattered: the Conservative Party still held 376 seats to Labour's 229, its share of the popular vote holding steady at 42.3 per cent.[67] On 3 January 1988, fresh from the General Election and with a new mandate for another five years, Thatcher contributed an article to the *Sunday Express* titled, 'Britain Counts for Something Good Again'. In it, she wrote that there had been 'great changes wrought during the 1980s'. For the first time since the Second World War, she wrote, 'our energies as a people are now increasingly concentrated on improving our national standing'. Britain in 1988, she claimed, was a 'different country – a country revitalised; a country of rising confidence; a country which counts for something again'. The issue was no longer 'whether Britain has a future but how we are going to make the most of it'. Claiming to know 'what the British people would like to see', she turned first to foreign affairs, arguing that they wanted a government 'which is able to exercise influence not merely in the European Community and the Commonwealth, but also in Moscow and Washington and elsewhere'. Within the EEC, the British people wanted to see 'order brought to the Community's financial affairs and its huge economic potential realised'.[68] Yet Britain was bigger than Europe. It was, once again, a global power.

Although she did not put a name to it, Thatcher was arguing that Britain had been restored to a time when it triumphed as an extra-European power, a golden age that existed before the loss of national confidence in the 1960s and before the economic travails of the 1970s. Whether consciously or not, she was looking back to Britain's imperial past, to a Victorian era in which Britain's navy ruled the waves; its economics were free; and its explorers, traders and missionaries 'civilised' the world, spreading across the globe as Europeans confident in their own future. Under the Conservative government of the 1980s, she claimed, chains that had once bound Britain had been cast off. A narrow vision of subsuming British sovereignty within a European super-state would return Britain to the state from which she had delivered it. Her worst fears and suspicions were confirmed when Delors addressed the European Parliament on 6 July 1988, calling for a 'European government in one form or another [by 1995]' and predicting that 'In ten years' time [or by 1998] 80 per cent of economic legislation and perhaps even fiscal and social legislation will be of Community origins'.[69] Were this to materialise, Thatcher's notion of a Britain happy and glorious would no longer hold true, and she immediately claimed that Delors's prophecies were 'absurd' and that the man himself had 'gone over the top'. The *Daily Mail* wrote that in her rebuttal she was '[f]izzling with patriotic pep [as she] ridicules the European dream of its Commission President'.[70]

And so it was that on 20 September 1988 she stood in Bruges to deliver what would become her defining speech on Britain and Europe. She began provocatively, challenging what many politicians in the Six had believed since the 1950s and, indeed, what many British statesmen had ever so subtly given their consent to over the previous three decades: that 'Europe' and the Community were one and the same. Thatcher disagreed. 'Europe', she said, 'is not the creation of the Treaty of Rome. Nor is the European idea the property of any group or institution. We British are as much heirs to the legacy of European culture as any other nation. Our links to the rest of Europe, the continent of Europe, have been the dominant factor in our history'. From the three-hundred-year Roman occupation, through invasions of the Saxons, Danes and Normans, to the invitation from Parliament to the Dutchman William of Orange to take the British crown, Britons were incontrovertibly European and proud to be so. On this point, Thatcher was quite clear: 'Too often, the history of Europe is described as a series of interminable wars and quarrels. Yet from our perspective today surely what strikes us most is our common experience. For instance, the story of how Europeans explored and colonised – and yes, without apology – civilised much of the world is an extraordinary tale of talent, skill and courage'. The British had 'in a very special way contributed to Europe' by making certain that Europe did not fall 'under the dominance of a single power. We have fought and have died for her freedom'. The United Kingdom, perhaps more so than any continental power, was committed to Europe's future. Yet the future of Europe and the future of the European Community could not be confused. The European Community was '*one* manifestation of that European identity, but it is not the only one'. Britain's 'destiny' was 'in Europe, as part of the Community', but this was 'not to say that our future lies only in Europe. . . . The Community is not an end in itself'.

After thus establishing that the British were as European as any of their neighbours on the continent but that Britons did not see 'Europe' and 'the Community' as synonymous, Thatcher provided her vision for Europe. Looking to the future, it must be a community of 'independent sovereign states'. To try to 'suppress nationhood and concentrate power at the centre of a European conglomerate would be highly damaging. . . . Europe will be stronger precisely because it has France as France, Spain as Spain, Britain as Britain, each with its own customs, traditions and identity'. It would be folly, she said, 'to try to fit them into some sort of identikit European personality'. Thatcher also dismissed the suggestion that 'working more closely together' required 'power to be centralised in Brussels or decisions to be taken by an appointed bureaucracy'. Taking a swipe at Delors, she said, 'We have not successfully rolled back the frontiers of the state in Britain, only to see them re-imposed at a European level with a European super-state exercising a new dominance from Brussels'. Certainly, she insisted, 'we want to see Europe more united and with a greater sense of common purpose. But it must be in a way which preserves the different traditions, parliamentary powers and sense of national pride in one's own country'.

She concluded by laying out the 'British approach' to Europe: 'Utopia never comes, because we know we should not like it if it did. Let Europe be a family of nations, understanding each other better, appreciating each other more, doing more together but relishing our national identity no less than our common European endeavour. Let us have a Europe which plays its full part in the wider world, which looks outward not inward, and which preserves that Atlantic community – that Europe on both sides of the Atlantic – which is our noblest inheritance and our greatest strength'.[71] That noblest inheritance was, of course, the United States of America, thirteen European colonies that had risen up to lead the mother country. For Thatcher, the European heritage, Britain's imperial past, and its shared future with the United States were inseparable.

When the speech was drafted, it had not been without its critics in the UK. The Foreign Secretary Sir Geoffrey Howe, on reading an early draft, sent to the Prime Minister a note highlighting a number of sections of the speech which he believed contained 'plain and fundamental errors'. He was disturbed by the suggestion that we were 'more successful colonialists than any other European countries' (a reference that was later softened to instead praise European colonialism as a single, civilising contribution to the world). He recommended that she 'delete the reference to "forget a United States of Europe, it will not come"' (she did remove the offending phrase) and he chafed at her notion that the EEC did not require some adjustments of sovereignty: '[it] does, has and will require the sacrifice of political independence and the rights of national parliaments. That is inherent in the treaties'.[72] John Kerr, Assistant Under-Secretary at the Foreign Office, agreed that 'a good deal of the drafting seemed offbeam, and in some cases unnecessarily provocative'. He recommended that it would be 'counterproductive to make the speech so controversial as to guarantee that it evokes replies/rebuttals'.[73] The Foreign Office composed an alternative draft and sent it to Charles Powell, Thatcher's Private Secretary, in early September.

Powell incorporated some of the Foreign Office recommendations but kept its original feel, and reported that the Prime Minister was 'broadly content with it'.[74] Kerr told Patrick Wright, the Permanent Under-Secretary at the Foreign Office, that the new version 'buys some 80 per cent of [our] suggestions' and reported that it 'thus looks as if our damage limitation exercise is heading for success'. He then said, in what is perhaps one of the greatest misjudgments of recent British history, 'I don't think the Bruges speech is now likely to cause trouble with Community partners'. He even recommended that there was 'no need for you to trouble' the Foreign Secretary, who was travelling in Africa.[75] As a result, Howe did not read the revised draft of the speech, having last looked at it prior to providing his critique. It would have made little difference if he had, for No. 10 altered the speech again before it was delivered. The paper from which Thatcher read in Bruges had not been seen by any of her cabinet colleagues, nor by officials outside of 10 Downing Street.[76]

The speech caused an immediate splash. A letter writer to the *Daily Mail*, still a broadly pro-European newspaper, thanked Thatcher for 'having the courage to stick up for the British people' and for showing 'the true British spirit', one which would lead Britain to be 'as it always has been, firm, decisive and unique, a Britain we can be proud of'.[77] In contrast, the editorial board of the *Daily Telegraph* described it as an 'untimely offensive' and argued that the speech was 'based on the presumption that there is some deeper and more immediate threat to our sovereignty than the incautiously phrased remarks of a European civil servant [Delors]'. It concluded: 'Britain's special concerns and reservations about the degree of European integration that is either feasible or desirable could have been conveyed by a speech in which there was less "No, because" and more "Yes, but"'.[78]

Not all agreed with the editorial board, however. Simon Heffer, writing in that same newspaper, characterised the speech as Thatcher's 'most uncompromising declaration yet of her intention to defend British parliamentary sovereignty against the EEC bureaucracy'. He said her speech was 'certain to appeal to a large contingent of the Conservative party'.[79] Bruce Anderson agreed, writing that the speech '[rode] roughshod over Continental hypocrisy' and praised Margaret Thatcher's 'combination of Anglo-Saxon pragmatism and swipes with the Prime Ministerial handbag'. He recognised, however, that 'the Tory party's Euro-enthusiasts were upset by the speech'. Presciently, he asked, 'Could it be that either Mrs Thatcher's lack of support for the institutions of the European Community, or her successor's excessive willingness to accommodate them, will lead to the Tory party splitting over Europe, as it did on the Corn Laws and on free trade?' He hoped this would not be the case because the 'pro-Europeans' seemed to be distinctly out-of-step with much of the British public which, '[A]fter a decade and a half of hacking at the Brussels coalface, wrangling about budgets, sheepmeat regimes, and food mountains', had received a 'good antidote to idealism'. Finally, as so many others had done over the years, he brought the subject back to the legacy of empire and Britain's post-imperial present:

> The commitment of the original Europeans was forged in 1945, on the ruins of old Europe. In the immediate post-war years, even Churchill seemed prepared to pay a price in sovereignty to bring Europe together. Other younger Tories saw Europe as
> a replacement for Empire, and a means of rebutting Dean Acheson's charge (lost an empire, not found a role). Later, in the locust years of decline, when there seemed to be no domestic means of salvaging the British economy, many Tories saw Europe as the only hope. . . . But none of those impulses has much political resonance today. The dreams of an Empire substitute and the fears of economic collapse are both defunct. Most younger Tories are happy to be little Englanders, especially now that England does not seem so little.[80]

Following the speech, one European Foreign Minister commented in private to Heath that 'You British have gone back to where you were before 1950'.[81] Yet this analysis falls somewhat short of the mark. In 1950, the Labour Government was sceptical of entering the European Coal and Steel Community both because of its strong industrial position and, even more so, because of its continuing leadership of an still-expansive British Empire and Commonwealth. By 1988, that empire was long gone. In contrast to the rhetoric of Ernest Bevin, which were the words of an imperialist who could not imagine a day in which British imperialism was not a force in international affairs, Thatcher's Bruges speech was born from post-imperial longing for days past, a nostalgia that had grown with the 1982 victory in the South Atlantic and had been largely responsible for Thatcher's re-election in 1983. Writing after the Bruges speech, Heath expressed incredulity that 'any British Prime Minister could make a speech as hostile and ill-informed as the one Mrs Thatcher delivered in Bruges'.[82] Many nineteenth-century Liberals had uttered similar accusations against Disraeli.

Thatcher's Bruges speech fundamentally altered the way the Conservative Party responded to Europe, providing a new lease on life for the anti-Marketeers, who would shortly become known as

Eurosceptics – a semantic evolution that seemed to suggest they were opposed to more than simply a trading arrangement. Her attacks on European socialism also provided Neil Kinnock the ammunition he needed within the Labour Party to finally reject withdrawal from the EEC, instead skilfully arguing that rather than being an enemy to British social democracy, the European Community in fact provided an important safeguard against the rampant market capitalism of the Tory Party. As the Eurosceptic Labour MP Nigel Spearing wrote in the aftermath of Thatcher's Bruges Speech, 'if Labour warm to Commissioner Delors and the floor at Brighton [where the Conservative conference was being held] back the "Bruges line", then our two major parties might be seen to change places on their broad approaches to the EEC'.[83] In one of the more remarkable turnarounds of twentieth-century British political history, within just a few years the Labour Party would become committed to 'Europe' whilst the Conservatives would become a party ripped apart by ideological battle, a war between an aging contingent of pro-European MPs who were increasingly marginalised within Parliament and a much more vocal Eurosceptic core.

* * *

When her fall came, it was quick, as tends to be the case in Conservative politics. That is not to say there were no warning signs. Ever since Thatcher's Bruges Speech, there were whispers amongst the pro-European Tory 'wets' that it was finally time to stand up to her policies. P. G. Sharp, a Conservative Party agent and himself a Eurosceptic, confessed to Enoch Powell (still the confidant of many anti-European Conservatives) that he did not 'wish Joan of Arc's fate upon her. She faces a hard struggle inside the Conservative Party if she wishes to extricate us from Brussels' web'.[84] Powell replied that it was 'as yet early to know what may be the practical and political outcome of the Prime Minister's initiative at Bruges. It may result in a crystallization of what I believe is the general and growing public dislike of the consequences of our membership of the EEC'.[85]

The *Daily Mail* was more certain. Long a supporter of the Prime Minister, it now found her 'blurred vision of Britain's future ... profoundly worrying'. With her head, she recognised 'the compelling economic logic of the single market in Europe. But in her heart she cherishes "the Special Relationship" with America'. It was time to choose: 'Does our destiny lie with Europe or doesn't it? The *Daily Mail* is passionately convinced that in Europe and only in Europe will we continue to flourish and proper'. It closed with a warning for the Conservative government: 'We are in Europe. We have under the governance of Margaret Thatcher recovered from decades of decline. We have the strength to shape the Europe of tomorrow. We have the confidence to lead. How tragic if the woman who has brought us this far were now to fail. She can and must carry us on to greatness in Europe. For if she persists in wanting it both ways – betting on Europe, but banking on America – then, ere long, Britain could end up with the worst of both worlds: Cast adrift between two continental super powers, without a paddle'.[86]

It was not only in Bruges that Thatcher was causing controversy. In late 1985, the Westland Helicopter Company, the only UK company to manufacture helicopters, was on the brink of bankruptcy. The Westland Board of Directors looked to the American firm Sikorsky for a rescue package. When the Defence Secretary Michael Heseltine learned of the package, he began to lobby for a European rescue package instead, even persuading the National Armaments Directors (NADs) of France, West Germany, Italy and the UK to buy only European helicopters, thus ensuring that if Westland went with Sikorsky, it would receive no European orders. This violated the government's policy of nonintervention in the economy and enraged certain ministers, particularly Leon Brittan from the Department of Trade and Industry. Thatcher refused to support Heseltine's plan, and, on 13 December, the Westland Board rejected the European bid. Despite this, Heseltine continued to lobby the European cause, even writing to Lloyd's Bank to campaign against the Sikorsky bid. In public, he described the matter as 'Europe versus America' and made no secret of the fact that he believed Britain's future lay with the former, in stark contrast to the Prime Minister's vision of a stronger Anglo–American partnership.[87] Thatcher instructed the Solicitor-General Sir Patrick Mayhew to inform Heseltine that his letter to Lloyd's Bank contained 'material inaccuracies'. Mayhew's letter was leaked to the Press Association, completely undermining Heseltine's credibility. At a cabinet meeting on 8 January 1986, Thatcher ruled that all future statements on Westland had to be cleared at the cabinet level. Heseltine resigned on the spot, walking out of the meeting into the glare of the waiting press cameras outside. The scandal was not yet over, however, as Brittan was forced to admit that it was he who leaked the letter, giving Thatcher no choice but to accept his resignation on 24 January.[88]

The Westland Affair, as it came to be known, was quickly followed by the government's failure to sell British car manufacturer British Leyland to American company General Motors (GM). The sticking point for the House of Commons was that British Leyland owned Land Rover, which Tory MPs wanted to remain British-made and owned. When GM refused to buy British Leyland without Land Rover, the deal collapsed. Shortly thereafter, the government suffered its first parliamentary defeat, when sixty-eight Conservative MPs rebelled and voted against the Sunday Trading Bill. There followed on 8 May 1986 a by-election defeat by the Alliance in Ryedale and the reduction of the Conservative vote from 15,000 to just 100 in a second by-election in West Derbyshire.[89] Across the board, Thatcher's government was entering a general period of malaise.

The most difficult issue, however, was the Community Charge, better known as the 'Poll Tax'. This was intended to replace the local council rates (which were based on the value of property) with a tax operated on a per capita basis, with the local authorities setting the level for each region. This would mean that people rather than property would be taxed (at that time, it was estimated that only 12 million out of the 35 million people eligible to vote paid the full council rates, the majority receiving reductions or complete exemptions). Thatcher believed that the poll tax would encourage all people to have a stake in their community whilst simultaneously highlighting the high spending of Labour councils – put simply, those councils that spent more would have to level a higher Community Charge to pay their bills, a charge that would be felt by all constituents.[90] The Chancellor of the Exchequer Nigel Lawson immediately opposed the idea, circulating a memorandum to the cabinet on 16 May 1985 that argued that the poll tax would be 'politically unsustainable' as '[t]he biggest gainers would be better off households in high rateable value properties; the losers would be poorer households, particularly larger ones'. Providing evidence for his argument, he demonstrated that a 'pensioner couple in Inner London could find themselves paying 22 per cent of their net income in poll tax, whereas a better off couple in the suburbs would pay only 1 per cent'. This would be 'completely unworkable and politically catastrophic'. It could spell the end of the Conservative government in Britain.[91]

Lawson, however, was overruled. In 1986, Thatcher introduced the tax on a test basis in Scotland and, after the 1987 General Election, introduced a bill in Parliament to extend it to the rest of the United Kingdom. John Major, having been promoted to Chief Secretary to the Treasury, was intimately involved in its introduction. He later recalled, 'Within Cabinet, Nigel Lawson continued to oppose the whole idea, and to warn that the tax would be unworkable and politically catastrophic. Although I warmed to the intellectual rationale of the tax, I was persuaded by Nigel's warnings; and as chief secretary I was often deputed by him to argue the Treasury case in Cabinet committees'. Major had no more success than Lawson, however: 'Even when I thought I had won the argument, I lost the decision. Defeated on substance, I remained involved in practical questions of implementation'.[92] Consequently, in July 1988 – against the wishes of the Chancellor of the Exchequer and ministers and officials throughout the Treasury – the poll tax became law. In overruling Lawson, Thatcher had relied for her economic advice on Sir Alan Walters, whom she brought to 10 Downing Street as her economic adviser. It was well known that Walters 'undermin[ed] the Chancellor in private'. His 'contempt for Nigel was undisguised, and was a common topic of conversation in both the City and Fleet Street'.[93] Lawson's defeat on the issue of the poll tax was a humiliation, but it was not his first nor would it be his last.

It was with the controversy over the poll tax coming to boil and rapidly rising interest rates suggesting an economic storm was once again brewing in Britain that the European elections were held in June 1989. Falling as they did on the tenth anniversary of Thatcher's election, Neil Kinnock wisely used the elections as a referendum 'on Thatcherism in general and the Bruges approach in particular'.[94] He was able to do so because he had completely transformed the Labour Party from a Eurosceptic party that in 1983 had pledged to withdraw from the EEC to a party that sought to unite more closely with continental Europe in the hopes of forging a uniquely European ideology of social democracy, an ideology which could act as a check on the rampant free-market capitalism of Thatcher and Reagan.[95] In the 1989 Labour Party Policy Review, the party concluded that 'Britain's role in the world must be based on a realistic assessment of our interests and influence. Our empire is long gone. We can no longer challenge the might or the influence of the superpowers'. Europe was the one area where British influence might be retained, and the report concluded that 'Some 60 per cent of Britain's trade is with our Community partners. We could not now withdraw without great damage to our economy'.[96] In the aftermath of the Policy Review, Nigel Spearing lamented that 'the new leadership of the Labour Party has appeared to be back pedalling fast [from the 1983 General Election promise of withdrawal] into toleration and active co-operation. There is thus a distinct likelihood that in the June Euro-elections Labour will be perceived as the "pro-European" grouping, whilst Mrs Thatcher in her Bruges costume will be projected as "sticking up for British interests"'.[97]

When the European election campaign began, it quickly became clear that Kinnock's strategy of portraying the Labour Party as no more hostile to Europe than the Conservatives and using the election as a general referendum on Thatcher's ten years in office was a successful one. During a press conference on 14 June, Thatcher struggled to keep the conversation on European policy, repeatedly having to pledge her support for the Chancellor of the Exchequer. In particular, Thatcher was asked, 'If you say that your policies and the Chancellor's policies are indivisible, and you are both in love with each other on the economy, why do you need Professor [Alan] Walters? ... He is pinpointed as the cause of the differences between you and No 11'. Thatcher dismissed such charges as 'absolute nonsense', yet the rumours of a falling out between herself and Lawson dogged the rest of the campaign, taking their inevitable toll on the Conservative message.[98]

When the results were released on 16 June, the Labour Party had overtaken the Conservatives in the European Parliament, winning forty-five seats to the Tories' thirty-two.[99] Four months later, Lawson became the first of Thatcher's cabinet to resign in protest at her policies, writing in his resignation letter that 'The successful conduct of economic policy is possible only if there is, and is seen to be, full agreement between the Prime Minister and the Chancellor of the Exchequer. Recent events have confirmed that this essential requirement cannot be satisfied so long as Alan Walters remains your personal economic adviser'.[100] Lawson's resignation caused an immediate bout of soul-searching within the Conservative Party, and, in November 1989, Sir Anthony Meyer decided to mount a leadership challenge. Meyer was a known pro-Europeanist, having served as a diplomat in the British Embassy in Paris from 1951 to 1956 before working at the Foreign Office on Britain's approach to the Common Market from 1958 to 1962. In 1962, he had resigned from diplomatic service to work for Gladwyn Jebb's Common Market Campaign and in 1964 entered Parliament as a Conservative MP.[101] It was Thatcher's stance on

Europe more than Lawson's resignation that caused him to mount a challenge, and, although he was defeated by 314 votes to 33, the contest revealed 'a certain amount of discontent'.[102]

On 6 December, the morning after the leadership challenge, the Conservative MPs George Younger, Ian Gow, Richard Ryder, Mark Lennox-Boyd, Tristan Garel-Jones and Gerry Neale (who had formed Thatcher's campaign team) met for a 'post mortem meeting'. Gow argued that 'Quite a number of people voted for the Prime Minister with considerable reluctance.... We would be mistaken if we thought that there was enthusiasm from everybody who voted for Mrs Thatcher'. The main issues for unease, he said, were Thatcher's leadership style (which he did not think could be changed), Europe and, finally, 'mistakes as far as the economy is concerned'. Garel-Jones agreed that style, Europe and the economy were the three main issues, noting that 'She is in a minority of the Party on Europe.... Her tone is very important. Somehow we have to find a role of leadership for her and Britain in the Community. This may mean using Chequers at the weekend to entertain potential allies in Europe. Young people are important here because young people believe we are the Party of Europe'. He added, in a remarkably candid moment, 'We are talking about the beginning of the end of the Thatcher Era. We have to try and ensure that that is managed in a way that enables her to go to the end of her Prime Ministership with dignity and honour'.[103]

In the end, it was the European issue rather than the economy or her style that brought about her downfall. In early 1989, the Hungarian government dismantled the barbed wire at the 'Iron Curtain' border with Austria, intended as a symbolic gesture of a gradually liberalising attitude towards the West. In an unintended consequence, however, East German holiday-makers in Hungary began to abandon their cars and belongings and walk across the open fields to Austria and the West, avoiding the official (and still-manned) border crossings. By August, 5,000 had done so. For 'humanitarian reasons' the Hungarian government therefore officially opened the border on 11 September. In the following three days alone, 15,000 East Germans left the German Democratic Republic, prompting the East German government to cancel permission for any of its citizens to visit Hungary. Following mass protests, on 9 November, the East German Politburo decided to lift the travel restrictions. When asked by a British journalist if this meant that East Germans could now cross the Berlin Wall into West Berlin, one

East German official replied 'yes'. This led to a spontaneous surge of people at the Berlin Wall, producing the now famous images of East and West Berliners chiselling the wall down inch by inch.[104]

The British Prime Minister declared that it was 'a great day for freedom'.[105] When the gathered press corps in 10 Downing Street began to question her about the implications of the wall's fall, particularly if it would lead to German reunification, Thatcher was less enthusiastic. 'You are going much too fast, much too fast', she chastised one journalist. 'The task now is to build a genuine democracy in East Germany'. When pressed again on her views on possible reunification, she insisted that the primary focus must be on building a 'proper, genuine democracy, a multi-party democracy, in East Germany', which would 'keep people rebuilding East Germany and staying there'. Asked a third time what a possible German reunification could mean for the future of NATO, she snapped, 'NATO is still vital'. Then, forestalling further questioning, she said: 'May I say this to you: had America stayed in Europe after the First World War and we had had a NATO then, I do not believe we should have had a Second World War. Let us learn that lesson! Thank you very much! Sorry it is raining!'[106] And with that, she stepped out of the drizzle into the offices of No. 10.

The events in Berlin that morning continued to dominate British foreign policy for the next eight months, until Saddam Hussein's invasion of Kuwait. Thatcher's first order of business was to telephone Kohl, who also had on his agenda calls with American President George H. W. Bush, French President François Mitterrand and the Soviet leader Mikhail Gorbachev. She succeeded in becoming the first foreign head of government to speak with him and immediately agreed to his request for a half-day special meeting of the twelve heads of government of the European Community.[107] Yet Thatcher's vision of what this meeting should entail differed greatly from Kohl's. Within a week of the East–West border being opened for free travel, Thatcher ordered her cabinet to present a more staid view on events in Germany, and, on 16 November, she instructed Foreign Secretary Douglas Hurd – in Berlin on a fact-finding mission – to announce before the Brandenburg Gate that the issue of German reunification was 'not immediate'.[108]

Thatcher also wrote to Gorbachev, ensuring that a copy of her letter was leaked to the West German foreign office, informing the Soviet president that a hasty reunification could lead to 'risky instability'; consequently, 'ordered steps for the maintenance of stability and prudence are necessary'. In this letter, she cleverly referenced her telephone conversation with Kohl, stating that she and the West German Chancellor were in agreement that the 'most solid foundation' for stability lay in political and economic reforms within East Germany, that Kohl and she believed 'destabilization must be avoided' and that 'Nobody in the West has the intention of interfering in the internal affairs of the GDR [German Democratic Republic] or endangering the security interests of the GDR or the Soviet Union'.[109] Having outlined their purported agreement on a steady approach, Thatcher was then able to express surprise when, on 28 November, the West German Chancellor unveiled a ten-point plan that would lead to the reunification of Germany.[110] She warned the sixteen NATO heads of government against a timetable for reunification, stressing that the stability of NATO and the European Community had to take precedence over what she saw as a symbolic and potentially dangerous gesture.[111] At a meeting of the European Council on 8 December, in the presence of Helmut Kohl, she then loudly informed the other European heads of government that 'We beat the Germans twice, and now they're back'.[112] If it were not so tragically mistaken in sentiment, it would have been funny, mimicking as it did the English football chant that still reverberates around stadiums whenever England plays Germany: 'Two world wars and one world cup'.[113]

Thatcher was not alone in her concerns about German reunification. On 20 January 1990, she met with French President Mitterrand for lunch at the Elysée Palace in Paris, together with her chief foreign policy advisor Charles Powell and the French diplomatic advisor Loic Hennekinne. In a letter written later that day from Powell to Stephen Wall, private secretary to the Foreign Secretary, Powell noted that the 'whole discussion was about German reunification and European security'. According to Powell, Thatcher accused West Germany of 'constantly pressing forward towards reunification', of using arguments for reunification that were 'not very convincing', and of assuming that they could 'bring East Germany into the European Community'. Thatcher claimed that East Germany was 'close to collapse' and reasserted her contention that the economic stability of the European Community had to trump sentimental notions of a united Germany. Mitterrand was blunter. As Powell related to Wall: 'Mitterrand agreed that German reunification was a central theme for both Britain and France. The sudden prospect of reunification had delivered a sort of mental shock to the Germans. Its effect had been to turn them once again into the "bad" Germans they used to be. They were behaving with a certain brutality and concentrating on reunification to the exclusion of everything else. It was difficult to maintain good relations with them in this sort of mood'. He added that Mitterrand 'did not think Europe was yet ready for German reunification: and he certainly could not accept that it had to take priority over everything else'.

With the prospect of a reunified German raising the spectre of 'bad Germans' once again, Mitterrand and Thatcher fell back into the language and assumptions of the Second World War. Mitterrand suggested that 'some of the demonstrations in East Germany in favour of reunification had been encouraged by West German "agents", who had provided the banners and other material calling for reunification'. He recommended that Thatcher and he approach Gorbachev to try to 'persuade the Soviet Union to stiffen East German resistance to reunification'. Thatcher assured him that Britain and France would 'stand together on this'.[114] Following this meeting, Thatcher launched what amounted to a propaganda campaign against German reunification. In an interview with the *Wall Street Journal* in late January 1990, she openly criticised Kohl, stating that he should 'subordinate [his] narrow nationalistic goals to the longer-term needs of Europe'. She declared that a united Germany would 'destroy the economic equilibrium of the EC, in which West Germany already predominates' and would undermine Gorbachev, which would be 'a catastrophe for all'.[115] Horst Teltschik, Kohl's foreign policy adviser, described in his diary that the West German Chancellor was 'astonished by this public criticism'.[116] Thatcher did not stop there, however. She suggested to other European leaders that there be a five-year transitional period with two German states, during which time East Germany could slowly be raised to the economic level of West Germany. On 2 February, she circulated an internal memo to her cabinet suggesting that 'The problems will not be overcome by strengthening the EC', which would only lead to 'Germany's ambitions' becoming the 'dominant and active factor'.[117]

Nevertheless, as the days of February passed into March, German reunification became more and more likely, and President Mitterrand issued a statement of contingent support. Thatcher, too, reluctantly informed the House of Commons that the reunification of Germany was 'probable'. Charles Powell tried to soften Thatcher's reputation, holding a three-hour conversation with Teltschik. In what is perhaps the most complete commentary on Thatcher's mind at this time, Powell explained that she belonged to a 'different generation' from he and Teltschik, one which was 'still marked by the time when there was a "cultural gap" between Great Britain and Germany'. He noted that Thatcher was very 'uneasy at the thought of a big strong Germany' and that for her the Soviet Union had to be consulted at every stage of a possible unification. NATO had to be preserved with a united Germany within it, and the financial stability of the European Community had to be safeguarded. Thatcher's absolute opposition to reunification was wavering, but she was adamant that it be done in a way that would preserve Western security, German democracy and European capitalism.[118] This point she had made to Helmut Kohl himself on 24 February, telling him for the first time that she accepted reunification but only under certain conditions.[119]

In late March, Thatcher instructed Powell to organise a meeting of academics and politicians at Chequers to discuss what she called 'the German problem'. In a memorandum sent on 19 March to all participants, Powell explained that Thatcher's objective was 'to use our knowledge and experience of Germany's past to help shape our policy towards Germany and Europe for the future'. Powell suggested that the participants use the first part of the meeting to explore 'Germany's past and the lessons to be learned from it' and the second part of the meeting to address 'wider questions about Germany's future role in Europe'. In particular, he wanted to know 'what does history tell us about the character and behaviour of the German-speaking people of Europe?'; 'have the Germans changed in the last 40 years (or 80 or 150 years), either as a result of some mutation in their national character or because of changes in their external environment?'; and 'in the light of history, how can we "satisfy" the Germans? Is there something they want and we can give them, which will neutralise their drive to extend their sway, whether politically or territorially?'[120]

In addressing the questions, the participants concluded that the German national characteristic was best distinguished by 'their insensitivity to the feelings of others (most noticeable in their behaviour over the Polish border), their obsession with themselves, a strong inclination to self-pity, and a longing to be liked. Some even less flattering attributes were also mentioned as an abiding part of the German character: in alphabetical order, angst, aggressiveness, assertiveness, bullying, egotism, inferiority complex, sentimentality'. The participants admitted that 'today's Germans were very different from their predecessors' but nevertheless questioned 'how a cultured and cultivated nation had allowed itself to be brain-washed into barbarism. If it had happened once, could it not happen again?' With regards to reunification, the participants argued that 'Germans would not necessarily think more dangerously, but they would think differently. There was already evident a kind of triumphalism in German thinking and attitudes which would be uncomfortable for the rest of us'. Given this, it would be better to try to keep the Germans 'on-side' than marginalise them. As Powell summarised in a report of the meeting: 'The overall message was unmistakable: we should be nice to the Germans'.[121]

Having received this advice, Thatcher arranged her first one-on-one meeting with Kohl in 10 Downing Street since the fall of the wall. The West German Chancellor assured the Prime Minister that he was 'not prepared to pay any price for the unity of Germany' and insisted that a united Germany would remain within NATO and the European Community. The meeting went a considerable distance to thawing relations between the British and West German governments, and, at the press conference following, Kohl pronounced that 'Margaret is a wonderful woman'. Horst Teltschik, present at the meeting, had a more guarded impression. He noted in his diary: 'As always, she was an impressive and stimulating, if difficult, partner in talks. Margaret Thatcher knows what she wants, holds to her positions fearlessly, and shows little consideration for the possible sensitivities of her interlocutor. . . . The famous saying applies to her: England knows neither friends nor enemies, England knows only its interests'.[122]

From that point forward, Thatcher began to recognise – grudgingly – that Britain's interests lay in supporting rather than opposing German reunification, if only to ensure that it occurred within the context of NATO and the European Community. At a series of meetings in April with American President Bush, Thatcher even argued that a united Germany ought to be given immediate and full membership of 'the North Atlantic Alliance, the American conventional and nuclear presence in Europe, and the future strategy of the alliance'. This she repeated to Kohl on 20 April as a 'gesture of good will'.[123] She thereafter worked tirelessly with Bush, Kohl and Mitterrand to ensure Soviet agreement that a united Germany would enter NATO, which Gorbachev conceded on 17 July.[124] Less than three months later, on 3 October 1990, West and East Germany became one and automatically entered both NATO and the European Community. It was one of the more remarkable political transitions of the twentieth century.

For Thatcher, however, the legacy of her initial hostility towards German reunification and her instinctive Euroscepticism was too much for many of her cabinet colleagues to bear. They had been horrified by her behaviour and the conclusions reached at the Chequers summit and embarrassed by the tone that was emanating from the Prime Minister in the name of all Britons. On October 31 1990, she provided the final straw, saying in a House of Commons debate, 'The President of the Commission, Mr Delors, said at a press conference the other day that he wanted the European Parliament to be a democratic body of the Community, he wanted the Commission to be the Executive and he wanted the Council of Ministers to be the Senate. No. No. No'.[125] John Major, now sitting beside her as the Chancellor of the Exchequer, 'nearly fell off the bench'.[126] The very next day, Sir Geoffrey Howe, the Leader of the House of Commons, Lord President and Deputy Prime Minister (who Thatcher had dismissed from the Foreign Office in July 1989 for his refusal to agree with her position on Europe), resigned, claiming that he felt his 'presence was no longer restraining her dangerous anti-Europeanism'.[127]

Howe's letter of resignation focussed entirely on the European issue. His vision for Europe, he wrote, had always been 'practical and hard-headed. I am not a Euro-idealist or federalist. My concern is less with grand schemes than with immediate realities'. Yet those immediate realities demanded British involvement in Europe. Too much British energy over the past decade had been 'devoted to correcting the consequences of our late start in Europe. It would be a tragedy, not just for our financial institutions and our industrial strength, but also for the aspirations of a younger generation, if we were to risk making the same mistake again'. He was 'deeply anxious' that the 'mood you have struck ... will make it more difficult for Britain to hold and retain a position of influence in this vital debate'.[128] When, on 13 November, Howe gave his resignation speech in the House of Commons, he told his parliamentary colleagues: 'The tragedy is ... that the Prime minister's perceived attitude towards Europe is running increasingly serious risks for the future of our nation. ... We have paid heavily in the past for late starts and squandered opportunities in Europe. We dare not let that happen again'.[129] He closed, saying, 'The time has come for others to consider their own response to the tragic conflict of loyalties with which I have myself wrestled for perhaps too long'.[130]

Howe's resignation speech made it all but certain that Thatcher would face another leadership challenge, and one which would have considerably more open support than the failed attempt by Meyer a year earlier.[131] It came sooner than most expected. The morning after Howe's speech, Michael Heseltine announced that he would be challenging Thatcher for the leadership of the Conservative Party.[132] He was immediately supported by both Lawson and Howe.[133] Like Howe, Heseltine was driven by his disagreements with the Prime Minister over Europe, later writing that Thatcher 'divided the Tory Party [over Europe] and unleashed the hounds that were to eat away at the vitals of party unity'. For Heseltine, Thatcher had opened a schism in the party by shifting it from being a united 'party of Europe' to one plagued with Eurosceptics. This was, in his mind, a dangerous trend and not one conducive to Britain playing a prominent role on the world stage. It was, indeed, a shift that would bring the party close to collapse and lead directly to an internecine civil war throughout the 1990s and its thirteen years in the political wilderness from 1997 to 2010.[134]

In the first round of voting on 20 November, Thatcher defeated Heseltine by 204 votes to 152 with sixteen abstentions. Under Tory Party rules, however, this was not enough to avoid a second ballot – she had fallen two votes shy.[135] After consultation with her cabinet colleagues, whose hesitation in supporting her was obvious, the Prime Minister decided to withdraw her name from the second ballot and resign as Prime Minister. Margaret Thatcher's reign was over.[136] In the second ballot, Douglas Hurd threw his name into the hat, claiming – as Heseltine had done – that Thatcher's views on Europe were 'deeply mistaken'. He later described how, as Foreign Secretary from 1989 onwards, he had listened to 'outbursts of her anxiety and irritation', particularly about Germany and its reunification.[137] John Major decided to do so likewise. In his memoirs, he wrote that although he had always publicly supported Thatcher, 'was pleased to serve in her government and defended her with conviction when criticisms were brought', in private he was 'uneasy' about her 'crude anti-Europeanism'.[138] Although he dispelled it as a 'myth' that 'she was brought down by a cabal of pro-European "wets"', he acknowledged that her 'gut reaction was much more hostile to Europe' than his.[139] In words that would make even her most fervent critics blush, he described her as 'like a shorting circuit [which] flickered and crackled. Intermittently the lamp of European statesmanship still glowed; then – fssst! – and a shower of vivid commentary would light up the Margaret who attracted the last-ditch Englander'.[140]

When the results of the second ballot were announced on 26 November, Major had secured 185 votes, Heseltine 131 and Hurd 56. Like Thatcher, he had fallen two votes short of being declared an outright winner. However, Heseltine and Hurd immediately announced that they would not stand in a third ballot, instead pledging their support to Major. With their announcements, John Major won the Prime Ministership, just thirteen days after Howe's speech to the House of Commons that had precipitated Thatcher's fall. That evening, he was cheered by Conservative members in Parliament, given champagne by his opponent Michael Heseltine and had his hand shaken by Neil Kinnock, the Labour leader who was gunning for his job. It was one of those rare moments in the House of Commons when all present, regardless of partisan divide, had only goodwill to dispense. Only Margaret Thatcher, in the dying hours of her premiership, dampened the mood, telling the baying press, 'I shan't be pulling the levers there, but I shall be a very good back-seat driver'.[141] In this, she had every intention of keeping her word.

* * *

If pro-European Conservatives had been wary of the 'tone' of Margaret Thatcher, they received a welcome surprise with John Major. Softspoken, polite to a fault and unassuming, he was in many ways the antithesis of his predecessor, the accountant rather than the demagogue, one who tended to act out of pragmatism rather than conviction, in search of consensus rather than conflict. As Chancellor of the Exchequer, he had persuaded Thatcher to finally give Britain's assent to join the European Exchange Rate Mechanism (ERM), which she did on 5 October 1990, only weeks before the resignation of Sir Geoffrey Howe and her own demise.[142] Speaking in Bonn in March 1991, Major claimed that Britain's place was to be 'at the very heart of Europe'.[143]

These were more than just words for Major, and he developed a very different relationship with his European colleagues than Thatcher had managed. He found Delors to be 'an able and sensitive man, if sometimes a little prickly'.[144] He and Kohl became 'firm friends and, on occasion, allies'. In contrast to the anti-German instincts of Thatcher, which had blinded her to Kohl's good intentions, Major described the German Chancellor as a man who 'had a ripe sense of humour and a deep interest in British politics' and who 'admired Winston Churchill and often spoke of him with great warmth'.[145] Mitterrand was an 'erudite student of history' with a 'formidable knowledge of Britain'.[146] Thatcher had held an instinctive hostility to continental European leaders. Major believed that 'With friendship and understanding can come a measure of trust that helps to make the world safer. It is cynical to believe that personal chemistry between leaders counts for nothing when the chips are down; only national interest counts. I don't agree'.[147] He also recognised that 'getting your way in Europe was a specialised affair. It had its own natural rhythms. It was better to play by club rules. Britain needed to raise its voice from within the charmed circle'.[148] This was not a view held by the previous government.

Upon leaving office, Thatcher's Euroscepticism only deepened. When Major announced in Bonn that Britain's place was to be 'at the very heart of Europe', Thatcher wrote that this was 'a plain impossibility in more than merely the geographical sense, since our traditions and interests diverged sharply in many areas from those of our Continental neighbours'.[149] Giving her first major public address since leaving 10 Downing Street, she released a shot across the bow of Major's government: 'A democratic Europe of nation states could be a force for liberty, enterprise and open trade. But, if creating a United States of Europe overrides these goals, the new Europe will be one of subsidy and protection'.[150] She then took a very symbolic step in opposition to Major's new policy of engagement, accepting the chair of the Bruges Group ('a ginger group hostile to many European developments') and the Conservative No Turning Back Group (also committed to the cause of Euroscepticism).[151]

Many agreed with her stance. Some even continued to refer back to the Commonwealth as a reason for their opposition to Europe, one voter writing in November 1991 that 'culturally and emotionally, we are not of one mind with Europe and are unlikely to ever be so. . . . I believe that in the ultimate choice it is best to do things that support Britain and our close friends, not things that support friends of occasional convenience'. He continued, 'I believe our closest ties are with America and the Commonwealth countries. My family has lived for 17 years in New Zealand and I was amazed at the closeness and goodwill from them to us. . . . It is the common heritage of the bulk of the population that creates this common set of free goals. I am afraid that Europe does not enjoy this heritage and never will'.[152]

Even so, the catalyst for many Eurosceptics was the proposed Treaty of European Union, better known as the Maastricht Treaty. At the Rome Summit of October 1990, European leaders had called for an intergovernmental conference on monetary and political union, to be held at Maastricht in December 1991.[153] Throughout the summer of 1991, following Major's 'heart of Europe' speech, Conservatives voiced unease about 'Europe'. Norman Tebbit in particular offered 'frequent advice in public and with maximum publicity', and '[e]very whisper from Margaret Thatcher' was being 'passed on to the waiting media. . . . She was invariably hostile to the single currency and the spectre of federalism, and her views continued to trigger a response from different factions of the party'.[154] Much of the hostility was mere grandstanding, however, and few MPs were yet prepared to defy their leader, given how few months he had been in No. 10. Consequently, when, on 20 November, Major held a Commons debate laying out the government's negotiating objectives at Maastricht – 'No federalism. No commitment to a single currency. No Social Chapter. No Community competence on foreign or home affairs or defence' – he received a majority of 101 in support of his position, with only six Conservative MPs voting against.[155]

Major travelled to Maastricht on 5 December, along with his Foreign Secretary Douglas Hurd and the Chancellor of the Exchequer Norman Lamont. However, the start of the conference was overshadowed when, on its eve, President Yeltsin of Russia, President Kravchuk of Ukraine and Mr Shushkevich of Byelorussia announced that they were creating the Commonwealth of Independent States (CIS) and that 'the USSR ceases to exist'. The Soviet Union was now dead, and the future Europe – particularly its Eastern half – was very much in doubt.[156] It was against this background that the Maastricht negotiations took place and that Major achieved what was arguably his greatest success in European policy during the seven years of his premiership. Over the course of two long days of negotiation (the second technically running into a third, with discussions only coming to a close at 1:30 a.m.), Major secured for Britain the freedom to decide whether or not to join a European common currency, the right to determine its own foreign and defence policy, an exemption from the European Social

Charter (which would be binding on the other eleven members), an elimination of the words 'federal vocation' to describe the work of the Community, and the power to determine its own immigration policy.[157] The Prime Minister had achieved all that he had promised Parliament. It was, as Stephen Wall has written, a 'serious success for John Major'.[158]

In Britain, the press was 'ecstatic'. *The Times* headlined its Wednesday edition with 'Major wins all he asks for at Maastricht', the *Daily Telegraph* reported that Major had taken Britain '[o]ut of the summit and into the light' and the *Economist* proclaimed that it was 'the deal Tory ministers and most backbenchers had been praying for'.[159] Major later recalled how when he made his statement in the House of Commons announcing the results, he was 'received with acclaim and the waving of order papers. In Cabinet all was sweetness and light, with Ken Baker particularly effusive. Douglas Hurd and Norman Lamont were received rapturously at meetings of Conservative backbenchers. It was the modern equivalent of a Roman triumph'.[160] When Parliament voted on the Treaty on 19 December 1991, only seven Conservatives rebelled and just three abstained.[161]

Forty-six years after Churchill had first called for a United States of Europe, the United Kingdom became a fully fledged member of the European Union. Just five years later, on 1 July 1997, the Union Flag was lowered for the last time over Hong Kong, which was reverting back to Chinese control following a deal struck by Thatcher in 1984. The historian Peter Clarke has written that with the lowering of the flag, 'Britain's dominion over palm and pine was reduced to a scattering of remote islands and rocky outposts'.[162] On that rainy evening in Hong Kong, the British Empire died its final death. As the *Evening Standard* proclaimed on its front page, 'It's All Over'.[163] Little did John Major know it in 1992, but the same could be said of Tory support for his European policies. When he was re-elected in the General Election of April 1992, the Conservative manifesto proudly proclaimed that 'The Conservatives have been the party of Britain in Europe for 30 years. . . . We have ensured that Britain is at the heart of Europe, a strong and respected partner'.[164] By the time of his defeat by the New Labour leader Tony Blair five years later, Britain had become a post-imperial, Eurosceptic nation. It is a legacy that endures to this day.

CONCLUSION: POST-IMPERIAL BRITAIN AND THE RISE OF EUROSCEPTICISM

'[M]ost of the problems the world has faced have come, in one fashion or another, from mainland Europe, and the solutions from outside it'. So proclaimed Lady Thatcher in 2002, writing in what was to become her last major intervention in public life, her book *Statecraft*. After tackling first the legacy of the Cold War, the rise of Asia and the tumult in the Middle East and Balkans, she turned to European 'Dreams and Nightmares'. It was, she said, 'the resolve of Britain, of the Commonwealth and, decisively, of America' that had restored sanity to the European continent, although some Europeans had 'resented it ever since'. She recommended against seeking solutions for the continent's problems, as 'Europe as a whole is fundamentally unreformable'.[1] It was far better to work around Europe. Finally, saving her strongest words for the conclusion, she wrote: '[T]he United States was based from its inception on a common language, culture and values – Europe has none of these things. ... "Europe" is the result of *plans*. It is, in fact, a classic utopian project, a monument to the vanity of intellectuals, a programme whose inevitable destiny is failure'.[2]

In the immediate aftermath of John Major's coming to power, Thatcher had been vocal – if somewhat cautious – about publicly criticising his European policy, on the one hand making known her displeasure but on the other not wishing to undermine his position in the way Heath had sought to undermine hers twenty years' earlier. The Conservative General Election victory in April 1992 'liberated' Thatcher to be far more assertive, no longer concerned that her comments might undermine the Prime Minister to the extent that she would risk allowing a Labour government under the stewardship of Neil Kinnock to come to power. Major himself seemed to sense this. After being congratulated by his private secretary Stephen Wall on winning his own mandate, the Prime Minister replied, 'You wait. This is where my troubles really begin'.[3]

Delivering an address at the Hague on 15 May 1992, only weeks after the election, Thatcher spoke with an unabashed Euroscepticism that was quite distinct from when she had been in government. Sarcastically referring to 'the vision of New European Man walking purposefully towards the Common Agricultural Policy', she said in strong terms: 'Our choice is clear. Either we exercise democratic control of Europe through cooperation between national governments and parliaments which have legitimacy, experience and closeness to the people. Or we transfer decisions to a remote multilingual parliament, accountable to no real European public opinion and thus increasingly subordinate to a powerful bureaucracy'. For Thatcher, it was clear that Maastricht was a bridge too far on the road to Europe.[4] That the former Prime Minister chose to include this speech as the only appendix (other than a political chronology) in her memoirs speaks volumes about how she perceived its importance. The House of Commons voted on the second reading of the Maastricht Bill six days later. This time, the number of Conservative rebels voting against had risen to twenty-four.[5] Given that the Tory majority in Parliament had been slashed at the General Election from 100 to only 21, this made Major reliant on the votes of Liberal Democrats and Labour MPs to pass his European policy.[6] On the eve of the vote, Thatcher published an article in *The European* arguing that 'Real progress comes not from more bureaucracy, but from the values and institutions of government by consent, through ministers seen to be accountable. These things are in tune with the instincts of the people. They are part of the heritage we have built up over the centuries'. It was no coincidence that, following this reference to British heritage, she chose to end her piece quoting lines from that bard of empire, Rudyard Kipling.[7]

Thatcher was not the only Conservative to have serious doubts about Maastricht. One voter told Enoch Powell that 'As a Tory I am very angry that the British government has agreed to the Maastricht Treaty ... without even the promise of a referendum'. He argued that there should be a new Eurosceptic party and that 'All those MPs, especially those Conservatives in critical marginal seats, must know if they vote for the Maastricht Treaty then they will be challenged by alternative [Eurosceptic] Tory and Unionist candidates'. He added, 'In the absence of a referendum many Tories are waiting to support such an endeavour'.[8] Another voter told Powell that the Maastricht Treaty had 'prompted my resignation from the Conservative Party'. He was now going to 'direct my efforts' into grass-roots campaigning with explicitly Eurosceptic organisations.[9] The chairman of the Central Suffolk Conservative Association reported in August 1992 that 'Strong reservations about our entanglement with Europe are now being expressed on every side – both deeply and earnestly and I think cracks are now appearing in the vast edifice'.[10] And the *Daily Mail* – which since the Maastricht negotiations had become noticeably cooler towards Europe – claimed that the Foreign Secretary Douglas Hurd 'look[ed] forward to [an] alternative vision of a wider association of European nations, enjoying a free market in goods and services and capital'.[11]

The situation became graver still when, on 16 September 1992, the United Kingdom crashed out of the European Exchange Rate Mechanism (ERM) less than two years after entering. When Britain joined, the government had done so largely for political rather than economic reasons. The timing was thus not advantageous for sterling, pegged at DM 2.95 (which translated to over $1.90 at times).[12] Under the mechanism, if the pound fell to the bottom of its permitted range (DM 2.773), the government would be required to intervene to prop it up. Over the summer of 1992, the pound began to fall, prompting the Chancellor of the Exchequer to raise interest rates to 10 per cent and spend billions of foreign currency buying sterling that was being sold on the currency markets. On 13 September (a Sunday), the Italian Prime Minister Giuliano Amato telephoned Major at the Queen's Balmoral Estate in Scotland to inform him that the Italian government planned to devalue the lira. The following day, the German Bundesbank cut German interest rates, the first reduction in five years. Each of these events had a negative effect on the value of sterling, which dropped still further, and, on the morning of 16 September – a day which later came to be known as 'Black Wednesday' – Major awoke to find there had been a massive sell-off of sterling. At 11.00 a.m., the Bank of England raised interest rates from 10 to 12 per cent but to no avail. A few hours later, it again raised the rate to 15 per cent, yet still the pound continued to be sold. Consequently, at 7.30 that evening Norman Lamont announced the suspension of Britain's membership of the ERM.[13]

The events of 'Black Wednesday' only confirmed for Eurosceptics that Europe was the cause of Britain's downfall. On the morning after the crash, Max Hastings, the editor of the *Daily Telegraph*, chose to follow the instincts of some of his colleagues at the newspaper and migrate the editorial opinion from supporting the government's 'middle-of-the-road European policy' to instead becoming an actively Eurosceptic newspaper, a journey soon followed by the *Daily Mail*.[14] That day – 17 September – Major drafted a resignation statement but Stephen Wall refused to read it and Major's sister, brother and cabinet colleagues persuaded him to stay (commenting on this, Wall simply says, 'I argued with him then that he should stay and, for what contribution I made to his decision to do so, I am glad that I did';[15] Major remembers it slightly differently: 'Only after I had left Number 10 did he [Wall] tell me that had he agreed [to read the letter], he would have been drawn into textual analysis that would have reinforced the likelihood of my going'[16]). Others were not so kind. Writing only weeks after 'Black Wednesday', Thatcher expressed her pleasure at British withdrawal from the ERM and directly linked it to the Maastricht Treaty, saying, 'The first [the ERM] is a prerequisite to the second. We found the confines of the first unbearable; the strait-jacket of the second would be ruinous'. Then, as so often before, she looked back to a time of British greatness: 'The Conservative Party needs to be united, not torn apart. Britain needs to regain the confidence that we can manage our own affairs successfully once more'.[17]

Meanwhile, in a referendum on 2 June 1992, the Danish electorate rejected the Maastricht Treaty. Given that the treaty had to be ratified unanimously by Community members, this meant that it could now come into force only if the Danes held a second referendum to approve the treaty. This vote corresponded with Britain taking the presidency of the Council of Ministers of the European Community, its chief responsibility being to ensure the treaty's successful ratification. As Major later wrote, 'Not since the heyday of the Vikings had the Danes precipitated such disruption'.[18] The government immediately delayed the committee stage of the bill in Westminster until the intentions of the Danes could be assessed. The consequence was that the issue was 'kicked into the long grass' and, in the Prime Minister's words, 'the virus of Euro-scepticism infected much fresh tissue'.[19] Before the month was out, sixty-nine Tory MPs had signed an Early Day Motion calling for the government to adopt a new approach to Europe. It was on the heels of this motion that the events of 'Black Wednesday' occurred, turning 'a quarter of a century of unease into a flat rejection of any wider involvement in Europe. Many Conservatives threw logic to one side; emotional rivers burst their banks'.[20] As Thatcher said, 'Britain must resist.... Britain was not like other European nations. Britain had won the war'.[21]

Four days after 'Black Wednesday', the French also held a referendum on ratification, which passed with a bare majority, thus relieving some of the pressure from Major's shoulders. For his part, the Prime Minister was 'determined to enact the Treaty. I had given my word on behalf of Britain, and I had done so only after having my negotiating aims overwhelmingly endorsed by Parliament'.[22] His persistence paid off. On 22 July 1993, the House of Commons ratified the Maastricht Treaty. In contrast to just twenty months before, however, when only seven Conservatives had voted against its first reading, it had not been an easy passage. At first, the bill was defeated by eight votes, when an 'unholy alliance of Conservatives determined to kill the agreement I had reached at Maastricht, and an opposition that had supported the negotiation but was keen to destroy the government' came together to thwart the legislation. The Prime Minister only resolved the crisis after tabling an emergency Motion of Confidence in the government, making it clear that 'if we were defeated through another rebellion, I would seek a dissolution of Parliament and an immediate general election'. As he later confessed, 'For any prime minister, it was the ultimate gamble'. The gamble paid off, and when the House again divided, the government won by thirty-nine votes.[23]

The following afternoon, Major gave back-to-back interviews to television and radio broadcasters, the last of which was with ITN's Michael Brunson. Once the interview was over, he and Brunson conversed casually about the current state of the Conservative Party. In response to a question Brunson asked about three ministers threatening to resign over Major's European policy, the Prime Minister replied: 'Just think it through from my perspective. You are the prime minister, with a majority of eighteen, a party that is still harking back to the golden age that never was and is now invented. I could bring in other people. But where do you think most of this poison is coming from? From the dispossessed and never-possessed. You and I can think of ex-ministers who are causing all sorts of trouble. Do we want three more of the bastards out there?'[24] Little did Major or Brunson know, but although the television cameras had been switched off, a 'feed' cable from an earlier interview with the BBC was still live, transmitting every word Major spoke back to the studios in Millbank. The Prime Minister and leader of the Conservative Party had, in essence, dismissed the Eurosceptics as 'bastards'.

Major's comments struck at the heart of the problem facing the British political classes in the aftermath of Maastricht. By 1994, many in the Conservative Party – both inside and outside Parliament – were uneasy with recent events in Europe. As the *Sunday Telegraph* wrote on 1 May of that year, 'If you are on the wrong bus, you do not make it less wrong by staying on it, and recent experience has shown that we are no good at turning the bus around. This much, at least, is clear: better to get off than go over the precipice towards which it is heading'.[25] Yet it was not only Conservatives who were sceptical of the European project. Despite the combined efforts of Neil Kinnock, his successor John Smith and the newly elected leader Tony Blair, many in the Labour Party were likewise uncomfortable with the European Union. As late as March 1996, a fifth of Labour MPs publicly challenged official party policy by raising 'the anti-European banner . . . in outright opposition'. On the twenty-ninth of that month, the *Daily Mail* reported that the rebellion had 'exposed Labour's deep divisions on Europe and posed a potentially lethal threat to a Blair administration. Unless the Labour leader were to command a massive Commons majority, the anti-European dissenters – who number far more than the band of Tory Euro-sceptics John Major has to deal with – could wreak havoc with his governing plans'.[26]

Shortly after the final passage of the Maastricht Bill and Britain's official entry into the European Union, new elections for the European Parliament were held in June 1994. That year, there was a new party on the ballot, one with little name recognition and even less support. It was called the United Kingdom Independence Party (UKIP). Founded on 3 September 1993 by the London School of Economics historian Alan Sked, it had evolved from the Anti-Federalist League, a party established in November 1991 to oppose the Maastricht Treaty.[27] As an early member explained to Enoch Powell in September 1993, its membership believed that the name UKIP 'better expressed our aspirations' than the Anti-Federalist

League.[28] In its manifesto the following year, it called for 'the repeal of all legislation giving EC law precedence over English & Scots law' and pledged to fight the European election on a 'boycott platform', where elected UKIP MEPs would not take their seats in the European Parliament, nor draw salaries or claim expenses from European institutions.[29] The party had little immediate impact on the European elections. Contesting only twenty-four seats in June 1994, its main contribution was to allow some Labour MEPs to triumph over their Conservative opponents by attracting the votes of 'disgruntled Tories'.[30] It was not a party to be taken seriously, and even those Eurosceptic Conservatives who were dismayed by John Major's European policies had no intention of leaving the Tory fold.

Less than two decades later, however, UKIP had experienced a phenomenal surge. In his autobiography, Conservative Eurosceptic David Heathcoat-Amery did not mention UKIP in the context of the 1994 European elections. By the 2010 General Election, however, he was blaming UKIP for his defeat because in his Wells Constituency the UKIP candidate secured 1,711 votes and he lost by 800, allowing the Liberal Democrat candidate to sneak into what had always been a fairly safe Conservative seat.[31] On 14 January 2013, a Comres Poll revealed that if the 2014 European Parliamentary Elections had been held that day, the Conservatives would sink to third place behind Labour and UKIP. As the *Daily Record and Sunday Mail* reported, it was 'the first time that UKIP, led by Nigel Farage, have beaten the Tories in a major poll'.[32] When at the Eastleigh by-election in February 2013 UKIP secured 27 per cent of the vote (suggesting that if mirrored across the country at a General Election, UKIP would win seventeen seats in Westminster), Farage predicted an 'earthquake in British politics' at the European elections.[33] Even he could not have anticipated how well his party would do.

The European Parliamentary Elections were held in Britain on 22 May 2014, the same day as the local council elections. In the latter, after having won 'only a handful of local council places in their 20-year history', UKIP awoke on the morning after the elections with 'more than 300 councillors, enough to make them a significant presence in town halls up and down the country'.[34] More importantly, in the European Elections, UKIP secured 27.5 per cent of the vote, compared to 25.4 per cent for the Labour Party, 23.9 per cent for the Conservatives and a dismal 6.87 per cent for the Liberal Democrats (which fell to fifth place behind the Green Party). Consequently, UKIP sent to the European Parliament twenty-four MEPs all committed to a British withdrawal from the European Union, more than the twenty Labour MEPs, the nineteen Conservatives, the three Greens and the single Liberal Democrat MEP.[35] For the first time since 1906, neither the Conservative nor Labour Party had won a national vote. It is yet to be seen whether UKIP can have a lasting presence in British politics, but what can be said with certainty is that the party has already had a lasting effect on the nation. When, in 2014, the British public were asked to have their say on 'Europe', they voted overwhelming for a party pledged to bring about British withdrawal from the European Union. Britain, a post-imperial country, had revealed itself to be a Eurosceptic nation.

* * *

At first blush, the rapid rise of Euroscepticism in the 1990s and 2000s could be seen as an immediate reaction to the formation of the European Union – with all its constitutional implications for sovereignty, the potential impact it might have on immigration and the stresses it would place on British foreign policy (e.g., over the adventures in Afghanistan and Iraq, when the United Kingdom was once again torn between its geographical closeness to the European continent and its ever-present allegiance to the United States, Britain's most successful colony). Yet as the story of the British and Europe has shown, since the Second World War there has always been an essential cultural aspect to Euroscepticism, where questions of national identity have loomed as large as pragmatic concerns. From its first incarnation in the form of the 'anti-Marketeers' to Nigel Farage's UKIP, Euroscepticism has been inseparable from a nostalgic rendering of Britain's past, from a desire to return to the 'golden age' of British history – an age that was defined by British imperialism, even if present-day Eurosceptics do not call the Empire by its name.

In December 1988, writing in the aftermath of Thatcher's Bruges Speech, Paul Johnson of the *Daily Mail* wondered why the British public had, in the 1980s, rediscovered a taste for the Edwardian Era, from Sir Edward Elgar reaching the top of the classical pops and a revival of interest in the architectural work of Sir Edwin Lutyens to renewed attention on Rudyard Kipling. This era represented, 'to most minds, the golden age of the British Empire' and the 'great

Edwardian triumvirate, Elgar, Lutyens and Kipling, were closely associated with it, celebrating its glories in music, stone, verse and prose'. Johnson recognised that the 'empire is gone and none of us wants it back' but nevertheless saw this revival of Edwardian interest as being kindled by 'the warming patriotic fires which Mrs Thatcher helped to ignite' and which were based on 'a belief that the British still have something noble and profoundly moral to give to the world'. This was, he wrote, 'undoubtedly linked to Britain's increasing integration with the European community and the spreading awareness that the coming of the Single Market in 1992 will be an irrevocable step'. Johnson predicted that the 'vast majority of the British people, being sensible and realistic, recognise that our future lies within Europe and are not daunted by the idea'. Nevertheless, they were also 'conscious of certain inalienable British characteristics, which express the noblest side of the national character, and which they are determined to retain and take with us. The Edwardian cult reflects this consciousness'. He closed with a warning 'to the politicians and the media alike, and indeed to our Community partners'. It was that 'the British, while loyal Europeans, have no intention whatsoever of abandoning their heritage of greatness'.[36]

This 'heritage of greatness' had developed within the minds of Britons a national consciousness that insisted that their country was set apart from others on the European continent, a habit of thought that gave no hesitation to sailing 8,000 miles through the South Atlantic to retake from Argentina a rocky colonial outpost. It was a deep-rooted pattern of behaviour that would later encourage British policymakers to see it as their 'duty' and 'responsibility' to engage in further wars to assert their global presence. Writing in the postscript of his autobiography, Tony Blair said, 'I believe we should be projecting strength and determination abroad, not weakness or uncertainty.... In short, we have become too apologetic, too feeble, too inhibited, too imbued with doubt and too lacking in mission. Our way of life, our values, the things that made us great, remain not simply as a testament to us as nations but as harbingers of human progress. They are not relics of a once powerful politics; they are the living spirit of the optimistic view of human history'.[37]

Blair would no doubt be horrified to hear his sentiments described as those of an imperialist (although certainly many have accused him of being such), and there is no evidence to suggest that he was consciously thinking of Britain's imperial past when dealing with matters of state. Yet it is difficult to separate the present worldwide of the British establishment from its history of empire, a history that forged the national character and developed national attributes which – whilst no longer explicitly described in imperial terms – are nevertheless the product of empire.[38] It is the fear of Britain losing its place in the world – a fear of this imperial heritage slipping away – that has more than anything else led to the rise of Euroscepticism. The story of Britain's relationship with the European continent in the post-war world, far from being distinct from British imperialism, has in fact had everything to do with Britain's empire and its collapse.

In his autobiography, published in 1998, Ted Heath resurrected his case for British involvement in Europe using words similar to those spoken by British leaders since the Second World War: 'Geographically, historically and culturally, Britain is a European country. Our history has been defined primarily by our relations with the countries of continental Europe. British culture is a part of European culture, whether in art, music, drama or literature. . . . Even the development of the British Empire, though it turned our attention and energies to some extent outside Europe, was in large measure a product of the expansion of European rivalries into a global setting'. He then described the passing of that empire as an essential catalyst to Britain 'joining Europe', saying, 'Now that the British Empire, great and often noble venture though it was, is indeed "one with Nineveh and Tyre", our future lies clearly and inescapably where our roots are, in Europe, and in membership of the European Union'.[39]

Ironically, it is the very collapse of the British Empire that has made Britain's role within Europe so much more difficult to square for the British public. Whilst empires existed, it was possible for those within the United Kingdom to be British, to be 'European' and, perhaps most importantly of all, to be 'great', with all that such language implied. With the dawning of a post-imperial Britain, it has been much more problematic for Britons to reconcile themselves with their neighbours across the Channel. This book has told the story of the British and Europe, from the collapse of the British Empire to the rise of Euroscepticism. It is a story with many chapters left unwritten, whose conclusion is as yet uncertain. It is a story that has shaped Britain's past, is central to its present and will, beyond a shadow of doubt, define its future.

Notes

Introduction

1. Winston Churchill, 'Congress of Europe Address', The Hague, The Netherlands, 7 May 1948, in Robert Rhodes James, ed., *Winston S. Churchill: His Complete Speeches, 1897–1963: Volume VII, 19493–1949* (New York/London: Chelsea House, 1974), 7635–7639.
2. Churchill Archives Centre, Churchill College, Cambridge [CAC], Churchill Papers [CHUR] 2/21A, The British Delegation to the Congress of Europe, The Hague, May 1948.
3. Martin Gilbert, *Winston S. Churchill: Volume VIII: 'Never Despair', 1945–1965* (London: Heinemann, 1988), 406.
4. CAC, CHUR 2/21A, 'Political Report', Congress of Europe, The Hague, May 1948.
5. CAC, CHUR 2/21A, 'Economic Report', Congress of Europe, The Hague, May 1948.
6. CAC, CHUR 2/21A, 'Political Report', Congress of Europe, The Hague, May 1948.
7. Bruno Waterfield, 'David Cameron "must embrace Churchill's vision of United States of Europe"', *The Daily Telegraph*, online edition, 8 November 2013, www.telegraph.co.uk/news/worldnews/europe/eu/10436218/David-Cameron-must-embrace-Churchills-vision-of-United-States-of-Europe.html.
8. Martin Beckford, 'General Election 2010: Britain still wedded to empire, says Nick Clegg', *The Daily Telegraph*, online edition, 29 April 2010, www.telegraph.co.uk/news/election-2010/7647835/General-Election-2010-Britain-still-wedded-to-empire-says-Nick-Clegg.html.
9. Tim Adams, 'Cultural hallmark: The interview: Stuart Hall', *The Observer Review*, 23 September 2007, 8.
10. For example, on 24 May 2011, Hannan blogged that on Empire Day 'we can take some pride in our fathers' deeds. Britain introduced whole civilizations to

the rule of law, to property rights, to open markets, to impartial administration. Yes, we took resources from our dependencies, but we also built infrastructure: schools and clinics, roads and law-courts. And, while we fought some brutal counter-insurgency campaigns, we brought many colonies to independence without a shot being fired in anger'. Daniel Hannan, 'On Empire Day, Remember our greatest export: Westminster Democracy', *The Daily Telegraph*, online edition, 24 May 2011, http://blogs.telegraph.co.uk/news/danielhannan/100089126/on-empire-day-remember-our-greatest-export-westminster-democracy/.

11. Niall Ferguson, 'The European farce', *Newsweek*, Volume 159, Number 21; and Andrew Roberts, 'Europe's hubristic imperial overstretch', *The Financial Times*, online edition, 18 May 2012, http://www.ft.com/cms/s/0/595fe1ec-9f69-11e1-8b84-00144feabdc0.html#axzz2gZiQUXI0.

12. Bagehot, 'The empire strikes back', *The Economist*, 24 November 2012.

13. See the Bibliographical Note at the end of this work for more on this.

14. The third leg of this historiographical stool is, of course, Cold War History. Perhaps not surprisingly, both studies concerned with the end of Britain's empire and those that look at Britain's relationship with the European continent have consistently incorporated the Cold War context into their stories, particularly in recent years. That decolonisation (in particular) and European integration (to a lesser extent, at least according to the current historiography) were both affected by the Cold War is not in doubt. The fault lies in bringing together the history of empire with the history of Europe.

15. The first full-length study of decolonisation came only in 1988, with John Darwin's *Britain and Decolonisation: The Retreat from Empire in the Post-War World* (Basingstoke: Macmillan, 1988), after which has followed a number of important studies, including David M. Anderson and David Killingray, eds., *Policing and Decolonisation: Politics, Nationalism and the Police, 1917–65* (Manchester: Manchester University Press, 1992); Nicholas J. White, *Decolonisation: The British Experience since 1945* (London: Longman, 1999); Georgina Sinclair, *At the End of the Line: Colonial Policing and the Imperial Endgame, 1945–1980* (Manchester: Manchester University Press, 2006); Ronald Hyam, *Britain's Declining Empire: The Road to Decolonisation, 1918–1968* (Cambridge: Cambridge University Press, 2006); Peter Clarke, *The Last Thousand Days of the British Empire* (London: Allen Lane, 2007); and my own *Imperial Endgame: Britain's Dirty Wars and the Empire of Empire* (Basingstoke: Palgrave Macmillan, 2011). Of particular interest to historians, and capturing the public's imagination more than anything else, has been Britain's end of empire in Kenya, including David Anderson, *Histories of the Hanged: Britain's Dirty War in Kenya and the End of Empire* (London: Weidenfeld & Nicolson, 2004); Caroline Elkins, *Britain's Gulag: The Brutal End of Empire in Kenya*

(London: Jonathan Cape, 2005); Daniel Branch, *Defeating Mau Mau, Creating Kenya: Counterinsurgency, Civil War and Decolonisation* (Cambridge: Cambridge University Press, 2009); and Huw C. Bennet, *Fighting the Mau Mau: The British Army and Counter-Insurgency in the Kenya Emergency* (Cambridge: Cambridge University Press, 2013). For the effect of decolonisation on Britain itself, see Antoinette Burton, ed., *After the Imperial Turn: Thinking with and through the Nation* (Durham, North Carolina: Duke University Press, 2006); Stuart Ward, ed., *British Culture and the End of Empire* (Manchester: Manchester University Press, 2001); Wendy Webster, *Englishness and Empire, 1939–1965* (Oxford: Oxford University Press, 2005); and Rachel Gilmour and Bill Schwarz, eds., *End of Empire and the English Novel since 1945* (Manchester: Manchester University Press, 2011).

16. In 1964, Miriam Camps wrote the first substantial work on Britain and Europe in the post-war period and described the 'European relationship as one of a set of three relationships: .... the relationship with the Commonwealth, the relationship with the United States, the relationship with Continental Europe' (*Britain and the European Community, 1955–1963*, Princeton: Princeton University Press, 1964). Yet this broader context is largely missing in her subsequent narrative of Britain's relationship with the emerging European Economic Community prior to 1963. She concludes that the British 'missed the opportunity to create the kind of Europe they later wanted' (507). This story of 'missed opportunity' has become the foremost interpretation of Britain's relationship with the European continent in the twentieth century, from Stephen George's account of a 'semi-detatched', 'awkward partner' (*Britain and European Integration since 1945*, Oxford: Basil Blackwell, 1991) and Edmund Dell's accusation of a British abdication of leadership in Europe (*The Schuman Plan and the British Abdication of Leadership in Europe*, Oxford: Oxford University Press, 1995) through Lord Beloff's 'dialogues of the deaf' (*Britain and the European Union: Dialogues of the Deaf*, Basingstoke: Macmillan, 1996) and James Ellison's British 'threat to Europe' (*Threatening Europe: Britain and the Creation of the European Community, 1955–58*, Basingstoke: Macmillan, 2000) to Roy Denman's *Missed Chances: Britain and Europe in the Twentieth Century* (London: Cassell, 1996) and David Gowland, Arthur Turner and Alex Wright's contention that Britain has been 'on the sidelines' of Europe (*Britain and European Integration since 1945: On the Sidelines*, London: Routledge, 2010). There are a few noticeable exceptions. Wolfram Kaiser rejects the 'awkward partner' school to instead argue that the story is more complex, using a rigorous analysis of the archival record to demonstrate that British considerations of Europe extended beyond the EEC and its predecessors/successors (*Using Europe, Abusing the Europeans: Britain and European Integration, 1945–63*, Basingstoke: Macmillan, 1996). Helen Parr, in her close study of Harold Wilson's policy towards European

integration, examines the complex balancing of British European and Commonwealth interests, concluding that at least one British Prime Minister – Harold Wilson – was favourable towards Europe, so long as it was the 'right sort' of Europe (*Britain's Policy Towards the European Community: Harold Wilson and Britain's World Role, 1964–1967*, London: Routledge, 2006, 188). Melissa Pine goes further, arguing that Wilson sought to take Britain into Europe 'as part of a deliberate strategy' and that he, along with his two Foreign Secretaries George Brown and Michael Stewart, 'made a positive commitment to its success and were determined to take Britain into Europe' (*Harold Wilson and Europe: Pursuing Britain's Membership of the European Community*, London: Tauris Academic Studies, 2007, 1). See also Lionel Bell, *The Throw That Failed: Britain's 1961 Application to Join the Common Market* (London: New European, 1995), George Wilkes, ed., *Britain's Failure to Enter the European Community 1961–3* (London: Frank Cass, 1997), N. Piers Ludlow, *Dealing with Britain: The Six and the First UK Application to the EEC* (Cambridge: Cambridge University Press, 1997), and Anthony Forster, 'No Entry: Britain and the EEC in the 1960s', *Contemporary British History*, Volume 12, Number 2 (Summer 1998), 139–146.

17. For example, in volume four of the *Oxford History of the British Empire: The Twentieth Century* (Judith M. Brown and Wm. Roger Louis, eds., Oxford: Oxford University Press, 1999), there are only two references to the EEC, the first of which simply notes that the end of empire also saw Britain's first application to join the EEC (29), the second of which states that the 'history of the British Empire as an economic phenomenon came to an end sometime between 1967, when the detrimental effects of sterling's devaluation ended the currency's role as a reserve asset, and 1973, when Britain finally joined the European Economic Community' (358). Likewise, Andrew Thompson's companion volume *Britain's Experience of Empire in the Twentieth Century* (Oxford: Oxford University Press, 2012) contains just two extended discussions of Britain's involvement in European integration, neither of which clearly shows how the government's visions of the Empire/Commonwealth and Europe worked together, nor the reaction of the British public to Europe once the empire was jettisoned. Historians of Britain's post-war relationship with Europe are equally reticent to look comparatively at British interaction with Europe and the decline of the British Empire. To take just a few of many examples, in his work *Britain and European Unity, 1945–1999* (Basingstoke: Palgrave Macmillan, 2000), John W. Young references specific Commonwealth considerations during British negotiations for entry into the EEC but does not take a broader view of the interaction between imperial ideology and European integration. Gowland, Turner and Wright make even fewer mentions of the empire and its decline, referencing New Zealand's concerns about British entry just three times, despite the fact that these were thought at the time to have been

one of the main contributing factors for the collapse of negotiations in 1963. Likewise, in George Wilkes's edited volume, *Britain's Failure to Enter the European Community, 1961–63* (New York: Routledge, 1997), just one of its twelve essays gives any attention to the empire. Sean Greenwood's *Britain and European Integration since the Second World War* (Manchester: Manchester University Press, 1996) gives no suggestion of a broader context including the Empire/Commonwealth and concludes by deeming Britons 'half-hearted Europeans' (158). Stuart Ward has looked in detail at the effects of the EEC on the Commonwealth but from the Australian perspective rather than the British (*Australia and the British Embrace: The Demise of the Imperial Ideal*, Victoria, Australia: Melbourne University Press, 2001), as has Alex May in his edited collection *Britain, the Commonwealth, and Europe* (Basingstoke: Palgrave Macmillan, 2001), likewise from the Commonwealth's point of view. The combined effect of decolonisation on the one hand and a movement towards European integration on the other on the British people has been surprisingly understudied.

18. For example, in 1950, James Joll wrote of the general tendencies – what he called 'certain psychological attitudes towards Europe' – in British thinking. He identified three. First, there was a 'natural insularity of temperament formed by geographical, religious and political separation from the main developments on the Continent', which had led to a 'popular distrust of foreigners'. Second, there were the 'traditional beliefs about what are essential British interests' (the chief being 'Britain's position as a maritime and commercial power'). Finally, there was the conviction that there must be a 'balance of power' on the continent, where 'no single Continental power must be able to dominate the whole of Europe'. Britain's role was to 'hold the balance between the two equally matched powers in Europe who will thus each be prevented from winning supremacy'. Beyond these three 'psychological attitudes' held by all Britons in common, Joll argued that there have been two further divisions in British foreign policy, between the isolationists and the internationalists. The former, whilst acknowledging that Britain has a role to play in Europe, nevertheless maintain that 'there are only a few traditional reasons and a few traditional areas for which Britain need become involved in Europe'. In contrast, the internationalists argue that 'Britain is irrevocably a part of Europe and that she has a duty to act in conjunction with the other states of Europe in maintaining certain political principles'. In neither account of British interaction with the European continent does the Empire figure particularly prominently. James Joll, 'Introduction', in James Joll, ed., *Britain and Europe: Pitt to Churchill, 1793–1940* (London: Adam & Charles Black, 1950), 4, 8–9, 19–20, and 23–24. Hans W. Gatzke, likewise, believes that maintaining the balance of power on an external European continent has been the most prominent British policy towards Europe, writing that, following the First World

War, Great Britain 'tried to maintain the freedom from continental entanglements that she thought she had enjoyed before 1914. Her ideal then had been one of "splendid isolation", to be *of* Europe but not *in* Europe, to be not part of a continental balance of power but to hold the decisive tie-breaking voice in such a balance' (Hans W. Gatzke, 'Introduction', in Hans W. Gatzke, ed., *European Diplomacy between Two Wars, 1919–1939*, Chicago: Quadrangle Books, 1972), 9.

19. Linda Colley, 'What is imperial history now?' in David Cannadine, ed., *What Is History Now?* (Basingstoke: Palgrave Macmillan, 2002), 132.
20. Idem, 139.
21. The volume that comes closest to doing so is John M. MacKenzie, ed., *European Empires and the People: Popular Responses to Imperialism in France, Britain, the Netherlands, Belgium, Germany, and Italy* (Manchester: Manchester University Press, 2011).
22. There are a few notable exceptions to this. For example, see Nicholas J. White, 'Reconstructing Europe through rejuvenating empire: The British, French, and Dutch experiences compared', *Past and Present* (2011), Supplement 6, 211–236.
23. For example, Derek Heater – seeking the origins of contemporary European integration – traces Britain in Europe from the early medieval period towards the 'realisation' of his subject in the creation of the EEC in the 1950s. By looking for 'early schemes for unity', however, Heater fails to understand the actual (and ever-changing) role of Britain in Europe throughout history, unity or no unity. In his work, he makes no mention of mercantilist trade, imperial competition or the British concept of the balance of power that so dominated Anglo–European relations in the seventeenth, eighteenth and nineteenth centuries, nor does he reference the increased nationalism and xenophobia that have so often run parallel to calls for a united Europe. That the Second World War is mentioned only in passing is astounding. Derek Heater, *The Idea of European Unity* (Leicester: Leicester University Press, 1992).
24. One of the first to draw attention to this problem was New Zealander J. G. A. Pocock, whose influential 1975 essay 'British history: A plea for a new subject' (*Journal of Modern History*, Volume 47, Number 4, December 1975) argued for a new treatment of British history as a holistic story rather than separate stories of England, Wales, Scotland and Ireland. He included in his 'British history' also the 'British World' of the American colonies prior to 1783 and Canada, New Zealand and Australia to the present day. Ironically, the motivation for Pocock's essay came from his belief that, in the 1970s, Britons were becoming forgetful of the Empire/Commonwealth and were becoming *too European*: 'the English have been increasingly willing to declare that neither empire nor commonwealth ever meant much in their consciousness, and that they were at heart Europeans all the time' (602). In his response to

Pocock's article, renowned historian A. J. P. Taylor wrote in a way that characterised the English cultural arrogance to which I refer, claiming that Pocock's suggestion that 'British history could be handled as a common cultural experience' was patently 'not true': 'The culture is and always has been exclusively English, with some contributions from the outposts that are on a very small scale.... English history makes sense; British history makes sense. What does not make sense is to imply that there is something called British history that is different from English history..... British history starts only when the Scotch and Irish became English speakers, in other words, a variant of Englishmen. So English history turns out to be the best phrase after all' (A. J. P. Taylor, 'Comments on "British history: A plea for a new subject"', *Journal of Modern History*, Volume 47, Number 4, December 1975, 622–623). Despite Taylor's criticism, Pocock was undeterred, writing in 1982 that 'much of what passes by that name [British history] is English history and makes little pretence of being anything else' (J. G. A. Pocock, 'The limits and divisions of British history: In search of the unknown subject', *American Historical Review*, Volume 87, Number 2, April 1982). He pushed his case twice more, in 1992 and 1999, although by that point most historians would have agreed with his basic argument, even if they did not always apply it in their own work (J. G. A. Pocock, 'History and sovereignty: The historiographical response to Europeanization in two British cultures', *Journal of British Studies*, Volume 31, Number 4, October 1992; and J. G. A. Pocock, 'The New British history in Atlantic perspective: An antipodean commentary', *American Historical Review*, Volume 104, Number 2, April 1999).

25. Richard J. Evans, *Cosmopolitan Islanders: British Historians and the European Continent* (Cambridge: Cambridge University Press, 2009), 1–2. The works Evans references are John Kenyon, *The History Men: The Historical Profession in England since the Renaissance* (London: Weidenfeld & Nicolson, 1983); Christopher Parker, *The English Historical Tradition since 1850* (Edinburgh: John Donald, 1990); and Michael Bentley, *Modernizing England's Past: English Historiography in the Age of Modernism, 1870–1970* (Cambridge: Cambridge University Press, 2005).

26. Idem, 232.

27. Idem, 234. For more on this, see Conal Condren, 'English historiography and the invention of Britain and Europe', in John Milfull, ed., *Britain in Europe: Prospects for Change* (Aldershot: Ashgate, 1999), 11–27.

28. See Michael J. Braddick, *State Formation in Early Modern England, c. 1550–1700* (Cambridge: Cambridge University Press, 2000); John Brewer, *The Sinews of Power: War and the English State, 1688–1783* (London: Unwin Hyman, 1989); and Linda Colley, *Britons: Forging the Nation, 1707–1838* (New Haven, CT: Yale University Press, 1992).

29. R. W. Seton-Watson, *Britain in Europe, 1789–1914: A Survey of Foreign Policy* (Cambridge: Cambridge University Press, 1937), 646.
30. See Paul Kennedy, *The Rise and Fall of British Naval Mastery* (London: Allen Lane, 1976).
31. Douglas Jerrold, writing in 1941, exemplifies this view: 'We live on an island; islanders are proverbially peculiar people. For that reason, the continental nations as a whole neither particularly like us nor understand us at all. The converse is also true. The Elizabethan religious settlement and the English liberal tradition have, for more than a century, divided us from political and intellectual Europe. ... when we say to Europe that we prefer a free government to a good government (something which is axiomatic to Englishmen of all parties except the revolutionary socialists), we are saying something which sounds not enlightened but cynically immoral to a continental European of any race or school of thought' (*Britain and Europe, 1900–1940*, London: Collins, 1941), 22, 25. He writes further: 'British liberalism is the peculiar pride and achievement of the English-speaking peoples. It never made much appeal, and to-day [in 1941] it makes no appeal at all, on the Continent. British liberalism has its roots deep in English history and English Protestantism. It venerates tradition, it is puritan in temper and conservative in feeling. Continental liberalism is anti-monarchical, anti-clerical and revolutionary' (163–164).
32. Jeremy Black writes that 'it is misleading to play down or ignore enormous differences between Continental states in order to compare them with England or Britain. In many respects and for much of its history, Britain had more in common with the rest of north-west Europe than did the latter with the remainder of Europe'. Jeremy Black, *Convergence or Divergence? Britain and the Continent* (Basingstoke: Macmillan, 1994), 3.
33. Paul Kennedy, *The Rise of Anglo–German Antagonism, 1860–1914* (London: George Allen & Unwin, 1980), xi.
34. It is unnecessary here to cast a glance back in time to periods before the seventeenth or eighteenth centuries, but the inextricable links between the nations that eventually came to make up the United Kingdom and the other countries of Europe have been well-documented. See, in particular, Donald Matthew, *Britain and the Continent, 1000–1300* (London: Hodder Arnold, 2005); Geoffrey Parker, *The Military Revolution: Military Innovation and the Rise of the West, 1500–1800*, second edition (Cambridge: Cambridge University Press, 1996); Jonathan Scott, *England's Troubles: Seventeenth Century English Political Instability in a European Context* (Cambridge: Cambridge University Press, 2000); Steve Pincus, *1688: The First Modern Revolution* (New Haven, CT: Yale University Press, 2009); and Tony Clayton, *Europe and the Making of England, 1660–1760* (Cambridge: Cambridge University Press, 2007).

35. Paul Kennedy, *The Rise and Fall of the Great Powers: Economic Change and Military Conflict from 1500 to 2000* (London: Unwin Hyman, 1988), 155.
36. See Paul Kennedy, *The Realities behind Diplomacy: Background Influences on British External Policy, 1865–1980* (London: George Allen & Unwin, 1981), 17–73.
37. Richard Shannon, *The Crisis of Imperialism, 1865–1915* (London: Hart-Davis, MacGibbon, 1974), 43–45.
38. This view was most forcefully expressed by Benjamin Disraeli in 1872, when he told his audience at the Crystal Palace that Britain faced a choice: 'whether you will be content to be a comfortable England, modelled and moulded upon Continental principles ... or whether you will be a great country, an Imperial country' (quoted in John Charmley, *Splendid Isolation? Britain, the Balance of Power and the Origins of the First World War*, London: Hodder & Stoughton, 1999, 397). That Britain was European was undisputed; but to be great, the United Kingdom had to move beyond Europe to also become an extra-European imperial power.
39. For a useful examination of the short-lived and incomplete nature of 'splendid isolation' as a British foreign policy, see Christopher Howard, *Splendid Isolation: A Study of the Ideas Concerning Britain's International Position and Foreign Policy during the Later Years of the Third Marquis of Salisbury* (London: Macmillan, 1967).
40. For the Suez Canal, see Hubert Bonin, *History of the Suez Canal Company, 1858–2008: Between Controversy and Utility* (Genève: Librairie Droz S.A., 2010). For the Berlin Conference, see Stig Förster, Wolfgang J. Mommsen and Ronald Robinson, eds., *Bismarck, Europe and Africa: The Berlin Africa Conference 1884–1885 and the Onset of Partition* (Oxford: Oxford University Press, 1988).
41. Quoted in Harold Macmillan, *Tides of Fortune, 1945–1955* (London: Macmillan, 1969), 151.
42. Ibid.
43. See Colley, *Britons*.

1 A world undone

1. This description is taken from a number of sources, including written accounts, audio recordings and visual imagery, some of which is available online on the websites of the National Archives, the Imperial War Museum and the BBC.
2. Robin Cross, *VE Day: Victory in Europe, 1945* (London: Sidgwick & Jackson, in association with The Imperial War Museum, 1985), 100–107.

3. Winston Churchill, 'This is your victory', Ministry of Health, London, 8 May 1945, in James, ed., *Winston S. Churchill: His Complete Speeches*, 7154. Pamela Chichele-Plowden, Countess of Lytton, described the speech as 'surely your finest utterance' and told Churchill that her heart was 'very fully at the thought of the happiness you have given, and received, to the world [which] is overwhelming in magnitude'. CAC, Chartwell Papers [CHAR] 2/533, Letter from Pamela Chichele-Plowden, Countess of Lytton, to Winston Churchill, 9 May 1945.
4. Cross, *VE Day*, 108.
5. Field Marshal Lord Alanbrooke, Diary Entries, 7 and 9 May 1945, in Field Marshal Lord Alanbrooke, *War Diaries, 1939–1945*, edited by Alex Danchev and Daniel Todman (London: Weidenfeld & Nicolson, 2001), 688–689.
6. Winston Churchill, 'Forward, till the whole task is done', Broadcast, London, 13 May 1945, in James, ed., *Winston S. Churchill: His Complete Speeches*, 7162.
7. John Colville, Diary Entries for 14 and 17 May 1945, *The Fringes of Power: Downing Street Diaries, 1939–1955* (London: Weidenfeld & Nicholson, 2004), 565.
8. David Kynaston, *Austerity Britain, 1945–51* (London: Bloomsbury, 2007), 20.
9. Idem, 63–64.
10. Quoted in Idem, 69.
11. Colville, Diary Entry, 18 June 1945, in *The Fringes of Power*, 573.
12. Jeffry M. Diefendorf, 'Introduction: New perspectives on a rebuilt Europe', in Jeffry M. Diefendorf, ed., *Rebuilding Europe's Bombed Cities* (London: Macmillan, 1990), 1.
13. Niels Gutschow, 'Hamburg: The "catastrophe" of July 1943', in Diefendorf, ed., *Rebuilding Europe's Bombed Cities*, 117–118.
14. Frederick Taylor, *Dresden: Tuesday, 13 February 1945* (London: Bloomsbury, 2005), 408–409.
15. Cross, *VE Day*, 149.
16. Ibid. For more on this, see Pieter Lagrou, *The Legacy of Nazi Occupation: Patriotic Memory and National Recovery in Western Europe, 1945–1965* (Cambridge: Cambridge University Press, 2000), 81–128.
17. Reginald Roy, Diary, 2–14 May 1945, quoted in David Stafford, *Endgame 1945: Victory, Retribution, Liberation* (London: Little, Brown, 2007), 365.
18. Robert Reid, BBC interview with B. Whitaker, 30 May 1945, WRU C/11616, Reid Papers, quoted in Ibid, 365.
19. See Menno Spiering, *A Cultural History of British Euroscepticism* (Basingstoke: Palgrave Macmillan, 2015), 9–19.
20. Winston Churchill, 'Election address', Woodford, 26 May 1945, in James, ed., *Winston S. Churchill: His Complete Speeches*, 7167–7168.

21. See, for example, his correspondence with Lord Queenborough. CAC, CHAR 2/236/170–171, Letter from Almeric Hugh Paget, 1st Baron Queenborough, to Winston Churchill, 26 August 1935.
22. CAC, CHAR 8/615, Copy of an article, 'Why not "The United States of Europe?"', published in the *News of the World*, 29 May 1938.
23. CAC, CHAR 8/613, Copy of an article, 'France, Britain and the future fate of Europe', published in the *Daily Telegraph*, 4 October 1938.
24. The National Archives [TNA], Cabinet Office [CAB] 65/7/64, Conclusions of a meeting of the War Cabinet held at 10 Downing Street on 16 June 1940, and copy of the Declaration of an Anglo–French Union to be dispatched to both Monsieur Reynaud and General de Gaulle without delay.
25. Ibid.
26. Quoted in Julian Jackson, *The Fall of France: The Nazi Invasion of 1940* (Oxford: Oxford University Press, 2003), 137–138.
27. For a full account of Vichy France, see Julian Jackson, *France: The Dark Years, 1940–1944* (Oxford University Press, 2001).
28. Miriam Camps writes: 'The British emerged from the war larger than life, the French far weaker than they knew themselves to be. The process of readjustment – both the building up and the contracting down to size – has inevitably affected national attitudes and has made agreement between the two countries particularly difficult'. (*Britain and the European Community, 1955–1963*, Princeton: Princeton University Press, 1964, 519).
29. Macmillan, *Tides of Fortune*, 152.
30. Anthony Eden, *The Reckoning* (London: Cassell, 1965), 74.
31. Quoted in Macmillan, *Tides of Fortune*, 153.
32. John W. Young, *Britain and European Unity, 1945–1999*, 2nd edition (Basingstoke: Macmillan, 2000), 6.
33. John Charmley, *Duff Cooper* (London: Weidenfeld and Nicolson, 1986), 130.
34. Duff Cooper, *Old Men Forget: The Autobiography of Duff Cooper (Viscount Norwich)* (London: Rupert Hart-Davis, 1953), 249.
35. Ibid. The second was from future Prime Minister Harold Macmillan, who wrote: 'It was the finest thing I've heard since I've been in the House; the deep sincerity gripped even those members who most disagreed with your argument. I can assure you that it has heartened a great many of us more than you know'.
36. Idem, 314.
37. CAC, Duff Cooper Papers [DUFC] 4/4, Letter from Winston Churchill to Duff Cooper, October [no date] 1943.
38. CAC, DUFC 4/4, Letter from Duff Cooper to Winston Churchill, 18 October 1943.
39. Duff Cooper, Diary Entry, 4 January 1944, in John Julius Norwich, ed., *The Duff Cooper Diaries, 1915–1951* (London: Weidenfeld & Nicholson, 2005), 283.

40. Cooper, Diary Entry, 12 January 1944, in Idem, 289.
41. CAC, DUFC 4/2, Record of a Luncheon taking place between Mr Churchill and General de Gaulle on 12 January 1944, at Marrakesh, prepared by Duff Cooper, Office of the British Representative with the French Committee of National Liberation, 16 January 1944.
42. Ibid.
43. Cooper, Diary Entry, 13 January 1944, in Norwich, *The Duff Cooper Diaries*, 290.
44. To take just one example, on 20 March 1944, Cooper explained to Eden: 'There exists a fundamental difference between the English and the French approach to justice. The English consider that the most important of all things is that the accused should have a fair trial. They would rather a guilty man should escape than that he should be convicted on insufficient evidence. The English law of evidence is strict, and breach of it can invalidate a trial, for the legal game, like all other English games, must be played according to the rules. The French, on the other hand, believe that the main purpose of justice is to establish the guilt or innocence of the accused, and that while laws of evidence may exist, it matters very little whether they are strictly observed, so long as this main purpose is achieved'. CAC, DUFC 4/4, Letter from Duff Cooper to Anthony Eden, 20 March 1944.
45. Cooper, *Old Men Forget*, 346–347.
46. Quoted in Idem, 347.
47. CAC, DUFC 4/7, Dispatch from Duff Cooper to Anthony Eden, 16 August 1944.
48. DUFC 2/7, Dispatch from Lord Halifax, British Embassy, Washington DC, to Anthony Eden, 16 September 1944. For more on the American attitude, see Geir Lundestad, *The United States and Western Europe since 1945: From 'Empire' by Invitation to Transatlantic Drift* (Oxford: Oxford University Press, 2003), 25–37.
49. Charmley, *Duff Cooper*, 190–191.
50. Cooper, Diary Entry, 7 March 1945, in Norwich, *The Duff Cooper Diaries*, 357.
51. CAC, DUFC 4/7, Despatch from Duff Cooper to Anthony Eden, 11 March 1945.
52. Cooper, *Old Men Forget*, 351.
53. Cooper, Diary Entry, 30 April 1945, in Norwich, *The Duff Cooper Diaries*, 363.
54. CAC, DUFC 4/5, Letter from Duff Cooper to Anthony Eden, 4 May 1945.
55. Charmley, *Duff Cooper*, 203.
56. Cooper, Diary Entry, 31 May 1945, in Norwich, *The Duff Cooper Diaries*, 370.
57. Note in Ibid.

58. Cooper, *Old Men Forget*, 352.
59. CAC, CHAR 20/218/28, Telegraph from President Harry S. Truman to Winston Churchill, 8 May 1945.
60. CAC, CHAR 20/227B/161, Telegram from King Haakon VII of Norway to Winston Churchill, 9 May 1945.
61. Orme Sargent, 'Stocktaking after VE-Day', July 1945, quoted in Young, *Britain and European Unity*, 7.
62. Alan S. Milward, *The UK and the European Community, Volume I: The Rise and Fall of a National Strategy, 1945–1963* (London: Routledge, 2012), 16.
63. CAC, CHAR 2/533, Letter from Harold Macmillan to Winston Churchill, 27 July 1945.
64. Alanbrooke, Diary Entry, 26 July 1945, in Alanbrooke, *War Diaries*.
65. Cooper, Diary Entries, 26 July 1945, and 27 July 1945, in Norwich, *The Duff Cooper Diaries*, 379. Ironically, given Cooper's diary entries, Churchill chose to confide in him once the dust had settled, writing on 17 September: 'there are some unpleasant features in this election which indicate the rise of bad elements. Conscientious objectors were preferred to candidates of real military achievement and service. All the Members of Parliament who had done most to hamper and obstruct the war were returned by enormously increased majorities. None of the values of two years before were preserved. .... The soldiers voted with mirthful irresponsibility. ... Also, there is the latent antagonism of the rank and file for the Officer class, and of course the hopes raised by Socialists that a vote for Labour would get them out of the Army more quickly. A period not only of great difficulty and hardship but of disillusionment and frustration awaits the country. The new Ministers will not have time or strength for revolutionary measures. They will be dominated by the daily pressure of administration and finance, in both of which they will fail to give satisfaction. We are back at the two-Party system, and must await in a patriotic state of mind the inevitable revulsion'. CAC, DUFC 4/4 Letter from Winston Churchill to Duff Cooper, 17 September 1945.
66. Cooper, Diary Entry, 27 July 1945, in Norwich, *The Duff Cooper Diaries*, 379.
67. For Eden's complete biography, see Robert James Rhodes, *Anthony Eden* (London: Weidenfeld & Nicholson, 1986) and David Dutton, *Anthony Eden: A Life and Reputation* (London: Arnold, 1997). For Bevin's complete biography, see Alan Bullock, *Ernest Bevin: A Biography*, edited by Brian Brivati (London: Politico's, 2002) and Peter Weiler, *Ernest Bevin* (Manchester: Manchester University Press, 1993).
68. Francis William, *Ernest Bevin: Portrait of a Great Englishman* (London: Hutchinson, 1952), 54.
69. Idem, 101–111.

70. Sir Roderick Barclay, *Ernest Bevin and the Foreign Office, 1932–1969* (London: Published by the Author, Printed by Butler & Tanner Ltd., 1975), 77, 93 and 84.
71. Idem, 80.
72. Quoted in Ibid.
73. Lord Woolton, *The Memoirs of the Rt. Hon. The Earl of Woolton* (London: Cassell, 1959), 359.
74. Alan Bullock, *Ernest Bevin: Foreign Secretary, 1945–1951* (London: Heinemann, 1983), 30.
75. Ibid.
76. Young, *Britain and European Unity*, 1.
77. John Saville, *The Politics of Continuity: British Foreign Policy and the Labour Government, 1945–46* (London: Verso, 1993), 25.
78. Telegram from Lord Halifax to Ernest Bevin, 25 August 1945, quoted in Ibid.
79. Quoted in Idem, 94.
80. CAC, DUFC 4/7, Despatch from Duff Cooper to Ernest Bevin, 19 March 1946.
81. Bullock, *Ernest Bevin: Foreign Secretary*, 121.
82. Alan P. Dobson, *US Wartime Aid to Britain, 1940–1946* (London: Croom Helm, 1986), 62.
83. Leon Martel, *Lend-Lease, Loans, and the Coming of the Cold War: A Study of the Implementation of Foreign Policy* (Boulder, CO: Westview Press, 1979), 7.
84. Idem, 212.
85. Historian Alan Dobson brings the British position in 1945 into a stark light: 'In March 1941 the British economy had been unable to provide the means to withstand the armed threat from Germany and Italy, and she had insufficient dollars to buy what she required from the US. In September 1945 Britain's economy was unable to meet her civilian needs, and she had insufficient dollars to buy what she required from the US. In 1941 she had been vulnerable to armed attack because of her economic weakness; in 1945 she was vulnerable to unpalatable economic demands from the Americans for the same reason' (*US Wartime Aid to Britain*, 223–224).
86. Walter Lipgens, *A History of European Integration: Volume I, 1945–1947*, translated from the German by P. S. Falla and A. J. Ryder (Oxford: Clarendon Press, 1982), 158.
87. Martel, *Lend-Lease, Loans, and the Coming of the Cold War*, 1.
88. Saville, *The Politics of Continuity*, 150.
89. Bullock, *Ernest Bevin: Foreign Secretary*, 121.
90. TNA, CAB 129/1, CP (45) 112, Annex, 'Our overseas financial prospects': Cabinet Memorandum by Lord Keynes, in Ronald Hyam, ed., *British Documents on the End of Empire [BDOEE]: Series A, Volume 2,*

The Labour Government and the End of Empire, 1945–1951: Part II: *Economics and International Relations* (London: HMSO, 1992), 1–5.
91. Martel, *Lend-Lease, Loans, and the Coming of the Cold War*, 212.
92. Kaiser, *Using Europe, Abusing the Europeans*, 1.
93. CAC, Paul Einzig Papers [ENZG] 1/14, Letter from Brendan Bracken to Paul Einzig, 18 December 1945.
94. N. J. Crowson, *Britain and Europe: A Political History since 1918* (London: Routledge), 59.
95. Idem, 53 and 169 n. 2.
96. Lipgens, *A History of European Integration*, 169–170.
97. Crowson, *Britain and Europe*, 56.
98. Benjamin Grob-Fitzgibbon, *Imperial Endgame: Britain's Dirty Wars and the End of Empire* (Basingstoke: Palgrave Macmillan, 2011), 5.
99. Michael J. Cohen, 'The genesis of the Anglo–American Committee on Palestine, November 1945: A case study in the assertion of American hegemony', *Historical Journal*, Volume 22, Number 1 (March 1979), 192.
100. Letter from Harry S. Truman to Clement Attlee, 31 August 1945, reprinted in Francis Williams, *Twilight of Empire: Memoirs of Prime Minister Clement Attlee* (New York: A. S. Barnes and Co., 1962), 187–189.
101. Letter from Clement Attlee to Harry S. Truman, 18 September 1945, reprinted in Williams, *Twilight of Empire*, 189–190.
102. Quoted in Bullock, *Ernest Bevin: Foreign Secretary*, 178.
103. Stanley Wolpert, *Shameful Flight: The Last Years of the British Empire in India* (Oxford: Oxford University Press, 2006), 93.
104. Quoted in Idem, 94.
105. Colville, Diary Entry, 6 August 1945, in Colville, *The Fringes of Power*, 612.
106. TNA, CAB 131/2, DO(46) 40, '[Defence in the Mediterranean, Middle East and Indian Ocean]: Memorandum by Ernest Bevin for Cabinet Defence Committee, 13 March 1946, in Ronald Hyam, ed., *British Documents on the End of Empire [BDOEE]: Series 2: The Labour Government and the End of Empire, 1945–1951: Part III: Strategy, Politics and Constitutional Change* (London: Her Majesty's Stationery Office, 1992), 215–218.

2 Mr Churchill's Europe

1. Gilbert, *Winston S. Churchill: Volume VIII*, 166.
2. Winston Churchill, 'A New Europe', Speech to the French Institute, Paris, 12 November 1945, in James, ed., *Winston S. Churchill: His Complete Speeches*, 7248.
3. Winston Churchill, 'The Future of Europe', Address to a Joint Meeting of the Senate and Chamber, Brussels, 16 November 1945, in Idem, 7252–7253.

4. CAC, CHUR 2/140, Letter from Leo Amery to Winston Churchill, 26 November 1945.
5. David Farber, *Speaking for England: Leo, Julian and John Amery – The Tragedy of a Political Family* (London: Free Press, 2005), 524–529.
6. CAC, CHUR 2/140, 'British Links with Europe', Address by Rt Hon L. S. Amery, University of London, 26 November 1945.
7. Raymond A. Callahan, *Churchill: Retreat from Empire* (Tunbridge Wells: D. J. Costello, 1984), 245–246.
8. Winston Churchill, 'The Sinews of Peace', Speech given at Westminster College, Fulton, Missouri, 5 March 1946, in James, ed., *Winston S. Churchill: His Complete Speeches*, 7285–7293.
9. *The Times*, 6 March 1946, quoted in Gilbert, *Winston S. Churchill: Volume VIII*, 204.
10. 'Churchill's call for world domination', *Chicago Sun*, 6 March 1946, quoted in Ibid.
11. All quoted in Idem, 205.
12. Letter from Winston Churchill to Clement Attlee, 7 March 1946, quoted in Idem, 197.
13. Idem, 206.
14. Gilbert, *Winston S. Churchill: Volume VIII*, 208.
15. Winston Churchill, 'The United States of Europe', Speech to the States-General of the Netherlands, The Hague, 9 May 1946, in James, ed., *Winston S. Churchill: His Complete Speeches*, 7318–7323.
16. Winston Churchill, 'Foreign Affairs', Speech in the House of Commons, 5 June 1946, in James, ed., *Winston S. Churchill: His Complete Speeches*, 7342–7354.
17. Letter from Leopold Amery to Winston Churchill, 7 June 1946, quoted in Gilbert, *Winston S. Churchill: Volume VIII*, 241.
18. Churchill confessed to Cooper that 'I should have been very hard hit in my feelings to France if the Communist deserter from the French Army in time of war [Maurice Thorez] had definitely appeared at the head of the French Government. That would indeed have been a blow'. (Letter from Winston Churchill to Duff Cooper, 8 June 1946, quoted in Idem, 242).
19. Letter from Winston Churchill to Viscount Cecil of Chelwood, 9 June 1946, quoted in Idem, 242–243.
20. Winston Churchill, 'France and Europe', Speech in Metz, France, 14 July 1946, in James, ed., Winston S. *Churchill: His Complete Speeches*, 7357–7359.
21. Gilbert, *Winston S. Churchill: Volume VIII*, 254.
22. Winston Churchill, 'The Tragedy of Europe', Speech at the University of Zurich, 19 September 1946, in James, ed., *Winston S. Churchill: His Complete Speeches*, 7379–7382.
23. CAC, Julian Amery Papers [AMEJ] 1/3/3, Winston Churchill, 'A united Europe: One way to stop a new war', *Collier's Weekly*, Copyright 1946 [no date].

24. Peter Weiler, *Ernest Bevin* (Manchester: Manchester University Press, 1993), 102.
25. Ibid.
26. For more on Bevin's time at the Ministry of Labour, see Alan Bullock, *The Life and Times of Ernest Bevin: Volume II: Minister of Labour, 1940–1945* (London: Heinemann, 1967).
27. John Barnes and David Nicholson, eds., *The Empire at Bay: The Leo Amery Diaries* (London: Hutchinson, 1988), 1030, quoted in Weiler, *Ernest Bevin*, 146.
28. Piers Dixon, *Double Diploma: The Life of Sir Pierson Dixon, Don and Diplomat* (London: Hutchinson, 1968), 170, quoted in Idem, 147.
29. TNA, FO 800/464/11–12, Note of a conversation after dinner at Chequers, 16 September 1945, between Prime Minister Clement Attlee, Foreign Secretary Ernest Bevin, British Ambassador to France Duff Cooper, French Foreign Minister Georges Bidault and French Ambassador to the Court of St James's René Massigli.
30. TNA, Board of Trade [BT] 11/3152, Letter from Sir Edmund Hall-Patch to James R. C. Helmore, 5 September 1946.
31. TNA, BT 11/3152, Draft Paper, attached to Ibid.
32. CAC, DUFC 4/5, Conversation between Ernest Bevin and George Bidault at dinner at the British Embassy, Paris, 11 October 1946. Report of Conversation written by P. Dixon, 12 October 1946.
33. Ibid.
34. TNA, FO 371/67578, Telegram from Washington to the Foreign Office, 18 January 1947.
35. TNA, FO 371/67578, Telegram from the Foreign Office to Washington, 1 February 1947.
36. These were listed as an 'active and vital' democracy; an 'emphasis on personal freedom' and the reconciliation of 'liberty and order'; a 'comprehensive system of social services and industrial welfare second to none'; the 'greatest experiment in a planned economy in a free society that the world has ever known'; and 'ideas, institutions, literature, sports, etc., [that] have exerted a major influence on modern civilisation'.
37. TNA, CAB 124/1007, no. 62, 'Projection of Britain Overseas': Proposed statement as revised by Mr Morrison for Committee on Overseas Information Services (OI(46)10), in Ronald Hyam, ed., *British Documents on the End of Empire [BDOEE]*, Series A, Volume 2: *The Labour Government and the End of Empire, 1945–1951*: Part 1: *High Policy and Administration* (London: HMSO, 1992), 306–309.
38. British Library Newspaper Collection, 'A plea to Europe', *The Daily Mail* (London), 20 September 1946, 2; 'A voice from Zurich', *The Times*, 20 September 1946, in Gilbert, *Winston S. Churchill: Volume VIII*, 266.

39. British Library Newspaper Collection, 'Let Europe arise', *Western Morning News* (Devon), 23 September 1946, 2.
40. CAC, CHUR 2/18, Letter from Leopold Amery to Winston Churchill, 20 September 1946.
41. CAC, Leopold Amery Papers [AMEL] 1/7/39, Letter from Leopold Amery to Duncan Sandys, 20 September 1946.
42. Wolfram Kaiser, *Using Europe, Abusing the Europeans: Britain and European Integration, 1945–65* (Basingstoke: Macmillan, 1966), 11.
43. CAC, CHUR 2/20A, Draft statement of aims for the European Union (British Branch), sent from Duncan Sandys to Winston Churchill, 11 October 1946.
44. CAC, CHUR 2/20A, Lists of persons attending meeting of 3 December 1946, sent from Duncan Sandys to Winston Churchill, 11 October 1946.
45. CAC, CHUR 2/22A, Agenda and meetings, Meeting of the United States of Europe (British Branch), 17 October 1946, prepared by Duncan Sandys, 17 October 1946.
46. CAC, CHUR 2/19, Letter from Winston Churchill to Lord Citrine, 20 October 1946; CAC, CHUR 2/19, Letter from Winston Churchill to Viscount Camrose, 9 November 1946.
47. CAC, CHUR 2/18, Letter from Winston Churchill to Clement Attlee, 27 November 1946.
48. CAC, CHUR 2/20A, Note from Duncan Sandys to Winston Churchill, 13 December 1946.
49. Lord Moran, *Winston Churchill: The Struggle for Survival, 1940–1965, Taken from the Diaries of Lord Moran* (London: Constable & Company, 1966), 317.
50. CAC, CHUR 2/18, L. S. Amery, 'European unity and world peace', the *Sunday Times*, 27 October 1946.
51. CAC, AMEL 1/7/39, Letter from Duncan Sandys to Leopold Amery, 6 November 1946.
52. CAC, AMEL 1/7/39, Letter from Leopold Amery to Duncan Sandys, 9 December 1946.
53. British Library Newspaper Collection, 'European unity worth striving for', *Hull Daily Main* (East Riding of Yorkshire), 7 December 1946, 3.
54. Macmillan, *Tides of Fortune*, 156.
55. CAC, CHUR 2/25A, Letter from Winston Churchill to Geoffrey Fisher, Archbishop of Canterbury, 28 December 1946.
56. CAC, CHUR 2/25A, 'Statement of Aims: United Europe: Revised Draft "E"'.
57. CAC, AMEL 1/7/39, Letter from Leopold Amery to Winston Churchill, 10 January 1947.
58. CAC, AMEL 1/7/39, Composition of the Provisional British Committee of the United Europe, 16 January 1946.
59. British Library Newspaper Collection, 'United Europe plan to prevent war', *The Press and Journal* (Aberdeen), 17 January 1947, 1; 'Plan for a United

Europe', *The Yorkshire Post* (West Yorkshire), 17 January 1947, 1; 'United Europe campaign launched', *Dundee Courier* (Dundee), 17 January 1947, 2; 'All-party plan for Europe', *Western Morning News* (Devon), 17 January 1947, 3.

60. British Library Newspaper Collection, Letter to the Editor, 'European unity', by G. I. Bennett, *The Yorkshire Post* (West Yorkshire), 27 January 1947, 3.
61. CAC, AMEL 1/7/39, Summary of discussion on 'Mr. Winston Churchill's Proposals for a United Europe', 22 January 1947.
62. TNA, FO 371/67578, Letter from the National Executive Committee of the Labour Party to all Labour Party Members, 22 January 1947.
63. CAC, CHUR 2/22A, Letter from Lord Lindsay of Birker to Winston Churchill, 5 February 1947.
64. CAC, CHUR 2/19, Letter from Count Richard Coudenhove-Kalargi to Duncan Sandys, 24 March 1947.
65. CAC, CHUR 2/19, Letter from Count Richard Coudenhove-Kalargi to Winston Churchill, 27 March 1947.
66. CAC, CHUR 2/18, Copy of the notes made at an informal meeting of the United Europe Committee, 30 April 1947.
67. CAC, Duncan Sandys Papers [DSND] 9/2/15, Final planning arrangements for the United Europe Meeting, Royal Albert Hall, 14 May 1947.
68. Winston Churchill, 'United Europe', Speech given at the Royal Albert Hall, London, 14 May 1947, in James, *Winston S. Churchill: His Complete Speeches*, 7483–7488.
69. British Library Newspaper Collection, 'Europe', *The Western Morning News* (Devon), 15 May 1947, 2.
70. Harold Macmillan, *Tides of Fortune*, 159.
71. CAC, AMEL 1/7/39, Letter from Leopold Amery to Sir Herbert Walker, 2 June 1947. Not all Conservatives shared Amery's views, however, although most who were uneasy waited until the late 1940s or early 1950s to voice their concerns, still reluctant in 1947 to criticise any initiative put forward by Churchill so soon after his stirring wartime leadership. See Sue Onslow, *Backbench Debate within the Conservative Party and Its Influence on British Foreign Policy, 1948–57* (Basingstoke: Macmillan, 1997), especially chapters 2 and 3, 12–54.
72. CAC, CHUR 2/22A, 'Mr Marshall calls on European countries to organise for U.S. aid', Memorandum from the US Information Service, 6 June 1947.
73. CAC, CHUR 2/22A, Draft statement from Winston Churchill on Secretary of State Marshall's Harvard Speech, for consideration by the United Europe Committee, no date.
74. CAC, CHUR 2/22A, Duncan Sandys' comments on Winston Churchill's draft statement, 10 June 1947.

75. Special Collections Department, Cadbury Research Library, University of Birmingham [CRL], Avon Papers [AP] 19/1/12, Letter from Winston Churchill to Anthony Eden, 19 April 1947.
76. CRL, AP 19/1/14A, Letter from Anthony Eden to Winston Churchill, 14 May 1947.
77. CAC, CHUR 2/22A, Anthony Eden's comments on Winston Churchill's draft statement, 9 June 1947.
78. Onslow, *Backbench Debate within the Conservative Party and Its Influence on British Foreign Policy*, 24–27. Like other Conservatives, however, at this time, Eden was still unwilling to openly contest Churchill's views. When the former Prime Minister asked him to serve on the Council of the United Europe Movement on 15 June, Eden readily agreed, although he declined to play a more involved role on the Executive. CRL, AP 19/1/16, Letter from Winston Churchill to Anthony Eden, 15 June 1947, and CRP, AP 19/1/16A, Letter from Anthony Eden to Winston Churchill, 19 June 1947.
79. CAC, AMEL 1/7/39, Letter from Richard Merton to Leopold Amery, 9 July 1947.
80. CAC, AMEL 1/7/39, Letter from Leopold Amery to Richard Merton, 28 July 1947.
81. CAC, AMEL 1/7/39, Letter from Duncan Sandys to Leopold Amery, 3 September 1947.
82. CAC, AMEL 1/7/39, Letter from Peter Fraser to Leopold Amery, 6 May 1947.
83. CAC, AMEL 1/7/39, Letter from Sir Shuldham Redfern to Leopold Amery, 9 September 1947.
84. CAC, AMEJ 1/3/1, 'Economic aspects of European unity', Memorandum prepared by the Economic Sub-Committee of United Europe Movement, March 1948.
85. James, ed., *Winston S. Churchill: The Complete Speeches*, 7528–7537.
86. Lipgens, *A History of European Integration, 1945–1947*, 657.
87. Duncan Sandys, Memorandum to all Members of the United Europe Movement Executive Committee, quoted in Idem, 661.
88. Idem, 659–664.
89. Idem, 684.
90. CAC, CHUR 2/20A, Agenda, Luncheon Meeting of the Executive Committee of the United Europe Movement, 3 March 1948.
91. CAC, CHUR 2/23, 'Memorandum on United Europe', written by Robert Boothby, 3 March 1948.
92. CAC, CHUR 2/19, 'Draft political report', Joint International Committee of the Movements for European Unity, 12 March 1948.
93. Letter from Emanuel Shinwell to Winston Churchill, quoted in Gilbert, *Winston S. Churchill: Volume VIII*, 398.

94. CHUR 2/18, 'Mr Churchill "too powerful": Blum explains Labour fears', *Glasgow Herald*, 27 March 1948.
95. CAC, CHUR 2/18, Open Letter from Winston Churchill to Léon Blum, 4 April 1948.
96. CAC, CHUR 2/21A, The British Delegation to the Congress of Europe, The Hague, May 1948.
97. Macmillan, *Tides of Fortune*, 158–159.
98. Gilbert, *Winston S. Churchill: Volume VIII*, 406.
99. CAC, CHUR 2/22A, Letter from Winston Churchill to Lord Layton, 25 May 1948.

3 Mr Bevin's response

1. TNA, FO 371/67578, Minute from Gladwyn Jebb to Sir Oliver Harvey, 28 January 1947.
2. TNA, FO 371/67578, Notes scribbled in the margins of Ibid.
3. TNA, FO 371/67578, Telegram from the Foreign Office to Paris and Washington, 3 February 1947.
4. See also Lundestad, *The United States and Western Europe since 1945*, 89–91.
5. TNA, FO 371/67579, Foreign Office circular sent to all HM Representatives in Europe, from Ernest Bevin, 10 April 1947.
6. TNA, FO 800/465/14, Note from Hector McNeil to Ernest Bevin, 14 March 1947.
7. TNA, FO 800/465/15, Letter from Ernest Bevin to Hector McNeil, 15 March 1947.
8. TNA, FO 800/465/16–17, Note on a meeting between Ernest Bevin and Vincent Auriol, 17 April 1947, prepared by Oliver Harvey.
9. Weiler, *Ernest Bevin*, 159.
10. Idem, 160.
11. Idem, 161–162.
12. CAC, CHUR 2/20A, Letter from Duff Cooper to Winston Churchill, 25 September 1946.
13. Bullock, *Ernest Bevin: Foreign Secretary*, 357–392.
14. See Ritchie Ovendale, 'The Palestine policy of the British Labour Government 1947: The decision of withdraw', *International Affairs*, Volume 56, Number 1 (January 1980); Wm. Roger Louis, 'British imperialism and the end of the Palestine mandate', in Wm. Roger Louis and Robert W. Stookey, eds., *The End of the Palestine Mandate* (Austin: University of Texas Press, 1986); and Martin Jones, *Failure in Palestine: British and United States Policy after the Second World War* (London: Mansell, 1986).

15. Memorandum from Ernest Bevin to Clement Attlee, 1 January 1947, quoted in Bullock, *Ernest Bevin: Foreign Secretary*, 360.
16. John Darwin, *Britain and Decolonisation: The Retreat from Empire in the Post-War World* (New York: St. Martin's, 1988), 94–95.
17. Quoted in Stanley Wolpert, *Shameful Flight: The Last Years of the British Empire in India* (Oxford/New York: Oxford University Press, 2006), 131.
18. Young, *Britain and European Unity*, 11.
19. TNA, FO 800/465/16-17, Note on the meeting between Ernest Bevin and Vincent Auriol, 17 April 1947, prepared by Oliver Harvey.
20. Bullock, *Ernest Bevin: Foreign Secretary*, 395–396.
21. TNA, FO 800/465/20, Telegram from Ernest Bevin to Duff Cooper, 9 June 1947.
22. TNA, FO 800/465/22, Telegram from Ernest Bevin to Duff Cooper, 14 June 1947.
23. Ernest Bevin, Speech at the Foreign Press Association Lunch, London, 13 June 1947, quoted in Bullock, *Ernest Bevin: Foreign Secretary*, 406.
24. Bullock, *Ernest Bevin: Foreign Secretary*, 407–409.
25. Michael J. Hogan, *The Marshall Plan: America, Britain and the Reconstruction of Western Europe, 1947–1952* (Cambridge: Cambridge University Press, 1987), 51–52.
26. Bullock, *Ernest Bevin: Foreign Secretary*, 422.
27. Idem, 425.
28. Hogan, *The Marshall Plan*, 127.
29. TNA, FO 371/62552, Memorandum from Sir Edmund Hall-Patch to Ernest Bevin, 7 August 1947.
30. Hogan, *The Marshall Plan*, 46.
31. Milward, *The United Kingdom and the European Community, Volume I: The Rise and Fall of a National Strategy, 1945–1963*, 25.
32. Hogan, *The Marshall Plan*, 46.
33. Milward, *The United Kingdom and the European Community*, 25.
34. Idem, 26.
35. Idem, 28–29.
36. TNA, FO 800/444, ff 29–31 [Trade Relations with Europe, America and the Empire]: Minute from Mr Bevin to Mr Attlee, 16 September 1947, in Hyam, ed., *BDOEE, Series A, Volume 2*, Part II, 314–315.
37. TNA, Colonial Office [CO] 537/1985, 'Customs Union: Minute from the President of the Board of Trade to the Prime Minister', 6 October 1947.
38. Milward, *The United Kingdom and the European Community*, 29.
39. TNA, CO 537/1985, Telegraph sent from the Dominions Office to the Colonies, 27 October 1947.
40. Milward, *The United Kingdom and the European Community*, 30.

41. TNA, FO 800/465/39, Telegram from Hector McNeil to Ernest Bevin, 7 October 1947.
42. TNA, FO 800/447/98–99, Record of a conversation between Ernest Bevin and Georges Bidault, 29 November 1947, prepared by P. Dixon, 1 December 1947.
43. TNA, FO 800/447/99–101, Record of a discussion between Ernest Bevin and Georges Bidault at the Foreign Office, 17 December 1947.
44. TNA, CO 537/1985, Telegram from Roger Stevens, Head of the Economic Relations Department of the Foreign Office, to Joint, 18 November 1947.
45. Quoted in Milward, *The United Kingdom and the European Community*, 31.
46. TNA, CAB 129/23, CP (48) 6, 'The first aim of British foreign policy': Cabinet Memorandum by Mr Bevin, 4 January 1948, in Hyam, ed., *BDOEE, Series A, Volume 2*, Part II, 317–318.
47. TNA, CAB 128/12, CM 2(48) 5, 'Foreign policy in Europe': Cabinet conclusions, 8 January 1948, in Hyam, ed., *BDOEE, Series A, Volume 2*, Part II, 326–328.
48. Milward, *The United Kingdom and the European Community*, 31–32.
49. TNA, CO 537/3151, no. 62 [The Anglo–French Colonial Talks, 17–20 February 1948]: Minute by Sir S. Caine, 24 March 1948, in Hyam, ed., *BDOEE, Series A, Volume 2*, Part II, 425–426.
50. TNA, CAB 129/25, CP (48) 72, 'The threat to Western civilisation': Cabinet memorandum by Mr Bevin, 3 March 1948, in Hyam, ed., *BDOEE, Series A, Volume 2*, Part II, 328–330.
51. Milward, *The United Kingdom and the European Community*, 33.
52. CAC, Papers of Mark Abrams (ABMS) 3/8, Public Opinion Survey: Marshall Plan: J.112: March 1948, prepared by Research Services Limited.
53. CAC, ABMS 3/20, Survey of Public Opinion on Current Politics: E.183, May 1948, prepared by Research Services Limited.
54. TNA, CO 537/2819, 'Facing facts at Brussels', *Foreign Report* of the Economist Intelligence Unit, 12 February 1948.
55. TNA, FO 800/440/16, Telegram, personal, from Ernest Bevin to Paul-Henri Spaak, 18 February 1948.
56. Ibid.
57. TNA, FO 800/447/110–141, Conversations during the Secretary of State's visits to Paris for the C.E.E.C. Meeting (15–16 March 1948) and to Brussels for the signature of the Five-Power Brussels Treaty (17–18 March 1948), Conversation between the Ministers for Foreign Affairs of the United Kingdom, France, Belgium, the Netherlands and Luxembourg, 17 March 1948.
58. TNA, FO 371/73038, no 5159, 'Notes on international colonial co-operation': CO Information Department Memorandum no. 20, June 1948, in Hyam, ed., *BDOEE, Series A, Volume 2*, Part II, 427–431.
59. TNA, FO 371/73038, no. 5307, 'International Study Conference on Overseas Territories of Western Europe', Amsterdam, 9–12 June 1948: Despatch from

B. E. F. Gage (The Hague) to Mr Bevin, 26 June 1948, in Hyam, ed., *BDOEE, Series A, Volume 2*, Part II, 431–435.
60. TNA, FO 371/73039, no. 5989 [Collaboration with the French in Africa]: Despatch from Mr Creech Jones to all West African governors, 9 August 1948, in Hyam, ed., *BDOEE, Series A, Volume 2*, Part II, 435–438.
61. For an in-depth study of Bevin's relations with Europe – particularly with France – during these years, see Sean Greenwood, *The Alternative Alliance: Anglo-French Relations before the Coming of NATO, 1944–48* (London: Minerva, 1996).

4 The German problem

1. Roger G. Miller, *To Save a City: The Berlin Airlift, 1948–1949* (College Station: Texas A&M University Press, 2000), 32.
2. Quoted in Idem, 18.
3. Idem, 31; and Bullock, *Ernest Bevin: Foreign Secretary*, 531–548.
4. Miller, *To Save a City*, 31–32.
5. Bullock, *Ernest Bevin: Foreign Secretary*, 575.
6. CM (48) 43 (extract) CAB 128/13, Conclusions of a meeting of the Cabinet, 25 June 1948, in Keith Hamilton, Patrick Salmon and Stephen Twigge, eds., *Documents on British Policy Overseas [DBPO], Series III, Volume VI: Berlin in the Cold War, 1948–90* (London: Routledge, 2009) Document No. 21, CD-ROM.
7. Despatch 914 to Washington, Conversation between the Secretary of State Ernest Bevin and the United States Ambassador, 25 June 1948, in *DBPO, Series III, Volume VI*, Document No. 24, CD-ROM.
8. Miller, *To Save a City*, 45–46.
9. Telegram 1966 from Foreign Office to Paris, 28 June 1948, in *DBPO, Series III, Volume VI*, Document No. 37, CD-ROM.
10. Letter from Winston Churchill to Clement Attlee, 21 July 1948; and Letter from Winston Churchill to General Dwight Eisenhower, 27 July 1948, both quoted in Idem, 422.
11. CRL, AP 19/1/33, Letter from Winston Churchill to Anthony Eden, 12 September 1948.
12. CAC, CHUR 2/22A/68–69, Letter from Captain Stephen King-Hall to Winston Churchill, June 1948.
13. TNA, CAB 21/1970, 'Note of deputation from the British Section of the International Committee of the Movements for European Unity, received by the Prime Minister and Foreign Secretary', 17 June 1948.
14. Bullock, *Ernest Bevin: Foreign Secretary*, 584.
15. Ibid.

16. Idem, 585.
17. Gilbert, *Winston S. Churchill: Volume VIII*, 424–425.
18. Geoffrey Warner, 'The Labour governments and the unity of Western Europe, 1945–51', in Ritchie Ovendale, ed., *The Foreign Policy of the British Labour Governments, 1945–1951* (Leicester: Leicester University Press, 1984), 68.
19. CAC, CHUR 2/20B, Enclosure sent from Kenneth Hare-Scott to Winston Churchill, 19 April 1948.
20. CAC, CHUR 2/18, Letter from Winston Churchill to Clement Attlee, 27 July 1948.
21. CAC, CHUR 2/18, Letter from Clement Attlee to Winston Churchill, 30 July 1948.
22. Letter from Clement Attlee to Winston Churchill, 21 August 1948; and Letter from Winston Churchill to Clement Attlee, 21 August 1948, both quoted in Gilbert, *Winston S. Churchill: Volume VIII*, 425.
23. Ian Turner, 'The British occupation and its impact on Germany', in Ian D. Turner, ed., *Reconstruction in Post-War Germany: British Occupation Policy and the Western Zones, 1945–55* (Oxford: Berg, 1989), 4.
24. Milward, *The United Kingdom and the European Community, Volume I*, 21.
25. TNA, FO 371/55586, Franklin Minute, 8 February 1946, quoted in Anne Deighton, 'Cold War diplomacy: British policy towards Germany's Role in Europe, 1945–9', in Turner, ed., *Reconstruction in Post-War Germany*, 22.
26. Miller, *To Save a City*, 15.
27. Deighton, 'Cold War Diplomacy', 32.
28. Ibid.
29. Idem, 31.
30. Despatch 239 to Berlin, Conversation between the Secretary of State for Foreign Affairs and German Social Democrat representatives, 6 July 1948, in *DBPO, Series III, Volume VI*, Document No. 55, CD-ROM.
31. Minute, Strang to Bevin, 8 July 1948, in *DBPO, Series III, Volume VI*, Document No. 72, CD-ROM.
32. Minutes, Extract from Chiefs of Staff Committee (48), 96th meeting, 9 July 1948, in *DBPO, Series III, Volume VI*, Document 73, CD-ROM.
33. Despatch 1078 to Washington, Record of a conversation between the Secretary of State for Foreign Affairs and the United States Ambassador, 22 July 1948, in *DBPO, Series III, Volume VI*, Document No. 80, CD-ROM.
34. Despatch 1105 to Washington, Record of a conversation between the Secretary of State for Foreign Affairs and the United States Ambassador, 26 July 1948, in *DBPO, Series III, Volume VI*, Document No. 82, CD-ROM.
35. Telegram 8758 to Washington, From Foreign Office to Washington, 9 August 1948, in *DBPO, Series III, Volume VI*, Document No. 92, CD-ROM.
36. Bullock, *Ernest Bevin: Foreign Secretary*, 590.

37. Idem, 591.
38. Idem, 592–593.
39. Telegram 10207, From Foreign Office to Washington, 10 September 1948, in *DBPO, Series III, Volume VI*, Document No. 107, CD-ROM.
40. Telegram 10208, From Foreign Office to Washington, 10 September 1948, in *DBPO, Series III, Volume VI*, Document No. 107, CD-ROM.
41. Bullock, *Ernest Bevin: Foreign Secretary*, 593.
42. Letter: Roberts to Strang, 14 September 1948, in *DBPO, Series III, Volume VI*, Document No. 110, CD-ROM.
43. Bullock, *Ernest Bevin: Foreign Secretary*, 594.
44. Cabinet Conclusions (extract), Cabinet 61 (48), 22 September 1948, in *DBPO, Series III, Volume VI*, Document No. 111, CD-ROM.
45. Letter, Robertson to Strang, 30 September 1948, in *DBPO, Series III, Volume VI*, Document No. 168, CD-ROM.
46. Letter, Kirkpatrick to Robertson, 14 October 1948, in *DBPO, Series III, Volume VI*, Document No. 170, CD-ROM.
47. Bullock, *Ernest Bevin: Foreign Secretary*, 626.
48. Miller, *To Save a City*, 180.
49. Memo by Bevin, GEN 241/4, Cabinet Committee of Ministers on Germany, 'Germany and Berlin', Memorandum by the Secretary of State for Foreign Affairs, 4 February 1949, in *DBPO, Series III, Volume VI*, Document No. 135, CD-ROM.
50. Ibid. See also GEN 241/9th meeting, Cabinet Committee of Ministers on Germany, Minutes of meeting held on 7 February 1949, in *DBPO, Series III, Volume VI*, Document No. 136, CD-ROM.
51. TNA, The British Council [BW] 1/56, 'Germany', A briefing report for the chairman, British Council, 1949.
52. TNA, FO 800/465/FR/47/31, Summary of Bevin's talk with Bidault, 17 December 1947, quoted in Bullock, *Ernest Bevin: Foreign Secretary*, 499.
53. Michael F. Hopkins, *Oliver Franks and the Truman Administration: Anglo–American Relations, 1948–1952* (London: Frank Cass, 2003), 90.
54. Bullock, *Ernest Bevin: Foreign Secretary*, 622–623. See also Peter Foot, 'Britain, European unity and NATO, 1947–1950', in Francis H. Heller and John R. Gillingham, eds., *NATO: The Founding of the Atlantic Alliance and the Integration of Europe* (Basingstoke: Macmillan, 1992), 57–69.
55. Bullock, *Ernest Bevin: Foreign Secretary*, 623; Hopkins, *Oliver Franks and the Truman Administration*, 95.
56. Bullock, *Ernest Bevin: Foreign Secretary*, 670.
57. Michael Hopkins writes: 'With Acheson's arrival there began a new and rich phase in Franks' ambassadorship. For the remaining four years the Ambassador and the Secretary of State were to enjoy a working relationship that was

exceptional, if not indeed unique, in the history of the two countries since 1945' (*Oliver Franks and the Truman Administration*, 106).
58. Bullock, *Ernest Bevin: Foreign Secretary*, 670–675. For a full account of these meetings and, in particular, the British role in them, see Hopkins, *Oliver Franks and the Truman Administration*, 108–114.
59. Hopkins, *Oliver Franks and the Truman Administration*, 114.
60. Crowson, *Britain and Europe*, 63. See also Geir Lundestad, *'Empire' by Integration: The United States and European Integration, 1945–1997* (Oxford: Oxford University Press, 1998), 29–31.
61. Washington Telegram 1854, From Ernest Bevin to Sir William Strang, 1 April 1949, in *DBPO, Series III, Volume VI*, Document No. 139, CD-ROM.
62. Telegram 3638 to Washington, From Clement Attlee to Ernest Bevin, 1 April 1949, in *DBPO, Series III, Volume VI*, Document No. 140, CD-ROM.
63. Washington Telegram 2413, From Sir Oliver Franks to Ernest Bevin, 28 April 1949, in *DBPO, Series III, Volume VI*, Document No. 152, CD-ROM.
64. John Lamberton Harper, *American Visions of Europe: Franklin D. Roosevelt, George F. Kennan, and Dean G. Acheson* (Cambridge: Cambridge University Press, 1994), 187 and 203.
65. Telegram 4671 to Washington, From Ernest Bevin to Sir Oliver Franks, 28 April 1949, in *DBPO, Series III, Volume VI*, Document No. 154, CD-ROM.
66. Washington telegram 2467, From Sir Oliver Franks to Ernest Bevin, in *DBPO, Series III, Volume VI*, Document No. 157, CD-ROM.
67. Miller, *To Save a City*, 181.
68. Idem, 184–185.
69. Idem, 186.
70. Idem, 187.

5 A disunited Europe?

1. CRL, AP 13/3/15, Notes on Mr Eden's visit to Germany, 12–17 July 1948, prepared by H. L. d'A. H., 20 July 1948.
2. CRL, AP 19/1/33, Letter from Winston Churchill to Anthony Eden, 12 September 1948.
3. CRL, AP 19/1/33B, Poll of Public Opinion, Questionnaire No. 100a, *Daily Express*, 8 September 1948.
4. CAC, AMEJ 1/3/1, 'Speakers' notes', United Europe Movement, 9 August 1948.

5. CAC, AMEL 1/7/29, 'At turning point in outlook on world', by Rt Hon L. S. Amery, President of the Empire Industries Association and the British Empire League, in *The British Australasian: The Australian and New Zealand Weekly: The Only Paper Published in Europe for Australians and New Zealanders*, Volume XXVIII, No. 3339, 8 October 1948, 1.
6. Duncan Sandys, 'Western unity: Britain's imperial commitments', *The Times*, October 18 1948.
7. CAC, AMEJ 1/3/1, *Financial Times*, 27 July 1948.
8. TNA, CO 875/24, No. 8, 'Notes on British colonial policy': CO circular memorandum No. 28. Annex: CO Information Dept. circular outline (CO 857/24, No. 22, nd), March 1949, in Hyam, ed., *BDOEE: Series A: Volume 2*: Part 1, 326–334.
9. CAC, DSND 9/2/1, 'The European Union', Press Release, no author, 25 October 1948.
10. CAC, CHUR 2/20A, 'The European Movement: Press release No. 4', 25 October 1948.
11. CAC, DSND 9/3/1, Speech by Rt Hon Duncan Sandys at a luncheon of the Anglo–American Press Association in Paris, 1 December 1948.
12. CAC, CHUR 2/20B, Summary of statement by the delegation of the European Movement to the Five-Power Committee on European unity, 9 December 1948.
13. CRL, AP 13/3/23, Notes from Mr. Macmillan's speech in the American Aid and European (Financial Provisions) Bill Debate, Friday, 28 January 1949.
14. CAC, CHUR 2/25A, Letter from Count Richard Coudenhove-Kalergi to Winston Churchill, 22 April 1949.
15. CAC, CHUR 2/25A, Letter from Duncan Sandys to Winston Churchill, 3 May 1949
16. CAC, CHUR 2/25A, Letter from Winston Churchill to Count Richard Coudenhove-Kalergi, 8 May 1949.
17. CAC, CHUR 2/25A, Letter from Count Richard Coudenhove-Kalergi to Winston Churchill, 17 May 1949.
18. TNA, FO 800/440/41, Telegram from Foreign Secretary to OEEC Paris (United Kingdom Delegation), 14 October 1948.
19. TNA, FO 800/440/42, Personal telegram from Ernest Bevin to Paul-Henri Spaak, 14 October 1948.
20. TNA, FO 800/440/43–48, Letter from Hector McNeil, Minister of State, to Ernest Bevin, 16 October 1948.
21. TNA, FO 800/447/200, Record of the third meeting of the Consultative Council, Paris, 25–26 October 1948; Private Session, 25 October 1948.
22. FCO, Treasury [T] 232/47, Letter from J. V. Robb, Foreign Office, to E. R. Warner, Villa la Fenetre, Geneva, cc'd to Paul Gore-Booth (Foreign Office), Atkinson (Economic Information Unit) and Geoffrey Wilson (Cabinet Office), 28 October 1948, including as attachment the memorandum, 'Publicity

to combat the critical attitude of certain newspapers and journalists towards the United Kingdom policy at Economic Commission for Europe', 27 October 1948.
23. TNA, FO 800/448/3, Meeting of the Consultative Council of the Five-Power Brussels Treaty, London, 27–29 January 1949.
24. TNA, CO 537/4611, '[Africa]: Closer co-ordination of Anglo–French policies in Africa: Minute by A B Cohen', 2 March 1949, in Hyam, ed, *BDOEE, Series A, Volume 2*, Part II, 440–443.
25. TNA, FO 800/448/222, Record of the sixth session of the Consultative Council of the Brussels Treaty, Luxembourg, 17–19 June 1949.
26. Macmillan, *Tides of Fortune*, 168.
27. TNA, FO 800/448, Record of conversation between Ernest Bevin and Paul van Zeeland, 14 September 1949.
28. Robert Boothby, *Boothby: Recollections of a Rebel* (London: Hutchinson, 1978), 217.
29. Idem, 217–218.
30. Bullock, *Ernest Bevin: Foreign Secretary*, 716.
31. Quoted in Ibid.
32. Harper, *American Visions of Europe*, 213–214.
33. TNA, FO 800/448/262, Record of a meeting held at the State Department, Washington DC, 15 September 1949.
34. See Hopkins, *Oliver Franks and the Truman Administration*, 119–135.
35. Bullock, *Ernest Bevin: Foreign Secretary*, 720–722.
36. Quoted in Idem, 722.
37. Ibid.
38. Quoted in Harper, *American Visions of Europe*, 289.
39. TNA, FO 371/80024, Minute from F. D. W. Brown, Foreign Office, 6 October 1949.
40. CAC, DSND 9/3/2, Note from Duncan Sandys to Winston Churchill, 24 September 1949.
41. TNA, CAB 129/37/1, CP (49) 208, 'European policy': Cabinet memorandum by Mr Bevin on creation of a 'third world power' or consolidation of the West, 18 October 1949, in Hyam, ed, *BDOEE, Series A, Volume 2*, Part II, 340–348.
42. TNA, CAB 129/37/1, CP (49) 204, 'Council of Europe': Cabinet memorandum by Mr Bevin, 24 October 1949, in Hyam, ed., *BDOEE, Series A, Volume 2*, Part II, 348–353.
43. CAC, DSND 9/2/15, Speech by Paul-Henri Spaak, President of the Strasbourg Assembly of Europe, at the European Movement Meeting, Kingsway Hall, London, 28 November 1949.
44. CAC, DSND, Speech by Winston Churchill, at the European Movement Meeting, Kingsway Hall, London, 28 November 1949.

45. CAC, DSND, Speech by Winston Churchill, at the European Movement Meeting, Kingsway Hall, London, 28 November 1949.
46. CAC, DSND, Speech by Winston Churchill, at the European Movement Meeting, Kingsway Hall, London, 28 November 1949.
47. TNA, FO 800/448/377, Record of conversation with Robert Schuman, 2 November 1949, during the second session of the Committee of Ministers of the Council of Europe.
48. TNA, FO 371/80024, Minute from J. J. S. Garner, Under-Secretary of State at the Commonwealth Relations Office, 24 November 1949.
49. CAC, AMEJ 1/3/6, Survey of Public Opinion of European Union, Undertaken by the Eric Stern Public Opinion Research Organisation, Spring 1950.
50. Graham L. Rees, *Britain and the Postwar European Payments Systems* (Cardiff: University of Wales Press, 1963), 89–93.
51. Idem, 99.
52. Barry Eichengreen, *Reconstructing Europe's Trade and Payments: The European Payments Union* (Manchester: Manchester University Press, 1993), 1.
53. Rees, *Britain and the Postwar European Payments Systems*, 102–103.
54. Hugh Gaitskell, Diary Entry, 26 May 1950, in *The Diary of Hugh Gaitskell, 1945–1956*, edited by Philip M. Williams (London: Jonathan Cape, 1983), 186.
55. Rees, *Britain and the Postwar European Payments Systems*, 103–105.
56. Gaitskell, Diary Entry, 11 August 1950, in *The Diary of Hugh Gaitskell*, 190–191.
57. Rees, *Britain and the Postwar European Payments Systems*, 105–106.
58. Gaitskell, Diary Entry, 11 August 1950, in *The Diary of Hugh Gaitskell*, 191.
59. Rees, *Britain and the Postwar European Payments Systems*, 110–111.
60. Gaitskell, Diary Entry, 11 August 1950, in *The Diary of Hugh Gaitskell*, 191. For more on the European Payments Union, see also Alan S. Milward, *The Reconstruction of Western Europe, 1945–51* (London: Methuen & Co., 1984), especially chapters 10 and 11, 299–361.

6 The continental surprise and the fall of the Labour government

1. TNA, FO 800/449/99, Record of conversation with the French Ambassador, 9 May 1950.
2. TNA, FO 800/449/99, French press statement on the Schuman Plan, 9 May 1950.
3. François Duchêne, *Jean Monnet: The First Statesman of Interdependence* (London: W. W. Norton, 1994), 157–166.
4. TNA, Treasury [T] 229/216, Note of four conversations held with Monsieur Jean Monnet at the Treasury, between 3 and 7 March 1949.

5. TNA, T 229/216, 'Conversations with Monsieur Monnet: A briefing paper', 18 March 1949.
6. See, for example: TNA, T 229/216, 'First thoughts on the Monnet discussions', by E. A. Hitchman, 6 April 1949; TNA, T 229/216, 'First thoughts about M. Monnet', A memorandum by R. L. Hall to Sir Edwin Plowden, 8 April 1949; TNA, T 229/216, 'First thoughts for M. Monnet', by R. Willis, 11 April 1949.
7. TNA, T 229/216, 'Note on conversations with M Monnet', by Sir Edwin Plowden, 26 April 1949.
8. Duchêne, *Jean Monnet*, 188.
9. TNA, FO 371/88632, Letter from Sir Oliver Harvey to Sir Gladwyn Jebb, 30 December 1949.
10. Charles Moore, *Margaret Thatcher: The Authorized Biography: Volume One: Not For Turning* (London: Allen Lane, 2013), 97.
11. CRL, AP 14/3/10A, Speech at Chislehurst by Leopold Amery, 6 February 1950, included with AP 14/3/10, Letter from Leopold Amery to Anthony Eden, 8 February 1950.
12. Bullock, *Ernest Bevin: Foreign Secretary*, 753.
13. Idem, 756.
14. Quoted in Kenneth O. Morgan, *Labour in Power, 1945–1951* (Oxford: Clarendon Press, 1984), 410.
15. Sir Cuthbert Headlam, *Parliament and Politics in the Age of Churchill and Attlee: The Headlam Diaries, 1935–51*, edited by Stuart Ball (Cambridge: Cambridge University Press, 1999), 613.
16. Idem, 769.
17. Duchêne, *Jean Monnet*, 201.
18. Bullock, *Ernest Bevin: Foreign Secretary*, 769.
19. Geoffrey Warner, ed., *In the Midst of Events: The Foreign Office Diaries and Papers of Kenneth Younger, February 1950–October 1951* (Abingdon: Routledge, 2005), 13.
20. Duchêne, *Jean Monnet*, 201.
21. Hopkins, *Oliver Franks and the Truman Administration*, 153.
22. TNA, FO 800/449, Record of a conversation with Dean Acheson and Robert Schuman, 11 May 1950.
23. Harper, *American Visions of Europe*, 297.
24. Younger, Diary Entry, in Warner, ed., *In the Midst of Events*, 14.
25. Ibid.
26. Idem, 16.
27. Idem, 17–18.
28. CAC, CHUR 2/27, Press statement on the Schuman Plan, United Europe Movement, 15 May 1950.
29. Macmillan, *Tides of Fortune*, 189.

30. Quoted in Hopkins, *Oliver Franks and the Truman Administration*, 153.
31. British Library Newspaper Archive, 'The pact of Steel', Comment, *The Daily Mail* (London), 11 May 1950, 1.
32. Quoted in Edmund Dell, *The Schuman Plan and the British Abdication of Leadership in Europe*, 235–236.
33. Idem, 236–237.
34. Quoted in Idem, 237.
35. Idem, 238.
36. Quoted in Idem, 240.
37. TNA, CAB 124/1981, Message from the Foreign Secretary to the French Foreign Minister, 25 May 1950.
38. TNA, CAB 124/1981, Memorandum from the French Foreign Minister to the Secretary of State, complete with a communique to be signed by the British Government pledging its commitment, 25 May 1950.
39. TNA, CAB 124/1981, Memorandum by the United Kingdom Government to the French Government, 27 May 1950.
40. TNA, CAB 124/1981, Memorandum from Robert Schuman to Ernest Bevin, 30 May 1950.
41. TNA, CAB 124/1981, Memorandum from Ernest Bevin to Robert Schuman, 31 May 1950.
42. Quoted in Dell, *The Schuman Plan and the British Abdication of Leadership in Europe*, 242.
43. TNA, CAB 124/1981, French memorandum to the British Government, 1 June 1950.
44. Young, *Britain and European Unity*, 29.
45. TNA, CAB 124/1981, British memorandum to the French Government, 2 June 1950.
46. Younger, Diary Entry, in Warner, ed., *In the Midst of Events*, 19.
47. Bullock, *Ernest Bevin: Foreign Secretary*, 780.
48. Quoted in Chris Gifford, *The Making of Eurosceptic Britain: Identity and Economy in a Post-Imperial State* (Aldershot: Ashgate, 2008), 30.
49. Crowson, *Britain and Europe*, 67.
50. Young, *Britain and European Unity*, 30.
51. Younger, Diary Entry, in Warner, *In the Midst of Events*, 20.
52. Idem, 24–25.
53. TNA, CAB 124/1981, Six Power communique, 3 June 1950.
54. TNA, CAB 124/1981, British communique, 3 June 1950.
55. TNA, CAB 124/1981, French communique, 3 June 1950.
56. CAC, AMEJ 1/3/18, 'European unity: A statement by the National Executive Committee of the Labour Party', May 1950.
57. Quoted in Dell, *The Schuman Plan and the British Abdication of Leadership in Europe*, 248.

58. Ibid.
59. Anthony Nutting, *Europe Will Not Wait: A Warning and a Way Out* (London: Hollis & Carter, 1960), 29.
60. Idem, 32.
61. CAC, CHUR 2/112, Letter from Anthony Eden to Winston Churchill, enclosing notes from a conversation with the French Ambassador, 23 June 1950.
62. Macmillan, *Tides of Fortune*, 191–192.
63. Hopkins, *Oliver Franks and the Truman Administration*, 154.
64. Younger, Diary Entry, in Warner, ed., *In the Midst of Events*, 25.
65. William Stueck, *The Korean War: An International History* (Princeton: Princeton University Press, 1995), 11.
66. Max Hastings, *The Korean War* (New York: Simon and Schuster, 1987), 60–61.
67. Idem, 70; and Stueck, *The Korean War*, 72.
68. Bullock, *Ernest Bevin: Foreign Secretary*, 783.
69. TNA, CAB 129/41, CP (50) 153, 'Integration with Western European coal and steel industries: Commonwealth implications': Cabinet memorandum by Gordon Walker, 3 July 1950, in Hyam, ed., *BDOEE, Series A, Volume 2*, Part II, 365–367.
70. TNA, T 232/194, Treasury Memorandum: 'Consequences of contemporary movements in Western Europe towards forms of economic integration having federal implications', 19 July 1950.
71. CRL, AP 19/1/54A, Letter from Winston Churchill to Clement Attlee, 2 August 1950.
72. Quoted in Macmillan, *Tides of Fortune*, 193–194.
73. CRL, AP 19/1/56, Letter from Winston Churchill to Anthony Eden, 8 August 1950.
74. CAC, DSND 9/3/2, Council of Europe: Report of the seventh meeting of the Conservative Parliamentary Inter-Committee Group, House of Commons, 19 October 1950.
75. Macmillan, *Tides of Fortune*, 202.
76. Quoted in Ibid.
77. TNA, CAB 21/1970, 'Second session of the Consultative Assembly of the Council of Europe, Strasbourg, 7–28 August 1950', Notes by Denis Healy, submitted to the International Sub-Committee of the National Executive Committee of the Labour Party.
78. CAC, CHUR 2/112, Telegram from Anthony Eden to Winston Churchill, 11 August 1950.
79. CAC, CHUR 2/32, 'European Army', Notes prepared by the Rapporteur, Committee on General Affairs, Consultative Assembly, Council of Europe, 15 August 1950, sent from Duncan Sandys to Winston Churchill, 15 August 1950.

80. CAC, CHUR 2/32, Letter from Winston Churchill to Harry S Truman, 13 August 1950.
81. TNA, FO 800/495/109, Telegram from Hugh Dalton to Ernest Bevin, 14 August 1950.
82. CRL, AP 14/3/1, Letter from Kenneth Lindsay to Anthony Eden, August 1950.
83. CAC, DSND 9/2/18, 'European Movement: Objectives and Constitution of the European Movement', 18 October 1950.
84. CAC, DSND 9/2/19, 'Survey of public opinion on the question of European Union', undertaken by the Eric Stern Public Opinion Research Organisation, 22 September 1950.
85. TNA, FO 800/465/245, Note from Ernest Davies to Sir Pierson Dixon, describing a meeting between Ernest Bevin and Guy Mollet, 1 November 1950.
86. Warner, ed., *In the Midst of Events*, 37.
87. Younger, Diary Entry, in Idem, 44.
88. TNA, CAB 21/1682, 'An appreciation of the military and political situation in Malaya', by General Harold Briggs, Director of Operations, forwarded to the Chief of Staffs Committee of the Cabinet, November 16 1950.
89. TNA, CAB 21/1682, Minutes of a meeting held by the Chiefs of Staff Committee of the Cabinet, November 23 1950.
90. TNA, CAB 21/1682, Minutes of a meeting held between General Harold Briggs, Director of Operations, and Clement Attlee, Prime Minister, with Sir Henry Gurney and Cabinet Secretaries present, November 24 1950.
91. Younger, Diary Entry, in Warner, ed., *In the Midst of Events*, 51.
92. Headlam, *Diaries*, 630.
93. Morgan, *Labour in Power*, 439–440.
94. Henry Pelling, *The Labour Governments 1945–51* (London: Macmillan, 1984), 247.
95. CRL, AP 14/3/9, Letter from Julian Amery to Anthony Eden, 21 December 1950.
96. CRL, AP 14/3/9A, Letter from Anthony Eden to Julian Amery, 29 December 1950.
97. Quoted in Pelling, *The Labour Governments*, 247.
98. Idem, 248.
99. Bullock, *Ernest Bevin: Foreign Secretary*, 835.
100. Crowson, *Britain and Europe*, 66.
101. Younger, Diary Entry, in Warner, ed., *In the Midst of Events*, 72
102. Idem, 68–69.
103. Pelling, *The Labour Governments*, 249–250.
104. CAC, DSND 9/3/1, 'Progress of the idea of a European Army: Chronological survey', Prepared by Duncan Sandys.

105. TNA, FO 800/465/268–269, Note from R. G. Y. to Clement Attlee, 31 January 1951.
106. TNA, FO 371, 96343, Foreign Secretary's conversation with Guy Mollet, 17 March 1951.
107. Younger, Diary Entry, in Warner, ed., *In the Midst of Events*, 69–70.
108. Ibid.
109. Pelling, *The Labour Governments*, 257.
110. CAC, AMEJ 1/3/20, Telegram from Winston Churchill to Commonwealth Prime Ministers, 24 June 1951.
111. CAC, AMEJ 1/3/20, Letter from Harold Macmillan to Commonwealth Prime Ministers, 26 June 1951.
112. CRC, AP 14/3/57A, Leopold Amery, 'Towards a balanced world', *European Review*, No. 9, July 1951, sent with a letter to Anthony Eden, 11 July 1951; and to Winston Churchill (CAC, CHUR 2/27).
113. CAC, AMEJ 1/3/20, Letter from Canadian Prime Minister to Harold Macmillan, 4 July 1951.
114. CAC, AMEJ 1/3/20, Letter from New Zealand Prime Minister to Harold Macmillan, 25 July 1951; CAC, AMEJ 1/3/20, Letter from Australian Prime Minister to Harold Macmillan, 24 August 1951.
115. CAC, AMEJ 1/3/5, Letter from Sir Frank Keith Officer to Julian Amery, 4 July 1951.
116. CAC, AMEJ 1/3/20, Letter from Harold Macmillan to the Australian Prime Minister, 10 September 1951.
117. CAC, AMEJ 1/3/20, Letter from Australian Prime Minister to Harold Macmillan, 4 October 1951.
118. TNA, FO 371/96344, Letter from G. C. Alchin to C. A. E. Shuckburgh, 27 September 1951.
119. TNA, FO 371/124968, No. 24/2, 'Some notes on British foreign policy': Memorandum by Sir Roger Makins (FO), 11 August 1951, in Hyam, ed., *BDOEE, Series A, Volume 2*, Part II, 373–379.
120. Morgan, *Labour in Power*, 485–486.
121. Pelling, *The Labour Governments*, 259.
122. CAC, AMEJ 1/3/21: Part 1, Letter from Julian Amery to Harold Macmillan, 12 November 1951.

7 The realities of government

1. Gilbert, *Winston S. Churchill: Volume VIII*, 657–658.
2. Idem, 658.
3. Idem, 659.
4. Idem, 660.

5. TNA, FO 371/96345, 'Paris talks: European integration', Minute by Pierson Dixon, 31 October 1951.
6. TNA, CAB 129/48, C (51) 32, 'United Europe': Cabinet note by Mr Churchill, 29 November 1951, in David Goldsworthy, ed., *British Documents on the End of Empire [BDOEE], Series A, Volume 3, The Conservative Government and the End of Empire, 1951–1957*: Part I, *International Relations* (London: HMSO, 1994), 3–4.
7. Boothby, *Boothby*, 211.
8. Macmillan, *Tides of Fortune*, 157.
9. CRL, AP 14/3/84, Letter from Monsieur H. Hayat, Chamber of Representatives, Brussels, to Anthony Eden, 26 November 1951.
10. CRL, AP 14/3/83, Letter from D. Fairbanks to Anthony Eden, 19 November 1951.
11. Quoted in Macmillan, *Tides of Fortune*, 220.
12. CAC, AMEJ 1/3/21: Part 1, Typed summary of Strasburg Summit, from Julian Amery to Harold Macmillan, 3 December 1951.
13. Quoted in Macmillan, *Tides of Fortune*, 220.
14. Ibid.
15. Ibid.
16. CAC, AMEJ 1/3/21: Part 1, Typed summary of Strasburg Summit from Julian Amery to Harold Macmillan, 3 December 1951.
17. Quoted in Macmillan, *Tides of Fortune*, 221–222.
18. Richard Crossman, Diary Entry, 6 December 1951, in Janet Morgan, ed., *The Backbench Diaries of Richard Crossman* (London: Jonathan Cape, 1981), 48. Crossman also noted the irony that the Labour opposition was unable to capitalise on the about-face of Conservative policy: 'Replying to Churchill, Attlee was not able to berate him for going back on his leadership of the European Movement for the simple reason that Labour has been wholly isolationist itself' (49).
19. CRL, AP 20/15/1, Letter from Dwight D. Eisenhower, Supreme Headquarters, Allied Powers Europe, to Anthony Eden, 8 December 1951.
20. TNA, FO 371/96346, Letter from Robert Boothby to Winston Churchill, 12 December 1951.
21. TNA, FO 371/96356, Letter from Winston Churchill to Anthony Eden, 13 December 1951.
22. TNA, FO 371/96346, Minute from Anthony Eden to Winston Churchill, 15 December 1951.
23. TNA, FO 371/95757, No. 5, 'French proposals for Anglo-French conversations at ministerial level': record by C. P. Hope of an FO interdepartmental meeting with the CO, 13 November 1951, in Goldsworthy, ed., *BDOEE, Series A, Volume 3*, Part I, 294–296.

24. TNA, CO 537/7148, No. 17, 'Anglo–French relations in West Africa': Memorandum by A. B. Cohen, 20 November 1951, in Goldsworthy, ed., *BDOEE, Series A, Volume 3*, Part I, 296–303.
25. Richard Crossman observed that the King's death had 'swamped politics', an event that not only affected the British public but also gained an editorial in the *New York Times* which 'could really have been composed in London by an Englishman' and sent the newly independent nation of India into mourning. Crossman, Diary Entry, 11 February 1952, in Morgan, ed., *The Backbench Diaries of Richard Crossman*, 72.
26. Crossman, Diary Entry, 27 March 1952, in Idem, 98.
27. TNA, FO 371/10360, No. 33, 'British and French colonial policies in Africa': Minute by C. P. Hope, 2 April 1952, Goldsworthy, ed., *BDOEE, Series A, Volume 3*, Part I, 303–306.
28. TNA, FO 371/108108, No. 7, 'Anglo-French co-operation in Africa: Minute by B. J. Garnett, Africa Department Foreign Office, 9 March 1954.
29. TNA, CO 936/327 [Differences between British and French colonial policies]: Minute by H. T. Bourdillon, 21 April 1954, in Goldsworthy, ed., *BDOEE, Series A, Volume 3*, Part I, 314.
30. TNA, FO 1009/67, Telegram from the Foreign Office to H.M. Ambassador Paris, to O.E.E.C. Paris (U.K. Delegation) and to U.K. Delegation U.N. General Assembly Paris, 15 December 1951.
31. CRL, Papers of Sir Evelyn Shuckburgh, MS 191/1/2/1, Diaries 1951–52, Diary Entry, 16 December 1951.
32. Ibid.
33. CAC, AMEJ 1/3/21: Part 1, Letter from Anthony Eden to Harold Macmillan, 19 December 1951.
34. CRL, AP 20/15/2, Letter from Harold Macmillan to Anthony Eden, 21 December 1921.
35. TNA, FO 371/102331, 'Notes for Secretary of State's speech at Columbia University', Prepared 21 December 1951.
36. CAC, DSND 9/3/22, 'European integration: Note by Minister of Housing and Local Government [Harold Macmillan]', 16 January 1952.
37. CAC, AMEJ 1/3/21: Part 1, Letter from Julian Amery to Robert Carr, 17 January 1952.
38. CAC, AMEJ 1/3/9, Letter from Robert Boothby to Julian Amery, 17 February 1952.
39. CRL, AP 20/16/33, Extract from a diary written by Sir Evelyn Shuckburgh, late February 1952.
40. CRL, AP 20/16/28, Letter from Winston Churchill to Anthony Eden, 21 February 1952.
41. CRL, AP 20/16/33, Extract from a diary written by Sir Evelyn Shuckburgh, late February 1952.

42. CRL, AP 20/16/32, 'External action', Draft memorandum by R. A. Butler, February 1952.
43. CRL, AP 20/16/29, Letter from R. A. Butler to Anthony Eden, 22 February 1952.
44. CRL, AP 20/16/33, Extract from a diary written by Sir Evelyn Shuckburgh, late February 1952.
45. Ibid.
46. CRL, AP 20/16/31, Letter from Lord Cherwell to Anthony Eden, 27 February 1952.
47. CRL, AP 20/16/33, Extract from a diary written by Sir Evelyn Shuckburgh, late February 1952.
48. CRL, MS 191/1/2/1, Papers of Sir Evelyn Shuckburgh, Diaries 1951–52, Diary Entry, 12 March 1952.
49. See Edward Fursdon, *The European Defence Community: A History* (London: Macmillan, 1980), 64–102.
50. Saki Dockrill, *Britain's Policy for West German Rearmament, 1950–1955* (Cambridge: Cambridge University Press, 1991), 89–91.
51. Idem, 94–95.
52. Quoted in Furson, *The European Defence Community*, 141.
53. Quoted in Dockrill, *Britain's Policy for West German Rearmament*, 99.
54. CRL, MS 191/1/2/1, Papers of Sir Evelyn Shuckburgh, Diaries 1951–52, Diary Entry, 24 May 1952.
55. Kevin Ruane, *The Rise and Fall of the European Defence Community: Anglo–American Relations and the Crisis of European Defence, 1950–55* (Basingstoke: Macmillan, 2000), 34.
56. Fursdon, *The European Defence Community*, 147.
57. Ruane, *The Rise and Fall of the European Defence Community*, 34.
58. CRL, MS 191/1/2/1, Papers of Sir Evelyn Shuckburgh, Diaries 1951–52, Diary Entry, 27 May 1952.
59. CRL, Anthony Eden Additional Papers [AELAdd] 9, Letter from Anthony Eden to Sir Ivonne Kirkpatrick, 4 June 1952.
60. CAC, AMEJ 1/3/9, Letter from E. Beddington-Behrens to Anthony Eden, 16 June 1952.
61. TNA, CAB 129/53, C (52) 202, 'British overseas obligations': Cabinet Memorandum by Mr Eden, 18 June 1952, in Goldsworthy, ed., *BDOEE, Series A, Volume 3*, Part I, 4–12.
62. TNA, CO 1027/69, 'The Overseas Information Services: Report by Committee of Enquiry', 14 July 1952.
63. CAC, AMEJ 1/3/9, Letter from Robert Boothby to Brian Goddard, 26 June 1952.
64. CRC, MS 191/1/2/1, Papers of Sir Evelyn Shuckburgh, Diaries 1951–52, Diary Entry, 28 September 1952,

65. CRL, MS 191/1/2/1, Papers of Sir Evelyn Shuckburgh, Diaries 1951–52, Diary Entry, 3 November 1952.
66. Ibid.
67. CAC, AMEJ 1/3/9, Letter from E. Beddington-Behrens to Richard Law, 30 October 1952.
68. CAC, AMEJ 1/3/9, Letter from E. Beddington-Behrens to Baron Rene Boel, 5 November 1952.
69. CAC, AMEJ 1/3/9, Letter from E. Beddington-Behrens to R. A. Butler, 25 November 1952.
70. CRL, MS 191/1/2/2, Papers of Sir Evelyn Schuckburgh, Diaries 1953, Diary Entry, 7 January 1953.

8 Perfidious Gaul

1. CRL, AP 20/16/37, Memorandum from Anthony Eden to Winston Churchill, 19 January 1953.
2. Ibid.
3. CAC, AMEJ 1/3/9, Letter from Edward Beddington-Behrens to Julian Amery, 3 February 1953.
4. CRL, AP 20/16/37, Memorandum from Anthony Eden to Winston Churchill, 19 January 1953.
5. Bodleian Library, University of Oxford [Bodleian], Harold Macmillan Papers [MS Macmillan] dep. c. 386, ff. 456–457, Letter from Lady Rhys-Williams to Harold Macmillan, 12 January 1953.
6. TNA, FO 371/107925, Telegram from Sir Roger Makins to Anthony Eden, 27 January 1953.
7. TNA, FO 371/107925, Brief on 'European unity' for Secretary of State for Foreign Affairs ahead of his talks with Mr. Dulles, prepared by F. G. K. Gallagher, Foreign Office, 30 January 1953.
8. See Jasmine Aimaq, *For Europe or Empire? French Colonial Ambitions and the European Army Plan* (Lund, Sweden: Lund University Press, 1996).
9. CRL, AP 20/16/50, Memorandum from Anthony Eden to Churchill, 26 February 1953.
10. CRC, AP 20/16/50, Memorandum from Eden to Churchill, 26 February 1953.
11. CRC, AP 20/16/53, Letter from Anthony Eden to Winston Churchill, 18 March, 1953.
12. Quoted in Dockrill, *Britain's Policy for West German Rearmament*, 116–117.
13. Idem, 117.
14. CRL, MS 191/1/2/2, Papers of Sir Evelyn Shuckburgh, Diaries 1953, Diary Entry, 23 March 1953.

15. CAC, AMEJ 1/3/21: Part 2, Letter from Julian Amery to Sir Cecil Weir, 26 May 1953.
16. CAC, AMEJ 1/3/21: Part 2, Letter from Sir Cecil Weir to Julian Amery, 30 May 1953.
17. Ibid.
18. Roy Jenkins, 'Churchill: The government of 1951–55', in Robert Blake and Wm. Roger Louis, eds., *Churchill* (Oxford: Oxford University Press, 1993), 494.
19. Lord Moran, Diary Entry, 23 June 1953, in Lord Moran, *The Struggle for Survival*, 406.
20. Lord Moran, Diary Entry, 24 June 1953, in Idem, 408–409.
21. Lord Moran, Diary Entry, 26 June 1953, in Idem, 410.
22. Jenkins, 'Churchill: The government of 1951–1955', 495.
23. CRL, AP 20/16/7C, 'Reflections', A memorandum by Anthony Eden, 4 August 1953.
24. CRL, AP 20/16/10, Note from Sir Evelyn Shuckburgh to Sir William Strang, 4 August 1953.
25. Bodleian, MS Macmillan, dep. c. 387, 'E. D. C. and European unity', summer 1953.
26. Quoted in Dockrill, *Britain's Policy for West German Rearmament*, 128.
27. Quoted in Ruane, *The Rise and Fall of the European Defence Community*, 47.
28. Macmillan, *Tides of Fortune*, 526.
29. Bodleian, MS Macmillan, dep. c. 392, Letter from Lady Rhys-Williams to Harold Macmillan, 22 September 1953.
30. CRL, AP 20/16/80, Letter from Anthony Eden to Winston Churchill, 6 November 1953.
31. Macmillan, *Tides of Fortune*, 527.
32. Ibid.
33. CRL, AP 20/16/85, 'Steering brief for Bermuda', circulated to the cabinet by Anthony Eden, 19 November 1953.
34. CRL, AP 29/16/90, Letter from Anthony Eden to Winston Churchill, 4 December 1953.
35. Ibid.
36. CRL, AP 20/16/91, Letter from Anthony Eden to Winston Churchill, 7 December 1953.
37. CRL, MS 191/1/2/2, Papers of Sir Evelyn Shuckburgh, Diaries 1953, Diary Entry, 5 December 1953.
38. Ibid.
39. MS 191/1/2/2, Papers of Sir Evelyn Shuckburgh, Diaries 1953, Diary Entry, 7 December 1953.
40. MS 191/1/2/2, Papers of Sir Evelyn Shuckburgh, Diaries 1953, Diary Entry, 13 December 1953.

41. CRL, MS 191/1/2/2, Papers of Sir Evelyn Shuckburgh, Diaries 1953, Diary Entry, 16 December 1953.
42. CAC, AMEJ 1/3/11, 'Memorandum', by L. S. Amery and Julian Amery, for the ELEC Conference at Westminster, 5 January 1954.
43. CAC, AMEJ 1/3/13, Letter from Lady Rhys-Williams to Duncan Sandys, 19 January 1954.
44. CRL, MS 191/1/2/3, Papers of Sir Evelyn Shuckburgh, Diaries 1954, Diary Entry, 19 January 1954.
45. CRL, AP 20/17/10A, Letter from Anthony Eden to Selwyn Lloyd, 6 February 1954.
46. CRL, AP 20/3/530, Letter from Birch, Ministry of Defence, to Anthony Eden, 22 February 1954.
47. CRL, AP 20/17/58, Letter from Anthony Eden to Winston Churchill, 11 March 1954.
48. CRL, MS 191/1/2/3, Papers of Sir Evelyn Shuckburgh, Diaries 1954, Diary Entry, 31 March 1954.
49. CRL, AP 20/17/18A, Letter from Sir Roger Makins to Anthony Eden, 21 May 1954.
50. CRL, AP 20/17/19, Letter from Sir Roger Makins to Anthony Eden, 18 June 1954.
51. CRL, AP 13/3/53J, Joint statement by President Dwight D. Eisenhower and Prime Minister Winston Churchill, 25 June 1954.
52. CRL, AP 20/17/25, Letter from Harold Macmillan to Anthony Eden, 17 August 1954.
53. CRL, AP 20/17/189, Letter from Winston Churchill to Anthony Eden, 29 August 1954.
54. CRL, AP 20/17/90, Letter from Anthony Eden to Winston Churchill, 6 September 1954.
55. Milward, *The Rise and Fall of a National Strategy*, 123–124.
56. Bodleian, MS Macmillan, dep. c. 387, Note from Harold Macmillan to Anthony Eden, 1 September 1954.
57. Bodleian, MS Macmillan dep. c. 387, Memorandum for the Cabinet, by Harold Macmillan, September 1954.
58. Anne Deighton, 'Britain and the creation of Western European Union, 1954', in Anne Deighton, ed., *Western European Union, 1954–1997: Defence, Security, Integration* (St Antony's College, Oxford: Published by the European Interdependence Research Unit, St Antony's College, Oxford, with the support of the Foreign and Commonwealth Office, and the WEU Institute for Security Studies, Paris, 1997), 19.
59. N. J. Crowson, *The Conservative Party and European Integration since 1945: At the Heart of Europe?* (London: Routledge, 2007), 24.

60. CRL, AP 20/17/6, Letter from Harold Macmillan to Anthony Eden, 30 September 1954. Also found in Bodleian, MS Macmillan, dep. c. 387.
61. CRL, AP 14/3/632, Letter from Gladwyn Jebb to Anthony Eden, 30 September 1954.
62. CRL, AP 14/3/661, Letter from Sir Victor Mallet to Anthony Eden, 5 October 1954.
63. CRL, AP 14/3/566, Letter from Ashley Clarke to Anthony Eden, 8 October 1954.
64. CAC, AMEJ 1/3/13, Letter from Edward Beddington-Behrens to Anthony Eden, 5 October 1954.
65. CRL, AP 14/3/671, Letter from R. G. A. Meade, British Consul-General in Marseille, to Sir Anthony Rumbold, 20 October 1954.
66. TNA, CAB 129/72, C (54) 402, 'Internal security in the Colonies': Cabinet Memorandum by Mr Macmillan, 29 December 1954, in Goldsworthy, ed., *BDOEE, Series A, Volume 3*, Part I, 58.
67. Deighton, 'Britain and the creation of WEU', 21.
68. CRL, AP 20/17/9, Letter from Gladwyn Jebb to Anthony Eden, 27 December 1954.
69. Nutting, *Europe Will Not Wait*, 80.
70. Henry Pelling, *Churchill's Peacetime Ministry, 1951–55* (Basingstoke: Macmillan, 1997), 134.
71. CRL, AP 20/17/9, Letter from Gladwyn Jebb to Anthony Eden, 27 December 1954.
72. CRL, AP 20/17/114, Memorandum from Anthony Eden to Winston Churchill, 29 December 1954.
73. Pelling, *Churchill's Peacetime Ministry*, 134.
74. Letter, Winston Churchill to Dwight D. Eisenhower, 12 January 1955, in Peter G. Boyle, ed., *The Churchill–Eisenhower Correspondence, 1953–1955* (Chapel Hill: University of North Carolina Press, 1990), 184–186.
75. CAC, CHUR 2/217, Letter from Dwight D. Eisenhower to Winston Churchill, 25 January 1955.
76. Evelyn Shuckburgh, *Descent to Suez: Diaries, 1951–56*, Selected for Publication by John Charmley (London: Weidenfeld and Nicolson, 1986), 46–47 and 62.
77. Richard Crossman, Diary Entry, 23 June 1952, in Morgan, ed., *The Backbench Diaries of Richard Crossman*, 112.
78. Idem, 129 and 145.
79. Pelling, *Churchill's Peacetime Ministry*, 169.
80. CRL, AP 20/18/7A, Telegram No. 539 from Roger Makins to Anthony Eden, 10 March 1955.
81. CRL, AP 20/18/1, Memorandum from Anthony Eden to Winston Churchill, 11 March 1955.

82. CRL, AP 20/18/5, Memorandum from Winston Churchill to Anthony Eden, 12 March 1955.
83. CRL, AP 20/18/8, Telegram from Anthony Eden to Sir Roger Makins, 15 March, 1955.
84. CRL, AP 14/3/60, Telegram from Sir Frank Hoyer Millar to Anthony Eden, 29 March, 1955.

9 The decline and fall of the imperial Europeans

1. CRL, AP 19/1/10, Letter from Winston Churchill to King George VI, 16 June 1942.
2. CRL, Papers of Sir Evelyn Shuckburgh, MS 191/1/2/4, Diary Entry, 6 April 1955.
3. D. R. Thorpe, *Eden: The Life and Times of Anthony Eden, First Earl of Avon, 1897–1977* (London: Chatto & Windus, 2003), 434–436.
4. Idem, 436–437.
5. Richard Crossman, Diary Entry, 3 May, 1955, in Morgan, *The Backbench Diaries of Richard Crossman*, 420.
6. Morgan, *The Backbench Diaries of Richard Crossman*, 420–421 (Editorial Comment).
7. Alistair Horne, *Macmillan, 1894–1956: Volume I of the Official Biography* (London: Macmillan, 1988), 358–361.
8. Idem, 371.
9. Lord Beloff, *Britain and the European Union: Dialogue of the Deaf*, 56.
10. The observer, Russell Bretherton, was an under-secretary in the Board of Trade and was – as one historian has described him – 'the wrong man in the wrong place, representing the wrong policy'. Thomas Raineau, 'Europeanising Whitehall? The British Civil Service and Europe, 1957–1972', in Matthieu Osmont, Emilia Robin-Hivert, Katja Seidel, Mark Spoerer and Christian Wenkel, eds., *Europeanisation in the 20th Century: The Historical Lens* (Brussels: P. I. E. Lang, 2012), 59. In determining that the British government should not enter the negotiations following the Messina Conference, the Treasury was of the utmost importance, its officials (along with those of the Board of Trade) always having been far more sceptical than the Foreign Office of schemes for European integration. See N. Piers Ludlow, 'A waning force: The treasury and British European policy, 1955–63', *Contemporary British History*, Volume 17, Number 4 (Winter 2003), 87–104 (see, in particular, pages 89–91).
11. Quoted in Horne, *Macmillan, 1894–1956*, 362–363.
12. Quoted in Idem, 363.
13. Quoted in Idem, 363.

14. Quoted in Thorpe, *Eden*, 453.
15. Quoted in Ibid, 453.
16. Bodleian, MS Macmillan, dep. c. 295, Note from Harold Macmillan to Antony Head, 11 November 1954; Bodleian, MS Macmillan, dep. c. 295, Letter from Harold Macmillan to Winston Churchill, December 1954.
17. TNA, FO 317/117642, 'Paper on the future of Cyprus', Colonial and Foreign Offices, 25 June 1955.
18. Robert Holland, *Britain and the Revolt in Cyprus, 1954–1959* (Oxford: Clarendon, 1998), 72.
19. Bodleian, MS Macmillan, dep. c. 301, Memorandum from Harold Macmillan to Anthony Eden, 29 August 1955; Stella Soulioti, *Fettered Independence: Cyprus, 1878–1964: Volume One: The Narrative* (Minneapolis: Minnesota Mediterranean and East European Monographs, Modern Greek Studies, University of Minnesota, 2006), 29–32.
20. Thorpe, *Eden*, 445–446.
21. For a more detailed account of this revolution in Egypt, see Joel Gordon, *Nasser's Blessed Movement: Egypt's Free Officers and the July Revolution* (Oxford: Oxford University Press, 1992).
22. Quoted in Horne, *Macmillan, 1894–1956*, 367.
23. Idem, 367–371.
24. CAC, CHUR 2/220, Letter from Harold Macmillan to Winston Churchill, 2 November 1955.
25. CRL, AP 14/4/57A, Letter from Robert Boothby to Anthony Eden, 27 April 1956.
26. Thorpe, *Eden*, 470.
27. Idem, 471–472.
28. TNA, CAB 134/1315, PR (56) 3, 'The future of the United Kingdom in world affairs': Memorandum by Officials of the Treasury, Foreign Office and Ministry of Defence for Cabinet Policy Review Committee, 1 June 1956, in Goldsworthy, ed., *BDOEE, Series A, Volume 3*, Part I, 61–81.
29. TNA, CAB 134/1315, PR (56) 11, 'Assumptions for future planning': Note by Sir A Eden for Cabinet Policy Review Committee, 15 June 1956, in Goldsworthy, ed., *BDOEE, Series A, Volume 3*, Part I, 91.
30. TNA, CO 1032/51, no. 112 [The Commonwealth and international relations]: CRO paper on the probable development of the Commonwealth over the next ten or fifteen years, June 1956, in Goldsworthy, ed., *BDOEE, Series A, Volume 3*, Part I, 92–100.
31. TNA, FO 371/122028, Letter from Harold Macmillan to Selwyn Lloyd, 15 May 1956; Letter from Harold Macmillan to Peter Thorneycroft, 15 May 1956.
32. Although Macmillan's original memorandum is not found in the archives, these six proposals are repeated in a memorandum by Peter Thorneycroft, 'Initiative

in Europe: Memorandum by the President of the Board of Trade', in TNA, FO 371/122028.
33. TNA, FO 371/122028, Minute from Selwyn Lloyd, 17 May 1956.
34. FO 371/122028, 'Initiative in Europe: Memorandum by the President of the Board of Trade', 22 May 1956.
35. FO 371/122029, Minutes of the first meeting of the Working Group on the United Kingdom Initiative in Europe, 21 June 1956.
36. FO 371/122029, Draft Statement contained in correspondence between Harold Macmillan and Peter Thorneycroft, 21 June 1956.
37. TNA, CAB 129/82, CP (56) 191, 'United Kingdom commercial policy': Joint Cabinet Note by Mr Macmillan and Mr Thorneycroft, 27 July 1956, in Goldsworthy, ed., *BDOEE, Series A, Volume 3*, Part III, 99–100.
38. TNA, CAB 129/82, CP (56) 191, Annex: Interim Report by Officials on 'United Kingdom initiative in Europe, Plan G', in Goldsworthy, ed., *BDOEE, Series A, Volume 3*, Part III, 99–118.
39. TNA, FO 371/122034, Letter from Lord Home to Harold Macmillan, 3 September 1956.
40. TNA, CAB 129/83, CP (56) 208, 'Plan G': Cabinet memorandum by Mr Macmillan on the proposed European Free Trade Area, 11 September 1956, Goldsworthy, ed., *BDOEE, Series A, Volume 3*, Part III, 122–123.
41. TNA, CAB 129/83, CP (56) 207, 'Plan G and the Commonwealth', Cabinet Memorandum by Home, 7 September 1956, in Goldsworthy, ed., *BDOEE, Series A, Volume 3*, Part III, 125, n. 2
42. TNA, CAB 128/30/2, CM 65 (56) 2, 'Commercial policy': Cabinet conclusions on the proposed European Free Trade Area', 14 September 1956, in Goldsworthy, ed., *BDOEE, Series A, Volume 3*, Part III, 124–129.
43. Ibid.
44. TNA, CAB 128/30/2, CM 66 (56) 2, 'Commercial policy': Cabinet conclusions on the proposed European free trade area and the colonies and broader considerations, 18 September 1956, in Goldsworthy, ed., *BDOEE, Series A, Volume 3*, Part III, 129–132.
45. TNA, FO 317/122034, 'Summary of Plan G', 21 September 1956.
46. TNA, PREM 11/1352, Cabinet: Franco–British Union: Draft report to the Cabinet, 24 September 1956.
47. TNA, PREM 11/1352, Notes on a meeting between Anthony Eden and Monsieur Mollet, 27 September 1956.
48. The cabinet did discuss the French offer of Commonwealth membership, but rejected it after concluding that the Commonwealth 'derives from the long historical association between the United Kingdom and other Commonwealth countries – all of which were at one time parts of the British Empire. . . . Thus, it is perhaps the essence of the Commonwealth that its members, though they are independent sovereign States with a developing system of separate citizenships,

do not regard themselves as "foreign" to one another'. French membership would 'entirely change the basis of their association'. TNA, PREM 11/1352, Cabinet: Anglo–French Union: Commonwealth Membership: Memorandum by the Secretary of the Cabinet, Norman Brook, 29 September 1956.
49. TNA, CAB 129/84, CP (56) 256, 'A mutual free trade area with Europe': Joint Cabinet memorandum by Mr Macmillan and Mr Thorneycroft, 6 November 1956, in Goldsworthy, ed., *BDOEE, Series A, Volume 3*, Part III, 132–134.
50. For more on the development of Plan G, see James R. V. Ellison, 'Perfidious Albion? Britain, Plan G and European integration, 1955–1956', *Contemporary British History*, Volume 10, No. 4 (Winter 1996), 1–34.
51. Grob-Fitzgibbon, *Imperial Endgame*, 338–340.
52. See Gordon, *Nasser's Blessed Movement*.
53. 'Extracts from speech by Colonial Nasser announcing the nationalisation of the Suez Canal Company', 26 July 1956, in D. C. Watt, ed., *Documents on the Suez Crisis, 26 July to 6 November 1956* (London: Royal Institute of International Affairs, 1957), 44–49.
54. CRL, AO 20/24/313, Telegram from Anthony Eden to Prime Ministers of Canada, Australia, New Zealand and South Africa, 28 July 1956.
55. 'Anglo–French ultimatum to the governments of Egypt and Israel', 30 October 1956, in Watt, ed., *Documents on the Suez Crisis*, 85–86.
56. For details on this invasion, see Keith Kyle, *Suez: Britain's End of Empire in the Middle East* (London: I. B. Tauris, 2003), 461–464; and Anthony Farrar-Hockley, 'The post-war army, 1945–1963', in David Chandler and Ian Beckett, eds., *The Oxford History of the British Army* (Oxford: Oxford University Press, 1994), 334–337.
57. For a first-hand account of this, see Shuckburgh, *Descent to Suez: Diaries 1951–6*, especially 362–366.
58. Grob-Fitzgibbon, *Imperial Endgame*, 345–347.
59. Kyle, *Suez*, 464–465.
60. Grob-Fitzgibbon, *Imperial Endgame*, 348–349.
61. CAC, CHUR 2/143, Letter from Viscount Montgomery of Alamein to Sir Winston Churchill, 6 December 1956.
62. David Carlton, *Anthony Eden: A Biography* (London: Allen Lane, 1981), 464.
63. Grob-Fitzgibbon, *Imperial Endgame*, 350.
64. TNA, FO 371/122040, Letter from F. E. Figgures, Treasury, to A. J. Eden, Foreign Office, 22 November 1956.
65. CAC, CHUR 2/217, Letter from Winston Churchill to Dwight D. Eisenhower, 23 November 1956.
66. TNA, FO 371/122040, Letter from Sir P. Mason, the Hague, to the Foreign Office, 3 December 1956; and Letter from Sir F. Hoyer Millar, Bonn, to the Foreign Office, 3 December 1956.

67. CRL, Papers of Sir Evelyn Shuckburgh, MS 191/1/2/5, Diaries 1956–57, Diary Entry, 5 December 1956.
68. TNA, CAB 129/84, CP (57) 6, '"The grand design" (co-operation with Western Europe)': Cabinet memorandum by Mr Selwyn Lloyd, 5 January 1957, in Goldsworthy, ed., *BDOEE, Series A, Volume 3*, Part I, 102–107.

10 At sixes and sevens

1. British Library, Newspaper Collections, Richard Crossman, 'Crossman says … Ike may like Macmillan – But will the folks at home?', *Daily Mirror*, 15 January 1957, p. 7.
2. Bodleian Library, Oxford University [Bodleian], MS Macmillan dep. c. 920, f. 50, Telegram from Rome to Foreign Office, Personal for Prime Minister from Foreign Secretary.
3. Bodleian, MS Macmillan dep. c. 920, ff. 2–18, 'European economic developments'.
4. Macmillan Diary Entry, 8 February 1957, in *The Macmillan Diaries: Volume II: Prime Minister and After, 1957–1966*, edited and with an introduction by Peter Catterall (Basingstoke: Macmillan, 2011), 3.
5. Ludlow, 'A waning force', 93.
6. Bodleian, MS Macmillan dep. c. 920, ff. 2–18, 'European economic developments'.
7. Macmillan Diary Entry, 17 February 1957, in *The Macmillan Diaries*, 6–7.
8. TNA, CO 852/1701, 'Closer economic association with Europe: Views of colonial governments of the conclusions of the meeting of colonial representatives held on the 27th March to 2nd April, 1957'; and TNA, CO 852/1701, Savingram from the Governor, Western Region of Nigeria, to the Colonial Secretary, 29 April 1957.
9. Ibid.
10. Bodleian, MS Macmillan dep. c. 920, f. 58, Personal minute from Prime Minister to Mr. Poole, 18 April 1957.
11. Bodleian, MS Macmillan, dep. c. 920, ff. 59–60, Letter from Harold Macmillan to Lord Layton, 26 April 1957.
12. Bodleian, MS Macmillan dep. c. 920, ff. 2–18, 'European economic developments'.
13. Bodleian, MS Macmillan dep. c. 920, f. 61, Telegram from Bonn to the Foreign Office, to Prime Minister from Secretary of State, 6 May 1957.
14. Bodleian, MS Macmillan dep. c. 920, ff. 2–18, 'European economic developments'.
15. Macmillan Diary Entry, 8 May 1957, in *The Macmillan Diaries*, 33–34.

16. TNA, Dominions Office [DO] 35/9623, Telegraph from Commonwealth Relations Office to UK High Commissioners in Canada, Australia, New Zealand, South Africa, India, Pakistan, Ceylon, Ghana, and the Federation of Rhodesia and Nyasaland, and sent to HM Ambassador in Dublin, 25 May 1957.
17. Bodleian, MS Macmillan dep. c. 920, f. 68, Personal minute from Prime Minister to Foreign Secretary, 26 May 1957.
18. British Library, Newspaper Collections, 'The six or the seven?' Daily Mail Comment, *The Daily Mail*, 20 June 1957, p. 1.
19. TNA, FO 371/130991, Draft of speech by Prime Minister to the United Kingdom Council of the European Movement at the Central Hall, London, 9 July 1957.
20. Bodleian, MS Macmillan dep. c. 920, f. 75, Personal minute from Prime Minister to Chancellor of the Exchequer, 15 July 1957.
21. Bodleian, MS Macmillan dep. c. 920, f. 77, Personal minute from Prime Minister to Chancellor of the Exchequer, 22 July 1957.
22. Bodleian, MS Macmillan dep. c. 920, ff. 2–18, 'European economic developments'.
23. Bodleian, MS Macmillan dep. c. 920, f. 94, Personal minute from Prime Minister to Maudling, 13 August 1957.
24. Bodleian, MS Macmillan dep. c. 920, ff. 2–18, 'European economic developments'.
25. Macmillan Diary Entry, 7 October 1957, in *The Macmillan Diaries*, 63.
26. Bodleian, MS Macmillan dep. c. 920, ff. 2–18, 'European economic developments'.
27. Ibid.
28. TNA, T 337/44, Letter from P. Gore-Booth, Foreign Office, to Sir John Coulson, Treasury, 7 November 1957.
29. TNA, T 337/44, 'The political significance of the European Free Trade Area: United Kingdom attitude to the Customs Union', November 1957.
30. TNA, T 337/21, Letter from Hugh Ellis-Rees, United Kingdom Delegation to OEEC, to Sir John Coulson, Paymaster General's Office, 13 January 1958.
31. Bodleian, MS Macmillan dep. c. 920, ff. 2–18, 'European economic developments'.
32. Macmillan Diary Entry, 15 December 1957, in *The Macmillan Diaries*, 76–77.
33. TNA, T 337/21, Note from E. E. Tomkins, British Embassy, Paris, to Sir John Coulson, 16 January 1958.
34. Bodleian, MS Macmillan dep. c. 920, ff. 2–18, 'European economic developments'.
35. Ibid.
36. Ibid.

37. Ibid.
38. Macmillan Diary Entry, 14 May 1957, in *The Macmillan Diaries*, 117.
39. Idem, 118.
40. Idem, 119.
41. For an in-depth study of the comings and goings of the numerous French governments in the post-war period, see Philip M. Williams, with David Goldey and Martin Harrison, *French Politicians and Elections, 1951–1969* (Cambridge: Cambridge University Press, 1970); and Jean-Pierre Rioux, *The Fourth Republic, 1944–1958*, translated by Godfrey Rogers (Cambridge: Cambridge University Press, 1987).
42. Tony Judt, *Postwar: A History of Europe since 1945* (London: William Heinemann, 2005), 287–288.
43. Crowson, *Britain and Europe*, 74.
44. Macmillan Diary Entry, 23 June 1958, in *The Macmillan Diaries*, 128.
45. Bodleian, MS Macmillan dep. c. 920, ff. 144–145, Personal minute from Prime Minister to Foreign Secretary, 24 June 1958.
46. Bodleian, MS Macmillan dep. c. 920, f. 146, Letter from Macmillan to Lady Rhys-Williams, 28 June 1958.
47. Bodleian, MS Macmillan, dep. c. 920, ff. 147–149, Letter from Macmillan to de Gaulle, 30 June 1958.
48. Macmillan Diary Entry, 30 June 1958, in *The Macmillan Diaries*, 130.
49. Harold Macmillan, *Riding the Storm, 1956–1959* (London: Macmillan, 1971), 447.
50. Macmillan Diary Entry, 4 July 1958, in *The Macmillan Diaries*, 131.
51. Bodleian, MS Macmillan dep. c. 920, f. 151, Letter from de Gaulle to Macmillan, 5 July 1958.
52. Bodleian, MS Macmillan dep. c. 920, ff. 2–18, 'European economic developments'.
53. Ibid.
54. Macmillan Diary Entry, 9 October 1958, in *The Macmillan Diaries*, 164.
55. Bodleian, MS Macmillan dep. c. 920, ff. 158–159, Personal minute from the Prime Minister to the Foreign Secretary, 1958. Writing a week later, Macmillan suggested that Britain ought also to 'denounce the Western European Union Treaty' if the European FTA failed. Whilst this would mean ending a Treaty that had been in force for fifty years, Macmillan felt that 'we could do so as a result of the extreme provocation of the Six threatening us with economic discrimination'. Bodleian, MS Macmillan, dep. c. 920, f. 160, Note from Prime Minister to Foreign Secretary, 26 October 1958.
56. Bodleian, MS Macmillan dep. c. 920, ff. 2–18, 'European economic developments'.
57. Macmillan Diary Entry, 26 October 1958, in *The Macmillan Diaries*, 167.

58. Bodleian, MS Macmillan dep. c. 920, ff. 164–166, Note by Prime Minister, 'European Free Trade Area', for the Cabinet, 4 November 1958.
59. Bodleian, MS Macmillan dep. c. 920, ff. 2–18, 'European economic developments'.
60. Macmillan Diary Entry, 6 November 1958, in *The Macmillan Diaries*, 169.
61. Bodleian, MS Macmillan dep. c. 920, ff. 168–171, Letter from Macmillan to de Gaulle, 7 November 1958.
62. Bodleian, MS Macmillan dep. c. 920, ff. 2–18, 'European economic developments'.
63. Ibid.
64. Crowson, *Britain and Europe*, 74.
65. Macmillan Diary Entry, 17 November 1958, in *The Macmillan Diaries*, 170.
66. Macmillan touches on this in his diary entry of 27 January 1959. Idem, 186.
67. Young, *Britain and European Unity*, 61–62.
68. Idem, 62; and Milward, *The Rise and Fall of a National Strategy*, 311.
69. Macmillan Diary Entry, 6 May 1959, in *The Macmillan Diaries*, 216–217.
70. Jacqueline Tratt, *The Macmillan Government and Europe: A Study in the Process of Policy Development* (Basingstoke: Macmillan, 1996), 50–51.
71. Macmillan Diary Entry, 7 July 1959, in *The Macmillan Diaries*, 230–231.
72. Bodleian, MS Macmillan dep. c. 925, ff. 1–8, 'The founding of E.F.T.A.'.
73. Bodleian, MS Macmillan dep. c. 311, ff. 52–61, Letter from David Eccles to Macmillan, 9 August 1959.
74. See Macmillan, *Riding the Storm*, chapter 4 'The Anglo–American schism, 89–179; chapter 6 'Aftermath of Suez', 206–239; and chapter 10, 'Honeymoon at Washington', 313–341.
75. TNA, FO 371/145608, Visit of the President of the United States, 20 August 1959: France: Brief by the Foreign Office, prepared by A. D. F. Pemberton-Pigott, 19 August 1959.
76. See Harold Macmillan, *Pointing the Way, 1959–1961* (London: Macmillan, 1972), chapter 1, 1–23.
77. Macmillan Diary Entry, 9 October 1959, in *The Macmillan Diaries*, 251.
78. Moore, *Margaret Thatcher*, 140–143.
79. Bodleian, MS Macmillan dep. c. 925, ff. 43–49, Personal minute from Macmillan to Foreign Secretary, 'The Organisation of Europe', 22 October 1959.
80. TNA, Prime Minister's Office [PREM] 11/2985, Memorandum from P. F. de Zulueta to Prime Minister, 30 October 1959.
81. TNA, PREM 11/2985, 'United Kingdom policy towards Western Europe: The six and the seven', Foreign Office Planning Section, 27 October 1959.
82. Bodleian, MS Macmillan dep. c. 925, ff. 1–8, 'The founding of E.F.T.A.'.
83. Bodleian, MS Macmillan dep. c. 925, f. 54, Letter from Macmillan to Foreign Secretary, 22 November 1959.

84. Macmillan Diary Entry, 29 November 1959, in *The Macmillan Diaries*, 259–260. For an excellent account of the confusion of British policy during the period in late 1959, see Tratt, *The Macmillan Government and Europe*, 55–70.
85. Macmillan, *Pointing the Way*, 58.
86. Bodleian, MS Macmillan dep. c. 925, ff. 58–60, Note from Harold Macmillan to Chancellor of the Exchequer, 10 December 1959.
87. Bodleian, MS Macmillan dep. c. 925, ff. 1–8, 'The founding of E.F.T.A.'.
88. TNA, PREM 11/2985, Memorandum from Foreign Secretary to Prime Minister, 13 December 1959.
89. Macmillan, *Pointing the Way*, 60.
90. Ibid.
91. For further exploration of this, see Grob-Fitzgibbon, *Imperial Endgame*. See also Philip E. Hemming, 'Macmillan and the end of the British Empire in Africa', in Richard Aldous and Sabine Lee, eds., *Harold Macmillan and Britain's World Role* (Basingstoke: Macmillan, 1996), 97–121. Hemming writes: 'Shedding the Empire was not, in Macmillan's eyes, tantamount to surrendering Britain's status as one of the world's great powers. Former British possessions would mark their coming of age on the global scene with formal membership of the Commonwealth. As *primus inter pares* in the Commonwealth, the United Kingdom would continue to exercise a political, economic and strategic leadership role among her erstwhile territories. In this manner Britain's international importance would be maintained' (97).
92. Macmillan wrote in his memoirs: 'There is a common illusion that this story [of decolonisation], begun during and after the First World War and concluded within less than twenty years of the Second, is one of weakness and decay, resulting from the loss of will govern inherent in a democratic system. This is an undeserved libel on a people who twice in my lifetime demonstrated their courage and tenacity, as well as against its leaders. . . . It is a vulgar but false jibe that the British people by a series of gestures unique in history abandoned their Empire in a fit of frivolity or impatience. They had not lost the will or even the power to rule. But they did not conceive of themselves as having the right to govern in perpetuity. It was rather their duty to spread to other nations those advantages which through the long course of centuries they had won for themselves'. Macmillan, *Pointing the Way*, 116–117.
93. For a first-hand account of this trip, see Macmillan, *Pointing the Way*, chapter 6, 116–177.
94. Sarah Stockwell and L. J. Butler, 'Introduction', in L. J. Butler and Sarah Stockwell, eds., *The Wind of Change: Harold Macmillan and British Decolonization* (Basingstoke: Palgrave Macmillan, 2013), 1.
95. Harold Macmillan, 'Wind of Change Speech', quoted in Macmillan, *Pointing the Way*, 473–482. For a full analysis of the context of this speech, see Saul

Debow, 'Macmillan, Verwoerd and the 1960 "Wind of Change" speech', in Butler and Stockwell, eds., *The Wind of Change*, 20–47.
96. Stockwell and Butler, 'Introduction', 4.
97. Macmillan, *Riding the Storm*, 200.
98. Stockwell and Butler, 'Introduction', 4.
99. Idem, 6. See also Dubow, 'Macmillan, Verwoerd and the 1960 "Wind and Change" speech', 22–23.
100. For an analysis of the generational nature of Macmillan's policy-making after the 1959 General Election, see Simon Ball, 'The wind of change as generational drama', in Butler and Stockwell, ed., *The Wind of Change*, 96–115.
101. Quoted in Stuart Ward, 'Whirlwind, hurricane, howling tempest: The wind of change and the British world', in Butler and Stockwell, ed., *The Wind of Change*, 58–59.
102. Idem, 59 and 61.
103. Idem, 61.
104. Quoted in Dubow, 'Macmillan, Verwoerd and the 1960 "Wind of Change" speech', 29.
105. Macmillan, *Pointing the Way*, 163–164.
106. Quoted in Richard Toye, 'Words of change: The rhetoric of Commonwealth, Common Market and Cold War, 1961–3', in Butler and Stockwell, eds., *The Wind of Change*, 144.

11 Towards the Common Market

1. British Library, Newspaper collections, George Murray, 'No matter how much this fact may shock you, our future is in Europe not in the Commonwealth', *The Daily Mail*, 16 June 1961.
2. Raineau, 'Europeanising Whitehall?', 64.
3. Macmillan Diary Entry, 20 December 1959, in *The Macmillan Diaries*, 264.
4. Don Cook, *Charles de Gaulle: A Biography* (London: Secker & Warburg, 1984).
5. Charles de Gaulle, *The Complete War Memoirs of Charles de Gaulle*, translated from the French by Jonathan Griffen and Richard Howard (New York: Carroll & Graf Publishers, 1998), 3.
6. Paul Reynaud, *The Foreign Policy of Charles de Gaulle: A Critical Assessment*, translated by Mervyn Savill (London: Paul Hamlyn, 1964), 9.
7. De Gaulle described these seventeen Prime Ministers as 'all men of worth and undoubtedly qualified for the affairs of State (six of the seventeen had been my ministers, four others would be later), but one after the other deprived, by the absurdity of the regime, of any real grip on events. How often, watching them from a distance struggling with the impossible, had I grieved over this waste!'

Charles de Gaulle, *Memoirs of Hope: Renewal, 1958–62; Endeavour, 1962–*, translated by Terence Kilmartin (London: Weidenfeld and Nicolson, 1971), 8.
8. Idem, 22–30.
9. Idem, 32.
10. Alexander Werth, *The de Gaulle Revolution* (London: Robert Hale Limited, 1960), 327.
11. De Gaulle, *Memoirs of Hope*, 34–35.
12. Idem, 171.
13. TNA, PREM 11/2985, Notes for the Prime Minister's conversations with President de Gaulle on 12 and 13 March 1960.
14. Bodleian, MS Macmillan dep. c. 925, ff. 1–8, 'The founding of E.F.T.A.'.
15. Macmillan, *Pointing the Way*, 313.
16. De Gaulle, *Memoirs of Hope*, 187.
17. Bodleian, MS Macmillan dep. c. 925, ff. 1–8, 'The founding of E.F.T.A.'.
18. Macmillan, *Pointing the Way*, 315.
19. TNA, FO 371/150269, Telegram from Sir Christopher Steel to the Foreign Office, 31 March 1960 (10.40 a.m.).
20. TNA, FO 371/150269, Telegram from Sir Gladwyn Jebb to the Foreign Office, 31 March 1960.
21. TNA, FO 371/150269, Telegram from Sir Christopher Steel to the Foreign Office, 31 March 1960 (6.32 p.m.).
22. Bodleian, MS Macmillan dep. c. 925, ff. 1–8, 'The founding of E.F.T.A.'.
23. TNA, FO 371/150273, Letter from Frank Lee to Rowley Cromer, 6 April 1960.
24. Bodleian, MS Macmillan dep. c. 942, ff. 135–138, Letter from Harold Macmillan to Charles de Gaulle, 7 April 1960.
25. Bodleian, MS Macmillan dep. c. 942, f. 151, Personal minute from Prime Minister to Foreign Secretary, 22 April 1960.
26. Bodleian, MS Macmillan dep. c. 925, ff. 1–8, 'The founding of E.F.T.A.'.
27. CAC, Papers of Paul Einzig [ENZG] 1/19, Letter from Harold Macmillan to Paul Einzig, 1 May 1960.
28. Bodleian, MS Macmillan dep. c. 942, ff. 152–153, Personal minute from Macmillan to Foreign Secretary, 8 May 1960.
29. Quoted in FO 371/150283, Minute by Sir Roger W. Jackling, 20 May 1960.
30. FO 371/150283, Minute by Sir Roger W. Jackling, 20 May 1960.
31. Peter Hennessy, *Whitehall* (London: Secker & Warburg, 1989), 160.
32. Bodleian, MS Macmillan dep. c. 942, ff. 116–123, 'Sixes and sevens in 1960'.
33. Bodleian, MS Macmillan, ff. 163–164, Letter from Macmillan to Lady Rhys-Williams, 12 June 1960.
34. Bodleian, MS Macmillan dep. c. 942, ff. 116–123, 'Sixes and sevens in 1960'. Throughout July, the retiring British Ambassador to France, Sir Gladwyn Jebb, argued to Macmillan that there was no 'half-way house' in Europe.

If the British government were to spurn the European Economic Community, there was no alternative and the United Kingdom would be left out in the cold. There is some evidence to suggest that Jebb was influential in converting Macmillan's thinking to favour British entry to the EEC. See Sean Greenwood, '"Not the 'general will' but the will of the general": The input of the Paris Embassy to the British "Great Debate" on Europe, Summer 1960', *Contemporary British History*, Volume 18, Number 3 (Autumn 2004), 177–188.

35. Bodleian, MS Macmillan dep. c. 942, ff. 116–123, 'Sixes and sevens in 1960'.
36. Tratt, *The Macmillan Government and Europe*, 124.
37. Ludlow, 'A waning force', 96.
38. Tratt, *The Macmillan Government and Europe*, 126.
39. Ibid.
40. Idem, 127.
41. Bodleian, MS Macmillan dep. c. 942, ff. 116–123, 'Sixes and sevens in 1960'.
42. Quoted in Macmillan, *Pointing the Way*, 317.
43. Interview Transcript in John P. S. Gearson, 'British policy and the Berlin Wall crisis, 1958–61', *Contemporary Record*, Volume 6, Number 1 (Summer 1992), 131.
44. Jack M. Schick, *The Berlin Crisis, 1958-1962* (Philadelphia: University of Pennsylvania Press, 1971), 10–17.
45. Gearson, 'British policy and the Berlin Wall crisis, 1958–61', 117–118.
46. Idem, 118.
47. Bodleian, MS Macmillan dep. c. 942, ff. 116–123, 'Sixes and sevens in 1960'.
48. Idem, 110.
49. Interview transcript in Gearson, 'British policy and the Berlin Wall crisis, 1958–61', 130.
50. Macmillan, *Pointing the Way*, 64.
51. Quoted in Idem, 66.
52. Idem, 92.
53. Memorandum from Selwyn Lloyd to Macmillan, 12 November 1959, quoted in Idem, 97.
54. Macmillan Diary Entry, 17 November 1959, in *The Macmillan Diaries*, 257–258.
55. Macmillan Diary Entry, 18 November 1959, in Idem, 258.
56. Macmillan Diary Entry, 19 November 1959, in Ibid.
57. Quoted in Macmillan, *Pointing the Way*, 98.
58. Macmillan, *Pointing the Way*, 195.
59. Gearson, 'British policy and the Berlin Wall crisis', 120.
60. Interview transcript, Sir Bernard Ledwidge, in Gearson, 'British policy and the Berlin Wall crisis, 1958–61', 144–145.
61. Schick, *The Berlin Crisis*, 139–145.

62. Gearson, 'British policy and the Berlin Wall crisis', 121.
63. For the most complete account of this invasion, see Howard Jones, *The Bay of Pigs* (Oxford: Oxford University Press, 2008).
64. For a detailed account of the events of these summer months, see Robert M. Slusser, *The Berlin Crisis of 1961: Soviet-American Relations and the Struggle for Power in the Kremlin, June-November 1961* (Baltimore/London: Johns Hopkins University Press, 1973).
65. Gearson, 'British policy and the Berlin Wall crisis', 114–115. For a fascinating first-hand account of this by Brigadier L. F. Richards, who at the time was assistant provost marshal as a lieutenant colonel at the British headquarters Berlin, British section, in charge of all military police operations in Berlin, see Idem, 149–159.
66. Bodleian, MS Macmillan dep. c. 951, ff. 81–96, 'The U.K. application to join E.E.C. – Part I'.
67. Bodleian, MS Macmillan dep. c. 942, ff. 116–123, 'Sixes and sevens in 1960'.
68. TNA, T 299/48, Letter from the Earl of Cromer, British Embassy, Washington DC, to Sir Dennis Rickett, HM Treasury, 7 December 1960; and TNA T 299/48, Letter from Norman Stratham, British Embassy, Bonn, to F. K. Gallagher, Foreign Office, 13 December 1960.
69. TNA, T 299/48, Letter from the Earl of Cromer, British Embassy, Washington DC, to Sir Dennis Rickett, HM Treasury, 7 December 1960
70. TNA T 299/48, Letter from R. E. Barclay, Foreign Office, to Sir Harold Caccia, Washington DC, 22 December 1960.
71. TNA 299/48, Letter from Sir Harold Caccia to Sir Roderick Barclay, 28 December 1960.
72. TNA 299/48, 'European unity and the Six/Seven problem: An analysis', Draft memorandum concerning the problems of European unity for transmissions to selected members of the US Administration: Note by Foreign Office, 23 January 1961.
73. Bodleian, MS Macmillan dep. c. 942, f. 66, Telegram from Foreign Office to Paris, from Heath to Macmillan, 27 January 1961.
74. British Library, Newspaper Collections, 'A look at ourselves', Daily Mail Comment, *The Daily Mail*, 27 January 1961, p. 1.
75. Bodleian, MS Macmillan dep. c. 942, ff. 2–19, 'East-West relations, January 1960 to June 1961'.
76. Macmillan Diary Entry, 29 January 1961, in *The Macmillan Diaries*, 358.
77. Bodleian, MS Macmillan dep. c. 942, f. 70, Telegram from the Prime Minister to Dr Adenauer, 31 January 1961.
78. Macmillan Diary Entry, 23 February 1961, in *The Macmillan Diaries*, 362.
79. Bodleian, MS Macmillan dep. c. 942, ff. 2–19, 'East-West relations, January 1960 to June 1961'.

80. TNA, DO 182/83, 'Briefing paper: Preparatory talks with Mr Dean Rusk: The development of the Commonwealth', 13 February 1961.
81. TNA, DO 182/83, 'Supplementary briefing paper: The competing claims of the Commonwealth and of Western Europe on the United Kingdom', 13 February 1961.
82. Macmillan Diary Entry, 8 April 1961, in *The Macmillan Diaries*, 372–373.
83. Bodleian, MS Macmillan, dep. c. 951, f. 104, Telegram from Macmillan to Menzies and Holyoake, 15 April 1961.
84. Bodleian, MS Macmillan dep. c. 951, f. 109, Telegram from Holyoake to Macmillan, 28 April 1961.
85. Bodleian, MS Macmillan dep. c. 951, ff. 105–106, Cabinet Conclusions, 20 April 1961.
86. Macmillan Diary Entry, 26 April 1961, in *The Macmillan Diaries*, 377.
87. Bodleian, MS Macmillan dep. c. 951, ff. 107–108, Cabinet Conclusions, 26 April 1961.
88. Macmillan makes this point in his diary on 17 May 1961. See *The Macmillan Diaries*, 383.
89. Macmillan Diary Entry, 19 May 1961, in *The Macmillan Diaries*, 383–384.
90. Macmillan Diary Entry, 22 May 1961, in Idem, 385.
91. Macmillan Diary Entry, 30 May 1961, in Ibid.
92. Macmillan Diary Entry, 18 June 1961, in Idem, 393.
93. Bodleian, MS Macmillan dep. c. 951, f. 140, 'The Commonwealth and Europe', A note from the Prime Minister to the Cabinet, 21 June 1961.
94. British Library, Newspaper Collections, William Pickles, 'The choice is the empire OR Europe: It cannot be both', *The Daily Express*, 5 June 1961, p. 8.
95. British Library, Newspaper Collections, Colin Lawson, 'Common Market: Germans give shock take-it-or-leave-it warning to Britain: Our terms or not at all', *The Daily Express*, 7 June 1961, front page.
96. Macmillan Diary Entry, 11 June 1961, in *The Macmillan Diaries*, 391–392.
97. TNA, T 299/136, Letter from Philip de Zulueta to Mr Bishop, 15 June 1961.
98. A copy of the White Paper can be found in TNA, T 299/136.
99. Macmillan Diary Entry, 15 July 1961, in *The Macmillan Diaries*, 399.
100. TNA, DO 165/69, Brief for visits by United Kingdom Ministers of Commonwealth countries: Political aspects of U.K. membership of the E.E.C.', June 1961.
101. Bodleian, MS Macmillan dep. c. 951, f. 152, Telegram from Thorneycroft to Prime Minister, 30 June 1961.
102. Bodleian, MS Macmillan dep. c. 951, f. 169, Telegram from Sandys to Prime Minister, 5 July 1961.
103. Bodleian, MS Macmillan dep. c. 951, f. 174, Telegram from Sandys to Prime Minister, 11 July 1961.

104. Bodleian, MS Macmillan dep. c. 951, f. 176, Telegram from Sandys to Prime Minister, 13 July 1961.
105. Bodleian, MS Macmillan dep. c. 951, f. 178, Telegram from Minister of Aviation to Prime Minister, 14 July 1961.
106. Bodleian, MS Macmillan dep. c. 951, f. 181, Telegram from Sandys to Prime Minister, 15 July 1961.
107. British Library, Newspaper Collections, Brendan Abbott, 'This Common Market will give us no quarter!' *The Daily Express*, 19 July 1961, p. 6.
108. British Library, Newspaper Collections, Brendan Abbott, 'This Common Market will give us no quarter!' *The Daily Express*, 19 July 1961, p. 6.
109. Macmillan Diary Entry, 22 July 1961, in *The Macmillan Diaries*, 399. See also Bodleian, MS Macmillan dep. c. 951, ff. 198–199, Cabinet Conclusions, 21 July 1961.
110. Bodleian, MS Macmillan dep. c. 951, Letter from Edward Boyle to Macmillan, 20 July 1961.
111. Harold Macmillan, *At the End of the Day, 1961–1963* (London: Macmillan, 1973), 1.
112. Quoted in Idem, 18.
113. Idem, 26.
114. Bodleian Library, MS Macmillan dep. c. 951, ff. 242–243, Macmillan Television Broadcast, 4 August 1961.
115. David Dutton, 'Anticipating Maastricht: The Conservative Party and Britain's First Application to Join the European Community', *Contemporary Record*, Volume 7, Number 3 (Winter 1993), 523.

12 The rise of the anti-Marketeers

1. Dutton, 'Anticipating Maastricht', 526–527.
2. TNA, PREM 11/3785, Letter from Anthony Montague Browne to Philip F. de Zulueta, 3 August 1961.
3. TNA, PREM 11/3785, Letter from Mrs Constance Hart to Winston Churchill, 30 July 1961.
4. TNA, PREM 11/3785, Letter from Winston Churchill to Mrs Doris Moss, Chairman of the Woodford Divisional Conservative Association, 14 August 1961.
5. Bodleian, MS Macmillan, dep. c. 951, ff. 245–250, Letter from Macmillan to Queen Elizabeth II, 5 August 1961.
6. Lord Salisbury's letter, quoted in CAC, Plowden Papers [PLDN] 5/3/1, Letter from Plowden to the Marquess of Salisbury, 16 August 1961.
7. CAC, PLDN 5/3/1, Letter from Plowden to the Marquess of Salisbury, 16 August 1961.

8. British Library, Newspaper Collections, 'Unnecessary choice', Daily Mail Comment, *The Daily Mail*, 27 September 1961, p. 1.
9. Macmillan Diary Entry, 8 October 1961, in *The Macmillan Diaries*, 418.
10. Macmillan Diary Entry, 13 October 1961, in Idem, 419.
11. Ibid.
12. CAC, PLDN 5/3/2, Statement of the Common Market Campaign, 25 May 1961.
13. TNA, PREM 11/4225, Letter from Lord Gladwyn to the Prime Minister, 24 November 1961.
14. CAC, Gladwyn Papers [GLAD] 1/3/9, Letter from Lord Gladwyn to Jean Monnet and other European leaders, 13 October 1961.
15. Statement by Ted Heath to the Governments of the Six, 10 October 1961, quoted in Lionel Bell, *The Throw that Failed*, 73.
16. Quoted in N. Piers Ludlow, *Dealing with Britain: The Six and the First UK Application to the EEC*, 79.
17. Bodleian, MS Macmillan dep. c. 951, ff. 273–284, Record of a conversation at Birch Grove between Macmillan and de Gaulle, 25 November 1961.
18. Macmillan Diary Entry, 28 November 1961, in *The Macmillan Diaries*, 431.
19. CAC, GLAD 1/3/9, Letter from Philip de Zulueta to Lord Gladwyn, 15 December 1961.
20. Bodleian, MS Macmillan dep. c. 957, f. 40, Letter from Macmillan to Lord Beaverbrook, 5 March 1962.
21. *Daily Express*, 6 March 1962, clipping in Bodleian, MS Macmillan dep. c. 957, f. 38.
22. Bodleian, MS Macmillan dep. c. 957, f. 36, Letter from Lord Beaverbrook to Macmillan, 7 March 1962.
23. CAC, PLDN 5/3/1, Address by Jean Monnet at the opening ceremony of the Second World Congress of Man-made Fibres, London, 1 May 1962.
24. Quoted in Dutton, 'Anticipating Maastricht', 525. Emphasis added.
25. Bodleian, MS Macmillan dep. c. 957, ff. 130–131, Personal minute from Prime Minister to Foreign Secretary, 16 May 1962.
26. Macmillan Diary Entry, 19 May 1962, in *The Macmillan Diaries*, 471–472.
27. Ibid.
28. Bodleian, MS Macmillan dep. c. 957, ff. 152–162, Notes of points made in discussion at Chequers, 19 May 1962, between the Prime Minister, Foreign Secretary and Lord Privy Seal.
29. Bodleian, MS Macmillan dep. c. 957, ff. 134–138, Record of a conversation at the Château de Champs, 2 June 1962, between Macmillan and de Gaulle.
30. Macmillan Diary Entry, 3 June 1962, in *The Macmillan Diaries*, 475. See also Bodleian, MS Macmillan dep. c. 957, ff. 139–146, Record of a conversation at the Château de Champs, 3 June 1962, between Macmillan and de Gaulle.

31. Bodleian, MS Macmillan dep. c. 310, f. 49, Letter from Philip de Zuleuta to Macmillan, 28 May 1962.
32. See Douglas Brinkley and Richard T. Griffiths, eds., *John F. Kennedy and Europe* (Baton Rouge: Louisiana State University Press, 1999), especially chapter 17, Stuart Ward, 'Kennedy, Britain, and the European Community', 317–332.
33. Note of a Call to the White House, 6 April 1961, quoted in Oliver Bange, *The EEC Crisis of 1963: Kennedy, Macmillan, de Gaulle and Adenauer in Conflict* (Basingstoke: Macmillan, in association with the Institute of Contemporary British History, 2000), 38.
34. TNA, PREM 11/3796, Letter from Jean Monnet to Macmillan, 27 June 1962.
35. Macmillan Diary Entry, 19 June 1962, in *The Macmillan Diaries*, 478–479.
36. Bodleian, MS Macmillan dep. c. 957, ff. 246–248, Letter from Macmillan to Lady Rhys-Williams, 2 August 1962.
37. Macmillan Diary Entry, 21 September 1962, in *The Macmillan Diaries*, 498.
38. Quoted in Dutton, 'Anticipating Maastricht', 531.
39. Dutton, 'Anticipating Maastricht', 527.
40. Quoted in Dutton, 'Anticipating Maastricht', 527.
41. Alistair Horne, *Macmillan, 1957–1986: Volume II of the Official Biography* (London: Macmillan, 1989), 339–350.
42. Bodleian, MS Macmillan dep. c. 957, ff. 2–15, 'The wooing of Europe – Part II'.
43. Ibid.
44. Bodleian, MS Macmillan dep. c. 957, ff. 260–262, Letter from Macmillan to Queen Elizabeth II, 7 August 1962.
45. CAC, GLAD 1/3/9, Letter from Jean Monnet to Lord Gladwyn, 6 September 1962.
46. Bodleian, MS Macmillan dep. e. 11, ff. 2–94, Macmillan speech at the opening of the Commonwealth Conference, September 1962.
47. Brian Brivati, *Hugh Gaitskell* (London: Richard Cohen, 1996), 404–408.
48. Bodleian, Harold Wilson Papers [MS Wilson] c. 873, Statement, Labour Common Market Committee, 19 September 1962. For more on the Labour Committee for Europe, see 'The Labour Committee for Europe', *Contemporary Record*, Volume 7, Number 2 (Autumn 1993), 386–416.
49. Bodleian, Uncatalogued papers of Lord Callaghan, 1962, Speech by James Callaghan on the Common Market at the annual dinner of the Edmonton Labour Party, 15 September 1962.
50. Bodleian, MS Wilson c. 873, Statement by Hugh Gaitskell, for transmission at 2130 on 21 September 1962.
51. Bodleian, Uncatalogued papers of Lord Callaghan, 1962, 'Labour and the Common Market: Statement by the National Executive Committee', 29 September 1962.
52. Quoted in Brivati, *Hugh Gaitskell*, 414.

53. Bodleian, MS Macmillan dep. c. 310, f. 104, Letter from Lord Balfour to Home, 23 September 1962.
54. Bodleian, MS Macmillan dep. c. 310, f. 103, Letter from Home to Lord Balfour, 28 September 1962.
55. CAC, ABMS 3/121, Public opinion survey: Follow-up Report No. 1: J. 3475, September 1962.
56. Macmillan Diary Entry, 4 October 1962, in *The Macmillan Diaries*, 502–503.
57. Quoted in Dutton, 'Anticipating Maastricht', 534.
58. Bodleian, MS Macmillan dep. c. 957, f. 308, Pamphlet, 'Britain, the Commonwealth and Europe', by Harold Macmillan, published by the Conservative and Unionist Central Office, October 1962.
59. Bodleian, MS Macmillan dep. e. 11, ff. 169–238, Prime Minister's speech to the Conservative Party Conference, Llandudno, 13 October 1962.
60. Quoted in Dutton, 'Anticipating Maastricht', 533.
61. Ibid.
62. Idem, 533–534.
63. Bodleian, MS Macmillan dep. c. 310, f. 323, Letter from Lord Casey to Macmillan, 17 October 1962.
64. Bodleian, MS Macmillan dep. c. 961, ff. 2–17, 'Europe – The third part'.
65. Macmillan Diary Entry, 1 December 1962, in *The Macmillan Diaries*, 521.
66. Bodleian, Uncatalogued papers of Lord Callaghan, 1962, 'Alternatives to the Common Market: Outline report', Labour Party, December 1962.
67. Quoted in Douglas Brinkley, *Dean Acheson: The Cold War Years, 1953–1971* (New Haven: Yale University Press, 1992), 176.
68. Macmillan Diary Entry, 7 December 1962, in *The Macmillan Diaries*, 523.
69. Macmillan Diary Entry, 9 December 1962, in Idem, 523.
70. Brinkley, *Dean Acheson*, 177.
71. Macmillan Diary Entry, 9 December 1962, in *The Macmillan Diaries*, 523.
72. Quoted in Brinkley, *Dean Acheson*, 178.
73. CAC, AMEJ 1/3/38, Summary of the Rambouillet Talks, 27 December 1962, prepared by Julian Amery for Edward Heath, 8 January 1963.
74. Macmillan Diary Entry, 16 December 1962, in *The Macmillan Diaries*, 526.
75. Macmillan Diary Entry, 1 January 1963, in Idem, 533.
76. Bodleian, MS Macmillan dep. c. 961, ff. 2–17, 'Europe – The third part'.
77. Quoted in Ludlow, *Dealing with Britain*, 207.
78. Macmillan Diary Entry, 28 January 1963, in *The Macmillan Diaries*, 536.
79. Ludlow, *Dealing with Britain*, 213–216.
80. Brivati, *Hugh Gaitskell*, 426–429.
81. Idem, 434–436.
82. Bodleian, MS Macmillan dep. c. 961, ff. 2–17, 'Europe – The third part'.
83. Quoted in Ludlow, *Dealing with Britain*, 224.
84. Ibid.

13 Empire eclipsed, Europe embraced, Britain rejected

1. Helen Parr, 'A question of leadership: July 1966 and Harold Wilson's European decision', *Contemporary British History*, Volume 19, Number 4 (December 2005), 438.
2. Quoted in Parr, 'A question of leadership', 439. See also Helen Parr, *Britain's Policy Towards the European Community*, 23–26.
3. British Library Newspaper Collections, 'All over? History will wait!' *The Daily Mirror*, 30 January 1963, front page.
4. Quoted in Telegram from Sir Pierson Dixon, Paris, to the Foreign Office, 1 February 1963.
5. TNA, T 312/371, Telegram from Mr Hainworth, Brussels, to the Foreign Office, 1 February 1963.
6. TNA, T 312/371, Telegram Sir Arthur Tandy, Strasbourg, to Foreign Office, 6 February 1963.
7. Ibid.
8. TNA, PREM 11/4220, Telegram from Edward Heath to Brussels (United Kingdom Delegation), 6 February 1963.
9. TNA, PREM 11/4220, 'A positive policy after Brussels', Memorandum by Sir Philip de Zulueta to the Prime Minister, 4 February 1963.
10. TNA, PREM 11/4220, Telegram from Foreign Office to Washington DC, 27 February 1963.
11. CAC, ABMS 3/139, 'Britain's economic future', July 1963, Prepared for *The Times*, by Research Services Limited.
12. CAC, ABMS 3/136, 'Britain today: Her international affiliations; Her standing in the world; Her daily newspapers: A study of the opinions of people listed in Who's Who', September 1963, A Survey by Research Services Limited.
13. FO 371/172610, no 13, 'The future of British colonial territories': CO memorandum. Annex: 'Likely future status', in Ronald Hyam and Wm Roger Louis, eds., *BDOEE: Series A, Volume 4, The Conservative Government and the End of Empire, 1957–1964*: Part I: *High Policy, Political and Constitutional Change* (London: The Stationery Office, 2000), 211–216.
14. Richard Lamb, *The Macmillan Years, 1957–1963: The Emerging Truth* (London: John Murray, 1995), 454–472. For the broader societal context of the affair, see R. P. T. Davenport-Hines, *An English Affair: Sex, Class and Power in the Age of Profumo* (London: HarperPress, 2013).
15. Quoted in Idem, 473.
16. Idem, 472.
17. Idem, 476.
18. Macmillan, *At the End of the Day*, 505.
19. Kenneth Young, *Sir Alec Douglas-Home* (Teaneck, NJ: Fairleigh Dickinson University Press, 1971), 167–168.

20. Quoted in Macmillan, *At the End of the Day*, 518–519.
21. Harold Wilson, *A Personal Record: The Labour Government, 1964–1970* (Boston: Little, Brown, 1971), 5.
22. Idem, 6–7.
23. Idem, 18–20. For another account of these events, see Anthony Shrimsley, *The First Hundred Days of Harold Wilson* (New York: Frederick A. Praeger, 1965), 9, 13–14 and 20–22.
24. These conditions are summarised in, amongst other documents, Bodleian Library, MS Wilson c. 873, Letter from George Elvin, General Secretary of the Association of Cinematograph Television and Allied Technicians, to Harold Wilson, 29 April 1963.
25. Bodleian Library, MS Wilson c. 873, Statement issued by the Deputy Leader of the Opposition, George Brown, 25 October 1963.
26. PREM 13/32, ff. 89–90, [UK economic situation]: Outward telegram No. 12331 from FO to Washington transmitting a message from Mr Wilson to President Johnson, 23 October 1964, in S. R. Ashton and Wm. Roger Louis, eds., *BDOEE: Series A: Volume 5: East of Suez and the Commonwealth, 1964–1971: Part 1: East of Suez* (London: The Stationery Office, 2004), 3–4.
27. LBJ Presidential Library, Austin, Texas [LBJ], National Security File [NSF], Head of State Correspondence [HSC], Box 9A, f. 87a, Letter from Harold Wilson to President Johnson.
28. LBJ, NSF, HSC, Box 9A, f. 85a, Telegram from President Johnson to Harold Wilson, 19 November 1964.
29. Jonathan Coleman, *A 'Special Relationship'? Harold Wilson, Lyndon B. Johnson and Anglo-American Relations 'at the Summit', 1964–86* (Manchester: Manchester University Press, 2004), 25.
30. LBJ, NSF, HSC, Box 6, f. 13, Letter from Harold Wilson to President Johnson, 22 July 1964.
31. LBJ, NSF, HSC, Box 9A, f. 71a, Letter from Harold Wilson to President Johnson, 9 December 1964.
32. CAC, GLAD 1/3/20, Letter from Lord Gladwyn to Harold Wilson, 8 February 1965.
33. CAC, GLAD 1/3/20, Letter from Harold Wilson to Lord Gladwyn, 13 February 1965.
34. PREM 13/316, ff. 2–5, 'Haute politique: Thoughts for the weekend': Minute by J. O. Wright to Mr Wilson on the importance of Europe, 12 February, 1965, in S. R. Ashton and Wm. Roger Louis, eds., *BDOEE: Series A: Volume 5: East of Suez and the Commonwealth, 1964–74: Part II: Europe, Rhodesia, Commonwealth* (London: The Stationery Office, 2004), 1–3.
35. CAC, GLAD 1/3/18, Note from Lord Gladwyn to Rt Hon J. Grimond, 15 February 1965.
36. Ibid.

37. House of Commons Debate, 16 February 1965, *Hansard*, Volume 706, 1003–1005.
38. CAC, DSND 9/9, 'A changing Commonwealth in a divided world', by Richard Hornby, MP, 5 March 1965.
39. CAC, DSND 9/9, 'Commonwealth and Common Market – A reconciliation?', by the Conservative Research Department, 5 March 1965.
40. TNA, DO 164/105, Note from L. B. Walsh Atkins to Sir Neil Pritchard, 15 April 1965.
41. TNA, DO 164/105, Note from H. A. F. Rumbold to Sir Neil Pritchard, 15 April 1965.
42. CAC, DSND 9/9, 'Britain and Europe', May 1965.
43. CAC, GLAD 1/3/18, Britain in Europe 'Declaration', 20 May 1965.
44. CAC, GLAD 1/3/18, Letter from Lord Gladwyn to Kenneth Keith, 27 May 1965.
45. CAC, GLAD 1/3/19, 'Britain in Europe: Campaign for a European Political Community: Policy declaration', July 1965.
46. CAC, GLAD 1/3/18, Letter from Beddington-Behrens to Lord Gladwyn, 29 July 1965.
47. CAC, GLAD 1/3/18, Letter from Lord Gladwyn to Beddington-Behrens, 4 August 1965.
48. See Parr, *Britain's Policy Towards the European Community*, 46–55.
49. Parr, 'A question of leadership', 442–443.
50. Quoted in Idem, 443.
51. Quoted in Idem, 444.
52. Parr, 'A question of leadership', 445.
53. Bodleian Library, MS Wilson c. 873, Newspaper clipping, 'Tory renewal of Common Market aim: Mr Heath ready for Brighton', *The Times*, 21 September 1965.
54. TNA, PREM 13/440, Note from the Labour Chief Whip to the Prime Minister, 16 December 1965.
55. LBJ, NSF, HSC, Box 9B, f. 3. Telegram from Harold Wilson to President Johnson, 27 February 1966.
56. Colman, *A 'Special Relationship'?*, 100–102.
57. Quoted in Wilson, *A Personal Record*, 218.
58. TNA, FO 371/188399, Letter from H. L. Lindo, High Commissioner for Jamaica, to Arthur Bottomley, Secretary of State for Commonwealth Relations, 1 February 1966.
59. TNA, FO 371/188399, Note from T. W. Keeble, Commonwealth Relations Office, to Norman Stratham, Foreign Office, 10 February 1966.
60. TNA, FO 371/188399, Telegram from Secretary of State for Commonwealth Relations to H. L. Lindo, no date.

61. TNA, FO 371/188399, Letter from Ian Maclennan, British High Commissioner to New Zealand to Godfrey E. Boyd Shannon, Commonwealth Relations Office, 16 February 1966.
62. TNA, FO 371/188399, Letter from H. Lintott, British High Commissioner in Canada, to Godfrey Shannon, Commonwealth Relations Office, 14 March 1966; and FO 371/188399, Letter from Charles Johnston, British High Commissioner in Australia, to G. E. B. Shannon, Commonwealth Relations Office, 25 March 1966.
63. TNA, FO 371/188388, Letter from New Zealand High Commissioner to Prime Minister, 28 March 1966.
64. CAC, GLAD 1/3/21, 'Franco–British discussion, Paris, 5–6 May', Summary of discussion prepared by the Royal Institute of International Affairs, Chatham House.
65. CAC, PLDN 5/3/4, Speech by Lord Gladwyn at press conference on the occasion of the launching of the 'Campaign for a European Political Community', 28 June 1966.
66. TNA, FO 371/188362, Letter from Sir Patrick Dean, British Ambassador, Washington DC, to Sir Burke Trend, Cabinet Office, 11 July 1966.
67. CAC, GLAD 1/3/1, Letter from Henry Kissinger to Lord Gladwyn, 12 August 1966.
68. Michael D. Bordo, Ronald MacDonald and Michael J. Oliver, 'Sterling in Crisis, 1964–1967', Working Paper 14657, National Bureau of Economic Research, 7–8.
69. CAC, PLDN, 2/3/1, Letter from Lord Plowden to Mr Jeffrey Pressman, Office of the Hon. Lee Metcalf, United States Senate, 10 August 1966.
70. Parr, 'A question of leadership', 437.
71. LBJ, NSF, HSC, Box 10A, Telegram from Harold Wilson to President Johnson, 11 November 1966.
72. LBJ, NSF, HSC, Box 10A, Telegram from President Johnson to Harold Wilson, 15 November 1966.
73. TNA, CAB 164/455, Summary of American view of British entry into the EEC, prepared by Sir Patrick Dean, British Ambassador to the United States, for Sir Con O'Neill, Foreign Office, 9 December 1966.
74. See Sylvia Ellis, *Britain, America, and the Vietnam War* (Westport, CT: Praeger, 2004), especially chapter 5, 'The collapse of the understanding: August 1966–February 1968', 199–265; and Colman, *A 'Special Relationship'?*, especially chapters 6 and 7, 121–166.
75. Parr, 'Britain, American, East of Suez and the EEC', 412.
76. TNA, CAB 164/455, Letter from A. M. Pallister, 10 Downing Street, to C. M. MacLehose, Foreign Office, 10 January 1967.
77. TNA, CAB 164/455, Memorandum from Sir Con O'Neill to the Permanent Under-Secretary A. M. Pallister, 10 Downing Street, 9 February 1967,

including as attachment 'Summary of guidance to United States diplomatic posts abroad on the attitude of the administration towards the British approach to the E.E.C.'.
78. CAC, DSND 9/9, Letter from the British Council of the European Movement to Duncan Sandys, 17 February 1967.
79. Quoted in Anne Deighton, 'The Labour Party, public opinion and "the second try" in 1967', in Oliver J. Daddow, ed., *Harold Wilson and European Integration: Britain's Second Application to Join the EEC* (London: Frank Cass, 2003), 39. For a detailed analysis of the CBI's position on European integration in the 1960s, see Neil Rollings, 'The Confederation of British Industry and European Integration in the 1960s', in Idem, 115–132.
80. For more on the Conservative Opposition's approach to Europe during the Wilson governments of the 1960s, see Philip Lynch, 'The Conservatives and the Wilson application', in Idem, 56–74.
81. CAC, DSND 9/9, The Rt Hon Edward Heath, Leader of the Opposition, speaking at the Central Council Meeting at Church House, Westminster, 4 March 1967.
82. Wilson, *A Personal Record*, 296.
83. CAB 129/128/2, C(67)33, 'The approach to Europe': Joint Cabinet memorandum by Mr Wilson and Mr Brown, 16 March, 1967, in Ashton and Louis, *BDOEE: Series A: Volume 5:* Part II, 3–14.
84. British Library, Newspaper collections, Gordon Jeffrey, 'Join us now, Europe urges', *Daily Mirror*, 17 March 1967, front page.
85. Ibid.
86. Bodleian Library, MS Wilson c. 873, 'Britain and the E.E.C.', Speech of the Secretary of State for Foreign Affairs to the Parliamentary Labour Party, 6 April 1967.
87. TNA, PREM 13/1473, Telegraph from Paris to the Foreign Office, 26 April 1967.
88. Bodleian Library, MS Wilson, c. 873, 'Possible proposals to de Gaulle regarding our EEC entry', no author, 26 April 1967.
89. TNA, CAB 164/108, 'An analysis of the EFTA communique: London: 28 April 1967', submitted by P. F. Hancock of the Foreign Office to W. A. Nield of the Cabinet Office, 9 June 1967.
90. Quoted in, Bodleian Library, MS Wilson c. 873, 'Labour and the Common Market: A statement by the National Executive Committee to the Annual Conference of the Labour Party', Scarborough, October 1967.
91. Anthony Adamthwaite, 'John Bull v. Marianne, round two: Anglo–French relations and Britain's second EEC membership bid', in Daddow, ed., *Harold Wilson and European Integration*, 166.
92. Parr, *Britain's Policy Towards the European Community*, 154–155.

93. CAC, GLAD 1/3/24, Letter from Dr Kurt Birrenbach, Dusseldorf, to Lord Gladwyn, 29 May 1967.
94. Bodleian Library, Sir Con O'Neill Papers, MS. Eng. c. 6065, f.1, 'The United Kingdom and the European Communities', Text of a statement made on behalf of Her Majesty's Government by the Secretary of State for Foreign Affairs at the meeting of the Council of Western European Union, the Hague, 4 July 1967.
95. Quoted in Parr, *Britain's Policy Towards the European Community*, 162.
96. Quoted in Helen Parr, 'Saving the Community: The French response to Britain's second EEC application in 1967', *Cold War History*, Volume 6, Number 4 (November 2006), 428.
97. Quoted in Idem, 430.
98. Quoted in Idem, 431.
99. See Idem, 432–433.
100. Quoted in Idem, 437.
101. TNA, FCO 30/107, Letter from J. A. Robinson to Sir Con O'Neill, 27 July 1967.
102. TNA, FCO 30/107, Note from S. J. G. Cambridge to Mr Hancock and Sir Con O'Neill, 16 August 1967.
103. CAB 129/134, C(67) 187, Annex A, [Britain and the European Community]: Text of President de Gaulle's statement at a press conference on 27 November, 28 November 1967, in Ashton and Louis, eds., *BDOEE: Series A: Volume 5: Part II* (London: The Stationery Office, 2004), 39–42.

14 Entering the promised land? Britain joins 'Europe'

1. Bordo, MacDonald and Oliver, 'Sterling in crisis: 1964–1967', 9.
2. Ibid.
3. Wilson, *A Personal Record*, 461.
4. LBJ, NSF, HSC, Box 10A, f. 17, Telegram from President Johnson to Harold Wilson, 22 November 1967.
5. Wilson, *A Personal Record*, 466.
6. LBJ, NSF, HSC, Box 10A, f. 52d, Telegram from Harold Wilson to President Johnson, 13 July 1967.
7. CAB 128/43, CC 1(68) 3, 'Public expenditure: Post-devaluation measures': Cabinet conclusions on withdrawal from east of Suez, 4 January 1968, in S. R. Ashton and Wm. Roger Louis, eds., *BDOEE: Series A: Volume 5: East of Suez and the Commonwealth, 1964–1971: Part I: East of Suez* (London: The Stationery Office, 2004), 120–127.
8. LBJ, NSF, HSC, Box 10A, f. 67B, Memorandum from Walt Rostow to President Johnson, 11 January 1968.

9. Ibid.
10. Ibid.
11. PREM 13/1999, no. 8a, '[Defence review]: Personal message from President Johnson to Mr Wilson on British plans to withdraw from East of Suez', 11 January 1968, in Ashton and Louis, eds., *BDOEE: Series A: Volume 5: Part I*, 127–128.
12. CAB 129/135, C(68)22, 'Public expenditure: Post-devaluation measures': telegram from Mr Brown on his discussions in Washington about the East of Suez defence cuts (circulated to Cabinet with a note by Sir B Trend), 12 January 1968, in Idem, 131–132.
13. PREM 13/1999, no. 17, [Defence review]: Outward FO telegram no. 544 to Washington transmitting the text of Mr Wilson's reply to President Johnson, 15 January 1968, in Idem 138–140.
14. FCO 24/102, no. 319, 'United States reactions to our withdrawal East of Suez': Despatch from Sir P Dean (Washington) to Mr Brown, 4 March 1968, in Idem 146–150.
15. Quoted in Colman, *A 'Special Relationship?'*, 159.
16. Helen Parr, 'Britain, America, East of Suez and the EEC', 409–410.
17. Quoted in Paul Gliddon, 'The British Foreign Office and domestic propaganda on the European Community, 1960–72', *Contemporary British History*, Volume 23, Number 2 (June 2009), 160.
18. Quoted in Idem, 161.
19. TNA, FCO 30/243, 'Briefing from the Commonwealth Secretary's visit to Malaysia, Singapore, New Zealand, and Australia: Policy in Europe: Post Veto', 3 January, 1968, prepared by F. G. K. Gallagher.
20. Bodleian Library, MS Wilson c. 873, 'Europe Rally', Held at the Royal Albert Hall, 22 February 1968.
21. CAC, AMEJ 1/3/16: Part 2, Memorandum on Britain's European policy, to be discussed at the British Council of the European Movement's Executive Committee Meeting, 25 April 1968, written by David Howell MP.
22. TNA, FCO 41/284, General Affairs Committee, Western European Union, 'The British application for membership of the European Communities and the next steps in the building of Europe: Draft report', Mr van der Stoel, Rapportuer, 7 May 1968.
23. TNA, PREM 13/2090, Speaking note for Prime Minister's visit with M Monnet, 15 July, 1968, prepared by Foreign Office, 12 July 1968.
24. TNA, PREM 13/2090, Record of a conversation between Prime Minister and M Jean Monnet at 10 Downing Street, 15 July 1968.
25. Duchêne, *Jean Monnet*, 284–288.
26. TNA, FCO 30/450, Press communique from the Action Committee for the United States of Europe, 25 October 1968.

27. TNA, FCO 30/450, Letter from Jean Monnet to Michael Stewart, Foreign Secretary, 4 November 1968.
28. TNA, PREM 13/2632, Record of a conversation between the Prime Minister and Monsieur Jean Monnet at 10 Downing Street, 29 January 1969.
29. Wilson, *A Personal Record*, 610.
30. Idem, 610–612.
31. Bernard Ledwidge, *De Gaulle* (New York: St Martin's, 1982), 365.
32. Idem, 366.
33. Idem, 366–367.
34. Jean Lacouture, *De Gaulle: The Ruler, 1945–1970*, translated from the French by Alan Sheridan (London: W. W. Norton, 1991), 575–576.
35. Idem, 594.
36. TNA, BT 241/2254, Folio 3, 'Britain's application to join the EEC: The German Attitude', Minute by B. C. Wells, 23 June 1969.
37. TNA, FCO 7/1427, Letter from John Freeman, British Embassy, Washington DC, to Michael Stewart, Foreign and Commonwealth Secretary, 26 June 1969.
38. TNA, FCO 7/1434, Memorandum, 'The economic effects on the United States of our entry into the EEC', from A. W. Snelling to Mr Wiggin, 14 July 1969.
39. TNA, T 312/2717, 'New Zealand, Britain and the EEC: The future?' A memorandum from the British High Commissioner in New Zealand to the Secretary of State for Foreign and Commonwealth Affairs, 23 May 1969.
40. TNA, T 312/2717, 'Impressions of a visit to New Zealand', by Sir Basil Engholm, September 1969.
41. British Library, Newspaper Collections, Wildfrid Sendall, 'Don't let them hustle Britain', *Daily Express*, 4 August 1969, p. 4.
42. CAC, AMEJ 1/3/16: Part 2, British Council of the European Movement: Minutes of a meeting for the Executive Committee held in the House of Commons, 22 July 1969.
43. TNA, FCO 30/496, 'Merger of British Council of the European Movement & Britain in Europe: Statement by Lord Harlech at press conference, Waldorf Hotel, 25 July 1969.
44. 'Note on the Author', in Sir Con O'Neill, *Britain's Entry into the European Community: Report by Sir Con O'Neill on the Negotiations of 1970–72*, edited and with a foreword by Sir David Hannay (London: Whitehall History Publishing, in association with Frank Cass, 2000), xx–xxi.
45. TNA, FCO 30/490, Note from J. B. Johnston, Foreign Office, 10 October 1969.
46. O'Neill, *Report on the Negotiations for UK Entry into the European Community, June 1970–January 1972*, 14.
47. William Rodgers, 'Thomson, George Morgan, Baron Thomson of Monifieth (1921–2008)', *The Oxford Dictionary of National Biography* (Oxford University Press, online edition, September 2012).

48. Haig Simonian, *The Privileged Partnership: Franco–German Relations in the European Community, 1969–1984* (Oxford: Clarendon, 1985), 79–80.
49. TNA, FCO 7/1427, Memorandum from Sir James Marjoribanks, UKDEL EEC, Brussels, to Mr Christofas and J. A. Robinson, European Integration Department, Foreign and Commonwealth Office, 16 December 1969.
50. TNA, FCO 7/1427, 'Implications for Anglo–U.S. relations of Britain's European policies', by the FCO Planning Staff, 29 December 1969.
51. TNA, BW 1/727, Speech delivered by Mr. Schuman, French Minister for Foreign Affairs, before the Anglo–French Society, London, 22 January 1970.
52. Stephen Wall, *The Official History of Britain and the European Community: Volume II: From Rejection to Referendum, 1963–1975* (London: Routledge, 2013), 359.
53. Wilson, *A Personal Record*, 778–781.
54. Wall, *The Official History of Britain and the European Community*, 360.
55. Idem, 360–361.
56. Roger Broad, Witness seminar with leading members of the Labour Committee for Europe, held at the London office of the Commission of the European Communities, 12 June 1990, transcribed in 'The Labour Committee for Europe', 387.
57. George Thomson, Witness seminar with leading members of the Labour Committee for Europe, held at the London office of the Commission of the European Communities, 12 June 1990, transcribed in 'The Labour Committee for Europe', 394.
58. Anthony Forster, *Euroscepticism in Contemporary British Politics: Opposition to Europe in the British Conservative and Labour Parties since 1945* (London: Routledge, 2002), 34.
59. Idem, 33.
60. Philip Lynch, 'The Conservatives and the Wilson application', 69.
61. Bodleian Library, Papers of Sir Neil Martin, MS. Eng. Hist. c. 1130, f. 1, February 1969 Newsletter, The Anti-Common Market League, 24 February 1969.
62. Bodleian Library, MS. Eng. Hist. c. 1130, ff. 2–3, August 1969 Newsletter, The Anti-Common Market League, August 1969.
63. Ibid.
64. Bodleian Library, MS Wilson c.873, article clipping, A. P. Herbert, 'All in our own good time', *Daily Telegraph*, 18 March 1967.
65. Bodleian, MS. Eng. Hist. c. 1130, ff-4–5, October 1969 Newsletter, The Anti-Common Market League, October 1969.
66. Ibid.
67. Bodleian, MS. Eng. Hist. c. 1130, ff. 174–178, 'The Common Market Safeguards Campaign', January 1970.

68. Bodleian, MS. Eng. Hist. c. 1130, f. 6, Letter from the Anti-Common Market League to all its members, February 1970.
69. Bodleian, MS. Eng. Hist. c. 1130, f. 180, 'The Common Market Safeguards Campaign', June 1970.
70. Bodleian, MS. Eng. Hist. c. 1130, ff. 261–262, 'Statement by the Common Market Safeguard Campaign', Press Conference, 29 June 1970.
71. Catherine Hynes, *The New Year that Never Was: Heath, the Nixon Administration, and the Year of Europe* (Dublin: University College Dublin Press, 2009).
72. CAC, AMEJ 1/3/16: Part 1, Minutes of the first annual general meeting of the European Forum, held on 22 July 1970, in the House of Commons.
73. Edward Heath, *Old World, New Horizons: Britain, the Common Market, and the Atlantic Alliance* (London: Oxford University Press, 1970), 34.
74. Wall, *The Official History of Britain and the European Community*, 361–362.
75. See O'Neill, *Report on the Negotiations for UK Entry into the European Community*, 17–24.
76. Idem, 140.
77. TNA, T 312/2717, 'Negotiating aims of New Zealand', A brief for the Chief Secretary by J. F. Slater, 19 May 1970.
78. TNA, T 312/2718, 'Negotiating aims on New Zealand', A cabinet brief, 5 June 1970.
79. TNA, T 312/2718, Record of meeting between British and New Zealand officials, 8 June 1970.
80. TNA, T 312/2718, 'U.K. entry to the E.E.C.: Opening statement by Mr M. J. Moriarty at official discussion in London, 8 June 1970'.
81. TNA, T 312/2718, 'Record of meeting between British and New Zealand officials, 9 June 1970.
82. TNA, T 312/2718, U.K. entry to the EEC: Statement by Mr M. J. Moriarty at official discussions in London on 17 June 1970.
83. Bodleian, MS. Eng. Hist. c. 1130, Statement by the Common Market Safeguards Campaign, 22 September 1970.
84. Ben Pimlott, *Harold Wilson* (London: HarperCollins, 1992), 580.
85. Ibid.
86. TNA, FCO 26/792, National Opinion Poll Bulletin, 'The Common Market', Fieldwork dates 13–18 October 1970.
87. TNA, FCO 26/250, 'Political Campaign', Memorandum sent from Lord Harlech to the Chancellor of the Duchy of Lancaster, 17 August 1970.
88. TNA, FCO 26/550, Record of Meeting between the Chancellor of the Duchy of Lancaster and Officers of the British Council of the European Movement, held at the Foreign and Commonwealth Office, 20 August 1970.

89. TNA, FCO 26/547, 'Themes for Europe (draft)', given to Caroline Petrie, European Communities Information Unit, by Michael Niblock, Conservative Research Department, 10 September 1970.
90. Pimlott, *Harold Wilson*, 581.
91. Roy Jenkins, Witness seminar with leading members of the Labour Committee for Europe, held at the London office of the Commission of the European Communities, 12 June 1990, transcribed in 'The Labour Committee for Europe', 391.
92. TNA, FCO 26/792, Memorandum from R. C. Beetham, News Department, to Miss Petrie (ECIU), cc'd to Con O'Neill, 22 January 1971.
93. Pimlott, *Harold Wilson*, 581.
94. Bodleian Library, Uncatalogued papers of Lord Callaghan, 1971, 'Speech, Bitterne Park School, Southampton, 25 May 1971', in Pamphlet, 'James Callaghan on the Common Market', Published by the Labour Committee for Safeguards on the Common Market, 1971.
95. Bodleian Library, Uncatalogued papers of Lord Callaghan, 1971, Letter from W. Thomson, Edinburgh, to Callaghan, 26 May 1971.
96. TNA, FCO 26/792, Memorandum from S. A. Budd, European Communities Information Unit, to Adams, Ford, O'Neill, Logan, and Tickell, 21 April 1971. For Tony Benn's campaign for a referendum, see Tony Benn, *Office without Power: Diaries, 1968–72* (London: Hutchinson, 1988), 295–393.
97. TNA, FCO 26/792, Note from S. A. Budd to Mr Adams and Mr Logan, 17 June 1971.
98. CAC, DSND 9/9, 'Britain in Europe Seminar', St Ermin's Hotel, London, 27 April 1971.
99. TNA, CAB 164/970, Message from the Prime Minister to President Nixon, 26 May 1971.
100. O'Neill, *Report on the Negotiations for UK Entry into the European Community*, 337.
101. CAC, Michael Wolff Papers [WLFF] 3/2/39, Letter from the Lord Privy Council to Cabinet Ministers, 21 June 1971.
102. Wall, *The Official History of Britain and the European Community*, 412.
103. British Library, Newspaper Collections, 'Now we can lead Europe', Daily Mail Comment, *The Daily Mail*, 24 June 1971, p. 1.
104. Wall, *The Official History of Britain and the European Community*, 415.
105. Crowson, *Britain and Europe*, 99.
106. Roy Jenkins, Witness seminar with leading members of the Labour Committee for Europe, held at the London office of the Commission of the European Communities, 12 June 1990, transcribed in 'The Labour Committee for Europe', 390.
107. Crowson, *Britain and Europe*, 99.

108. Bodleian, MS Wilson c. 1294, Broadcast statement by Harold Wilson, 8 July 1971.
109. TNA, PREM 15/601, Letter from Lord Drogheda to Robert Armstrong, 29 July 1971.
110. TNA, PREM 15/601, Letter from Harold Wilson to Lord Drogheda, 26 July 1971.
111. CAC, WLFF 3/6/2, Note from Mr Croft, Cabinet Office, to Mr Stratham, 20 August 1971, included 'Common Market: N.E.C. background paper', 28 July 1971.
112. George Thomson, witness seminar with leading members of the Labour Committee for Europe, held at the London office of the Commission of the European Communities, 12 June 1990, transcribed in 'The Labour Committee for Europe', 395. He later claimed that 'If we had won the election, my profound conviction is that negotiations would have taken very broadly the course that they did finally take, because the pre-negotiations had established the amount of room for manoeuvre that there was. And the reality was known by anybody who followed the negotiations closely. I believe the Labour government would have taken Britain into the Community on roughly the terms that the Conservatives had got'.
113. Bodleian Library, Uncatalogued papers of Lord Callaghan, 1971, Speech, St George's Hall, Bradford, 8 September 1971, in Pamphlet, 'James Callaghan on the Common Market', Published by the Labour Committee for Safeguards on the Common Market, 1971.
114. Bodleian Library, Uncatalogued papers of Lord Callaghan, 1971, Speech, Cory Hall, Cardiff, 17 September 1971; and Speech, Wesley Central Hall, Portsmouth, 21 September 1971; both in Ibid.
115. See Pimlott, *Harold Wilson*, 579–602.
116. Wall, *The Official History of Britain and the European Community*, 419.
117. CAC, DSND 9/12, Letter from James R. H. Hutchinson to Duncan Sandys, 1 November 1971.
118. CAC, DSND 9/12, Letter from Duncan Sandys to Hutchinson, 5 November 1971.
119. Gowland, Turner and Wright, *Britain and European Integration since 1945*, 75.
120. Niklas H. Rossbach, *Heath, Nixon and the Rebirth of the Special Relationship: Britain, the US and the EC, 1969–74* (Basingstoke: Palgrave Macmillan, 2009), 10.
121. TNA, CAB 193/23, Extract from a talk given by Mr Pallister to the Civil Service College, 24 July 1972.
122. Kenneth O. Morgan, *The People's Peace: British History, 1945–1989* (Oxford: Oxford University Press, 1990), 342.

15 Seasons of discontent

1. TNA, FCO 30/1644, Opinion polls, January–August 1973.
2. Edward Heath, *The Course of My Life: My Autobiography* (London: Hodder & Stoughton, 1998), 380–383 and photo plates after p. 450.
3. Margaret Thatcher, *The Path to Power* (London: HarperCollins, 1995), 211.
4. Idem, 381.
5. David Heathcote-Amory, *Confessions of a Eurosceptic* (Barnsley: Pen & Sword Politics, 2012), 4.
6. Thatcher, *The Path to Power*, 207–211.
7. Heath, *The Course of My Life*, 394–395.
8. Quoted in Wall, *The Official History of Britain and the European Community*, 454.
9. Ibid.
10. TNA, FCO 30/1644, Opinion polls, January–August 1973, 'Gallup Poll, August 1973'.
11. Wall, *The Official History of Britain and the European Community*, 457.
12. See Rossbach, *Heath, Nixon and the Rebirth of the Special Relationship*, 44–78.
13. Quoted in Harold Wilson, *Final Term: The Labour Government, 1974–1976* (London: Weidenfeld and Nicolson, 1979), 2.
14. Timothy Heppell, *The Tories: From Winston Churchill to David Cameron* (London: Bloomsbury, 2014), 54.
15. Idem, 54–57.
16. Idem, 55.
17. Harold Wilson, *Final Term*, 3.
18. Arthur Marwick, *British Society since 1945, fourth edition* (London: Penguin, 2003), 152.
19. Alan Sked and Chris Cook, *Post-War Britain: A Political History, second edition* (London: Penguin, 1984), 258.
20. Wall, *The Official History of Britain and the European Community*, 470.
21. CAC, WLFF 3/2/43, Memorandum from Douglas Hurd to the Prime Minister, 19 September 1973.
22. CAC, WLFF 3/2/43, Cabinet Ministerial Committee on Europe, Public relations aspect of EEC work, Note by the Parliamentary Secretary, 25 September 1973.

---

123. Bodleian Library, Uncatalogued papers of Lord Callaghan, 1972, 'Statement to party conference', October 1972.
124. TNA, FCO 49/398, 'The Commonwealth after accession', Memorandum from Sir Denis Greenhill to all heads of mission, 5 December 1972.

23. TNA, FCO 30/1644, Letter from G. R. Denman, Department of Trade and Industry, to B. C. Cubbon, Cabinet Office, 28 September 1973.
24. Michael J. Turner, *Britain's International Role, 1970–1991* (Basingstoke: Palgrave Macmillan, 2010), 19.
25. Heath, *The Course of My Life*, 501.
26. Idem, 500.
27. TNA, FCO 30/1644, Minute from J. O. Wright to J. A. Robinson, 25 October 1973,
28. TNA, FCO 30/1644, Minute from J. A. Robinson to J. O. Wright, 26 October 1973.
29. Philip Ziegler, *Edward Heath: The Authorised Biography* (London: HarperPress, 2010), 411–416.
30. Quoted in Idem, 414.
31. Heath, *The Course of My Life*, 466.
32. Ziegler, *Edward Heath*, 416.
33. TNA, FCO 30/1644, Letter from Robert Carr, Home Secretary, to the Chief Whip, 16 November 1973.
34. TNA, FCO 30/1645, 'Europe – Presentation', Minute sent to all Government Ministers from the Prime Minister, 27 November 1973.
35. Thatcher, *The Path to Power*, 231.
36. Sked and Cook, *Post-War Britain*, 281.
37. CAC, AMEJ 1/3/38, 'Political co-operation by the member states of the European Communities: The European identity', Approved by the Foreign Ministers of the Nine Member States of the European Communities and published on the occasion of the European Summit Meeting in Copenhagen on 14 December 1973.
38. UKREP Brussels Diplomatic Report 149/74, MWP 1/1, '1973: Year One in the European Communties', in Keith Hamilton and Patrick Salmon, eds., *Documents on British Policy Overseas, Series III, Volume IV*: The Year of Europe: America, Europe and the Energy Crisis, 1972–1974 (Abingdon: Routledge, 2006), CD-ROM, document 517.
39. Heath, *The Course of My Life*, 511–516.
40. CAC, WLFF 3/2/43, Note from Robin Haydon, Chief Press Secretary, 10 Downing Street, to 'Minister', 9 January 1974.
41. Pimlott, *Harold Wilson*, 611.
42. Tony Benn, Diary Entry, 8 June 1973, in Tony Benn, *Against the Tide: Diaries, 1973–76* (London: Hutchinson, 1989), 44.
43. Ibid.
44. Simon Heffer, 'Powell, (John) Enoch (1912–1998)', *Oxford Dictionary of National Biography* (Oxford University Press, 2004, online edition, May 2008).
45. Ibid.

46. Quoted in Grob-Fitzgibbon, *Imperial Endgame*, 365.
47. Ibid.
48. For a full account of Powell's life, see Simon Heffer, *Like the Roman: The Life of Enoch Powell* (London: Faber and Faber, 2008).
49. Quoted in Camilla Schofield, *Enoch Powell and the Making of Postcolonial Britain* (Cambridge: Cambridge University Press, 2013), 296.
50. Tony Benn, Diary Entry, 27 July 1973, in Benn, *Against the Tide*, 56.
51. Pimlott, *Harold Wilson*, 611.
52. Tony Benn, Diary Entry, 7 February 1973, in Benn, *Against the Tide*, 105.
53. Bernard Donoughue, Diary Entry, 20 February 1974, in Bernard Donoughue, *Downing Street Diary: With Harold Wilson in No. 10* (London: Jonathan Cape, 2005), 29.
54. Donoughue, Diary Entry, 21 February 1974, in *Downing Street Diary*, 30–31.
55. Pimlott, *Harold Wilson*, 611–612.
56. Tony Benn, Diary Entry, 23 February 1974, in Benn, *Against the Tide*, 109.
57. Hynes, *The Year that Never Was* 224–225.
58. Thatcher, *The Path to Power*, 237.
59. Heath, *The Course of My Life*, 516.
60. Bodleian Library, MS Castle 306, f. 1, 'Labour and the EEC: Jim Callaghan spells it out', *Today*, No. 11, 21 February 1974, Published by the Labour Party.
61. Heath, *The Course of My Life*, 517–518.
62. Pimlott, *Harold Wilson*, 612–615.
63. Donoughue, Diary Entry, 4 March 1974, in *Downing Street Diary*, 54.
64. Wilson, *Final Term*, 10–11.
65. Bodleian Library, MS. Eng. Hist. c. 1131, f. 60, 'One year into the EEC: Common Market – The way out', Pamphlet published by the Common Market Safeguards Campaign, March 1974.
66. Record of meeting: Callaghan/Sonnefeldt, MWP 3/304/1, in Hamilton and Salmon, eds., *DPBO, Series III, Volume IV*, CD-ROM, document 568.
67. CAC, GLAD 1/3/47, 'Statement of the situation in the U.K. to the Political Committee', by Lord Gladwyn, 22 March 1974.
68. Tony Benn, Diary Entry, 8 April 1974, in Benn, *Against the Tide*, 135.
69. Bodleian Library, Uncatalogued papers of Lord Callaghan, 1974, 'Renegotiation of the terms of entry into the European Economic Community: Text of a statement by the Secretary of State for Foreign and Commonwealth Affairs in the Council of Ministers of the European Communities in Luxembourg', 1 April 1974.
70. Wilson, *Final Term*, 50–51.
71. Idem, 51.

72. British Library, Newspaper Collections, 'Good ... or bad?' Letters to the Editor, *Daily Mail*, 5 April 1974, p. 31.
73. CAC, AMEJ 1/10/16: Part 1, Letter from Julian Amery to Edward Heath, May 1974.
74. Donoughue, Diary Entry, 25 April 1974, in *Downing Street Diary*, 106.
75. Idem, 106–107. Tony Benn noted this encounter in the following way: 'Roy Jenkins said that if we went for a quick solution, the future of the Government would be in grave danger, which was a sort of vague threat of resignation'. Diary Entry, 25 April 1974, in Benn, *Against the Tide*, 142.
76. Idem, 107.
77. Ibid.
78. Tony Benn, Diary Entry, 24 April 1974, in Benn, *Against the Tide*, 143.
79. Wilson, *Final Term*, 56.
80. Sked and Cook, *Post-War Britain*, 297.
81. Quoted in Heath, *The Course of My Life*, 525.
82. Bernard Donoughue, Diary Entry, 16 September 1974, in Donoughue, *Downing Street Diary*, 186–187.
83. Heath, *The Course of My Life*, 525.
84. Bernard Donoughue, Diary Entry, 3 December 1974, in Donoughue, *Downing Street Diary*, 252–253.
85. Quoted in Wilson, *Final Term*, 91.
86. Bodleian Library, Uncatalogued papers of Lord Callaghan, 1974, 'Facts: Published monthly by the European Movement', December 1974.
87. Wilson, *Final Term*, 94–95.
88. Quoted in Idem, 95.
89. Bodleian Library, MS. Eng. Hist. c. 1131, ff. 140–143, National Referendum Campaign, Minutes of a meeting held in the House of Commons, 17 December 1974.
90. Tony Benn, Diary Entry, 12 December 1974, in Benn, *Against the Tide*, 283.
91. Quoted in Ibid.
92. Bodleian Library, MS. Eng. Hist. c. 1131, f. 245, 'The Common Market ... Loss of self-government', The Full Text of Rt Hon Anthony Benn's New Year Message to his Constituents, 29 December 1974.
93. Tony Benn, Diary Entry, 29 December 1974, in Benn, *Against the Tide*, 291.
94. Tony Benn, Diary Entry, 30 December 1974, in Ibid.
95. Tony Benn, Diary Entry, 1 January 1975, in Idem, 292.
96. Bodleian Library, MS. Eng. Hist. c. 1131, ff. 150–151, Statement by Neil Marten, M.P., Chairman of the National Referendum Campaign, 7 January 1975.
97. Bodleian Library, MS. Eng. Hist. c. 1131, ff. 185–190, 'Some thoughts on the referendum campaign', 7 January 1975.

98. Bernard Donoughue, Diary Entry, 2 January 1975, in Donoughue, *Downing Street Diary*, 271.
99. This was not the first time Wilson had disciplined Benn in this fashion. See Pimlott, *Harold Wilson*, 638–643.
100. Bodleian Library, MS. Eng. Hist. c. 1131, f. 199, 'Worse off in the Common Market', Text of the Speech by the Rt Hon Peter Shore, MP, Secretary of State for Trade, 19 January 1975, at the Co-operative Hall, Brighton.
101. Bodleian Library, MS Castle 306, Newspaper clipping, 'Midsummer madness', *The Daily Mail*, 24 January 1975, front page.
102. Bodleian Library, MS. Eng. Hist. c. 1131, f. 158, 'National Referendum campaign press release, 4 February 1975.
103. Bodleian Library, Uncatalogued papers of Lord Callaghan, 1975, Summary of the renegotiations, from the Labour Committee for Europe, 6 February 1975.
104. Bodleian Library, Uncatalogued papers of Lord Callaghan, 1975, 'Developments in Europe', published by the Labour Committee for Europe, 27 February 1975.
105. Bodleian Library, MS Castle 306, ff. 123–124, Newspaper clipping, 'At last, Wilson delivers his verdict on Europe: YES', *The Sun*, 18 March, front page.
106. Bodleian Library, MS Castle, 306, ff. 127–131, Newspaper clipping, 'Yes to Europe, but no to unity: Cabinet Revolt gathers force', *The Guardian*, 19 March 1975, front page.
107. Bernard Donoughue, Diary Entry, 18 March 1975, in Donoughue, *Downing Street Diary*, 339.
108. Bodleian Library, Uncatalogued papers of Lord Callaghan, 1975, Speech by Ian Mikardo at the annual dinner of the Wythenshawe Constituency Labour Party, 21 March 1975.
109. For an account of this leadership campaign, see Moore, *Margaret Thatcher*, 266–295.
110. US Embassy in London to State Department, 'Margaret Thatcher: Some first impressions', 16 February 1975, Margaret Thatcher Foundation, Online Archive, document 111068.
111. Quoted in Heath, *The Course of My Life*, 535.
112. Heath, *The Course of My Life*, 537–538.
113. Tony Benn, Diary Entry, 18 February 1974, in Benn, *Against the Tide*, 319.
114. Ibid.
115. Tony Benn, Diary Entry, 12 March 1975, in Benn, *Against the Tide*, 339.
116. Thatcher, *The Path to Power*, 330.
117. Idem, 330–331.
118. Bodleian Library, MS Castle 306, 'The Common Market: Why we object', Statement by the dissenting ministers, signed by Peter Shore, Michael Foot, Tony Benn, Barbara Castle, John Silken and Judith Hart, March 1975.

119. Bodleian Library, MS. Eng. Hist. c. 1132, ff. 26–27, Statement by Neil Marten, 16 May 1975.
120. Bodleian Library, MS Castle 306, Text of Commonwealth Heads of Government statement on the European Community, May 1975.
121. Thatcher, *The Path to Power*, 333–335.
122. Heath, *The Course of My Life*, 546.
123. Quoted in Thatcher, *The Path to Power*, 335.
124. Thatcher, *The Path to Power*, 336.
125. Bodleian Library, MS Castle 307, f. 52, National Referendum Campaign press release, 4 June 1975.
126. CAC, WLFF 3/8/12, Michael Wolff, 'When did we ever go it alone?' *Evening Standard*, 22 May 1975, p. 15.
127. Heath, *The Course of My Life*, 549.
128. Bernard Donoughue, Diary Entry, 6 June 1975, in Donoughue, *Downing Street Diary*, 401.
129. Idem, 402.
130. Tony Benn, Diary Entry, 6 June 1975, in Benn, *Against the Tide*, 387.

16 Half-hearted Europeans

1. TNA, PREM 19/53/155, Incoming brief, 'European issues', by the Cabinet Secretary, 4 May 1979.
2. Ibid.
3. Quoted in Margaret Thatcher, *The Downing Street Years* (London: HarperCollins Publishers, 1993), 35.
4. Bodleian Library, MS. Eng. Hist. c. 1132, ff. 134–135, Letter from Sir Cyril Black to Neil Marten, 13 June 1975.
5. Bodleian Library, MS. Eng. Hist. c. 1132, f. 136, Letter from Neil Marten to Sir Cyril Black, 17 June 1975.
6. Bodleian Library, MS. Eng. Hist. c. 1133, ff. 115–120, Report on public opinion and the EEC, February 1977.
7. Pimlott, *Harold Wilson*, 679.
8. Kenneth O. Morgan, *Callaghan: A Life* (Oxford: Oxford University Press, 1997), 469–475.
9. Thatcher, *The Path to Power*, 313.
10. Idem, 339.
11. Margaret Thatcher, 'Europe as I see it', Speech to the Centro Italiano di Studi per la Conciliazione Internazionale, Rome, 24 June 1977, Margaret Thatcher Foundation Online Archive, document 103403.
12. Moore, *Margaret Thatcher*, 378–379.
13. Morgan, *Callaghan*, 614.

14. Idem, 615.
15. Thatcher, *The Path to Power*, 339.
16. Bodleian Library, Geoffrey Howe Papers (MS Howe), dep. 145, Letter from John Nott to Margaret Thatcher, 10 July 1978.
17. Bodleian Library, MS Howe, dep. 145, 'EMU and all that', by Adam Ridley, Conservative Research Department, 12 July 1978, sent to Thatcher, and copied to Howe, Davies, Nott, Hurd, Tapsell, Wealker and Joynes.
18. Bodleian Library, MS Howe, dep. 145, Letter from Geoffrey Howe to Margaret Thatcher, 31 October 1978.
19. Thatcher, *The Path to Power*, 339–340.
20. Morgan, *Callaghan*, 615.
21. Quoted in Moore, *Margaret Thatcher*, 381.
22. For more on the Labour Party's approach to Europe under Callaghan, see Michael Newman, *Socialism and European Unity: The Dilemma of the Left in Britain and France* (London: Junction, 1983), 235–258.
23. Marwick, *British Society since 1945*, 228.
24. Tony Benn, *Conflicts of Interest: Diaries, 1977–80* (London: Hutchinson, 1990), 443.
25. For an account of the election campaign, see Morgan, *Callaghan*, 686–700.
26. Bodleian Library, MS Howe, dep. 145, Extract from a speech by John Nott, Opposition Spokesman for Trade, at the annual dinner of the Manufacturing Stationers Association, London, 14 March 1979.
27. Moore, *Margaret Thatcher*, 407–408.
28. Idem, 414.
29. Heppell, *The Tories*, 78.
30. Margaret Thatcher, *The Downing Street Years*, 19.
31. TNA, PREM 19/53, Note for the record: Extract from conversation between the Prime Minister, the Foreign and Commonwealth Secretary and the Lord Privy Seal in 10 Downing Street, 8 May 1979.
32. Margaret Thatcher, 'Speech at "Youth for Europe" rally', National Exhibition Centre, Birmingham, 2 June 1979, Margaret Thatcher Foundation, Online Archive, document 104088.
33. Thatcher, *The Downing Street Years*, 61.
34. Bodleian Library, Uncatalogued papers of Lord Callaghan, 1979, 'E.E.C. draft press statement', Labour Party, May 1979.
35. Margaret Thatcher, 'Speech at "Youth for Europe" rally', National Exhibition Centre, Birmingham, 2 June 1979, Margaret Thatcher Foundation, Online Archive, document 104088.
36. Bodleian Library, Uncatalogued papers of Lord Callaghan, 1979, Article clipping, 'The ballot of nine', *Yorkshire Post*, 7 June 1979.
37. Heath, *The Course of My Life*, 696.

38. TNA, PREM 19/54/74, Minute from the Foreign Secretary to Margaret Thatcher, 8 June 1979.
39. Margaret Thatcher, 'Europe – the obligations of liberty', Winston Churchill Memorial Lecture, Luxembourg, 18 October 1979, Margaret Thatcher Foundation, Online Archive, document 104149.
40. Ian Gilmour, *Dancing with Dogma: Britain under Thatcherism* (London: Simon & Schuster, 1992), 3.
41. Sked and Cook, *Post-War Britain*, 329–330.
42. See Richard Wade, *Conservative Party Economic Policy: From Heath in Opposition to Cameron in Coalition* (Basingstoke, Hampshire: Palgrave Macmillan, 2013), especially 114–144.
43. Eric J. Evans, *Thatcher and Thatcherism, second edition* (Abingdon, Oxon: Routledge, 2004), 21.
44. Sked and Cook, *Post-War Britain*, 332; and Anthony Seldon and Daniel Collings, *Britain under Thatcher* (Harlow: Longman, 2000), 7–8.
45. Seldon and Collings, *Britain under Thatcher*, 10.
46. Evans, *Thatcher and Thatcherism*, 19–20.
47. Seldon and Collings, *Britain under Thatcher*, 10.
48. Quoted in Thatcher, *The Downing Street Years*, 43.
49. Seldon and Collings, *Britain under Thatcher*, 14.
50. Evans, *Thatcher and Thatcherism*, 21.
51. Gilmour, *Dancing with Dogma*, 22–23.
52. Idem, 25.
53. Evans, *Thatcher and Thatcherism*, 21.
54. TNA, FCO 30/4302, Memorandum from M.G. Dougal, Overseas Information Department, to Lord N. Gordon Lennox and Mr. Blaker, Private Secretary, 28 February 1980.
55. Moore, *Margaret Thatcher*, 532–533.
56. Idem, 533.
57. Sked and Cook, *Post-War Britain*, 351–353.
58. Tony Benn, Diary Entry, 28 July 1981, in Tony Benn, *The End of an Era: Diaries, 1980–90*, edited by Ruth Winstone (London: Hutchinson, 1992), 141.
59. Tony Benn, Diary Entry, 29 July 1981, in Idem, 141–142.
60. Morgan, *The People's Peace*, 457–458.
61. Moore, *Margaret Thatcher*, 644–645.
62. Nicholas Henderson, 'Britain's decline: It's causes and consequences', Diplomatic Report No. 129/79, 31 March 1979, reprinted in *The Economist*, 2 June 1979, Margaret Thatcher Foundation, Online Archive, document 110961.
63. Seldon and Collings, *Britain under Thatcher*, 12.
64. Gilmour, *Dancing with Dogma*, 289.
65. Quoted in Sked and Cook, *Post-War Britain*, 376–377.

66. Gilmour, *Dancing with Dogma*, 290.
67. Quoted in Moore, *Margaret Thatcher*, 494.
68. Seldon and Collings, *Britain under Thatcher*, 13.
69. Gimour, *Dancing with Dogma*, 292.
70. Idem, 293.
71. Thatcher, *The Downing Street Years*, 86.
72. Gilmour, *Dancing with Dogma*, 294–295.
73. Quoted in Moore, *Margaret Thatcher*, 495.
74. Ibid.
75. TNA, CAB 193/282/2, Note from Secretary of State for Employment to Lord Carrington, 12 June 1980.
76. TNA, CAB 193/282/2, 'Public opinion polls on the EC', Cabinet Briefing Document, 19 June 1980.
77. TNA, CAB 193/282/2, Letter from Lord Carrington to the Prime Minister, 20 June 1980.
78. TNA, CAB 193/282/2, Letter from Michael Alexander, 10 Downing Street, to George Walden, Foreign and Commonwealth Office, 27 June 1980.
79. CAC, Nigel Spearing Papers [SPRG] 3, Safeguard Britain Campaign, 'International Project 1980', by Nigel Spearing, 21 June 1980.
80. Andrew Thorpe, *A History of the British Labour Party* (New York: St. Martin's Press, 1997), 204.
81. Idem, 205–206.
82. Ivor Crewe and Anthony King, *SDP: The Birth, Life and Death of the Social Democratic Party* (Oxford: Oxford University Press, 1995), 85–103. See also Bill Rodgers, 'SDP', in Andrew Adonis and Keith Thomas, eds., *Roy Jenkins: A Retrospective* (Oxford: Oxford University Press, 2004, 211–235).
83. Thorpe, *A History of the British Labour Party*, 206.
84. John Stevenson, *Third Party Politics since 1945: Liberals, Alliance and Liberal Democrats* (Oxford: Blackwell, 1993), 74–116.
85. CAC, Neil Kinnock Papers [KNNK] 8/8, 'Labour's case for withdrawal', Foreword by Michael Foot, Published by the Glasgow District Labour Party, 1981.
86. Bodleian Library, MS. Eng. Hist. c. 1131, f. 101, 'Opinion polls', *Common Market Watchdog*, No. 24, Summer 1981, Safeguard Britain Campaign.
87. Bodleian Library, MS. Eng. Hist. c. 1131, f. 97, 'Plan for withdrawal', *Common Market Watchdog*, No. 25, Autumn 1981, Safeguard Britain Campaign.
88. CAC, THCR 1/10/16, Farewell call on the Chancellor, by Oliver Wright, British Ambassador, Bonn, to Foreign Office, 17 February 1981.
89. CAC, THCR 1/10/16, Valedictory despatch, from Oliver Wright, British Ambassador, Bonn, to the Foreign Secretary, 27 February 1981.
90. CAC, THCR 1/10/44, Valedictory despatch, from Reginald Hibbert, British Ambassador, Paris, to the Foreign Secretary, 15 February 1982.

552 / Notes to pages 421–427

91. Moore, *Margaret Thatcher*, 651.
92. Tony Benn, Diary Entry, 3 April 1982, in Benn, *The End of an Era*, 204.
93. Tony Benn, Diary Entries, 5 April and 2 April 1982, in Idem, 205 and 202.
94. Martin Middlebrook, *Task Force: The Falklands War, 1982* (London: Penguin, 1987), 62–84.
95. Thatcher, *Downing Street Years*, 186.
96. Quoted in Idem, 184.

17 Mrs Thatcher, John Major and the road to European Union

1. Quoted in Moore, *Margaret Thatcher*, 673.
2. Quoted in Idem, 682.
3. Idem, 755.
4. Quoted in Thatcher, *The Downing Street Years*, 235.
5. Moore, *Margaret Thatcher*, 755.
6. Margaret Thatcher, Written statement on the tenth anniversary of British accession to the European Community, 29 December 1982, Margaret Thatcher Foundation, Online Archive, document 105080.
7. Stephen Wall, *A Stranger in Europe: Britain and the EU from Thatcher to Blair* (Oxford: Oxford University Press, 2008), 12–17.
8. 'Monthly warning assessment: Western Europe', CIA National Intelligence Council Memorandum, 24 May 1982, Margaret Thatcher Foundation, Online Archive, document 114311.
9. Middlebrook, *Task Force*, 155–64, 243–44 and 353–55.
10. Thatcher, *The Downing Street Years*, 227.
11. CAC, THCR 1/10/44, 'Paris Summit, 4–5 November 1982', Memorandum by A. S. C. for Margaret Thatcher, 3 November 1982.
12. Moore, *Margaret Thatcher*, 653.
13. Thatcher's biographer Charles Moore lists Mitterrand as amongst those who were placed 'in her good books for ever more' due to their conduct during the Falklands War, alongside Ronald Reagan, Caspar Weinberger, President Pinochet of Chile, Robert Muldoon of New Zealand, King Hussein of Jordan, Rex Hunt the Governor of the Falklands and David Owen of the SDP. *Margaret Thatcher*, 754.
14. George R. Urban, *Diplomacy and Disillusion at the Court of Margaret Thatcher* (London: I.B. Tauris, 1996), 131.
15. Quoted in Evans, *Thatcher and Thatcherism*, 104.
16. CAC, THCR 1/10/49, 'Draft speaking notes for Prime Minister – German Summit', 22 April 1983.
17. Simonian, *The Privileged Partnership*, 327–330.

18. Peter Clarke, *Hope and Glory: Britain 1900–2000* (London: Penguin, 2004), 372.
19. Idem, 376.
20. Sked and Cook, *Post-War Britain*, 430–431.
21. Idem, 431.
22. Quoted in Seldon and Collings, *Britain under Thatcher*, 23.
23. Sked and Cook, *Post-War Britain*, 432.
24. Tony Benn, Diary Entry, 11 June 1983, in Benn, *The End of an Era*, 295.
25. Thorpe, *A History of the British Labour Party*, 212–213.
26. Robert Harris, *The Making of Neil Kinnock* (London: Faber and Faber, 1984), 237.
27. Thatcher, *The Downing Street Years*, 306.
28. Idem, 306–311.
29. Idem, 875.
30. John Major, *The Autobiography* (London: HarperCollins, 1999), 77–81.
31. CAC, Enoch Powell Papers [POLL] 7/1. Part 2, 'An open letter to European Democrats – Who are you really?', League of Concerned Conservatives, March 1984.
32. CAC, POLL 7/1, Part 2, Letter from K. W. Haylett, 26 April 1984.
33. CAC, POLL 7/1, Part 2, Letter from Jonathan Poulton, Vice-Chairman, Bournemouth East Young Conservatives, 11 May 1984.
34. CAC, POLL 7/1, Part 2, Letter from Enoch Powell to Jonathan Poulton, 15 May 1984.
35. Margaret Thatcher, Forward to the Conservative European Manifesto, 21 May 1984, Margaret Thatcher Foundation, Online Archive, document 105684.
36. Thatcher, *The Downing Street Years*, 538–539.
37. Quoted in Idem, 540.
38. CAC, POLL 7/1, Part 2, Letter from Jim McBrearty to Enoch Powell, 6 June 1984.
39. CAC, POLL 7/1, Part 2, Letter from Enoch Powell to Jim McBrearty, 11 June 1984.
40. CAC, KNNK 21/3, Neil Kinnock, MP, speaking to the Socialist Group at the European Assembly, 15 September 1983, European Parliament Building, Strasbourg.
41. Forster, *Euroscepticism in Contemporary British Politics*, 69
42. Wall, *A Stranger in Europe*, 36.
43. Thatcher, *The Downing Street Years*, 543.
44. Idem, 544.
45. Wall, *A Stranger in Europe*, 36–37.
46. Idem, 38–39.

47. Letter, David Hannay to John Kerr, 29 March 1988, Margaret Thatcher Foundation, Online Archive, document 111772.
48. Ibid.
49. Margaret Thatcher, Speech to the College of Europe, Bruges, Belgium, 20 September 1988, Margaret Thatcher Foundation, Online Archive, document 107332.
50. CAC, POLL 7/10, Part 2, 'Britain', Printed and published by the Anti-Common Market League, Autumn Issue, 1984.
51. CAC, POLL 7/1, Part 2, Letter from T. G. Salmon, Scottish Anti-Common Market Council, to Enoch Powell, 26 July 1985.
52. George Ross, *Jacques Delors and European Integration* (New York: Oxford University Press, 1995), 29.
53. Thatcher, *The Downing Street Years*, 547.
54. Quoted in Ross, *Jacques Delors*, 30.
55. Idem, 30–31.
56. Thatcher, *The Downing Street Years*, 556.
57. Ross, *Jacques Delors*, 33.
58. Thatcher, *The Downing Street Years*, 547.
59. CAC, POLL 7/1, Part 2, Letter from R. E. G. Simmerson, Chairman, Conservatives Against the Common Market, to Enoch Powell, 1 August 1985.
60. CAC, SPRG 1, 'The Single European Act: A summary of contents', by Nigel Spearing, June 1986.
61. Thatcher, *The Downing Street Years*, 556.
62. CAC, POLL 7/2, Letter from Guy Esnouf, Conservative Central Office, to Mrs S. J. Donaldson, 21 July 1986, forwarded to Enoch Powell.
63. Thatcher, *The Downing Street Years*, 558.
64. Idem, 727.
65. Thatcher, *The Path to Power*, 337.
66. Thatcher, *The Downing Street Years*, 586–587.
67. Evans, *Thatcher and Thatcherism*, 26.
68. Margaret Thatcher, 'Britain counts for something again', *Sunday Express*, 3 January 1988, Margaret Thatcher Foundation, Online Archive, document 107136.
69. CAC, KNNK 8/28, Concluding section of M Jacques Delors's Speech to the European Parliament, 6 July 1988.
70. British Library, Newspaper Collections, 'Margaret Thatcher does a de Gaulle', Daily Mail Comment, *Daily Mail*, 28 July 1988, p. 6.
71. Margaret Thatcher, 'Speech to the College of Europe', Bruges, Belgium, Margaret Thatcher Foundation, Online Archive, document 107332.
72. Minute from Stephen Wall to John Kerr, providing Geoffrey Howe's criticism of the No. 10 Draft Speech, 1 September 1988, Margaret Thatcher Foundation, Online Archive, document 111793.

73. Letter from John Kerr to Patrick Wright, Permanent Under-Secretary at the Foreign and Commonwealth Office, 6 September 1988, Margaret Thatcher Foundation, Online Archive, document 111806.
74. Letter from Charles Powell to the Foreign and Commonwealth Office, 14 September 1988, Margaret Thatcher Foundation, Online Archive.
75. Letter from John Kerr to Patrick Wright, 16 September 1988, Margaret Thatcher Foundation, Online Archive.
76. Wall, *A Stranger in Europe*, 79.
77. British Library, Newspaper Collections, Letter to the Editor, 'Bravo, Maggie', *Daily Mail*, 1 October 1988, p. 39.
78. Editorial, 'Untimely offensive', *The Daily Telegraph*, 22 September 1988, p. 12.
79. Simon Heffer, 'Thatcher signals fight to stop EEC Superstate', *The Daily Telegraph*, 21 September 1988, p.1.
80. Bruce Anderson, 'Riding roughshod over Continental hypocrisy', *The Daily Telegraph*, 21 September 1988.
81. Heath, *The Course of My Life*, 710.
82. Idem, 706.
83. CAC, KNNK 8/28, Nigel Spearing, 'The treaties that lie behind the speeches', October 1988.
84. CAC, POLL 7/4, Letter from P. G. Sharp to Enoch Powell, 15 October 1988.
85. CAC, POLL 7/4, Letter from Enoch Powell to P. G. Sharp, 20 October 1988.
86. British Library, Newspaper collections, 'Caught between two continents', Daily Mail Comment, *The Daily Mail*, 2 December 1988.
87. Heathcote-Amery, *Confessions of a Eurosceptic*, 12–13.
88. Seldon and Collings, *Britain under Thatcher*, 35–36.
89. Idem, 36–37.
90. Idem, 48.
91. Nigel Lawson, Memorandum on the Community Charge, 16 May 1985, in Idem, Document 24, 110–111.
92. Major, *The Autobiography*, 171.
93. Idem, 131.
94. Thatcher, *The Downing Street Years*, 749.
95. Thorpe, *A History of the British Labour Party*, 223.
96. CAC, POLL 7/5, Part 1, Labour Party Policy Review 1989, Discussion Paper Seven, 'Britain in the World', February 1989.
97. CAC, SPRG 1, 'Labour and the EEC, Some crucial decisions', by Nigel Spearing, March 1989.
98. Transcript of a press conference with Margaret Thatcher concluding the European Election Campaign, 14 June 1989, Margaret Thatcher Foundation, document 107700.
99. Thatcher, *The Downing Street Years*, 750.

100. Letter from Nigel Lawson to Margaret Thatcher, 27 October 1989, Margaret Thatcher Foundation, Online Archive, document 107805.
101. Mark Stuart, 'Meyer, Sir Anthony John Charles, third baronet (1920–2004)', *Oxford Dictionary of National Biography*, online edn, January 2009.
102. Thatcher, *The Downing Street Years*, 830.
103. George Younger's 'Post mortem meeting notes', 6 December 1989, Margaret Thatcher Foundation, Online Archive, document 111437.
104. Harold James, *Europe Reborn: A History, 1914–2000* (Harlow: Pearson Education Ltd., 2003), 375–376. For a more in-depth look at this sequence of events, see Gale Stokes, *The Walls Came Tumbling Down: The Collapse of Communism in Eastern Europe* (Oxford: Oxford University Press, 1993).
105. Margaret Thatcher, Remarks on the Berlin Wall (fall thereof), Outside No. 10 Downing Street, Friday, 10 November 1989, Margaret Thatcher Foundation, Online Archive, document 107819.
106. Ibid.
107. Diary entry of Horst Teltschik, Friday, 10 November 1989, in Horst Teltschik (Foreign Policy advisor to Helmut Kohl), *329 Tage: Innenansichten der Einigung* [*329 Days: Inside View of Unification*], Siedler Publishing, 1991, translated for and available at the Margaret Thatcher Foundation, Online Archive, document 111021.
108. Diary entry of Horst Teltschik, Thursday, 16 November 1989, in Idem, document 111022.
109. Ibid.
110. Diary entry of Horst Teltschik, Saturday, 18 November 1989, in Idem, document 111023.
111. Diary entry of Horst Teltschik, Monday, 4 December 1989, in Idem, document 111025.
112. Carsten Volkery, '"The Germans are back!": The Iron Lady's views of German reunification', *Spiegel Online*, www.speigel.de/international/europe/0,1518,648364,00.html, 11 September 2009. Thatcher's comments were first reported in the autobiography of Helmut Kohl.
113. The wars, of course, were the First and Second World Wars of 1914–1918 and 1939–1945, respectively. The sole English world cup final victory, against Germany, was played in 1966.
114. Letter from Charles Powell, foreign policy adviser to Prime Minister Margaret Thatcher, to Stephen Wall, private secretary to Foreign Secretary Douglas Hurd, 20 January 1990, reprinted as attachment to the BBC news story, 'Thatcher's Fight against German Unity', news.bbc.co.uk/go/pr/fr/-/2/hi/Europe/8251211.stm.
115. Diary entry of Horst Teltschik, Friday, 26 January 1990, in Teltschik, *329 Tage: Innenansichten der Einigung*, Margaret Thatcher Foundation, Online Archive, document 111027.

116. Ibid.
117. Carsten Volkery, '"The Germans are back!": The Iron Lady's views of German reunification', *Spiegel Online.*
118. Diary entry of Horst Teltschik, Friday, 9 February 1990, in Teltschik, *329 Tage: Innenansichten der Einigung.* Margaret Thatcher Foundation, Online Archive, document 111030
119. Diary entry of Horst Teltschik, Friday, 24 February 1990, in Idem, document 111031.
120. Memorandum from Charles Powell to participants in the German Meeting, 19 March 1990, Margaret Thatcher Foundation, Online Archive, document 111046.
121. Charles Powell, 'Seminar on Germany: Summary record', 25 March 1990, available at the Margaret Thatcher Foundation, Online Archive, document 111047.
122. Diary entry of Horst Teltschik, Friday, 30 March 1990, in Teltschik, *329 Tage: Innenansichten der Einigung*, Margaret Thatcher Foundation, Online Archive, document 111034.
123. Diary entry of Horst Teltschik, Friday, 20 April 1990, in Idem, document 111038
124. Diary entry of Horst Teltschik, Tuesday, 17 July 1990, in Idem, document 111045.
125. Quoted in Major, *The Autobiography*, 176.
126. Ibid.
127. Geoffrey Howe, *Conflict of Loyalty* (London: Macmillan, 1994), 645.
128. Resignation letter from Sir Geoffrey Howe to Margaret Thatcher, 1 November 1990, Margaret Thatcher Foundation, Online Archive, document 108236.
129. Quoted in Howe, *Conflict of Loyalty*, 667.
130. Quoted in Evans, *Thatcher and Thatcherism*, 118-119.
131. Clarke, *Hope and Glory*, 398-399.
132. Evans, *Thatcher and Thatcherism*, 119.
133. Clarke, *Hope and Glory*, 399.
134. Michael Heseltine, *Life in the Jungle: My Autobiography* (London: Hodder & Stoughton, 2000), 348-349.
135. Thatcher, *The Downing Street Years*, 844.
136. Idem, 850-860.
137. Douglas Hurd, *Memoirs* (London: Little, Brown, 2003), 381-382.
138. Major, *The Autobiography*, 169.
139. Idem, 174-175.
140. Idem, 175.
141. Quoted in Idem, 200.

142. Press conference announcing decision to join the ERM, 5 October 1990, Margaret Thatcher Foundation, Online Archive, document 108212.
143. Quoted in Crowson, *The Conservative Party and European Integration since 1945*, 55.
144. Major, *The Autobiography*, 266.
145. Idem, 267.
146. Idem, 268.
147. Idem, 267.
148. Idem, 268.
149. Thatcher, *The Path to Power*, 475.
150. Quoted in Thatcher, *The Path to Power*, 475.
151. Major, *The Autobiography*, 268.
152. CAC, POLL 7/7, Part 1, Letter from Geoff Lezemore to Margaret Thatcher, 23 November 1991.
153. Crowson, *Britain and Europe*, 121–122.
154. Major, *The Autobiography*, 274.
155. Wall, *A Stranger in Europe*, 132.
156. Major, *The Autobiography*, 277.
157. Wall, *A Stranger in Europe*, 135.
158. Idem, 136.
159. Quoted in Idem, 288.
160. Ibid.
161. Crowson, *Britain and Europe*, 122–123.
162. Clarke, *Hope and Glory*, 403.
163. 'It's all over', *Evening Standard*, 30 June, 1997, front page.
164. Quoted in Wall, *A Stranger in Europe*, 137.

Conclusion   Post-imperial Britain and the rise of Euroscepticism

1. Margaret Thatcher, *Statecraft: Strategies for a Changing World* (London: HarperCollins, 2002), 320–321.
2. Idem, 359.
3. Quoted in Wall, *A Stranger in Europe*, 138.
4. 'Speech by Rt Hon Mrs Margaret Thatcher OM FRS to the Global Panel in The Hague, Friday, 15 May 1992', full speech in Appendix I, Thatcher, *The Path to Power*, 609–624.
5. Wall, *A Stranger in Europe*, 138.
6. Clarke, *Hope and Glory*, 407.
7. Margaret Thatcher, 'No substitute for the nation state', *The European*, 19 May 1992.

8. CAC, POLL 7/7, Part 2, Letter from David Neil-Smith to Enoch Powell, 14 December 1991.
9. CAC, POLL 7/14, Letter from Cam Poulter to Enoch Powell, 4 January 1992.
10. CAC, POLL 7/8, Part 2, Letter from Vivian T. C. Davies, Association Chairman, Central Suffolk Conservative Association, to Enoch Powell, 5 August 1992.
11. British Library, Newspaper Collections, 'Why Europe is not what it was', Daily Mail Comment, *Daily Mail*, 30 April 1992.
12. Clarke, *Hope and Glory*, 407.
13. Major, *The Autobiography*, 326–335.
14. Idem, 335.
15. Wall, *A Stranger in Europe*, 141.
16. Major, *The Autobiography*, 336.
17. Margaret Thatcher, 'Maastricht', *The European*, 8 October 1992.
18. Major, *The Autobiography*, 348.
19. Idem, 349.
20. Idem, 352.
21. Urban, *Diplomacy and Disillusionment at the Court of Margaret Thatcher*, 194.
22. Major, *The Autobiography*, 362.
23. Idem, 342–343.
24. Quoted in Idem, 343.
25. CAC, POLL 7/12, Newspaper clipping, Comment: 'Should we get out?', *The Sunday Telegraph*, 1 May 1994, p. 31.
26. CAC, SPRG 38, Part 5, Newspaper clipping, David Hughes, 'Blair is hit by Labour Euro-revolt', *The Daily Mail*, 28 March 1996, p. 11.
27. CAC, POLL 7/15, Part 1, 'The UK Independence Party', Campaign material, 1996. For a first-hand account of its founding, see Alan Sked, 'Reflections of a Eurosceptic', in Mark Bainbridge, ed., *The 1975 Referendum of Europe: Volume 1, Reflections of the Participants* (Exeter: Imprint Academic, 2007), 145–147.
28. CAC, POLL 7/8, Part 1, Letter from Gerard Batten to Enoch Powell, 29 September 1993.
29. CAC, POLL 7/8, Part 1, UK Independence Party and the 1994 European Parliamentary Elections (Draft Manifesto).
30. Stephen Goodwin, 'Disgruntled defect to anti-Brussels Sked-ites', *The Independent*, 14 June 1994.
31. Heathcoat-Amery, *Confessions of a Eurosceptic*, 156.
32. 'UKIP beat Tories in European Poll', *Daily Record and Sunday Mail*, 14 January 2013, p. 2.
33. Joe Murphy, 'Farage: Result will lead to an earthquake in Euro elections', *Evening Standard*, 1 March 2013, pp. 3–4.

34. Robert Ford and Fan Warren, 'UKIP have torn up the map: After their success in the local elections, UKIP are poised to wreak havoc in 2015', *The Daily Telegraph*, 27 May 2014, p. 17.
35. 'UK European Election Results', www.bbc.co.uk/news/events/vote2014/eu-uk-results.
36. British Library, Newspaper Collections, Paul Johnson, 'Why we've rediscovered Elgar's Era', *Daily Mail*, 5 December 1988, p. 6.
37. Tony Blair, *A Journey: My Political Life* (New York: Alfred A. Knopf, 2010), 656.
38. See Linda Colley, *Britons: Forging the Nation, 1707–1837*.
39. Heath, *The Course of My Life*, 724.

BIBLIOGRAPHY

Unpublished primary sources

Bodleian Library, University of Oxford

Papers of:
Castle, Barbara
Callaghan, James
Howe, Geoffrey
Macmillan, Harold
Marten, Sir Neil
O'Neill, Sir Con
Wilson, Harold

British Library

Newspaper Collections

Churchill Archives Centre, Churchill College, Cambridge

Papers of:
Abrams, Mark
Amery, Julian
Amery, Leopold
Churchill, Sir Winston (Chartwell Papers and Churchill Papers)
Cooper, Alfred Duff
Einzig, Paul
Jebb, Gladwyn (Lord Gladwyn)
Kinnock, Neil
Plowden, Edwin Noel

Powell, Enoch
Sandys, Duncan
Spearing, Nigel
Thatcher, Margaret
Wolff, Michael

Lyndon B. Johnson Presidential Library, Austin, Texas

Lyndon B. Johnson Papers

National Archives, Kew, Richmond-upon-Thames

Board of Trade
BT 11, Commercial Relations and Exports Department and Predecessors: Registered Files
BT 241, Commercial Relations and Export Division: Registered Files

British Council
BW 1, Registered Files, General Series

Cabinet Office
CAB 21, Registered Files, 1916–1965
CAB 65, War Cabinet and Cabinet Minutes, 1939–1945
CAB 124, Office of the Minister of Reconstruction, Lord President of the Council and Minister for Science: Records
CAB 128, Cabinet Minutes, 1945–1986
CAB 129, Cabinet Memoranda, 1945–1986
CAB 131, Defence Committee: Minutes and Papers, 1946–1963
CAB 134, Miscellaneous Committees: Minutes and Papers (General Series), 1945–1986
CAB 164, Subject (Theme Series) Files, 1963–1986
CAB 193, European Unit Files, 1971–1985

Colonial Office
CO 537, Confidential General and Confidential Original Print, 1759–1955
CO 852, Economic General Department and Predecessors, 1935–1966
CO 936, International and General Department and Predecessors: Original Correspondence, 1944–1967

CO 1027, Information Department: Registered Files, 1952–1967
CO 1032, Defence and General Department and Successors: Registered Files, General Colonial Policy, 1950–1968

Dominions Office
DO 35, Dominions Office and Commonwealth Relations Office: Original Correspondence, 1944–1967
DO 164, Commonwealth Relations Office: Defence: Registered Files, 1957–1967
DO 165, Commonwealth Relations Office: Economic Policy: Registered Files, 1951–1967
DO 182, Commonwealth Relations Office: Western and Middle East Department and Successors: Registered Files, 1960–1966

Foreign Office
FO 371, Political Department: General Correspondence from 1906 to 1966
FO 800 / 434–522, Private Papers of Ernest Bevin
FO 1009, Organisation for European Economic Cooperation, United Kingdom Delegation, 1948–1970

Foreign and Commonwealth Office
FCO 7, Commonwealth Office: American and Latin American Department: Registered Files, 1967–1982
FCO 24, Far East and Pacific Department and Foreign and Commonwealth Office, South West Pacific Department: Registered Files, 1967–1978
FCO 26, Information, News and Guidance Departments: Registered Files, 1967–1980
FCO 30, European Economic Organisations Department and Successors: Registered Files, 1967–1981
FCO 41, Western Organisations Department: Registered Files, 1967–1975
FCO 49, Planning Staff and Commonwealth Policy and Planning Department: Registered Files, 1965–1981

Prime Minister's Office
PREM 11, Correspondence and Papers, 1951–1964
PREM 13, Correspondence and Papers, 1964–1970
PREM 15, Correspondence and Papers, 1970–1974
PREM 16, Correspondence and Papers, 1974–1979

PREM 19, Correspondence and Papers, 1979–1997

Treasury
T 229, Central Economic Planning Staff: Registered Files: 1939–1956
T 232, European Economic Co-operation Committee (Rowan Committee): Registered Files, 1948–1955
T 299, Overseas Co-ordination Division: Registered Files, 1960–1962
T 312, Finance Overseas and Co-ordination Division: Registered Files, 1954–1974
T 337, Free Trade Area Office: Private Office Files, 1956–1959

Special Collections Department, Cadbury Research Library, University of Birmingham

Papers of:
Dixon, Pierson
Eden, Anthony (the Avon Papers and the Additional Papers)
Shuckburgh, Sir Evelyn

Newspapers

The Daily Express
The Daily Mail
The Daily Mirror
Daily Record and Sunday Mail
The Daily Telegraph
Dundee Courier
The Economist
The Evening Standard
The Financial Times
Hull Daily Main
The Independent
Newsweek
The Observer Review
The Press and Journal
The Sunday Telegraph
Western Morning News
The Yorkshire Post

Published primary sources, memoirs and autobiographies

Alanbrooke, Field Marshal Lord, *War Diaries, 1939–1945*, edited by Alex Danchev and Daniel Todman (London: Weidenfeld & Nicolson, 2001).
Ashton, S. R., and Louis, W. R., eds., *BDOEE: Series A: Volume 5: East of Suez and the Commonwealth, 1964–1971: Part 1: East of Suez* (London: The Stationery Office, 2004).
Barnes, John, and Nicholson, David, eds., *The Empire at Bay: The Leo Amery Diaries* (London: Hutchinson, 1988).
Benn, Tony, *Office without Power: Diaries, 1968–72* (London: Hutchinson, 1988).
Benn, Tony, *Against the Tide: Diaries, 1973–76* (London: Hutchinson, 1989).
Benn, Tony, *Conflicts of Interest: Diaries, 1977–80* (London: Hutchinson, 1990).
Benn, Tony, *The End of an Era: Diaries, 1980–90*, edited by Ruth Winstone (London: Hutchinson, 1992).
Blair, Tony, *A Journey: My Political Life* (New York: Alfred A. Knopf, 2010).
Boothby, Robert, *Boothby: Recollections of a Rebel* (London: Hutchinson, 1978).
Boyle, Peter G., ed., *The Churchill–Eisenhower Correspondence, 1953–1955* (Chapel Hill: University of North Carolina Press, 1990).
Colville, John, *The Fringes of Power: Downing Street Diaries, 1939–1955* (London: Weidenfeld & Nicolson, 2004).
Cooper, Duff, *Old Men Forget: The Autobiography of Duff Cooper (Viscount Norwich)* (London: Rupert Hart-Davis, 1953).
de Gaulle, Charles, *Memoirs of Hope: Renewal, 1958–62; Endeavour, 1962–*, translated by Terence Kilmartin (London: Weidenfeld and Nicholson, 1971).
de Gaulle, Charles, *The Complete War Memoirs of Charles de Gaulle*, translated from the French by Jonathan Griffen and Richard Howard (New York: Carroll & Graf, 1998).
Dixon, Piers, *Double Diploma: The Life of Sir Pierson Dixson, Don and Diplomat* (London: Hutchinson, 1968).
Donoughue, Bernard, *Downing Street Diary: With Harold Wilson in No. 10* (London: Jonathan Cape, 2005).
Eden, Anthony, *The Reckoning* (London: Cassell, 1965).
Gaitskell, Hugh, *The Diary of Hugh Gaitskell, 1945–1956*, edited by Philip M. Williams (London: Jonathan Cape, 1983).
Gilmour, Ian, *Dancing with Dogma: Britain under Thatcherism* (London: Simon & Schuster, 1992).
Goldsworthy, David, ed., *British Documents on the End of Empire: Series A, Volume 3: The Conservative Government and the End of Empire,*

1951–1957: Part 1, International Relations (London: Her Majesty's Stationery Office, 1994).

Hamilton, Keith, and Salmon, Patrick, eds., *Documents on British Policy Overseas: Series III, Volume IV: The Year of Europe: America, Europe and the Energy Crisis, 1972–1974* (Abingdon: Routledge, 2006).

Hamilton, Keith, Salmon, Patrick, and Twigge, Stephen, eds., *Documents on British Policy Overseas: Series III, Volume VI: Berlin in the Cold War, 1948–90* (London: Routledge, 2009).

Headlam, Sir Cuthbert, *Parliament and Politics in the Age of Churchill and Attlee: The Headlam Diaries, 1935–51*, edited by Stuart Ball (Cambridge: Cambridge University Press, 1999).

Heath, Edward, *Old World, New Horizons: Britain, the Common Market, and the Atlantic Alliance* (London: Oxford University Press, 1970).

Heath, Edward, *The Course of My Life: My Autobiography* (London: Hodder & Stoughton, 1998).

Heathcote-Amery, David, *Confessions of a Eurosceptic* (Barnsley: Pen & Sword Politics, 2012).

Heseltine, Michael, *Life in the Jungle: My Autobiography* (London: Hodder & Stoughton, 2000).

Howe, Geoffrey, *Conflict of Loyalty* (London: Macmillan, 1994).

Hurd, Douglas, *Memoirs* (London: Little, Brown, 2003).

Hyam, Ronald, ed., *British Documents on the End of Empire: Series 2: The Labour Government and the End of Empire, 1945–1951: Part III: Strategy, Politics and Constitutional Change* (London: Her Majesty's Stationery Office, 1992).

Hyam, Ronald, and Louis, Wm. Roger, eds., *British Documents on the End of Empire: Series A: Volume 4: The Conservative Government and the End of Empire, 1957–1964: Part I: High Policy, Political and Constitutional Change* (London: The Stationery Office, 2000).

James, Robert Rhodes, ed., *Winston S. Churchill: His Complete Speeches, 1897–1963: Volume VIII, 1950–1963* (New York and London: Chelsea House, 1974).

Macmillan, Harold, *Tides of Fortune, 1945–1955* (London: Macmillan, 1969)

Macmillan, Harold, *Riding the Storm, 1956–1959* (London: Macmillan, 1971).

Macmillan, Harold, *Pointing the Way, 1959–1961* (London: Macmillan, 1972).

Macmillan, Harold, *At the End of the Day, 1961–1963* (London: Macmillan, 1973).

Macmillan, Harold, *The Macmillan Diaries: Volume II: Prime Minister and After, 1957–1966*, edited and with an introduction by Peter Catterall (Basingstoke: Macmillan, 2011).

Major, John, *The Autobiography* (London: HarperCollins, 1999).
Moran, Lord, *Winston Churchill: The Struggle for Survival, 1940–1965, Taken from the Diaries of Lord Moran* (London: Constable & Company, 1966).
Morgan, Janet, ed., *The Backbench Diaries of Richard Crossman* (London: Jonathan Cape, 1981).
Norwich, John Julius, ed., *The Duff Cooper Diaries, 1915–1951* (London: Weidenfeld & Nicholson, 2005).
Nutting, Anthony, *Europe Will Not Wait: A Warning and a Way Out* (London: Hollis & Carter, 1960).
O'Neill, Sir Con, *Britain's Entry into the European Community: Report by Sir Con O'Neill on the Negotiations of 1970–72*, edited and with a forward by David Hannay (London: Whitehall History Publishing, in association with Frank Cass, 2000).
Reynaud, Paul, *The Foreign Policy of Charles de Gaulle: A Critical Assessment*, translated by Mervyn Savill (London: Paul Hamlyn, 1964).
Shuckburgh, Evelyn, *Descent to Suez: Diaries, 1951–56*, selected for Publication by John Charmley (London: Weidenfeld and Nicolson, 1986).
Sked, Alan, 'Reflections of a Eurosceptic', in Bainbridge, Mark, ed., *The 1975 Referendum of Europe: Volume 1, Reflections of the Participants* (Exeter: Imprint Academic, 2007).
Thatcher, Margaret, *The Downing Street Years* (London: HarperCollins, 1993).
Thatcher, Margaret, *The Path to Power* (London: HarperCollins, 1995).
Thatcher, Margaret, *Statecraft: Strategies for a Changing World* (London: HarperCollins, 2002).
Urban, George R., *Diplomacy and Disillusion at the Court of Margaret Thatcher* (London: I.B. Tauris, 1996).
Warner, Geoffrey, ed., *In the Midst of Events: The Foreign Office Diaries and Papers of Kenneth Younger, February 1950–October 1951* (Abingdon: Routledge, 2005).
Watt, D. C., ed., *Documents on the Suez Crisis, 26 July to 6 November 1956* (London: Royal Institute of International Affairs, 1957).
Williams, Francis, *Twilight of Empire: Memoirs of Prime Minister Clement Attlee* (New York: A. S. Barnes and Co., 1962).
Wilson, Harold, *A Personal Record: The Labour Government, 1964–1970* (Boston: Little, Brown, 1971).
Wilson, Harold, *Final Term: The Labour Government, 1974–1976* (London: Weidenfeld and Nicolson, 1979).
Woolton, Lord, *The Memoirs of the Rt. Hon. The Earl of Woolton* (London: Cassell, 1959).

Secondary sources
Books

Adonis, Andrew, and Thomas, Keith, eds., *Roy Jenkins: A Retrospective* (Oxford: Oxford University Press, 2004).

Aimaq, Jasmine, *For Europe or Empire? French Colonial Ambitions and the European Army Plan* (Lund, Sweden: Lund University Press, 1996).

Aldous, Richard, and Lee, Sabine, eds., *Harold Macmillan and Britain's World Role* (Basingstoke: Macmillan, 1996).

Anderson, David, *Histories of the Hanged: Britain's Dirty War in Kenya and the End of Empire* (London: Weidenfeld & Nicolson, 2004).

Anderson, David M., and Killingary, David, eds., *Policing and Decolonisation: Politics, Nationalism and the Police, 1917–65* (Manchester: Manchester University Press, 1992).

Anderson, Peter, and Weymouth, Tong, *Insulting the Public? The British Press and the European Union* (London: Longman, 1999).

Bainbridge, Mark, ed., *The 1975 Referendum of Europe: Volume 1, Reflections of the Participants* (Exeter: Imprint Academic, 2007).

Bange, Oliver, *The EEC Crisis of 1963: Kennedy, Macmillan, de Gaulle and Adenauer in Conflict* (Basingstoke: Macmillan, in association with the Institute of Contemporary British History, 2000).

Barclay, Sir Roderick, *Ernest Bevin and the Foreign Office, 1932–1969* (London: Published by the Author, Printed by Butler & Tanner Ltd, 1975).

Bell, Lionel, *The Throw that Failed: Britain's 1961 Application to Join the Common Market* (London: New European Publications, 1995).

Beloff, Lord, *Britain and the European Union: Dialogues of the Deaf* (Basingstoke: Macmillan, 1996).

Bennet, Huw C., *Fighting the Mau Mau: The British Army and Counter-Insurgency in the Kenya Emergency* (Cambridge: Cambridge University Press, 2013).

Bentley, Michael, *Modernizing England's Past: English Historiography in the Age of Modernism, 1870–1970* (Cambridge: Cambridge University Press, 2005).

Black, Jeremy, *Convergence or Divergence? Britain and the Continent* (Basingstoke: Macmillan, 1994).

Blake, Robert, and Louis, Wm. Roger, eds., *Churchill* (Oxford: Oxford University Press, 1993).

Bonin, Hubert, *History of the Suez Canal Company, 1858–2008: Between Controversy and Utility* (Genève: Librairie Droz S.A., 2010).

Braddick, Michael J., *State Formation in Early Modern Britain, c. 1550–1700* (Cambridge: Cambridge University Press, 2000).

Branch, Daniel, *Defeating Mau Mau, Creating Kenya: Counterinsurgency, Civil War and Decolonisation* (Cambridge: Cambridge University Press, 2009).
Brewer, John, *The Sinews of Power: War and the English State, 1688–1783* (London: Unwin Hyman, 1989).
Brinkley, Douglas, *Dean Acheson: The Cold War Years, 1953–1971* (New Haven: Yale University Press, 1992).
Brinkley, Douglas, and Griffiths, Richard T., eds., *John F. Kennedy and Europe* (Baton Rouge: Louisiana State University Press, 1999).
Brivati, Brian, *Hugh Gaitskell* (London: Richard Cohen, 1996).
Brown, Judith M., and Louis, Wm. Roger, eds., *Oxford History of the British Empire: Volume IV: The Twentieth Century* (Oxford: Oxford University Press, 1999).
Bullock, Alan, *The Life and Times of Ernest Bevin: Volume II: Minister of Labour, 1940–1945* (London: Heinemann, 1967).
Bullock, Alan, *Ernest Bevin: Foreign Secretary, 1945–1951* (London: Heinemann, 1983).
Bullock, Alan, *Ernest Bevin: A Biography*, edited by Brian Brivati (London: Politico's, 2002).
Burton, Antoinette, ed., *After the Imperial Turn: Thinking with and through the Nation* (Durham, NC: Duke University Press, 2006).
Butler, David, and Kitzinger, Uwe, *The 1975 Referendum, Second Edition* (Basingstoke: Macmillan, 1996).
Butler, L. J., and Stockwell, Sarah, eds., *The Wind of Change: Harold Macmillan and British Decolonization* (Basingstoke: Palgrave Macmillan, 2013).
Callahan, Raymond A., *Churchill: Retreat from Empire* (Tunbridge Wells: D. J. Costello, 1984).
Camps, Miriam, *Britain and the European Community, 1955–1963* (Princeton: Princeton University Press, 1964).
Cannadine, David, ed., *What Is History Now?* (Basingstoke: Palgrave Macmillan, 2002).
Carlton, David, *Anthony Eden: A Biography* (London: Allen Lane, 1981).
Chandler, David, and Beckett, Ian, eds., *The Oxford History of the British Army* (Oxford: Oxford University Press, 1994).
Charmley, John, *Duff Cooper* (London: Weidenfeld & Nicolson, 1986).
Charmley, John, *Splendid Isolation? Britain, the Balance of Power and the Origins of the First World War* (London: Hodder & Stoughton, 1999).
Clarke, Peter, *Hope and Glory: Britain 1900–2000* (London: Penguin, 2004).
Clarke, Peter, *The Last Thousand Days of the British Empire* (London: Allen Lane, 2007).
Clayton, Tony, *Europe and the Making of England, 1660–1760* (Cambridge: Cambridge University Press, 2007).

Coleman, Jonathan, *A 'Special Relationship'? Harold Wilson, Lyndon B. Johnson and Anglo–American Relations 'At the Summit', 1964–1968* (Manchester: Manchester University Press, 2004).

Colley, Linda, *Britons: Forging the Nation, 1707–1838* (New Haven, CT: Yale University Press, 1992).

Cook, Don, *Charles de Gaulle: A Biography* (London: Secker & Warburg, 1984).

Crewe, Ivor, and King, Anthony, *SDP: The Birth, Life and Death of the Social Democratic Party* (Oxford: Oxford University Press, 1995).

Cross, Robin, *VE Day: Victory in Europe, 1945* (London: Sidgewick & Jackson, in association with The Imperial War Museum, 1985).

Crowson, N. J., *The Conservative Party and European Integration since 1945: At the Heart of Europe?* (London: Routledge, 2007).

Crowson, N. J., *Britain and Europe: A Political History since 1918* (London: Routledge, 2011).

Daddow, Oliver J., ed., *Harold Wilson and European Integration: Britain's Second Application to Join the EEC* (London: Frank Cass, 2003).

Darwin, John, *Britain and Decolonisation: The Retreat from Empire in the Post-War World* (New York: St. Martin's Press, 1988).

Davenport-Hines, R. P. T., *An English Affair: Sex, Class and Power in the Age of Profumo* (London: HarperPress, 2013).

Davies, Norman, *The Isles: A History* (Oxford: Oxford University Press, 1999).

Deighton, Anne, ed., *Western European Union, 1954–1997: Defence, Security, Integration* (St. Antony's College, Oxford: Published by the European Interdependence Research Unit, St. Antony's College, Oxford, with support of the Foreign and Commonwealth Office, and the WEU Institute for Security Studies, Paris, 1997).

Dell, Edmund, *The Schuman Plan and the British Abdication of Leadership in Europe* (Oxford: Oxford University Press, 1995).

Denman, Roy, *Missed Chances: Britain and Europe in the Twentieth Century* (London: Cassell, 1996).

Diefendorf, Jeffry M., ed., *Rebuilding Europe's Bombed Cities* (London: Macmillan, 1990).

Dobson, Alan P., *US Wartime Aid to Britain, 1940–1946* (London: Croom Helm, 1986).

Dockrill, Saki, *Britain's Policy for West German Rearmament, 1950–1955* (Cambridge: Cambridge University Press, 1991).

Duchêne, François, *Jean Monnet: The First Statesman of Interdependence* (London: W. W. Norton, 1994).

Dutton, David, *Anthony Eden: A Life and Reputation* (London: Arnold, 1997).

Eichengreen, Barry, *Reconstructing Europe's Trade and Payments: The European Payments Union* (Manchester: Manchester University Press, 1993).

Elkins, Caroline, *Britain's Gulag: The Brutal End of Empire in Kenya* (London: Jonathan Cape, 2005).

Ellis, Sylvia, *Britain, America, and the Vietnam War* (Westport, CT: Praeger, 2004).

Ellison, James, *Threatening Europe: Britain and the Creation of the European Community, 1955–58* (Basingstoke: Macmillan, 2000).

Evans, Eric J., *Thatcher and Thatcherism*, second edition (Abingdon: Routledge, 2004).

Evans, Richard J., *Cosmopolitan Islanders: British Historians and the European Continent* (Cambridge: Cambridge University Press, 2009).

Farber, David, *Speaking for England: Leo, Julian and John Amery—The Tragedy of a Political Family* (London: Free Press, 2005).

Forster, Anthony, *Euroscepticism in Contemporary British Politics: Opposition to Europe in the British Conservative and Labour Parties since 1945* (London: Routledge, 2002).

Förster, Stig, Mommsen, Wolfgang J., and Robinson, Ronald, eds., *Bismarck, Europe and Africa: The Berlin Africa Conference 1884–1885 and the Onset of Partition* (Oxford: Oxford University Press, 1988).

Fursdon, Edward, *The European Defence Community: A History* (London: Macmillan, 1980).

Gatzke, Hans W., ed., *European Diplomacy between Two Wars, 1919–1939* (Chicago: Quadrangle, 1972).

George, Stephen, *Britain and European Integration since 1945* (Oxford: Basil Blackwell, 1991).

Gifford, Chris, *The Making of Eurosceptic Britain: Identity and Economy in a Post-Imperial State* (Aldershot: Ashgate, 2008).

Gilbert, Martin, *Winston S. Churchill: Volume VIII: 'Never Despair', 1945–1965* (London: Heinemann, 1988).

Gilmour, Rachel, and Schwarz, Bill, eds., *End of Empire and the English Novel since 1945* (Manchester: Manchester University Press, 2011).

Gordon, Joel, *Nasser's Blessed Movement: Egypt's Free Officers and the July Revolution* (Oxford: Oxford University Press, 1992).

Gowland, David, Turner, Arthur, and Wright, Alex, *Britain and European Integration since 1945: On the Sidelines* (London: Routledge, 2010).

Grayson, Richard S., *Austen Chamberlain and the Commitment to Europe: British Foreign Policy, 1924–29* (London: Frank Cass, 1997).

Greenwood, Sean, *The Alternative Alliance: Anglo–French Relations before the Coming of NATO, 1944–48* (London: Minerva, 1996).

Greenwood, Sean, *Britain and European Integration since the Second World War* (Manchester: Manchester University Press, 1996).

Grob-Fitzgibbon, Benjamin, *Imperial Endgame: Britain's Dirty Wars and the End of Empire* (Basingstoke: Palgrave Macmillan, 2011).

Harper, John Lamberton, *American Visions of Europe: Franklin D. Roosevelt, George F. Kennan, and Dean D. Acheson* (Cambridge: Cambridge University Press, 1994).
Harris, Robert, *The Making of Neil Kinnock* (London: Faber and Faber, 1984).
Hastings, Max, *The Korean War* (New York: Simon and Schuster, 1987).
Heater, Derek, *The Idea of European Unity* (Leicester: Leicester University Press, 1992).
Heffer, Simon, *Like the Roman: The Life of Enoch Powell* (London: Faber and Faber, 2008).
Heller, Francis H., and Gillingham, John R., eds., *NATO: The Founding of the Atlantic Alliance and the Integration of Europe* (Basingstoke: Macmillan, 1992).
Hennessy, Peter, *Whitehall* (London: Secker & Warburg, 1989).
Heppell, Timothy, *The Tories: From Winston Churchill to David Cameron* (London: Bloomsburg, 2014).
Hogan, Michael J., *The Marshall Plan: America, Britain and the Reconstruction of Western Europe, 1947–1952* (Cambridge: Cambridge University Press, 1987).
Holland, Robert, *Britain and the Revolt in Cyprus, 1954–59* (Oxford: Clarendon, 1998).
Hopkins, Michael F., *Oliver Franks and the Truman Administration: Anglo-American Relations, 1948–1952* (London: Frank Cass, 2003).
Horne, Alistair, *Macmillan, 1894–1956: Volume I of the Official Biography* (London: Macmillan, 1988).
Horne, Alistair, *Macmillan, 1957–1986: Volume II of the Official Biography* (London: Macmillan, 1989).
Howard, Christopher, *Splendid Isolation: A Study of the Ideas Concerning Britain's International Position and Foreign Policy during the Later Years of the Third Marquis of Salisbury* (London: Macmillan, 1967).
Howard, Michael, *The Continental Commitment: The Dilemma of British Defence Policy in the Era of the Two World Wars: The Ford Lectures in the University of Oxford, 1971* (London: Temple Smith, 1972).
Hyam, Ronald, *Britain's Declining Empire: The Road to Decolonisation, 1918–1968* (Cambridge: Cambridge University Press, 2006).
Hynes, Catherine, *The Year that Never Was: Heath, the Nixon Administration and the Year of Europe* (Dublin: University College Dublin Press, 2009).
Jackson, Julian, *France: The Dark Years, 1940–1944* (Oxford: Oxford University Press, 2001).
Jackson, Julian, *The Fall of France: The Nazi Invasion of 1940* (Oxford: Oxford University Press, 2003).
James, Harold, *Europe Reborn: A History, 1914–2000* (Harlow: Pearson Education Limited, 2003).

Jerrold, Douglas, *Britain and Europe, 1900–1940* (London: Collins, 1941).
Joll, James, ed., *Britain and Europe: Pitt to Churchill, 1793–1940* (London: Adam & Charles Black, 1950).
Jones, Howard, *The Bay of Pigs* (Oxford: Oxford University Press, 2008).
Jones, Martin, *Failure in Palestine: British and United States Policy after the Second World War* (London: Mansell, 1986).
Judt, Tony, *Postwar: A History of Europe since 1945* (London: William Heinemann, 2005).
Kaiser, Wolfram, *Using Europe, Abusing the Europeans: Britain and European Integration, 1945–63* (Basingstoke: Macmillan, 1966).
Kennedy, Paul, *The Rise of Anglo-German Antagonism, 1860–1914* (London: George Allen & Unwin, 1980).
Kennedy, Paul, *The Realities behind Diplomacy: Background Influences on British External Policy, 1865–1980* (London: George Allen & Unwin, 1981).
Kennedy, Paul, *The Rise and Fall of the Great Powers: Economic Change and Military Conflict from 1500 to 2000* (London: Unwin Hyman, 1988).
Kenyon, John, *The History Men: The Historical Profession in England since the Renaissance* (London: Weidenfeld & Nicolson, 1983).
Krein, David F., *The Last Palmerston Government: Foreign Policy, Domestic Politics, and the Genesis of 'Splendid Isolation'* (Ames: Iowa State University Press, 1978).
Kyle, Keith, *Suez: Britain's End of Empire in the Middle East* (London: I. B. Tauris, 2003).
Kynaston, David, *Austerity Britain, 1945–51* (London: Bloomsbury, 2007).
Lacouture, Jean, *De Gaulle: The Ruler, 1945–1970*, translated from the French by Alan Sheridan (London: W. W. Norton, 1991).
Lagrou, Peiter, *The Legacy of Nazi Occupation: Patriotic Memory and National Recovery in Western Europe, 1945–1965* (Cambridge: Cambridge University Press, 2000).
Lamb, Richard, *The Macmillan Years, 1957–1963: The Emerging Truth* (London: John Murray, 1995).
Ledwidge, Bernard, *De Gaulle* (New York: St. Martin's, 1982).
Lipgens, Walter, *A History of European Integration: Volume I, 1945–1947*, translated from the German by P. S. Falla and A. J. Ryder (Oxford: Clarendon, 1982).
Louis, Wm. Roger, and Stookey, Robert W., eds., *The End of the Palestine Mandate* (Austin: University of Texas Press, 1986).
Ludlow, N. Piers, *Dealing with Britain: The Six and the First UK Application to the EEC* (Cambridge: Cambridge University Press, 1997).
Lundestad, Geir, *'Empire' by Integration: The United States and European Integration, 1945–1997* (Oxford: Oxford University Press, 1998).

Lundestad, Geir, *The United States and Western Europe since 1945: From 'Empire' by Invitation to Transatlantic Drift* (Oxford: Oxford University Press, 2003).
MacKenzie, John W., ed., *European Empires and the People: Popular Responses to Imperialism in France, Britain, the Netherlands, Belgium, Germany, and Italy* (Manchester: Manchester University Press, 2011).
Martel, Leon, *Lend-Lease, Loans, and the Coming of the Cold War: A Study in the Implementation of Foreign Policy* (Boulder, CO: Westview Press, 1979).
Marwick, Arthur, *British Society since 1945, fourth edition* (London: Penguin, 2003).
Matthew, Donald, *Britain and the Continent, 1000–1300* (London: Hodder Arnold, 2005).
May, Alex, ed., *Britain, the Commonwealth, and Europe* (Basingstoke: Palgrave Macmillan, 2001).
Middlebrook, Martin, *Task Force: The Falklands War, 1982* (London: Penguin, 1987).
Milfull, John, ed., *Britain in Europe: Prospects for Change* (Aldershot: Ashgate, 1999).
Miller, Roger G., *To Save a City: The Berlin Airlift, 1948–1949* (College Station: Texas A&M University Press, 2000).
Milward, Alan S., *The Reconstruction of Western Europe, 1945–51* (London: Methuen & Co. Ltd., 1984).
Milward, Alan S., *The United Kingdom and the European Community, Volume I: The Rise and Fall of a National Strategy, 1945–1963* (London: Routledge, 2012).
Moore, Charles, *Margaret Thatcher: The Authorized Biography: Volume One: Not for Turning* (London: Allen Lane, 2013).
Morgan, Kenneth O., *Labour in Power, 1945–1951* (Oxford: Clarendon, 1984).
Morgan, Kenneth O., *The People's Peace: British History, 1945–1989* (Oxford: Oxford University Press, 1990).
Morgan, Kenneth O., *Callaghan: A Life* (Oxford: Oxford University Press, 1997).
Newman, Michael, *Socialism and European Unity: The Dilemma of the Left in Britain and France* (London: Junction, 1983).
Onslow, Sue, *Backbench Debate within the Conservative Party and Its Influence on British Foreign Policy, 1948–57* (Basingstoke: Macmillan, 1997).
Osmont, Matthieu, Robin-Hivert, Emilia, Seidel, Katja, Spoerer, Mark, and Wenkel, Christian, eds., *Europeanisation in the 20th Century: The Historical Lens* (Brussels: P. I. E. Lang, 2012).
Ovendale, Ritchie, ed., *The Foreign Policy of the British Labour Governments, 1945–1951* (Leicester: Leicester University Press, 1984).

Parker, Christopher, *The English Historical Tradition since 1850* (Edinburgh: John Donald, 1990).
Parker, Geoffrey, *The Military Revolution: Military Innovation and the Rise of the West, 1500–1800, second edition* (Cambridge: Cambridge University Press, 1996).
Parr, Helen, *Britain's Policy Towards the European Community: Harold Wilson and Britain's World Role, 1964–1967* (London: Routledge, 2006).
Pegg, Carl H., *Evolution of the European Idea, 1914–1932* (Chapel Hill: University of North Carolina Press, 1983).
Pelling, Henry, *The Labour Governments, 1945–51* (London: Macmillan, 1984).
Pelling, Henry, *Churchill's Peacetime Ministry, 1951–55* (Basingstoke: Macmillan, 1997).
Pimlott, Ben, *Harold Wilson* (London: HarperCollins, 1992).
Pincus, Steve, *1688: The First Modern Revolution* (New Haven, CT: Yale University Press, 2009).
Pine, Melissa, *Harold Wilson and Europe: Pursuing Britain's Membership of the European Community* (London: Tauris Academic Studies, 2007).
Rees, Graham L., *Britain and the Postwar European Payments System* (Cardiff: University of Wales Press, 1963).
Rhodes, Robert James, *Anthony Eden* (London: Weidenfeld & Nicholson, 1986).
Rioux, Jean-Pierre, *The Fourth Republic, 1944–1958*, translated by Godfrey Rogers (Cambridge: Cambridge University Press, 1987).
Ross, George, *Jacques Delors and European Integration* (New York: Oxford University Press, 1995).
Rossbach, Niklas H., *Heath, Nixon and the Rebirth of the Special Relationship: Britain, the US and the EC, 1969–74* (Basingstoke: Palgrave Macmillan, 2009).
Ruane, Kevin, *The Rise and Fall of the European Defence Community: Anglo-American Relations and the Crisis of European Defence, 1950–55* (Basingstoke: Macmillan, 2000).
Saville, John, *The Politics of Continuity: British Foreign Policy and the Labour Government, 1945–46* (London: Verdo, 1993).
Schick, Jack M., *The Berlin Crisis, 1958–1962* (Philadelphia: University of Pennsylvania Press, 1971).
Schofield, Camilla, *Enoch Powell and the Making of Postcolonial Britain* (Cambridge: Cambridge University Press, 2013).
Scott, Jonathan, *England's Troubles: Seventeenth Century English Political Instability in a European Context* (Cambridge: Cambridge University Press, 2000).
Seldon, Anthony, and Collings, Daniel, *Britain under Thatcher* (Harlow: Longman, 2000).

Seton-Watson, R.W., *Britain in Europe, 1789–1914: A Survey of Foreign Policy* (Cambridge: Cambridge University Press, 1937).
Shannon, Richard, *The Crisis of Imperialism, 1865–1915* (London: Hart-Davis, MacGibbon, 1974).
Shrimsley, Anthony, *The First Hundred Days of Harold Wilson* (New York: Frederick A. Praegar, 1965).
Simonian, Haig, *The Privileged Partnership: Franco-German Relations in the European Community, 1969–1984* (Oxford: Clarendon, 1985).
Sinclair, Georgina, *At the End of the Line: Colonial Policing and the Imperial Endgame, 1945–1980* (Manchester: Manchester University Press, 2006).
Sked, Alan and Cook, Chris, *Post-War Britain: A Political History*, second edition (London: Penguin, 1984).
Slusser, Robert M., *The Berlin Crisis of 1961: Soviet-American Relations and the Struggle for Power in the Kremlin, June–November 1961* (Baltimore and London: The Johns Hopkins University Press, 1973).
Soulioti, Stella, *Fettered Independence: Cyprus, 1878–1964: Volume One: The Narrative* (Minneapolis: Minnesota Mediterranean and East European Monographs, Modern Greek Studies, University of Minnesota, 2006).
Spiering, Menno, *A Cultural History of Euroscepticism* (Basingstoke: Palgrave Macmillan, 2015).
Stafford, David, *Endgame 1945: Victory, Retribution, Liberation* (London: Little, Brown, 2007).
Stevenson, John, *Third Party Politics since 1945: Liberals, Alliance and Liberal Democrats* (Oxford: Blackwell, 1993).
Stokes, Gale, *The Walls Came Tumbling Down: The Collapse of Communism in Eastern Europe* (Oxford: Oxford University Press, 1993).
Stueck, William, *The Korean War: An International History* (Princeton: Princeton University Press, 1995).
Taylor, Frederick, *Dresden: Tuesday, 13 February 1945* (London: Bloomsbury, 2005).
Thompson, Andrew, *Britain's Experience of Empire in the Twentieth Century* (Oxford: Oxford University Press, 2012).
Thorpe, Andrew, *A History of the British Labour Party* (New York: St. Martin's Press, 1997).
Thorpe, D. R., *Eden: The Life and Times of Anthony Eden, First Earl of Avon, 1897–1977* (London: Chatto & Windus, 2003).
Tratt, Jacqueline, *The Macmillan Government and Europe: A Study in the Process of Policy Development* (Basingstoke: Macmillan, 1996).
Turner, Ian, ed., *Reconstruction in Post-War Germany: British Occupation Policy and the Western Zones, 1945–55* (Oxtord: Berg, 1989).
Turner, Michael J., *Britain's International Role, 1970–1991* (Basingstoke: Palgrave Macmillan, 2010).

Wade, Richard, *Conservative Party Economic Policy: From Heath in Opposition to Cameron in Coalition* (Basingstoke: Palgrave Macmillan, 2013).
Wall, Stephen, *A Stranger in Europe: Britain and the EU from Thatcher to Blair* (Oxford: Oxford University Press, 2008).
Wall, Stephen, *The Official History of Britain and the European Community: Volume II: From Rejection to Referendum, 1963–1975* (London: Routledge, 2013).
Ward, Stuart, *Australia and the British Embrace: The Demise of the Imperial Ideal* (Victoria, Australia: Melbourne University Press, 2001).
Ward, Stuart, ed., *British Culture and the End of Empire* (Manchester: Manchester University Press, 2001).
Webster, Wendy, *Englishness and Empire, 1939–1965* (Oxford: Oxford University Press, 2005).
Weiler, Peter, *Ernest Bevin* (Manchester: Manchester University Press, 1993).
Werth, Alexander, *The de Gaulle Revolution* (London: Robert Hale, 1960).
White, Nicholas J., *Decolonisation: The British Experience since 1945* (London: Longman, 1999).
Wilkes, George, ed., *Britain's Failure to Enter the European Community, 1961–63* (London: Frank Cass, 1997).
William, Francis, *Ernest Bevin: Portrait of a Great Englishman* (London: Hutchinson, 1952).
Williams, Philip M., with Goldey, David and Harrison, Martin, *French Politicians and Elections, 1951–1969* (Cambridge: Cambridge University Press, 1970).
Wolpert, Stanley, *Shameful Flight: The Last Years of the British Empire in India* (Oxford: Oxford University Press, 2006).
Young, John W., *Britain and European Unity, 1945–1999, second edition* (Basingstoke: Macmillan, 2000).
Young, Kenneth, *Sir Alec Douglas-Home* (Teaneck, NJ: Fairleigh Dickinson University Press, 1971).
Ziegler, Philip, *Edward Heath: The Authorised Biography* (London: HarperPress, 2010).

Articles, essays and chapters

Adamthwaite, Anthony, 'John Bull v. Marianne, round two: Anglo–French relations and Britain's second EEC membership bid', in Daddow, Oliver J., ed., *Harold Wilson and European Integration: Britain's Second Application to Join the EEC* (London: Frank Cass, 2003).
Ball, Simon, 'The wind of change as generational drama', in Butler, L. J. and Stockwell, Sarah, eds., *The Wind of Change: Harold Macmillan and British Decolonization* (Basingstoke: Palgrave Macmillan, 2013).

Bordo, Michael D., MacDonald, Ronald, and Oliver, Michael J., 'Sterling in crisis, 1964–1967', Working Paper 14657, National Bureau of Economic Research.

Cohen, Michael J., 'The genesis of the Anglo–American Committee on Palestine, November 1945: A case study in the assertion of American hegemony', *The Historical Journal*, Volume 22, Number 1 (March 1979).

Colley, Linda, 'What is imperial history now?' in David Cannadine, ed., *What Is History Now?* (Basingstoke: Palgrave Macmillan, 2002).

Condren, Conal, 'English historiography and the invention of Britain and Europe', in Milfull, John, ed., *Britain in Europe: Prospects for Change* (Aldershot: Ashgate, 1999).

Debow, Saul, 'Macmillan, Verwoerd and the 1960 "Wind of Change" speech', in Butler, L. J., and Stockwell, Sarah, eds., *The Wind of Change: Harold Macmillan and British Decolonization* (Basingstoke: Palgrave Macmillan, 2013).

Deighton, Anne, 'Cold War diplomacy: British policy towards Germany's role in Europe, 1945–9', in Turner, Ian, ed., *Reconstruction in Post-War Germany: British Occupation Policy and the Western Zones, 1945–55* (Oxford: Berg, 1989).

Deighton, Anne, 'Britain and the creation of Western European Union, 1954', in Deighton, Anne, ed., *Western European Union, 1954–1997: Defence, Security, Integration* (St Antony's College, Oxford: Published by the European Interdependence Research Unit, St Antony's College, Oxford, with support of the Foreign and Commonwealth Office, and the WEU Institute for Security Studies, Paris, 1997).

Deighton, Anne, 'The Labour Party, public opinion and "the second try" in 1967', in Daddow, Oliver J., ed., *Harold Wilson and European Integration: Britain's Second Application to Join the EEC* (London: Frank Cass, 2003).

Diefendorf, Jeffry M., 'Introduction: New perspectives on a rebuilt Europe', in Jeffry M. Diefendorf, ed., *Rebuilding Europe's Bombed Cities* (London: Macmillan, 1990).

Dutton, David, 'Anticipating Maastricht: The Conservative Party and Britain's first application to join the European Community', *Contemporary Record*, Volume 7, Number 3 (Winter 1993).

Ellison, James R. V., 'Perfidious Albion? Britain, Plan G and European integration, 1955–1956', *Contemporary British History*, Volume 10, Number 4 (Winter 1996).

Farrar-Hockley, Anthony, 'The post-war army, 1945–1963', in Chandler, David, and Beckett, Ian, eds., *The Oxford History of the British Army* (Oxford: Oxford University Press, 1994).

Foot, Peter, 'Britain, European unity and NATO, 1947–1950', in Heller, Francis H., and Gillingham, John R., eds., *NATO: The Founding of the Atlantic Alliance and the Integration of Europe* (Basingstoke: Macmillan, 1992).

Forster, Anthony, 'No entry: Britain and the EEC in the 1960s', *Contemporary British History*, Volume 12, Number 2 (Summer 1998).
Gatzke, Hans W., 'Introduction', in Hans W. Gatzke, ed., *European Diplomacy between Two Wars, 1919–1939* (Chicago: Quadrangle, 1972).
Gearson, John P. S., 'British policy and the Berlin Wall crisis, 1958–61', *Contemporary Record*, Volume 6, Number 1 (Summer 1992).
Gliddon, Paul, 'The British Foreign Office and domestic propaganda on the European Community, 1960–72', *Contemporary British History*, Volume 23, Number 2 (June 2009).
Greenwood, Sean, '"Not the 'general will' but the will of the general": The input of the Paris Embassy to the British "Great Debate" on Europe, Summer 1960', *Contemporary British History*, Volume 18, Number 3 (Autumn 2004).
Gutschow, Niels, 'Hamburg: The "catastrophe" of July 1943', in Jeffry M. Diefendorf, ed., *Rebuilding Europe's Bombed Cities* (London: Macmillan, 1990).
Heffer, Simon, 'Powell, (John) Enoch (1912–1998)', *Oxford Dictionary of National Biography* (Oxford University Press, 2004, online edition, May 2008).
Hemming, Philip E., 'Macmillan and the end of the British Empire in Africa', in Aldous, Richard, and Lee, Sabine, eds., *Harold Macmillan and Britain's World Role* (Basingstoke: Macmillan, 1996).
Jenkins, Roy, 'Churchill: The government of 1951–55', in Blake, Robert, and Louis, Wm. Roger, eds., *Churchill* (Oxford: Oxford University Press, 1993).
Joll, James, 'Introduction', in James Joll, *Britain and Europe: Pitt to Churchill, 1793–1940* (London: Adam & Charles Black, 1950).
Ludlow, N. Piers, 'A waning force: The treasury and British European policy, 1955–63', *Contemporary British History*, Volume 17, Number 4 (Winter 2003).
Lynch, Philip, 'The Conservatives and the Wilson application', in Daddow, Oliver J., ed., *Harold Wilson and European Integration: Britain's Second Application to Join the EEC* (London: Frank Cass, 2003).
Ovendale, Ritchie, 'The Palestine policy of the British Labour Government 1947: The decision of withdraw', *International Affairs*, Volume 56, Number 1 (January 1980).
Parr, Helen, 'A question of leadership: July 1966 and Harold Wilson's European decision', *Contemporary British History*, Volume 19, Number 4 (December 2005).
Parr, Helen, 'Britain, America, east of Suez and the EEC: Finding a role in British foreign policy, 1964–67', *Contemporary British History*, Volume 20, Number 3 (September 2006).

Parr, Helen, 'Saving the Community: The French response to Britain's second EEC application in 1967', *Cold War History*, Volume 6, Number 4 (November 2006).
Pocock, J. G. A., 'British history: A plea for a new subject', *Journal of Modern History*, Volume 47, Number 4 (December 1975).
Pocock, J. G. A., 'The limits and divisions of British History: In search of the unknown subject', *American Historical Review*, Volume 87, Number 2 (April 1982).
Pocock, J. G. A., 'History and sovereignty: The historiographical response to Europeanization in two British cultures', *Journal of British Studies*, Volume 31, Number 4 (October 1992).
Pocock, J. G. A., 'The new British history in Atlantic perspective: An antipodean commentary', *American Historical Review*, Volume 104, Number 2 (April 1999).
Raineau, Thomas, 'Europeanising Whitehall? The British Civil Service and Europe, 1957–1972', in Osmont, Matthieu, Robin-Hivert, Emilia, Seidel, Katja, Spoerer, Mark, and Wenkel, Christian, eds., *Europeanisation in the 20th Century: The Historical Lens* (Brussels, Belgium: P. I. E. Lang, 2012).
Rodgers, Bill, 'SDP', in Adonis, Andrew, and Thomas, Keith, eds., *Roy Jenkins: A Retrospective* (Oxford: Oxford University Press, 2004).
Rodgers, William, 'Thomson, George Morgan, Baron Thomson of Monifieth (1921–2008)', *The Oxford Dictionary of National Biography* (Oxford University Press, online edition, September 2012).
Rollings, Neil, 'The confederation of British Industry and European integration in the 1960s', in Daddow, Oliver J., ed., *Harold Wilson and European Integration: Britain's Second Application to Join the EEC* (London: Frank Cass, 2003).
Stockwell, Sarah, and Butler, L. J., 'Introduction', in Butler, L. J., and Stockwell, Sarah, eds., *The Wind of Change: Harold Macmillan and British Decolonization* (Basingstoke: Palgrave Macmillan, 2013).
Stuart, Mark, 'Meyer, Sir Anthony John Charles, third baronet (1920–2004), *Oxford Dictionary of National Biography* (Online edition, January 2009).
Taylor, A. J. P., 'Comments on "British history: A plea for a new subject"', *Journal of Modern History*, Volume 47, Number 4 (December 1975).
Toye, Richard, 'Words of change: The rhetoric of Commonwealth, Common Market and Cold War, 1961–3', in Butler, L. J., and Stockwell, Sarah, eds., *The Wind of Change: Harold Macmillan and British Decolonization* (Basingstoke: Palgrave Macmillan, 2013).
Turner, Ian, 'The British occupation and its impact on Germany', in Turner, Ian, ed., *Reconstruction in Post-War Germany: British Occupation Policy and the Western Zones, 1945–55* (Oxford: Berg, 1989).

Ward, Stuart, 'Kennedy, Britain, and the European Community', in Brinkley, Douglas, and Griffiths, Richard T., eds., *John F. Kennedy and Europe* (Baton Rouge: Louisiana State University Press, 1999).

Ward, Stuart, 'Whirlwind, hurricane, howling tempest: The wind of change and the British world', in Butler, L. J., and Stockwell, Sarah, eds., *The Wind of Change: Harold Macmillan and British Decolonization* (Basingstoke: Palgrave Macmillan, 2013).

Warner, Geoffrey, 'The Labour governments and the unity of Western Europe, 1945–51', in Ovendale, Ritchie, ed., *The Foreign Policy of the British Labour Governments, 1945–1951* (Leicester: Leicester University Press, 1984).

White, Nicholas J., 'Reconstructing Europe through rejuvenating empire: The British, French, and Dutch experiences compared', *Past and Present* (2006), Supplement 6.

Index

Acheson, Dean, 36, 95, 96, 97, 112, 123, 128, 129, 138, 170, 263, 297
Action Committee for the United States of Europe, 338
Adenauer, Konrad, 1, 128, 132, 170, 178, 179, 182, 190, 200, 227, 232, 236, 259, 261, 266
Alanbrooke, Field Marshal Lord, 14, 26
Alchin, Geoffrey, 150
Algeria, 95
Amato, Giuliano, 463
Amery, Julian, 145, 152, 156, 165, 169, 179, 183, 190, 290, 298, 384
Amery, Leopold, 1, 35, 37, 44, 45, 46, 54, 114, 127, 149, 190
Amory, Heathcoat, 237, 242
Anderson, Bruce, 442
Ansiaux, Hubert, 121
Anti-Common Market Campaign, 350
Anti-Common Market League, 347, 434
Antigua, 226
Armitage, David, 4
Armstrong, Robert, 385
Atkins, Humphrey, 422
Atkins, LB Walsh, 313
Attlee, Clement, 30, 32, 45, 63, 65, 69, 83, 86, 96, 140, 144, 146, 148, 152
Auchinleck, Field Marshal Sir Claude, 281
Auriol, Vincent, 63, 65
Australia, 70, 72, 219, 233, 268, 271, 274, 336, 387
Austria, 71, 203, 239

Baker, Ken, 460
Ball, George, 321
Barnes, John, 316
Barroso, José Manuel, 2
Bech, Joseph, 105, 107
Beddington-Behrens, Edward, 172, 176, 177, 179, 197, 315, 336
Beetham, R.C., 358
Begin, Menachem, 31
Belgium, 19, 23, 34, 56, 66, 71, 76, 95, 100, 110, 135, 146, 172, 282
Benn, Tony, 355, 376, 378, 379, 382, 385, 388, 392, 398, 402, 413, 422, 428
Berlin Blockade, 80, 81, 85, 87, 90, 95, 98, 102
Berlin, Sir Isaiah, 281
Berlin Wall
  building of, 263
Bermuda, 226
Bermuda Conference, 187–190
Berry, Sidney, 48
Berthoud, Eric, 166
Bevan, Aneurin, 146
Bevin, Ernest, 26, 31, 32, 42, 60, 65, 68, 70–71, 76, 79, 80, 84, 86, 87, 88, 92, 94, 96, 102, 104, 106, 110, 118, 128, 138, 143, 144
  and European Coal and Steel Community, 123–124
  and Potsdam conference, 27
  death of, 146
  illnesses of, 130, 134

relationship with Winston Churchill, 39–40
response to the European Coal and Steel Community, 132
views on Europe, 28, 61–62, 66, 72–73, 114–116
views on the British Empire, 33, 42–43, 64–65
Bidault, Georges, 41, 42, 62, 66, 70–71, 76, 85, 95, 124, 178, 182, 192
  at Bermuda Conference, 189
Biffen, John, 411
Biggs-Davidson, John, 277
Birrenbach, Kurt, 328
Black, Sir Cyril, 401
Blair, Tony, 466, 469
Blum, Léon, 1, 58, 102
Boggs, Hale, 50
Bonham-Carter, Lady Violet, 1
Bonnet, Henri, 95
Boothby, Robert, 1, 45, 48, 56, 111, 146, 152, 155, 156, 158, 166, 169, 174, 177, 207
Bottomley, Arthur, 318
Boyle, Edward, 275, 290
Bracken, Brendan, 30
Brandt, Willy, 324, 326, 344, 372
Bretton Woods Agreement, 30, 369
Briand, Aristide, 37
Briggs, Sir Harold, 144
Britain in Europe
  launch of, 315
Brittan, Leon, 429
Brooke, Henry, 290
Brookes, Sir Norman, 243, 247
Brown, Ernest, 45, 48
Brown, George, 300, 306, 325, 327, 328, 333, 336, 419
Browne, Anthony Montague, 277
Brownjohn, General Nevil, 80
Bruce, David, 324
Brussels, Treaty of (1948), 74, 103
Bryant, Sir Arthur, 350
Bulganin, Nikolai, 207
Bush, George H.W., 450, 454
Butler, R.A., 153, 166, 202, 270, 290

Caccia, Sir Harold, 264, 267
Cadogan, Sir Alexander, 27

Caine, Sir Sydney, 73
Callaghan, James, 292, 300, 306, 359, 361, 363, 379, 381, 385, 387, 402, 403, 405, 409, 413, 423
  becomes Prime Minister, 402
Cameron, David, 2
Campaign for a European Political Community, 320
Camrose, Viscount, 45
Canada, 55, 70, 72, 95, 147, 218, 226, 271, 274
Carlisle, Mark, 413
Carr, Robert, 165, 373
Carrington, Lord, 408, 410, 411, 416, 417, 422, 429
Castle, Barbara, 305, 392
Central African Federation, 246
Ceylon, 271
Chamberlain, Neville, 17
Chambers, Sir Paul, 337
Chelwood, Viscount Cecil of, 37
Cheysson, Claude, 432
Churchill, Winston, 20, 23, 25, 37, 47, 55, 57, 77, 83, 85, 102, 103, 110, 117, 138, 140, 148, 152, 159, 163, 166, 175, 182, 185, 194, 199, 215, 220, 247, 278
  Albert Hall speech, 51–52
  and Congress of Europe, 1
  and Fulton, Missouri, speech, 1946, 36–37
  and proposal to form Anglo–French Union, 18
  and VE-Day, 13
  and Zurich Speech on United States of Europe, 43–44
  at Bermuda Conference, 188–189
  becomes Prime Minister, 1940, 18
  on appeasement, 17
  proposal for a European Army, 141–142
  resignation of, 201
  strokes of, 184
  views on de Gaulle, 20
  views on Europe, 16–17, 19, 25, 34–35, 154–155
  Zurich speech on the United States of Europe, 44
Citrine, Lord, 45

Clark, Alan, 423
Clark, Sir Kenneth, 281
Clarke, Sir Ashley, 197, 204
Clay, Lucius, 82
Clegg, Nick, 2
Cockfield, Arthur, 435, 436
Colley, Linda, 4
Colombo, Emilio, 330
Colville, John, 14, 33
Committee of European Economic Co-operation (CEEC), 67, 68
Common Market Safeguards Campaign, 350, 354
Congress of Europe, 1, 58, 77, 84
Conservative Party, 63, 103, 111, 127, 130, 137, 145, 146, 151, 152, 156, 203, 281, 291, 295, 313, 325, 357, 369, 384, 393, 404, 409, 427, 443
Cooper, Duff, 19–21, 25, 26, 28, 33, 37, 38, 63, 66, 82
  correspondence with Anthony Eden, 21–22, 23–24
Coudenhove-Kalergi, Richard, 50, 103
Coulson, Sir John, 232
Council of Europe, 110
Couve de Murville, Maurice, 237, 298, 299
Creech Jones, Arthur, 77
Cripps, Sir Stafford, 68, 101, 120, 125, 146
Crossland, Tony, 402
Crossman, Richard, 65, 158, 225, 305, 347
Cuba, 263
Curtis, Lionel, 48
Cyprus, 205, 226, 271
Czechoslovakia, 66, 206

Dalton, Hugh, 68, 127, 142, 148
de Besche, Hubert, 239
de Freitas, Geoffrey, 315, 317
de Gasperi, Alcide, 102
de Gaulle, Charles, 18, 20, 23, 24, 42, 45, 250, 251–253, 261, 265, 282, 287, 316, 327, 328, 330, 339
  becomes French Prime Minister (1958), 234
  becomes President of the French Fifth Republic, 252
  death of, 341
  resignation of, 341
  state visit to Britain, 255
de Margerie, Emmanuel Jacquin, 425
de Zuleuta, Philip, 242, 253, 273, 277, 284, 303
Dean, Sir Patrick, 321, 323, 335
Delors, Jacques, 435, 436, 437, 439
Dench, Judi, 368
Denmark, 66, 71, 95, 110, 239
Diamond, John, 352
Diefenbaker, John, 268
Dillon, C. Douglas, 243, 254
Disraeli, Benjamin, 217
Dixon, Sir Pierson, 67, 154, 186, 286
Donoughue, Bernard, 385, 386, 397
Douglas, Lewis, 80
Douglas-Home, Alec, 212, 214, 258, 263, 286, 306, 352, 374
du Cann, Edward, 317
Dulles, John Foster, 179, 192, 231
Dunkirk, Treaty of (1947), 65

Eccles, David, 141, 152, 240, 290
Eden, Anthony, 19, 20, 22, 25, 26, 53, 83, 99, 127, 137, 138, 141, 145, 152, 153, 191, 201, 217, 288, 289, 294, 377
  and the European Defence Community, 169–172
  at Bermuda Conference, 188–189
  becomes Prime Minister, 201, 202
  illnesses of, 183
  relationship with R. A. Butler, 166–168
  resignation of, 220
  views on British foreign policy, 173–174, 184–185, 207–210
  views on Europe, 155, 180–181, 215
Edwards, Bob, 1
Egypt, 153, 163, 177, 206, 217, 372
Einzig, Paul, 30, 256
Eisenhower, Dwight D., 83, 158, 179, 186, 194, 198, 219, 220, 240, 248, 261
  at Bermuda Conference, 188–189
Elisabeth Schwarzkopf, 368
Elliot, T. S., 281

Ellis-Rees, Hugh, 232
Engholm, Sir Basil, 342
European Coal and Steel Community (ECSC), 164, 183
  founding of, 146
European Defence Community (EDC), 147, 157, 164, 169–172, 178, 182, 191
European Economic Community (EEC)
  Britain votes to join (1971), 361
  Britain's application to join (1961), 250
  Britain's second application to join (1967), 328
  British decision to join (1961), 276
  British public's views on joining, 367
  British renegotiation of, 387
  founding of, 227
  referendum on continued British membership in, 391–398
European Elections, 1979, 408–410
European Free Trade Area (EFTA), 225
European Free Trade Association (EFTA), 328
  founding of, 238–240, 243
European League for Economic Cooperation (ELEC), 172, 177, 190
European Payments Union (EPU), 120
Evans, Geraint, 368
Evans, Richard, 5

Falklands War, 422, 423
Farage, Nigel, 2, 467
'Fanfare for Europe', 368
Fell, Anthony, 277
Ferguson, Niall, 3
Fisher, Geoffrey, 47
Foot, Michael, 65, 305, 350, 358, 359, 385, 392, 402, 413, 418, 421, 428
Forrestal, James, 82
France, 19, 24, 28, 34, 37, 62, 66, 71, 86, 90, 93, 95, 97, 100, 102, 103, 110, 124, 135, 146, 172, 178, 181, 187, 191, 194, 203, 228, 262, 282, 425
Franks, Sir Oliver, 90, 95, 96, 97, 131, 137
Fraser, Peter, 55
Freeman, John, 146, 341
Frere-Smith, Christopher, 388
Friedman, Milton, 411
Fulbright, J. William, 50

Gaillard, Felix, 234
Gaitskell, Hugh, 120–122, 146, 291, 293
  death of, 300
Galsworthy, Sir Arthur, 342
Garel-Jones, Tristan, 449
General Election, 1945, 15, 16, 26
General Election, 1950 (February), 127
General Election, 1951 (October), 151
General Election, 1955, 203
General Election, 1959, 241
General Election, 1966, 317
General Election, 1970, 341, 346
General Election, 1974, 375, 380
General Election, 1974 (September), 385
General Election, 1979, 407
General Election, 1983, 427
General Election, 1987, 438
Germany, 31, 37, 54, 61, 63, 79, 84, 86, 87, 92, 94, 99, 103, 110, 112, 124, 135, 142, 146, 172, 178, 182, 185, 194, 203, 206, 254, 259, 262, 282, 340
Ghana, 246, 272
Gibraltar, 226
Gibson, George, 45,
Gilmour, Ian, 408, 411, 413, 416, 430
Giscard, Valery, 416
Gobbi, Tito, 368
Goddard, Brian, 174
Goldsmith, James, 394
Gollancz, Victor, 45, 48
Gorbachev, Mikhail, 450
Gore-Booth, Sir Paul, 336
Goschen, George, 217
Gow, Ian, 424, 449
Gower, Raymond, 152, 311
Greece, 71, 96, 110, 206
Greenhill, Sir Denis, 365
Griffiths, James, 144
Grimond, Jo, 310, 336
Gurney, Sir Henry, 144

Haakon VII, King, 25
Hale, Leslie, 1
Halifax, Lord, 22, 28
Hall, Stuart, 2
Hall-Patch, Sir Edmund, 41, 68
Hallstein, Walter, 227, 275, 302
Hannan, Daniel, 3

Hannay, David, 434
Hare, John, 271
Harris, John, 370
Harrison, Earl G., 32
Harrod, Roy, 289
Hart, Judith, 385
Harvey, Sir Oliver, 60, 82, 126, 150, 179
Hastings, Max, 464
Hayday, Sir Frederick, 337
Headlam, Sir Cuthbert, 128
Healy, Denis, 402
Heath, Edward, 139, 142, 152, 258, 264, 265, 268, 271, 281, 286, 296, 298, 302, 325, 332, 351, 364, 367, 372, 375, 393, 395, 399, 410, 443, 470
   becomes Conservative Party leader, 315
   becomes Prime Minister, 341, 347
   resignation of, 380
Heathcoat-Amery, David, 367, 467
Heffer, Simon, 442
Henderson, Sir Nicholas, 414
Hennekinne, Loic, 451
Henry, Sir Oliver, 190
Herriot, Édouard, 56, 105
Herter, Christian, 254
Heseltine, Michael, 411, 445, 456, 457
Hibbert, Reginald, 421
Hicks, George, 45
Hitler, Adolf, 17
Holland, Sidney, 149
Holyoake, Keith, 268
Hong Kong, 227, 460
Hopkinson, Henry, 1
Hornby, Richard, 312
Howard, Michael, 281
Howe, Sir Geoffrey, 368, 405, 411, 429, 437, 441, 455
Howell, David, 411, 429
Hoyer Millar, Sir Frank, 200
Hunt, John, 373
Hurd, Douglas, 368, 370, 450, 456, 459, 460, 463

Iceland, 71, 95, 110, 177
India, 32, 64, 72, 271, 274, 376
Ireland, 71, 95, 110, 424
Irgun Zvai Leumi, 31
Ismay, Lord, 190

Israel, 153, 372
Italy, 71, 95, 110, 135, 146, 172, 225, 240, 282, 424

Jackling, Sir Roger, 257
Jamaica, 318
Jay, Douglas, 134, 292, 388
Jebb, Gladwyn, 60, 72, 126, 197, 198, 204, 254, 280, 284, 309, 314, 320, 328, 382
Jenkins, Peter, 421
Jenkins, Roy, 291, 333, 358, 361, 385, 402, 419, 428
Johnson, Donald, 305
Johnson, Lyndon B., 308, 318, 323, 332, 334
Jopling, Michael, 421
Joseph, Keith, 411, 429

Kaufman, Gerald, 428
Keeler, Christine, 305
Keith, Kenneth, 315
Kennan, George, 112
Kennedy, John F., 262, 263, 264, 268, 288
Kenya, 177, 205, 272
Kerr, John, 441
Kerstens, Pieter, 56
Keynes, John Maynard, 30
Khrushchev, Nikita, 260, 262, 263
Kiesinger, Kurt, 340
King, Evelyn, 48
King-Hall, Commander Stephen, 45, 84
Kinnock, Neil, 428, 431, 444, 447, 457, 466
Kirkpatrick, Sir Ivone, 82, 172, 204
Kissinger, Henry, 322
Knatchbull-Hugessen, Sir Hughe, 23
Kohl, Helmut, 426, 437, 450, 453
Korean War, 138, 144
Krushchev, Nikita, 207

Labour Party, 26, 37, 50, 57, 101, 103, 111, 114, 127, 135, 145, 203, 291, 313, 347, 354, 355, 363, 369, 383, 409, 418, 428, 444, 447
   National Executive Committee of, 15, 292, 362, 419
Lamont, Norman, 459, 460
Lang, Gordon, 48

Lawson, Nigel, 413, 429, 446, 448
Layton, Sir Walter, 1, 45, 48, 117
Lebanon, 24–25
Ledwidge, Sir Bernard, 261
Lee, Sir Frank, 255, 257
LeMay, Curtis, 82
Lend-Lease program, 29
Lennox-Boyd, Alan, 160, 202, 205, 246, 294
Lennox-Boyd, Mark, 449
Lewis, Douglas, 88
Liberal Democrats, 419
Liddell Hart, Basil, 281
Lie, Trygve, 19
Lindo, Sir Laurence, 318
Lindsay of Birker, Lord, 48, 50
Lindsay, Kenneth, 1, 142
Lloyd, Selwyn, 186, 191, 202, 210, 218, 221, 225, 227, 231, 241, 243, 256, 258, 260, 261, 290
Luce, Richard, 422
Łukaszewski, Jerzy, 434
Luxembourg, 71, 100, 110, 135, 146, 172
Lyttelton, Oliver, 23, 153, 160, 162, 294

MacKenzie King, William, 100
MacKenzie, John, 4
Maclennan, Ian, 319
Macleod, Ian, 246
Macmillan, Harold, 10, 18, 23, 25, 26, 47, 58, 103, 110, 117, 126, 127, 130, 137, 140, 141, 149, 152, 155, 164, 169, 179, 185, 194, 195, 197, 202, 203, 207, 216, 219, 227, 239, 256, 261, 265, 271, 272, 283, 287, 298, 367, 377
  and Commonwealth tour (1958), 234
  and decision to join the EEC, 275
  and the Profumo Affair, 305
  and 'Wind of Change' speech, 245–248
  becomes Prime Minister, 220, 225
  resignation of, 306
  views on Europe, 165, 229–231, 278
Major, John, 429, 447, 464
  becomes Prime Minister, 456
  views on Europe, 457
Makins, Sir Roger, 134, 137, 151, 180, 192, 200, 239, 243

Malaya, 144, 154, 205, 271
Malaysia, 333, 336
Mallet, Sir Victor, 197
Mansholt, Sicco, 302
Marie, André, 84
Marshall, George, 52, 66, 79, 87, 90, 92, 95
Marten, Neil, 348, 349, 350, 379, 388, 390, 395, 401
Massigli, René, 41, 123, 137, 226
Maude, Angus, 412
Maudling, Francis, 394
Maudling, Reginald, 230, 233, 238, 242, 269, 290, 336
Maxwell-Fyfe, Sir David, 45, 48, 152, 156, 169
Mayer, René, 178
Mayhew, Sir Patrick, 445
McEwan, John, 233
McLeannan, Sir Ian, 247
McNamara, Bob, 333
McNeil, Hector, 62, 70, 76, 105
Mendès-France, Pierre, 195
Menzies, Robert, 100, 149, 247, 268
Merton, Richard, 54
Messina Conference, 204
Metcalf, Lee, 322
Meyer, Sir Anthony, 425, 448
Mikardo, Ian, 65, 392
Millar, Sir Frederick Robert Hoyer, 243
Mitterrand, François, 424, 426, 450
Mollet, Guy, 143, 147, 156, 175, 215, 326
Molotov, Vyacheslav, 31, 67, 89, 96
Monnet, Jean, 1, 59, 125, 128, 205, 272, 280, 281, 285, 288, 291, 338, 339
Montgomery, Field Marshal Montgomery, 179
Moriarty, M.J., 353
Morrison, Herbert, 134, 146, 147, 150
Motz, Roger, 179
Murray, George, 249
Murray, Gilbert, 48, 50

Nasser, General Gamal Abdel, 206, 217
National Referendum Campaign, 388, 390, 391
Neale, Gerry, 449
Neave, Airey, 407

Netherlands, the, 19, 24, 37, 66, 71, 95, 100, 110, 135, 146, 171, 172, 282
New Zealand, 55, 72, 218, 233, 268, 271, 274, 319, 336, 342, 352, 353, 361, 387
Niblock, Michael, 357
Nicholls, Hamar, 277
Nigeria, 226, 246, 272
'Night of the Long Knives', the, 290
Nixon, Richard, 360, 364
Noel, Andre, 56
North Atlantic Treaty Organisation (NATO), 95, 96, 147, 194
Norway, 19, 71, 95, 110, 239
Nott, John, 404, 406, 411, 417
Nutting, Anthony, 137, 198
Nyasaland, 247

O'Neill, Sir Con, 316, 323, 324, 344, 352, 353, 359, 360, 395
Oliver, Laurence, 368
Organisation for Economic Cooperation and Development (OECD), 68
Organisation for European Economic Cooperation, 125, 172, 175, 210, 221
Organisation of Petroleum Exporting Countries (OPEC), 372
Ormsby-Gore, Sir David, 315, 343
Owen, David, 419

Pakistan, 271
Palestine, 31, 64
Pallister, Sir Michael, 364, 375
Pallister, A.M., 324
Park, Trevor, 311
Parkinson, Cecil, 429
Pétain, Marshall Philippe, 18
Petrie, Caroline, 358
Pfimlin, Pierre, 234
Pinay, Antoine, 178
'Plan G', 211–217
Pleven, René, 128, 147
Plowden, Sir Edwin, 125, 168, 278, 322
Poland, 66
Pompidou, Georges, 341, 344, 360
Portugal, 71, 96, 239
Poulton, Jonathan, 430
Powell, Charles, 441, 451, 452

Powell, Enoch, 349, 376–378, 379, 398, 422, 430, 431, 444, 462
Prior, James, 411, 413, 417
Pritchard, Sir Neil, 313
Profumo, John, 304
Pym, Francis, 373, 375, 411, 429

Ramadier, Paul, 66, 70
Reagan, Ronald, 438
Redfern, Sir Shuldham, 55
Reynaud, Paul, 1, 59
Rhodesia, 247
Rhys-Williams, Lady, 1, 48, 179, 186, 191, 236, 257, 289
Ridley, Adam, 404
Ridley, Nicholas, 414
Rippon, Geoffrey, 354, 356, 394
Roberts, Andrew, 3
Roberts, Frank, 91
Roberts, Sir Frank, 259
Robertson, General Sir Brian, 82, 92
Rodgers, William, 419
Rostow, Walt, 333
Rumbold, Sir Algernon, 313
Rumbold, Sir Anthony, 197
Rusk, Dean, 267, 288, 333
Russell, Bertrand, 48
Ryder, Richard, 449
Rys-Williams, Lady, 45

Safeguard Britain Campaign, 418, 420
Salisbury, Lord, 10
Salter, Sir James, 157
Sandys, Duncan, 44, 45, 47, 50, 53, 56, 101, 102, 103, 104, 110, 114, 152, 191, 202, 225, 258, 259, 264, 269, 270, 271, 274, 279, 312, 324, 337, 360, 363
Sargent, Orme, 25
Sargent, Sir Orme, 281
Saudi Arabia, 219
Schmidt, Helmut, 388, 400, 416, 420
Schröder, Gerhard, 300
Schuman, Maurice, 345
Schuman, Robert, 84, 85, 102, 105, 106, 112, 118, 124, 128, 129, 132, 170, 171
Schwarzkopf, Elisabeth, 368
Second World War

effects on Europe of, 16
Seton-Watson, R.W., 7
Shepherd, Rob, 417
Shertok, Moshe, 32
Shinwell, Emanuel, 57, 144, 350
Shore, Peter, 378, 385, 389, 390, 392
Short, Edward, 317
Shuckburgh, Sir Evelyn, 150, 163, 166, 171, 177, 199, 202, 220
Sierra Leone, 226, 272
Singapore, 274, 333, 336
Single European Act, 436
Sked, Alan, 466
Smith, John, 466
Snelling, Sir Arthur, 341
Soames, Christopher, 258, 269, 271, 339, 413
Social Democratic Party (SDP), 419
Sokolovsky, Vasily, 80
Sonnefeldt, Helmut, 381
South Africa, 72, 245, 246
Soviet Union, 31, 63, 66, 70, 79, 84, 86, 87, 97, 102, 191, 206, 262
Spaak, Paul-Henri, 1, 19, 59, 76, 102, 105, 108, 116, 300
Spain, 96
Spearing, Nigel, 418, 436, 444, 448
Spinelli, Altiero, 434
St John-Stevas, Norman, 413
St. Laurent, Louis, 100, 149
Stalin, Joseph, 23, 88, 90, 93, 96
Stanley, Oliver, 23, 45, 48
Steel, David, 419
Steel, Sir Christopher, 254
Stewart, Michael, 316, 338, 341, 344
Stikker, Dirk, 105, 107
Strang, Sir William, 88, 134
Stratchey, John, 144
Suez Crisis, 217–220
Sweden, 71, 95, 110, 238
Switzerland, 38, 71, 239
Syria, 24–25

Tandy, Sir Arthur, 302
Tanganyika, 226
te Kanawa, Kiri, 368
Tebbit, Norman, 414, 429, 459
Teltschik, Horst, 452
Templer, General Sir Gerald, 205

Thatcher, Margaret, 127, 241, 367, 368, 374, 379, 399, 402, 405, 409, 413, 429, 448, 453, 461
  and 1975 Referendum on British EEC membership, 395–396
  and Britain's EEC budget contribution, 416–417, 426–427, 431, 432
  and the Single Europe Act, 437
  becomes leader of the Conservative Party, 393
  becomes Prime Minister, 400, 408
  on Britain's place in the world, 438
  on the fall of the Berlin Wall, 450
  resignation of, 456
  speech in Bruges, 433, 439–443
  views on Europe, 403, 424
Thomas, Elbert, 50
Thome-Patenôtre, Jacqueline, 309
Thomson, George, 336, 344, 347, 362, 382
Thorneycroft, Peter, 152, 202, 210, 213, 216, 225, 258, 271, 274, 290, 377
Treaty of European Union (Maastricht Treaty), 459
Treaty of Rome, 227
Trend, Sir Burke, 321, 373
Trevor-Roper, Hugh, 281
Truman, Harry S., 25, 27, 29, 31, 36, 38, 64, 82, 95, 138, 142
Tucker, Geoffrey, 370
Turkey, 67, 71, 96, 110
Turton, Robert, 277, 290, 350

Uganda, 226
Ulbricht, Walter, 263
United Europe Movement, 50, 77, 100, 102, 111, 114, 116, 130, 143, 174, 177
  and Albert Hall Rally, 1947, 51–52
  launch of, 48
United Kingdom Independence Party (UKIP), 2, 466
United Nations, 64, 70, 89, 93, 102
United States, 19, 30, 70, 80, 82, 86, 88, 93, 95, 97, 102, 104, 118, 124, 131, 147, 164, 175, 191, 194, 203, 219, 228, 243, 254, 266, 268, 288, 318, 323, 345
  views on European unity, 22–23
Urban, George, 426

van Boetzelaar, Baron, 76
van der Stoel, Max, 337
van Kleffens, Eelco, 19
van Zeeland, Paul, 1, 56, 59, 105, 110
Vishinsky, Andrey, 96

Walker, Peter, 394, 411
Walker-Smith, Sir Derek, 277
Wall, Stephen, 369, 433, 451, 464
Walters, Sir Alan, 447
Ward, Stephen, 305
Watkinson, Harold, 290
Wavell, Sir Archibald, 32
Weir, Sir Cecil, 183
Weizmann, Chaim, 32
Welensky, Roy, 247
Western European Union (WEU), 204, 221, 264, 268, 337
Westland Affair, 445
Whitelaw, William, 360, 375, 393, 395, 429
Wiley, Alexander, 179
Williams, Shirley, 419, 421

Wilson, Harold, 69, 146, 291, 312, 325, 328, 334, 338, 339, 362, 376, 387, 389, 392, 399
  and devaluation of the Pound Sterling, 333
  becomes leader of the Labour Party, 300
  becomes Prime Minister, 301, 306
  re-elected as Prime Minister (1974), 380
  resignation of (1976), 402
  views on Europe, 307–308
Wolff, Michael, 397
Woolton, Lord, 27
Wormser, Olivier, 329
Wright, Oliver, 310, 420
Wright, Patrick, 441

Yew, Lee Kuan, 274
Yom Kippur War (1973), 372
Young, Janet, 429
Younger, George, 449
Younger, Kenneth, 128, 134, 146, 148
Yugoslavia, 175

Zanzibar, 226